SUPERMAN
REIGN OF THE SUPERMEN

SUPERMAN
REIGN OF THE SUPERMEN

SUPERMAN created by JERRY SIEGEL and JOE SHUSTER.
SUPERBOY created by JERRY SIEGEL.
SUPERGIRL based on the characters created by JERRY SIEGEL and JOE SHUSTER.

writers DAN JURGENS KARL KESEL LOUISE SIMONSON ROGER STERN

pencillers JON BOGDANOVE TOM GRUMMETT JACKSON GUICE DAN JURGENS DAVID LAPHAM EDDY NEWELL

inkers MIKE BARREIRO BRETT BREEDING DOUG HAZLEWOOD Dennis JANKE MIKE MACHLAN DENIS RODIER

colorist GLENN WHITMORE

letterers JOHN COSTANZA ALBERT De GUZMAN BILL OAKLEY

collection cover artists DAN JURGENS, BRETT BREEDING and HI-FI

STEEL created by LOUISE SIMONSON and JON BOGDANOVE.

MYRIAD created by DAN JURGENS.

Mike Carlin Editor - Original Series **Jennifer Frank** Assistant Editor - Original Series
Jeb Woodard Group Editor - Collected Editions **Steve Cook** Design Director - Books **Damian Ryland** Publication Design

Bob Harras Senior VP - Editor-in-Chief, DC Comics

Diane Nelson President
Dan DiDio and **Jim Lee** Co-Publishers
Geoff Johns Chief Creative Officer
Amit Desai Senior VP - Marketing & Global Franchise Management
Nairi Gardiner Senior VP - Finance
Sam Ades VP - Digital Marketing
Bobbie Chase VP - Talent Development
Mark Chiarello Senior VP - Art, Design & Collected Editions
John Cunningham VP - Content Strategy
Anne DePies VP - Strategy Planning & Reporting
Don Falletti VP - Manufacturing Operations
Lawrence Ganem VP - Editorial Administration & Talent Relations

Alison Gill Senior VP - Manufacturing & Operations
Hank Kanalz Senior VP - Editorial Strategy & Administration
Jay Kogan VP - Legal Affairs
Derek Maddalena Senior VP - Sales & Business Development
Jack Mahan VP - Business Affairs
Dan Miron VP - Sales Planning & Trade Development
Nick Napolitano VP - Manufacturing Administration
Carol Roeder VP - Marketing
Eddie Scannell VP - Mass Account & Digital Sales
Courtney Simmons Senior VP - Publicity & Communications
Jim (Ski) Sokolowski VP - Comic Book Specialty & Newsstand Sales
Sandy Yi Senior VP - Global Franchise Management

Color reconstruction by **Rick Keene**

SUPERMAN: REIGN OF THE SUPERMEN

Published by DC Comics. Compilation and all new material Copyright © 2016 DC Comics. All Rights Reserved. Originally published in single magazine form in ACTION COMICS 687-688, ADVENTURES OF SUPERMAN 500-502, SUPERMAN 78-79, SUPERMAN ANNUAL 5, SUPERMAN: THE MAN OF STEEL 22-23 and SUPERMAN: THE MAN OF STEEL ANNUAL 2. Copyright © 1993 DC Comics. All Rights Reserved. All characters, their distinctive likenesses and related elements featured in this publication are trademarks of DC Comics. The stories, characters and incidents featured in this publication are entirely fictional. DC Comics does not read or accept unsolicited submissions of ideas, stories or artwork.

DC Comics, 2900 West Alameda Ave., Burbank, CA 91505. Printed by RR Donnelley, Owensville, MO, USA. 3/18/16. First Printing. ISBN: 978-1-4012-6663-9

Library of Congress Cataloging-in-Publication Data is available.

PEFC Certified

Printed on paper from
sustainably managed
forests and controlled
sources

PEFC/29-31-75   www.pefc.org

FIRST SIGHTING...

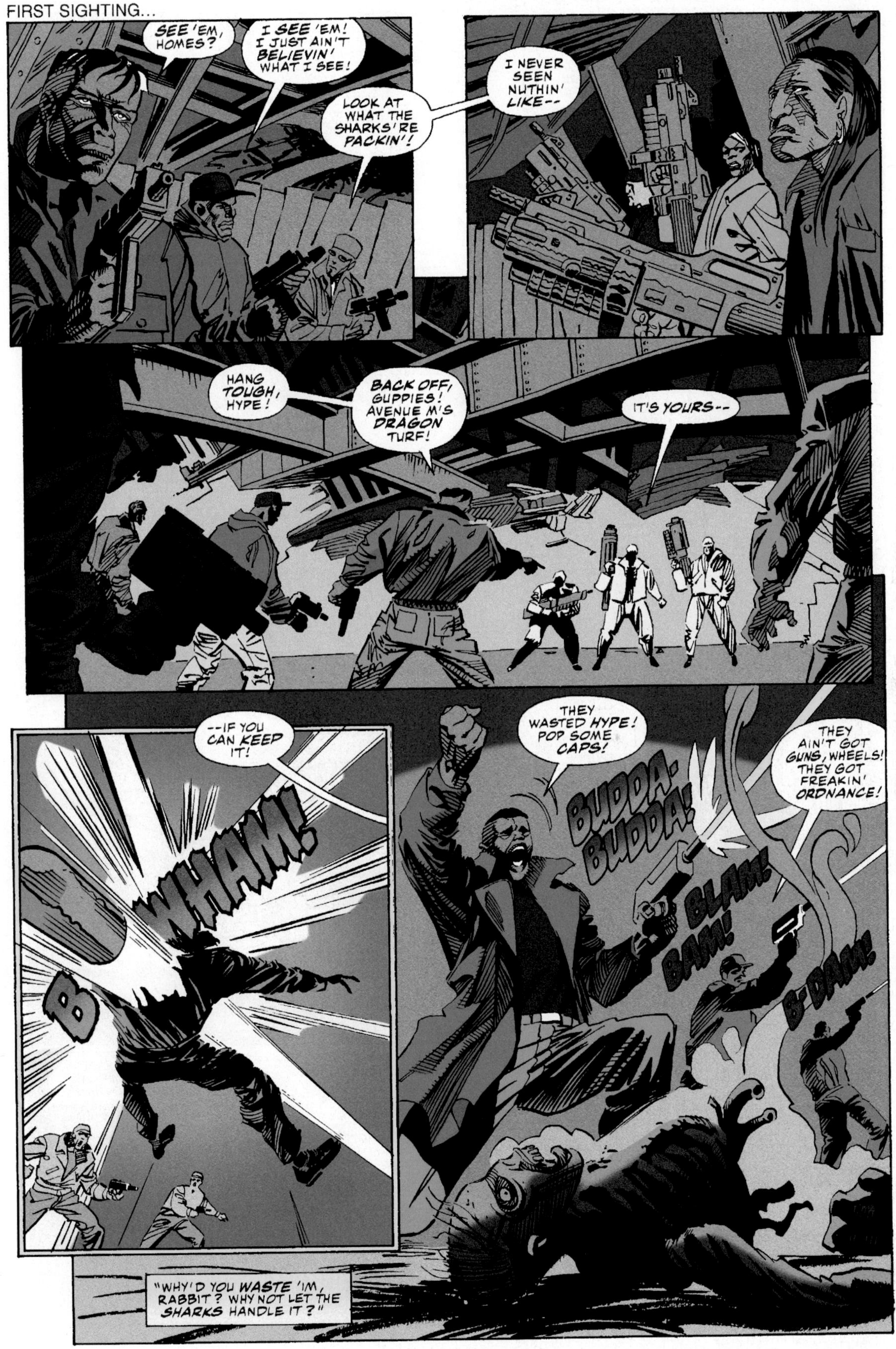
SEE 'EM, HOMES?
I SEE 'EM! I JUST AIN'T BELIEVIN' WHAT I SEE!
LOOK AT WHAT THE SHARKS'RE PACKIN'!
I NEVER SEEN NUTHIN' LIKE--
HANG TOUGH, HYPE!
BACK OFF, GUPPIES! AVENUE M'S DRAGON TURF!
IT'S YOURS--
--IF YOU CAN KEEP IT!
B-WHAM!
THEY WASTED HYPE! POP SOME CAPS!
BUDDA-BUDDA!
THEY AIN'T GOT GUNS, WHEELS! THEY GOT FREAKIN' ORDNANCE!
BLAM!
BAM!
B-DAM!
"WHY'D YOU WASTE 'IM, RABBIT? WHY NOT LET THE SHARKS HANDLE IT?"

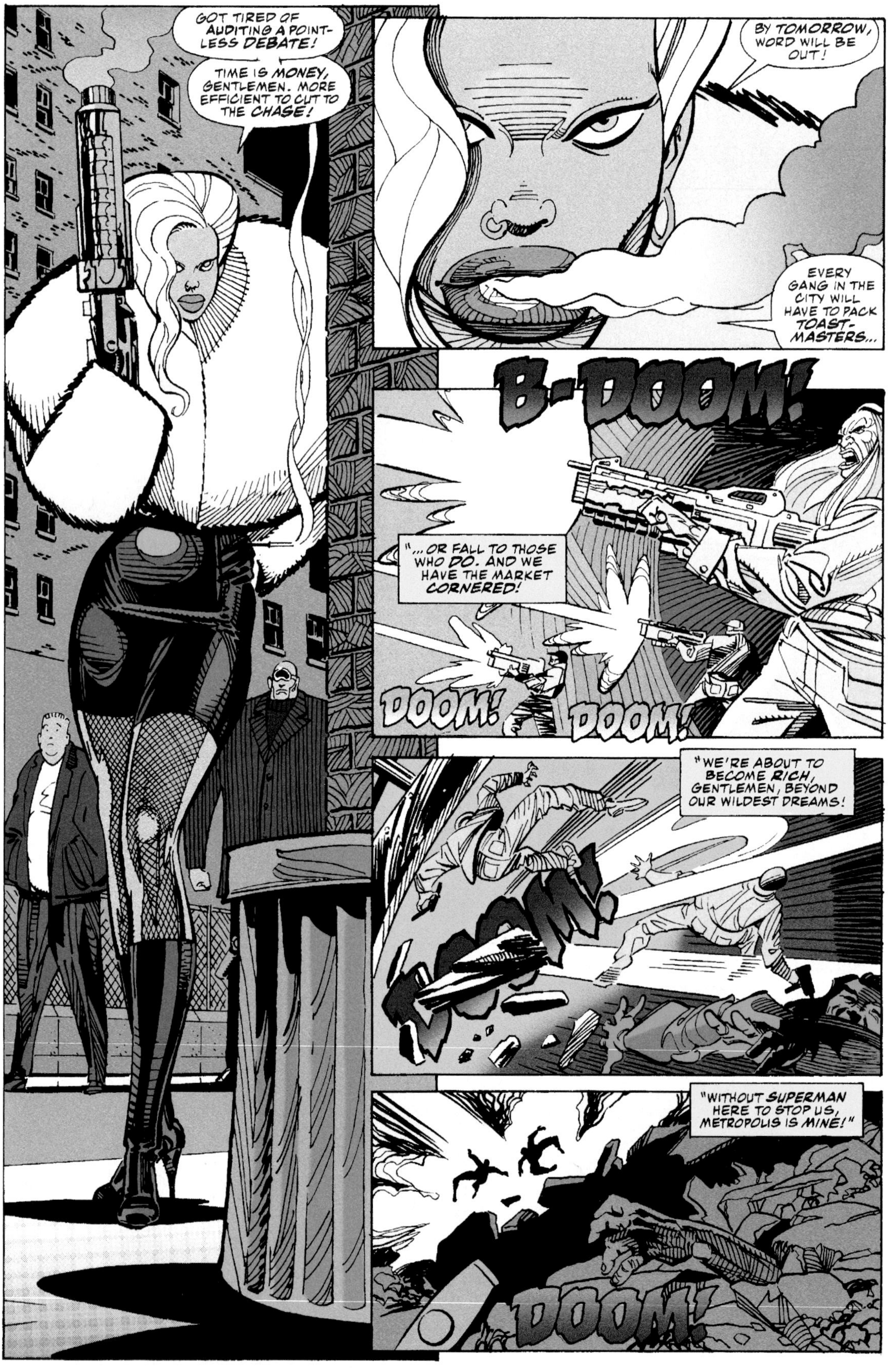
GOT TIRED OF AUDITING A POINTLESS DEBATE!
TIME IS MONEY, GENTLEMEN. MORE EFFICIENT TO CUT TO THE CHASE!
BY TOMORROW, WORD WILL BE OUT!
EVERY GANG IN THE CITY WILL HAVE TO PACK TOASTMASTERS...
B-DOOM!
"...OR FALL TO THOSE WHO DO. AND WE HAVE THE MARKET CORNERED!
DOOM! DOOM!
"WE'RE ABOUT TO BECOME RICH, GENTLEMEN, BEYOND OUR WILDEST DREAMS!
DOOM!
"WITHOUT SUPERMAN HERE TO STOP US, METROPOLIS IS MINE!"
DOOM!

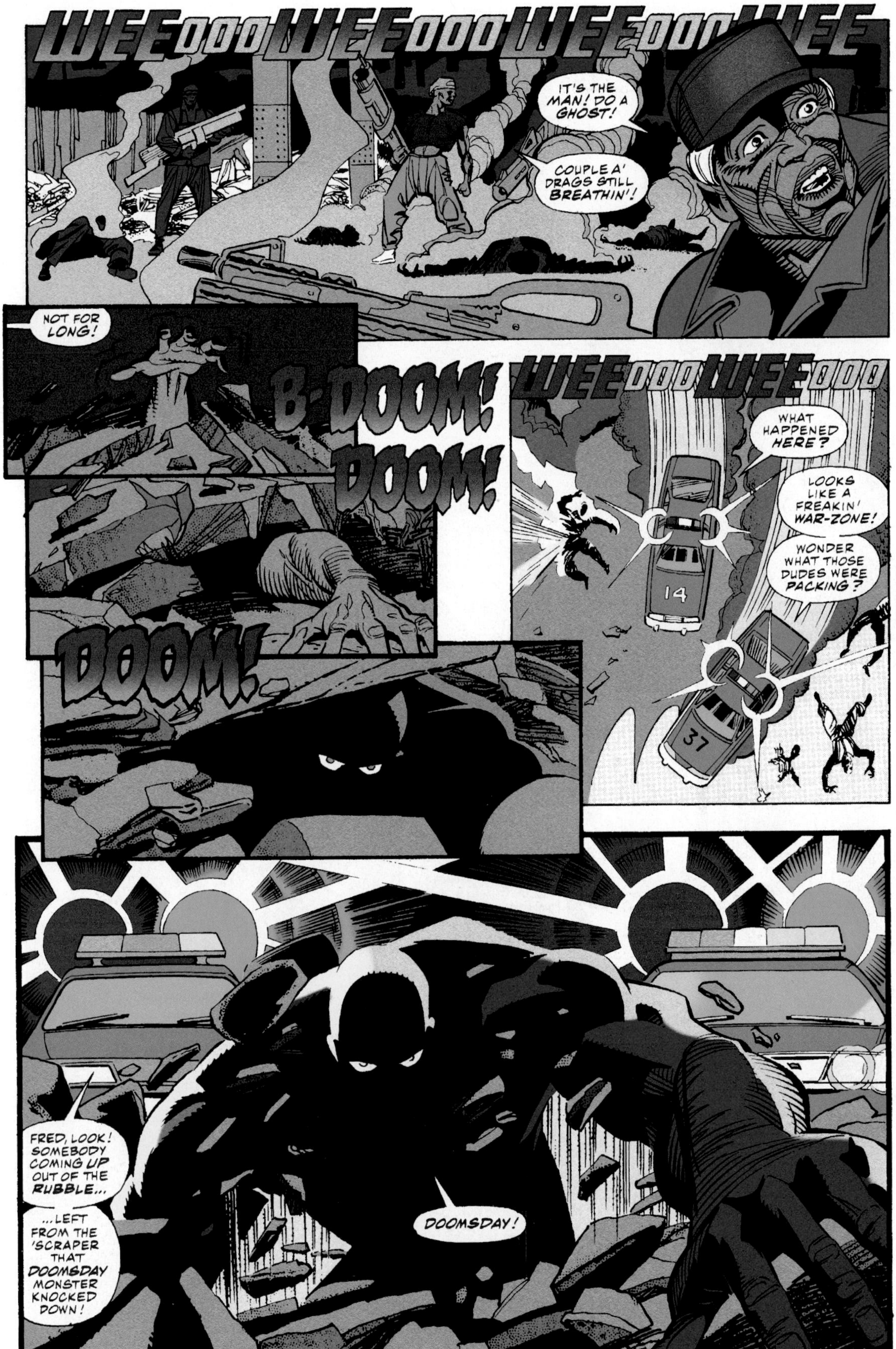
WEEOOOWEEOOOWEEOOOWEE
IT'S THE MAN! DO A GHOST!
COUPLE A' DRAGS STILL BREATHIN'!
NOT FOR LONG!
B-DOOM!
DOOM!
DOOM!
WEEOOOWEEOOO
WHAT HAPPENED HERE?
LOOKS LIKE A FREAKIN' WAR-ZONE!
WONDER WHAT THOSE DUDES WERE PACKING?
14
37
FRED, LOOK! SOMEBODY COMING UP OUT OF THE RUBBLE...
...LEFT FROM THE 'SCRAPER THAT DOOMSDAY MONSTER KNOCKED DOWN!
DOOMSDAY!

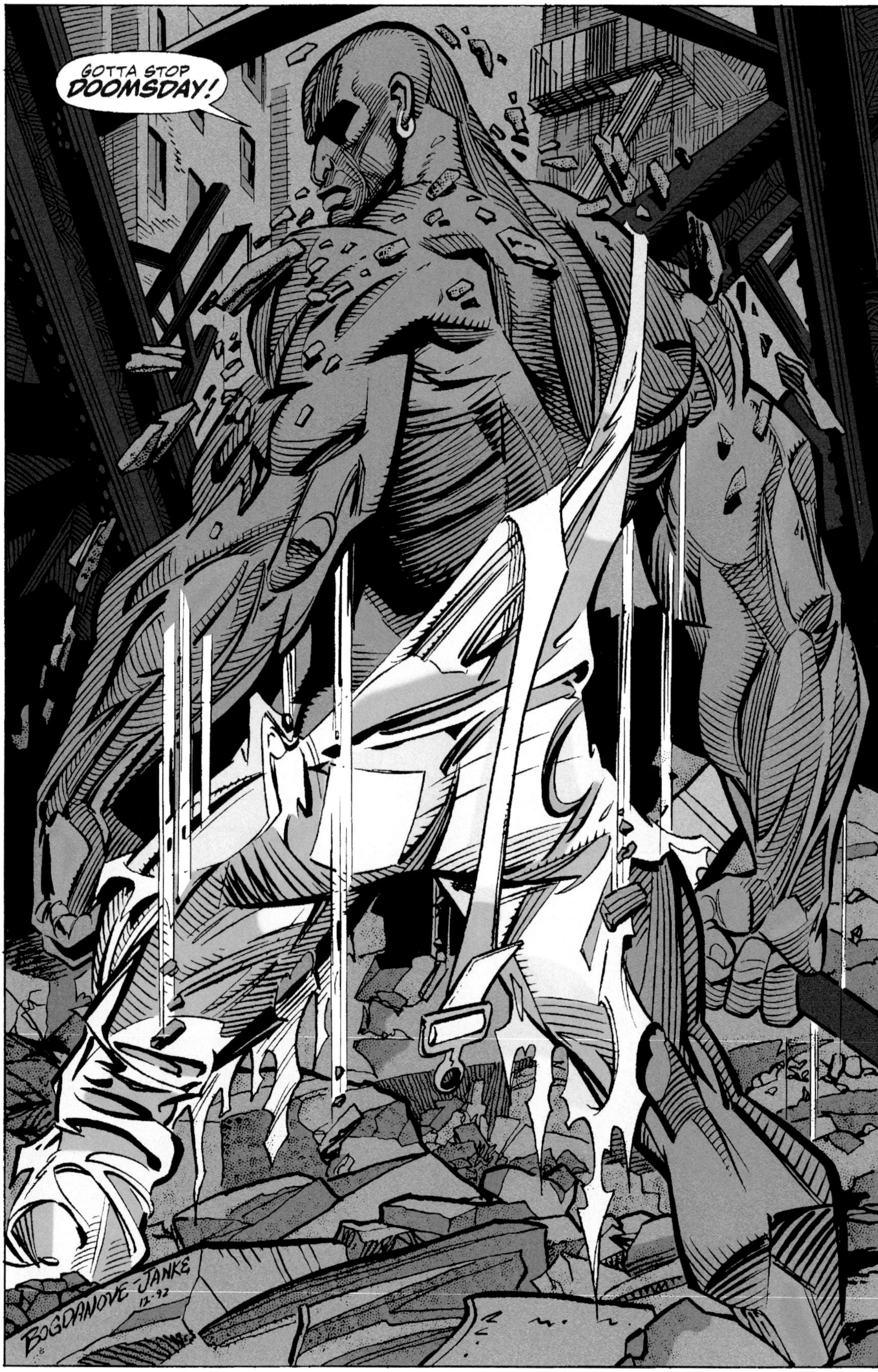
GOTTA STOP DOOMSDAY!
BOGDANOVE-JANKE 12-92

Louise Simonson: writer/Jon Bogdanove: penciller/Dennis Janke: inker

FIRST SIGHTING...

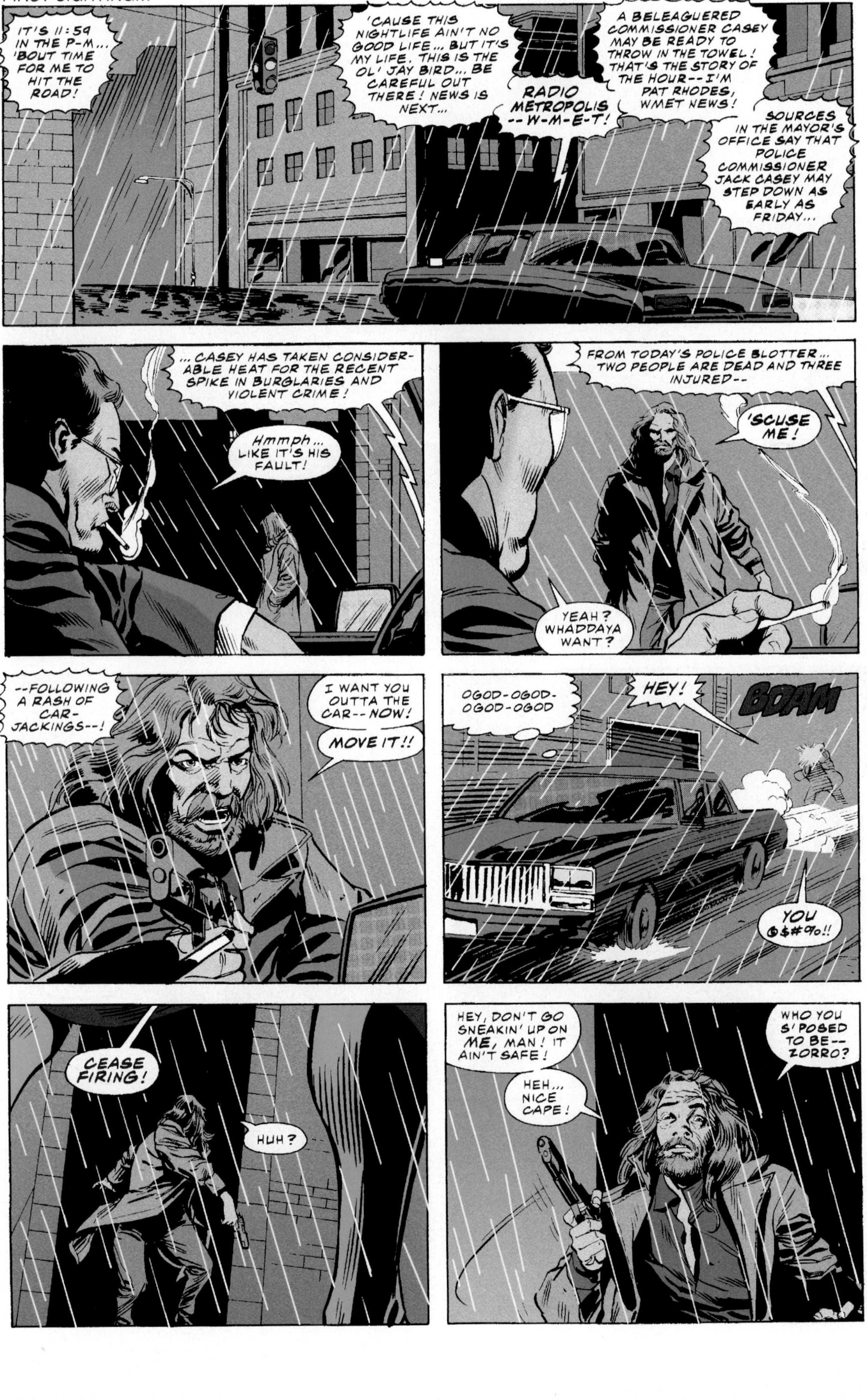

IT'S 11:59 IN THE P-M... 'BOUT TIME FOR ME TO HIT THE ROAD!
'CAUSE THIS NIGHTLIFE AIN'T NO GOOD LIFE... BUT IT'S MY LIFE. THIS IS THE OL' JAY BIRD... BE CAREFUL OUT THERE! NEWS IS NEXT...
RADIO METROPOLIS --W-M-E-T!
A BELEAGUERED COMMISSIONER CASEY MAY BE READY TO THROW IN THE TOWEL! THAT'S THE STORY OF THE HOUR--I'M PAT RHODES, WMET NEWS!
SOURCES IN THE MAYOR'S OFFICE SAY THAT POLICE COMMISSIONER JACK CASEY MAY STEP DOWN AS EARLY AS FRIDAY...
...CASEY HAS TAKEN CONSIDER-ABLE HEAT FOR THE RECENT SPIKE IN BURGLARIES AND VIOLENT CRIME!
Hmmph... LIKE IT'S HIS FAULT!
FROM TODAY'S POLICE BLOTTER... TWO PEOPLE ARE DEAD AND THREE INJURED--
'SCUSE ME!
YEAH? WHADDAYA WANT?
--FOLLOWING A RASH OF CAR-JACKINGS--!
I WANT YOU OUTTA THE CAR--NOW!
MOVE IT!!
OGOD-OGOD-OGOD-OGOD
HEY!
BLAM
YOU @$#%!!
CEASE FIRING!
HUH?
HEY, DON'T GO SNEAKIN' UP ON ME, MAN! IT AIN'T SAFE!
HEH... NICE CAPE!
WHO YOU S'POSED TO BE--ZORRO?

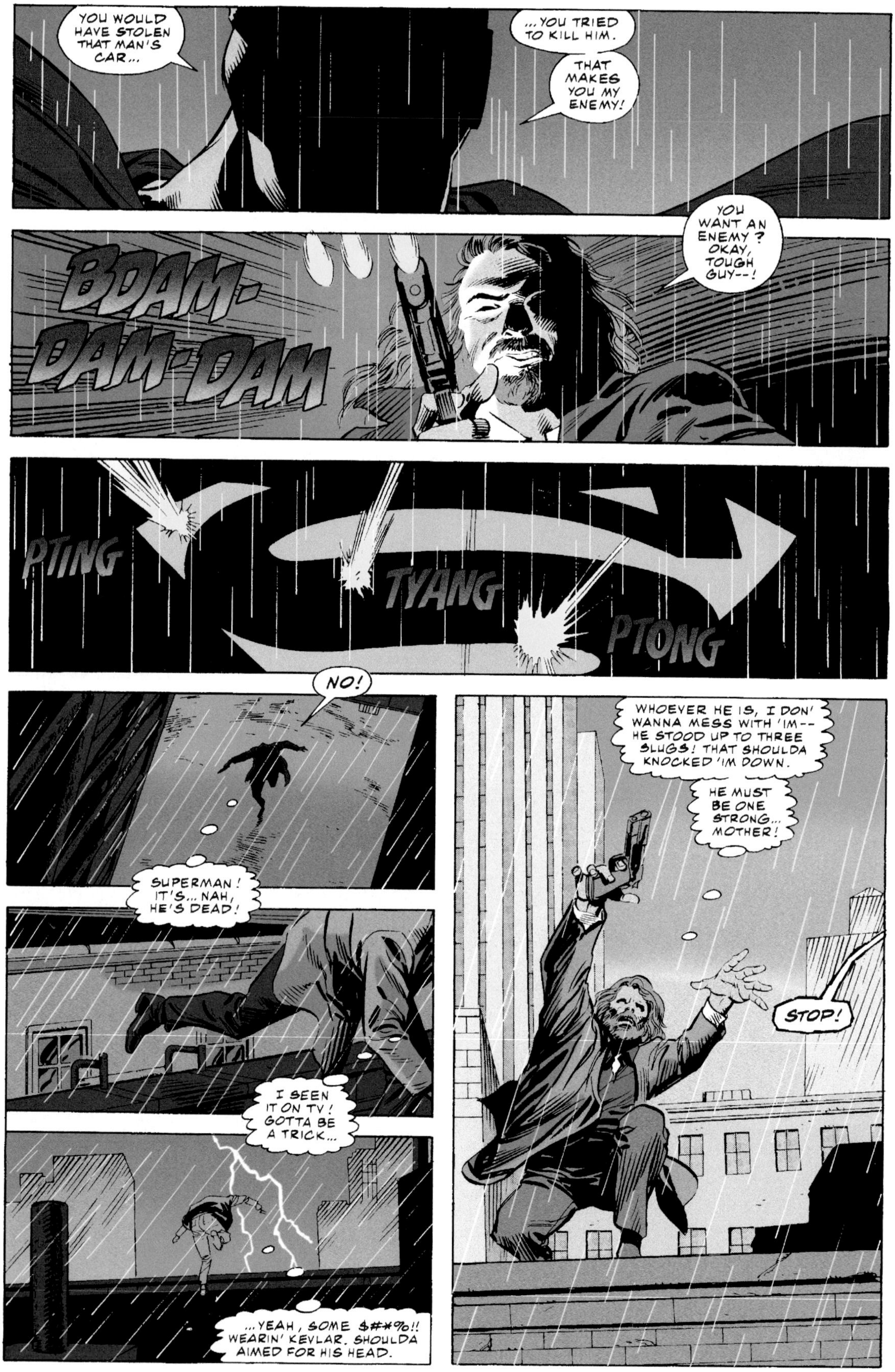
YOU WOULD HAVE STOLEN THAT MAN'S CAR...
...YOU TRIED TO KILL HIM.
THAT MAKES YOU MY ENEMY!
YOU WANT AN ENEMY? OKAY, TOUGH GUY--!
BDAM-DAM-DAM-DAM
PTING
TYANG
PTONG
NO!
SUPERMAN! IT'S... NAH, HE'S DEAD!
I SEEN IT ON TV! GOTTA BE A TRICK...
...YEAH, SOME $#*%!! WEARIN' KEVLAR. SHOULDA AIMED FOR HIS HEAD.
WHOEVER HE IS, I DON' WANNA MESS WITH 'IM-- HE STOOD UP TO THREE SLUGS! THAT SHOULDA KNOCKED 'IM DOWN.
HE MUST BE ONE STRONG... MOTHER!
STOP!

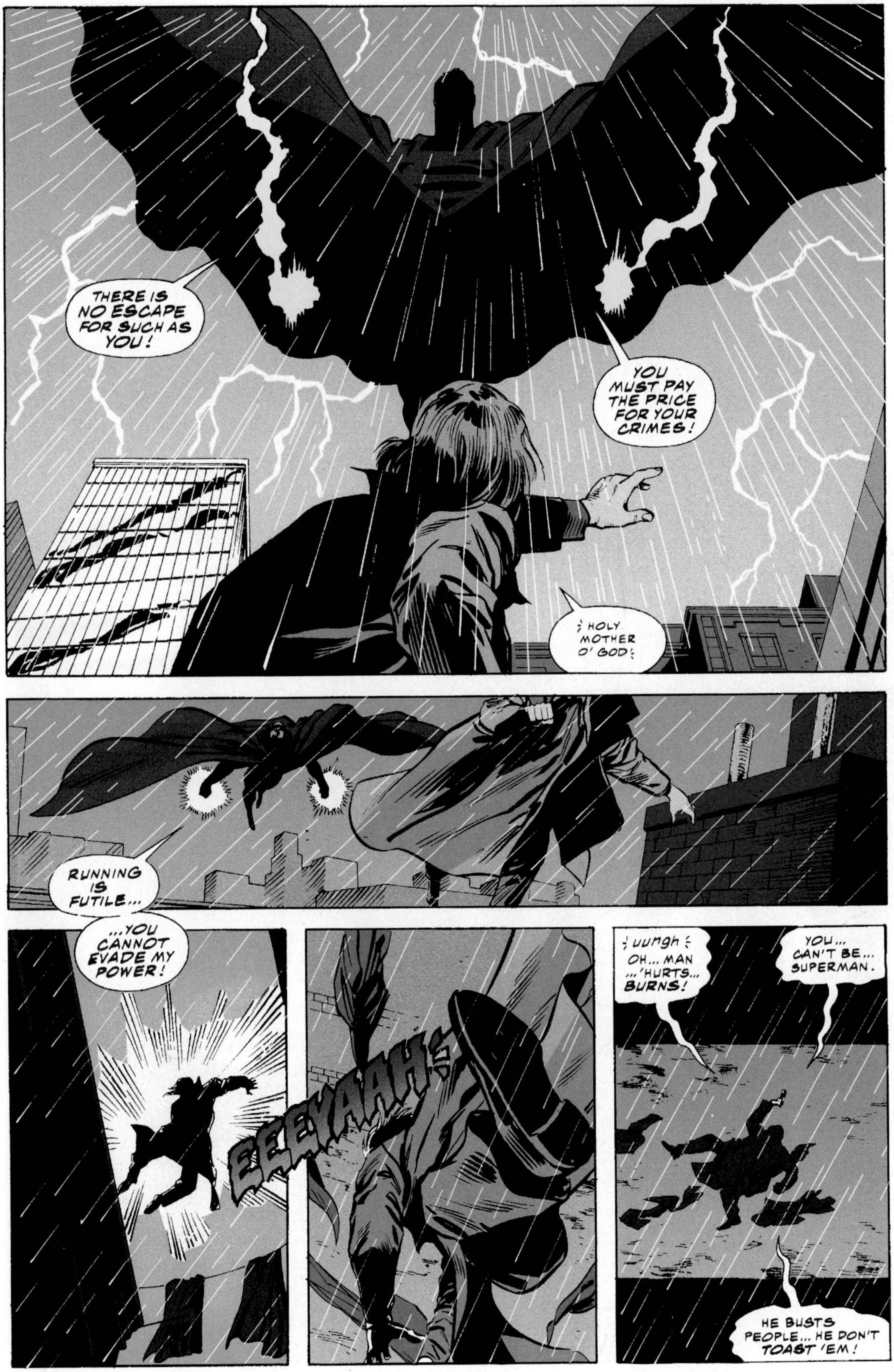
THERE IS NO ESCAPE FOR SUCH AS YOU!
YOU MUST PAY THE PRICE FOR YOUR CRIMES!
¡HOLY MOTHER O' GOD!
RUNNING IS FUTILE...
...YOU CANNOT EVADE MY POWER!
EEEYAAH!
¡uungh! OH... MAN ...'HURTS... BURNS!
YOU... CAN'T BE... SUPERMAN.
HE BUSTS PEOPLE... HE DON'T TOAST 'EM!

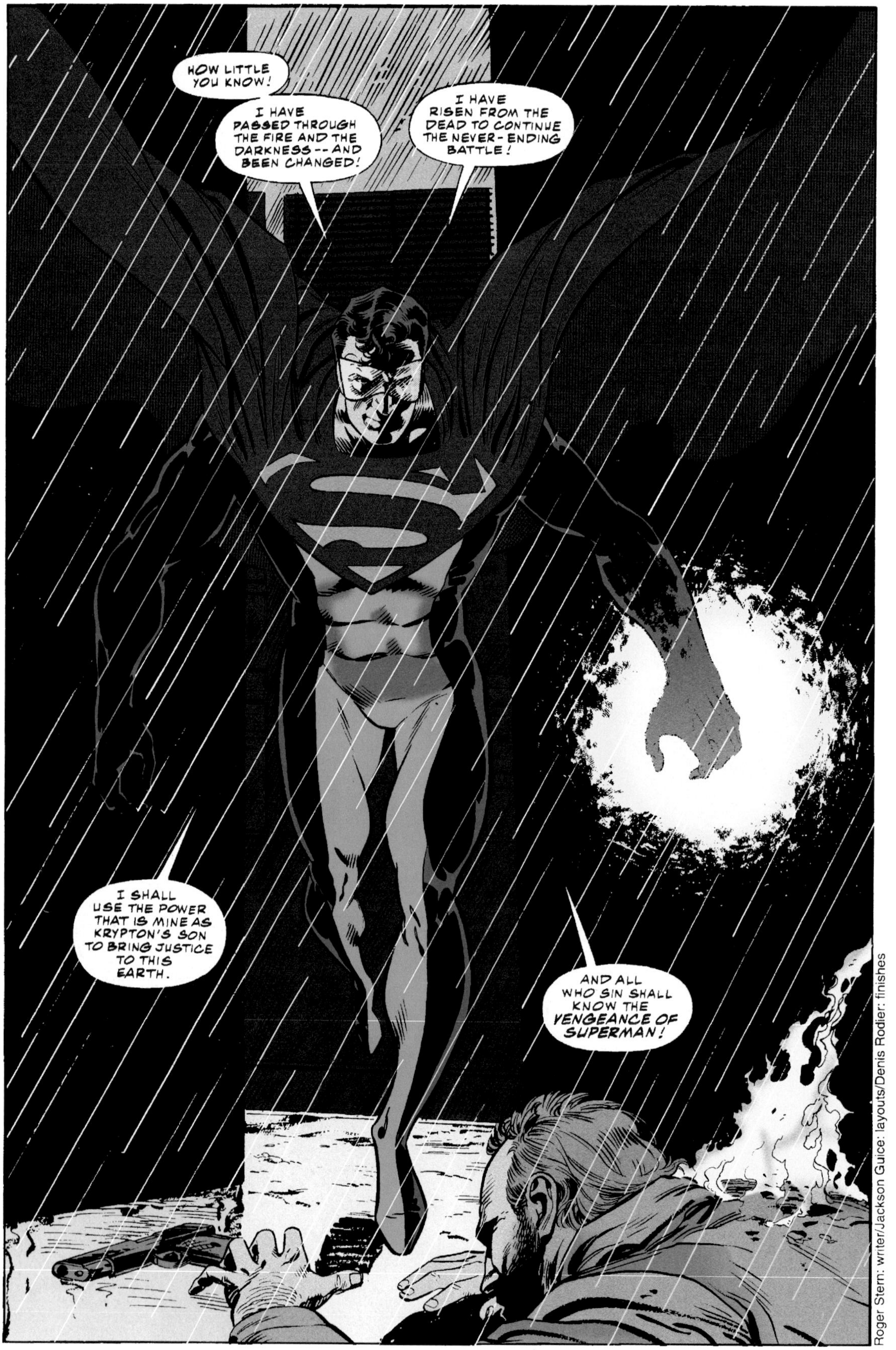
HOW LITTLE YOU KNOW!
I HAVE PASSED THROUGH THE FIRE AND THE DARKNESS -- AND BEEN CHANGED!
I HAVE RISEN FROM THE DEAD TO CONTINUE THE NEVER-ENDING BATTLE!
I SHALL USE THE POWER THAT IS MINE AS KRYPTON'S SON TO BRING JUSTICE TO THIS EARTH.
AND ALL WHO SIN SHALL KNOW THE VENGEANCE OF SUPERMAN!

Roger Stern: writer/Jackson Guice: layouts/Denis Rodier: finishes

FIRST SIGHTING...

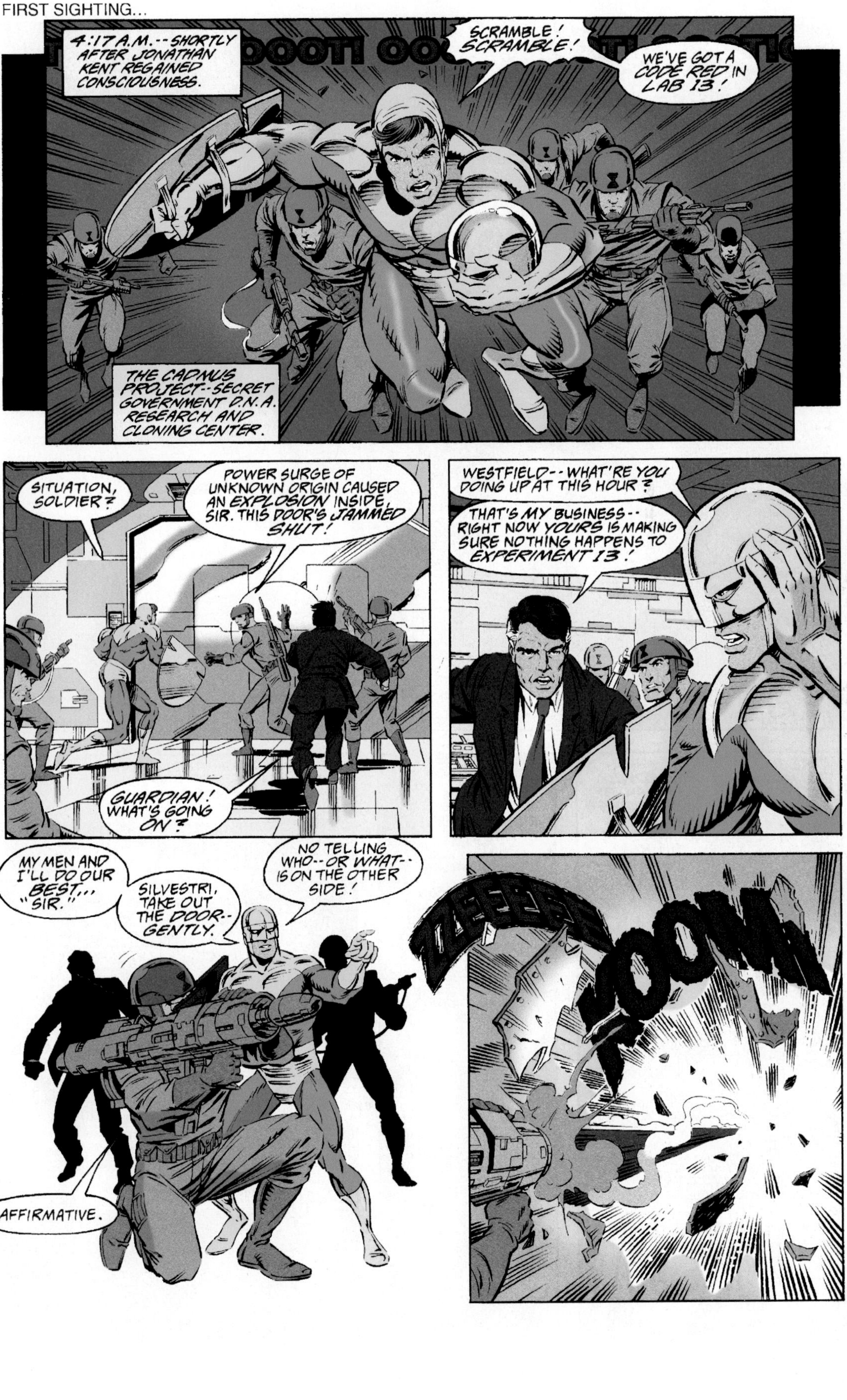

4:17 A.M.--SHORTLY AFTER JONATHAN KENT REGAINED CONSCIOUSNESS.
SCRAMBLE! SCRAMBLE!
WE'VE GOT A CODE RED IN LAB 13!
THE CADMUS PROJECT--SECRET GOVERNMENT D.N.A. RESEARCH AND CLONING CENTER.
SITUATION, SOLDIER?
POWER SURGE OF UNKNOWN ORIGIN CAUSED AN EXPLOSION INSIDE, SIR. THIS DOOR'S JAMMED SHUT!
GUARDIAN! WHAT'S GOING ON?
WESTFIELD--WHAT'RE YOU DOING UP AT THIS HOUR?
THAT'S MY BUSINESS--RIGHT NOW YOURS IS MAKING SURE NOTHING HAPPENS TO EXPERIMENT 13!
MY MEN AND I'LL DO OUR BEST... "SIR."
SILVESTRI, TAKE OUT THE DOOR--GENTLY.
NO TELLING WHO--OR WHAT--IS ON THE OTHER SIDE!
AFFIRMATIVE.

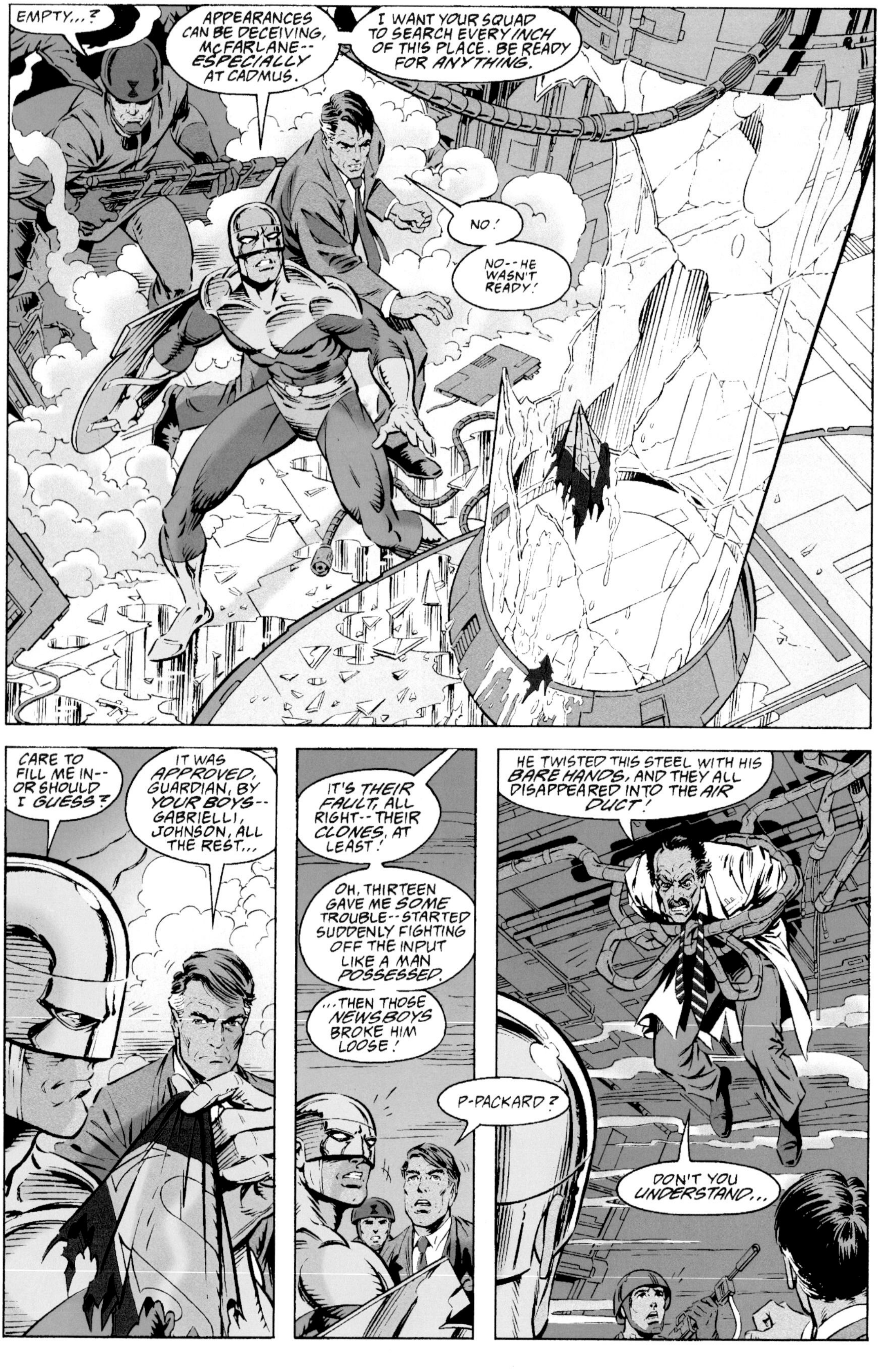
EMPTY...?
APPEARANCES CAN BE DECEIVING, McFARLANE-- ESPECIALLY AT CADMUS.
I WANT YOUR SQUAD TO SEARCH EVERY INCH OF THIS PLACE. BE READY FOR ANYTHING.
NO!
NO--HE WASN'T READY!
CARE TO FILL ME IN-- OR SHOULD I GUESS?
IT WAS APPROVED, GUARDIAN, BY YOUR BOYS-- GABRIELLI, JOHNSON, ALL THE REST...
IT'S THEIR FAULT, ALL RIGHT--THEIR CLONES, AT LEAST!
OH, THIRTEEN GAVE ME SOME TROUBLE--STARTED SUDDENLY FIGHTING OFF THE INPUT LIKE A MAN POSSESSED.
...THEN THOSE NEWSBOYS BROKE HIM LOOSE!
P-PACKARD?
HE TWISTED THIS STEEL WITH HIS BARE HANDS, AND THEY ALL DISAPPEARED INTO THE AIR DUCT!
DON'T YOU UNDERSTAND...

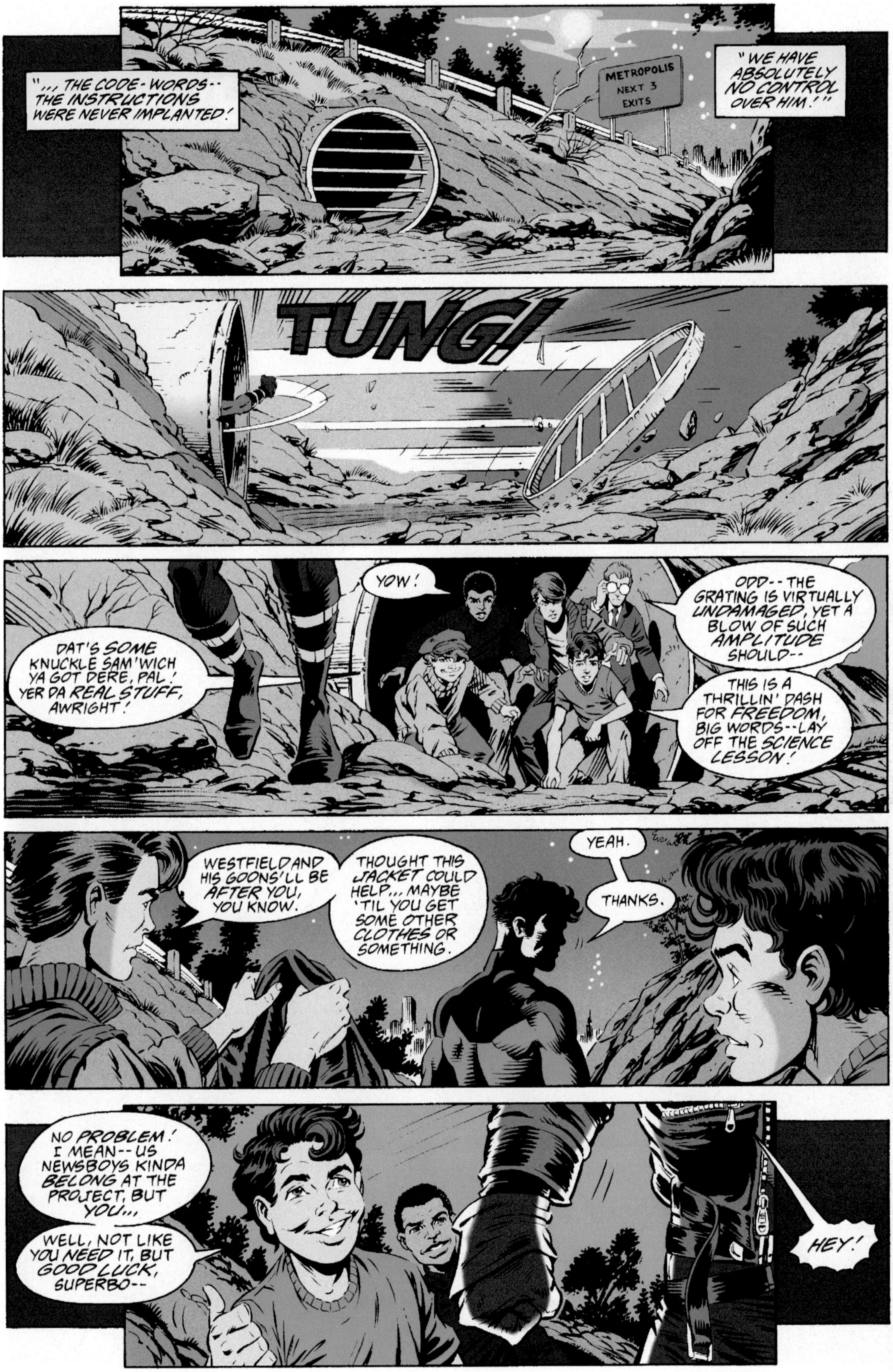
"... THE CODE-WORDS-- THE INSTRUCTIONS WERE NEVER IMPLANTED!
METROPOLIS NEXT 3 EXITS
"WE HAVE ABSOLUTELY NO CONTROL OVER HIM!"
TUNG!
YOW!
DAT'S SOME KNUCKLE SAM'WICH YA GOT DERE, PAL! YER DA REAL STUFF, AWRIGHT!
ODD--THE GRATING IS VIRTUALLY UNDAMAGED, YET A BLOW OF SUCH AMPLITUDE SHOULD--
THIS IS A THRILLIN' DASH FOR FREEDOM, BIG WORDS--LAY OFF THE SCIENCE LESSON!
WESTFIELD AND HIS GOONS'LL BE AFTER YOU, YOU KNOW.
THOUGHT THIS JACKET COULD HELP... MAYBE 'TIL YOU GET SOME OTHER CLOTHES OR SOMETHING.
YEAH.
THANKS.
NO PROBLEM! I MEAN--US NEWSBOYS KINDA BELONG AT THE PROJECT, BUT YOU...
WELL, NOT LIKE YOU NEED IT, BUT GOOD LUCK, SUPERBO--
HEY!

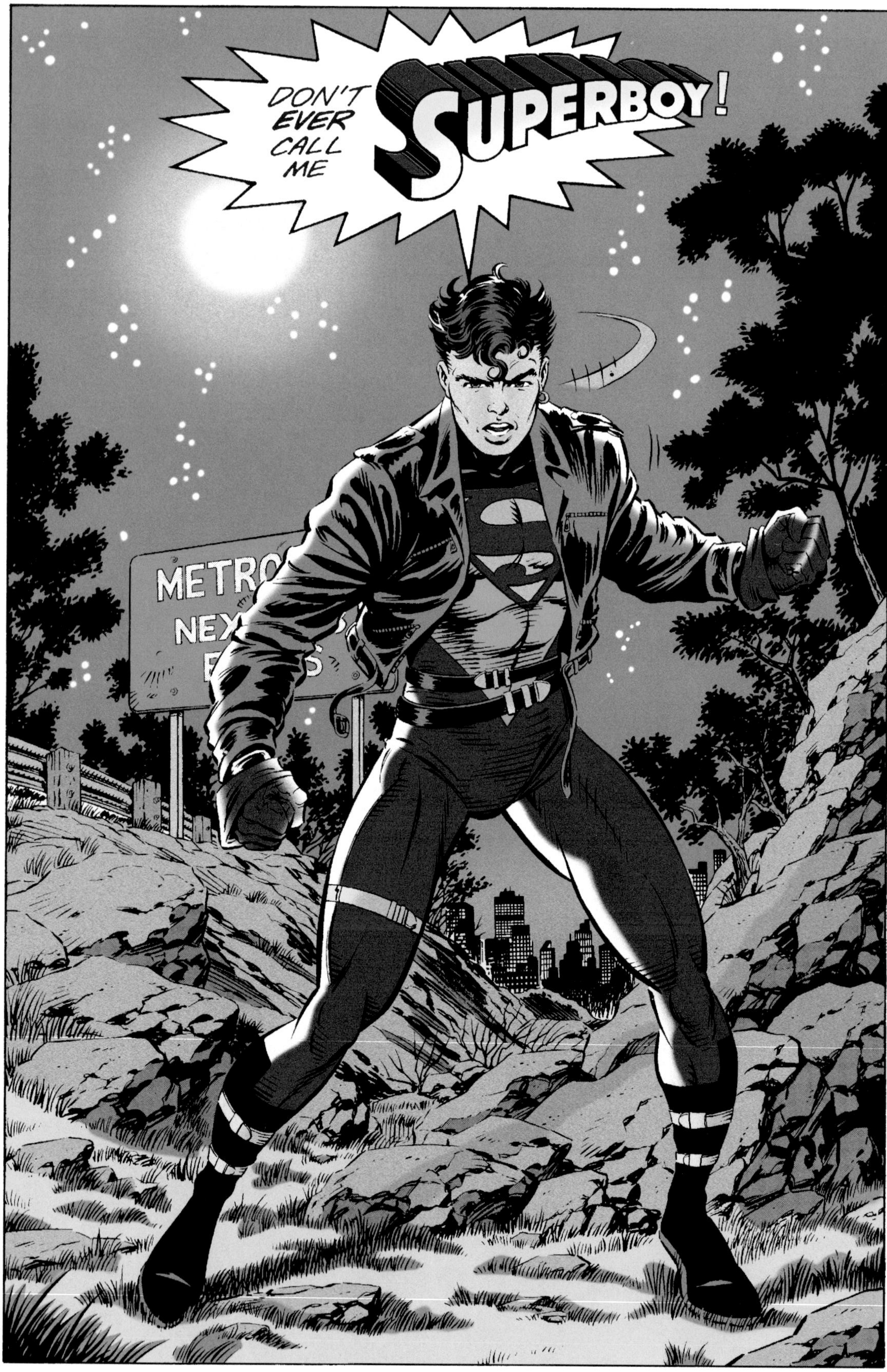
DON'T EVER CALL ME SUPERBOY!

Karl Kesel: writer/Tom Grummett: penciller/Doug Hazlewood: inker

FIRST SIGHTING...

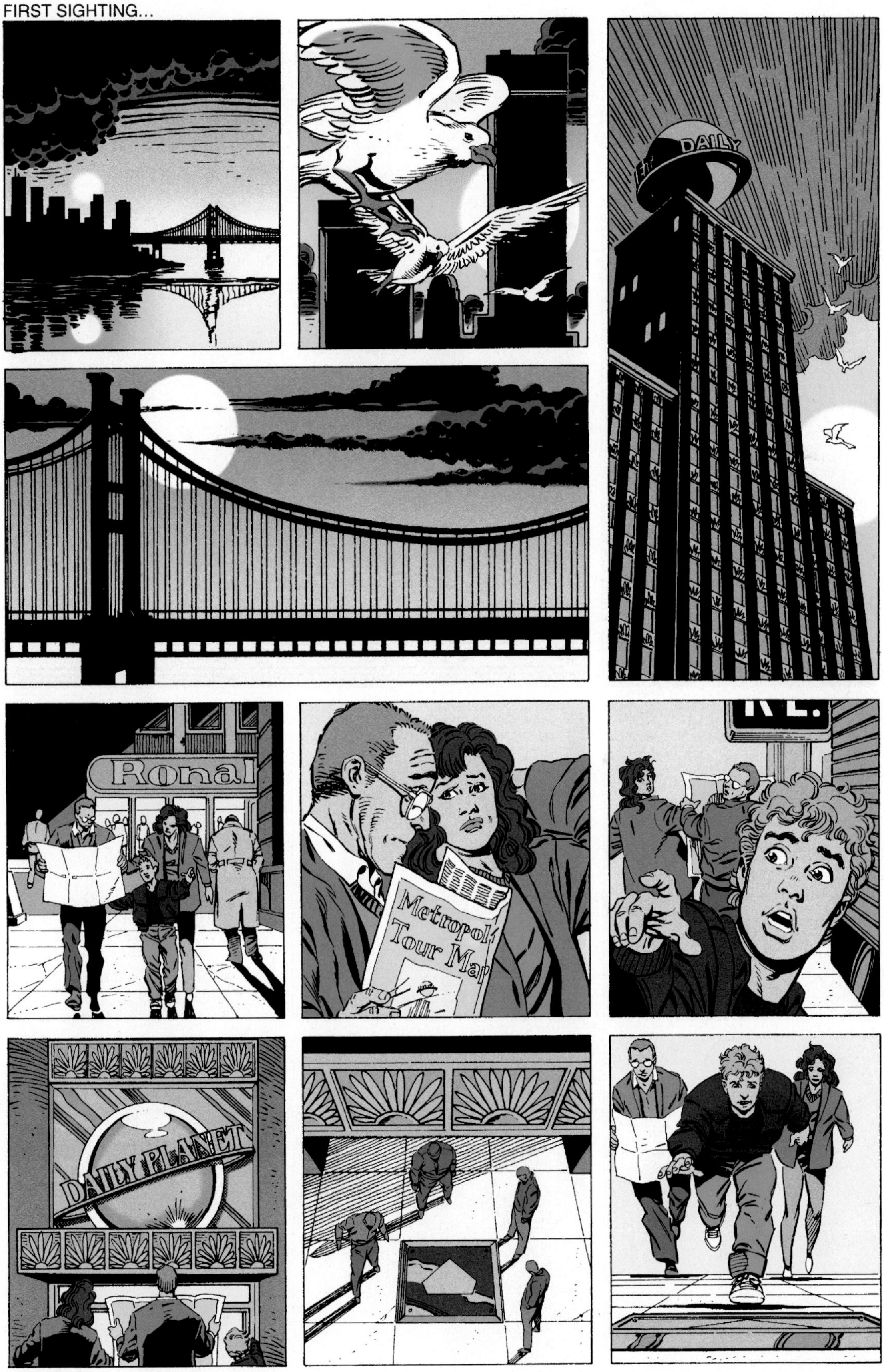
DAILY
Tour Map
DAILY PLANET

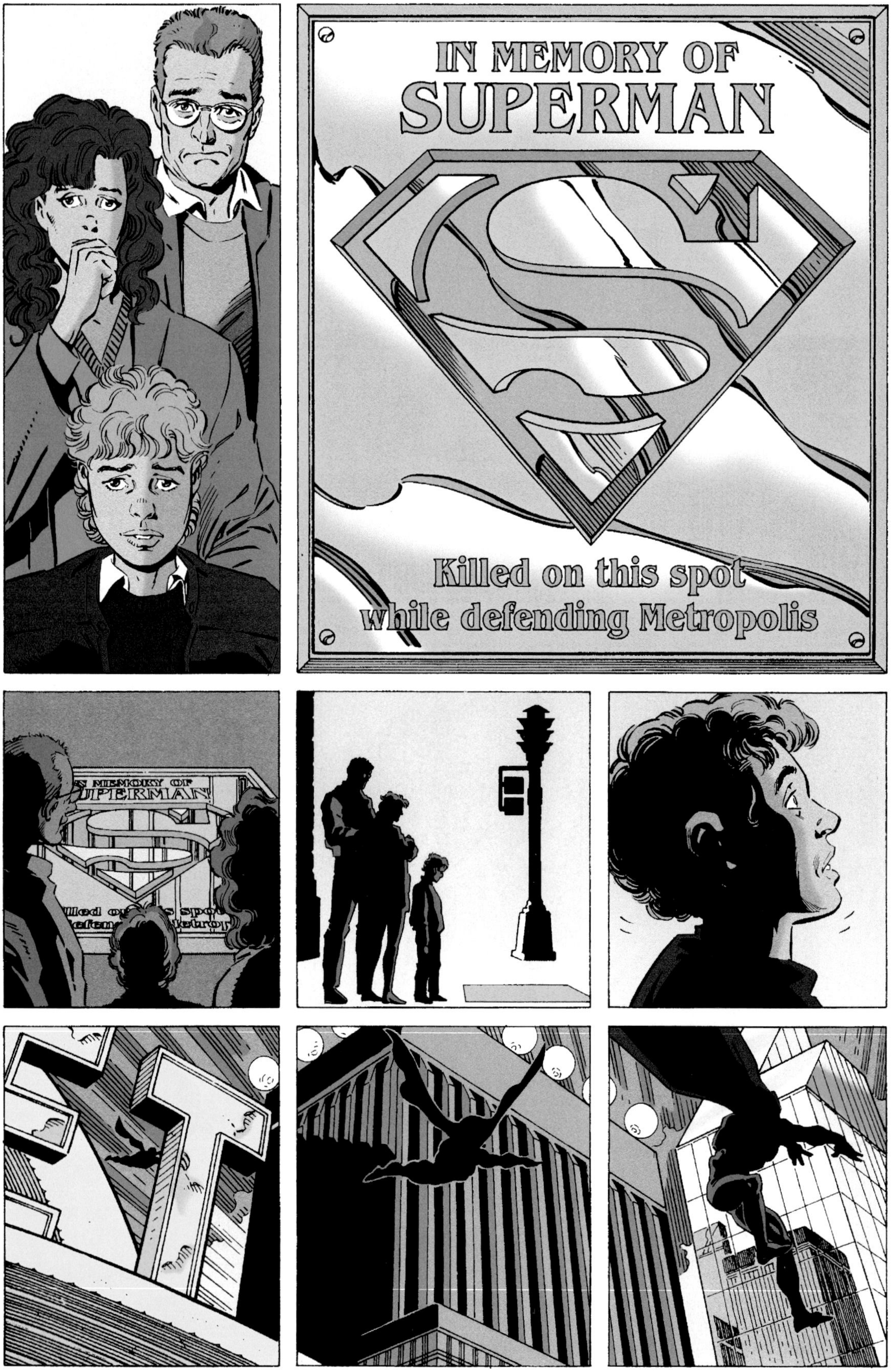
IN MEMORY OF
SUPERMAN
Killed on this spot
while defending Metropolis

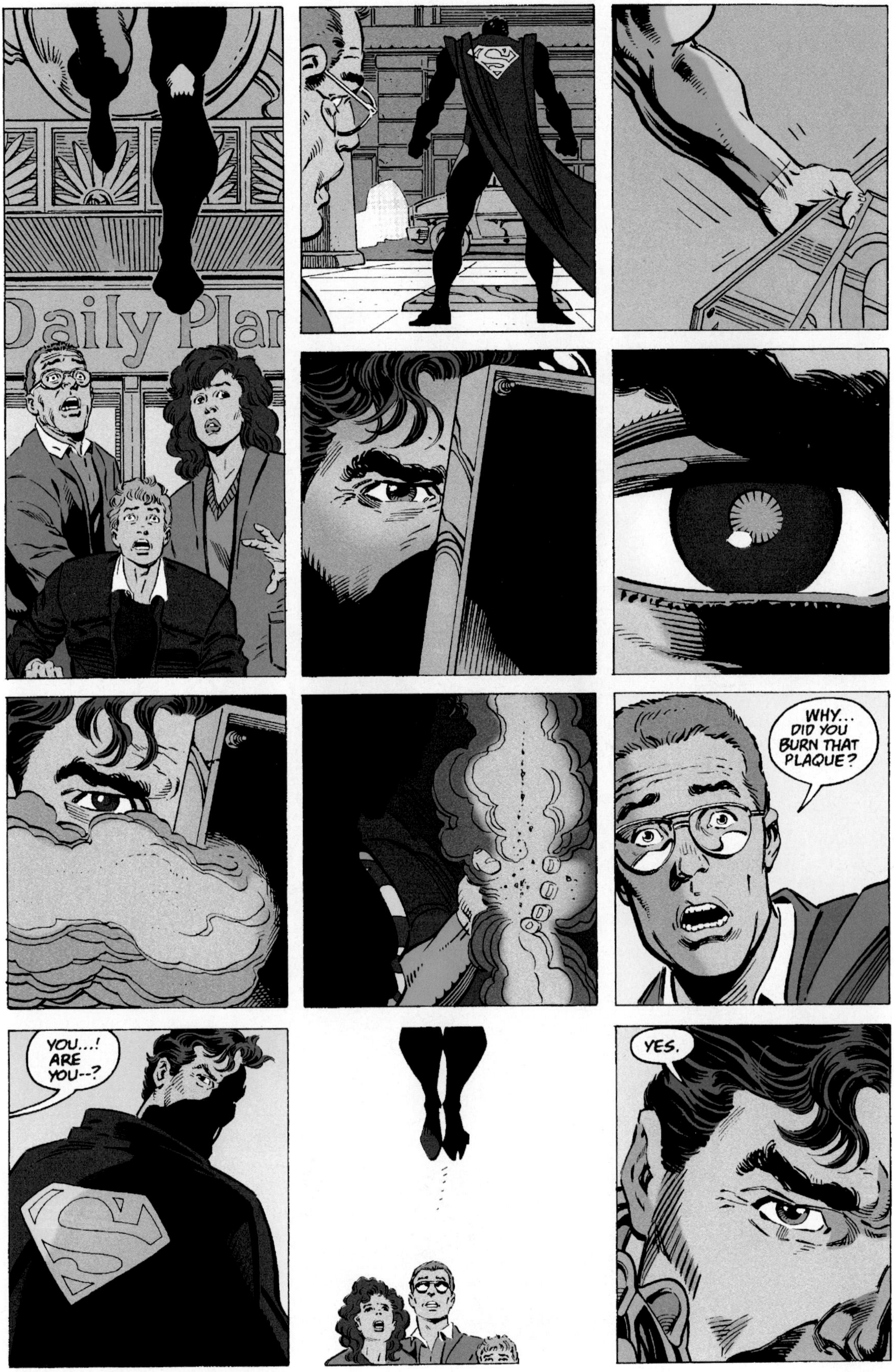
Daily Plan
WHY... DID YOU BURN THAT PLAQUE?
YOU...! ARE YOU--?
YES.

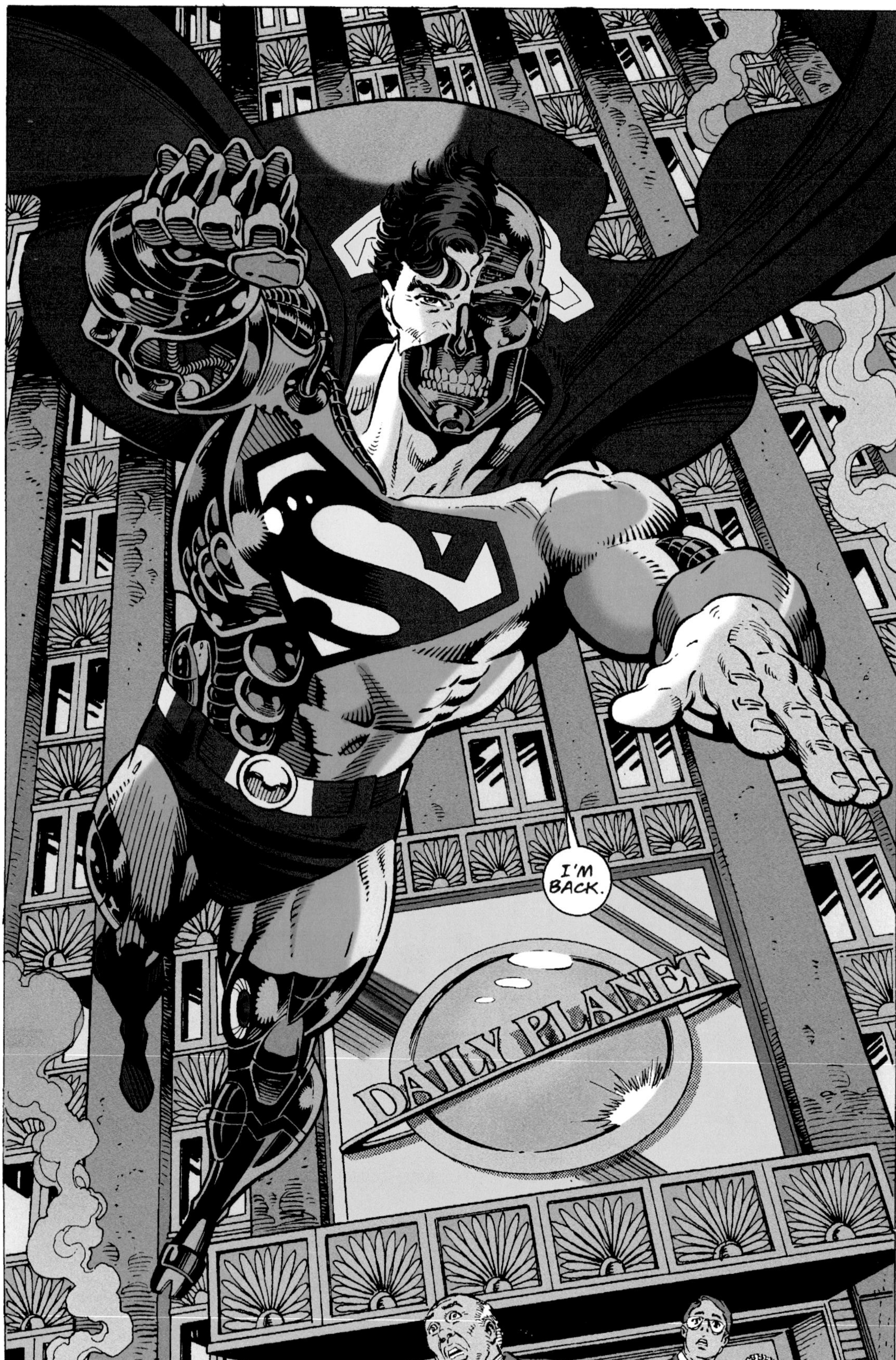
I'M BACK.
DAILY PLANET

Dan Jurgens: writer/Dan Jurgens: layouts/Brett Breeding: finishes

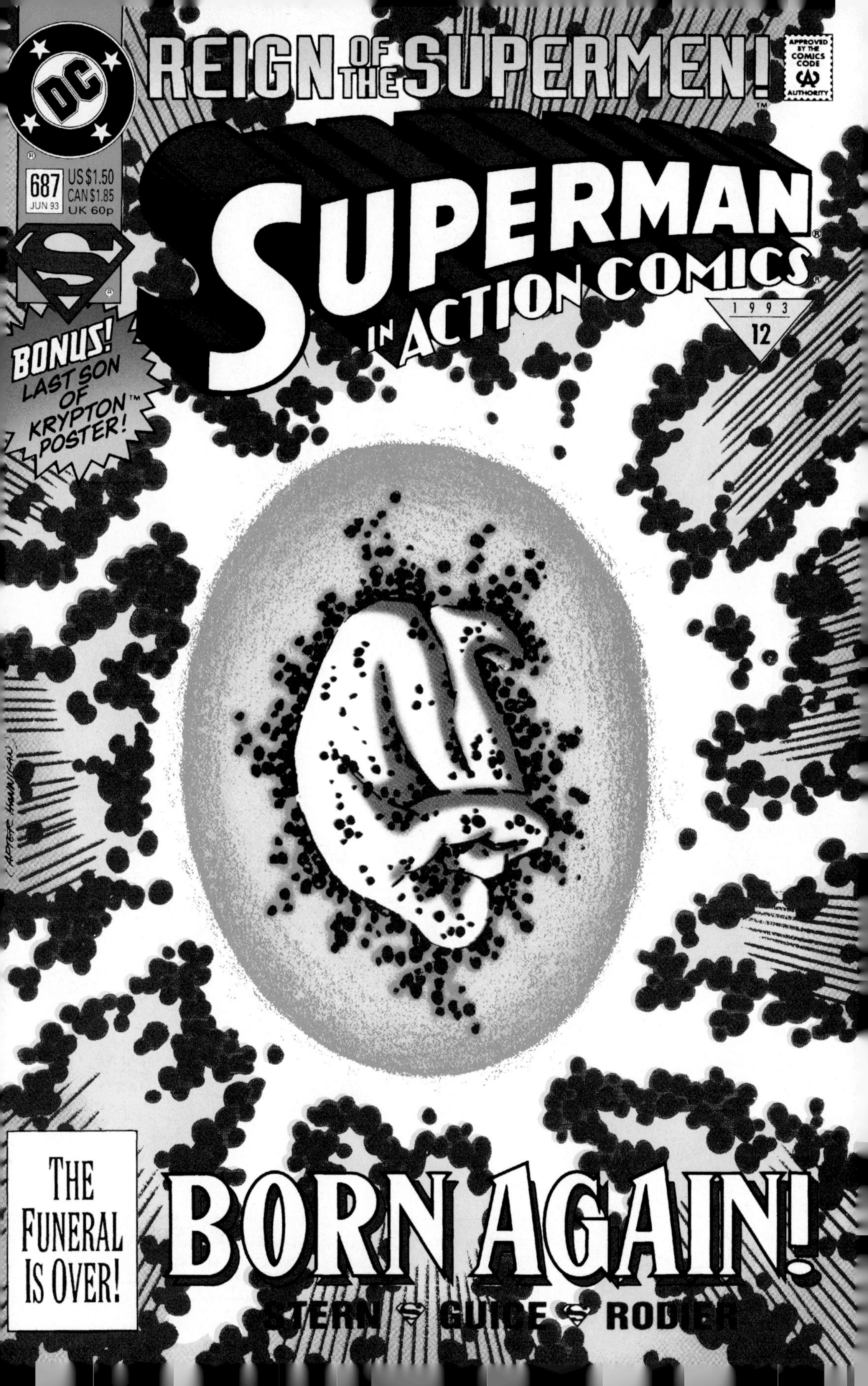
DC
REIGN OF THE SUPERMEN!
APPROVED BY THE COMICS CODE AUTHORITY
687 JUN 93
US $1.50 CAN $1.85 UK 60p
SUPERMAN IN ACTION COMICS
1993 12
BONUS! LAST SON OF KRYPTON™ POSTER!
THE FUNERAL IS OVER!
BORN AGAIN!
STERN GUICE RODIER

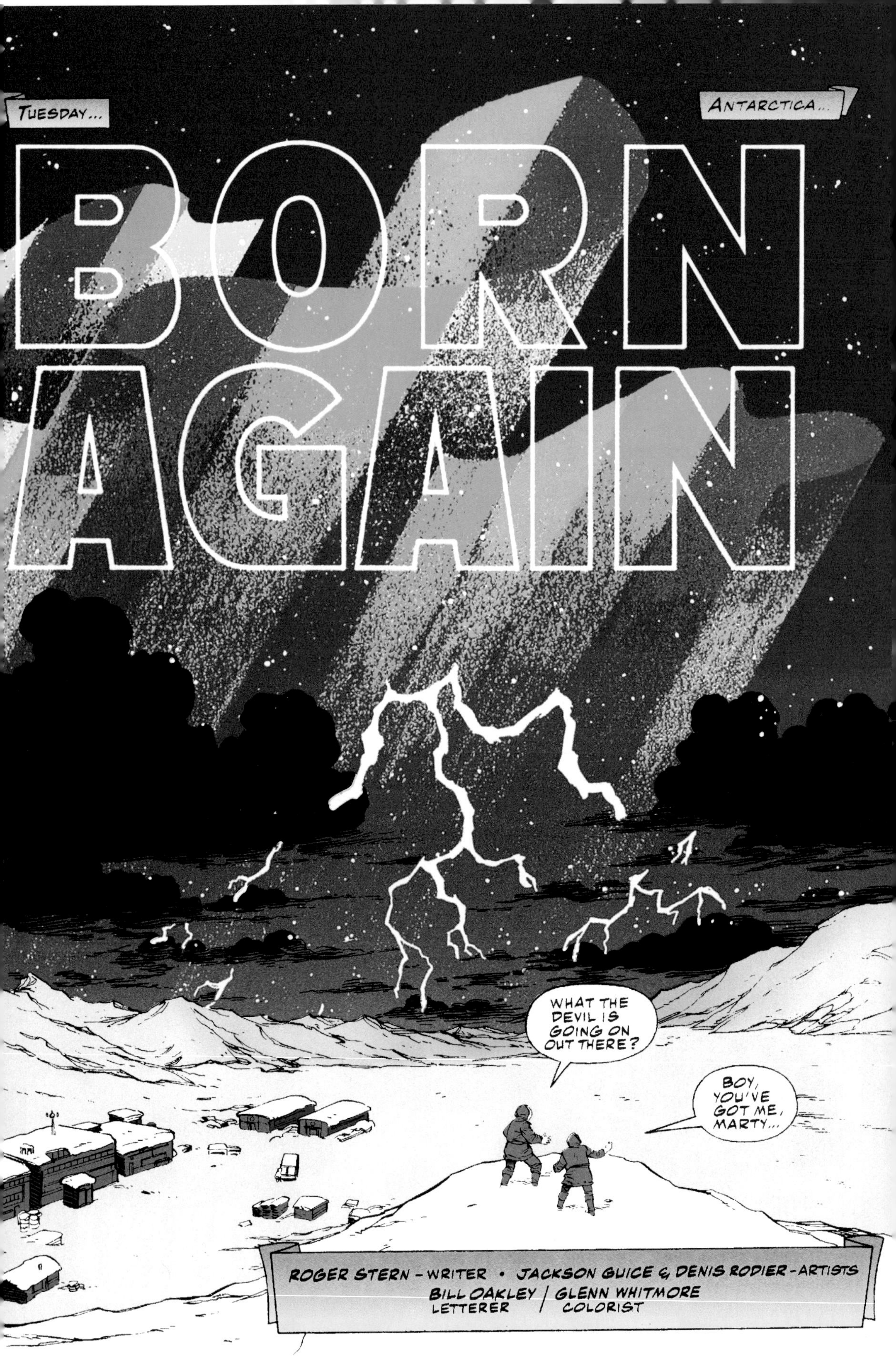
TUESDAY...
ANTARCTICA...
BORN AGAIN
WHAT THE DEVIL IS GOING ON OUT THERE?
BOY, YOU'VE GOT ME, MARTY...
ROGER STERN - WRITER • JACKSON GUICE & DENIS RODIER - ARTISTS
BILL OAKLEY LETTERER / GLENN WHITMORE COLORIST

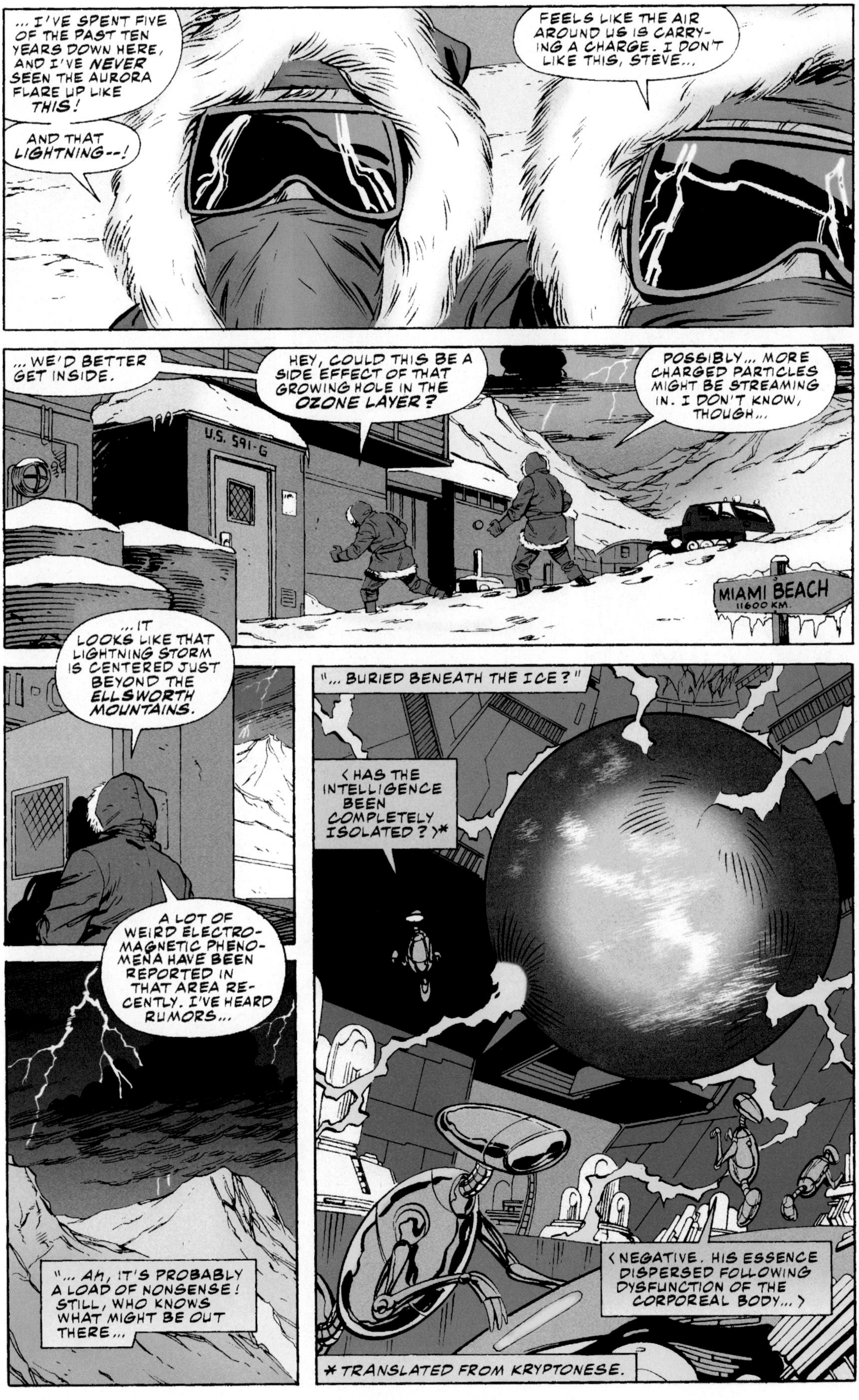

... I'VE SPENT FIVE OF THE PAST TEN YEARS DOWN HERE, AND I'VE NEVER SEEN THE AURORA FLARE UP LIKE THIS!
AND THAT LIGHTNING--!
FEELS LIKE THE AIR AROUND US IS CARRYING A CHARGE. I DON'T LIKE THIS, STEVE...
... WE'D BETTER GET INSIDE.
HEY, COULD THIS BE A SIDE EFFECT OF THAT GROWING HOLE IN THE OZONE LAYER?
POSSIBLY... MORE CHARGED PARTICLES MIGHT BE STREAMING IN. I DON'T KNOW, THOUGH...
U.S. 591-G
MIAMI BEACH
11600 KM.
... IT LOOKS LIKE THAT LIGHTNING STORM IS CENTERED JUST BEYOND THE ELLSWORTH MOUNTAINS.
A LOT OF WEIRD ELECTROMAGNETIC PHENOMENA HAVE BEEN REPORTED IN THAT AREA RECENTLY. I'VE HEARD RUMORS...
"... AH, IT'S PROBABLY A LOAD OF NONSENSE! STILL, WHO KNOWS WHAT MIGHT BE OUT THERE...
"... BURIED BENEATH THE ICE?"
< HAS THE INTELLIGENCE BEEN COMPLETELY ISOLATED? >*
< NEGATIVE. HIS ESSENCE DISPERSED FOLLOWING DYSFUNCTION OF THE CORPOREAL BODY... >
* TRANSLATED FROM KRYPTONESE.

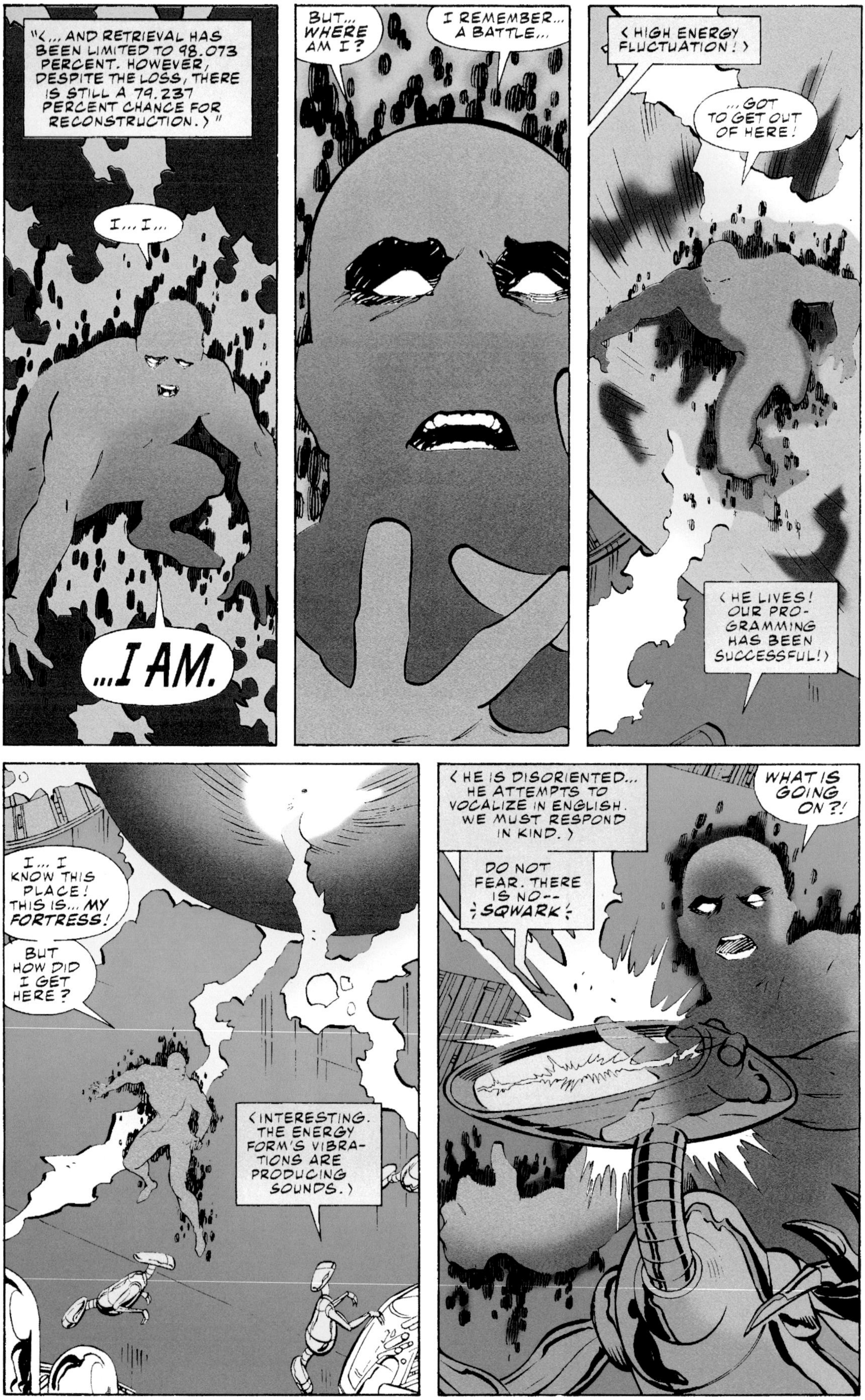
"<... AND RETRIEVAL HAS BEEN LIMITED TO 98.073 PERCENT. HOWEVER, DESPITE THE LOSS, THERE IS STILL A 79.237 PERCENT CHANCE FOR RECONSTRUCTION.>"
I... I...
...I AM.
BUT... WHERE AM I?
I REMEMBER... A BATTLE...
<HIGH ENERGY FLUCTUATION!>
...GOT TO GET OUT OF HERE!
<HE LIVES! OUR PROGRAMMING HAS BEEN SUCCESSFUL!>
I... I KNOW THIS PLACE! THIS IS... MY FORTRESS!
BUT HOW DID I GET HERE?
<INTERESTING. THE ENERGY FORM'S VIBRATIONS ARE PRODUCING SOUNDS.>
<HE IS DISORIENTED... HE ATTEMPTS TO VOCALIZE IN ENGLISH. WE MUST RESPOND IN KIND.>
WHAT IS GOING ON?!
DO NOT FEAR. THERE IS NO-- SQWARK

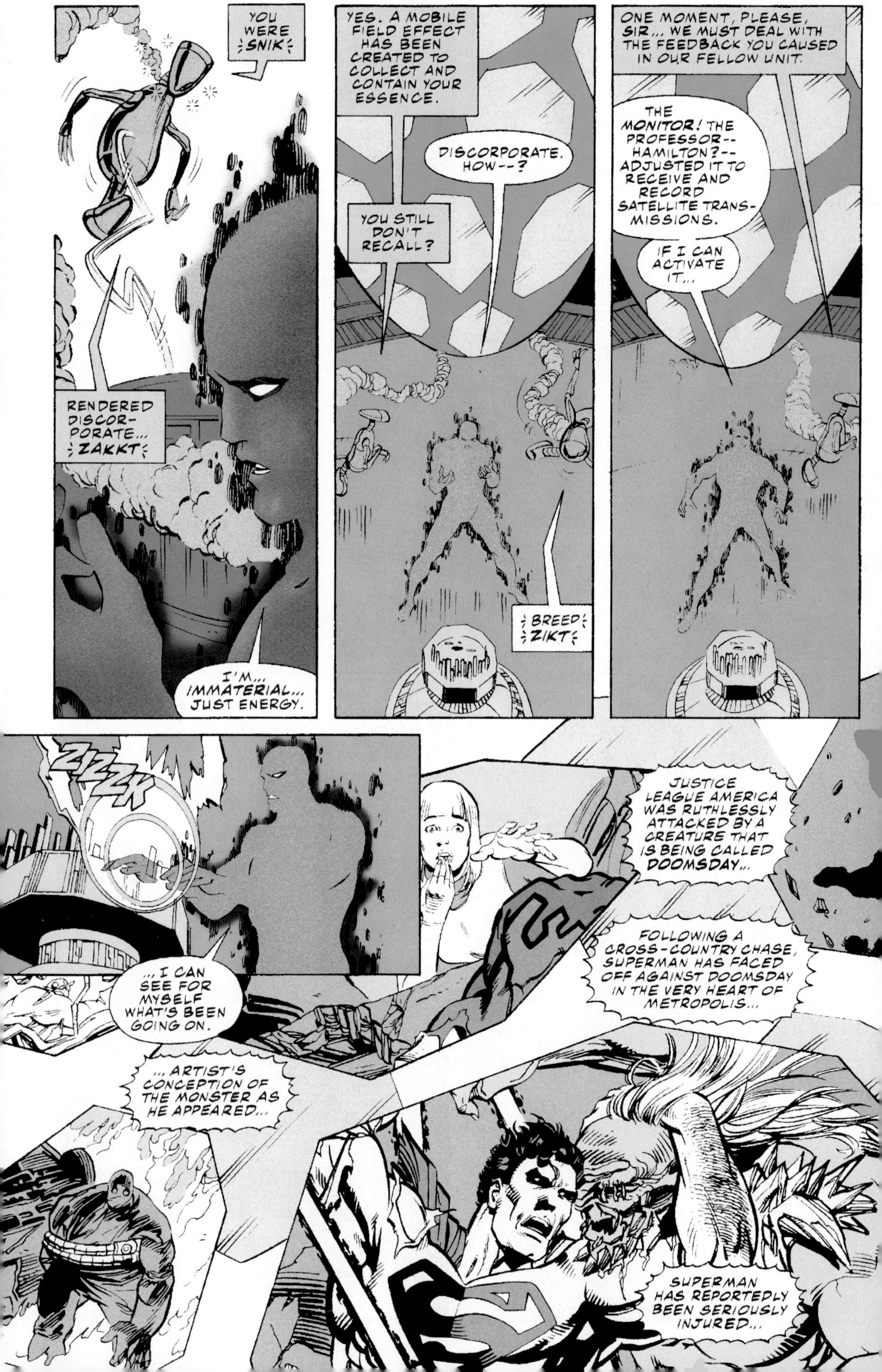
YOU WERE SNIK
RENDERED DISCOR-PORATE... ZAKKT
I'M... IMMATERIAL... JUST ENERGY.
YES. A MOBILE FIELD EFFECT HAS BEEN CREATED TO COLLECT AND CONTAIN YOUR ESSENCE.
DISCORPORATE. HOW--?
YOU STILL DON'T RECALL?
BREED ZIKT
ONE MOMENT, PLEASE, SIR... WE MUST DEAL WITH THE FEEDBACK YOU CAUSED IN OUR FELLOW UNIT.
THE MONITOR! THE PROFESSOR-- HAMILTON?-- ADJUSTED IT TO RECEIVE AND RECORD SATELLITE TRANS-MISSIONS.
IF I CAN ACTIVATE IT...
ZZZK
...I CAN SEE FOR MYSELF WHAT'S BEEN GOING ON.
JUSTICE LEAGUE AMERICA WAS RUTHLESSLY ATTACKED BY A CREATURE THAT IS BEING CALLED DOOMSDAY...
FOLLOWING A CROSS-COUNTRY CHASE, SUPERMAN HAS FACED OFF AGAINST DOOMSDAY IN THE VERY HEART OF METROPOLIS...
...ARTIST'S CONCEPTION OF THE MONSTER AS HE APPEARED...
SUPERMAN HAS REPORTEDLY BEEN SERIOUSLY INJURED...

...SUPERMAN WAS DECLARED DEAD AT APPROXIMATELY 6:23 P.M.

...THE SOLEMN DRUM BEAT AS THE WORLD'S GREAT HEROES MARCH ALONG IN TRIBUTE, FOLLOWING THEIR GALLANT LEADER ONE LAST TIME.

DEAD?

THE WORLD WILL LONG REMEMBER THIS GREAT MAN, WHO SACRIFICED HIS OWN LIFE TO END THE THREAT OF DOOMSDAY... GOD BLESS HIM.

DEAD.

MOURNERS CONTINUE TO VISIT HIS TOMB IN METROPOLIS'S CENTENNIAL PARK, LEAVING TRIBUTES TO THIS LAST SON OF KRYPTON WHO GREW UP TO BECOME THE MOST AMERICAN OF HEROES...

NO! IT CAN'T END THIS WAY!

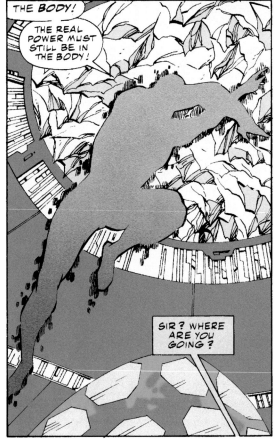

THE BODY! THE REAL POWER MUST STILL BE IN THE BODY!

SIR? WHERE ARE YOU GOING?

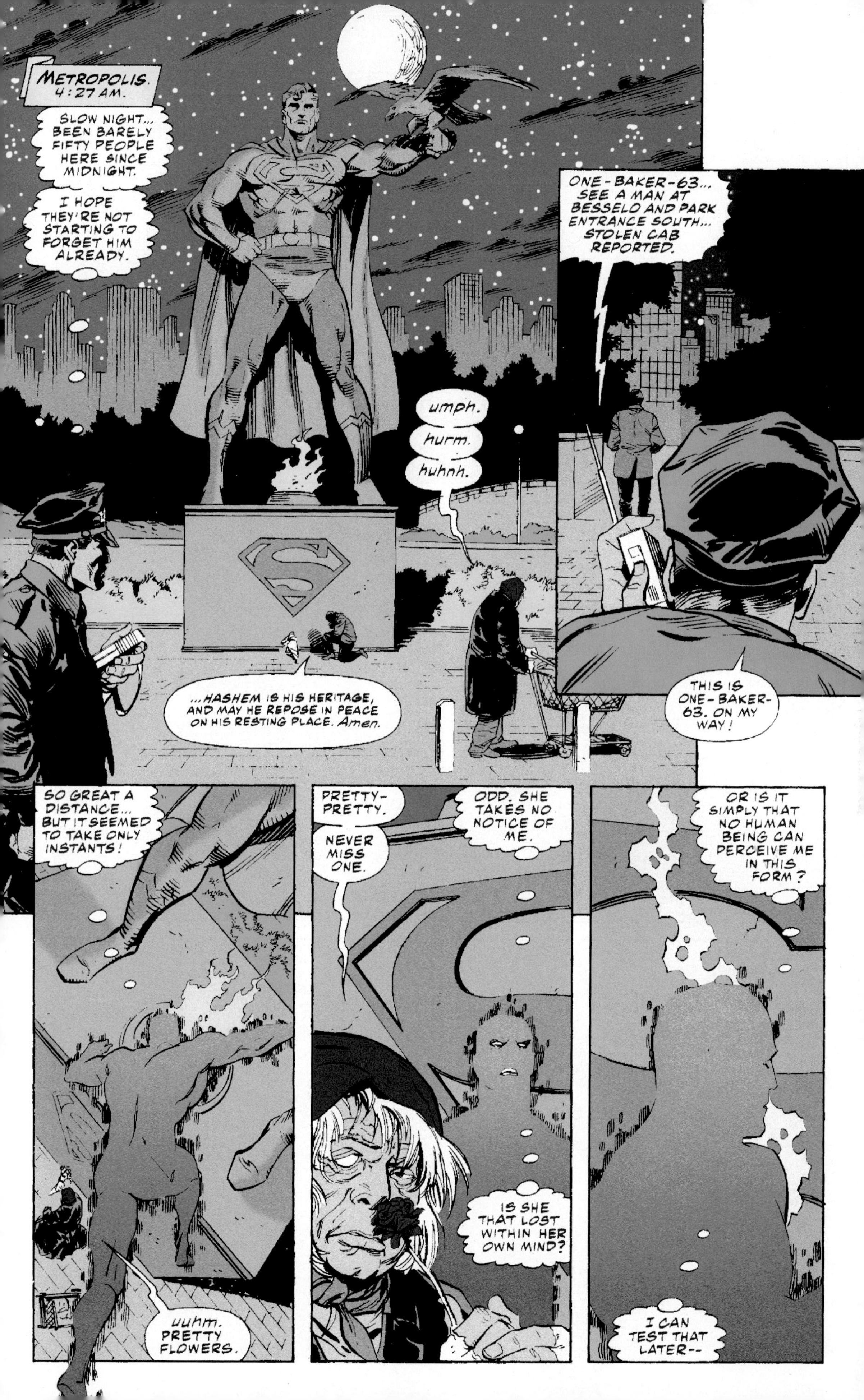
METROPOLIS. 4:27 AM.
SLOW NIGHT... BEEN BARELY FIFTY PEOPLE HERE SINCE MIDNIGHT.
I HOPE THEY'RE NOT STARTING TO FORGET HIM ALREADY.
umph.
hurm.
huhnh.
...HASHEM IS HIS HERITAGE, AND MAY HE REPOSE IN PEACE ON HIS RESTING PLACE. Amen.
ONE-BAKER-63... SEE A MAN AT BESSELO AND PARK ENTRANCE SOUTH... STOLEN CAB REPORTED.
THIS IS ONE-BAKER-63. ON MY WAY!
SO GREAT A DISTANCE... BUT IT SEEMED TO TAKE ONLY INSTANTS!
uuhm. PRETTY FLOWERS.
PRETTY-PRETTY.
NEVER MISS ONE.
ODD. SHE TAKES NO NOTICE OF ME.
IS SHE THAT LOST WITHIN HER OWN MIND?
OR IS IT SIMPLY THAT NO HUMAN BEING CAN PERCEIVE ME IN THIS FORM?
I CAN TEST THAT LATER--

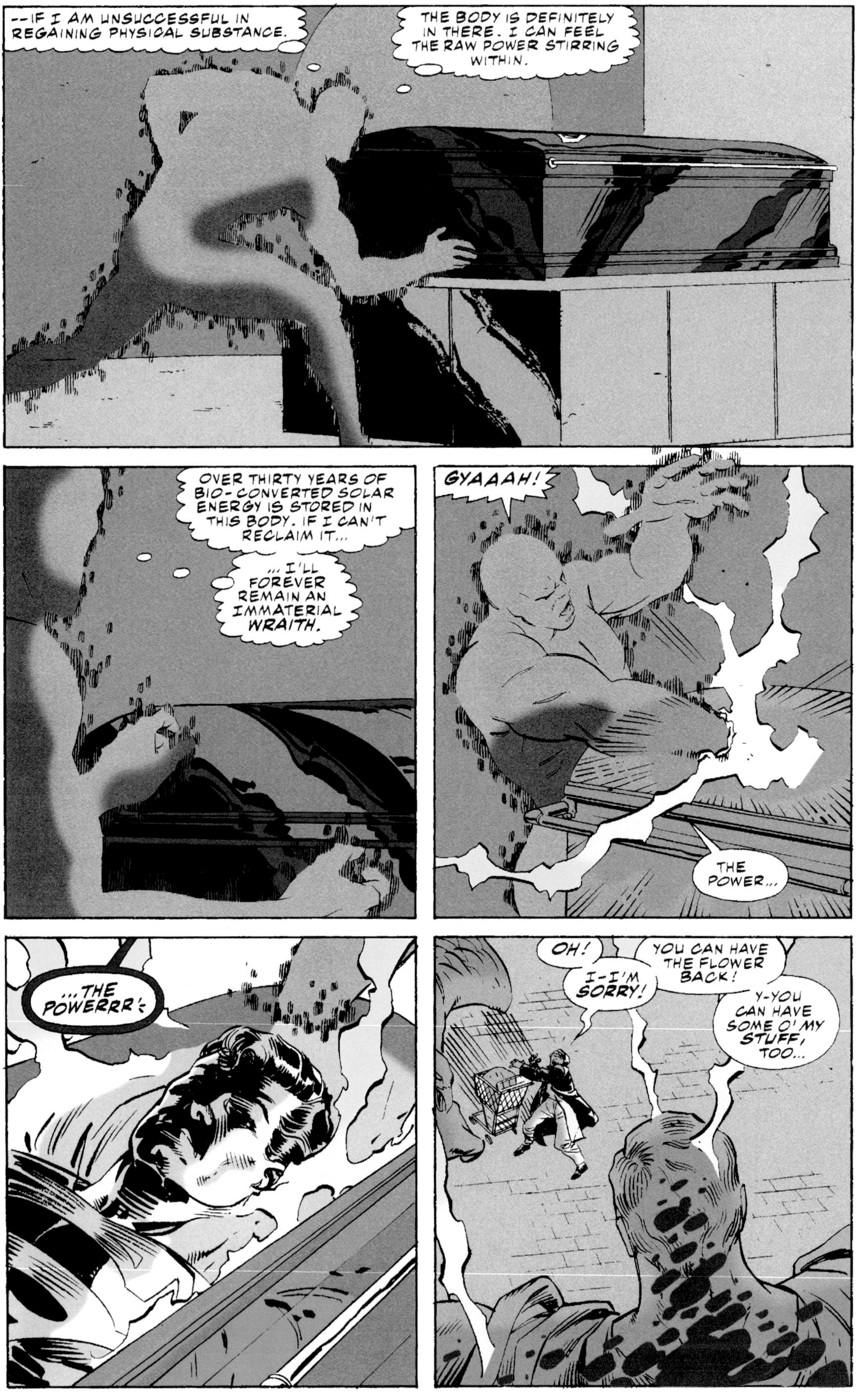
--IF I AM UNSUCCESSFUL IN REGAINING PHYSICAL SUBSTANCE.
THE BODY IS DEFINITELY IN THERE. I CAN FEEL THE RAW POWER STIRRING WITHIN.
OVER THIRTY YEARS OF BIO-CONVERTED SOLAR ENERGY IS STORED IN THIS BODY. IF I CAN'T RECLAIM IT...
...I'LL FOREVER REMAIN AN IMMATERIAL WRAITH.
GYAAAH!
THE POWER...
...THE POWERRR!
OH!
I-I'M SORRY!
YOU CAN HAVE THE FLOWER BACK!
Y-YOU CAN HAVE SOME O' MY STUFF, TOO...

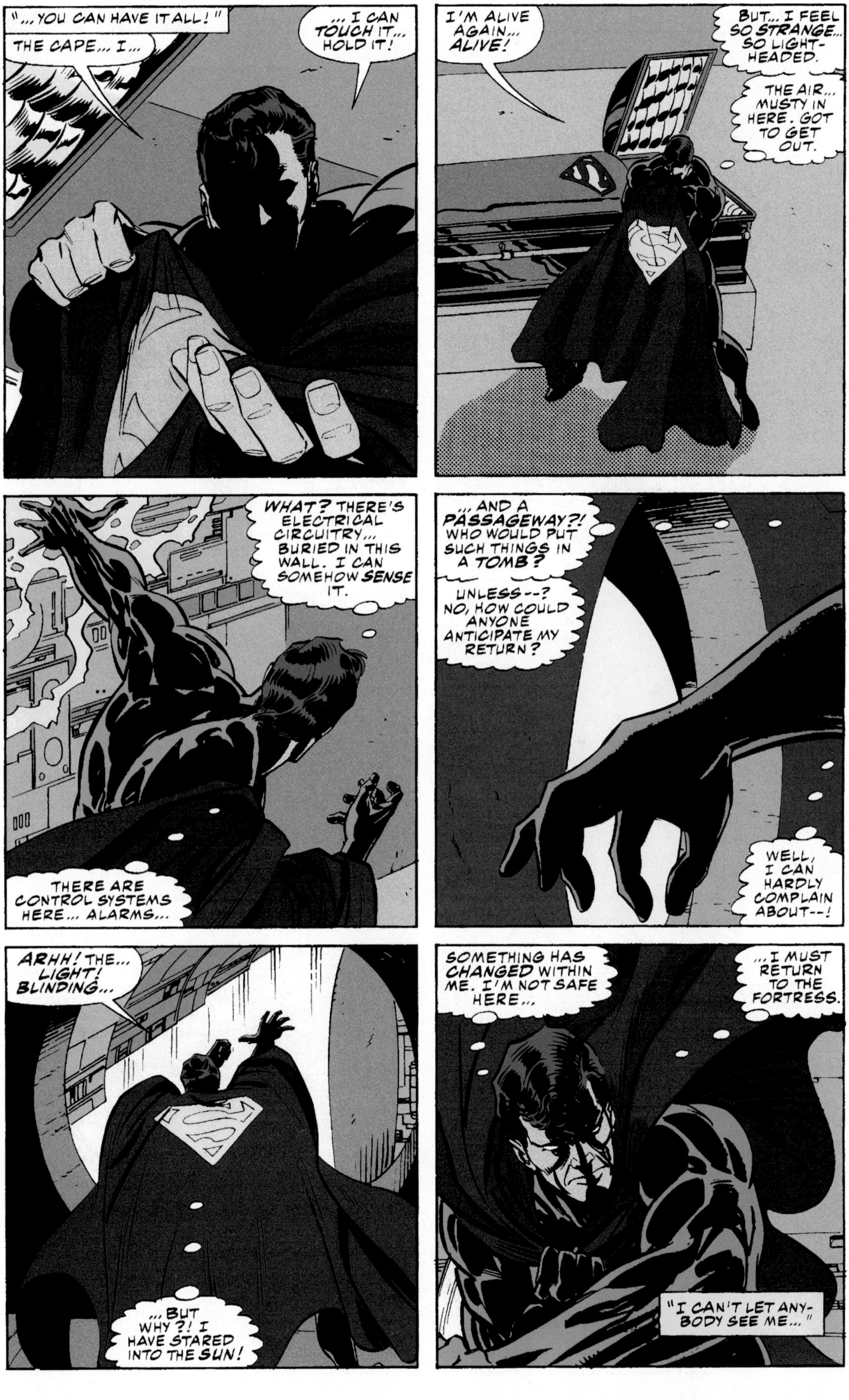
"...YOU CAN HAVE IT ALL!"
THE CAPE... I...
...I CAN TOUCH IT... HOLD IT!
I'M ALIVE AGAIN... ALIVE!
BUT... I FEEL SO STRANGE... SO LIGHT-HEADED.
THE AIR... MUSTY IN HERE. GOT TO GET OUT.
WHAT? THERE'S ELECTRICAL CIRCUITRY... BURIED IN THIS WALL. I CAN SOMEHOW SENSE IT.
THERE ARE CONTROL SYSTEMS HERE... ALARMS...
...AND A PASSAGEWAY?! WHO WOULD PUT SUCH THINGS IN A TOMB?
UNLESS--? NO, HOW COULD ANYONE ANTICIPATE MY RETURN?
WELL, I CAN HARDLY COMPLAIN ABOUT--!
ARHH! THE... LIGHT! BLINDING...
...BUT WHY?! I HAVE STARED INTO THE SUN!
SOMETHING HAS CHANGED WITHIN ME. I'M NOT SAFE HERE...
...I MUST RETURN TO THE FORTRESS.
"I CAN'T LET ANYBODY SEE ME..."

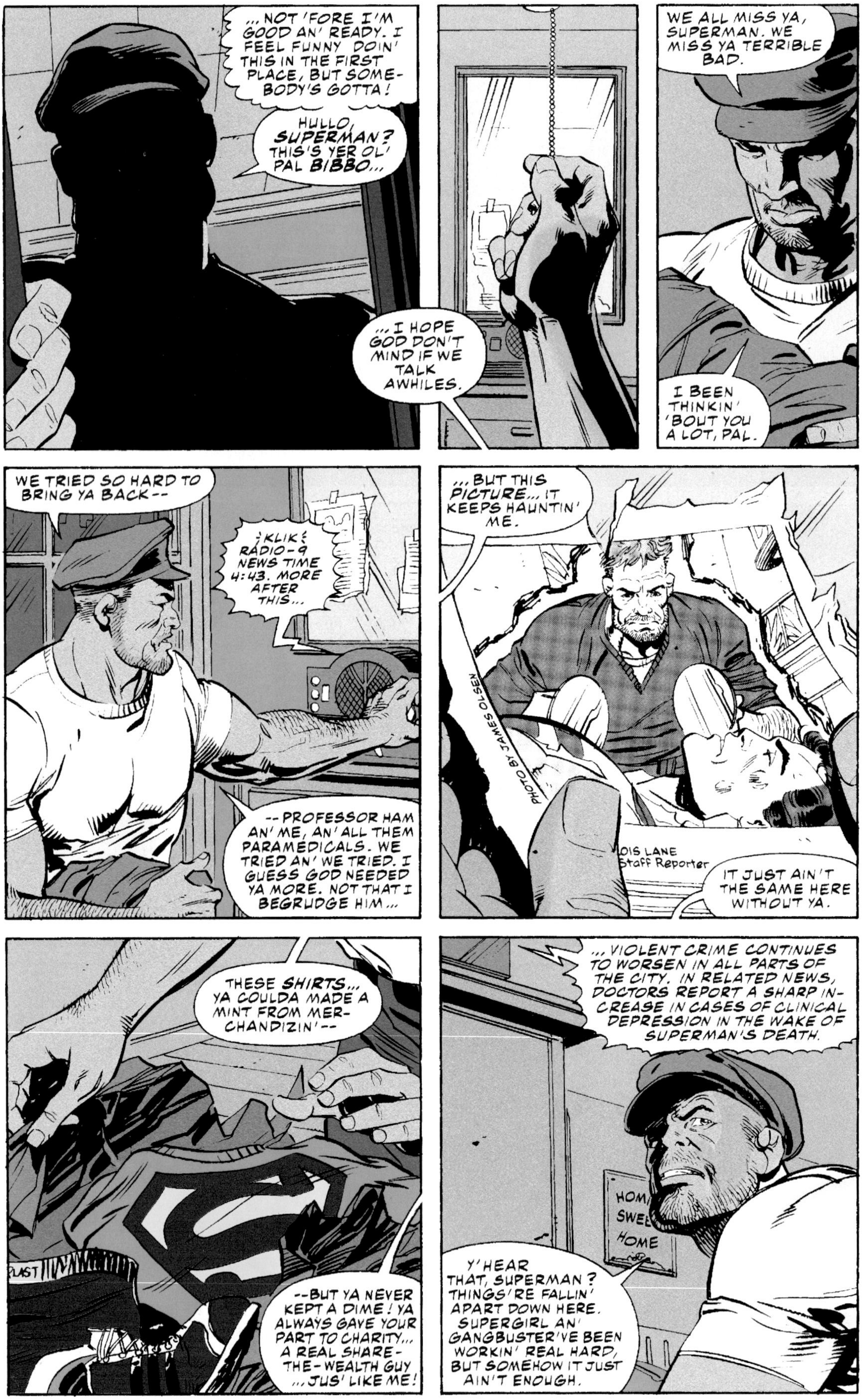
...NOT 'FORE I'M GOOD AN' READY. I FEEL FUNNY DOIN' THIS IN THE FIRST PLACE, BUT SOME-BODY'S GOTTA!
HULLO, SUPERMAN? THIS'S YER OL' PAL BIBBO...
...I HOPE GOD DON'T MIND IF WE TALK AWHILES.
WE ALL MISS YA, SUPERMAN. WE MISS YA TERRIBLE BAD.
I BEEN THINKIN' 'BOUT YOU A LOT, PAL.
WE TRIED SO HARD TO BRING YA BACK--
:KLIK: RADIO-9 NEWS TIME 4:43. MORE AFTER THIS...
--PROFESSOR HAM AN' ME, AN' ALL THEM PARAMEDICALS. WE TRIED AN' WE TRIED. I GUESS GOD NEEDED YA MORE. NOT THAT I BEGRUDGE HIM...
...BUT THIS PICTURE... IT KEEPS HAUNTIN' ME.
PHOTO BY JAMES OLSEN
LOIS LANE Staff Reporter
IT JUST AIN'T THE SAME HERE WITHOUT YA.
THESE SHIRTS... YA COULDA MADE A MINT FROM MER-CHANDIZIN'--
--BUT YA NEVER KEPT A DIME! YA ALWAYS GAVE YOUR PART TO CHARITY... A REAL SHARE-THE-WEALTH GUY ...JUS' LIKE ME!
...VIOLENT CRIME CONTINUES TO WORSEN IN ALL PARTS OF THE CITY. IN RELATED NEWS, DOCTORS REPORT A SHARP IN-CREASE IN CASES OF CLINICAL DEPRESSION IN THE WAKE OF SUPERMAN'S DEATH.
Y'HEAR THAT, SUPERMAN? THINGS'RE FALLIN' APART DOWN HERE. SUPERGIRL AN' GANGBUSTER'VE BEEN WORKIN' REAL HARD, BUT SOMEHOW IT JUST AIN'T ENOUGH.

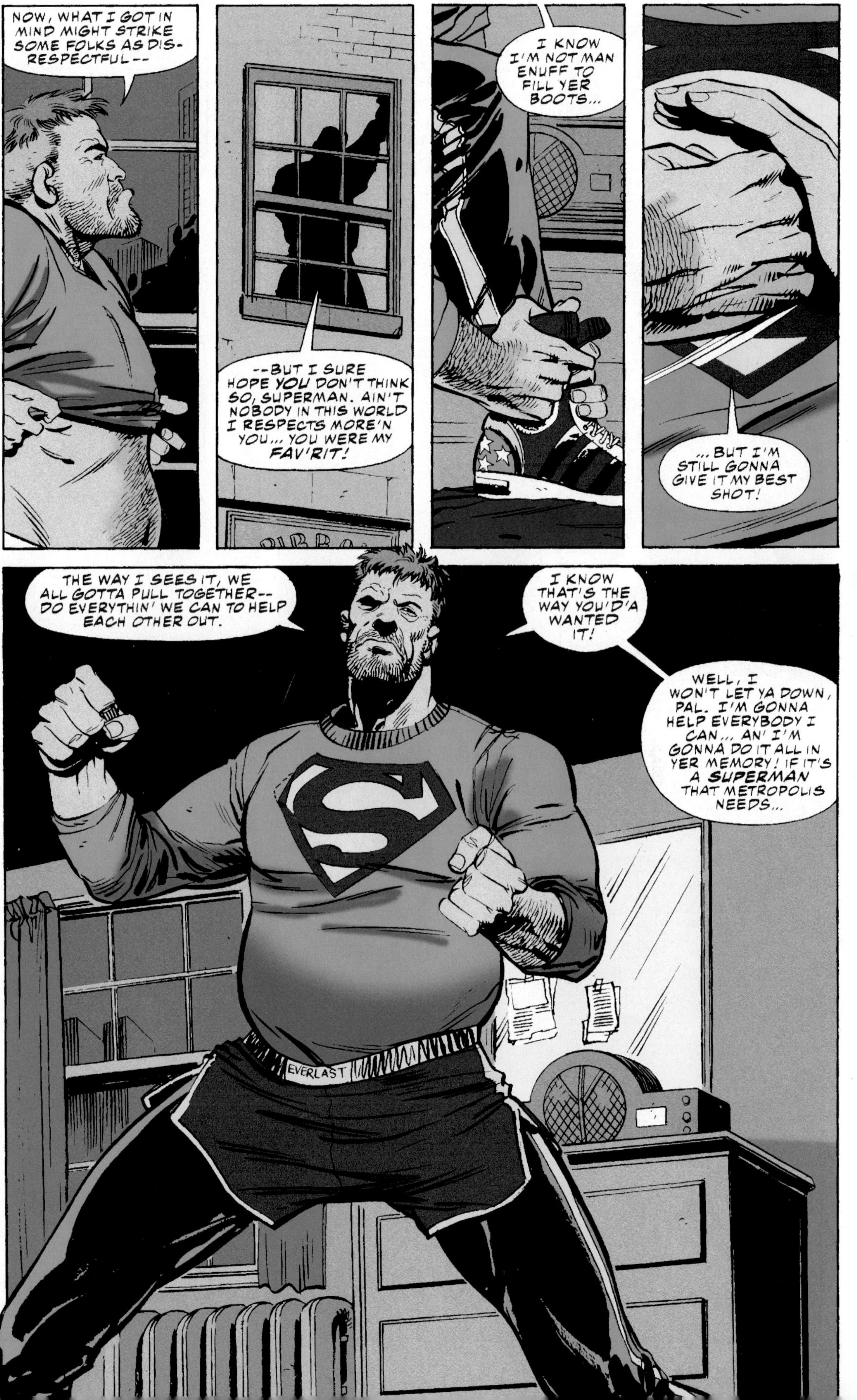

NOW, WHAT I GOT IN MIND MIGHT STRIKE SOME FOLKS AS DIS-RESPECTFUL --
--BUT I SURE HOPE YOU DON'T THINK SO, SUPERMAN. AIN'T NOBODY IN THIS WORLD I RESPECTS MORE'N YOU... YOU WERE MY FAV'RIT!
I KNOW I'M NOT MAN ENUFF TO FILL YER BOOTS...
...BUT I'M STILL GONNA GIVE IT MY BEST SHOT!
THE WAY I SEES IT, WE ALL GOTTA PULL TOGETHER-- DO EVERYTHIN' WE CAN TO HELP EACH OTHER OUT.
I KNOW THAT'S THE WAY YOU'D'A WANTED IT!
WELL, I WON'T LET YA DOWN, PAL. I'M GONNA HELP EVERYBODY I CAN... AN' I'M GONNA DO IT ALL IN YER MEMORY! IF IT'S A SUPERMAN THAT METROPOLIS NEEDS...
EVERLAST

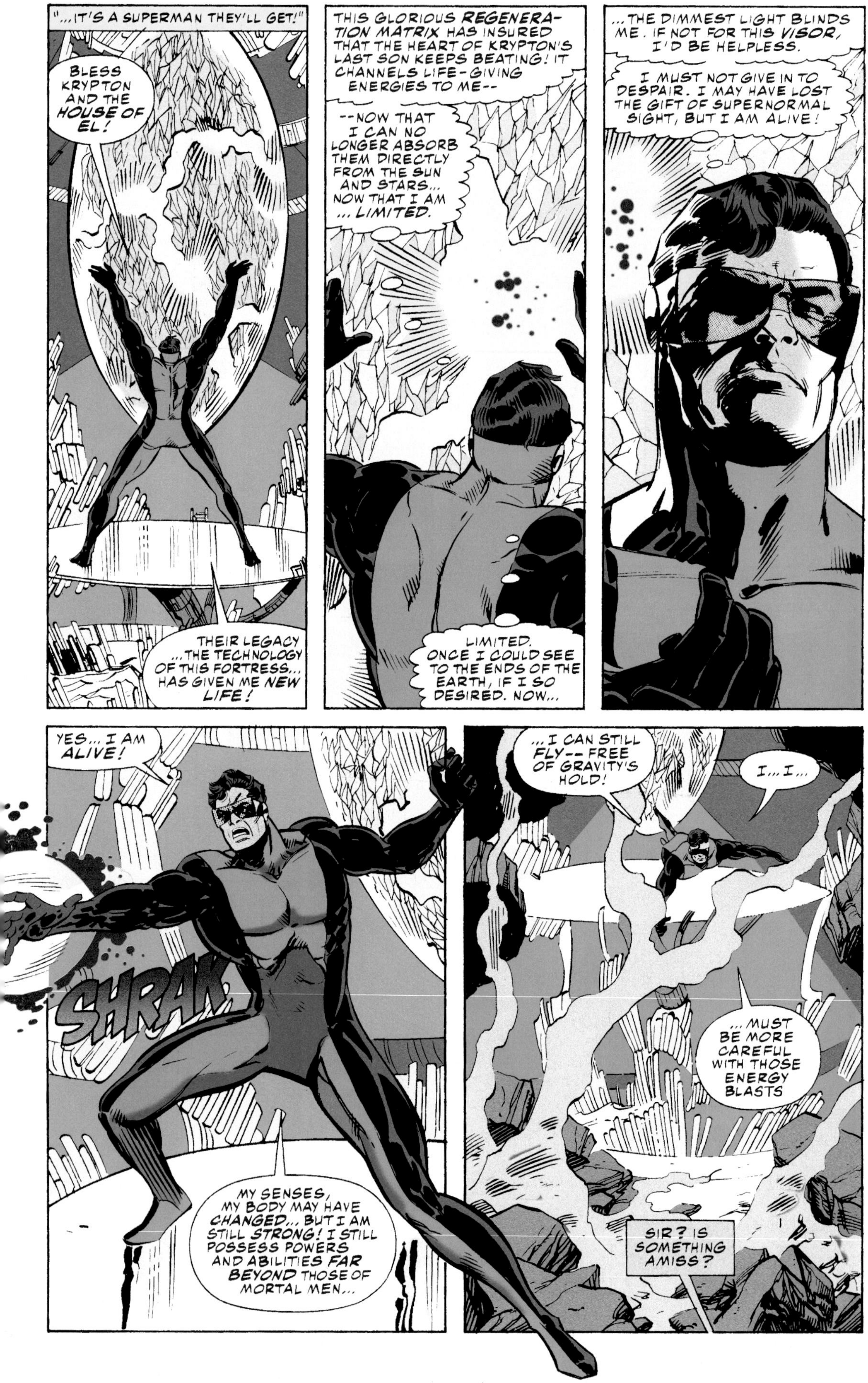
"...IT'S A SUPERMAN THEY'LL GET!"
BLESS KRYPTON AND THE HOUSE OF EL!
THEIR LEGACY ...THE TECHNOLOGY OF THIS FORTRESS... HAS GIVEN ME NEW LIFE!
THIS GLORIOUS REGENERATION MATRIX HAS INSURED THAT THE HEART OF KRYPTON'S LAST SON KEEPS BEATING! IT CHANNELS LIFE-GIVING ENERGIES TO ME--
--NOW THAT I CAN NO LONGER ABSORB THEM DIRECTLY FROM THE SUN AND STARS... NOW THAT I AM ...LIMITED.
LIMITED. ONCE I COULD SEE TO THE ENDS OF THE EARTH, IF I SO DESIRED. NOW...
...THE DIMMEST LIGHT BLINDS ME. IF NOT FOR THIS VISOR, I'D BE HELPLESS.
I MUST NOT GIVE IN TO DESPAIR. I MAY HAVE LOST THE GIFT OF SUPERNORMAL SIGHT, BUT I AM ALIVE!
YES... I AM ALIVE!
SHRAK
MY SENSES, MY BODY MAY HAVE CHANGED... BUT I AM STILL STRONG! I STILL POSSESS POWERS AND ABILITIES FAR BEYOND THOSE OF MORTAL MEN...
...I CAN STILL FLY-- FREE OF GRAVITY'S HOLD!
I... I...
...MUST BE MORE CAREFUL WITH THOSE ENERGY BLASTS
SIR? IS SOMETHING AMISS?

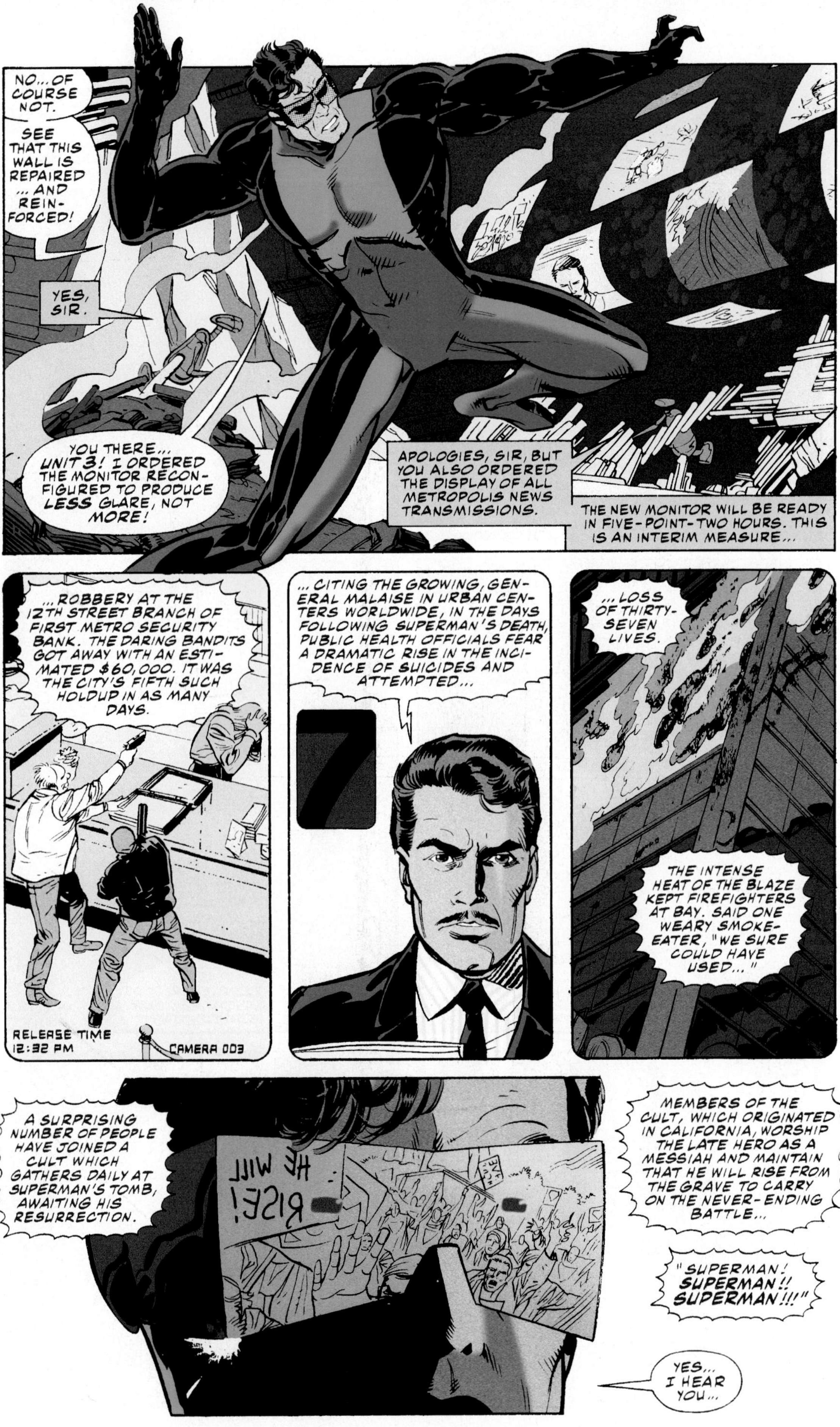
NO... OF COURSE NOT.
SEE THAT THIS WALL IS REPAIRED ... AND REIN-FORCED!
YES, SIR.
YOU THERE... UNIT 3! I ORDERED THE MONITOR RECON-FIGURED TO PRODUCE LESS GLARE, NOT MORE!
APOLOGIES, SIR, BUT YOU ALSO ORDERED THE DISPLAY OF ALL METROPOLIS NEWS TRANSMISSIONS.
THE NEW MONITOR WILL BE READY IN FIVE-POINT-TWO HOURS. THIS IS AN INTERIM MEASURE...
...ROBBERY AT THE 12TH STREET BRANCH OF FIRST METRO SECURITY BANK. THE DARING BANDITS GOT AWAY WITH AN ESTI-MATED $60,000. IT WAS THE CITY'S FIFTH SUCH HOLDUP IN AS MANY DAYS.
RELEASE TIME 12:32 PM
CAMERA 003
...CITING THE GROWING, GEN-ERAL MALAISE IN URBAN CEN-TERS WORLDWIDE, IN THE DAYS FOLLOWING SUPERMAN'S DEATH, PUBLIC HEALTH OFFICIALS FEAR A DRAMATIC RISE IN THE INCI-DENCE OF SUICIDES AND ATTEMPTED...
...LOSS OF THIRTY-SEVEN LIVES.
THE INTENSE HEAT OF THE BLAZE KEPT FIREFIGHTERS AT BAY. SAID ONE WEARY SMOKE-EATER, "WE SURE COULD HAVE USED..."
A SURPRISING NUMBER OF PEOPLE HAVE JOINED A CULT WHICH GATHERS DAILY AT SUPERMAN'S TOMB, AWAITING HIS RESURRECTION.
HE WILL RISE!
MEMBERS OF THE CULT, WHICH ORIGINATED IN CALIFORNIA, WORSHIP THE LATE HERO AS A MESSIAH AND MAINTAIN THAT HE WILL RISE FROM THE GRAVE TO CARRY ON THE NEVER-ENDING BATTLE...
"SUPERMAN! SUPERMAN!! SUPERMAN!!!"
YES... I HEAR YOU...

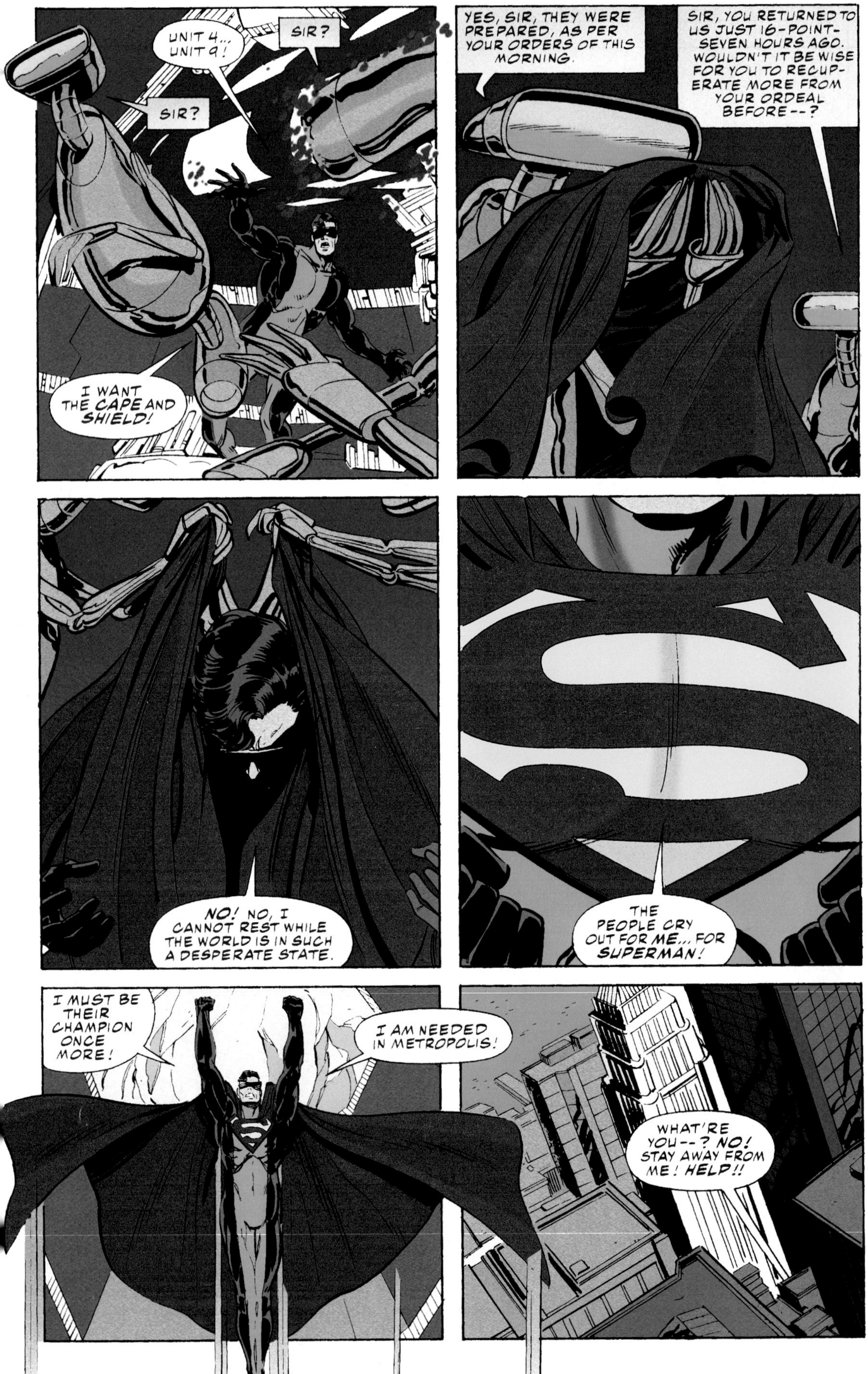
UNIT 4... UNIT 9!
SIR?
SIR?
I WANT THE CAPE AND SHIELD!
YES, SIR, THEY WERE PREPARED, AS PER YOUR ORDERS OF THIS MORNING.
SIR, YOU RETURNED TO US JUST 16-POINT-SEVEN HOURS AGO. WOULDN'T IT BE WISE FOR YOU TO RECUPERATE MORE FROM YOUR ORDEAL BEFORE--?
NO! NO, I CANNOT REST WHILE THE WORLD IS IN SUCH A DESPERATE STATE.
THE PEOPLE CRY OUT FOR ME... FOR SUPERMAN!
I MUST BE THEIR CHAMPION ONCE MORE!
I AM NEEDED IN METROPOLIS!
WHAT'RE YOU--? NO! STAY AWAY FROM ME! HELP!!

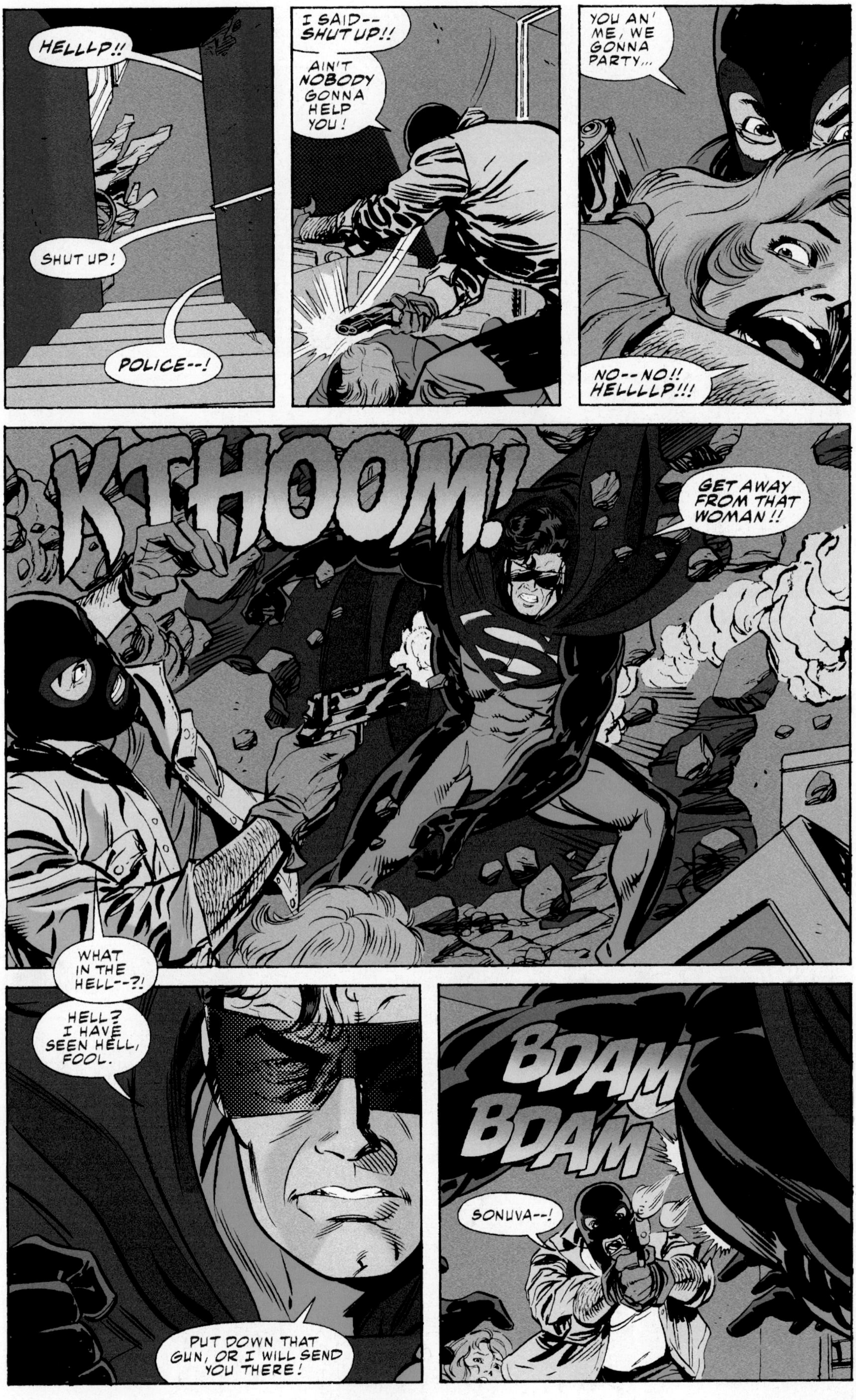
HELLLP!!
SHUT UP!
POLICE--!
I SAID-- SHUT UP!!
AIN'T NOBODY GONNA HELP YOU!
YOU AN' ME, WE GONNA PARTY...
NO--NO!! HELLLLP!!!
KTHOOM!
GET AWAY FROM THAT WOMAN!!
WHAT IN THE HELL--?!
HELL? I HAVE SEEN HELL, FOOL.
PUT DOWN THAT GUN, OR I WILL SEND YOU THERE!
BDAM BDAM
SONUVA--!

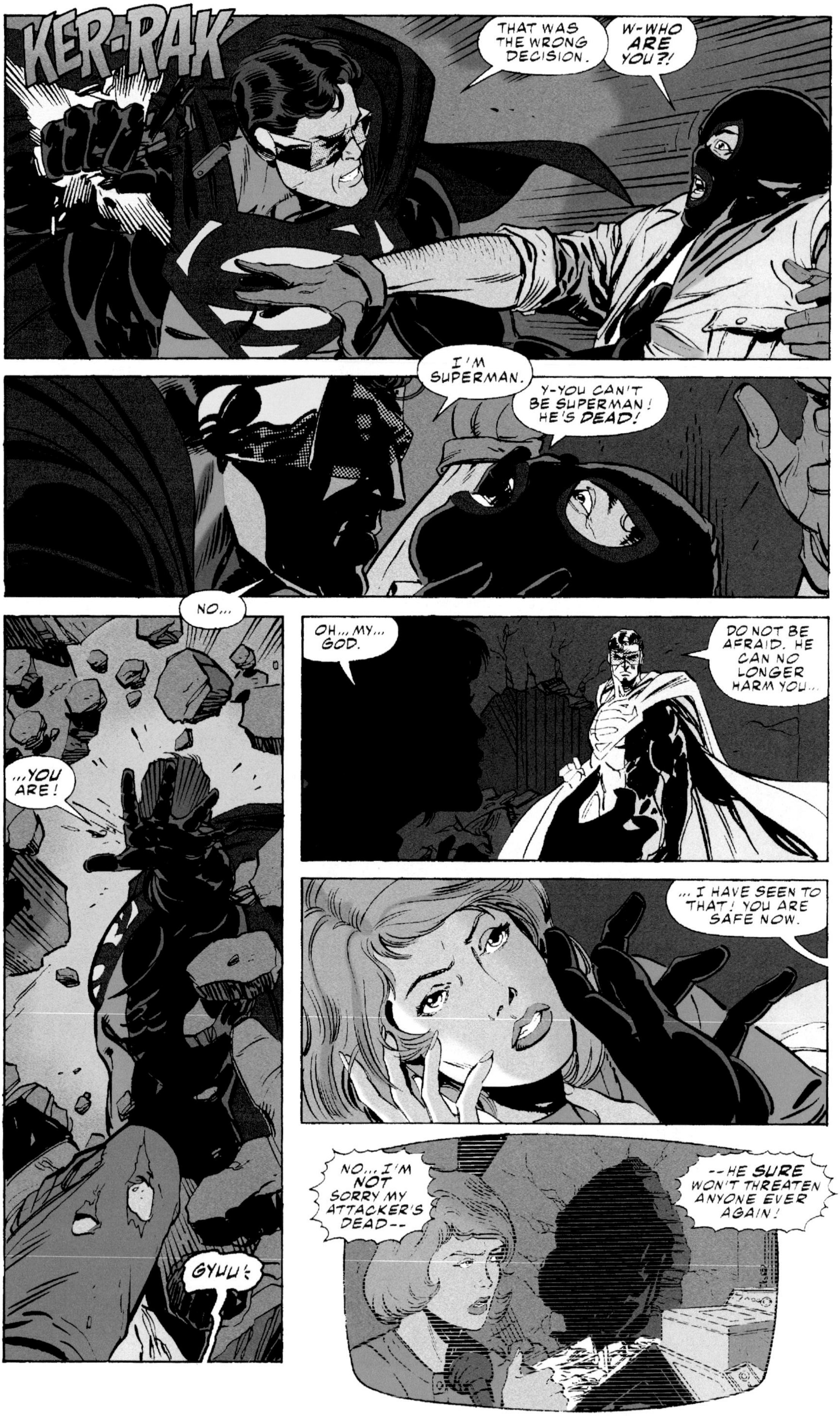
KER-RAK
THAT WAS THE WRONG DECISION.
W-WHO ARE YOU?!
I'M SUPERMAN.
Y-YOU CAN'T BE SUPERMAN! HE'S DEAD!
NO...
...YOU ARE!
GYUU!
OH... MY... GOD.
DO NOT BE AFRAID. HE CAN NO LONGER HARM YOU...
... I HAVE SEEN TO THAT! YOU ARE SAFE NOW.
NO... I'M NOT SORRY MY ATTACKER'S DEAD--
--HE SURE WON'T THREATEN ANYONE EVER AGAIN!

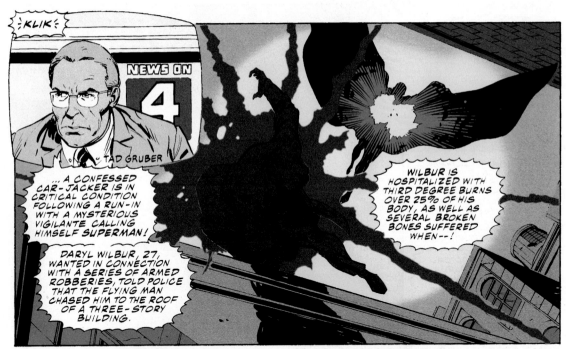

KLIK

NEWS ON 4

TAD GRUBER

...A CONFESSED CAR-JACKER IS IN CRITICAL CONDITION FOLLOWING A RUN-IN WITH A MYSTERIOUS VIGILANTE CALLING HIMSELF SUPERMAN!

DARYL WILBUR, 27, WANTED IN CONNECTION WITH A SERIES OF ARMED ROBBERIES, TOLD POLICE THAT THE FLYING MAN CHASED HIM TO THE ROOF OF A THREE-STORY BUILDING.

WILBUR IS HOSPITALIZED WITH THIRD DEGREE BURNS OVER 25% OF HIS BODY, AS WELL AS SEVERAL BROKEN BONES SUFFERED WHEN--!

KLIK

10 SPECIAL REPORT

METROPOLIS HARBOR. HERE, JUST BEFORE DAWN...

...A BOAT CARRYING THREE MEN AND AN UNSPECIFIED QUANTITY OF HEROIN--

--WAS REPORTEDLY STOPPED BY A MAN WEARING THE CAPE AND INSIGNIA OF THE LATE SUPERMAN! AND A CITY WONDERS... HAS THEIR HERO RETURNED FROM THE BEYOND?

KLIK

LIVE ON 6:

RON, A CAT BURGLAR GOT THE SURPRISE OF HIS LIFE LATE LAST NIGHT, WHEN HE ATTEMPTED TO BREAK INTO A 26TH FLOOR APARTMENT.

A MASKED MAN WHOM ONE WITNESS CALLED "DIRTY HARRY WITH A CAPE," DANGLED THE BURGLAR HIGH ABOVE THE STREETS FOR SEVERAL MINUTES BEFORE LEAVING HIM TIED TO A SEVENTH-STORY FLAG POLE.

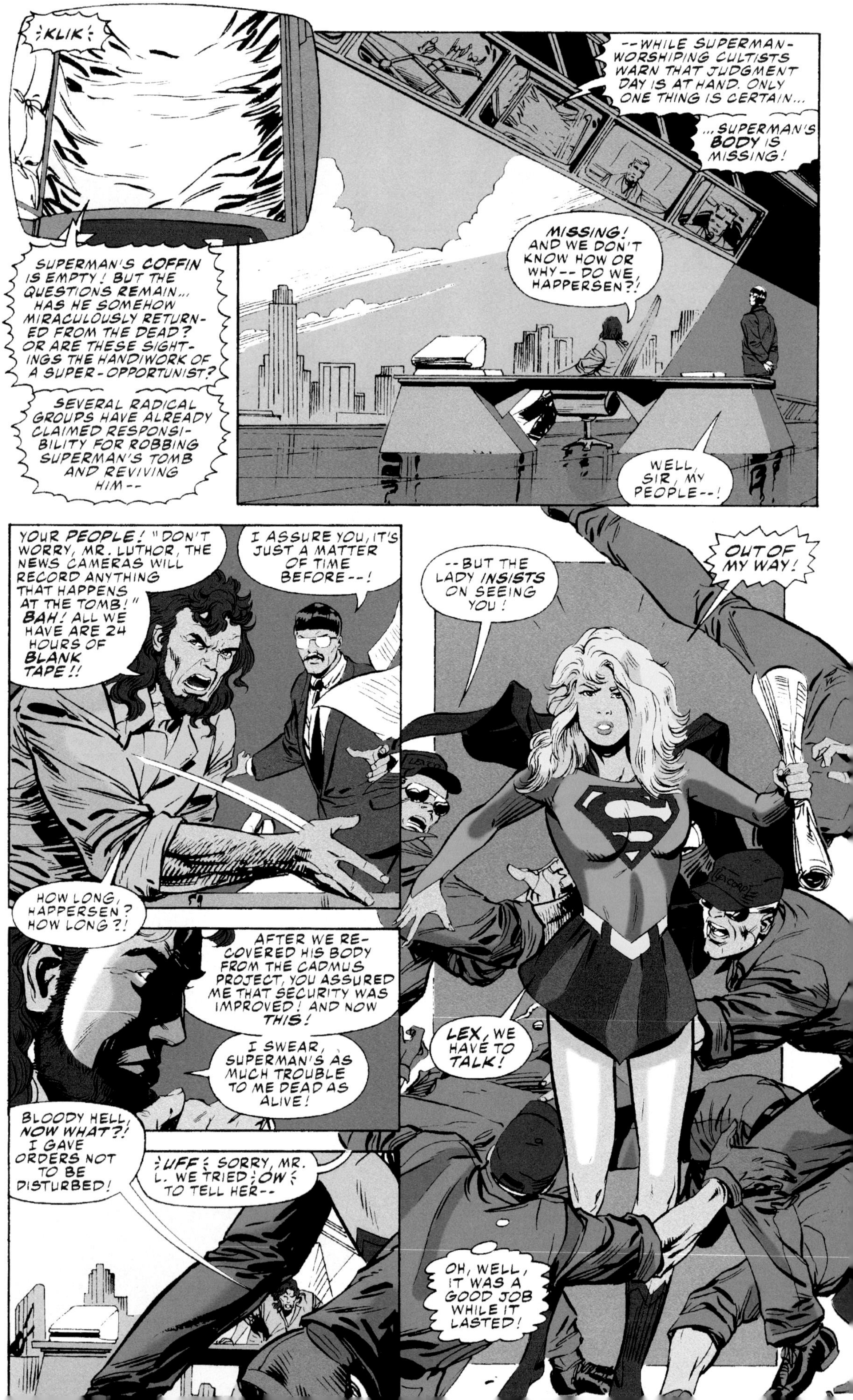

KLIK
--WHILE SUPERMAN-WORSHIPING CULTISTS WARN THAT JUDGMENT DAY IS AT HAND. ONLY ONE THING IS CERTAIN...
...SUPERMAN'S BODY IS MISSING!
SUPERMAN'S COFFIN IS EMPTY! BUT THE QUESTIONS REMAIN... HAS HE SOMEHOW MIRACULOUSLY RETURNED FROM THE DEAD? OR ARE THESE SIGHTINGS THE HANDIWORK OF A SUPER-OPPORTUNIST?
SEVERAL RADICAL GROUPS HAVE ALREADY CLAIMED RESPONSIBILITY FOR ROBBING SUPERMAN'S TOMB AND REVIVING HIM--
MISSING! AND WE DON'T KNOW HOW OR WHY-- DO WE, HAPPERSEN?!
WELL, SIR, MY PEOPLE--!
YOUR PEOPLE! "DON'T WORRY, MR. LUTHOR, THE NEWS CAMERAS WILL RECORD ANYTHING THAT HAPPENS AT THE TOMB!" BAH! ALL WE HAVE ARE 24 HOURS OF BLANK TAPE!!
I ASSURE YOU, IT'S JUST A MATTER OF TIME BEFORE--!
HOW LONG, HAPPERSEN? HOW LONG?!
AFTER WE RECOVERED HIS BODY FROM THE CADMUS PROJECT, YOU ASSURED ME THAT SECURITY WAS IMPROVED! AND NOW THIS!
I SWEAR, SUPERMAN'S AS MUCH TROUBLE TO ME DEAD AS ALIVE!
BLOODY HELL, NOW WHAT?! I GAVE ORDERS NOT TO BE DISTURBED!
UFF SORRY, MR. L. WE TRIED OW TO TELL HER--
--BUT THE LADY INSISTS ON SEEING YOU!
OUT OF MY WAY!
LEX, WE HAVE TO TALK!
OH, WELL, IT WAS A GOOD JOB WHILE IT LASTED!

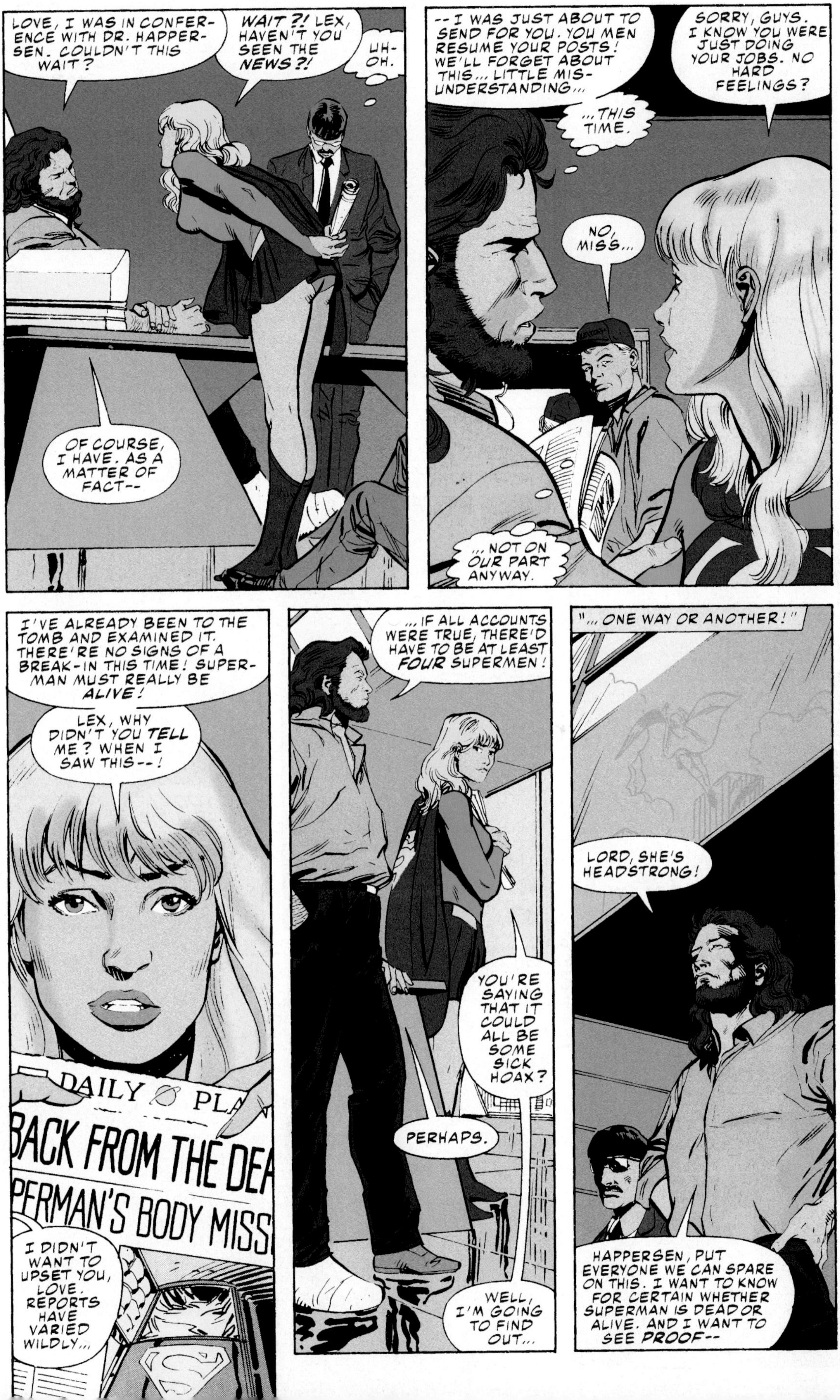
LOVE, I WAS IN CONFERENCE WITH DR. HAPPERSEN. COULDN'T THIS WAIT?
WAIT?! LEX, HAVEN'T YOU SEEN THE NEWS?!
UH-OH.
OF COURSE, I HAVE. AS A MATTER OF FACT--
--I WAS JUST ABOUT TO SEND FOR YOU. YOU MEN RESUME YOUR POSTS! WE'LL FORGET ABOUT THIS... LITTLE MISUNDERSTANDING...
SORRY, GUYS. I KNOW YOU WERE JUST DOING YOUR JOBS. NO HARD FEELINGS?
...THIS TIME.
NO, MISS...
...NOT ON OUR PART ANYWAY.
I'VE ALREADY BEEN TO THE TOMB AND EXAMINED IT. THERE'RE NO SIGNS OF A BREAK-IN THIS TIME! SUPERMAN MUST REALLY BE ALIVE!
LEX, WHY DIDN'T YOU TELL ME? WHEN I SAW THIS--!
DAILY PLA
BACK FROM THE DEA
PERMAN'S BODY MISS
I DIDN'T WANT TO UPSET YOU, LOVE. REPORTS HAVE VARIED WILDLY...
...IF ALL ACCOUNTS WERE TRUE, THERE'D HAVE TO BE AT LEAST FOUR SUPERMEN!
YOU'RE SAYING THAT IT COULD ALL BE SOME SICK HOAX?
PERHAPS.
WELL, I'M GOING TO FIND OUT...
"...ONE WAY OR ANOTHER!"
LORD, SHE'S HEADSTRONG!
HAPPERSEN, PUT EVERYONE WE CAN SPARE ON THIS. I WANT TO KNOW FOR CERTAIN WHETHER SUPERMAN IS DEAD OR ALIVE. AND I WANT TO SEE PROOF--

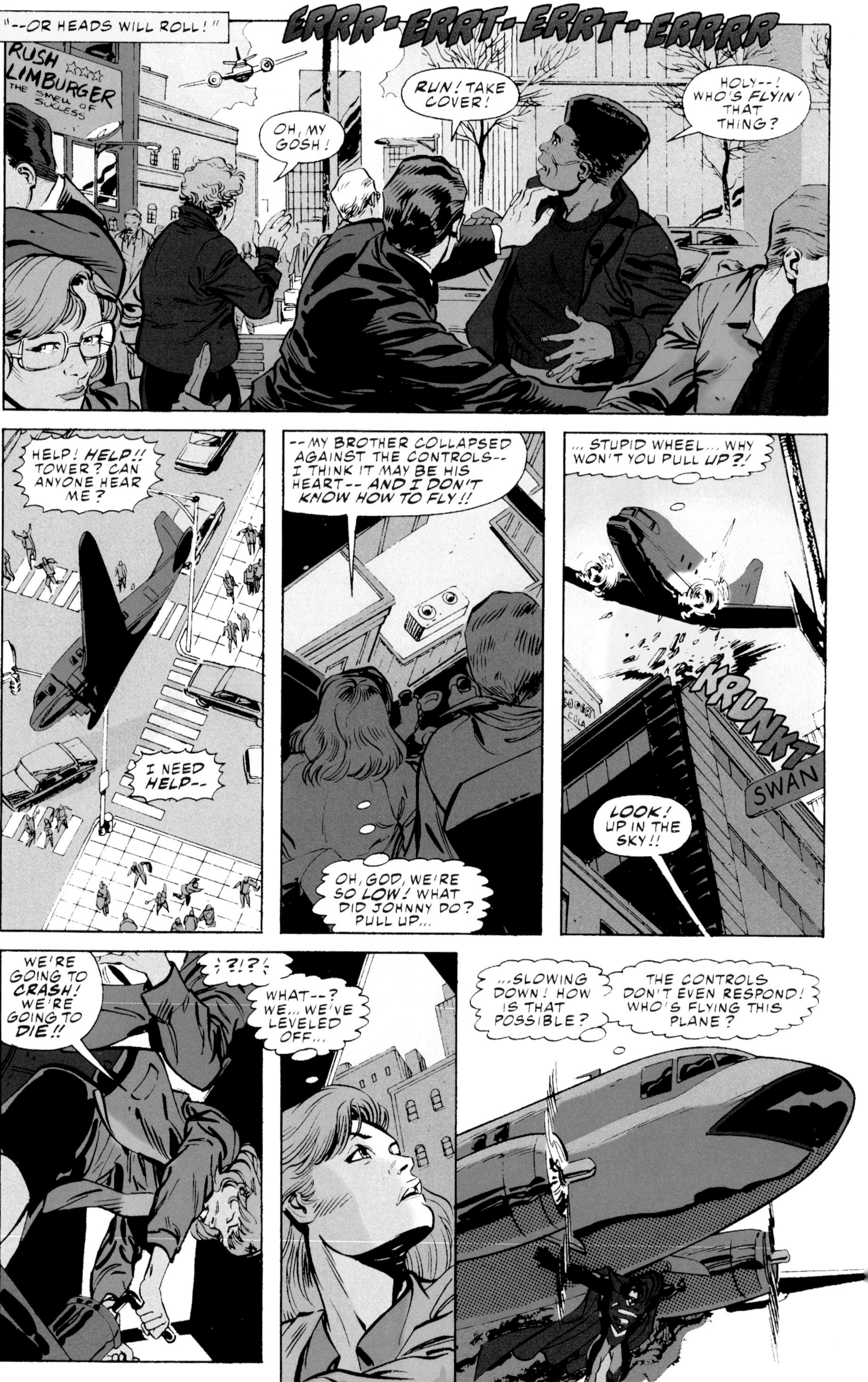
"--OR HEADS WILL ROLL!"
ERRR-ERRT-ERRT-ERRRR
RUSH LIMBURGER THE SMELL OF SUCCESS
OH, MY GOSH!
RUN! TAKE COVER!
HOLY--! WHO'S FLYIN' THAT THING?
HELP! HELP!! TOWER? CAN ANYONE HEAR ME?
I NEED HELP--
--MY BROTHER COLLAPSED AGAINST THE CONTROLS-- I THINK IT MAY BE HIS HEART-- AND I DON'T KNOW HOW TO FLY!!
OH, GOD, WE'RE SO LOW! WHAT DID JOHNNY DO? PULL UP...
... STUPID WHEEL... WHY WON'T YOU PULL UP?!
KRUNKT
SWAN
LOOK! UP IN THE SKY!!
WE'RE GOING TO CRASH! WE'RE GOING TO DIE!!
¿?!?¿
WHAT--? WE... WE'VE LEVELED OFF...
...SLOWING DOWN! HOW IS THAT POSSIBLE?
THE CONTROLS DON'T EVEN RESPOND! WHO'S FLYING THIS PLANE?

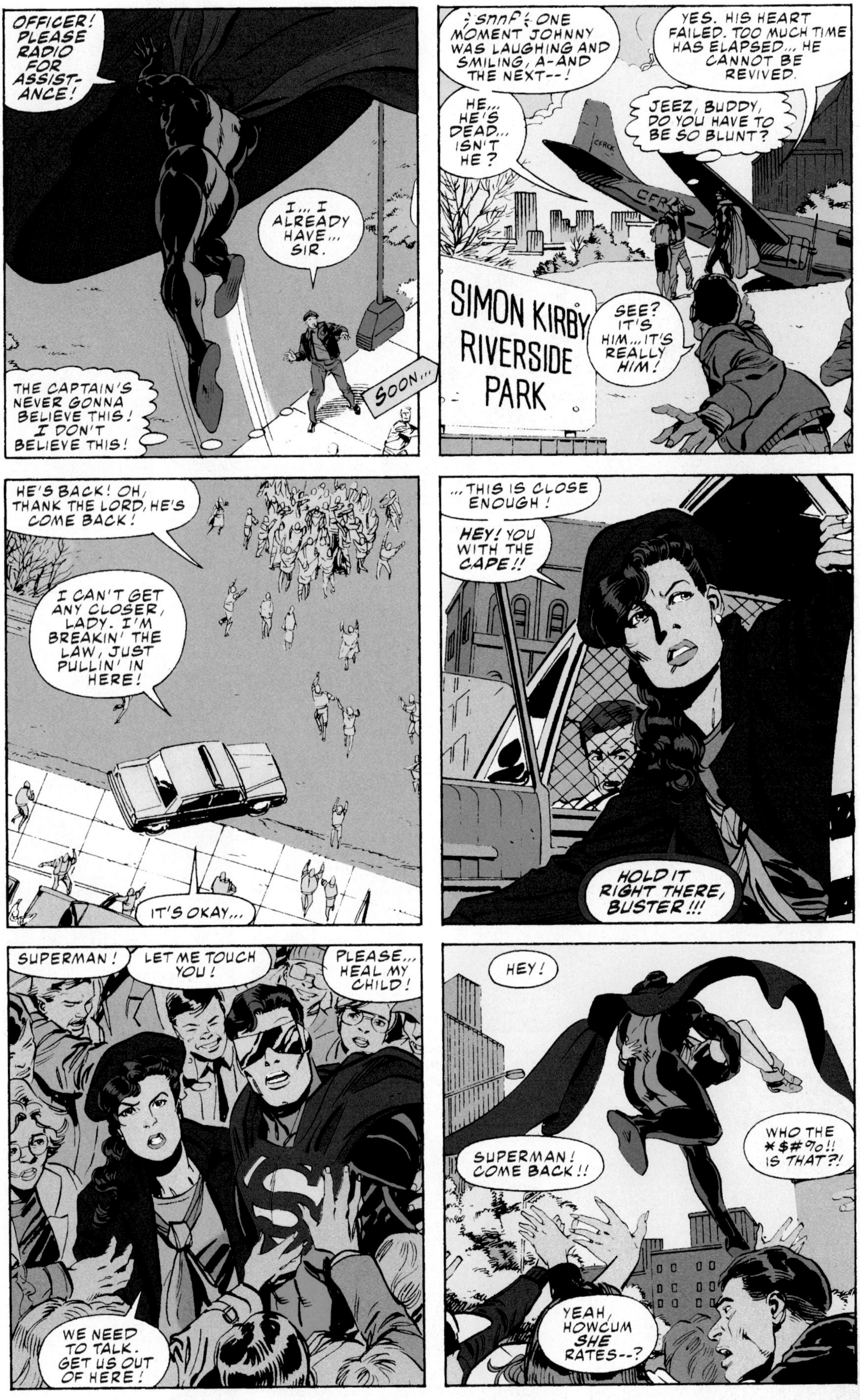
OFFICER! PLEASE RADIO FOR ASSIST-ANCE!
I... I ALREADY HAVE... SIR.
THE CAPTAIN'S NEVER GONNA BELIEVE THIS! I DON'T BELIEVE THIS!
SOON...
SNNF ONE MOMENT JOHNNY WAS LAUGHING AND SMILING, A-AND THE NEXT--!
HE... HE'S DEAD... ISN'T HE?
YES. HIS HEART FAILED. TOO MUCH TIME HAS ELAPSED... HE CANNOT BE REVIVED.
JEEZ, BUDDY, DO YOU HAVE TO BE SO BLUNT?
SIMON KIRBY RIVERSIDE PARK
SEE? IT'S HIM... IT'S REALLY HIM!
HE'S BACK! OH, THANK THE LORD, HE'S COME BACK!
I CAN'T GET ANY CLOSER, LADY. I'M BREAKIN' THE LAW, JUST PULLIN' IN HERE!
IT'S OKAY...
...THIS IS CLOSE ENOUGH!
HEY! YOU WITH THE CAPE!!
HOLD IT RIGHT THERE, BUSTER!!!
SUPERMAN!
LET ME TOUCH YOU!
PLEASE... HEAL MY CHILD!
WE NEED TO TALK. GET US OUT OF HERE!
HEY!
SUPERMAN! COME BACK!!
WHO THE *$#%!! IS THAT?!
YEAH, HOWCUM SHE RATES--?

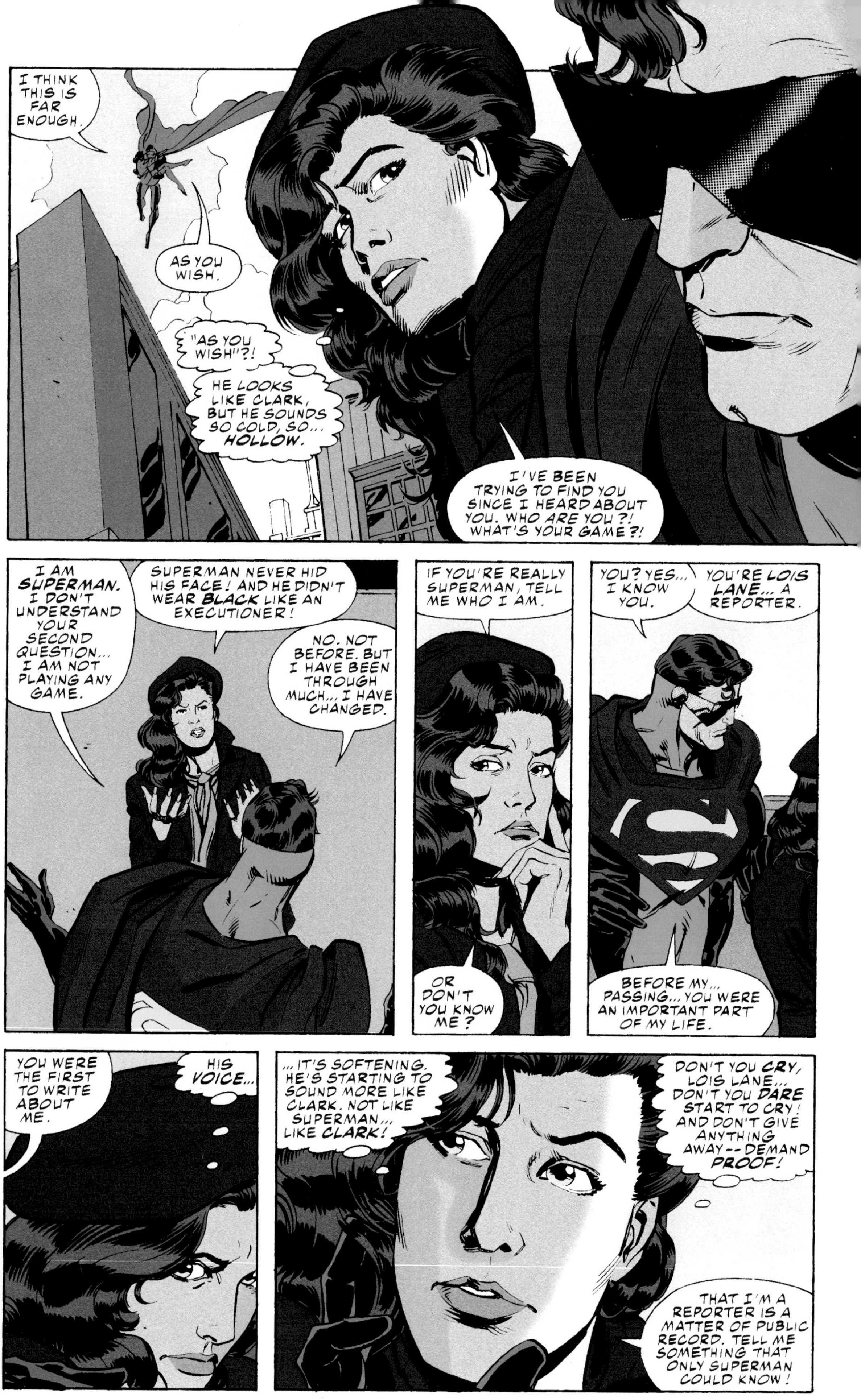

I THINK THIS IS FAR ENOUGH.
AS YOU WISH.
"AS YOU WISH"?!
HE LOOKS LIKE CLARK, BUT HE SOUNDS SO COLD, SO... HOLLOW.
I'VE BEEN TRYING TO FIND YOU SINCE I HEARD ABOUT YOU. WHO ARE YOU?! WHAT'S YOUR GAME?!
I AM SUPERMAN. I DON'T UNDERSTAND YOUR SECOND QUESTION... I AM NOT PLAYING ANY GAME.
SUPERMAN NEVER HID HIS FACE! AND HE DIDN'T WEAR BLACK LIKE AN EXECUTIONER!
NO. NOT BEFORE. BUT I HAVE BEEN THROUGH MUCH... I HAVE CHANGED.
IF YOU'RE REALLY SUPERMAN, TELL ME WHO I AM.
OR DON'T YOU KNOW ME?
YOU? YES... I KNOW YOU.
YOU'RE LOIS LANE... A REPORTER.
BEFORE MY... PASSING... YOU WERE AN IMPORTANT PART OF MY LIFE.
YOU WERE THE FIRST TO WRITE ABOUT ME.
HIS VOICE...
...IT'S SOFTENING. HE'S STARTING TO SOUND MORE LIKE CLARK. NOT LIKE SUPERMAN... LIKE CLARK!
DON'T YOU CRY, LOIS LANE... DON'T YOU DARE START TO CRY! AND DON'T GIVE ANYTHING AWAY -- DEMAND PROOF!
THAT I'M A REPORTER IS A MATTER OF PUBLIC RECORD. TELL ME SOMETHING THAT ONLY SUPERMAN COULD KNOW!

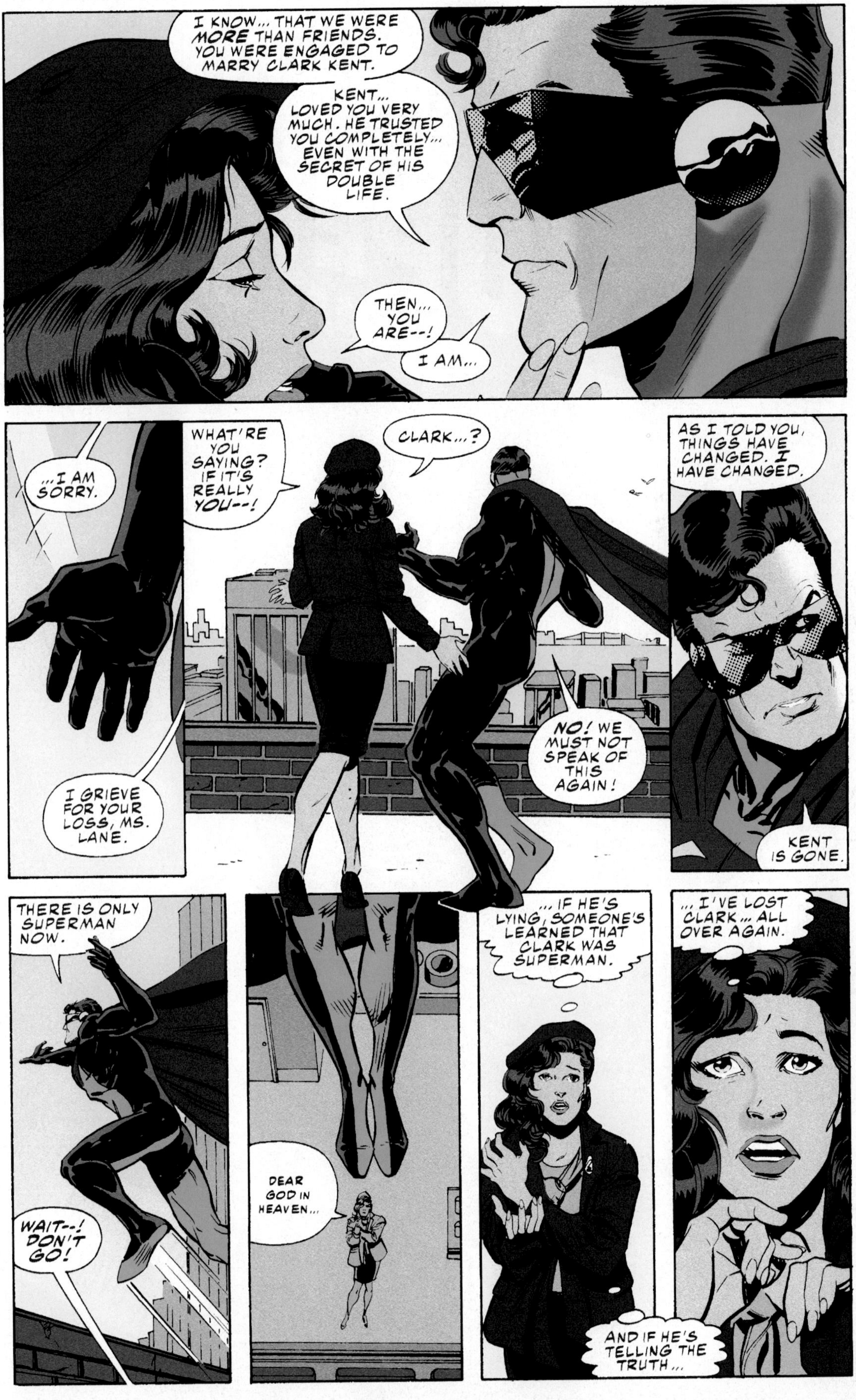

I KNOW... THAT WE WERE MORE THAN FRIENDS. YOU WERE ENGAGED TO MARRY CLARK KENT.
KENT... LOVED YOU VERY MUCH. HE TRUSTED YOU COMPLETELY... EVEN WITH THE SECRET OF HIS DOUBLE LIFE.
THEN... YOU ARE--!
I AM...
...I AM SORRY.
I GRIEVE FOR YOUR LOSS, MS. LANE.
WHAT'RE YOU SAYING? IF IT'S REALLY YOU--!
CLARK...?
NO! WE MUST NOT SPEAK OF THIS AGAIN!
AS I TOLD YOU, THINGS HAVE CHANGED. I HAVE CHANGED.
KENT IS GONE.
THERE IS ONLY SUPERMAN NOW.
WAIT--! DON'T GO!
DEAR GOD IN HEAVEN...
... IF HE'S LYING, SOMEONE'S LEARNED THAT CLARK WAS SUPERMAN.
AND IF HE'S TELLING THE TRUTH...
... I'VE LOST CLARK... ALL OVER AGAIN.

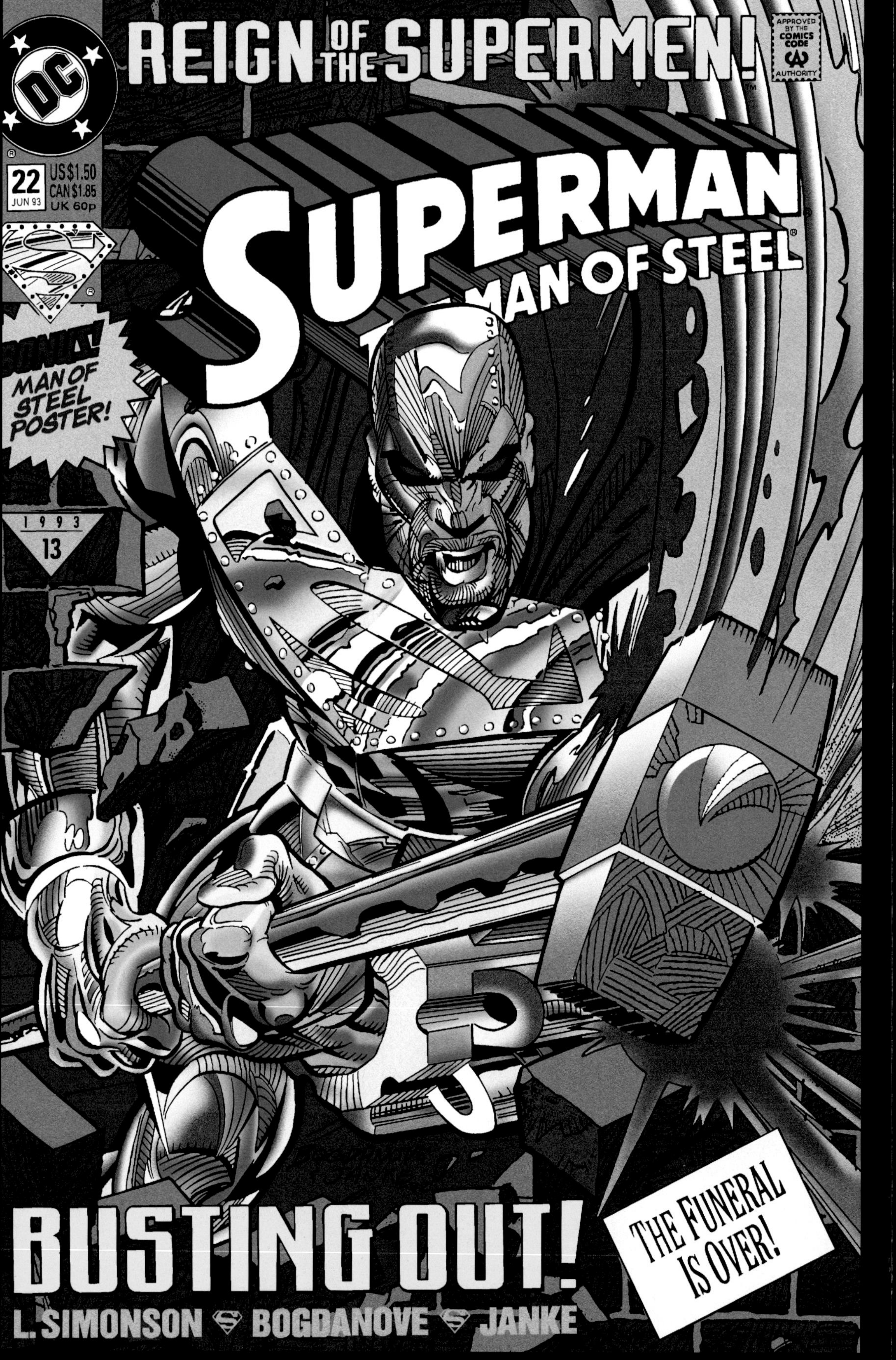
REIGN OF THE SUPERMEN!
APPROVED BY THE COMICS CODE AUTHORITY
DC
22 JUN 93
US $1.50
CAN $1.85
UK 60p
SUPERMAN
THE MAN OF STEEL
BONUS! MAN OF STEEL POSTER!
1993
13
BUSTING OUT!
THE FUNERAL IS OVER!
L. SIMONSON
BOGDANOVE
JANKE

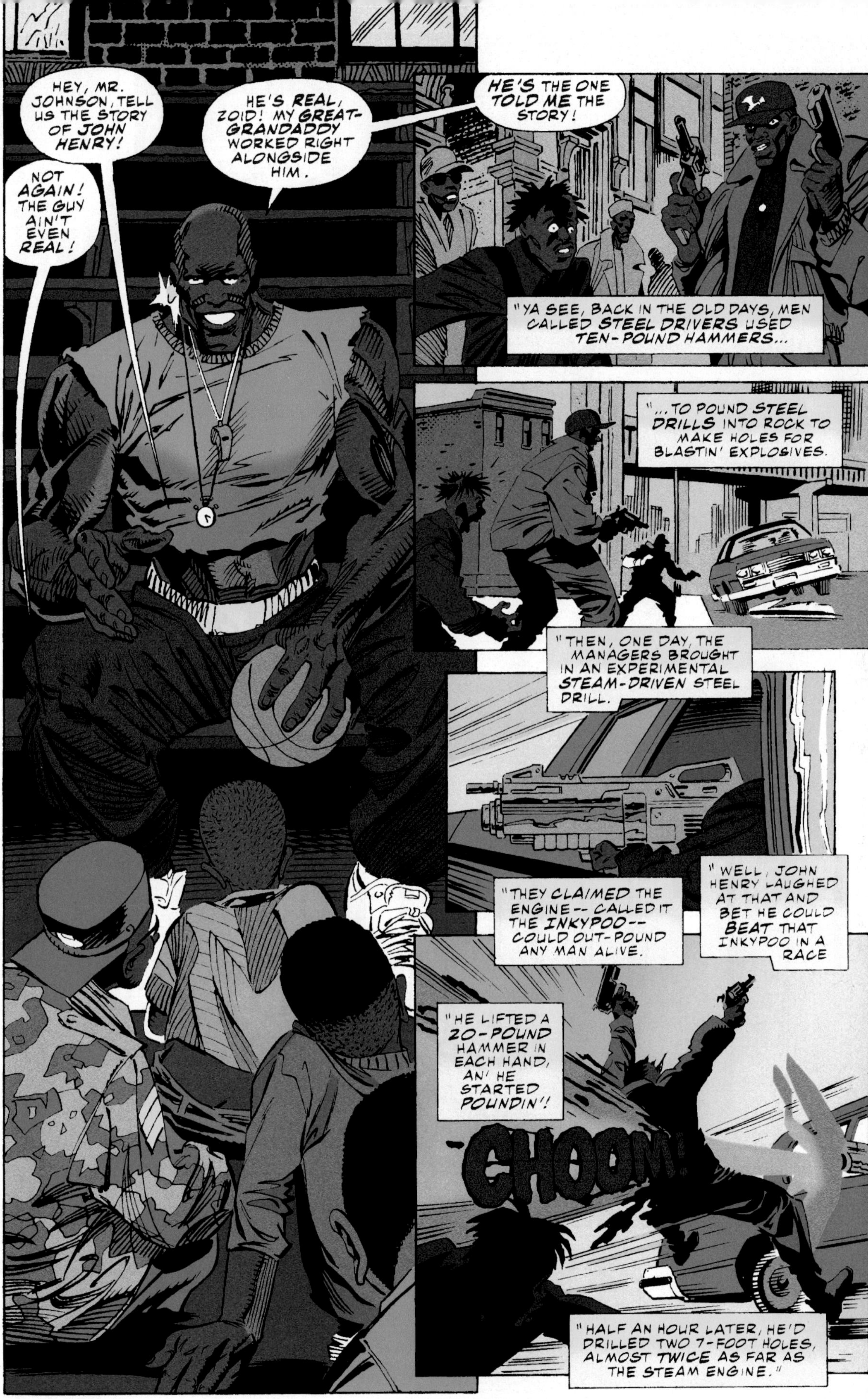
HEY, MR. JOHNSON, TELL US THE STORY OF JOHN HENRY!
NOT AGAIN! THE GUY AIN'T EVEN REAL!
HE'S REAL, ZOID! MY GREAT-GRANDADDY WORKED RIGHT ALONGSIDE HIM.
HE'S THE ONE TOLD ME THE STORY!
"YA SEE, BACK IN THE OLD DAYS, MEN CALLED STEEL DRIVERS USED TEN-POUND HAMMERS...
"...TO POUND STEEL DRILLS INTO ROCK TO MAKE HOLES FOR BLASTIN' EXPLOSIVES.
"THEN, ONE DAY, THE MANAGERS BROUGHT IN AN EXPERIMENTAL STEAM-DRIVEN STEEL DRILL.
"THEY CLAIMED THE ENGINE -- CALLED IT THE INKYPOO -- COULD OUT-POUND ANY MAN ALIVE.
"WELL, JOHN HENRY LAUGHED AT THAT AND BET HE COULD BEAT THAT INKYPOO IN A RACE
"HE LIFTED A 20-POUND HAMMER IN EACH HAND, AN' HE STARTED POUNDIN'!
CHOOM!
"HALF AN HOUR LATER, HE'D DRILLED TWO 7-FOOT HOLES, ALMOST TWICE AS FAR AS THE STEAM ENGINE."

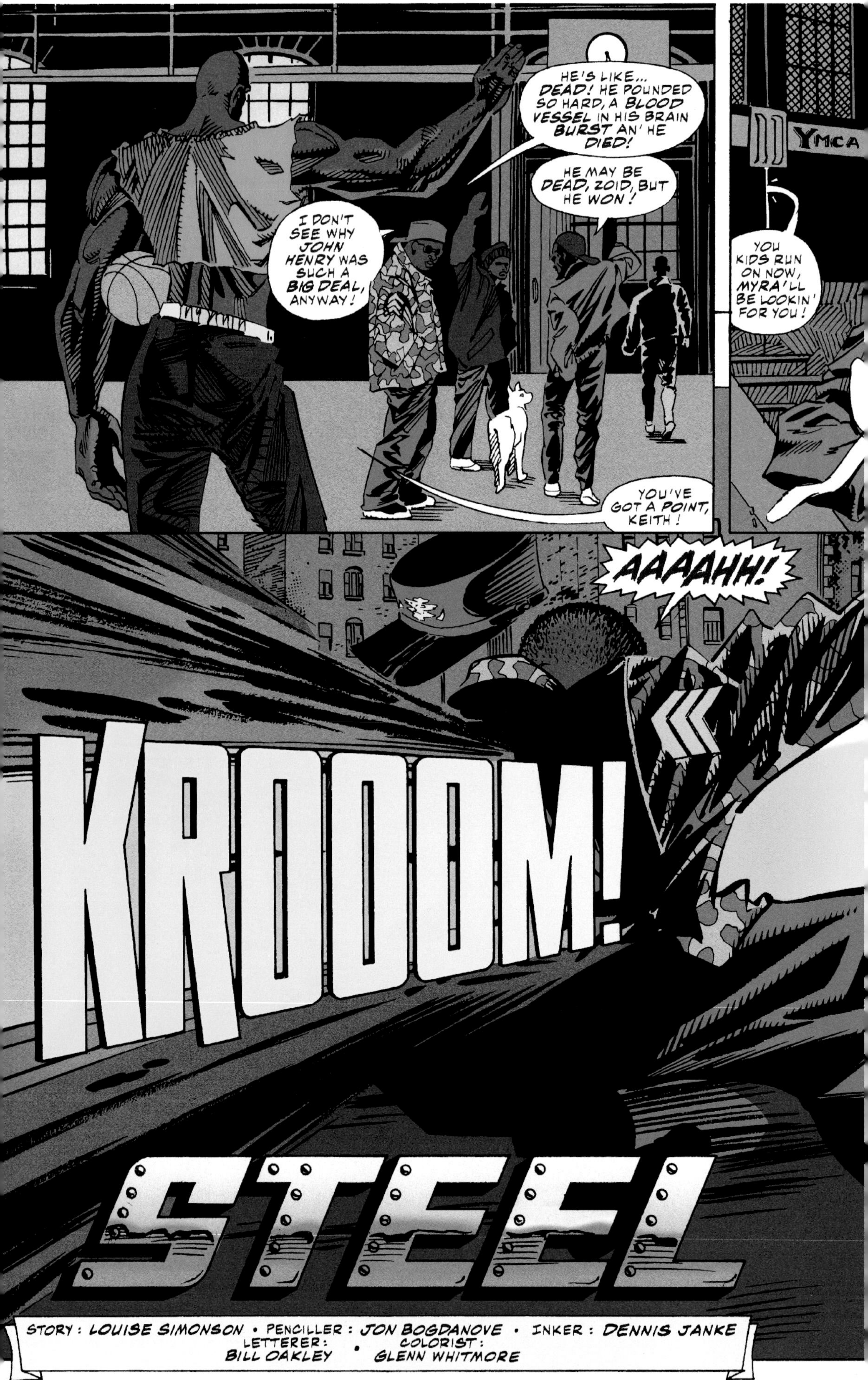
HE'S LIKE... DEAD! HE POUNDED SO HARD, A BLOOD VESSEL IN HIS BRAIN BURST AN' HE DIED!
HE MAY BE DEAD, ZOID, BUT HE WON!
I DON'T SEE WHY JOHN HENRY WAS SUCH A BIG DEAL, ANYWAY!
YOU'VE GOT A POINT, KEITH!
YMCA
YOU KIDS RUN ON NOW, MYRA'LL BE LOOKIN' FOR YOU!
AAAAHH!
KROOOM!
STEEL
STORY: LOUISE SIMONSON • PENCILLER: JON BOGDANOVE • INKER: DENNIS JANKE
LETTERER: BILL OAKLEY • COLORIST: GLENN WHITMORE

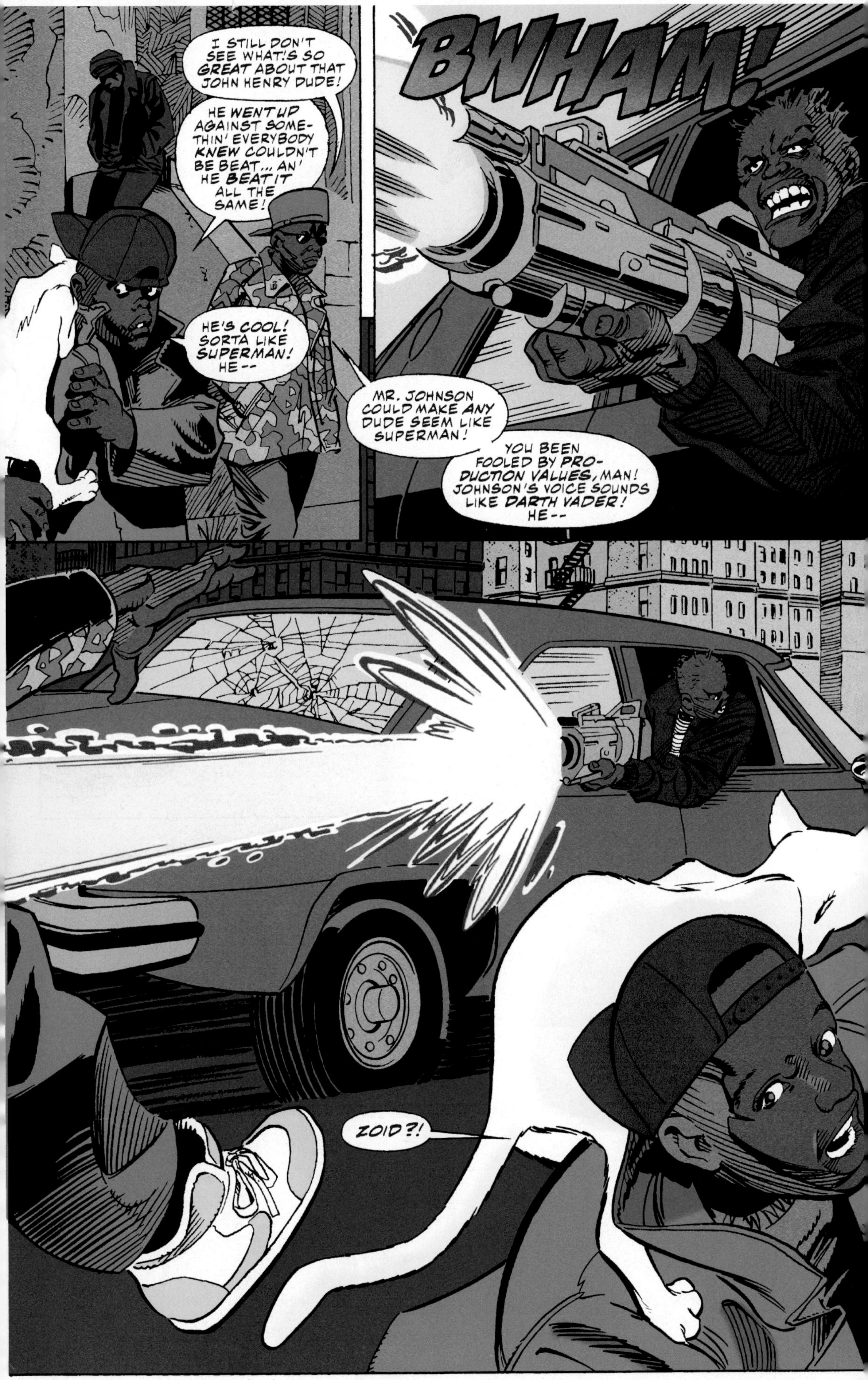
I STILL DON'T SEE WHAT'S SO GREAT ABOUT THAT JOHN HENRY DUDE!
HE WENT UP AGAINST SOMETHIN' EVERYBODY KNEW COULDN'T BE BEAT... AN' HE BEAT IT ALL THE SAME!
HE'S COOL! SORTA LIKE SUPERMAN! HE--
MR. JOHNSON COULD MAKE ANY DUDE SEEM LIKE SUPERMAN!
BWHAM!
YOU BEEN FOOLED BY PRODUCTION VALUES, MAN! JOHNSON'S VOICE SOUNDS LIKE DARTH VADER! HE--
ZOID?!

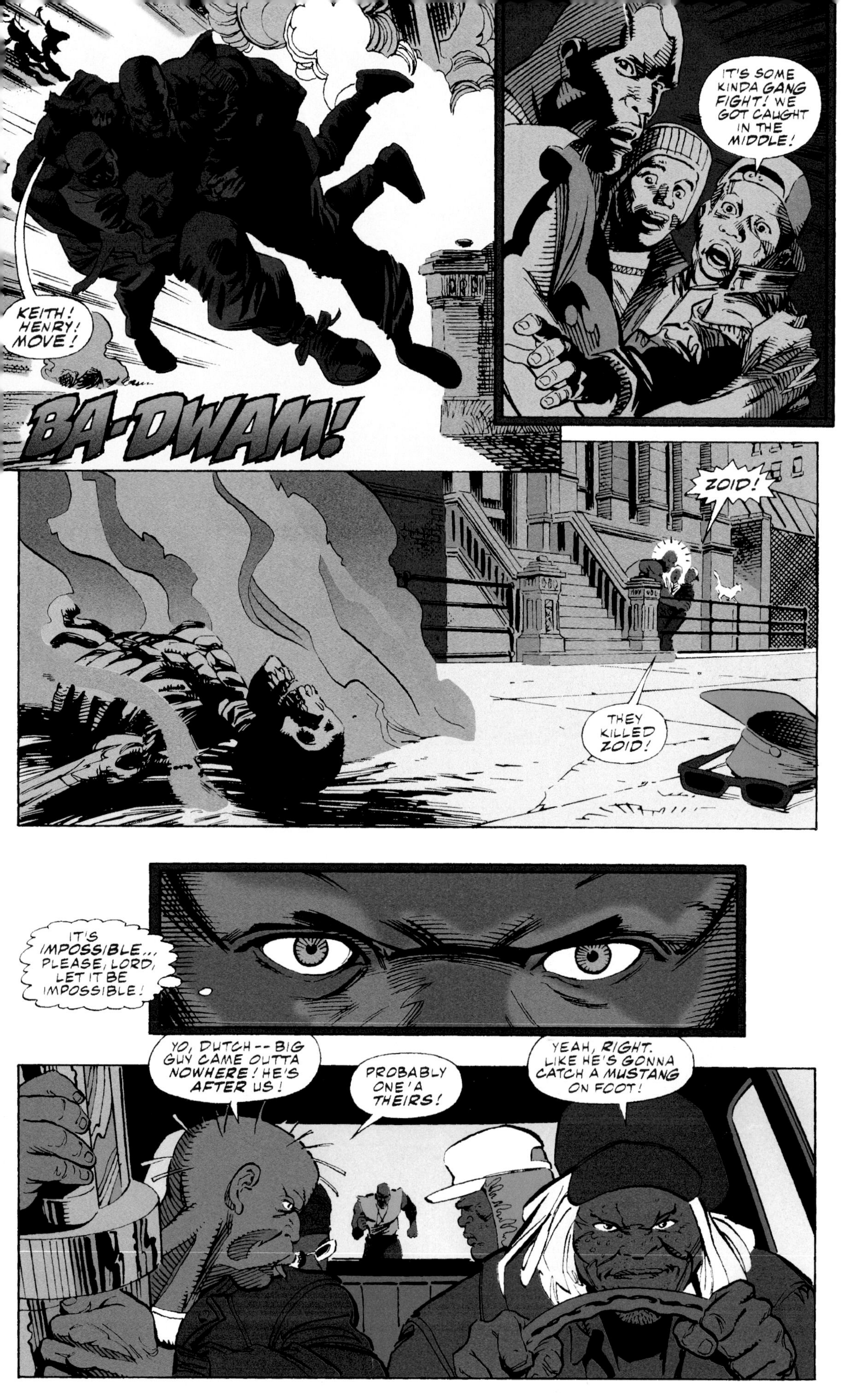
KEITH! HENRY! MOVE!
BA-DWAM!
IT'S SOME KINDA GANG FIGHT! WE GOT CAUGHT IN THE MIDDLE!
ZOID!
THEY KILLED ZOID!
IT'S IMPOSSIBLE... PLEASE, LORD, LET IT BE IMPOSSIBLE!
YO, DUTCH -- BIG GUY CAME OUTTA NOWHERE! HE'S AFTER US!
PROBABLY ONE 'A THEIRS!
YEAH, RIGHT. LIKE HE'S GONNA CATCH A MUSTANG ON FOOT!

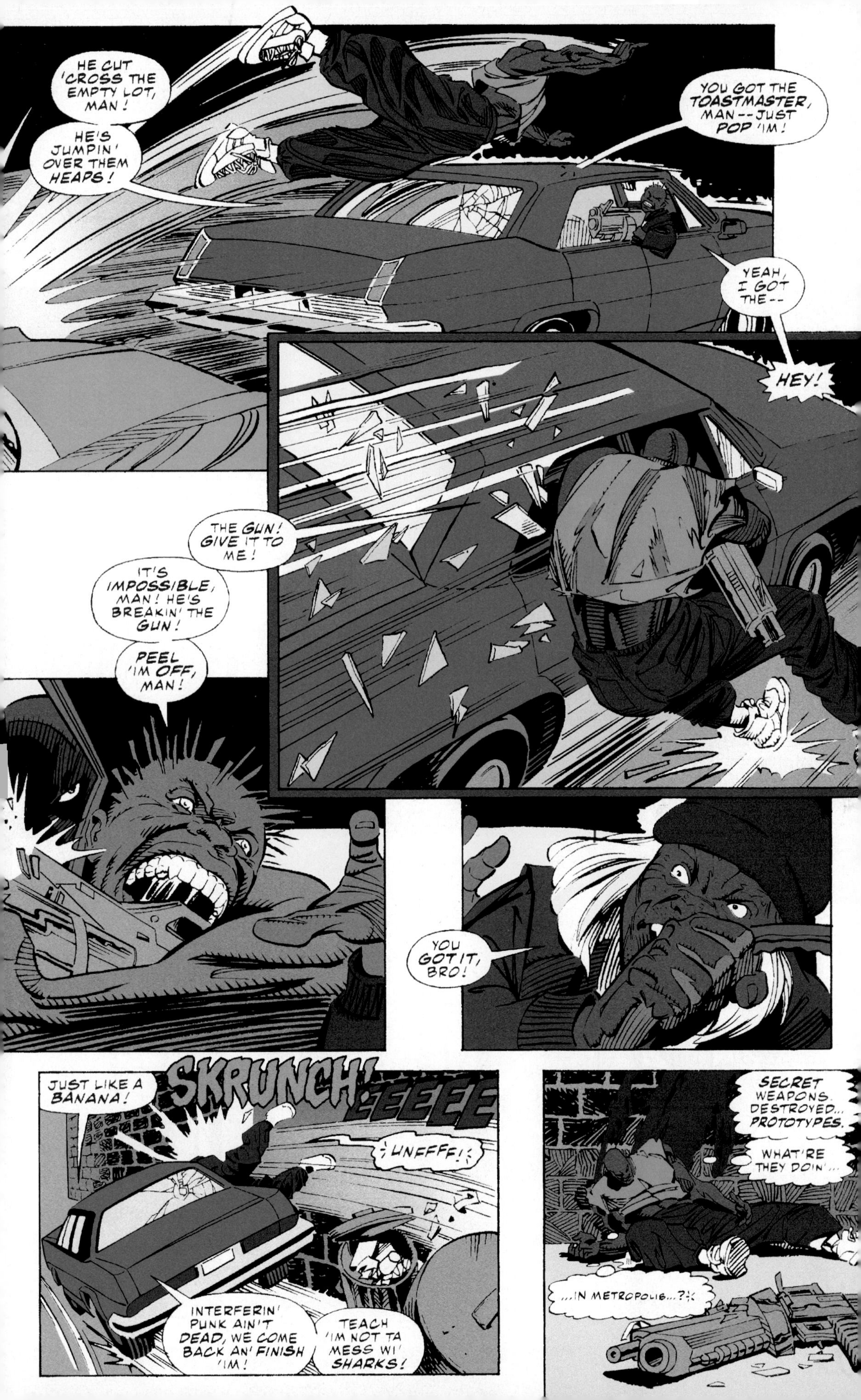
HE CUT 'CROSS THE EMPTY LOT, MAN!
HE'S JUMPIN' OVER THEM HEAPS!
YOU GOT THE TOASTMASTER, MAN--JUST POP 'IM!
YEAH, I GOT THE--
HEY!
THE GUN! GIVE IT TO ME!
IT'S IMPOSSIBLE, MAN! HE'S BREAKIN' THE GUN!
PEEL 'IM OFF, MAN!
YOU GOT IT, BRO!
JUST LIKE A BANANA!
SKRUNCH!
EEEEE
UNFFFF!
INTERFERIN' PUNK AIN'T DEAD, WE COME BACK AN' FINISH 'IM!
TEACH 'IM NOT TA MESS WI' SHARKS!
SECRET WEAPONS. DESTROYED... PROTOTYPES.
WHAT'RE THEY DOIN'...
...IN METROPOLIS...?

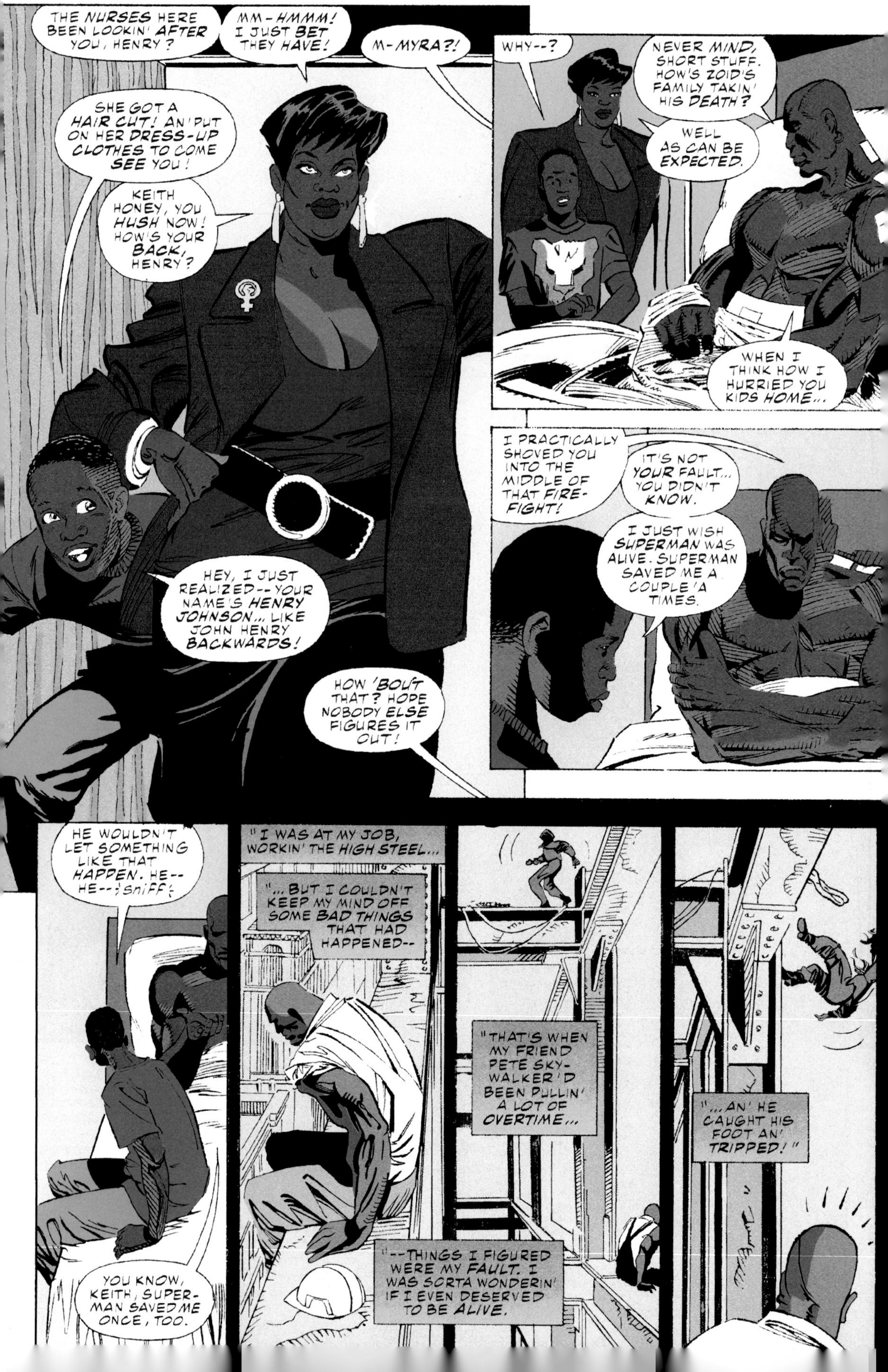

THE NURSES HERE BEEN LOOKIN' AFTER YOU, HENRY?
MM-HMMM! I JUST BET THEY HAVE!
M-MYRA?!
SHE GOT A HAIR CUT! AN' PUT ON HER DRESS-UP CLOTHES TO COME SEE YOU!
KEITH HONEY, YOU HUSH NOW! HOW'S YOUR BACK, HENRY?
HEY, I JUST REALIZED-- YOUR NAME'S HENRY JOHNSON... LIKE JOHN HENRY BACKWARDS!
HOW 'BOUT THAT? HOPE NOBODY ELSE FIGURES IT OUT!
WHY--?
NEVER MIND, SHORT STUFF. HOW'S ZOID'S FAMILY TAKIN' HIS DEATH?
WELL AS CAN BE EXPECTED.
WHEN I THINK HOW I HURRIED YOU KIDS HOME...
I PRACTICALLY SHOVED YOU INTO THE MIDDLE OF THAT FIRE-FIGHT!
IT'S NOT YOUR FAULT... YOU DIDN'T KNOW.
I JUST WISH SUPERMAN WAS ALIVE. SUPERMAN SAVED ME A COUPLE 'A TIMES.
HE WOULDN'T LET SOMETHING LIKE THAT HAPPEN. HE-- HE-- ¡sniff¡
YOU KNOW, KEITH, SUPER-MAN SAVED ME ONCE, TOO.
"I WAS AT MY JOB, WORKIN' THE HIGH STEEL...
"...BUT I COULDN'T KEEP MY MIND OFF SOME BAD THINGS THAT HAD HAPPENED--
"--THINGS I FIGURED WERE MY FAULT. I WAS SORTA WONDERIN' IF I EVEN DESERVED TO BE ALIVE.
"THAT'S WHEN MY FRIEND PETE SKY-WALKER'D BEEN PULLIN' A LOT OF OVERTIME...
"...AN' HE CAUGHT HIS FOOT AN' TRIPPED!"

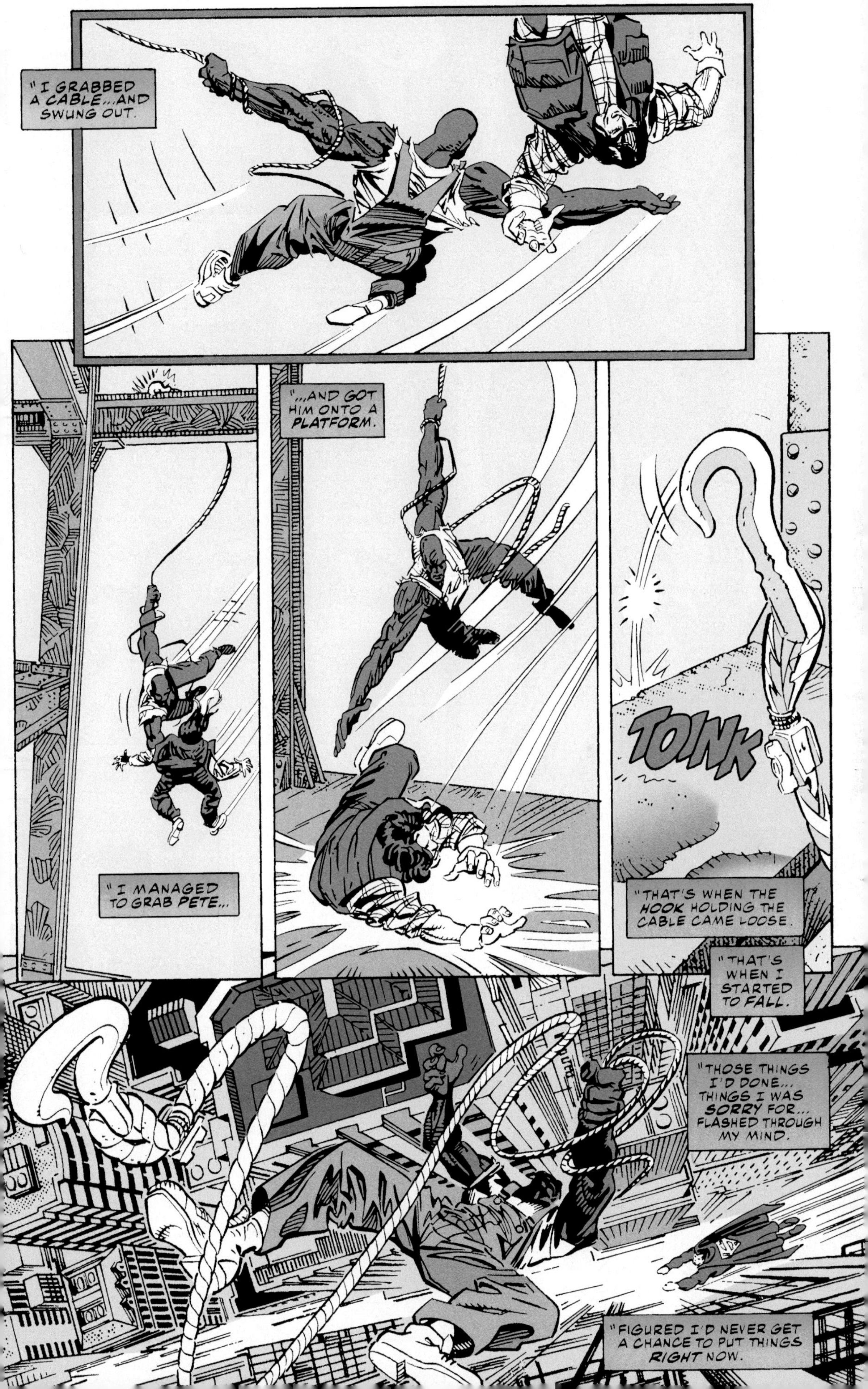
"I GRABBED A CABLE...AND SWUNG OUT.
"I MANAGED TO GRAB PETE...
"...AND GOT HIM ONTO A PLATFORM.
TOINK
"THAT'S WHEN THE HOOK HOLDING THE CABLE CAME LOOSE.
"THAT'S WHEN I STARTED TO FALL.
"THOSE THINGS I'D DONE... THINGS I WAS SORRY FOR... FLASHED THROUGH MY MIND.
"FIGURED I'D NEVER GET A CHANCE TO PUT THINGS RIGHT NOW.

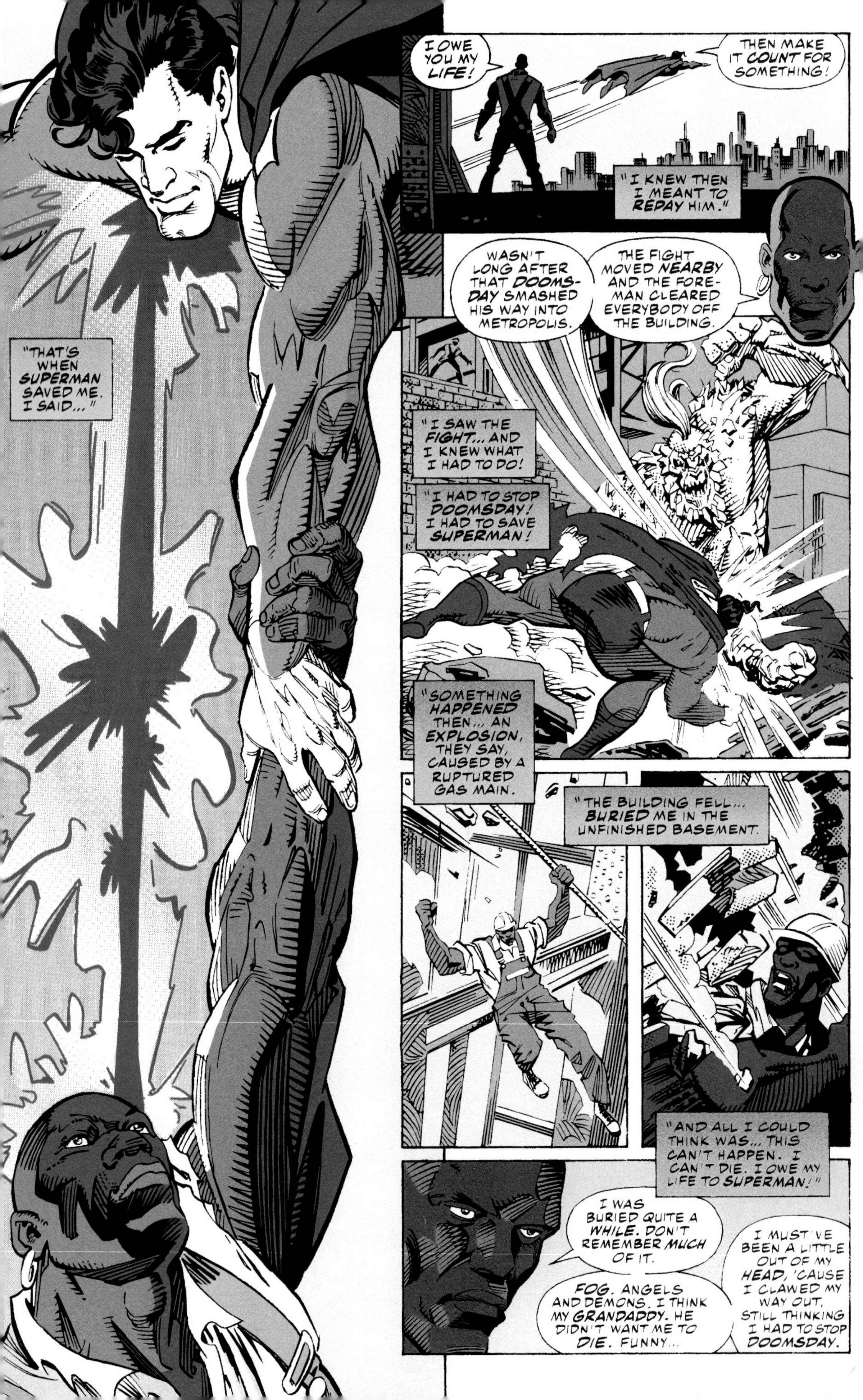
"THAT'S WHEN SUPERMAN SAVED ME. I SAID..."
I OWE YOU MY LIFE!
THEN MAKE IT COUNT FOR SOMETHING!
"I KNEW THEN I MEANT TO REPAY HIM."
WASN'T LONG AFTER THAT DOOMSDAY SMASHED HIS WAY INTO METROPOLIS.
THE FIGHT MOVED NEARBY AND THE FOREMAN CLEARED EVERYBODY OFF THE BUILDING.
"I SAW THE FIGHT... AND I KNEW WHAT I HAD TO DO!
"I HAD TO STOP DOOMSDAY! I HAD TO SAVE SUPERMAN!
"SOMETHING HAPPENED THEN... AN EXPLOSION, THEY SAY, CAUSED BY A RUPTURED GAS MAIN.
"THE BUILDING FELL... BURIED ME IN THE UNFINISHED BASEMENT.
"AND ALL I COULD THINK WAS... THIS CAN'T HAPPEN. I CAN'T DIE. I OWE MY LIFE TO SUPERMAN!"
I WAS BURIED QUITE A WHILE. DON'T REMEMBER MUCH OF IT.
FOG. ANGELS AND DEMONS. I THINK MY GRANDADDY. HE DIDN'T WANT ME TO DIE. FUNNY...
I MUST'VE BEEN A LITTLE OUT OF MY HEAD, 'CAUSE I CLAWED MY WAY OUT, STILL THINKING I HAD TO STOP DOOMSDAY.

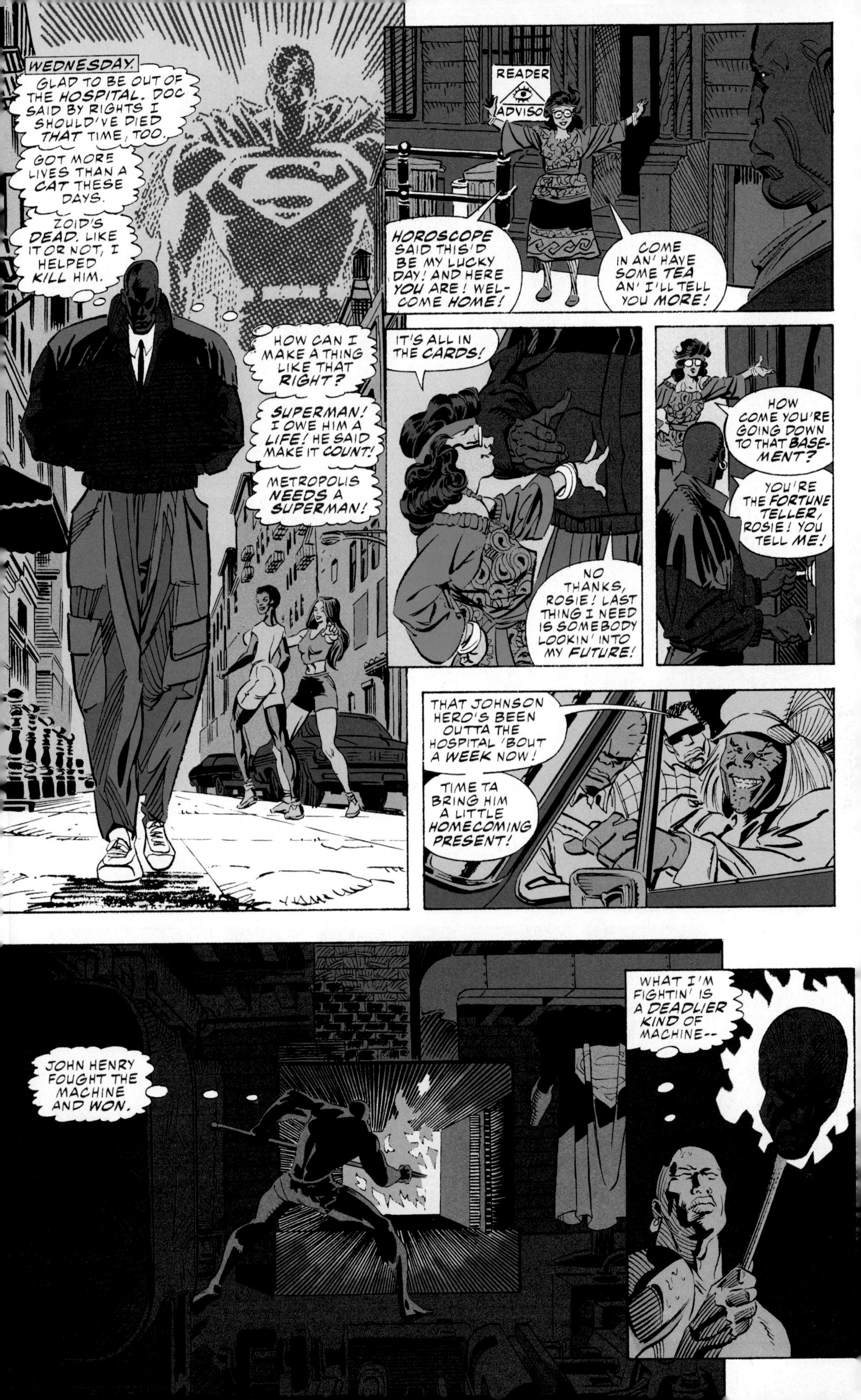
WEDNESDAY.
GLAD TO BE OUT OF THE HOSPITAL. DOC SAID BY RIGHTS I SHOULD'VE DIED THAT TIME, TOO.
GOT MORE LIVES THAN A CAT THESE DAYS.
ZOID'S DEAD. LIKE IT OR NOT, I HELPED KILL HIM.
HOW CAN I MAKE A THING LIKE THAT RIGHT?
SUPERMAN! I OWE HIM A LIFE! HE SAID MAKE IT COUNT!
METROPOLIS NEEDS A SUPERMAN!
READER
ADVISO
HOROSCOPE SAID THIS'D BE MY LUCKY DAY! AND HERE YOU ARE! WEL-COME HOME!
COME IN AN' HAVE SOME TEA AN' I'LL TELL YOU MORE!
IT'S ALL IN THE CARDS!
NO THANKS, ROSIE! LAST THING I NEED IS SOMEBODY LOOKIN' INTO MY FUTURE!
HOW COME YOU'RE GOING DOWN TO THAT BASE-MENT?
YOU'RE THE FORTUNE TELLER, ROSIE! YOU TELL ME!
THAT JOHNSON HERO'S BEEN OUTTA THE HOSPITAL 'BOUT A WEEK NOW!
TIME TA BRING HIM A LITTLE HOMECOMING PRESENT!
JOHN HENRY FOUGHT THE MACHINE AND WON.
WHAT I'M FIGHTIN' IS A DEADLIER KIND OF MACHINE--

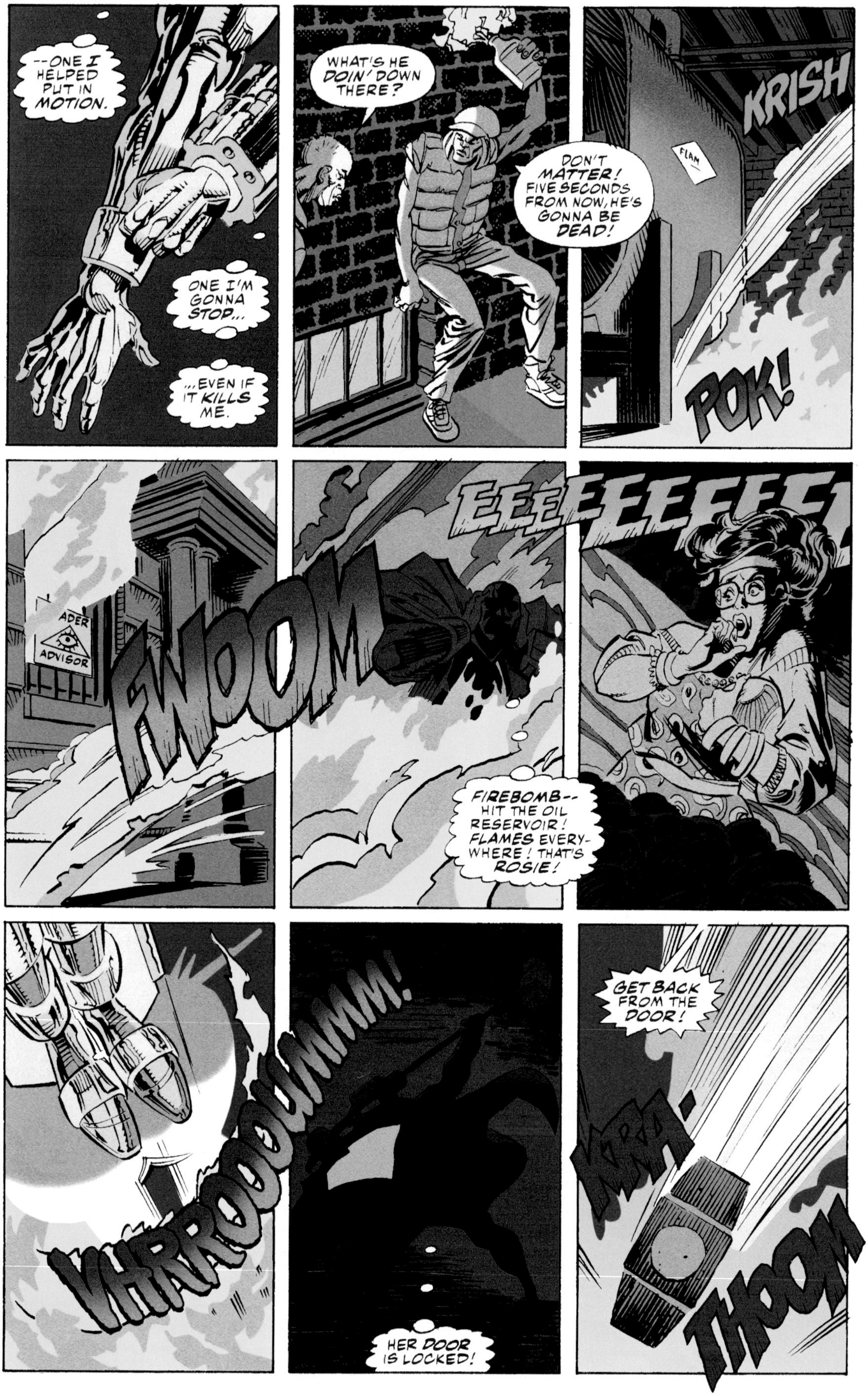

--ONE I HELPED PUT IN MOTION.
ONE I'M GONNA STOP...
...EVEN IF IT KILLS ME.
WHAT'S HE DOIN' DOWN THERE?
DON'T MATTER! FIVE SECONDS FROM NOW, HE'S GONNA BE DEAD!
KRISH
FLAM
POK!
ADER
ADVISOR
FWOOM
EEEEEEEEE
FIREBOMB-- HIT THE OIL RESERVOIR! FLAMES EVERY-WHERE! THAT'S ROSIE!
VHRROOUMMM!
HER DOOR IS LOCKED!
GET BACK FROM THE DOOR!
KRRA-THOOM

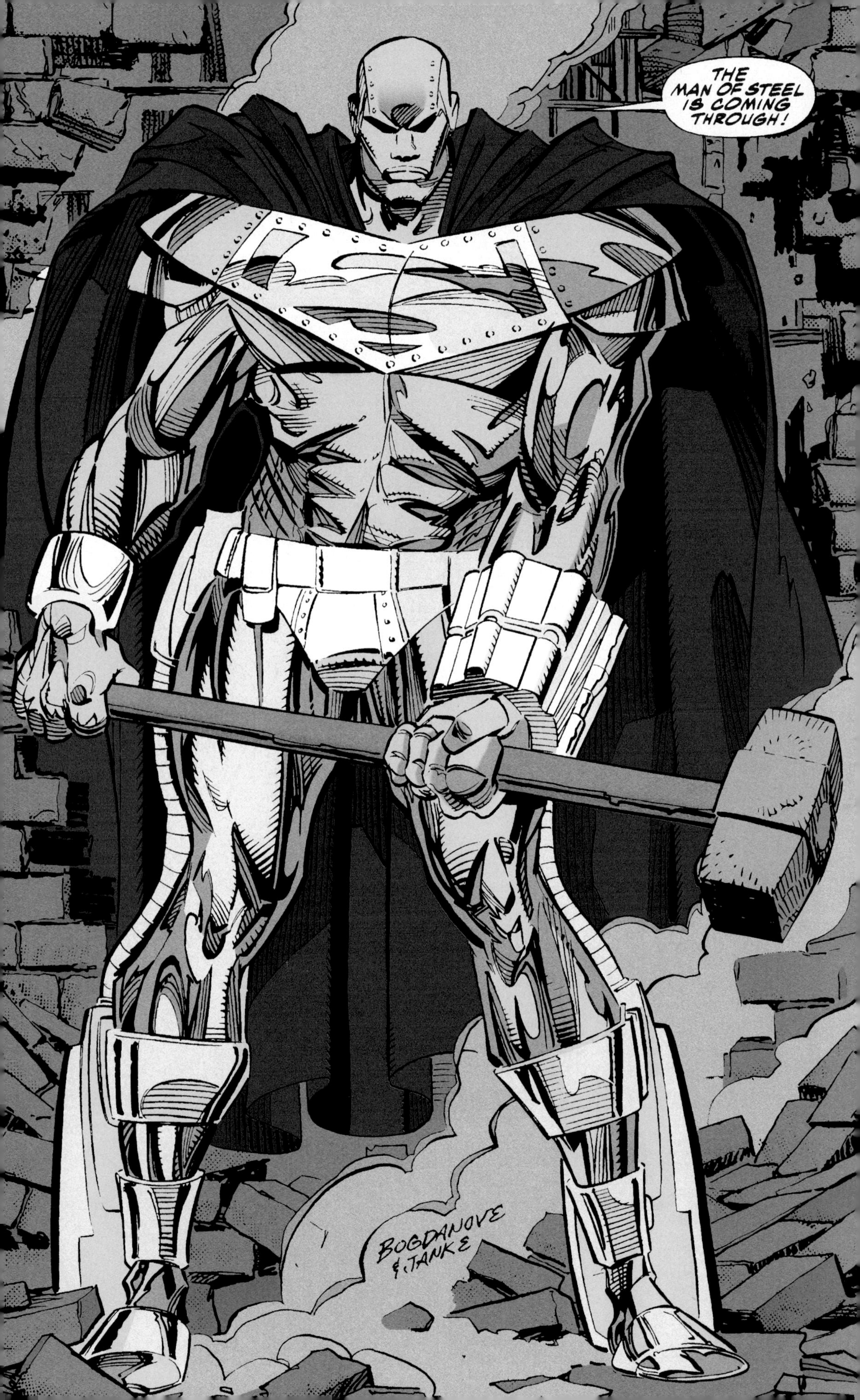
THE MAN OF STEEL IS COMING THROUGH!
BOGDANOVE & JANKE

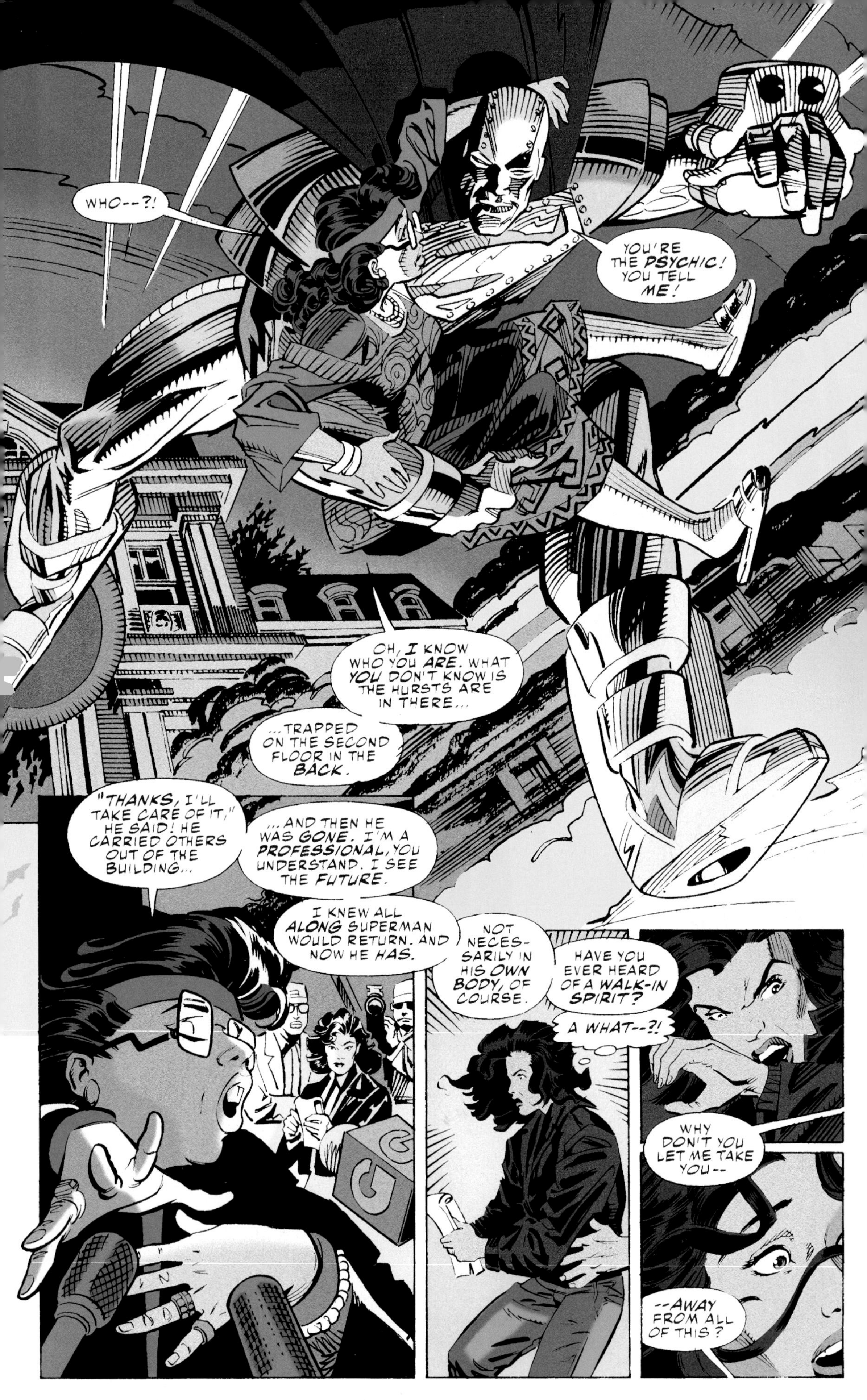
WHO--?!
YOU'RE THE PSYCHIC! YOU TELL ME!
OH, I KNOW WHO YOU ARE. WHAT YOU DON'T KNOW IS THE HURSTS ARE IN THERE...
...TRAPPED ON THE SECOND FLOOR IN THE BACK.
"THANKS, I'LL TAKE CARE OF IT," HE SAID! HE CARRIED OTHERS OUT OF THE BUILDING...
...AND THEN HE WAS GONE. I'M A PROFESSIONAL, YOU UNDERSTAND. I SEE THE FUTURE.
I KNEW ALL ALONG SUPERMAN WOULD RETURN. AND NOW HE HAS.
NOT NECES-SARILY IN HIS OWN BODY, OF COURSE.
HAVE YOU EVER HEARD OF A WALK-IN SPIRIT?
A WHAT--?!
WHY DON'T YOU LET ME TAKE YOU--
--AWAY FROM ALL OF THIS?

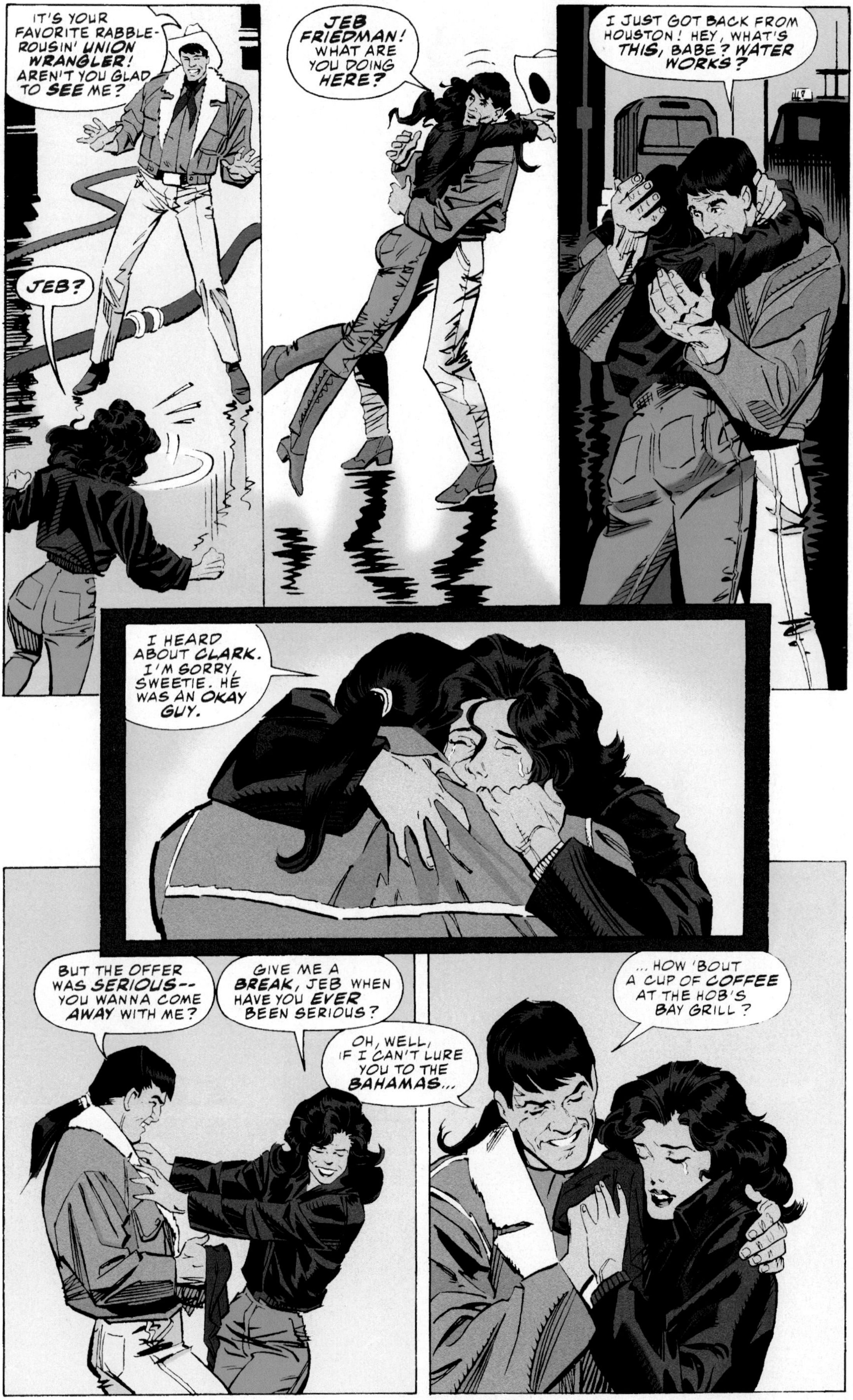
IT'S YOUR FAVORITE RABBLE-ROUSIN' UNION WRANGLER! AREN'T YOU GLAD TO SEE ME?
JEB?
JEB FRIEDMAN! WHAT ARE YOU DOING HERE?
I JUST GOT BACK FROM HOUSTON! HEY, WHAT'S THIS, BABE? WATER WORKS?
I HEARD ABOUT CLARK. I'M SORRY, SWEETIE. HE WAS AN OKAY GUY.
BUT THE OFFER WAS SERIOUS-- YOU WANNA COME AWAY WITH ME?
GIVE ME A BREAK, JEB WHEN HAVE YOU EVER BEEN SERIOUS?
OH, WELL, IF I CAN'T LURE YOU TO THE BAHAMAS...
...HOW 'BOUT A CUP OF COFFEE AT THE HOB'S BAY GRILL?

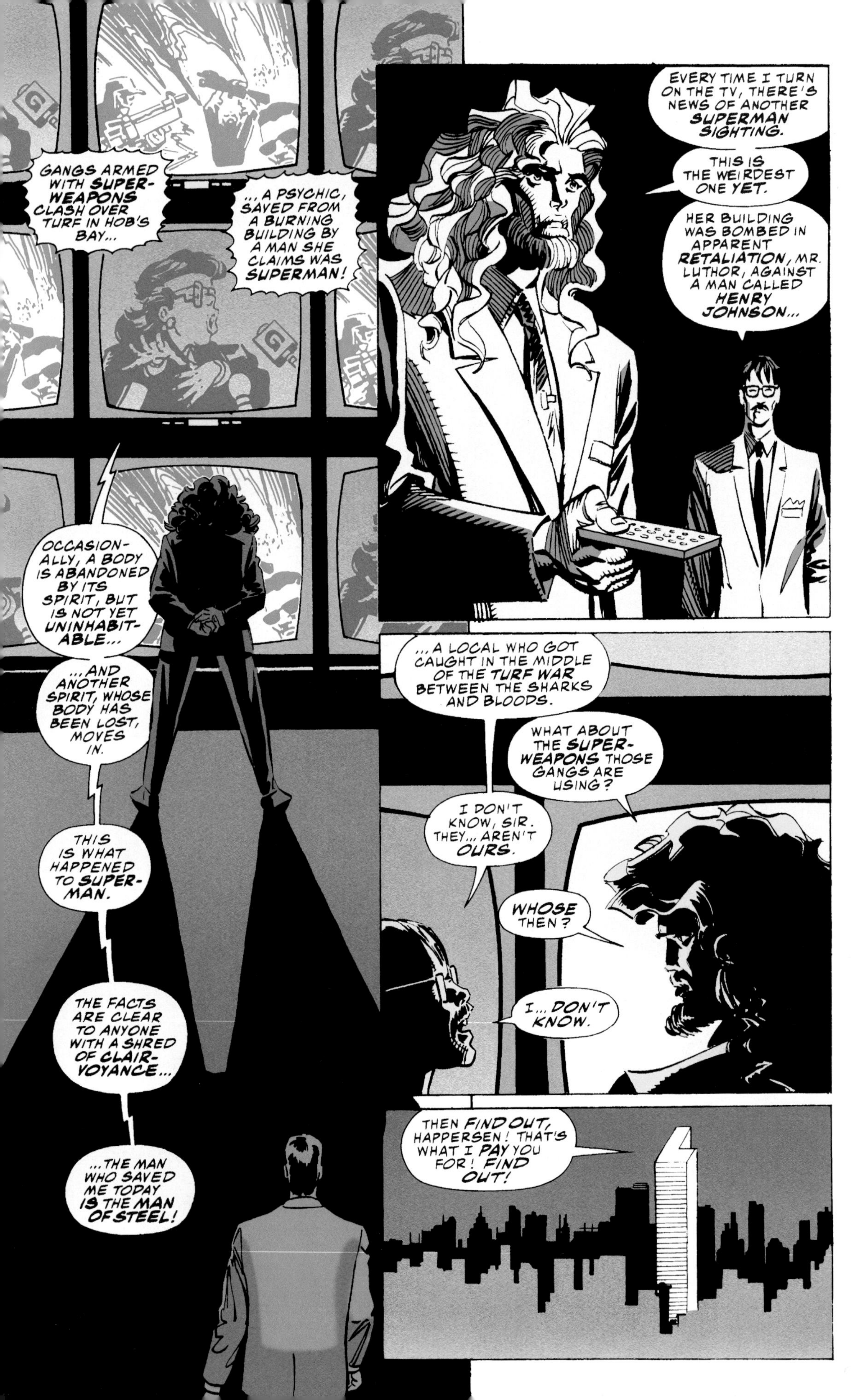

GANGS ARMED WITH SUPER-WEAPONS CLASH OVER TURF IN HOB'S BAY...
...A PSYCHIC, SAVED FROM A BURNING BUILDING BY A MAN SHE CLAIMS WAS SUPERMAN!
EVERY TIME I TURN ON THE TV, THERE'S NEWS OF ANOTHER SUPERMAN SIGHTING.
THIS IS THE WEIRDEST ONE YET.
HER BUILDING WAS BOMBED IN APPARENT RETALIATION, MR. LUTHOR, AGAINST A MAN CALLED HENRY JOHNSON...
OCCASION-ALLY, A BODY IS ABANDONED BY ITS SPIRIT, BUT IS NOT YET UNINHABIT-ABLE...
...AND ANOTHER SPIRIT, WHOSE BODY HAS BEEN LOST, MOVES IN.
THIS IS WHAT HAPPENED TO SUPER-MAN.
THE FACTS ARE CLEAR TO ANYONE WITH A SHRED OF CLAIR-VOYANCE...
...THE MAN WHO SAVED ME TODAY IS THE MAN OF STEEL!
...A LOCAL WHO GOT CAUGHT IN THE MIDDLE OF THE TURF WAR BETWEEN THE SHARKS AND BLOODS.
WHAT ABOUT THE SUPER-WEAPONS THOSE GANGS ARE USING?
I DON'T KNOW, SIR. THEY... AREN'T OURS.
WHOSE THEN?
I... DON'T KNOW.
THEN FIND OUT, HAPPERSEN! THAT'S WHAT I PAY YOU FOR! FIND OUT!

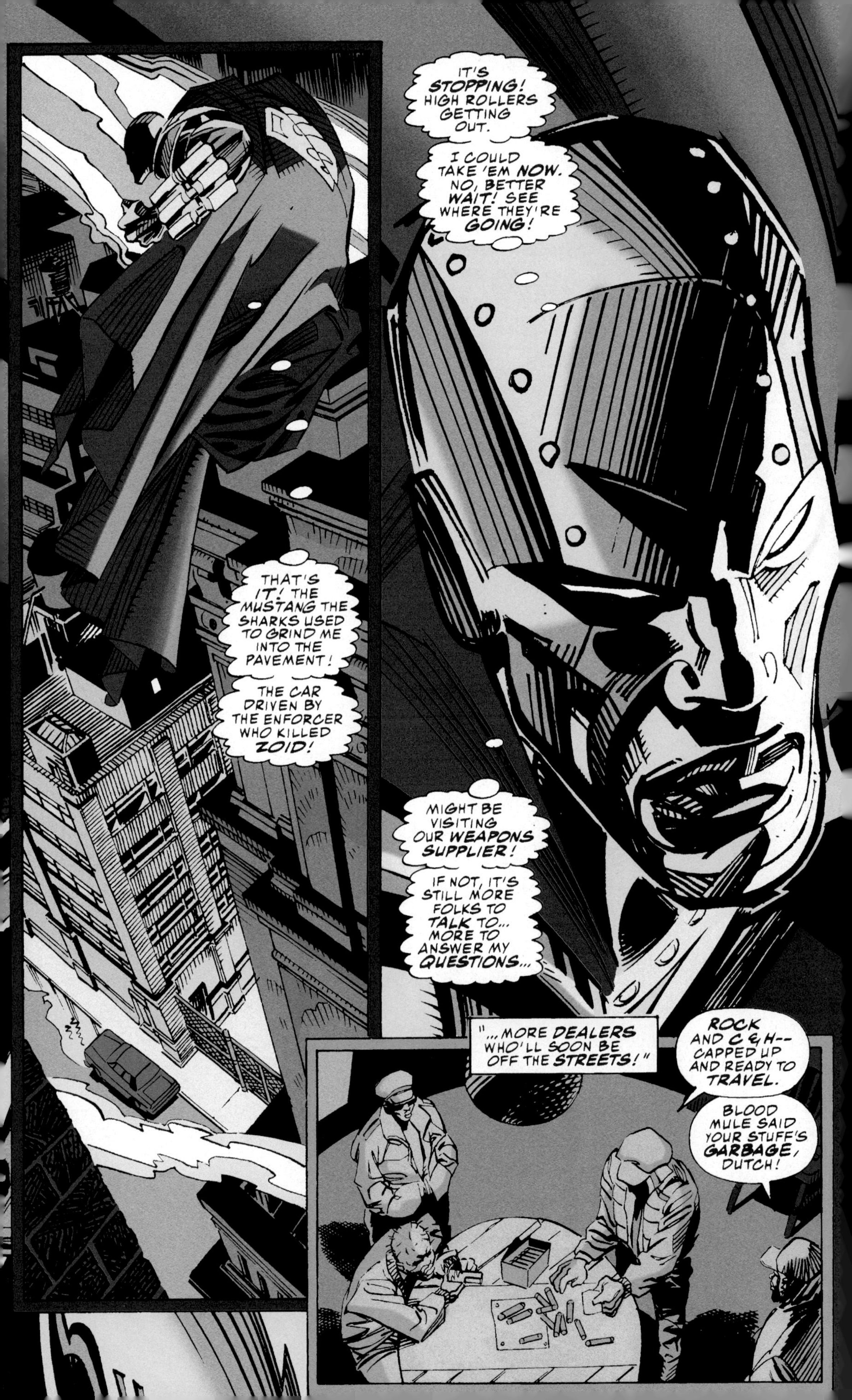
IT'S STOPPING! HIGH ROLLERS GETTING OUT.
I COULD TAKE 'EM NOW. NO, BETTER WAIT! SEE WHERE THEY'RE GOING!
THAT'S IT! THE MUSTANG THE SHARKS USED TO GRIND ME INTO THE PAVEMENT!
THE CAR DRIVEN BY THE ENFORCER WHO KILLED ZOID!
MIGHT BE VISITING OUR WEAPONS SUPPLIER!
IF NOT, IT'S STILL MORE FOLKS TO TALK TO... MORE TO ANSWER MY QUESTIONS...
"...MORE DEALERS WHO'LL SOON BE OFF THE STREETS!"
ROCK AND C & H-- CAPPED UP AND READY TO TRAVEL.
BLOOD MULE SAID YOUR STUFF'S GARBAGE, DUTCH!

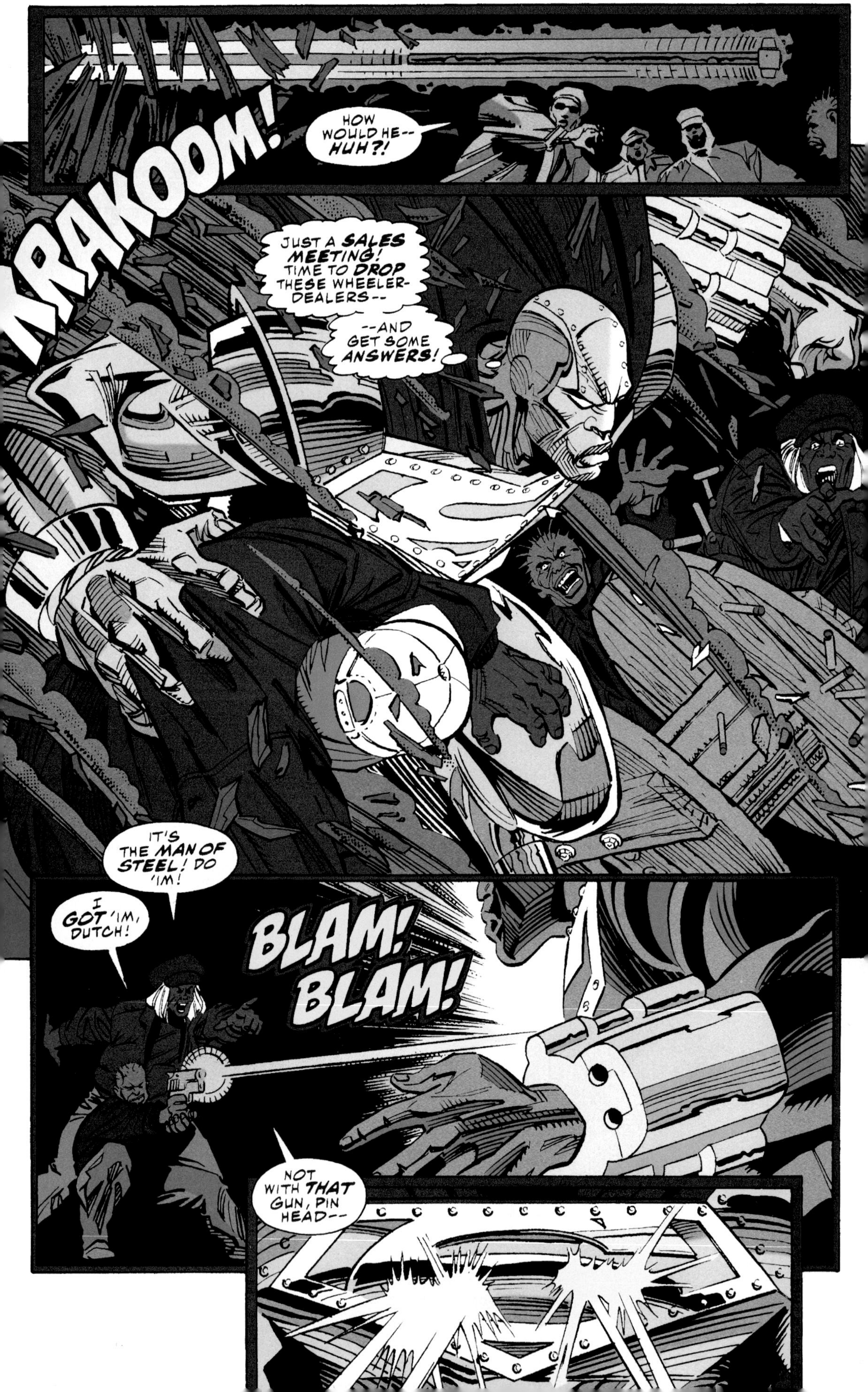
KRAKOOM!
HOW WOULD HE-- HUH?!
JUST A SALES MEETING! TIME TO DROP THESE WHEELER-DEALERS--
--AND GET SOME ANSWERS!
IT'S THE MAN OF STEEL! DO 'IM!
I GOT 'IM, DUTCH!
BLAM! BLAM!
NOT WITH THAT GUN, PIN HEAD--

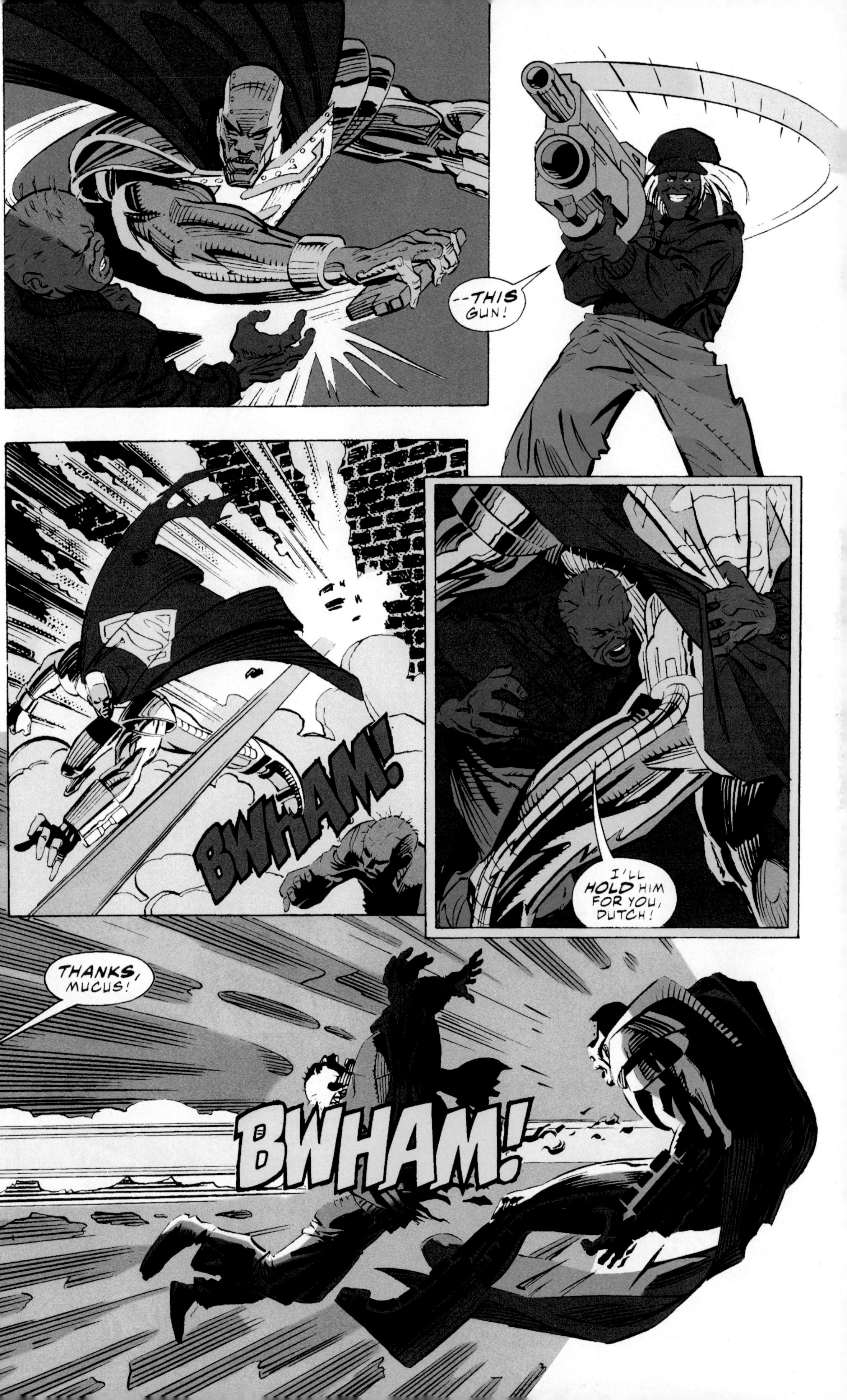
--THIS GUN!
BWHAM!
I'LL HOLD HIM FOR YOU, DUTCH!
THANKS, MUCUS!
BWHAM!

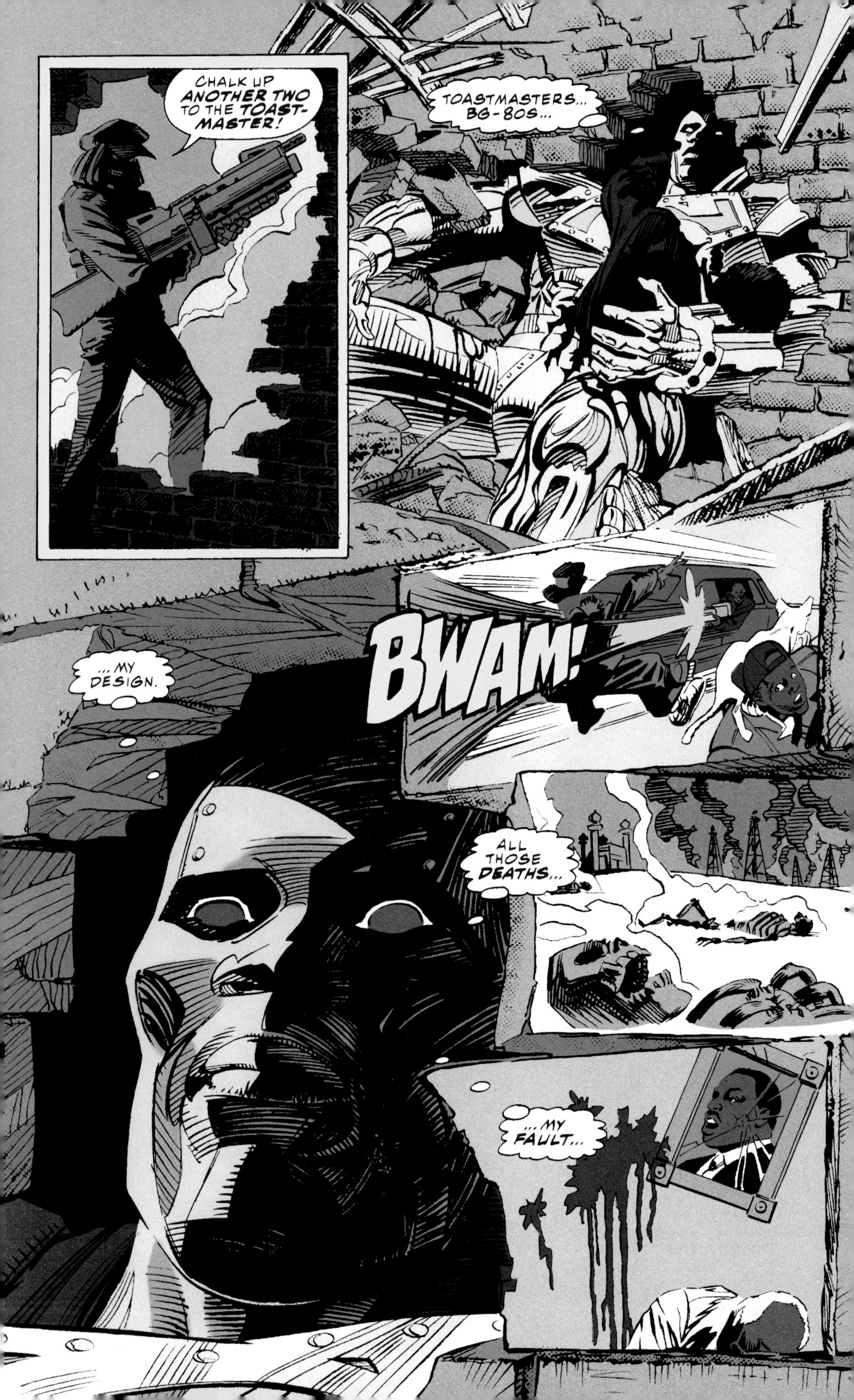
CHALK UP ANOTHER TWO TO THE TOAST-MASTER!
TOASTMASTERS... BG-80S...
...MY DESIGN.
BWAM!
ALL THOSE DEATHS...
...MY FAULT...

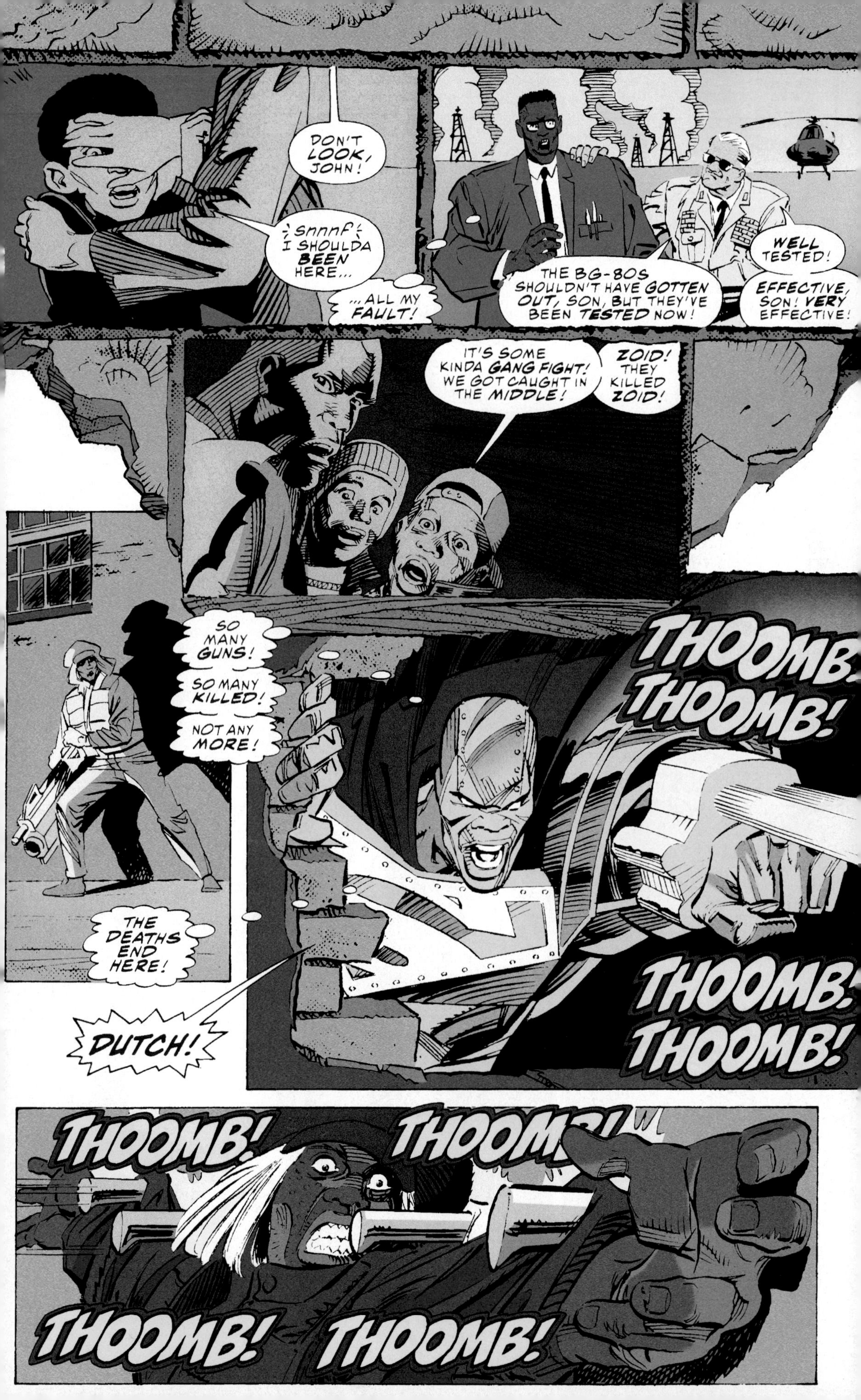
DON'T LOOK, JOHN!
snnnf! I SHOULDA BEEN HERE...
...ALL MY FAULT!
THE BG-80S SHOULDN'T HAVE GOTTEN OUT, SON, BUT THEY'VE BEEN TESTED NOW!
WELL TESTED!
EFFECTIVE, SON! VERY EFFECTIVE!
IT'S SOME KINDA GANG FIGHT! WE GOT CAUGHT IN THE MIDDLE!
ZOID! THEY KILLED ZOID!
SO MANY GUNS!
SO MANY KILLED!
NOT ANY MORE!
THE DEATHS END HERE!
DUTCH!
THOOMB! THOOMB!
THOOMB! THOOMB!
THOOMB!
THOOMB!
THOOMB!
THOOMB!

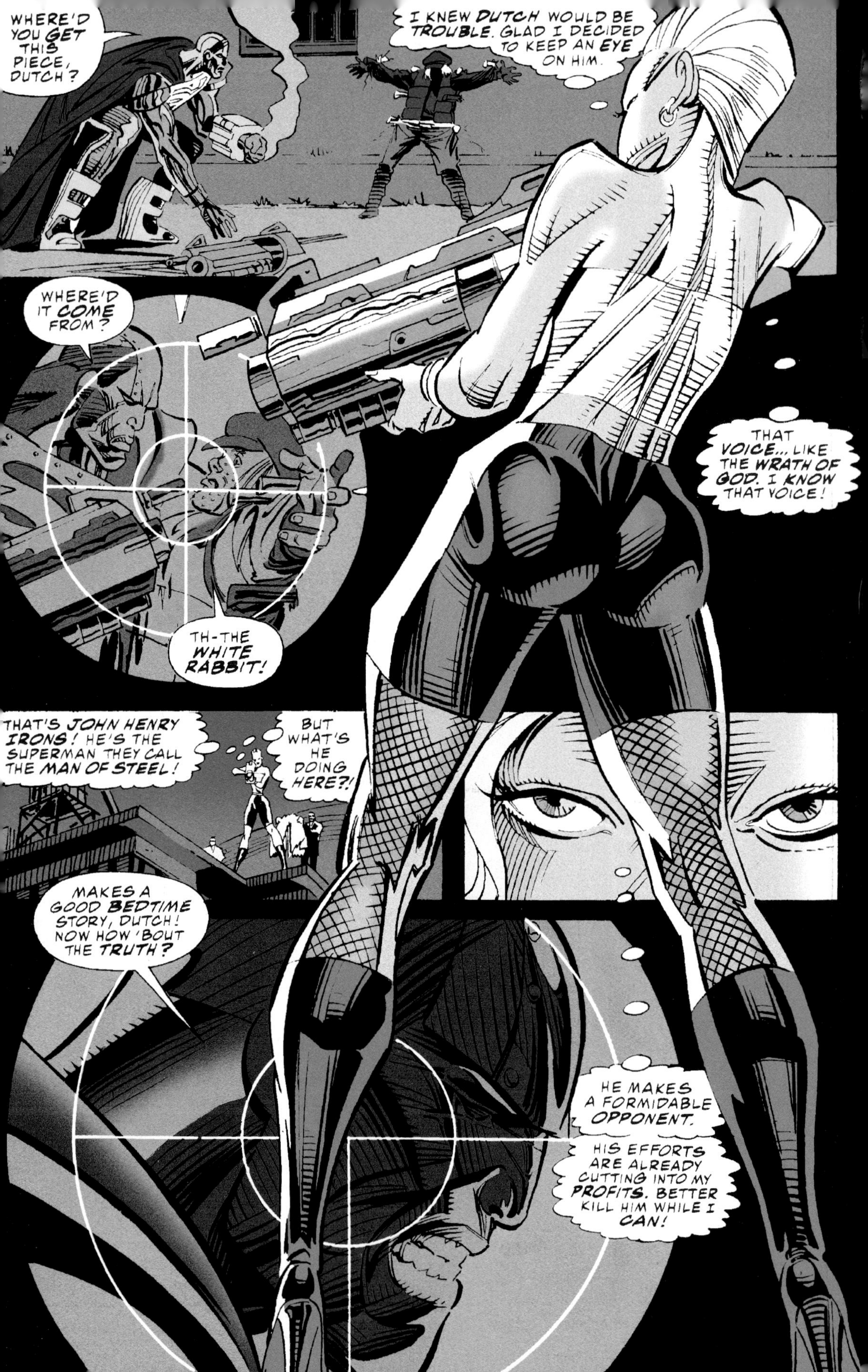
WHERE'D YOU GET THIS PIECE, DUTCH?
I KNEW DUTCH WOULD BE TROUBLE. GLAD I DECIDED TO KEEP AN EYE ON HIM.
WHERE'D IT COME FROM?
TH-THE WHITE RABBIT!
THAT VOICE... LIKE THE WRATH OF GOD. I KNOW THAT VOICE!
THAT'S JOHN HENRY IRONS! HE'S THE SUPERMAN THEY CALL THE MAN OF STEEL!
BUT WHAT'S HE DOING HERE?!
MAKES A GOOD BEDTIME STORY, DUTCH! NOW HOW 'BOUT THE TRUTH?
HE MAKES A FORMIDABLE OPPONENT.
HIS EFFORTS ARE ALREADY CUTTING INTO MY PROFITS. BETTER KILL HIM WHILE I CAN!

IT'S THE TRUTH! IT'S THE BUNNY-- **KPOK!**

YOU HAD A BEAD ON THE MAN OF STEEL, RABBIT! WHY'D YOU POP DUTCH?!

DUTCH WAS SINGING HIS HEART OUT, LUG. AND IF THERE'S ONE THING I HATE, IT'S A PIGEON!

B-BUT THE MAN OF STEEL...?

HE'S POTENTIALLY MORE PROFITABLE THAN BOTH OF YOU COMBINED.

"HE MIGHT LISTEN TO REASON...OR TO BLACKMAIL. NO, THERE'S NO POINT IN KILLING HIM...YET."

DAILY PLANET

THERE ARE FOUR GUYS OUT THERE WHO CLAIM TO BE SUPERMAN--!

THE KID WHO SAYS HE'S A CLONE OF SUPERMAN, THE CYBORG WHO CLAIMS HE'S SUPERMAN REBUILT...

...THE FASCIST IN SHADES. AND THE MAN OF STEEL THE FORTUNE TELLER SAID IS SUPERMAN RETURNED IN A DIFFERENT BODY.

SHE CALLED HIM A WALK-IN SPIRIT.

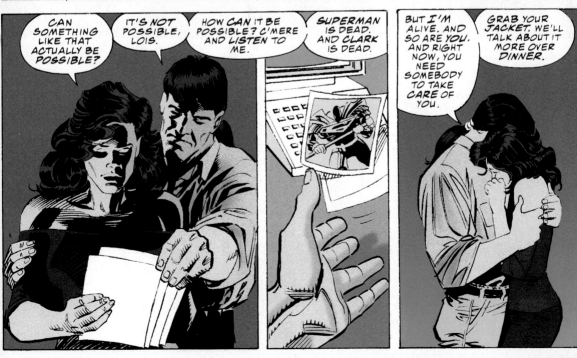

CAN SOMETHING LIKE THAT ACTUALLY BE POSSIBLE?

IT'S NOT POSSIBLE, LOIS.

HOW CAN IT BE POSSIBLE? C'MERE AND LISTEN TO ME.

SUPERMAN IS DEAD. AND CLARK IS DEAD.

BUT I'M ALIVE. AND SO ARE YOU. AND RIGHT NOW, YOU NEED SOMEBODY TO TAKE CARE OF YOU.

GRAB YOUR JACKET. WE'LL TALK ABOUT IT MORE OVER DINNER.

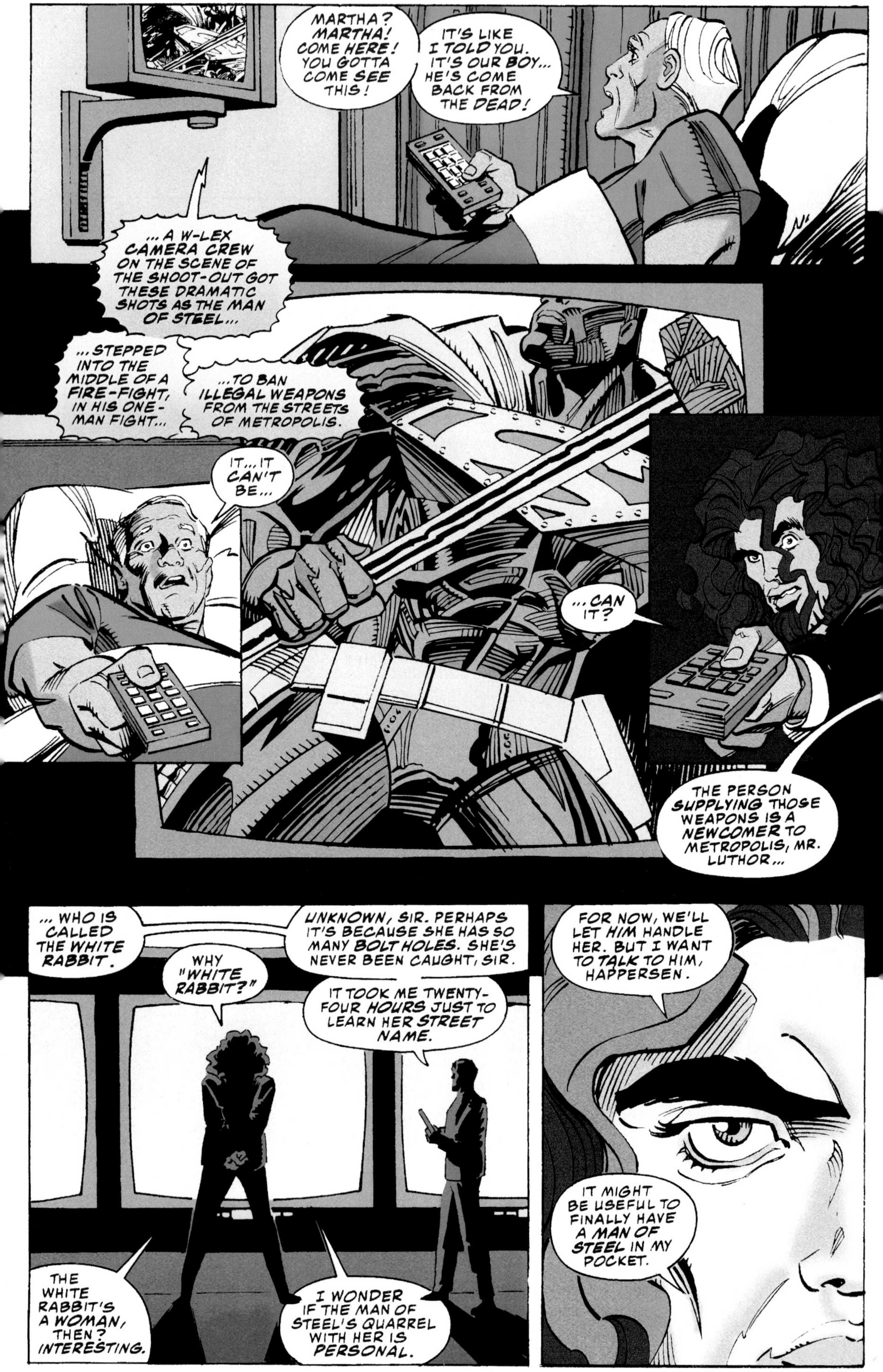
MARTHA? MARTHA! COME HERE! YOU GOTTA COME SEE THIS!
IT'S LIKE I TOLD YOU. IT'S OUR BOY... HE'S COME BACK FROM THE DEAD!
... A W-LEX CAMERA CREW ON THE SCENE OF THE SHOOT-OUT GOT THESE DRAMATIC SHOTS AS THE MAN OF STEEL...
...STEPPED INTO THE MIDDLE OF A FIRE-FIGHT, IN HIS ONE-MAN FIGHT...
...TO BAN ILLEGAL WEAPONS FROM THE STREETS OF METROPOLIS.
IT... IT CAN'T BE...
...CAN IT?
THE PERSON SUPPLYING THOSE WEAPONS IS A NEWCOMER TO METROPOLIS, MR. LUTHOR...
... WHO IS CALLED THE WHITE RABBIT.
WHY "WHITE RABBIT?"
UNKNOWN, SIR. PERHAPS IT'S BECAUSE SHE HAS SO MANY BOLT HOLES. SHE'S NEVER BEEN CAUGHT, SIR.
IT TOOK ME TWENTY-FOUR HOURS JUST TO LEARN HER STREET NAME.
THE WHITE RABBIT'S A WOMAN, THEN? INTERESTING.
I WONDER IF THE MAN OF STEEL'S QUARREL WITH HER IS PERSONAL.
FOR NOW, WE'LL LET HIM HANDLE HER. BUT I WANT TO TALK TO HIM, HAPPERSEN.
IT MIGHT BE USEFUL TO FINALLY HAVE A MAN OF STEEL IN MY POCKET.

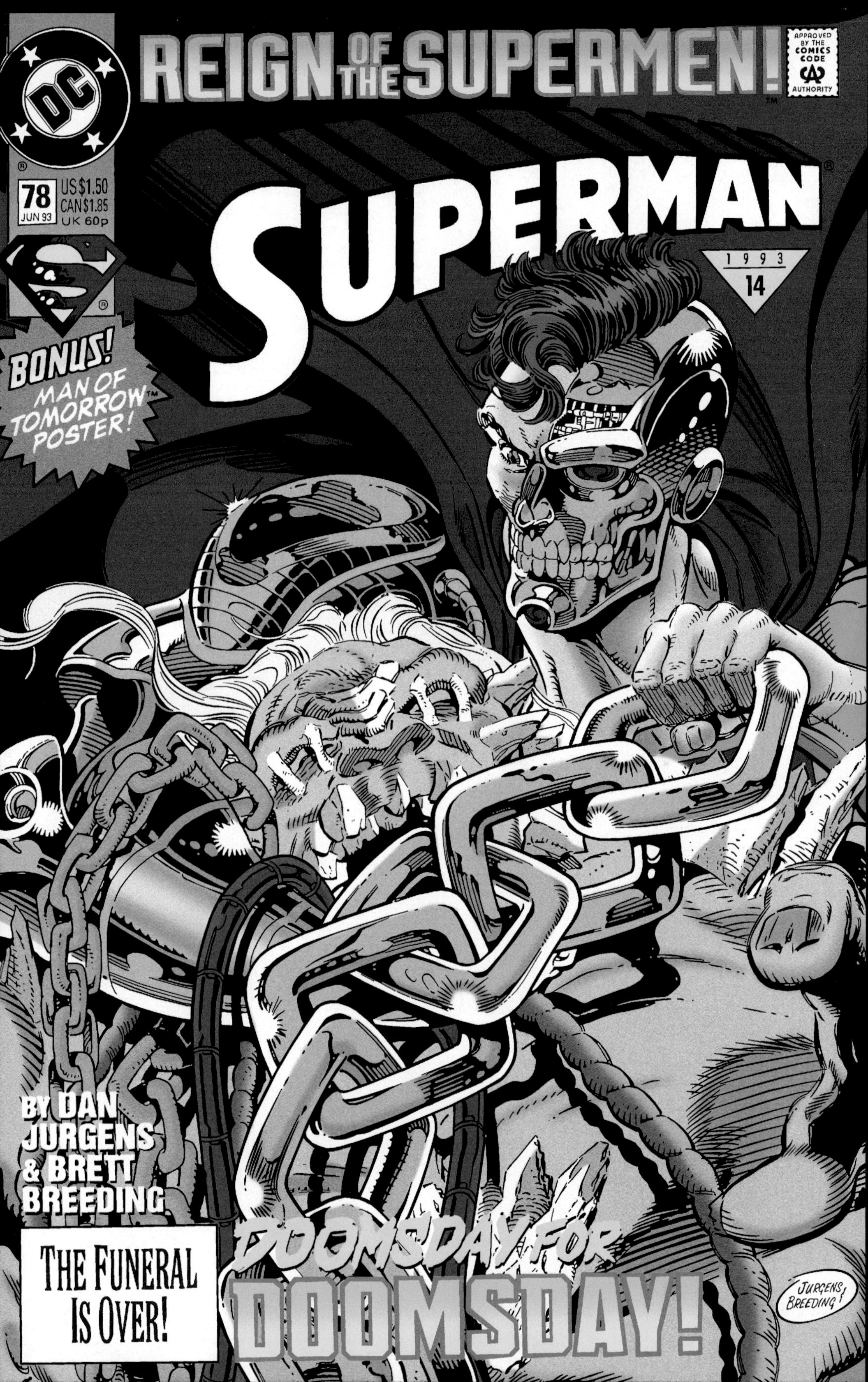
REIGN OF THE SUPERMEN!
APPROVED BY THE COMICS CODE AUTHORITY
DC
78
JUN 93
US $1.50
CAN $1.85
UK 60p
SUPERMAN
1993
14
BONUS! MAN OF TOMORROW POSTER!
BY DAN JURGENS & BRETT BREEDING
THE FUNERAL IS OVER!
DOOMSDAY FOR DOOMSDAY!
JURGENS BREEDING

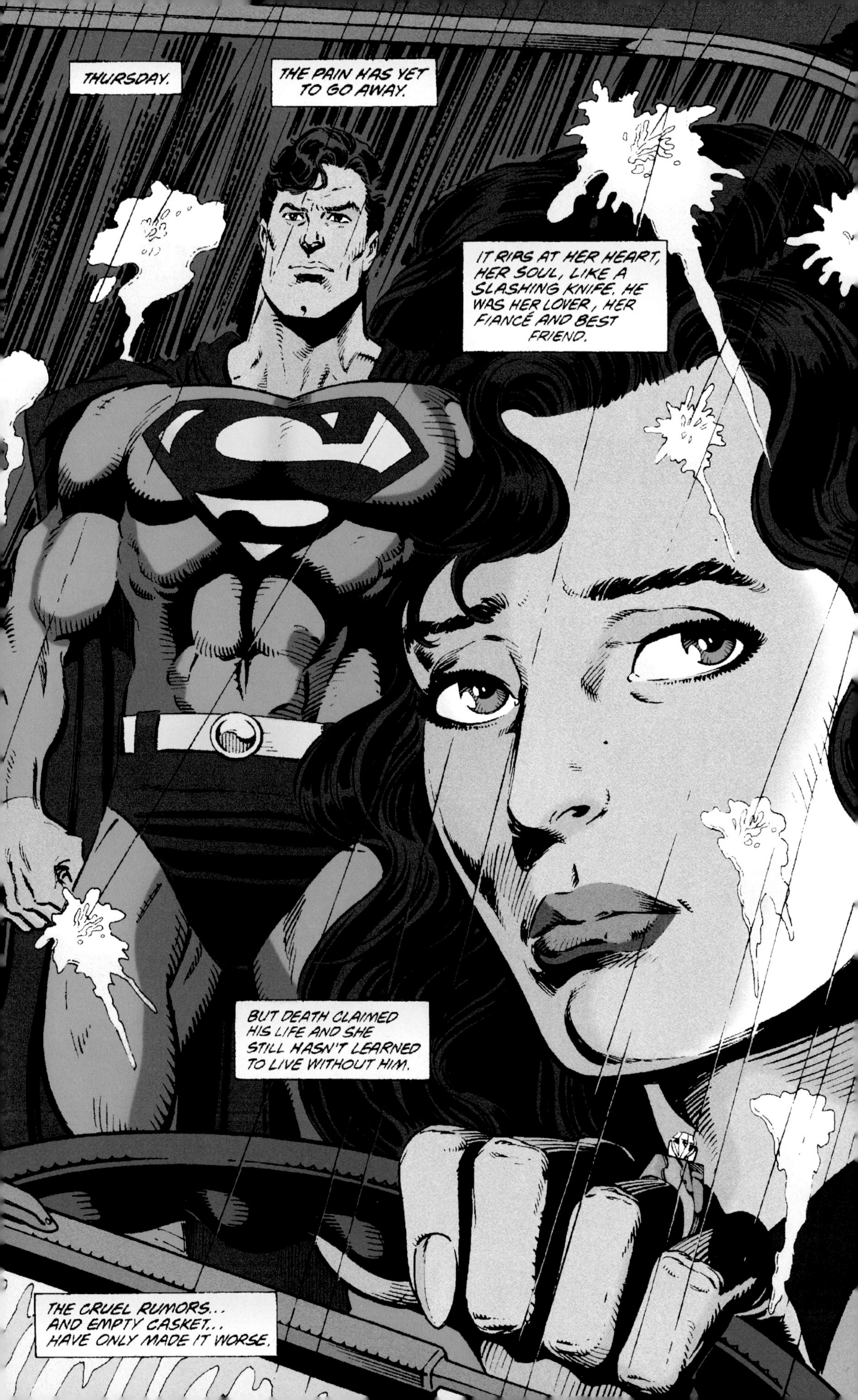
THURSDAY.
THE PAIN HAS YET TO GO AWAY.
IT RIPS AT HER HEART, HER SOUL, LIKE A SLASHING KNIFE. HE WAS HER LOVER, HER FIANCÉ AND BEST FRIEND.
BUT DEATH CLAIMED HIS LIFE AND SHE STILL HASN'T LEARNED TO LIVE WITHOUT HIM.
THE CRUEL RUMORS... AND EMPTY CASKET... HAVE ONLY MADE IT WORSE.

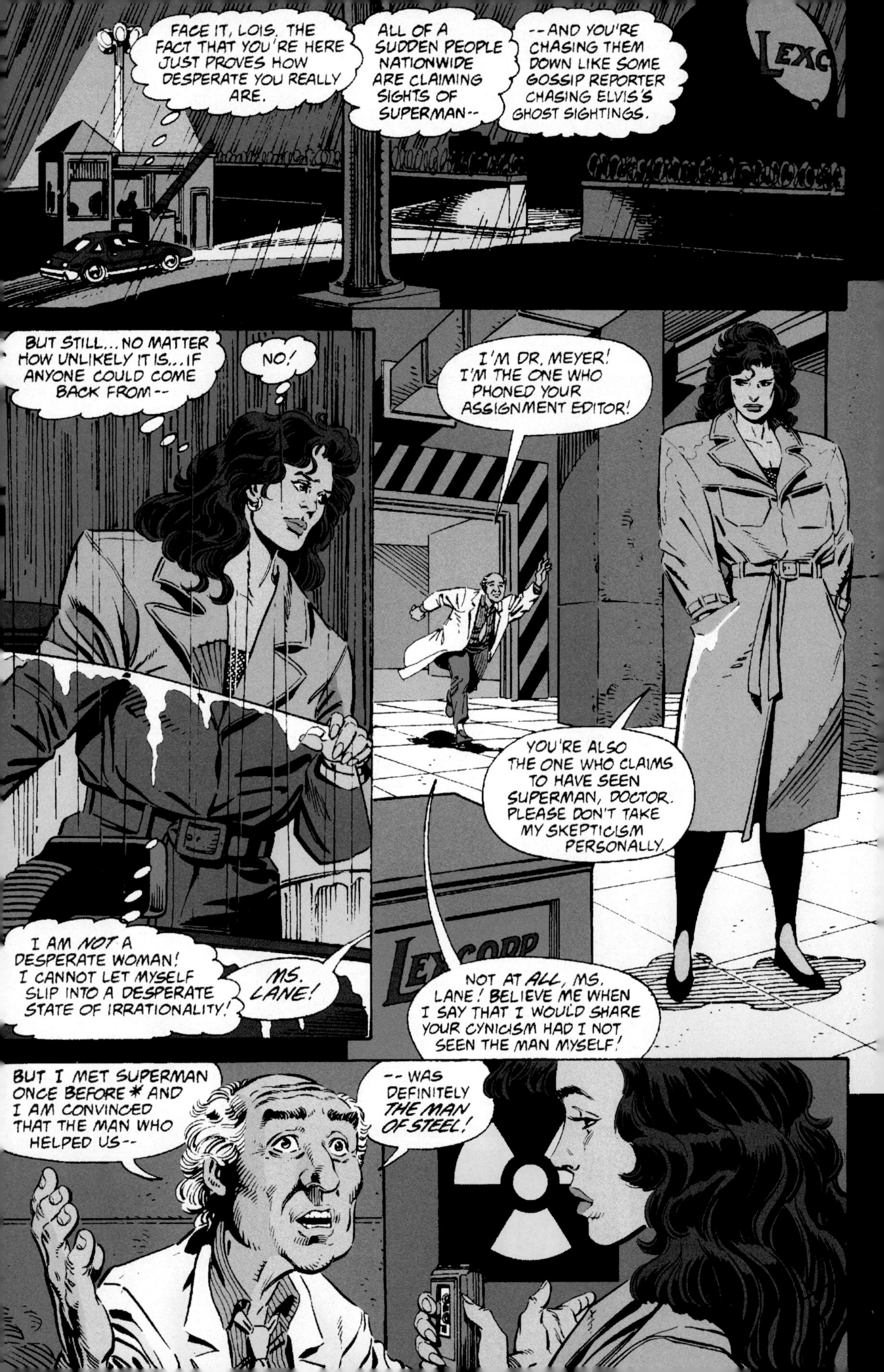
FACE IT, LOIS. THE FACT THAT YOU'RE HERE JUST PROVES HOW DESPERATE YOU REALLY ARE.
ALL OF A SUDDEN PEOPLE NATIONWIDE ARE CLAIMING SIGHTS OF SUPERMAN--
--AND YOU'RE CHASING THEM DOWN LIKE SOME GOSSIP REPORTER CHASING ELVIS'S GHOST SIGHTINGS.
LEXC
BUT STILL... NO MATTER HOW UNLIKELY IT IS... IF ANYONE COULD COME BACK FROM--
NO!
I AM NOT A DESPERATE WOMAN! I CANNOT LET MYSELF SLIP INTO A DESPERATE STATE OF IRRATIONALITY!
MS. LANE!
I'M DR. MEYER! I'M THE ONE WHO PHONED YOUR ASSIGNMENT EDITOR!
YOU'RE ALSO THE ONE WHO CLAIMS TO HAVE SEEN SUPERMAN, DOCTOR. PLEASE DON'T TAKE MY SKEPTICISM PERSONALLY.
NOT AT ALL, MS. LANE! BELIEVE ME WHEN I SAY THAT I WOULD SHARE YOUR CYNICISM HAD I NOT SEEN THE MAN MYSELF!
BUT I MET SUPERMAN ONCE BEFORE* AND I AM CONVINCED THAT THE MAN WHO HELPED US--
--WAS DEFINITELY THE MAN OF STEEL!

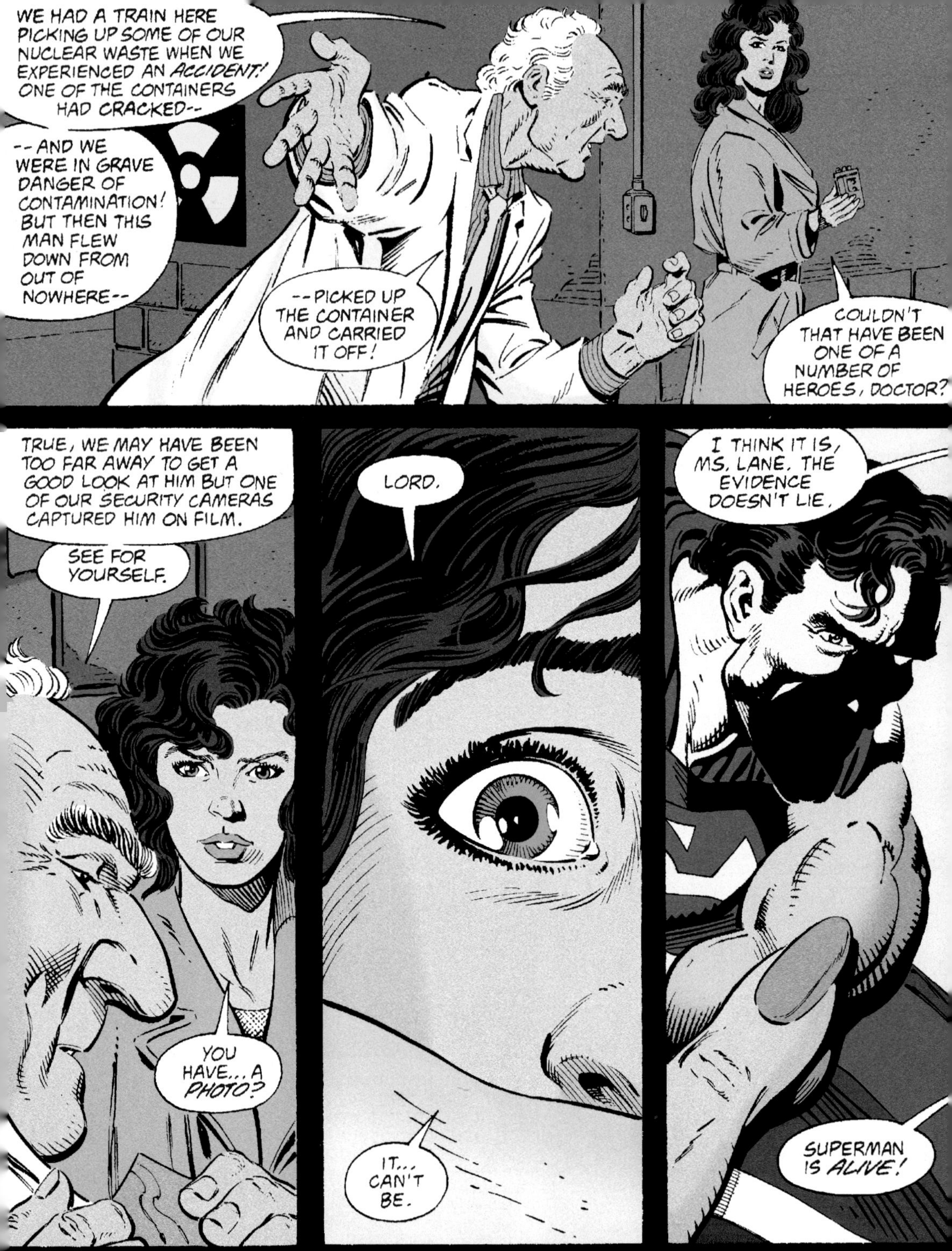

WE HAD A TRAIN HERE PICKING UP SOME OF OUR NUCLEAR WASTE WHEN WE EXPERIENCED AN ACCIDENT! ONE OF THE CONTAINERS HAD CRACKED--
--AND WE WERE IN GRAVE DANGER OF CONTAMINATION! BUT THEN THIS MAN FLEW DOWN FROM OUT OF NOWHERE--
--PICKED UP THE CONTAINER AND CARRIED IT OFF!
COULDN'T THAT HAVE BEEN ONE OF A NUMBER OF HEROES, DOCTOR?
TRUE, WE MAY HAVE BEEN TOO FAR AWAY TO GET A GOOD LOOK AT HIM BUT ONE OF OUR SECURITY CAMERAS CAPTURED HIM ON FILM.
SEE FOR YOURSELF.
YOU HAVE... A PHOTO?
LORD.
IT... CAN'T BE.
I THINK IT IS, MS. LANE. THE EVIDENCE DOESN'T LIE.
SUPERMAN IS ALIVE!

ALIVE

DAN JURGENS story & layout
BRETT BREEDING finished art
JOHN COSTANZA letterer
GLENN WHITMORE colorist

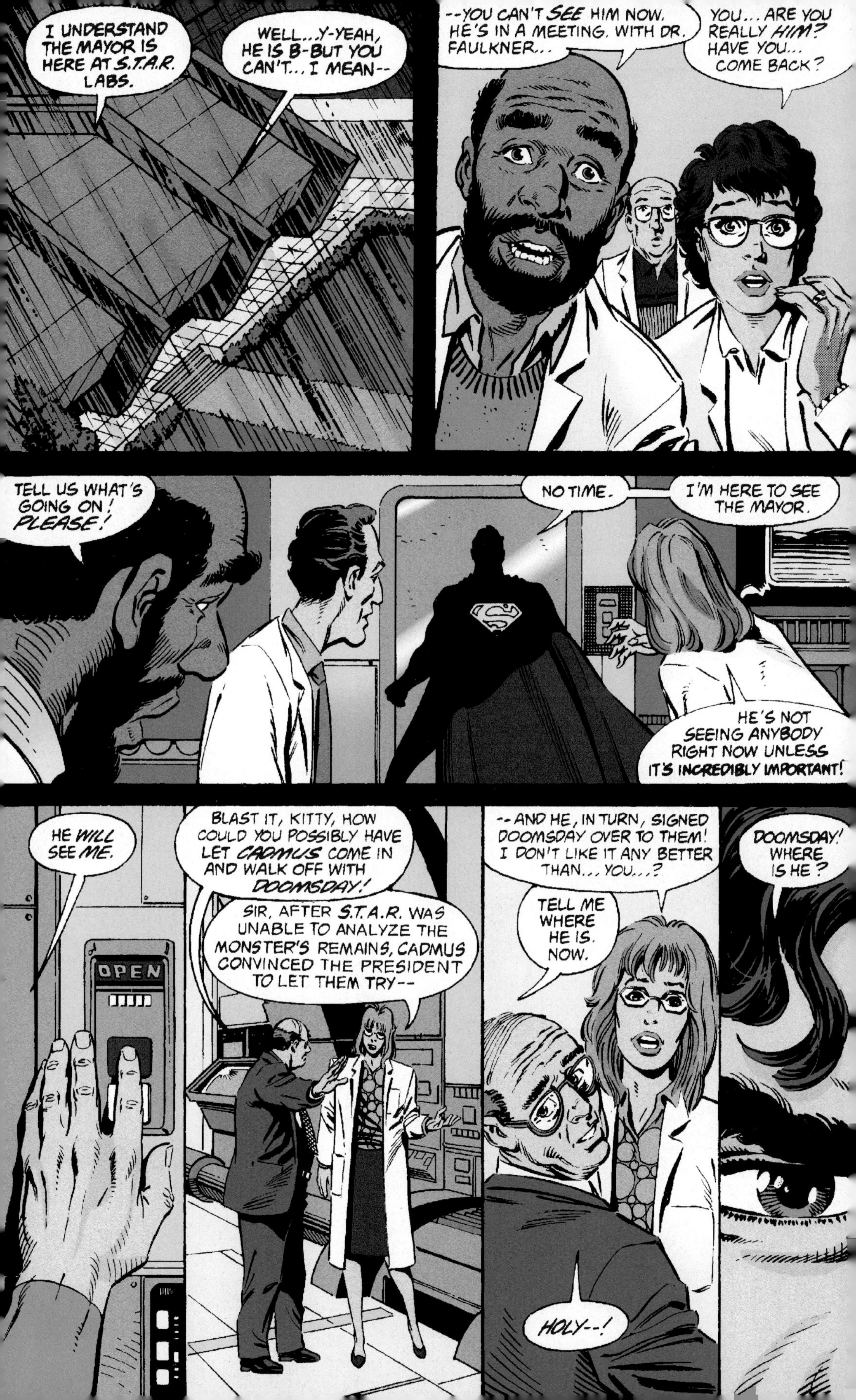
I UNDERSTAND THE MAYOR IS HERE AT S.T.A.R. LABS.
WELL... Y-YEAH, HE IS B-BUT YOU CAN'T... I MEAN--
--YOU CAN'T SEE HIM NOW. HE'S IN A MEETING. WITH DR. FAULKNER...
YOU... ARE YOU REALLY HIM? HAVE YOU... COME BACK?
TELL US WHAT'S GOING ON! PLEASE!
NO TIME.
I'M HERE TO SEE THE MAYOR.
HE'S NOT SEEING ANYBODY RIGHT NOW UNLESS IT'S INCREDIBLY IMPORTANT!
HE WILL SEE ME.
OPEN
BLAST IT, KITTY, HOW COULD YOU POSSIBLY HAVE LET CADMUS COME IN AND WALK OFF WITH DOOMSDAY!
SIR, AFTER S.T.A.R. WAS UNABLE TO ANALYZE THE MONSTER'S REMAINS, CADMUS CONVINCED THE PRESIDENT TO LET THEM TRY--
--AND HE, IN TURN, SIGNED DOOMSDAY OVER TO THEM! I DON'T LIKE IT ANY BETTER THAN... YOU...?
TELL ME WHERE HE IS. NOW.
HOLY--!
DOOMSDAY! WHERE IS HE?

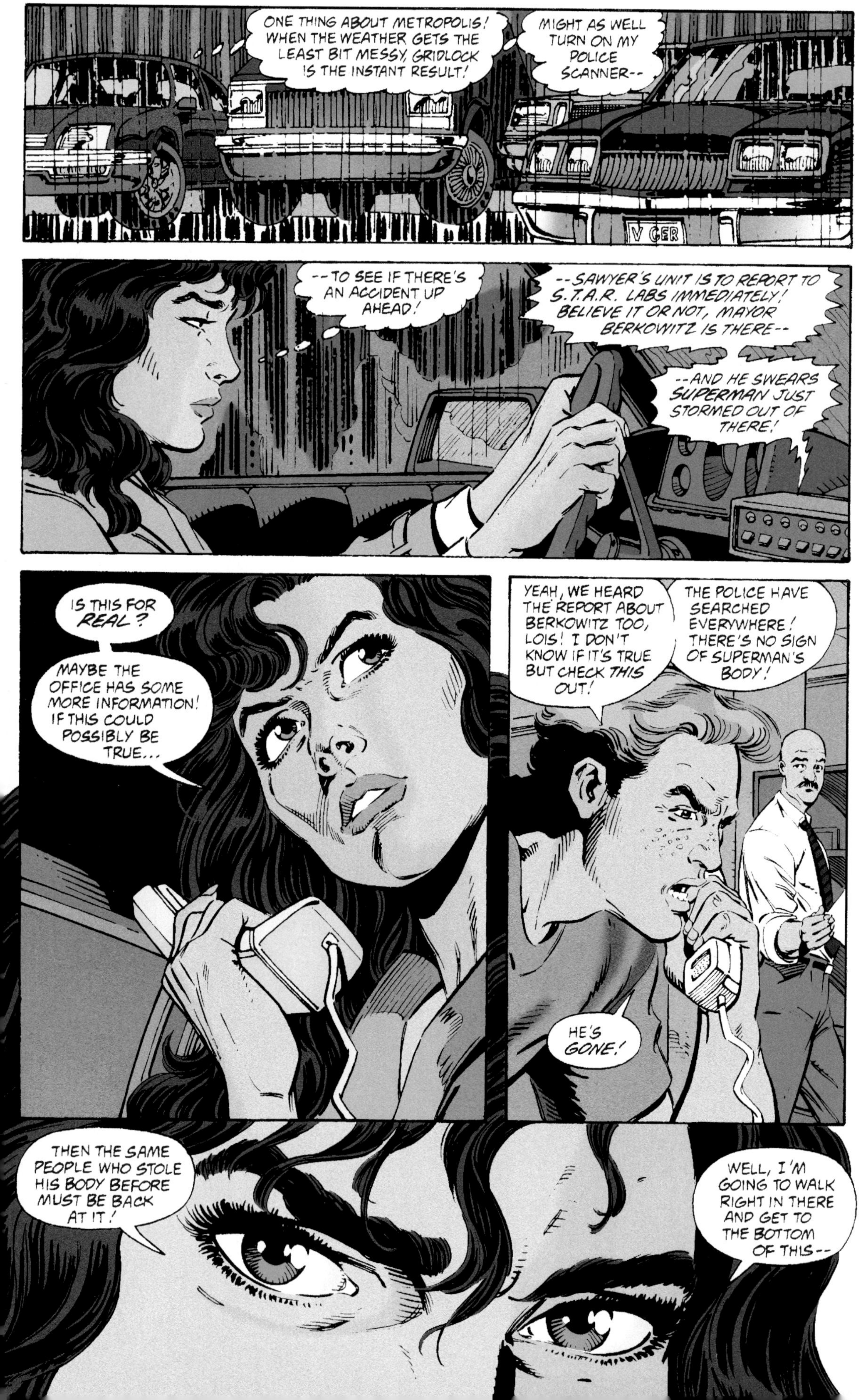

ONE THING ABOUT METROPOLIS! WHEN THE WEATHER GETS THE LEAST BIT MESSY, GRIDLOCK IS THE INSTANT RESULT!
MIGHT AS WELL TURN ON MY POLICE SCANNER--
--TO SEE IF THERE'S AN ACCIDENT UP AHEAD!
--SAWYER'S UNIT IS TO REPORT TO S.T.A.R. LABS IMMEDIATELY! BELIEVE IT OR NOT, MAYOR BERKOWITZ IS THERE--
--AND HE SWEARS SUPERMAN JUST STORMED OUT OF THERE!
IS THIS FOR REAL?
MAYBE THE OFFICE HAS SOME MORE INFORMATION! IF THIS COULD POSSIBLY BE TRUE...
YEAH, WE HEARD THE REPORT ABOUT BERKOWITZ TOO, LOIS! I DON'T KNOW IF IT'S TRUE BUT CHECK THIS OUT!
THE POLICE HAVE SEARCHED EVERYWHERE! THERE'S NO SIGN OF SUPERMAN'S BODY!
HE'S GONE!
THEN THE SAME PEOPLE WHO STOLE HIS BODY BEFORE MUST BE BACK AT IT!
WELL, I'M GOING TO WALK RIGHT IN THERE AND GET TO THE BOTTOM OF THIS--

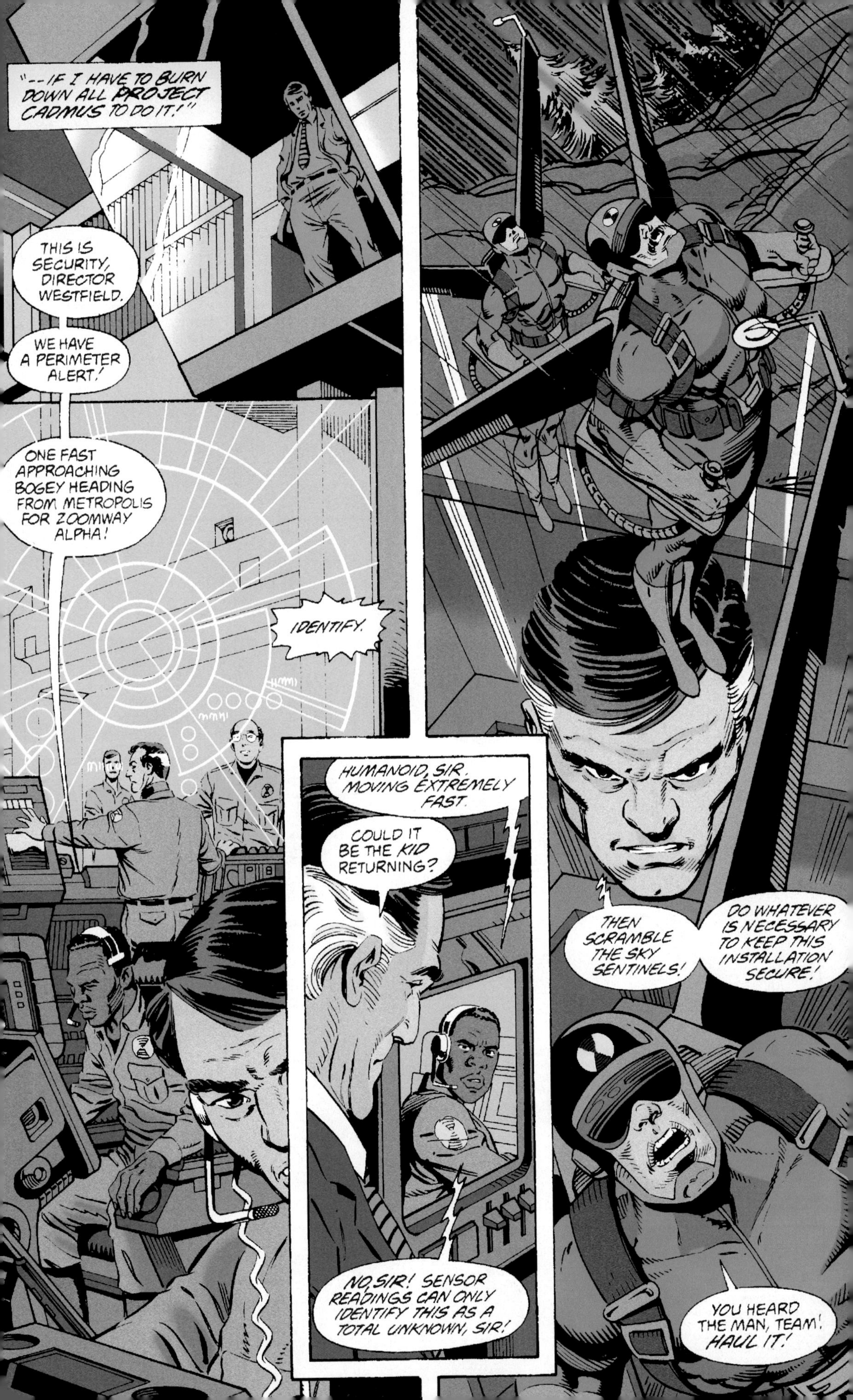
"--IF I HAVE TO BURN DOWN ALL PROJECT CADMUS TO DO IT!"
THIS IS SECURITY, DIRECTOR WESTFIELD.
WE HAVE A PERIMETER ALERT!
ONE FAST APPROACHING BOGEY HEADING FROM METROPOLIS FOR ZOOMWAY ALPHA!
IDENTIFY.
HUMANOID, SIR. MOVING EXTREMELY FAST.
COULD IT BE THE KID RETURNING?
NO, SIR! SENSOR READINGS CAN ONLY IDENTIFY THIS AS A TOTAL UNKNOWN, SIR!
THEN SCRAMBLE THE SKY SENTINELS!
DO WHATEVER IS NECESSARY TO KEEP THIS INSTALLATION SECURE!
YOU HEARD THE MAN, TEAM! HAUL IT!

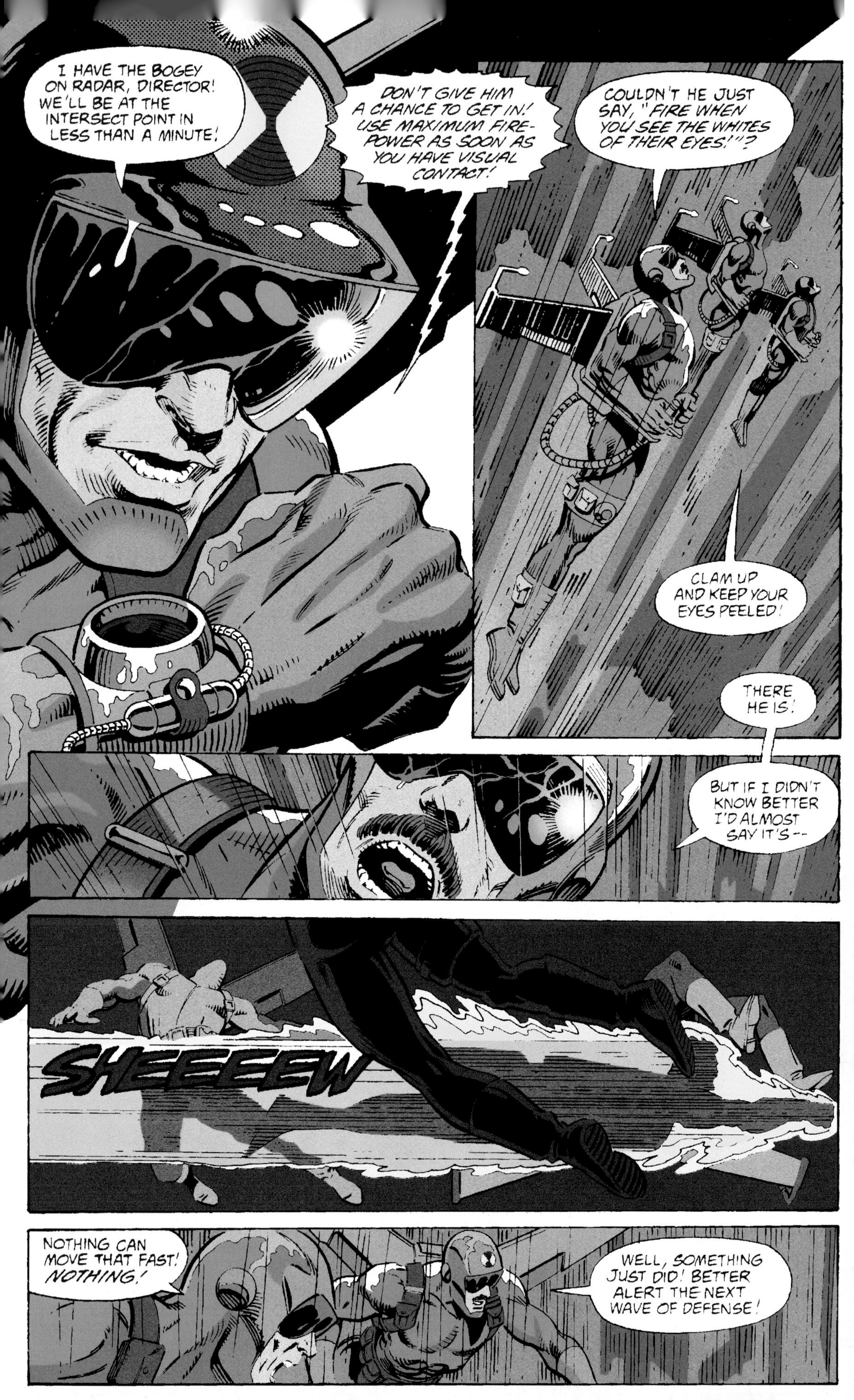
I HAVE THE BOGEY ON RADAR, DIRECTOR! WE'LL BE AT THE INTERSECT POINT IN LESS THAN A MINUTE!
DON'T GIVE HIM A CHANCE TO GET IN! USE MAXIMUM FIRE-POWER AS SOON AS YOU HAVE VISUAL CONTACT!
COULDN'T HE JUST SAY, "FIRE WHEN YOU SEE THE WHITES OF THEIR EYES!"?
CLAM UP AND KEEP YOUR EYES PEELED!
THERE HE IS!
BUT IF I DIDN'T KNOW BETTER I'D ALMOST SAY IT'S--
SHEEEEEW
NOTHING CAN MOVE THAT FAST! NOTHING!
WELL, SOMETHING JUST DID! BETTER ALERT THE NEXT WAVE OF DEFENSE!

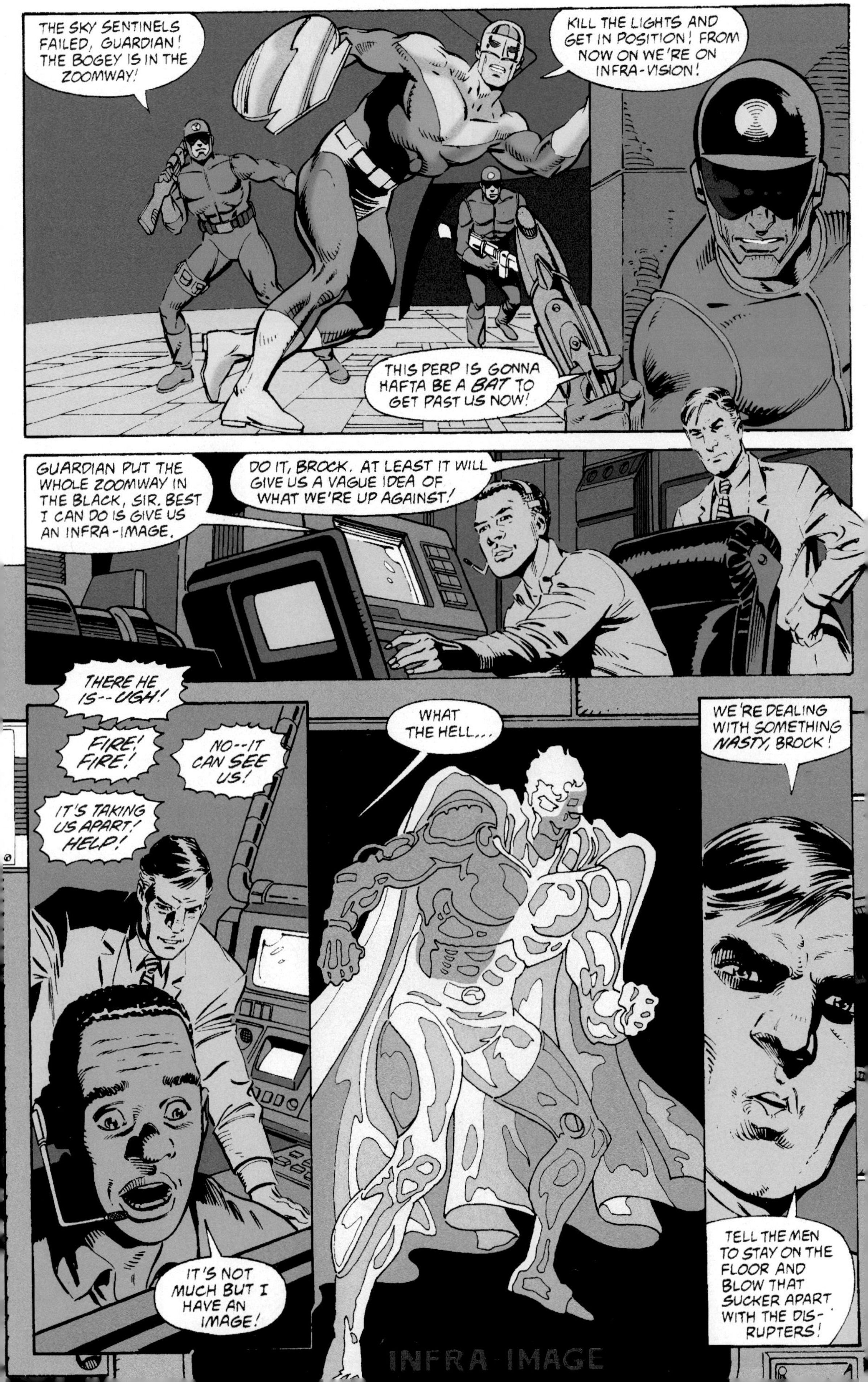
THE SKY SENTINELS FAILED, GUARDIAN! THE BOGEY IS IN THE ZOOMWAY!
KILL THE LIGHTS AND GET IN POSITION! FROM NOW ON WE'RE ON INFRA-VISION!
THIS PERP IS GONNA HAFTA BE A BAT TO GET PAST US NOW!
GUARDIAN PUT THE WHOLE ZOOMWAY IN THE BLACK, SIR. BEST I CAN DO IS GIVE US AN INFRA-IMAGE.
DO IT, BROCK. AT LEAST IT WILL GIVE US A VAGUE IDEA OF WHAT WE'RE UP AGAINST!
THERE HE IS--UGH!
FIRE! FIRE!
NO--IT CAN SEE US!
IT'S TAKING US APART! HELP!
IT'S NOT MUCH BUT I HAVE AN IMAGE!
WHAT THE HELL...
WE'RE DEALING WITH SOMETHING NASTY, BROCK!
TELL THE MEN TO STAY ON THE FLOOR AND BLOW THAT SUCKER APART WITH THE DIS-RUPTERS!
INFRA-IMAGE

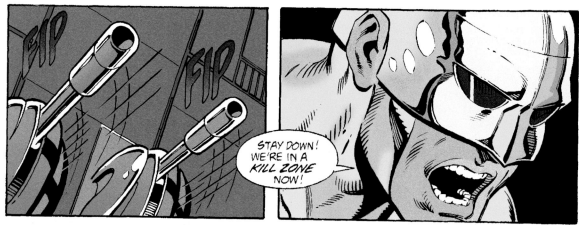

STAY DOWN! WE'RE IN A KILL ZONE NOW!

FIRE!

MAXIMUM POWER ON TARGET! THIS'LL SHAKE HIM APART FOR SURE!

YOUR WEAPONS CAN'T HURT ME! GIVE ME WHAT I WANT AND I'LL LEAVE!

DAMN! TURN THE LIGHTS BACK ON SO I CAN SEE WHO I'M UP AGAINST!

THERE'S NO WAY YOU'RE GOING TO STOP ME!

KCHUNNG

I'VE COME FOR DOOMSDAY!

IT... CAN'T... BE...

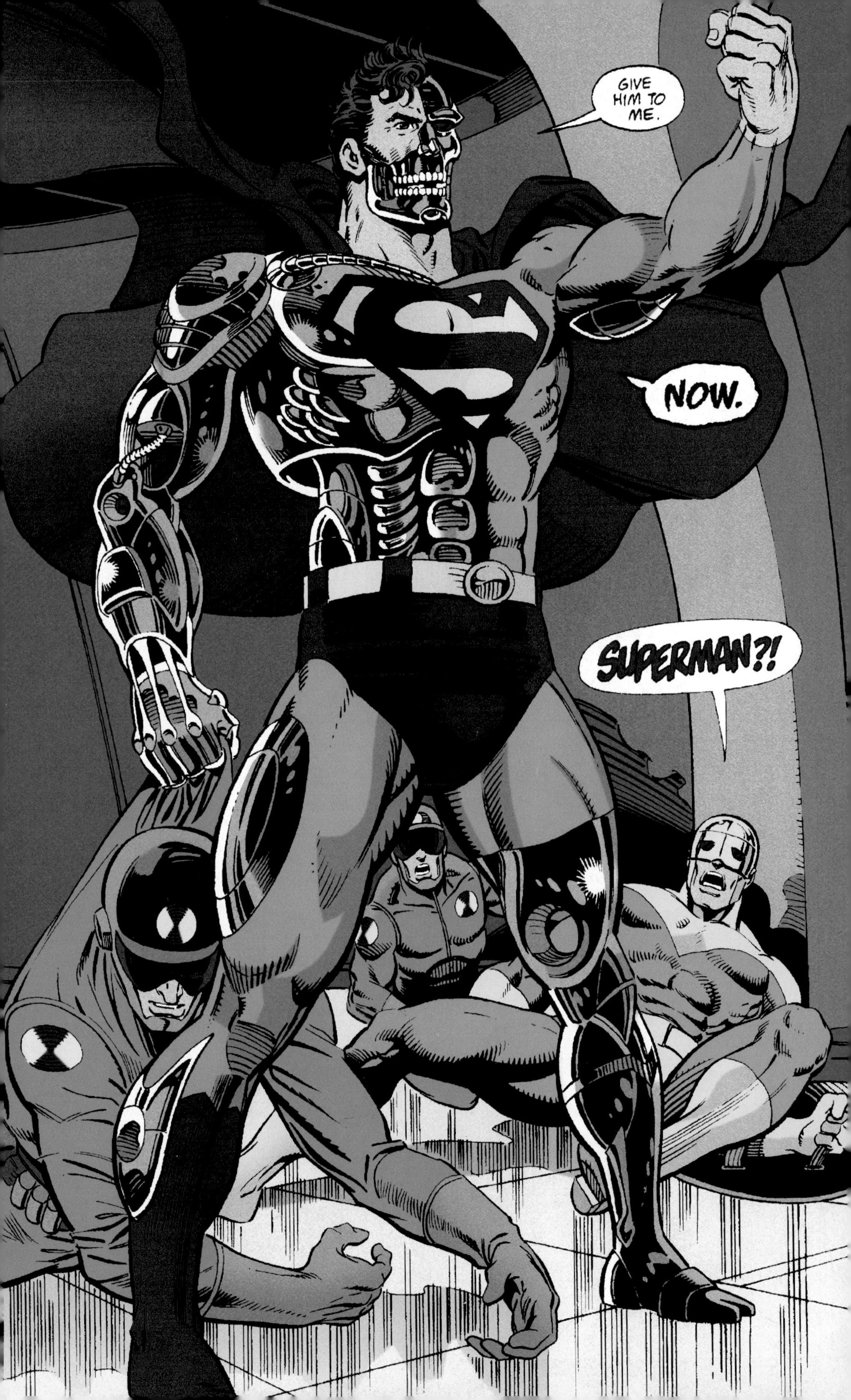

GIVE HIM TO ME.
NOW.
SUPERMAN?!

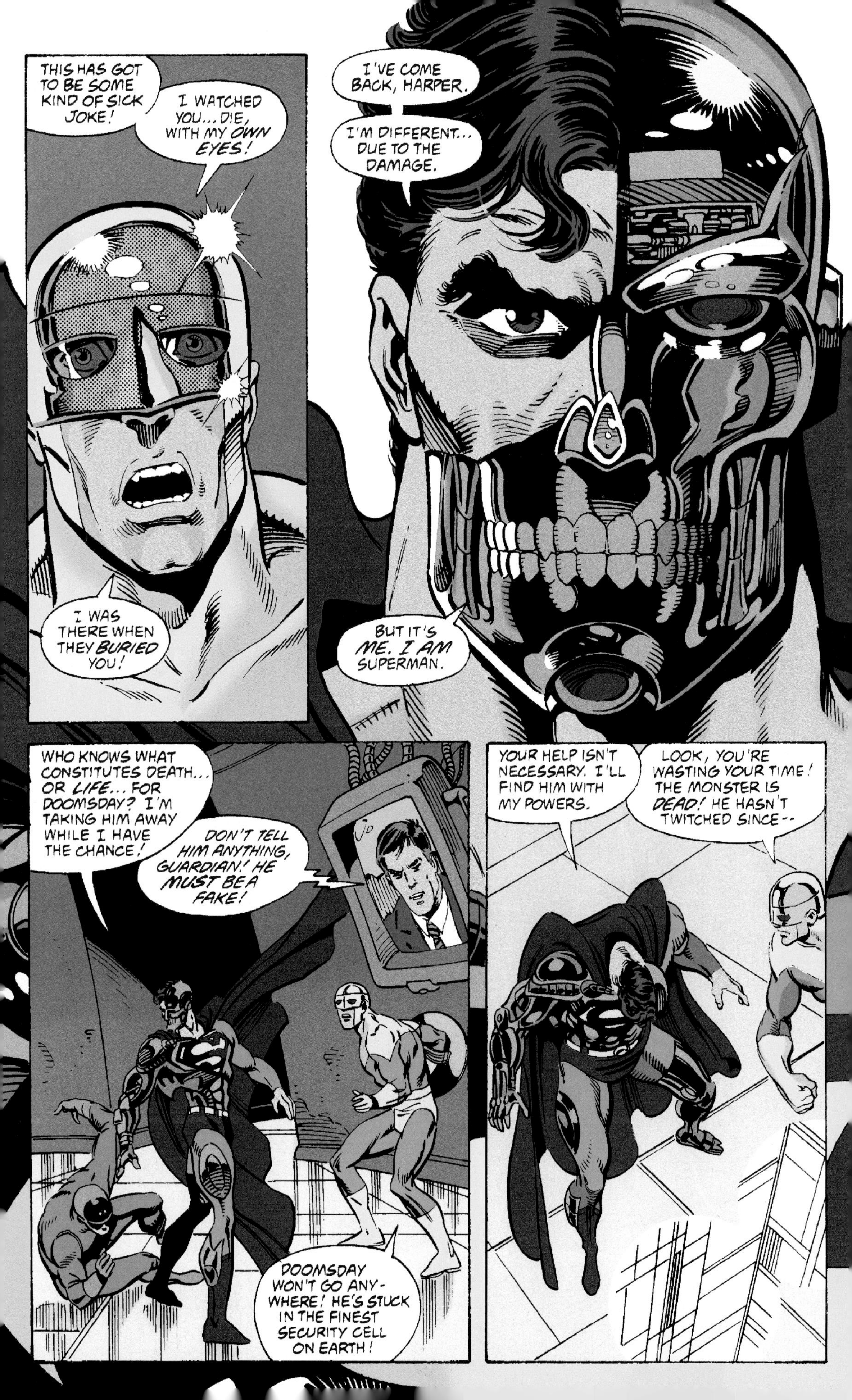
THIS HAS GOT TO BE SOME KIND OF SICK JOKE!
I WATCHED YOU... DIE, WITH MY OWN EYES!
I WAS THERE WHEN THEY BURIED YOU!
I'VE COME BACK, HARPER.
I'M DIFFERENT... DUE TO THE DAMAGE.
BUT IT'S ME. I AM SUPERMAN.
WHO KNOWS WHAT CONSTITUTES DEATH... OR LIFE... FOR DOOMSDAY? I'M TAKING HIM AWAY WHILE I HAVE THE CHANCE!
DON'T TELL HIM ANYTHING, GUARDIAN! HE MUST BE A FAKE!
DOOMSDAY WON'T GO ANY-WHERE! HE'S STUCK IN THE FINEST SECURITY CELL ON EARTH!
YOUR HELP ISN'T NECESSARY. I'LL FIND HIM WITH MY POWERS.
LOOK, YOU'RE WASTING YOUR TIME! THE MONSTER IS DEAD! HE HASN'T TWITCHED SINCE--

SINCE HE *"KILLED"* ME, HARPER?

THERE.

WAIT!

DOOMSDAY IS *WAR* COME TO LIFE!

HE'S FAR TOO DANGEROUS TO BE KEPT HERE!

YOU GENETIC MANIPULATION FREAKS ARE LIKELY TO TRY CLONING AN *ARMY* OF DOOMSDAYS!

I WON'T ALLOW IT!

YOU'RE BREAKING A WHOLE SLEW OF FEDERAL LAWS, MISTER! AND NOT EVEN THE REAL SUPERMAN WAS POWERFUL ENOUGH TO OPEN THAT VAULT!

I'M MORE THAN I USED TO BE, WESTFIELD. I'M PART *MACHINE.*

FIP SHP SHWIP

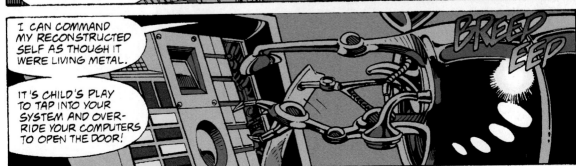

I CAN COMMAND MY RECONSTRUCTED SELF AS THOUGH IT WERE LIVING METAL.

IT'S CHILD'S PLAY TO TAP INTO YOUR SYSTEM AND OVER-RIDE YOUR COMPUTERS TO OPEN THE DOOR!

BREEP EEP

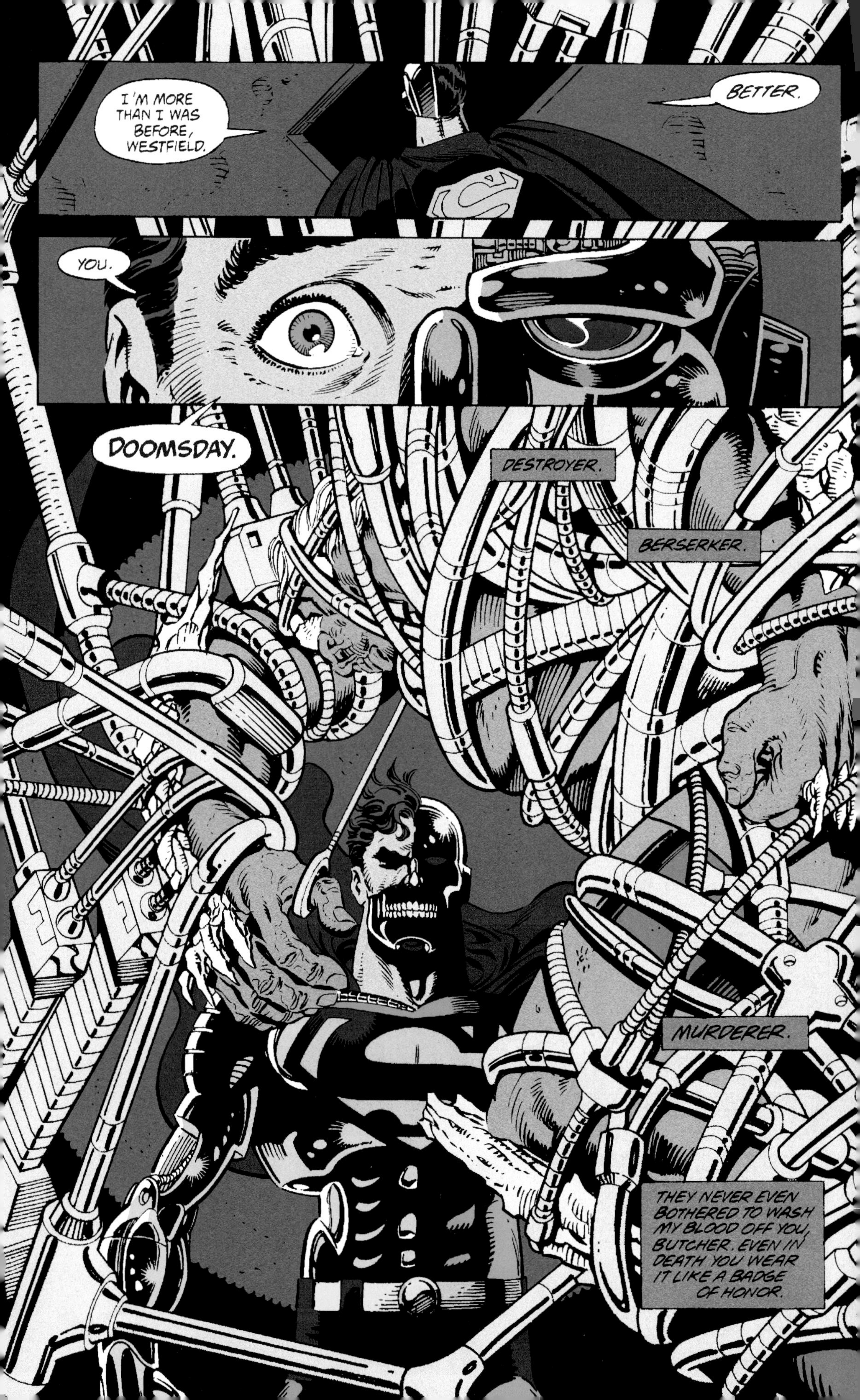
I'M MORE THAN I WAS BEFORE, WESTFIELD.
BETTER.
YOU.
DOOMSDAY.
DESTROYER.
BERSERKER.
MURDERER.
THEY NEVER EVEN BOTHERED TO WASH MY BLOOD OFF YOU, BUTCHER. EVEN IN DEATH YOU WEAR IT LIKE A BADGE OF HONOR.

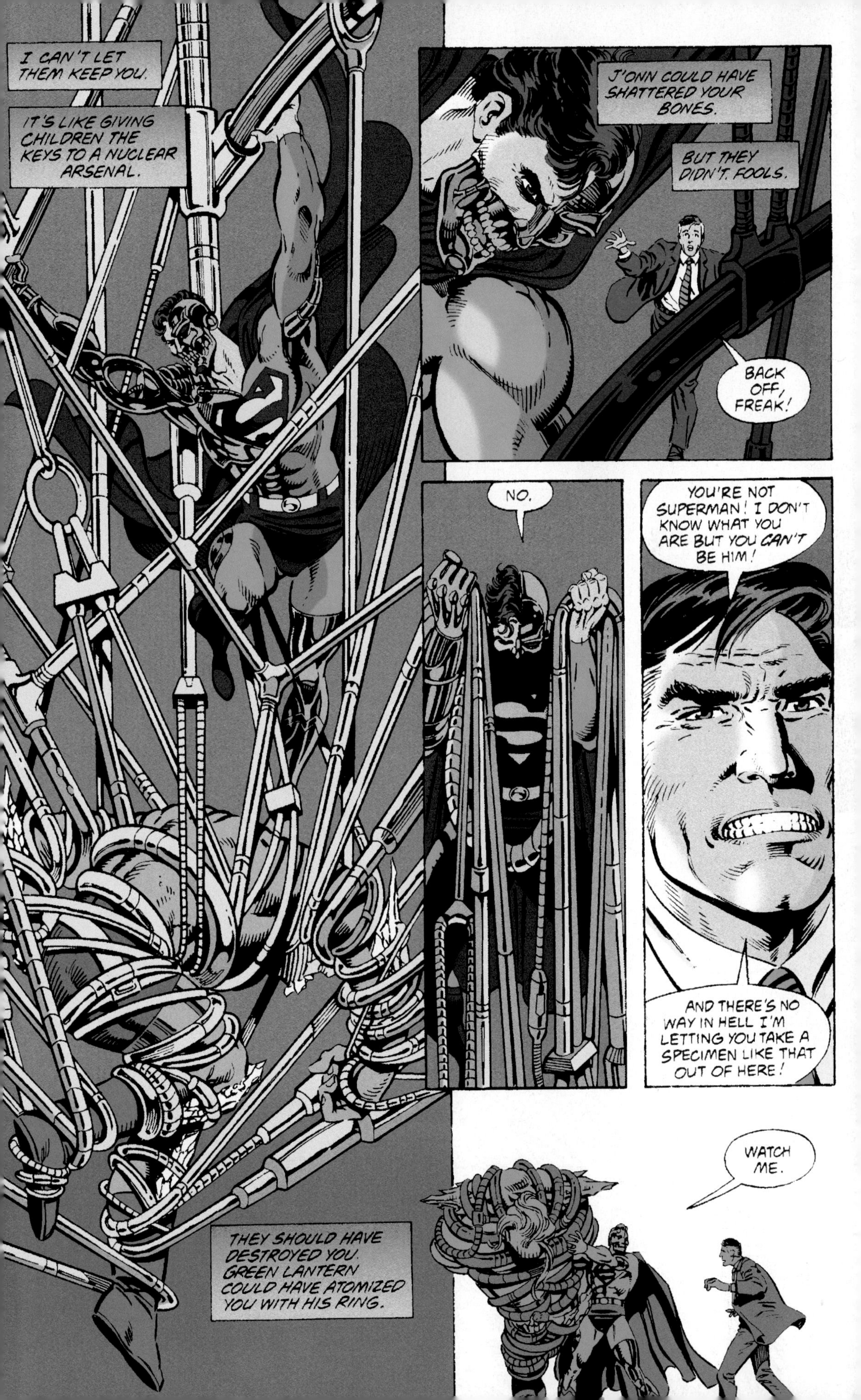
I CAN'T LET THEM KEEP YOU.
IT'S LIKE GIVING CHILDREN THE KEYS TO A NUCLEAR ARSENAL.
J'ONN COULD HAVE SHATTERED YOUR BONES.
BUT THEY DIDN'T. FOOLS.
BACK OFF, FREAK!
NO.
YOU'RE NOT SUPERMAN! I DON'T KNOW WHAT YOU ARE BUT YOU CAN'T BE HIM!
AND THERE'S NO WAY IN HELL I'M LETTING YOU TAKE A SPECIMEN LIKE THAT OUT OF HERE!
THEY SHOULD HAVE DESTROYED YOU. GREEN LANTERN COULD HAVE ATOMIZED YOU WITH HIS RING.
WATCH ME.

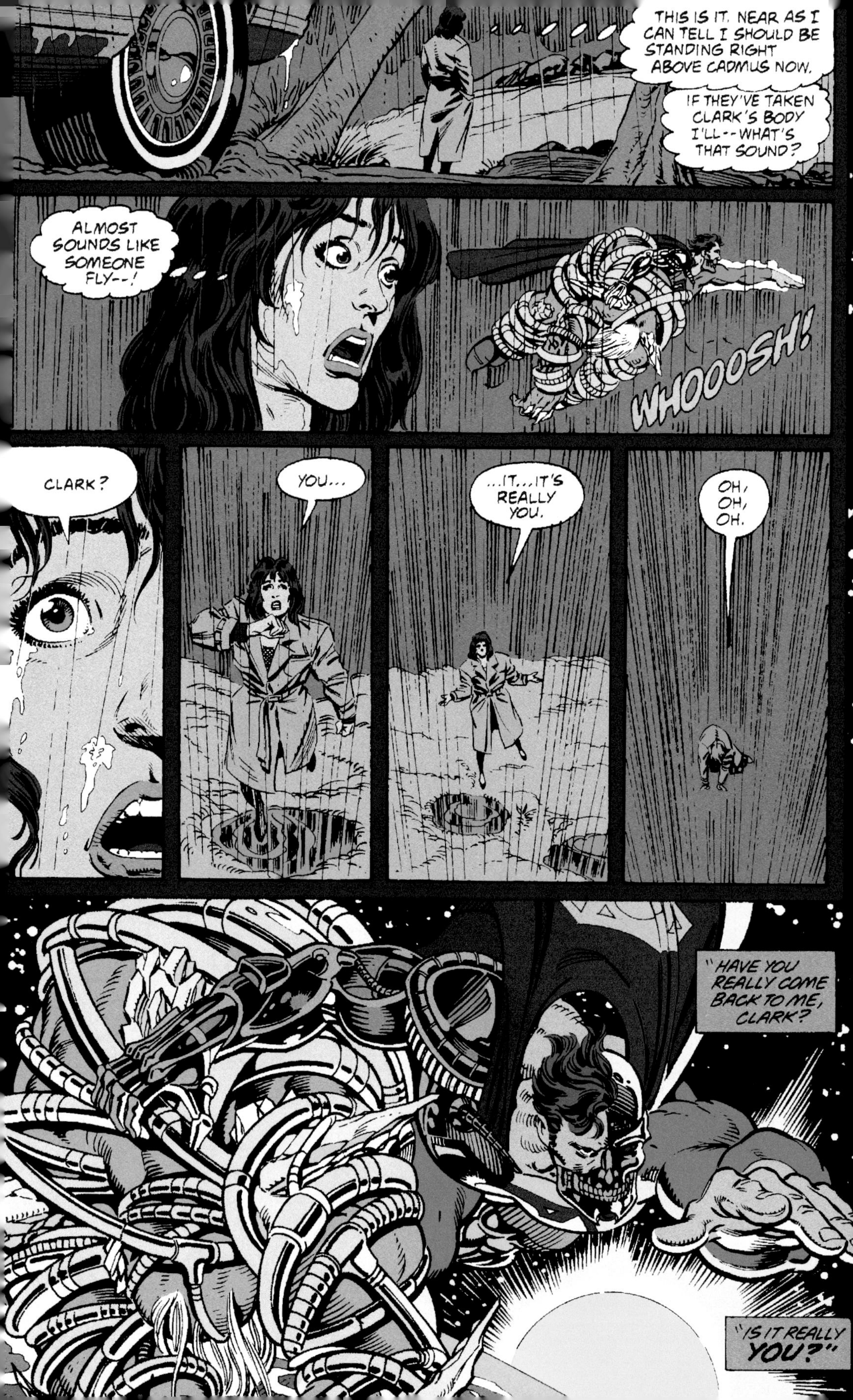
THIS IS IT. NEAR AS I CAN TELL I SHOULD BE STANDING RIGHT ABOVE CADMUS NOW.
IF THEY'VE TAKEN CLARK'S BODY I'LL--WHAT'S THAT SOUND?
ALMOST SOUNDS LIKE SOMEONE FLY--!
WHOOOOSH!
CLARK?
YOU...
...IT...IT'S REALLY YOU.
OH, OH, OH.
"HAVE YOU REALLY COME BACK TO ME, CLARK?
"IS IT REALLY YOU?"

PERFECT.

THAT ASTEROID IS JUST WHAT I NEED.

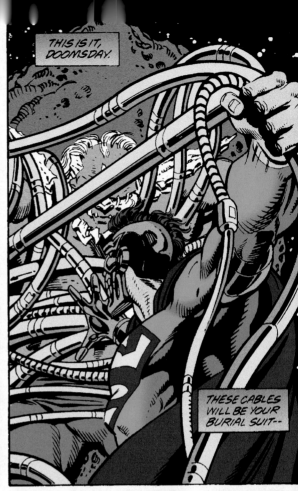

THIS IS IT, DOOMSDAY.

THESE CABLES WILL BE YOUR BURIAL SUIT--

--AND THIS ASTEROID'S FROZEN ORE, MELTED AROUND YOU, WILL BE YOUR CASKET.

LET THE COLD VACUUM OF SPACE BE YOUR ETERNAL RESTING PLACE.

IT'S MORE THAN YOU DESERVE.

WHIRR

A PRECAUTION.

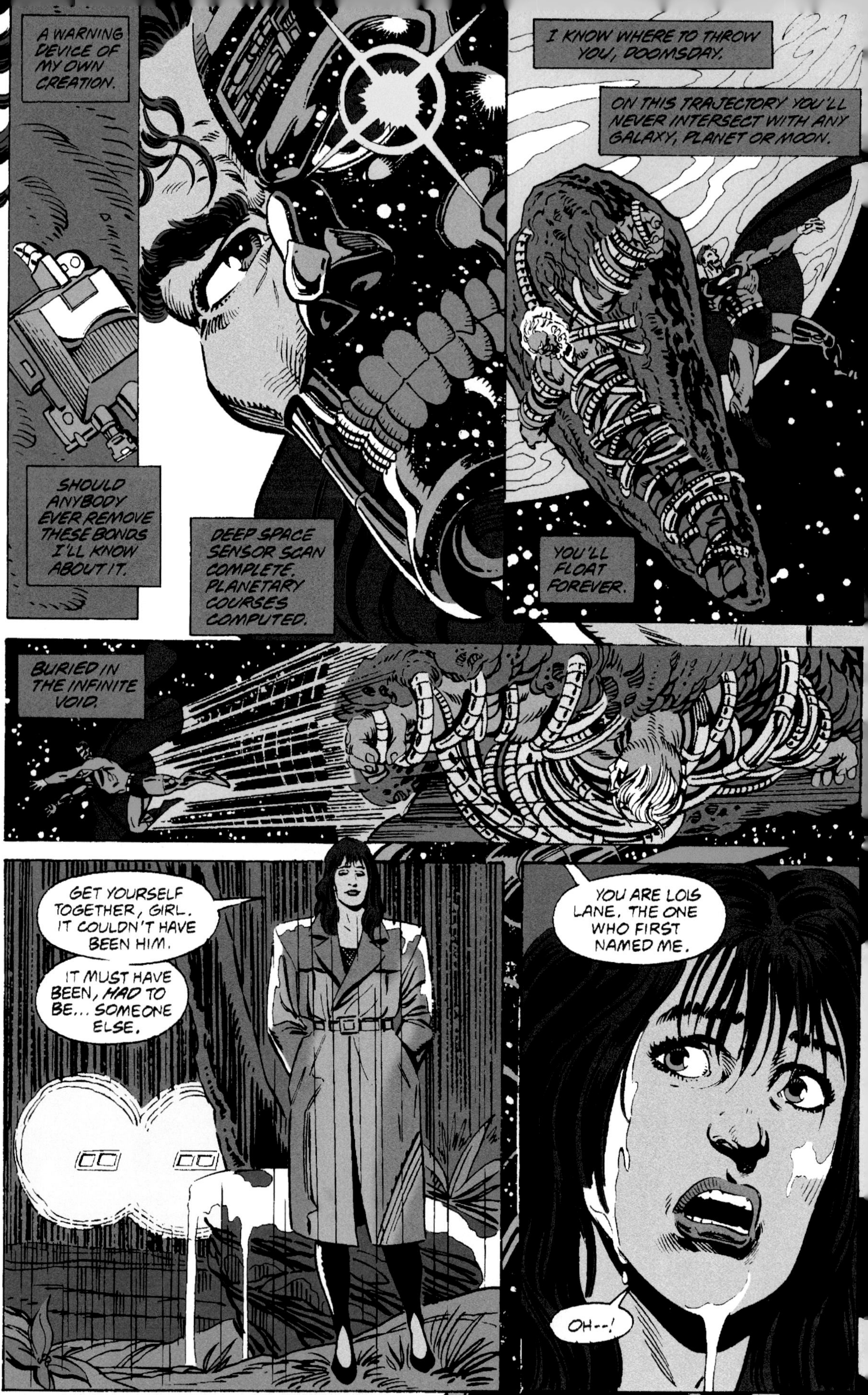
A WARNING DEVICE OF MY OWN CREATION.
SHOULD ANYBODY EVER REMOVE THESE BONDS I'LL KNOW ABOUT IT.
DEEP SPACE SENSOR SCAN COMPLETE. PLANETARY COURSES COMPUTED.
I KNOW WHERE TO THROW YOU, DOOMSDAY.
ON THIS TRAJECTORY YOU'LL NEVER INTERSECT WITH ANY GALAXY, PLANET OR MOON.
YOU'LL FLOAT FOREVER.
BURIED IN THE INFINITE VOID.
GET YOURSELF TOGETHER, GIRL. IT COULDN'T HAVE BEEN HIM.
IT MUST HAVE BEEN, HAD TO BE... SOMEONE ELSE.
YOU ARE LOIS LANE. THE ONE WHO FIRST NAMED ME.
OH--!

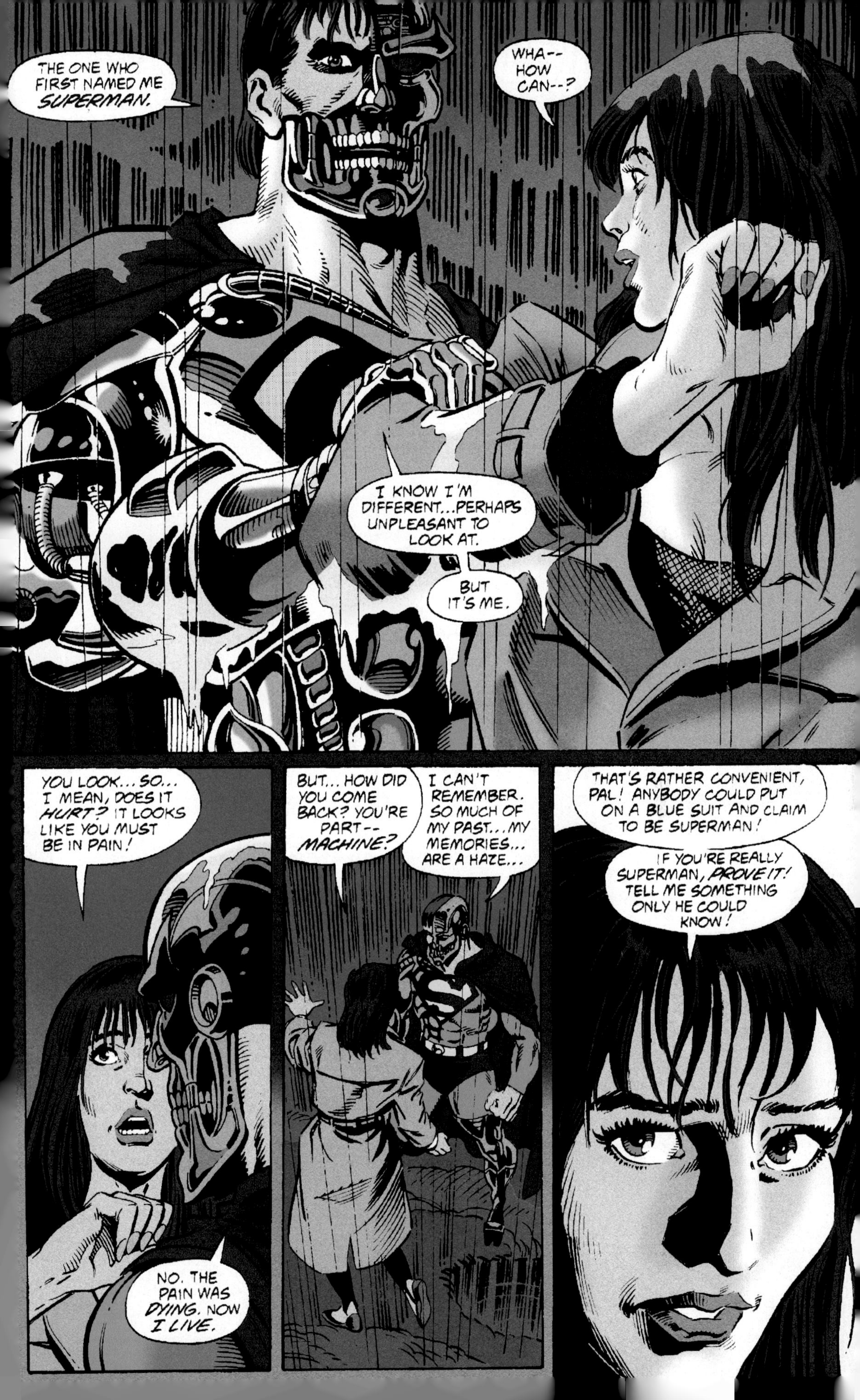
THE ONE WHO FIRST NAMED ME SUPERMAN.
WHA-- HOW CAN--?
I KNOW I'M DIFFERENT...PERHAPS UNPLEASANT TO LOOK AT.
BUT IT'S ME.
YOU LOOK... SO... I MEAN, DOES IT HURT? IT LOOKS LIKE YOU MUST BE IN PAIN!
NO. THE PAIN WAS DYING. NOW I LIVE.
BUT... HOW DID YOU COME BACK? YOU'RE PART-- MACHINE?
I CAN'T REMEMBER. SO MUCH OF MY PAST... MY MEMORIES... ARE A HAZE...
THAT'S RATHER CONVENIENT, PAL! ANYBODY COULD PUT ON A BLUE SUIT AND CLAIM TO BE SUPERMAN!
IF YOU'RE REALLY SUPERMAN, PROVE IT! TELL ME SOMETHING ONLY HE COULD KNOW!

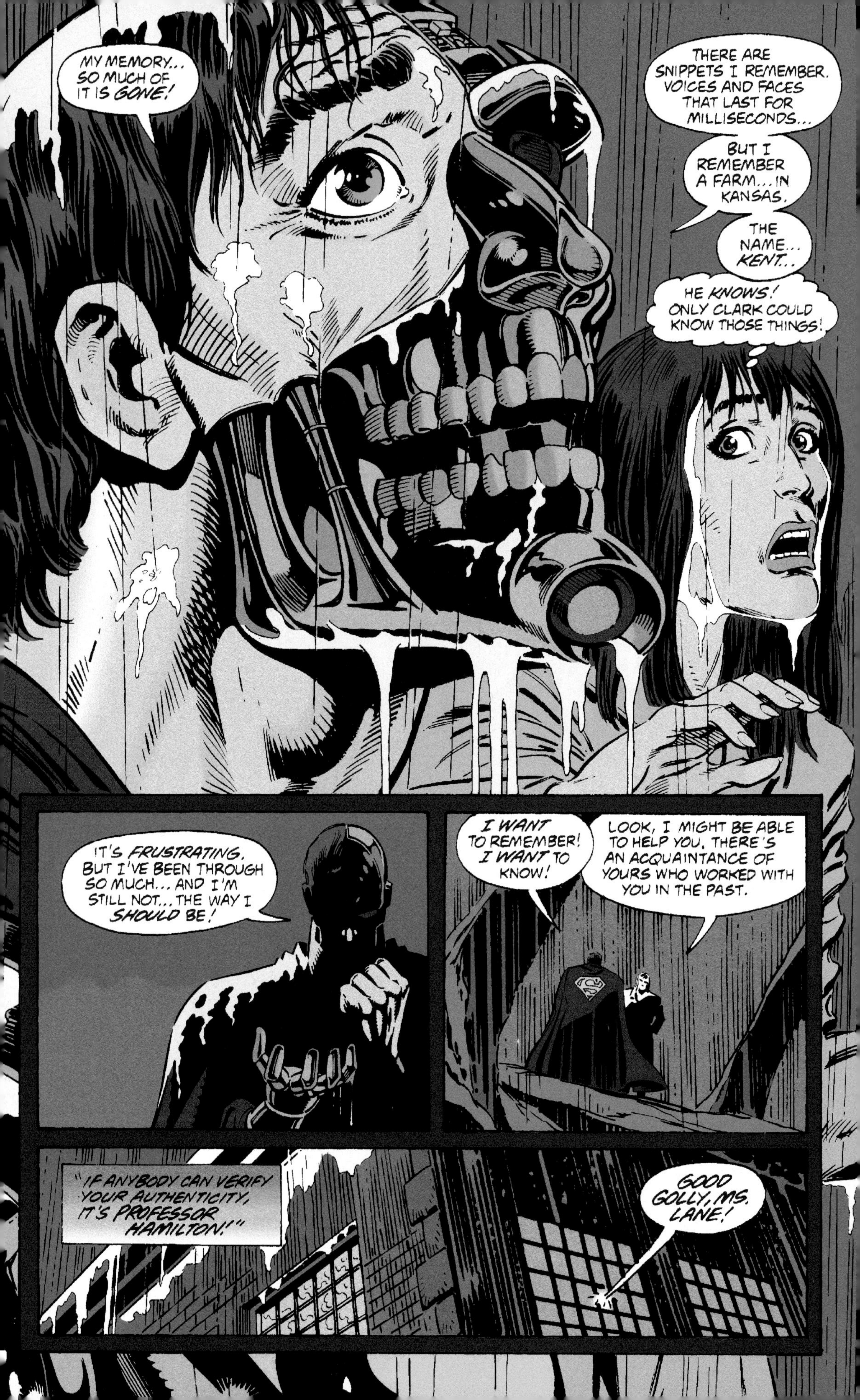
MY MEMORY... SO MUCH OF IT IS GONE!
THERE ARE SNIPPETS I REMEMBER. VOICES AND FACES THAT LAST FOR MILLISECONDS...
BUT I REMEMBER A FARM... IN KANSAS.
THE NAME... KENT...
HE KNOWS! ONLY CLARK COULD KNOW THOSE THINGS!
IT'S FRUSTRATING. BUT I'VE BEEN THROUGH SO MUCH... AND I'M STILL NOT... THE WAY I SHOULD BE!
I WANT TO REMEMBER! I WANT TO KNOW!
LOOK, I MIGHT BE ABLE TO HELP YOU. THERE'S AN ACQUAINTANCE OF YOURS WHO WORKED WITH YOU IN THE PAST.
"IF ANYBODY CAN VERIFY YOUR AUTHENTICITY, IT'S PROFESSOR HAMILTON!"
GOOD GOLLY, MS. LANE!

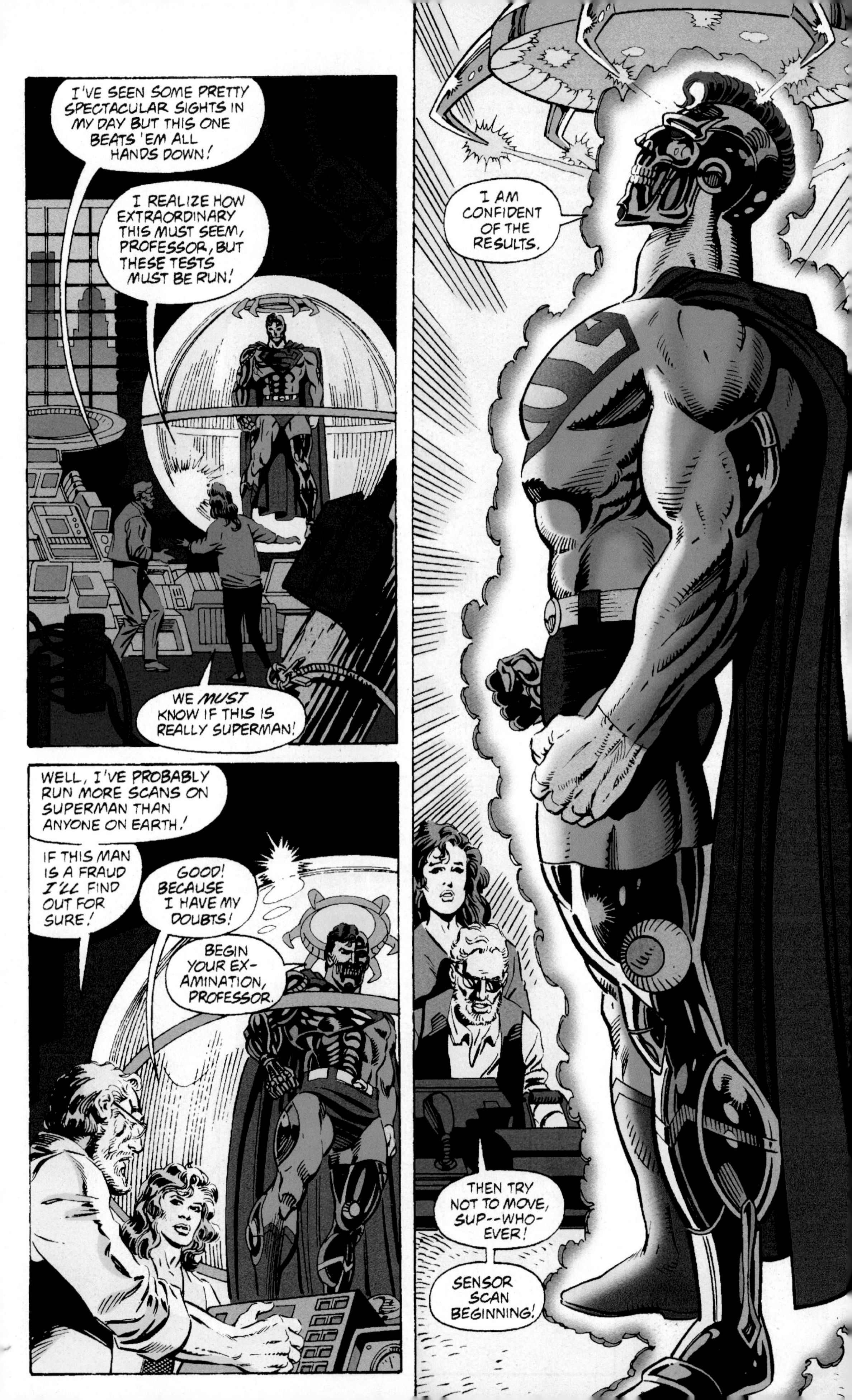
I'VE SEEN SOME PRETTY SPECTACULAR SIGHTS IN MY DAY BUT THIS ONE BEATS 'EM ALL HANDS DOWN!
I REALIZE HOW EXTRAORDINARY THIS MUST SEEM, PROFESSOR, BUT THESE TESTS MUST BE RUN!
WE *MUST* KNOW IF THIS IS REALLY SUPERMAN!
WELL, I'VE PROBABLY RUN MORE SCANS ON SUPERMAN THAN ANYONE ON EARTH!
IF THIS MAN IS A FRAUD *I'LL* FIND OUT FOR SURE!
GOOD! BECAUSE I HAVE MY DOUBTS!
BEGIN YOUR EX-AMINATION, PROFESSOR.
I AM CONFIDENT OF THE RESULTS.
THEN TRY NOT TO MOVE, SUP--WHO-EVER!
SENSOR SCAN BEGINNING!

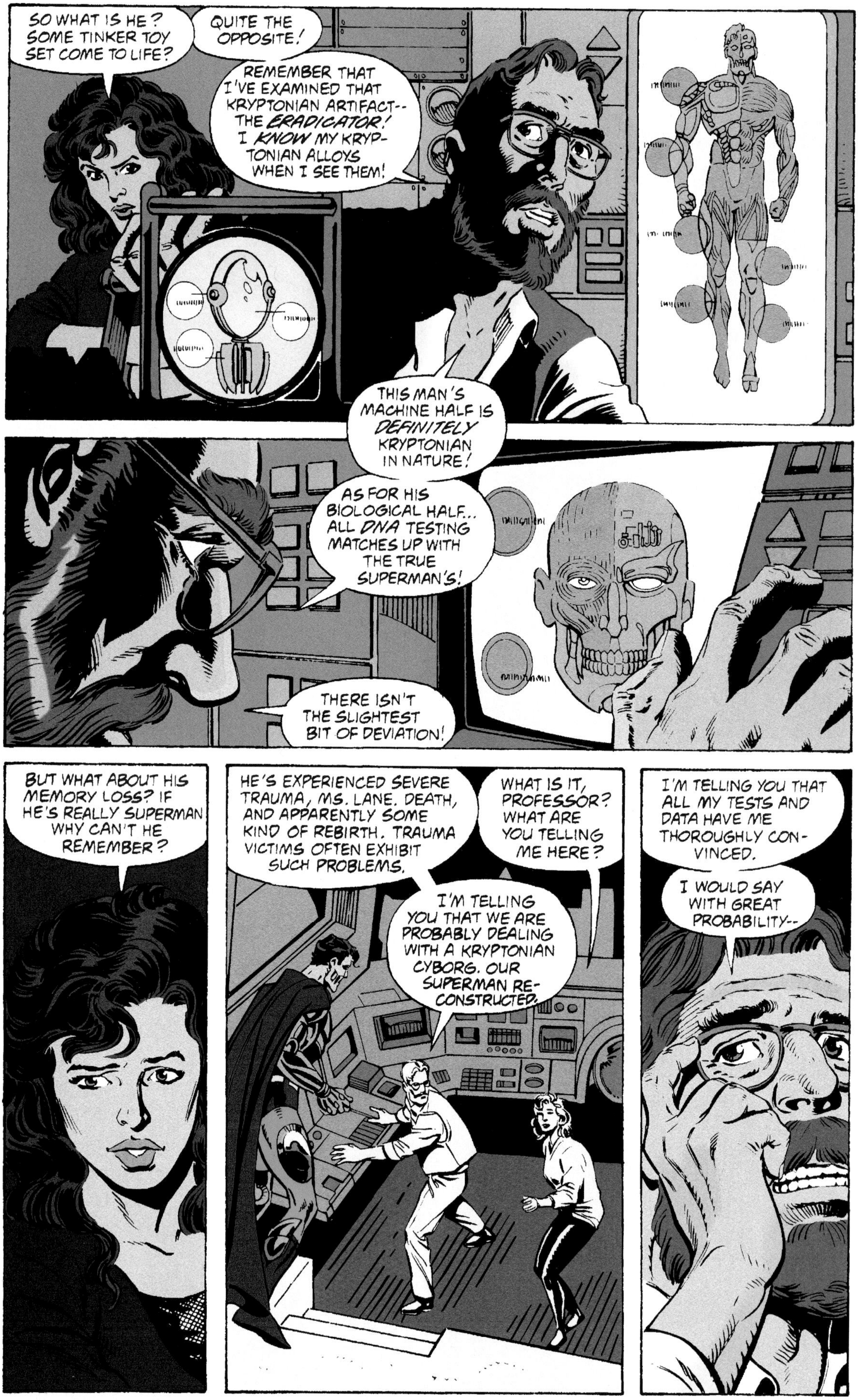
SO WHAT IS HE? SOME TINKER TOY SET COME TO LIFE?
QUITE THE OPPOSITE!
REMEMBER THAT I'VE EXAMINED THAT KRYPTONIAN ARTIFACT-- THE ERADICATOR! I KNOW MY KRYPTONIAN ALLOYS WHEN I SEE THEM!
THIS MAN'S MACHINE HALF IS DEFINITELY KRYPTONIAN IN NATURE!
AS FOR HIS BIOLOGICAL HALF... ALL DNA TESTING MATCHES UP WITH THE TRUE SUPERMAN'S!
THERE ISN'T THE SLIGHTEST BIT OF DEVIATION!
BUT WHAT ABOUT HIS MEMORY LOSS? IF HE'S REALLY SUPERMAN WHY CAN'T HE REMEMBER?
HE'S EXPERIENCED SEVERE TRAUMA, MS. LANE. DEATH, AND APPARENTLY SOME KIND OF REBIRTH. TRAUMA VICTIMS OFTEN EXHIBIT SUCH PROBLEMS.
WHAT IS IT, PROFESSOR? WHAT ARE YOU TELLING ME HERE?
I'M TELLING YOU THAT WE ARE PROBABLY DEALING WITH A KRYPTONIAN CYBORG. OUR SUPERMAN RECONSTRUCTED.
I'M TELLING YOU THAT ALL MY TESTS AND DATA HAVE ME THOROUGHLY CONVINCED.
I WOULD SAY WITH GREAT PROBABILITY--

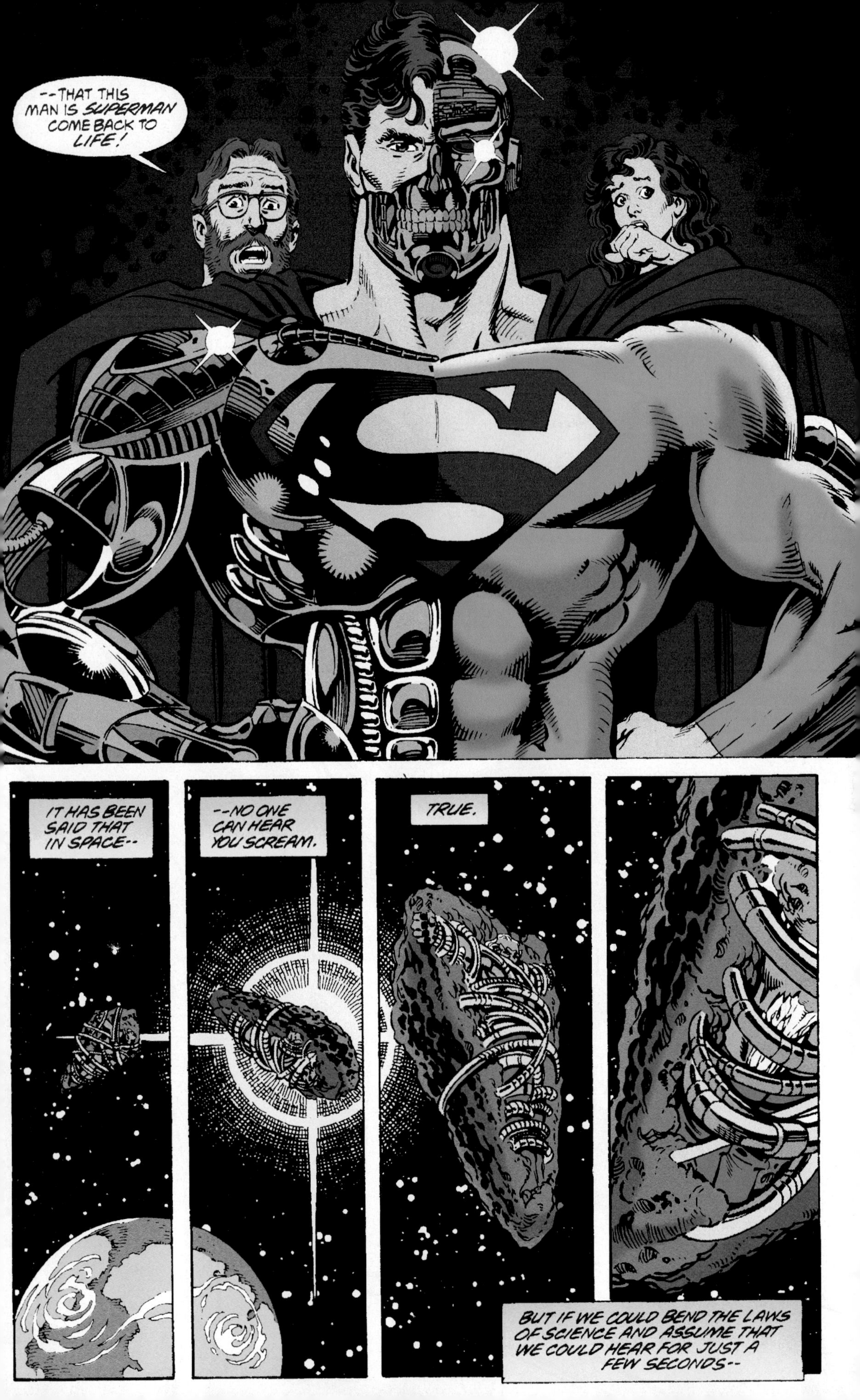
--THAT THIS MAN IS SUPERMAN COME BACK TO LIFE!
IT HAS BEEN SAID THAT IN SPACE--
--NO ONE CAN HEAR YOU SCREAM.
TRUE.
BUT IF WE COULD BEND THE LAWS OF SCIENCE AND ASSUME THAT WE COULD HEAR FOR JUST A FEW SECONDS--

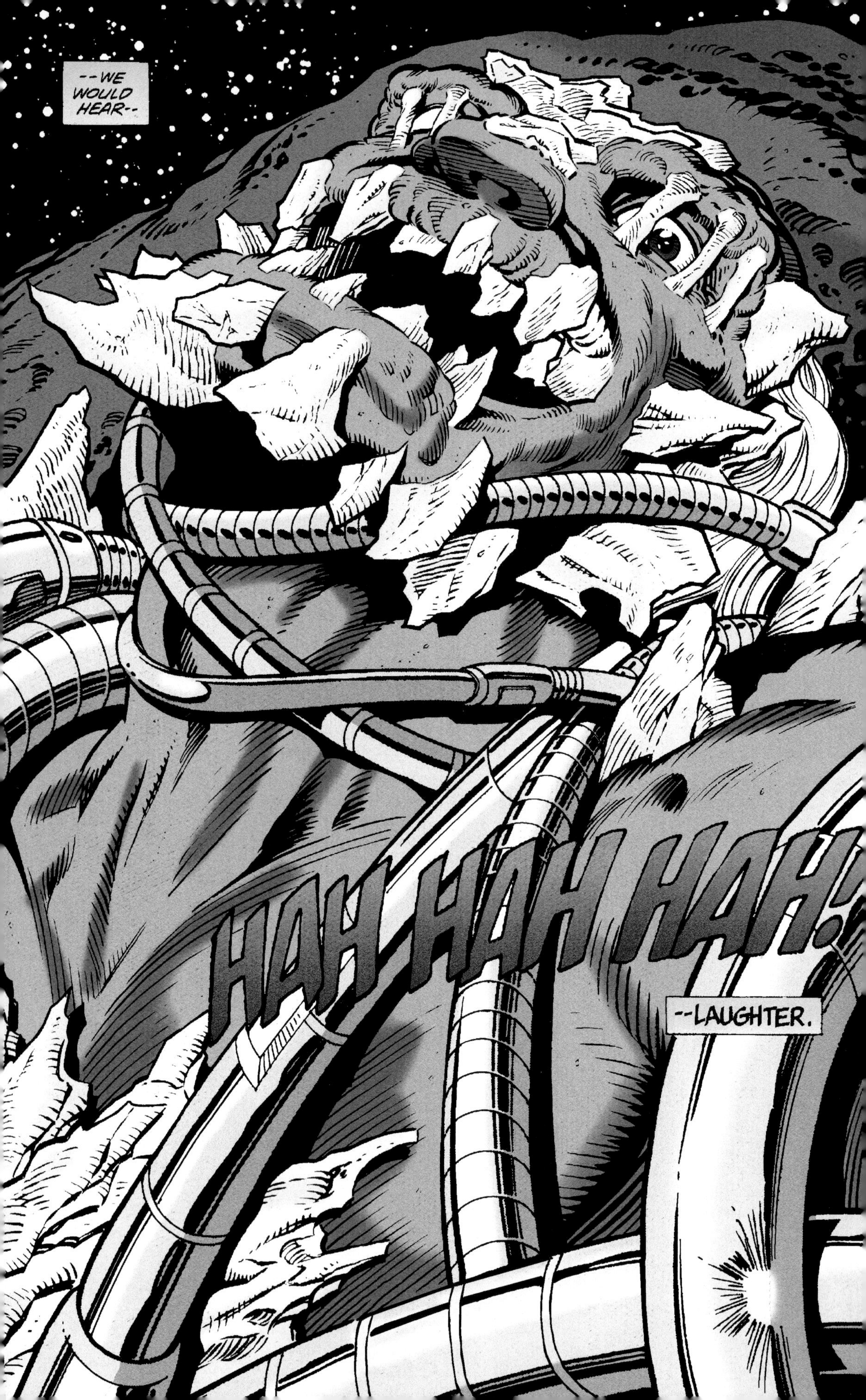
--WE WOULD HEAR--
HAH HAH HAH HAH!
--LAUGHTER.

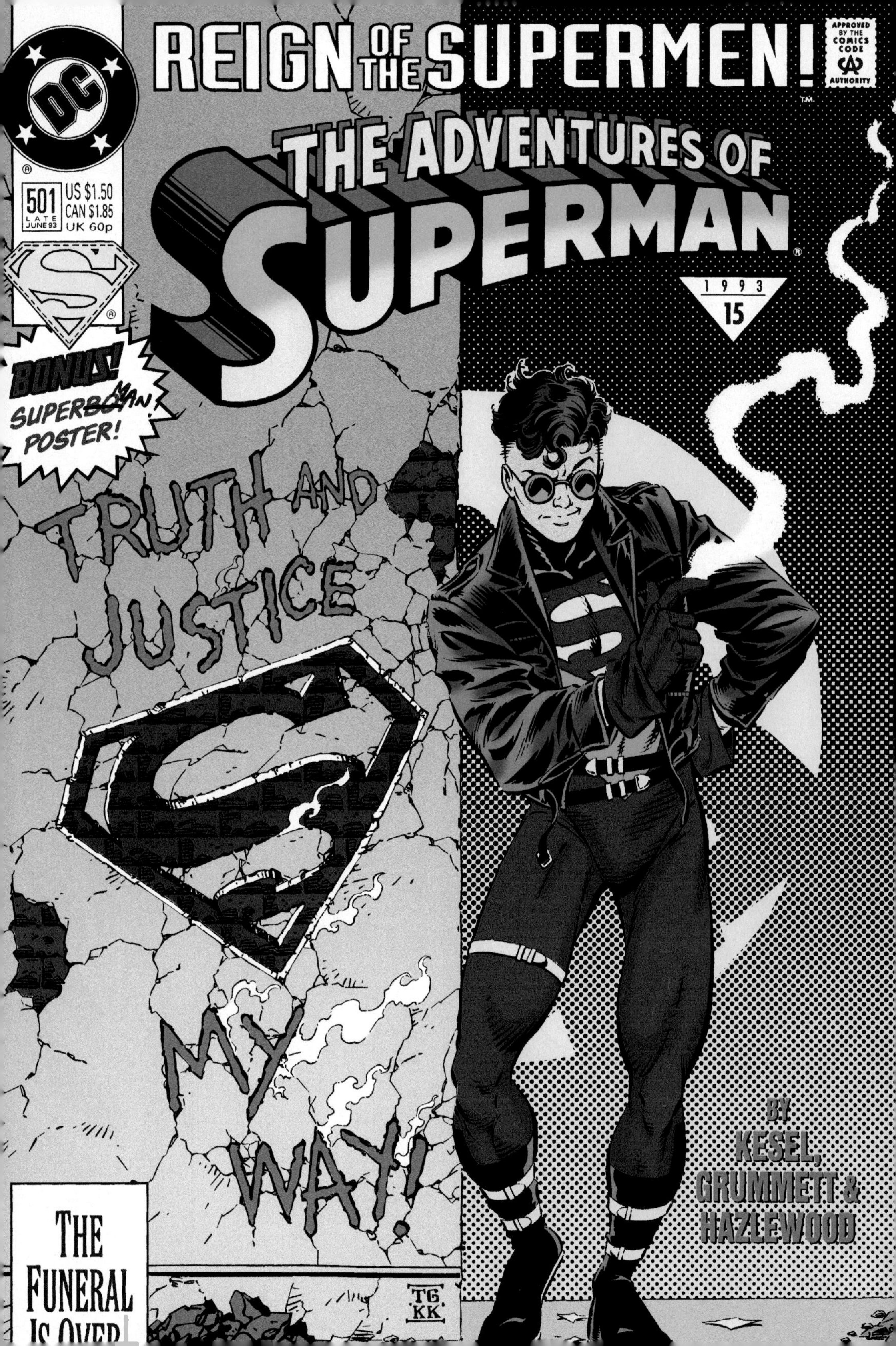

REIGN OF THE SUPERMEN!
APPROVED BY THE COMICS CODE AUTHORITY
DC
501
LATE JUNE 93
US $1.50
CAN $1.85
UK 60p
THE ADVENTURES OF SUPERMAN
1993
15
BONUS!
SUPERBOY MAN POSTER!
TRUTH AND JUSTICE
MY WAY!
BY KESEL, GRUMMETT & HAZLEWOOD
TG KK
THE FUNERAL IS OVER

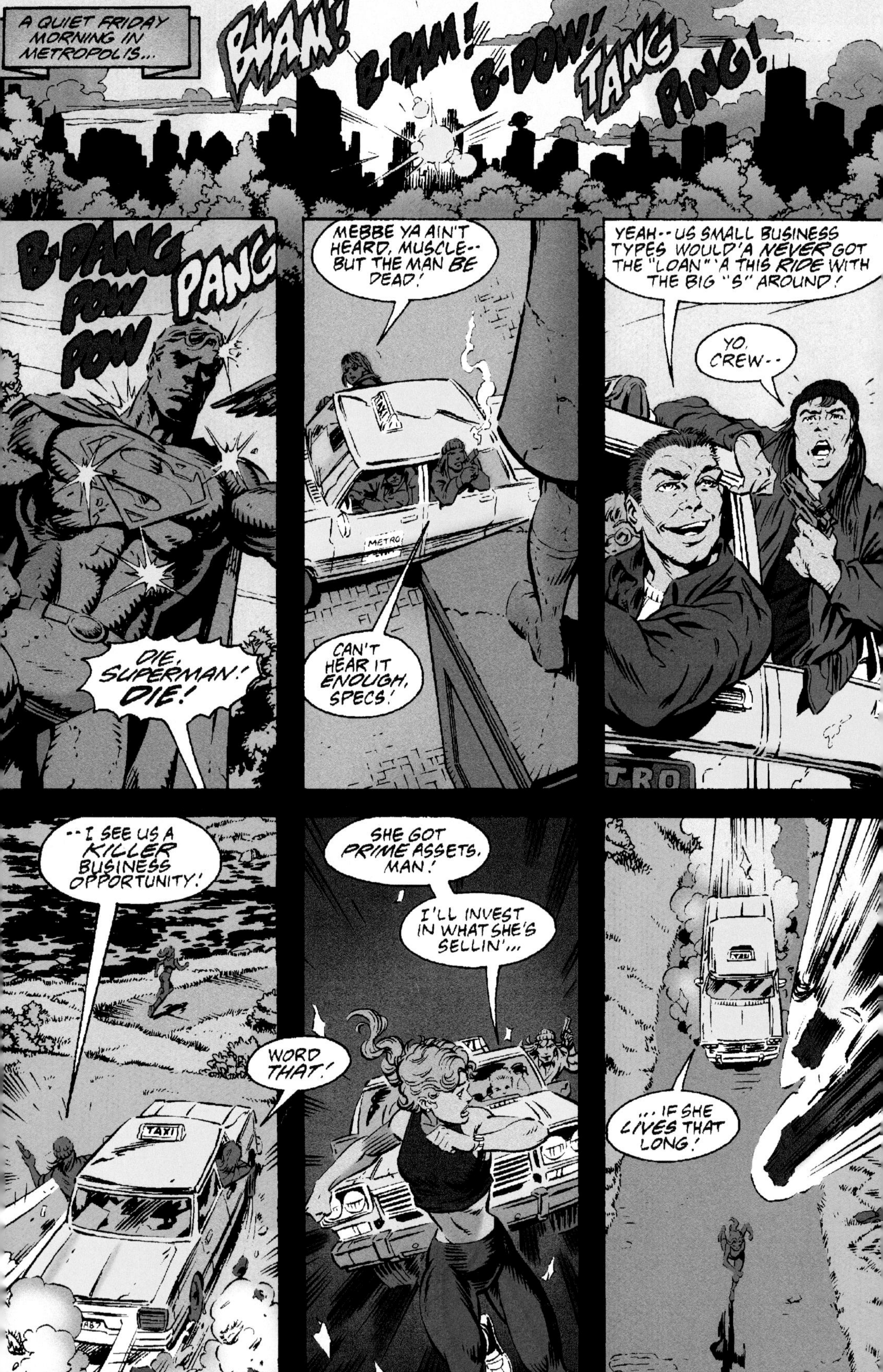
A QUIET FRIDAY MORNING IN METROPOLIS...
BLAM!
B-DAM!
B-DOW!
TANG
PING!
B-DANG
POW
POW
PANG
DIE, SUPERMAN! DIE!
MEBBE YA AIN'T HEARD, MUSCLE-- BUT THE MAN BE DEAD!
CAN'T HEAR IT ENOUGH, SPECS!
YEAH--US SMALL BUSINESS TYPES WOULD'A NEVER GOT THE "LOAN" 'A THIS RIDE WITH THE BIG "S" AROUND!
YO, CREW--
--I SEE US A KILLER BUSINESS OPPORTUNITY!
WORD THAT!
SHE GOT PRIME ASSETS, MAN!
I'LL INVEST IN WHAT SHE'S SELLIN'...
...IF SHE LIVES THAT LONG!

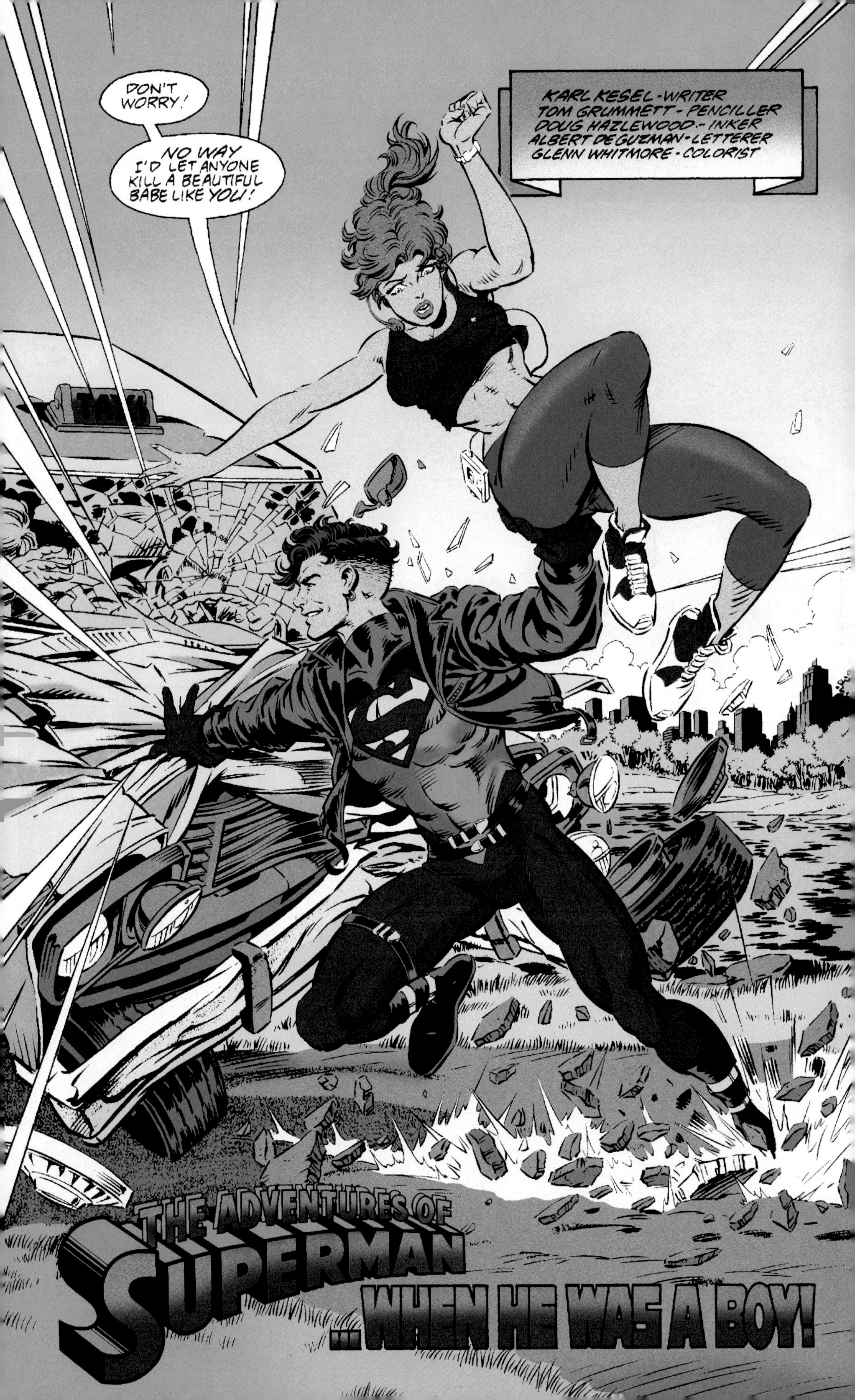

DON'T WORRY!
NO WAY I'D LET ANYONE KILL A BEAUTIFUL BABE LIKE YOU!
KARL KESEL - WRITER
TOM GRUMMETT - PENCILLER
DOUG HAZLEWOOD - INKER
ALBERT DEGUZMAN - LETTERER
GLENN WHITMORE - COLORIST
TAXI
THE ADVENTURES OF SUPERMAN
...WHEN HE WAS A BOY!

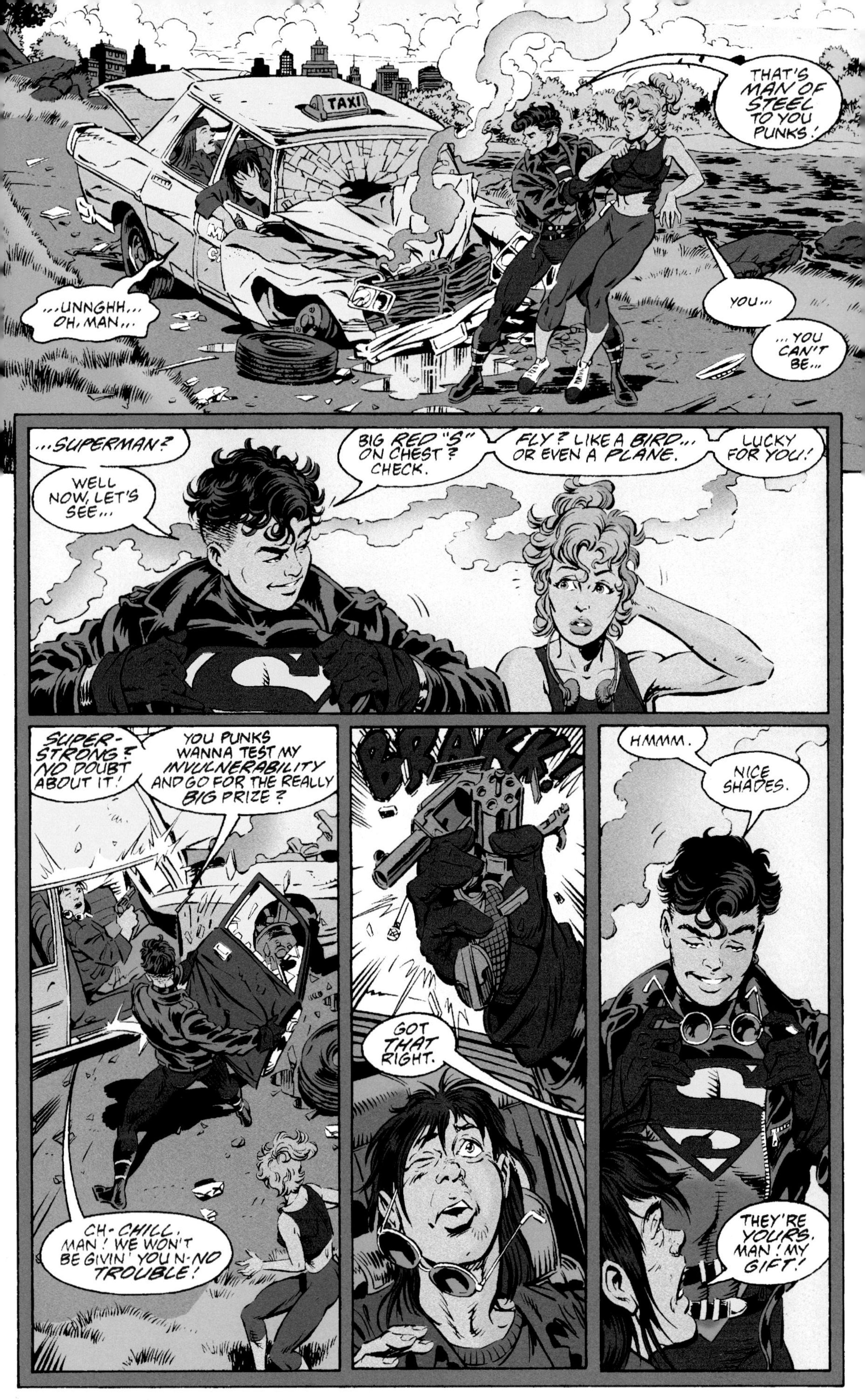
THAT'S MAN OF STEEL TO YOU PUNKS!
...UNNGHH... OH, MAN...
YOU...
...YOU CAN'T BE...
...SUPERMAN?
WELL NOW, LET'S SEE...
BIG RED "S" ON CHEST? CHECK.
FLY? LIKE A BIRD... OR EVEN A PLANE.
LUCKY FOR YOU!
SUPER-STRONG? NO DOUBT ABOUT IT!
YOU PUNKS WANNA TEST MY INVULNERABILITY AND GO FOR THE REALLY BIG PRIZE?
CH-CHILL, MAN! WE WON'T BE GIVIN' YOU N-NO TROUBLE!
BRAKK!
GOT THAT RIGHT.
HMMM.
NICE SHADES.
THEY'RE YOURS, MAN! MY GIFT!

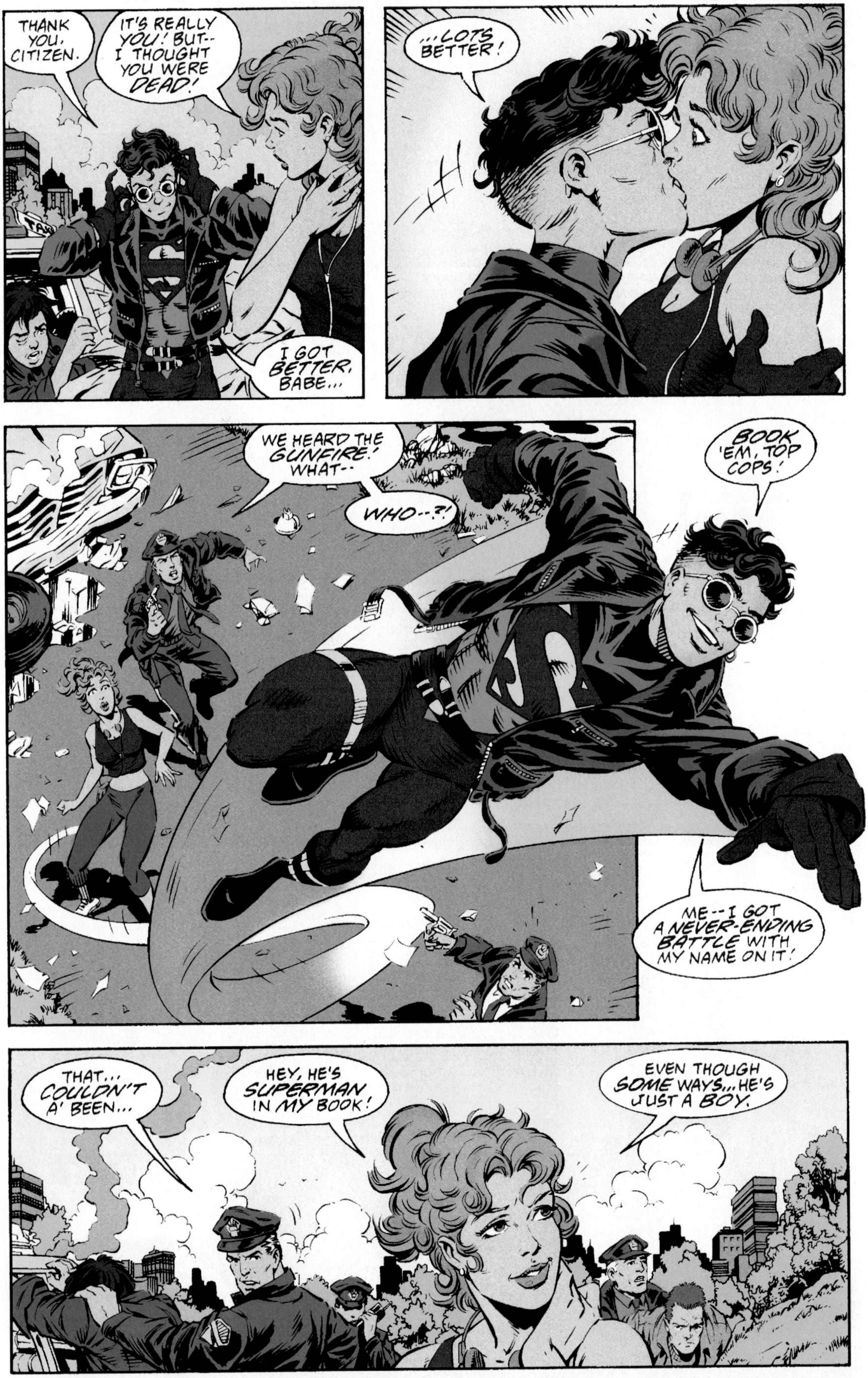
THANK YOU, CITIZEN.
IT'S REALLY YOU! BUT-- I THOUGHT YOU WERE DEAD!
I GOT BETTER, BABE...
...LOTS BETTER!
WE HEARD THE GUNFIRE! WHAT--
WHO--?!
BOOK 'EM, TOP COPS!
ME--I GOT A NEVER-ENDING BATTLE WITH MY NAME ON IT!
THAT... COULDN'T A' BEEN...
HEY, HE'S SUPERMAN IN MY BOOK!
EVEN THOUGH SOME WAYS...HE'S JUST A BOY.

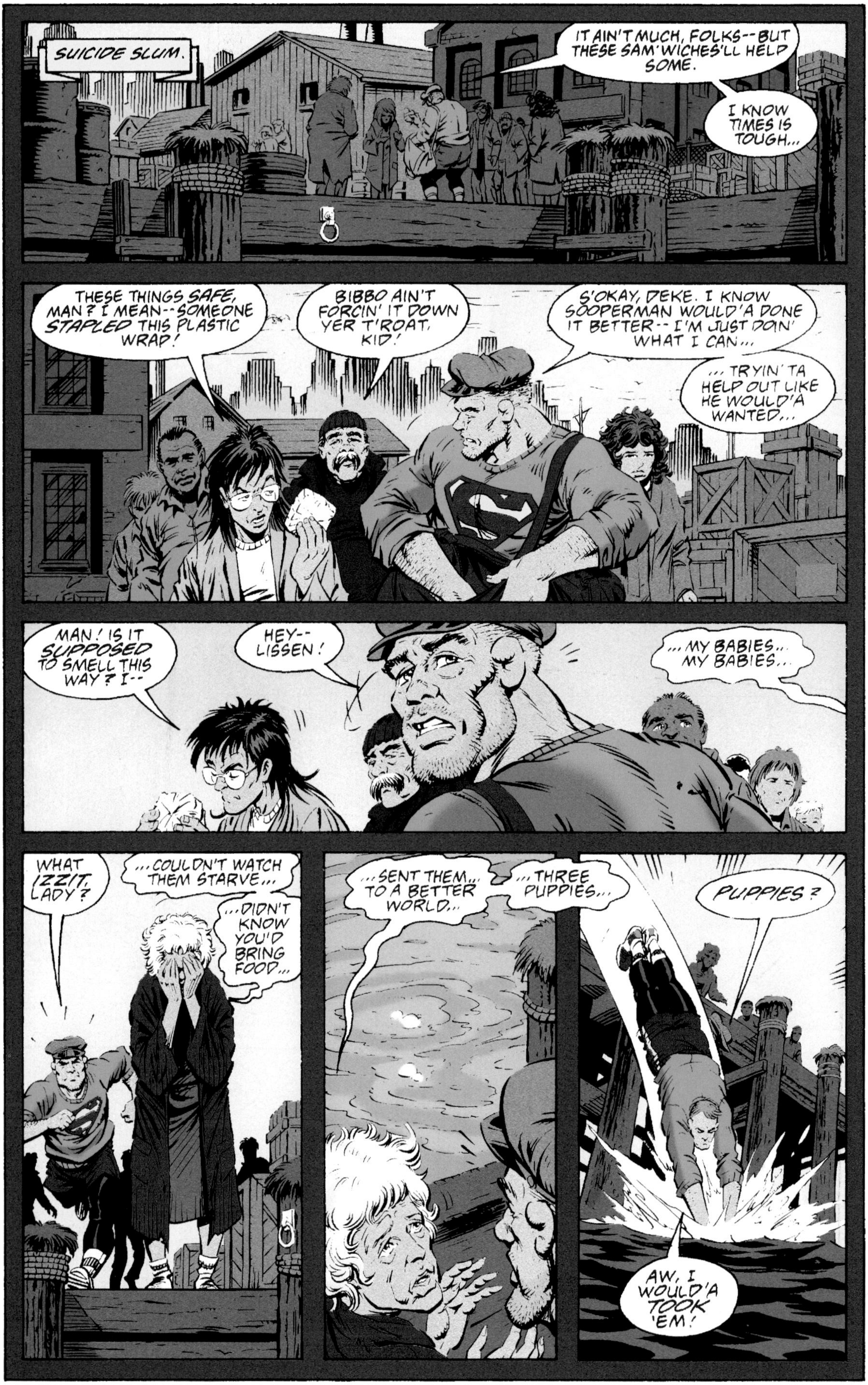
SUICIDE SLUM.
IT AIN'T MUCH, FOLKS-- BUT THESE SAM'WICHES'LL HELP SOME.
I KNOW TIMES IS TOUGH...
THESE THINGS SAFE, MAN? I MEAN--SOMEONE STAPLED THIS PLASTIC WRAP!
BIBBO AIN'T FORCIN' IT DOWN YER T'ROAT, KID!
S'OKAY, DEKE. I KNOW SOOPERMAN WOULD'A DONE IT BETTER-- I'M JUST DOIN' WHAT I CAN...
...TRYIN' TA HELP OUT LIKE HE WOULD'A WANTED...
MAN! IS IT SUPPOSED TO SMELL THIS WAY? I--
HEY-- LISSEN!
...MY BABIES... MY BABIES...
WHAT IZZIT, LADY?
...COULDN'T WATCH THEM STARVE...
...DIDN'T KNOW YOU'D BRING FOOD...
...SENT THEM... TO A BETTER WORLD...
...THREE PUPPIES...
PUPPIES?
AW, I WOULD'A TOOK 'EM!

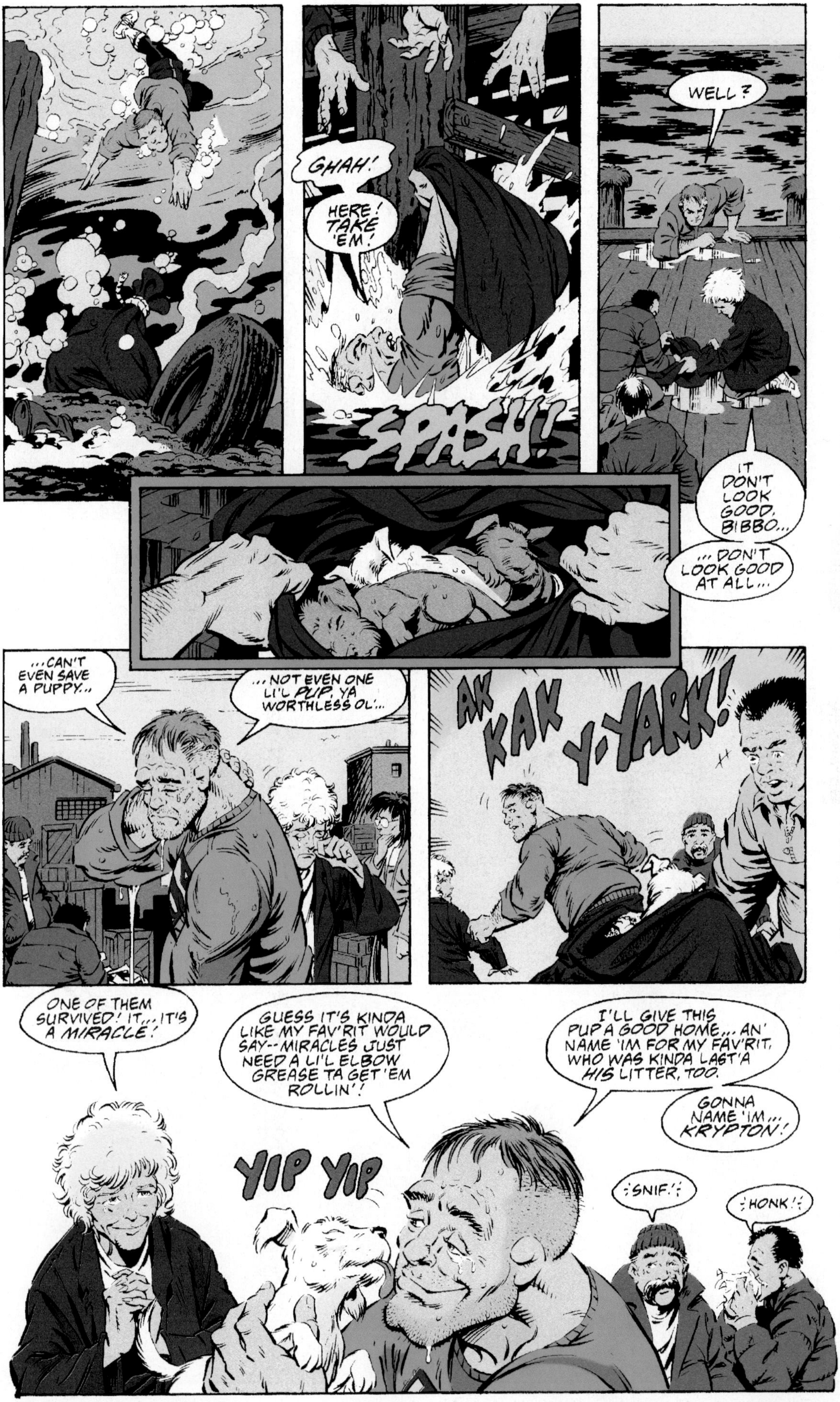

GHAH!
HERE! TAKE 'EM!
SPASH!
WELL?
IT DON'T LOOK GOOD, BIBBO...
...DON'T LOOK GOOD AT ALL...
...CAN'T EVEN SAVE A PUPPY...
...NOT EVEN ONE LI'L PUP, YA WORTHLESS OL'...
AK KAK Y-YARK!
ONE OF THEM SURVIVED! IT... IT'S A MIRACLE!
GUESS IT'S KINDA LIKE MY FAV'RIT WOULD SAY--MIRACLES JUST NEED A LI'L ELBOW GREASE TA GET 'EM ROLLIN'!
I'LL GIVE THIS PUP A GOOD HOME... AN' NAME 'IM FOR MY FAV'RIT, WHO WAS KINDA LAST'A HIS LITTER, TOO.
GONNA NAME 'IM... KRYPTON!
YIP YIP
SNIF.
HONK!

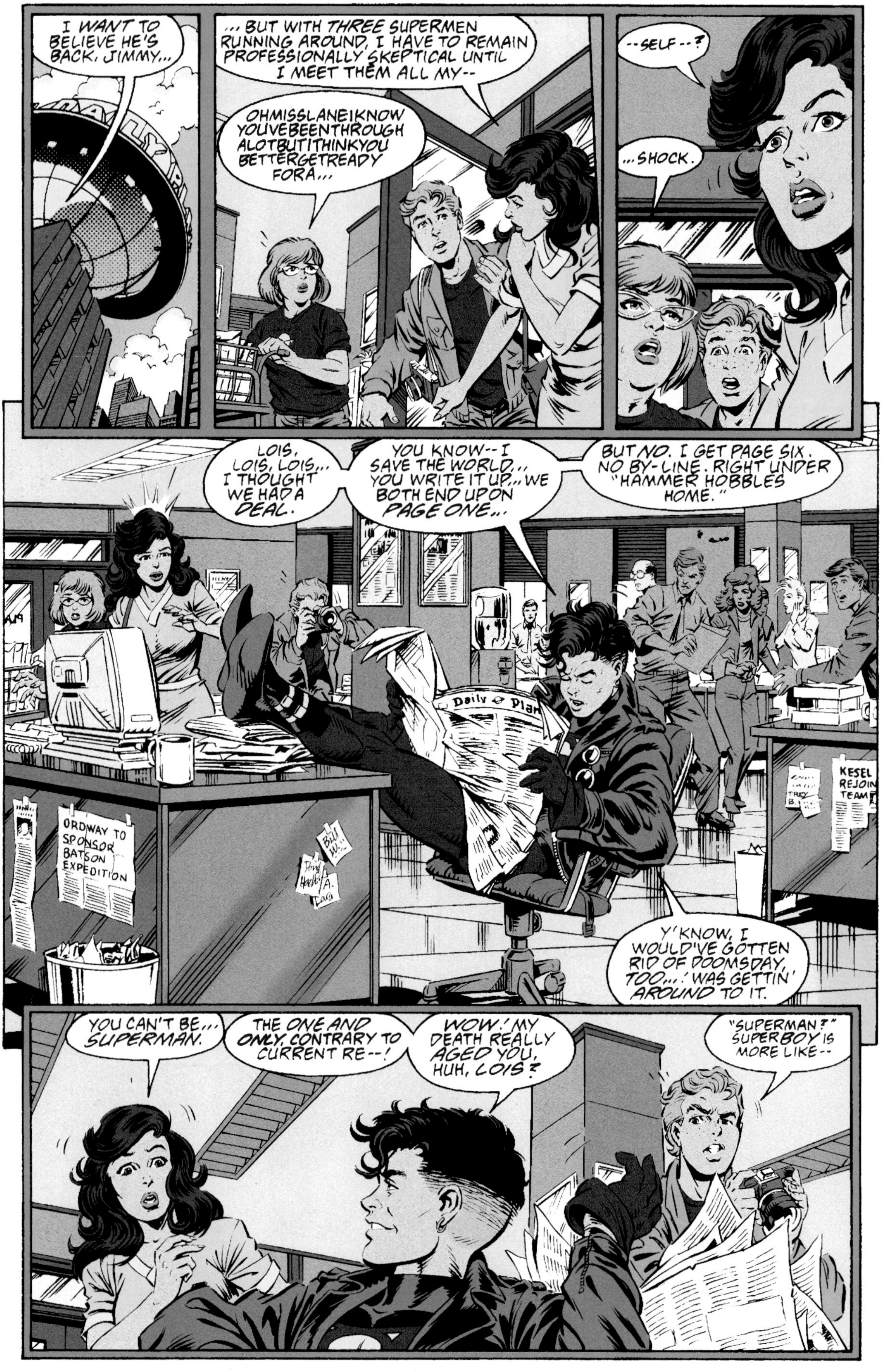
I WANT TO BELIEVE HE'S BACK, JIMMY...
...BUT WITH THREE SUPERMEN RUNNING AROUND, I HAVE TO REMAIN PROFESSIONALLY SKEPTICAL UNTIL I MEET THEM ALL MY--
OHMISSLANEIKNOW YOUVEBEENTHROUGH ALOTBUTITHINKYOU BETTERGETREADY FORA...
--SELF--?
...SHOCK.
LOIS, LOIS, LOIS... I THOUGHT WE HAD A DEAL.
YOU KNOW--I SAVE THE WORLD... YOU WRITE IT UP... WE BOTH END UP ON PAGE ONE...
BUT NO. I GET PAGE SIX. NO BY-LINE. RIGHT UNDER "HAMMER HOBBLES HOME."
ORDWAY TO SPONSOR BATSON EXPEDITION
KESEL REJOIN TEAM
Y'KNOW, I WOULD'VE GOTTEN RID OF DOOMSDAY, TOO... 'WAS GETTIN' AROUND TO IT.
YOU CAN'T BE... SUPERMAN.
THE ONE AND ONLY, CONTRARY TO CURRENT RE--!
WOW! MY DEATH REALLY AGED YOU, HUH, LOIS?
"SUPERMAN?" SUPERBOY IS MORE LIKE--

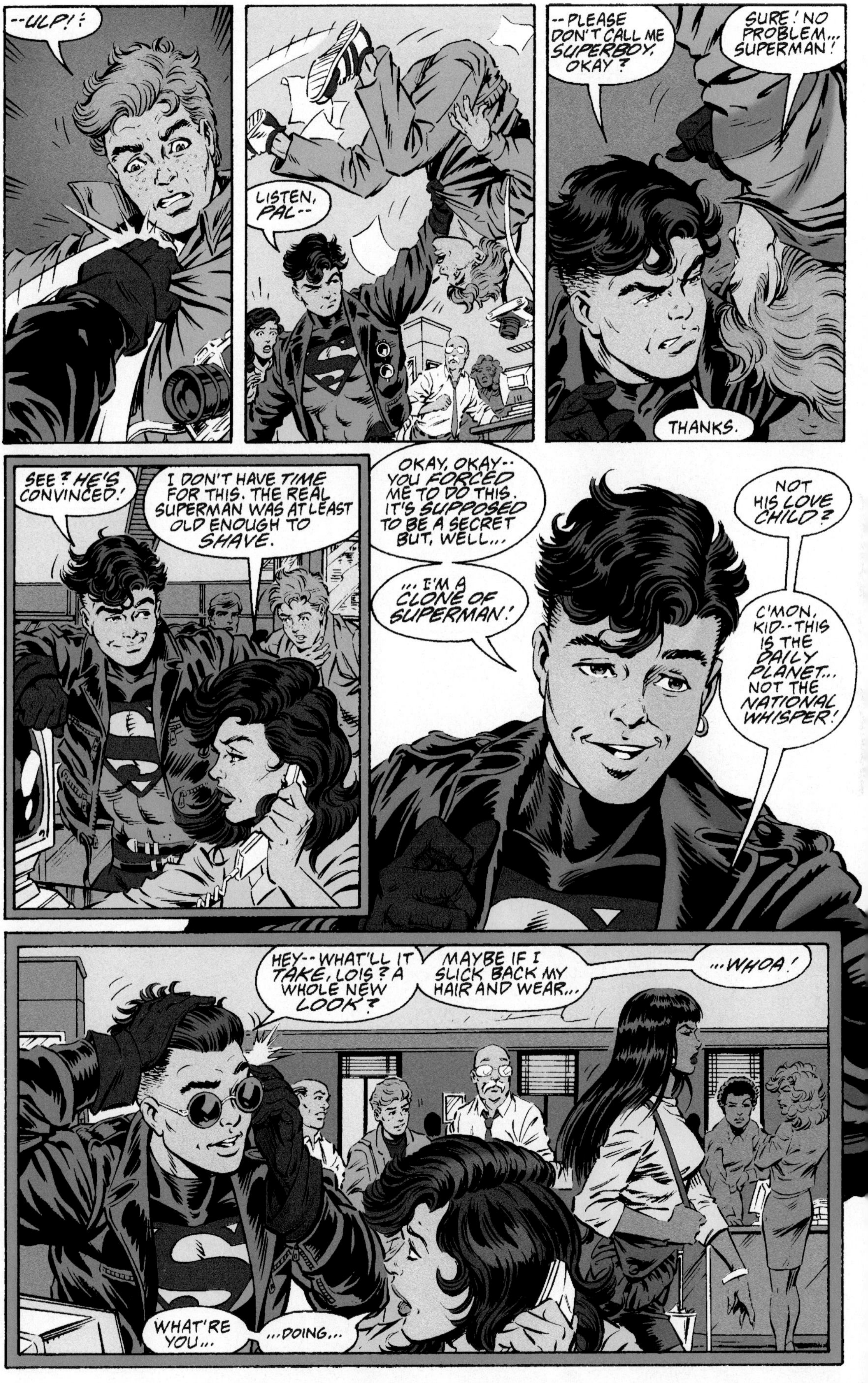
--ULP!--
LISTEN, PAL--
--PLEASE DON'T CALL ME SUPERBOY, OKAY?
SURE! NO PROBLEM... SUPERMAN!
THANKS.
SEE? HE'S CONVINCED!
I DON'T HAVE TIME FOR THIS. THE REAL SUPERMAN WAS AT LEAST OLD ENOUGH TO SHAVE.
OKAY, OKAY-- YOU FORCED ME TO DO THIS. IT'S SUPPOSED TO BE A SECRET BUT, WELL...
...I'M A CLONE OF SUPERMAN!
NOT HIS LOVE CHILD?
C'MON, KID--THIS IS THE DAILY PLANET... NOT THE NATIONAL WHISPER!
HEY--WHAT'LL IT TAKE, LOIS? A WHOLE NEW LOOK?
MAYBE IF I SLICK BACK MY HAIR AND WEAR...
...WHOA!
WHAT'RE YOU...
...DOING...

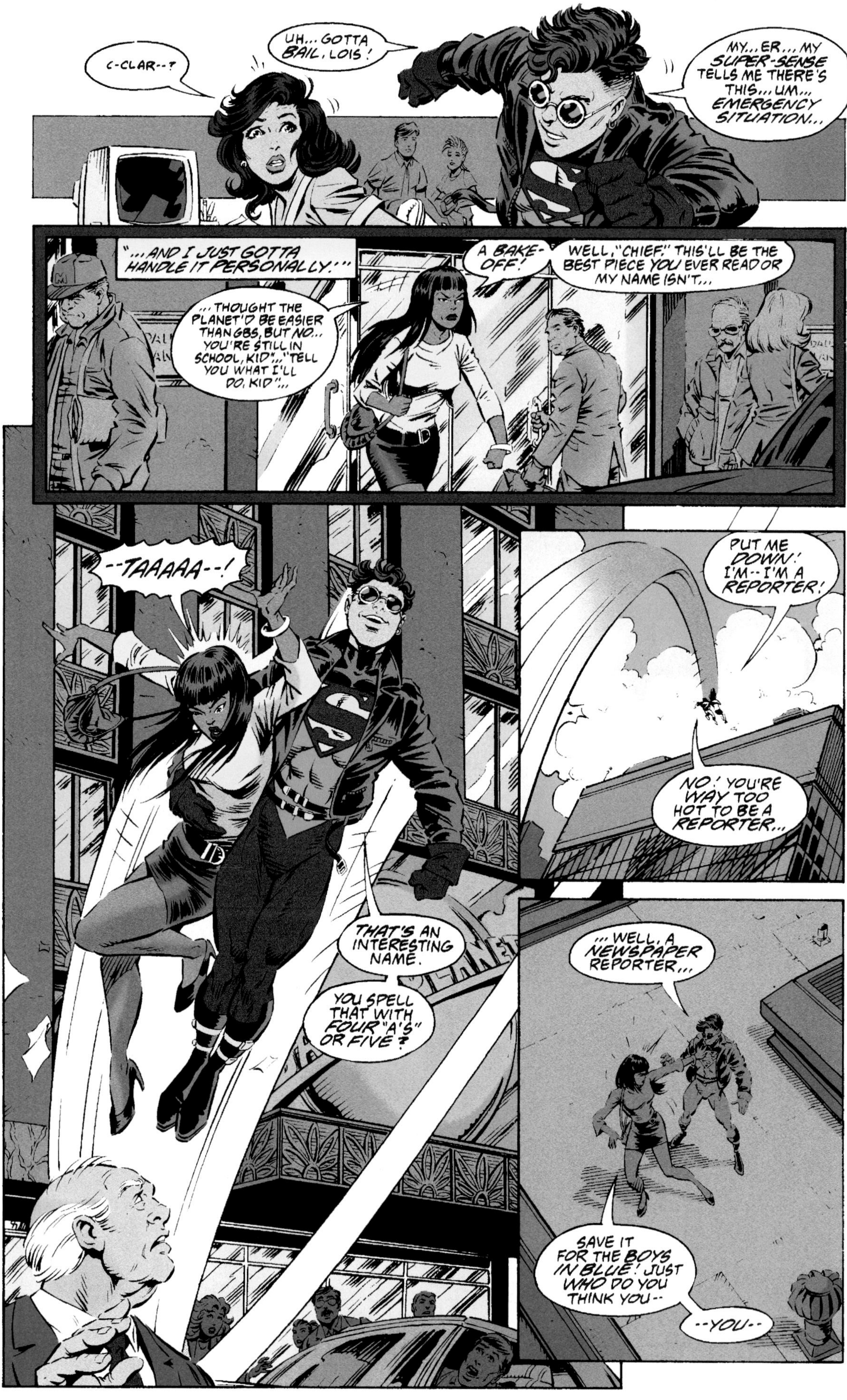

C-CLAR--?
UH... GOTTA BAIL, LOIS!
MY... ER... MY SUPER-SENSE TELLS ME THERE'S THIS... UM... EMERGENCY SITUATION...
"...AND I JUST GOTTA HANDLE IT PERSONALLY."
...THOUGHT THE PLANET'D BE EASIER THAN GBS, BUT NO... "YOU'RE STILL IN SCHOOL, KID"... "TELL YOU WHAT I'LL DO, KID"...
A BAKE-OFF!
WELL, "CHIEF," THIS'LL BE THE BEST PIECE YOU EVER READ OR MY NAME ISN'T...
--TAAAAA--!
THAT'S AN INTERESTING NAME.
YOU SPELL THAT WITH FOUR "A'S" OR FIVE?
PUT ME DOWN! I'M--I'M A REPORTER!
NO! YOU'RE WAY TOO HOT TO BE A REPORTER...
...WELL, A NEWSPAPER REPORTER...
SAVE IT FOR THE BOYS IN BLUE! JUST WHO DO YOU THINK YOU--
--YOU--

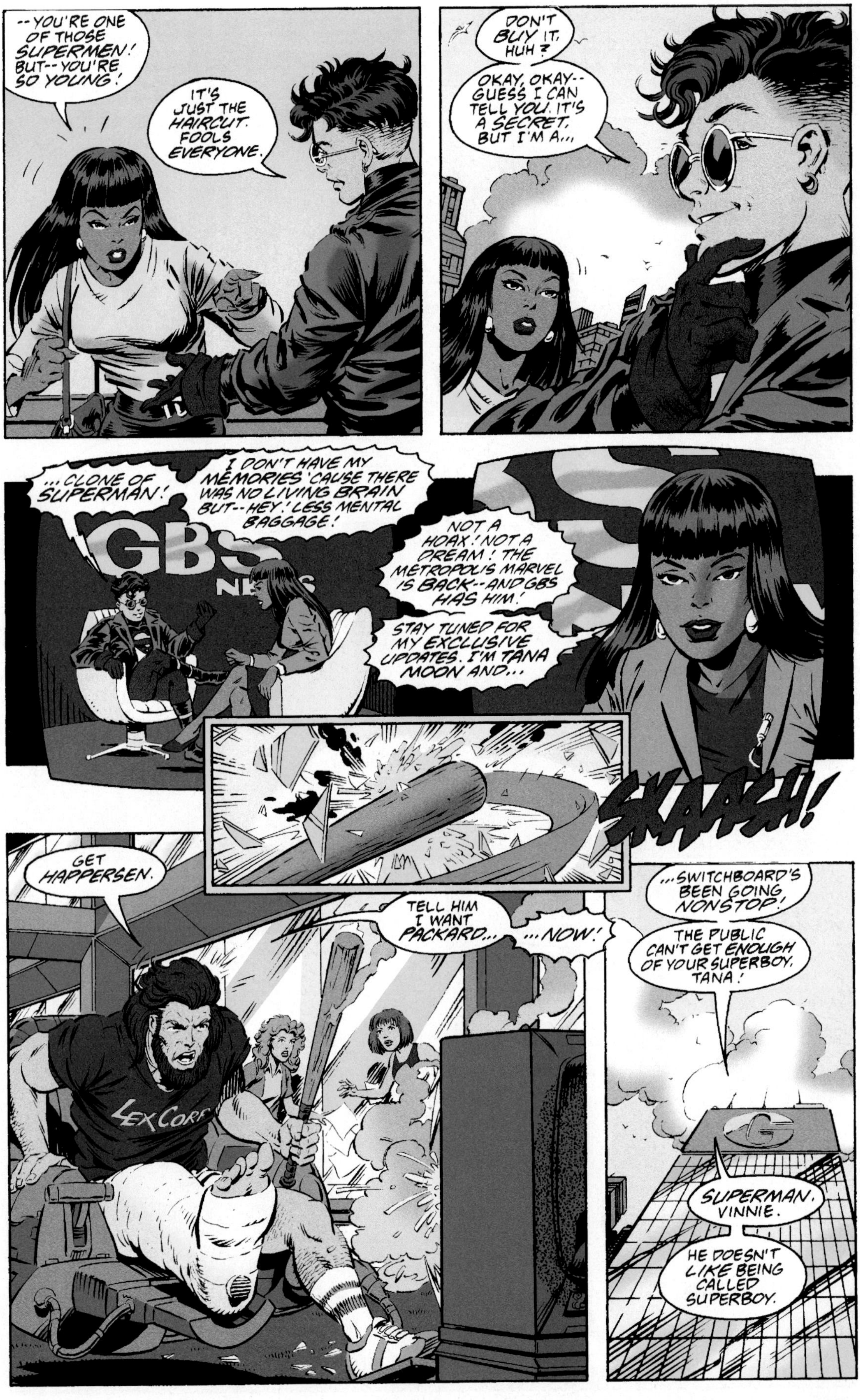
--YOU'RE ONE OF THOSE SUPERMEN! BUT--YOU'RE SO YOUNG!
IT'S JUST THE HAIRCUT. FOOLS EVERYONE.
DON'T BUY IT, HUH?
OKAY, OKAY--GUESS I CAN TELL YOU. IT'S A SECRET. BUT I'M A...
...CLONE OF SUPERMAN!
I DON'T HAVE MY MEMORIES 'CAUSE THERE WAS NO LIVING BRAIN BUT--HEY! LESS MENTAL BAGGAGE!
GBS NEWS
NOT A HOAX! NOT A DREAM! THE METROPOLIS MARVEL IS BACK--AND GBS HAS HIM!
STAY TUNED FOR MY EXCLUSIVE UPDATES. I'M TANA MOON AND...
SMASH!
GET HAPPERSEN.
TELL HIM I WANT PACKARD...
...NOW!
LEX CORP
...SWITCHBOARD'S BEEN GOING NONSTOP!
THE PUBLIC CAN'T GET ENOUGH OF YOUR SUPERBOY, TANA!
SUPERMAN, VINNIE.
HE DOESN'T LIKE BEING CALLED SUPERBOY.

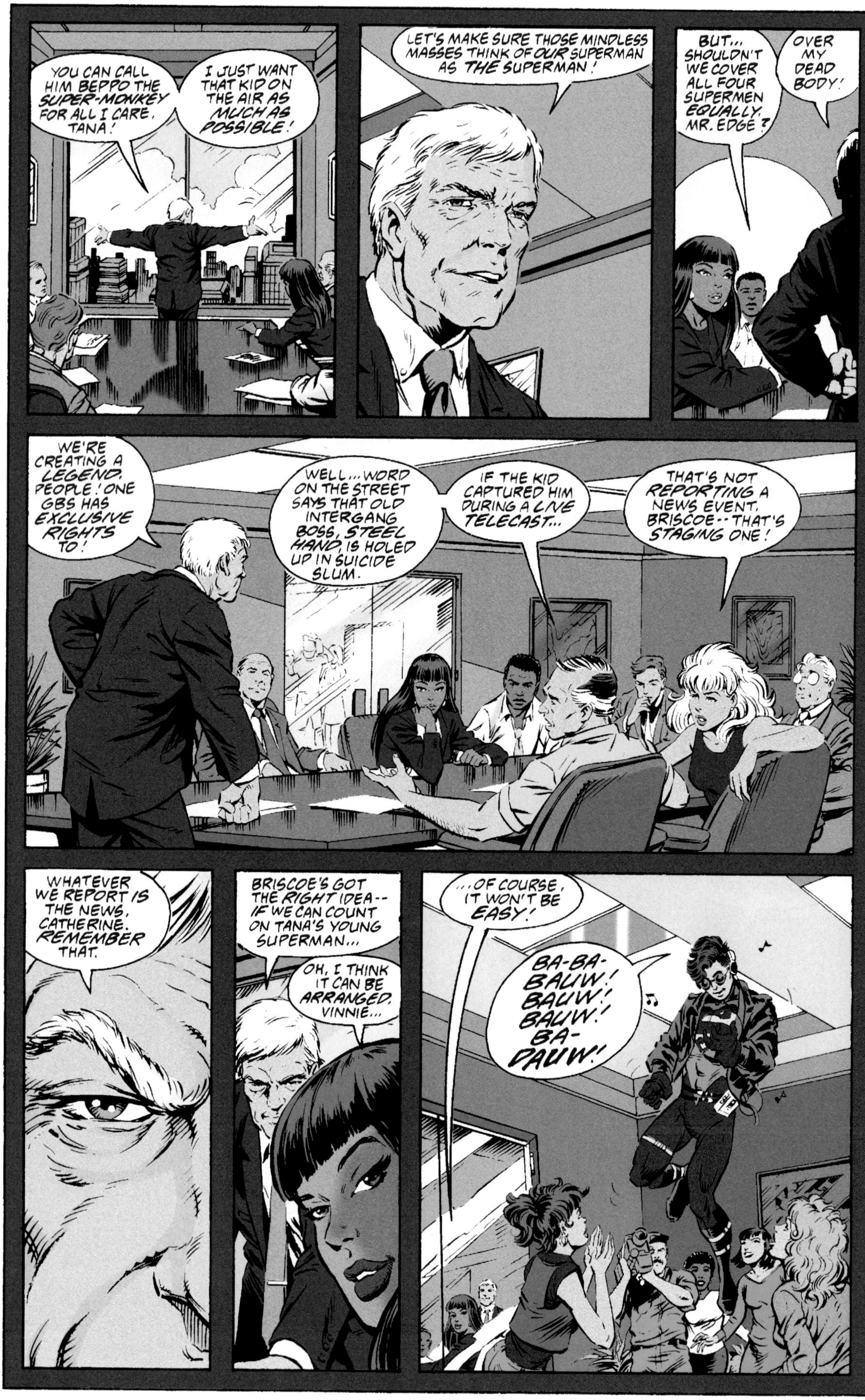
YOU CAN CALL HIM BEPPO THE SUPER-MONKEY FOR ALL I CARE, TANA!
I JUST WANT THAT KID ON THE AIR AS MUCH AS POSSIBLE!
LET'S MAKE SURE THOSE MINDLESS MASSES THINK OF OUR SUPERMAN AS THE SUPERMAN!
BUT... SHOULDN'T WE COVER ALL FOUR SUPERMEN EQUALLY, MR. EDGE?
OVER MY DEAD BODY!
WE'RE CREATING A LEGEND, PEOPLE! ONE GBS HAS EXCLUSIVE RIGHTS TO!
WELL... WORD ON THE STREET SAYS THAT OLD INTERGANG BOSS, STEEL HAND, IS HOLED UP IN SUICIDE SLUM.
IF THE KID CAPTURED HIM DURING A LIVE TELECAST...
THAT'S NOT REPORTING A NEWS EVENT, BRISCOE -- THAT'S STAGING ONE!
WHATEVER WE REPORT IS THE NEWS, CATHERINE. REMEMBER THAT.
BRISCOE'S GOT THE RIGHT IDEA -- IF WE CAN COUNT ON TANA'S YOUNG SUPERMAN...
OH, I THINK IT CAN BE ARRANGED, VINNIE...
...OF COURSE, IT WON'T BE EASY!
BA-BA-BAUW! BAUW! BAUW! BA-DAUW!

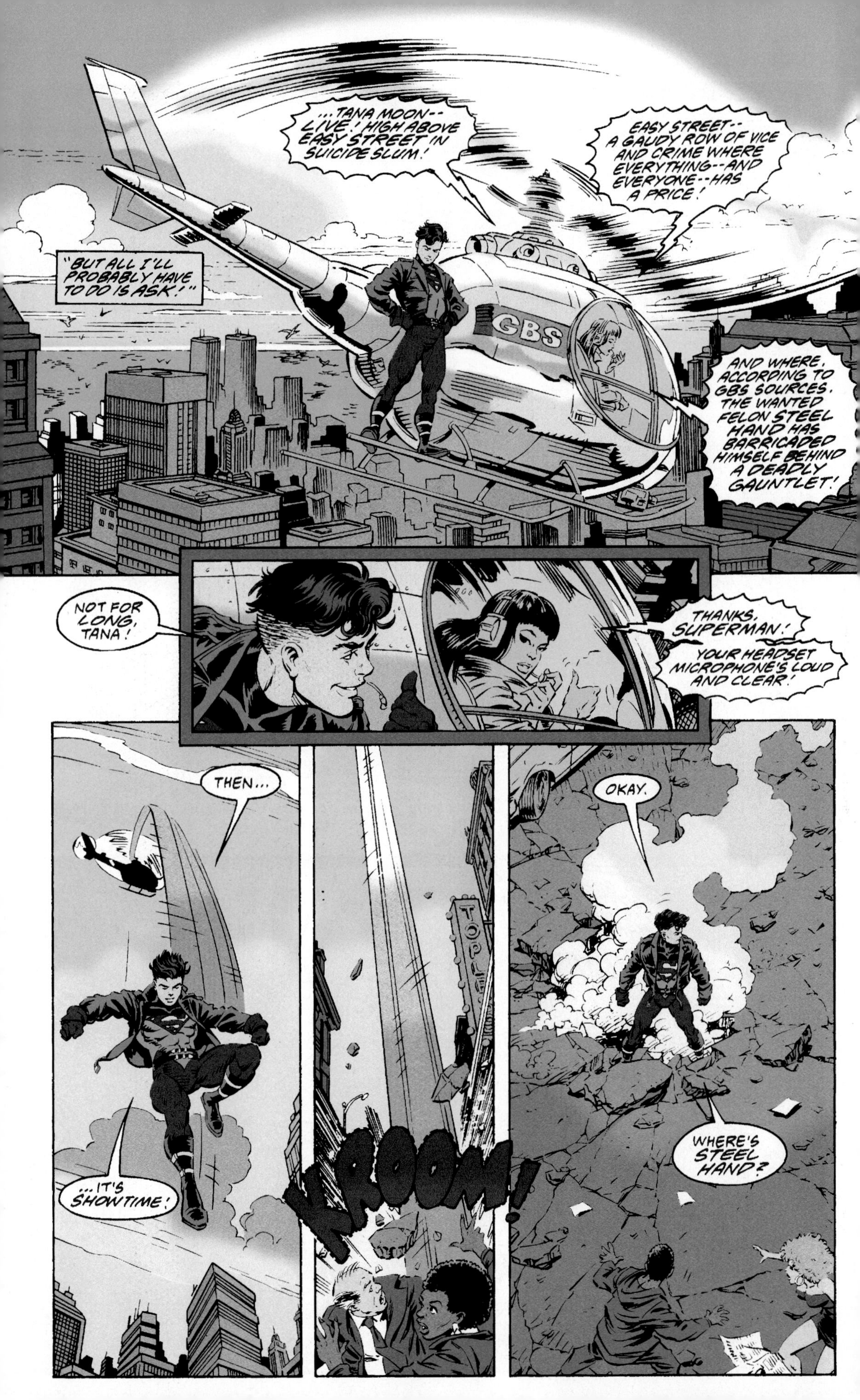
...TANA MOON--LIVE! HIGH ABOVE EASY STREET IN SUICIDE SLUM!
EASY STREET--A GAUDY ROW OF VICE AND CRIME WHERE EVERYTHING--AND EVERYONE--HAS A PRICE!
"BUT ALL I'LL PROBABLY HAVE TO DO IS ASK!"
GBS
AND WHERE, ACCORDING TO GBS SOURCES, THE WANTED FELON STEEL HAND HAS BARRICADED HIMSELF BEHIND A DEADLY GAUNTLET!
NOT FOR LONG, TANA!
THANKS, SUPERMAN!
YOUR HEADSET MICROPHONE'S LOUD AND CLEAR!
THEN...
...IT'S SHOWTIME!
TOPLE
KROOOM!
OKAY.
WHERE'S STEEL HAND?

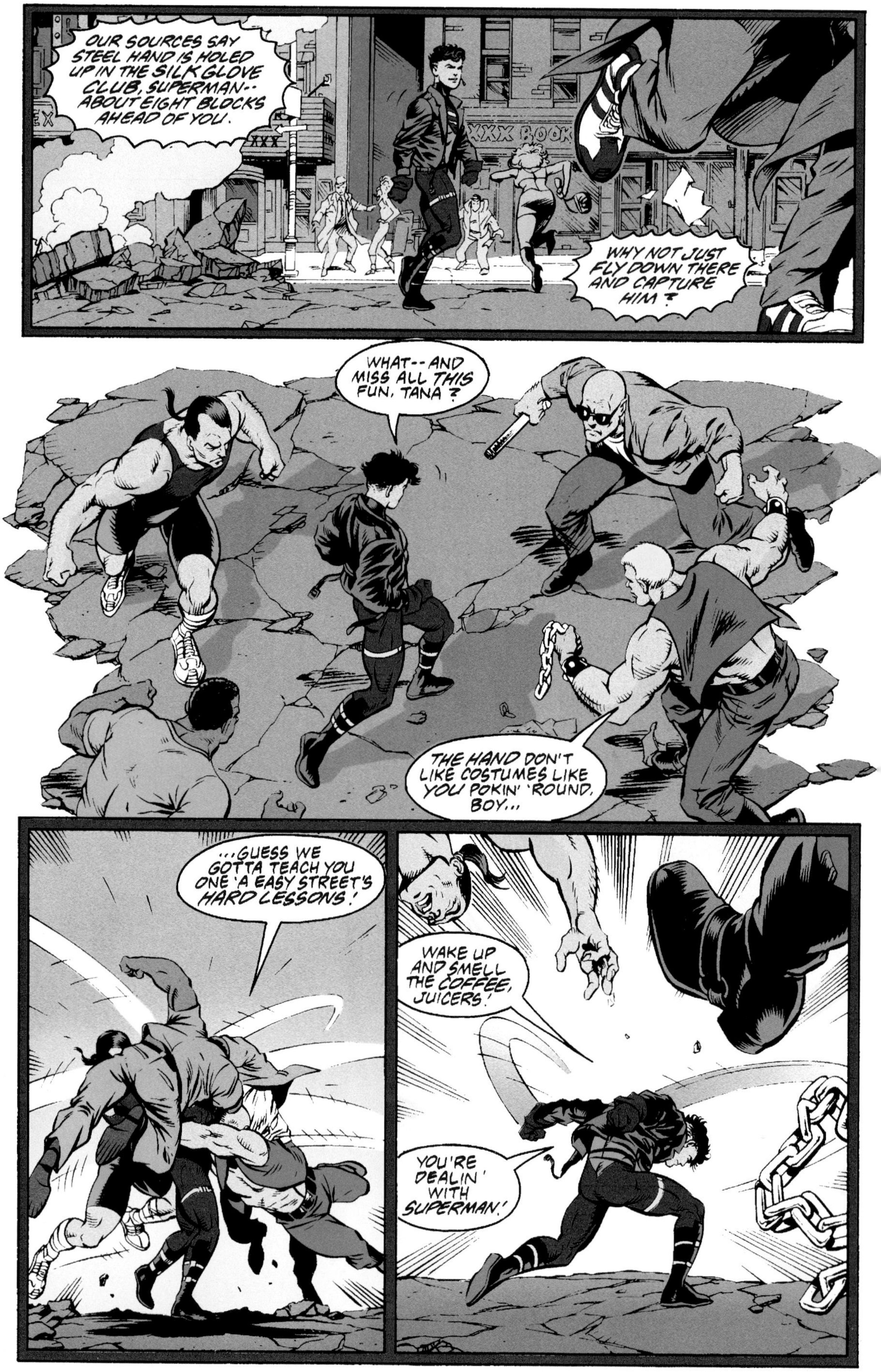
OUR SOURCES SAY STEEL HAND IS HOLED UP IN THE SILK GLOVE CLUB, SUPERMAN-- ABOUT EIGHT BLOCKS AHEAD OF YOU.
WHY NOT JUST FLY DOWN THERE AND CAPTURE HIM?
WHAT-- AND MISS ALL THIS FUN, TANA?
THE HAND DON'T LIKE COSTUMES LIKE YOU POKIN' 'ROUND, BOY...
...GUESS WE GOTTA TEACH YOU ONE 'A EASY STREET'S HARD LESSONS!
WAKE UP AND SMELL THE COFFEE, JUICERS!
YOU'RE DEALIN' WITH SUPERMAN!

SOOPERMAN, HUH? HEARD YOUSE WAS BACK! MEBBE YOUSE SHOULDA *STAYED DEAD!*

AT AT AT AT

BUT THEN I WOULDN'T HAVE MET *YOU* CHARMING GALS!

LOOK, I'M SURE IT'S *SOCIETY'S* FAULT YOU'RE HERE, AND I WISH I HAD TIME TO GET TO KNOW EACH OF YOU *PERSONALLY...*

...BUT *BUSINESS* BEFORE *PLEASURE!*

KRAK-AK KOOM!

THE REST OF EASY STREET LOOKS *CLEAR,* SUPERMAN.

KEEP THE CAMERA TIGHT ON HIM, GORDON.

SOME *GAUNTLET,* HUH, TANA?

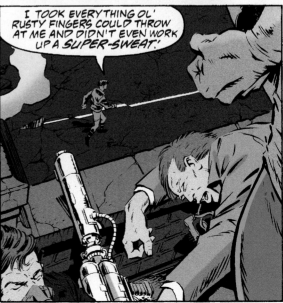

I TOOK EVERYTHING OL' RUSTY FINGERS COULD THROW AT ME AND DIDN'T EVEN WORK UP A *SUPER-SWEAT!*

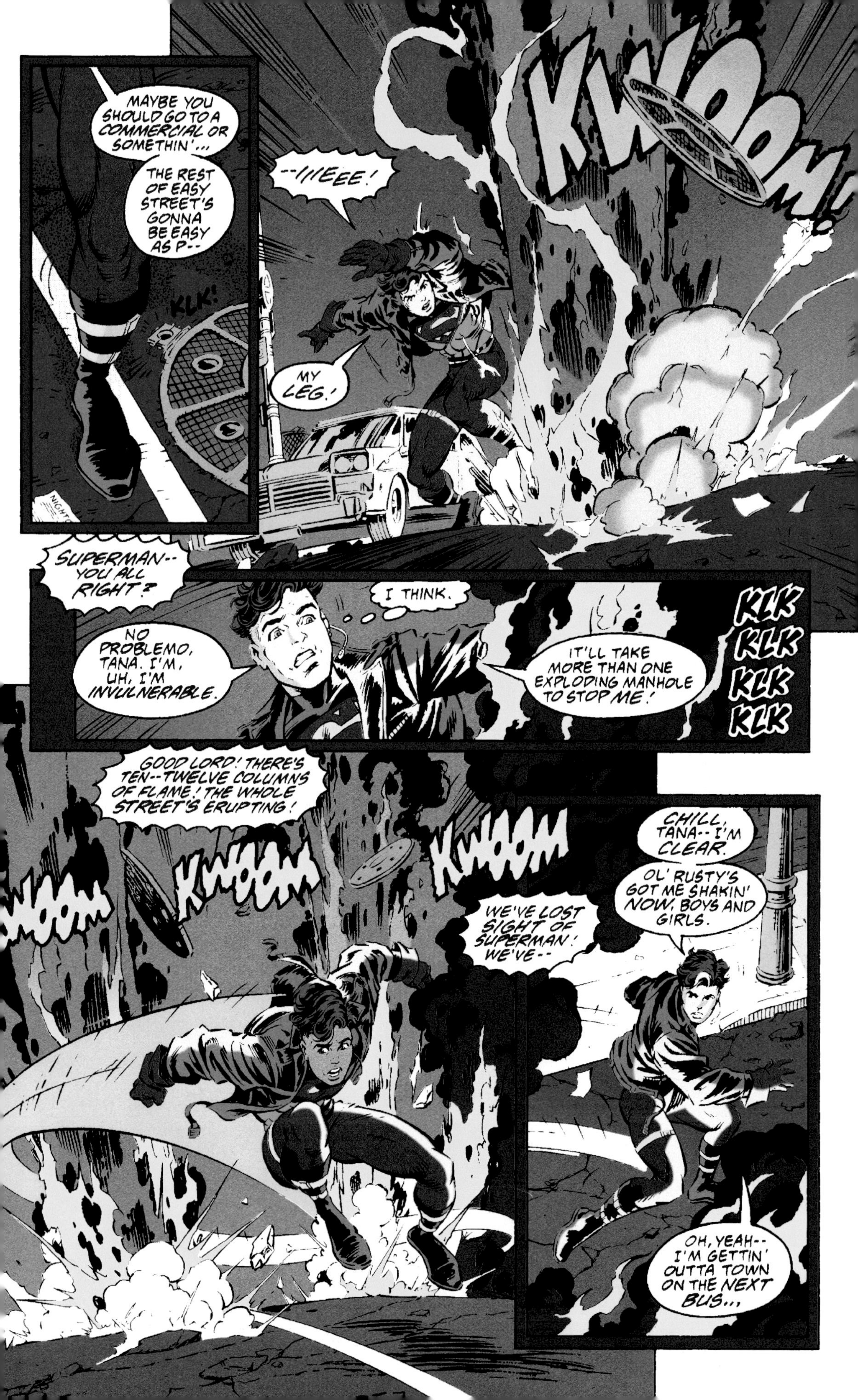
MAYBE YOU SHOULD GO TO A COMMERCIAL OR SOMETHIN'...
THE REST OF EASY STREET'S GONNA BE EASY AS P--
KLK!
--IIIEEE!
KWOOM!
MY LEG!
SUPERMAN-- YOU ALL RIGHT?
I THINK.
NO PROBLEMO, TANA. I'M, UH, I'M INVULNERABLE.
IT'LL TAKE MORE THAN ONE EXPLODING MANHOLE TO STOP ME!
KLK KLK KLK KLK
GOOD LORD! THERE'S TEN--TWELVE COLUMNS OF FLAME! THE WHOLE STREET'S ERUPTING!
WHOOM
KWOOM
KWOOM
WE'VE LOST SIGHT OF SUPERMAN! WE'VE--
CHILL, TANA-- I'M CLEAR.
OL' RUSTY'S GOT ME SHAKIN' NOW, BOYS AND GIRLS.
OH, YEAH-- I'M GETTIN' OUTTA TOWN ON THE NEXT BUS...

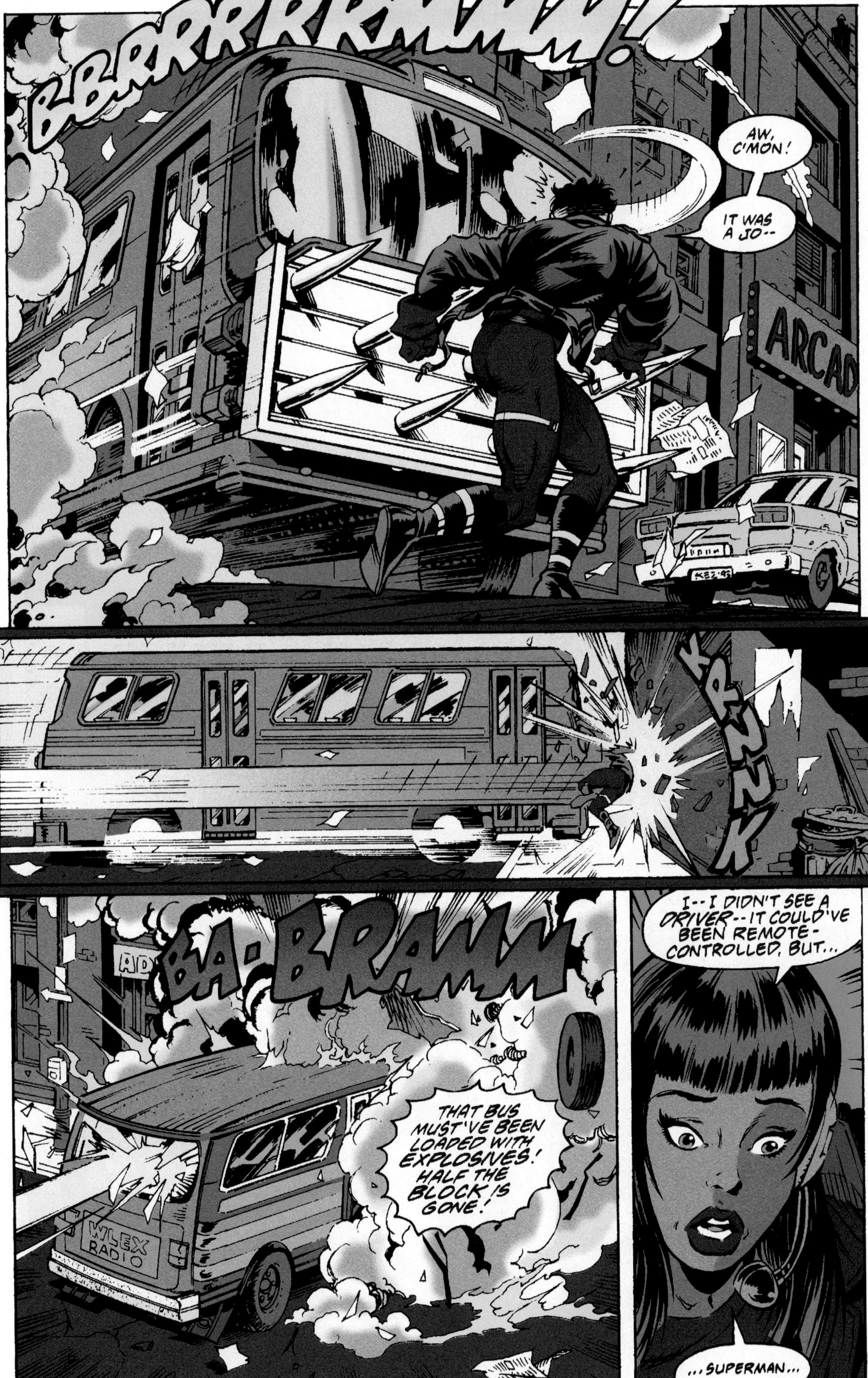
BBRRRRRRMMMM!
AW, C'MON!
IT WAS A JO--
ARCAD
KRUNNK
BA-BRAMM
WLEX RADIO
THAT BUS MUST'VE BEEN LOADED WITH EXPLOSIVES! HALF THE BLOCK IS GONE!
I--I DIDN'T SEE A DRIVER--IT COULD'VE BEEN REMOTE-CONTROLLED, BUT...
...SUPERMAN...

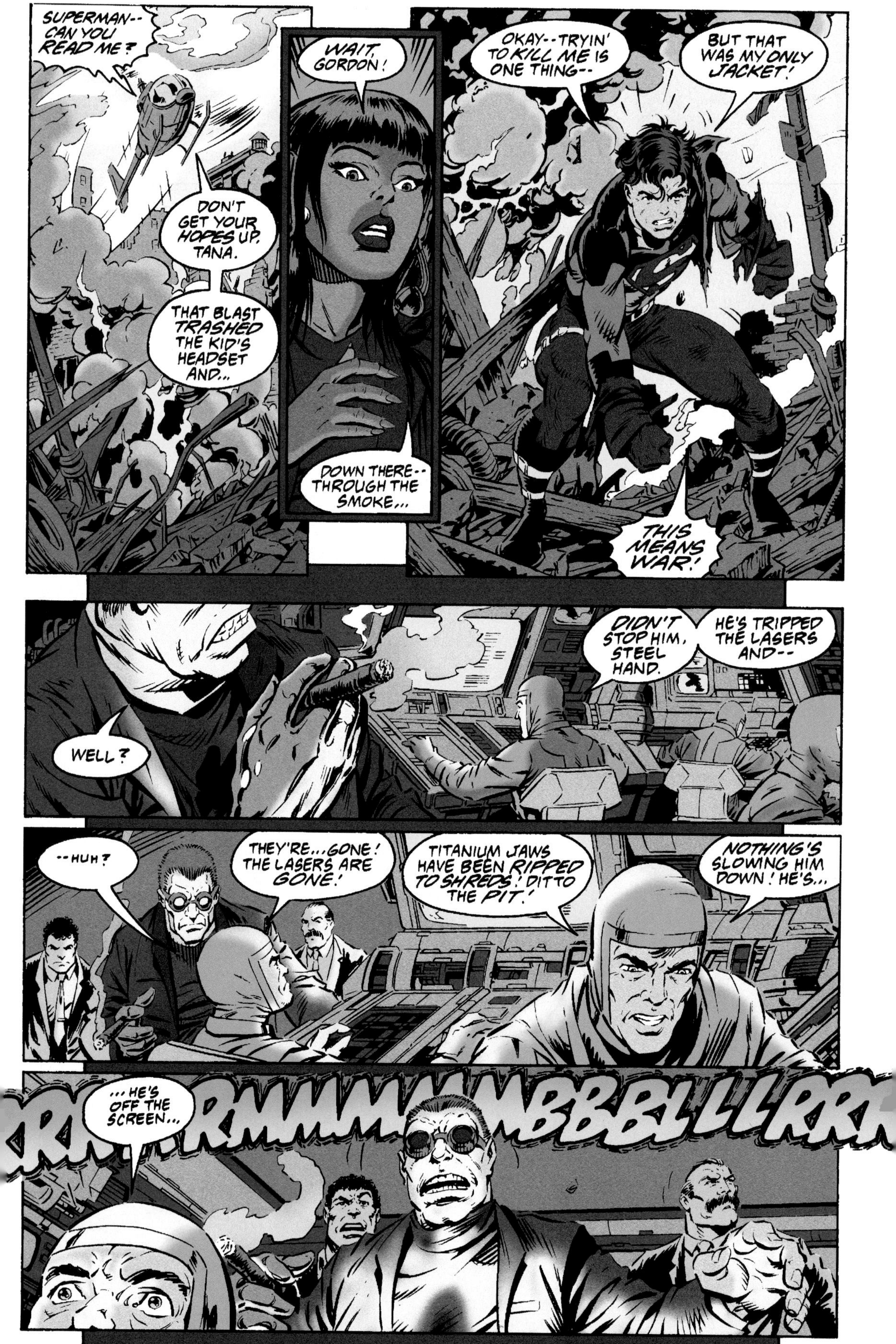
SUPERMAN--CAN YOU READ ME?
WAIT, GORDON!
DON'T GET YOUR HOPES UP, TANA.
THAT BLAST TRASHED THE KID'S HEADSET AND...
DOWN THERE--THROUGH THE SMOKE...
OKAY--TRYIN' TO KILL ME IS ONE THING--
BUT THAT WAS MY ONLY JACKET!
THIS MEANS WAR!
WELL?
DIDN'T STOP HIM, STEEL HAND.
HE'S TRIPPED THE LASERS AND--
--HUH?
THEY'RE...GONE! THE LASERS ARE GONE!
TITANIUM JAWS HAVE BEEN RIPPED TO SHREDS! DITTO THE PIT!
NOTHING'S SLOWING HIM DOWN! HE'S...
...HE'S OFF THE SCREEN...
RRRMMMMMBBBLLLRRR

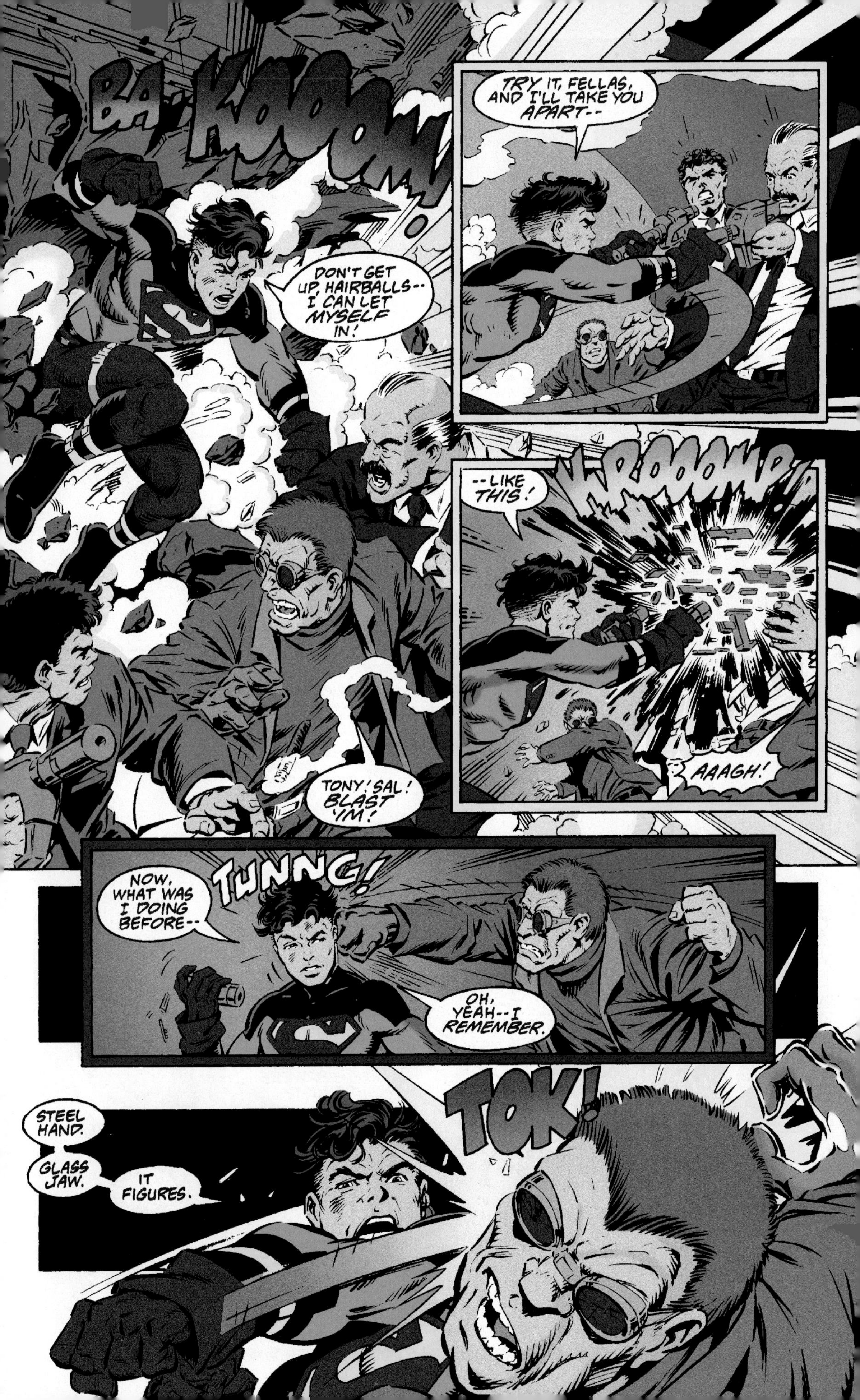
BA-KOOOM!
DON'T GET UP, HAIRBALLS-- I CAN LET MYSELF IN!
TONY! SAL! BLAST 'IM!
TRY IT, FELLAS, AND I'LL TAKE YOU APART--
--LIKE THIS!
KROOOOM!
AAAGH!
NOW, WHAT WAS I DOING BEFORE--
TUNNG!
OH, YEAH--I REMEMBER.
TOK!
STEEL HAND.
GLASS JAW.
IT FIGURES.

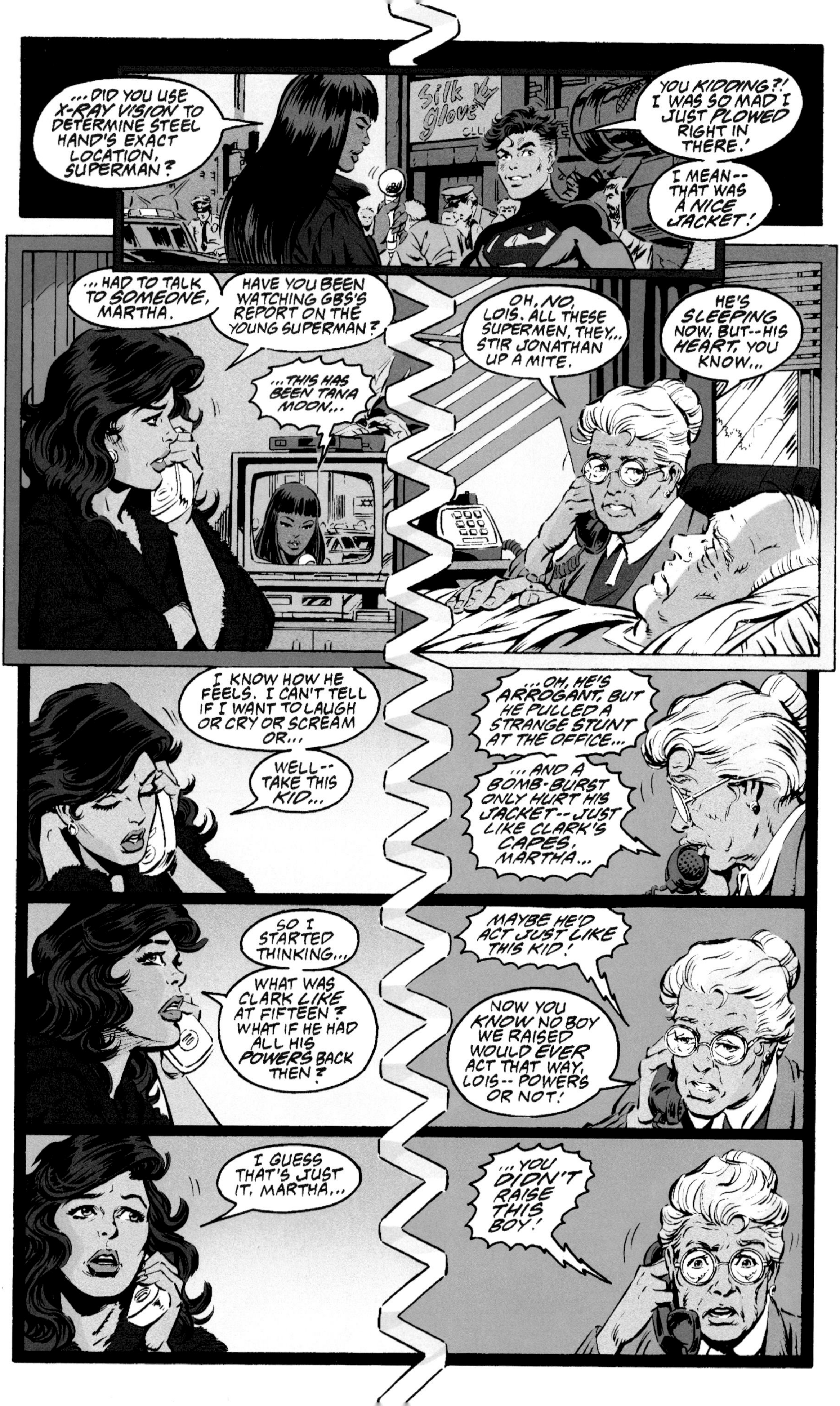

...DID YOU USE X-RAY VISION TO DETERMINE STEEL HAND'S EXACT LOCATION, SUPERMAN?
YOU KIDDING?! I WAS SO MAD I JUST PLOWED RIGHT IN THERE!
I MEAN-- THAT WAS A NICE JACKET!
...HAD TO TALK TO SOMEONE, MARTHA.
HAVE YOU BEEN WATCHING GBS'S REPORT ON THE YOUNG SUPERMAN?
...THIS HAS BEEN TANA MOON...
OH, NO, LOIS. ALL THESE SUPERMEN, THEY... STIR JONATHAN UP A MITE.
HE'S SLEEPING NOW, BUT--HIS HEART, YOU KNOW...
I KNOW HOW HE FEELS. I CAN'T TELL IF I WANT TO LAUGH OR CRY OR SCREAM OR...
WELL-- TAKE THIS KID...
...OH, HE'S ARROGANT, BUT HE PULLED A STRANGE STUNT AT THE OFFICE...
...AND A BOMB-BURST ONLY HURT HIS JACKET-- JUST LIKE CLARK'S CAPES, MARTHA...
SO I STARTED THINKING...
WHAT WAS CLARK LIKE AT FIFTEEN? WHAT IF HE HAD ALL HIS POWERS BACK THEN?
MAYBE HE'D ACT JUST LIKE THIS KID!
NOW YOU KNOW NO BOY WE RAISED WOULD EVER ACT THAT WAY, LOIS-- POWERS OR NOT!
I GUESS THAT'S JUST IT, MARTHA...
...YOU DIDN'T RAISE THIS BOY!

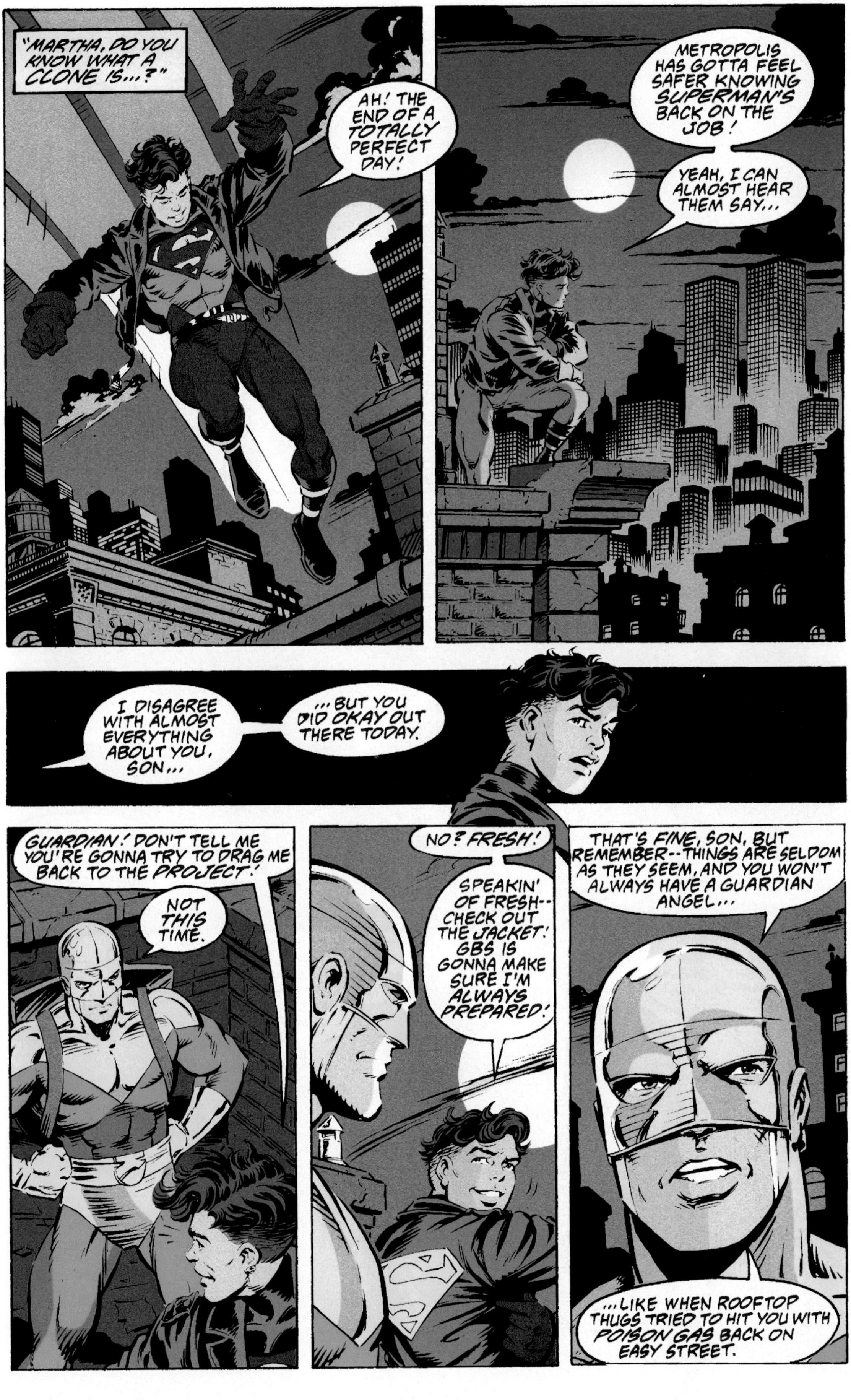
"MARTHA, DO YOU KNOW WHAT A CLONE IS...?"
AH! THE END OF A TOTALLY PERFECT DAY!
METROPOLIS HAS GOTTA FEEL SAFER KNOWING SUPERMAN'S BACK ON THE JOB!
YEAH, I CAN ALMOST HEAR THEM SAY...
I DISAGREE WITH ALMOST EVERYTHING ABOUT YOU, SON...
...BUT YOU DID OKAY OUT THERE TODAY.
GUARDIAN! DON'T TELL ME YOU'RE GONNA TRY TO DRAG ME BACK TO THE PROJECT!
NOT THIS TIME.
NO? FRESH!
SPEAKIN' OF FRESH-- CHECK OUT THE JACKET! GBS IS GONNA MAKE SURE I'M ALWAYS PREPARED!
THAT'S FINE, SON, BUT REMEMBER--THINGS ARE SELDOM AS THEY SEEM, AND YOU WON'T ALWAYS HAVE A GUARDIAN ANGEL...
...LIKE WHEN ROOFTOP THUGS TRIED TO HIT YOU WITH POISON GAS BACK ON EASY STREET.

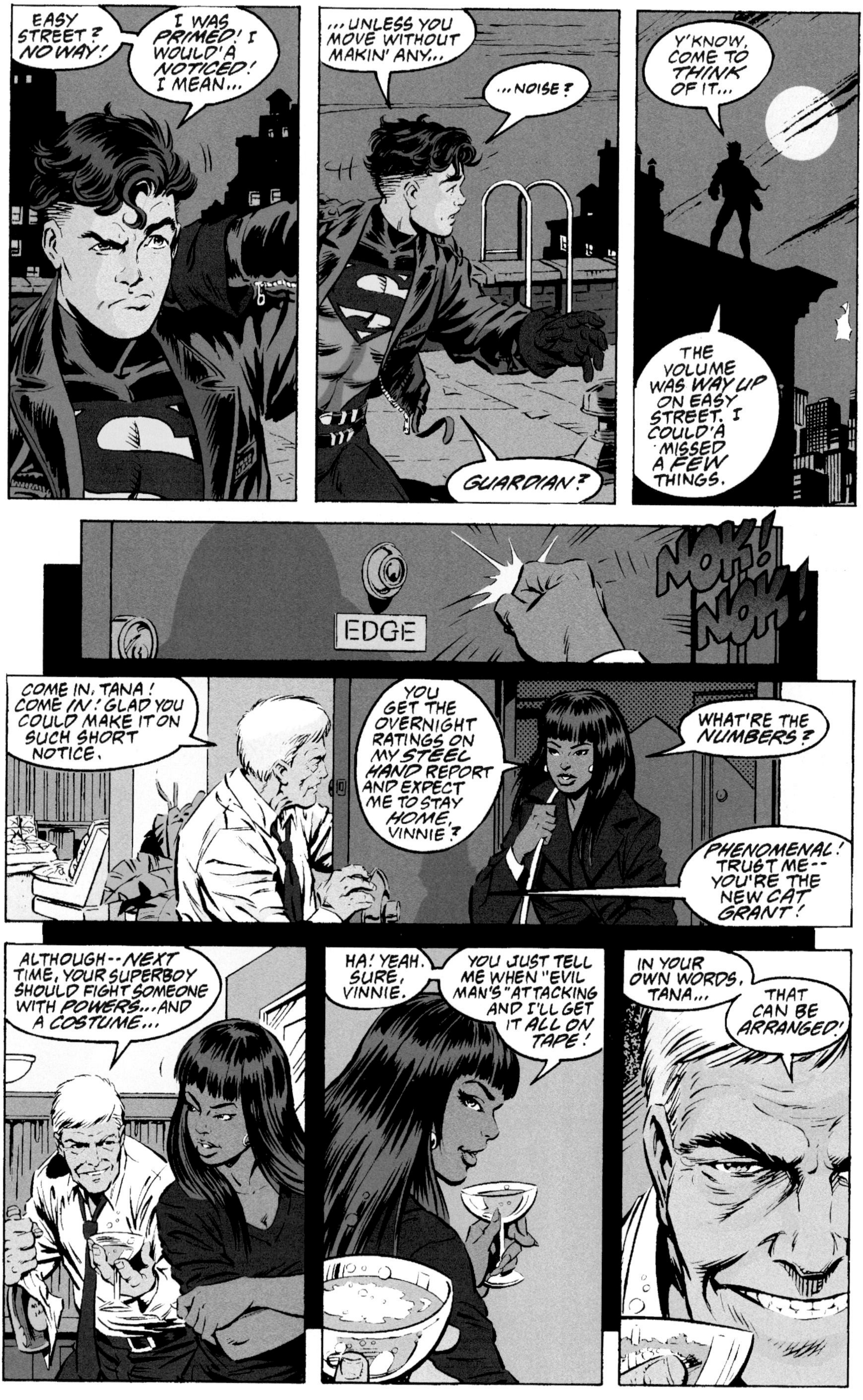
EASY STREET? NO WAY!
I WAS PRIMED! I WOULD'A NOTICED! I MEAN...
...UNLESS YOU MOVE WITHOUT MAKIN' ANY...
...NOISE?
GUARDIAN?
Y'KNOW, COME TO THINK OF IT...
THE VOLUME WAS WAY UP ON EASY STREET. I COULD'A MISSED A FEW THINGS.
EDGE
NOK! NOK!
COME IN, TANA! COME IN! GLAD YOU COULD MAKE IT ON SUCH SHORT NOTICE.
YOU GET THE OVERNIGHT RATINGS ON MY STEEL HAND REPORT AND EXPECT ME TO STAY HOME, VINNIE?
WHAT'RE THE NUMBERS?
PHENOMENAL! TRUST ME-- YOU'RE THE NEW CAT GRANT!
ALTHOUGH--NEXT TIME, YOUR SUPERBOY SHOULD FIGHT SOMEONE WITH POWERS...AND A COSTUME...
HA! YEAH. SURE, VINNIE.
YOU JUST TELL ME WHEN "EVIL MAN'S" ATTACKING AND I'LL GET IT ALL ON TAPE!
IN YOUR OWN WORDS, TANA...
THAT CAN BE ARRANGED!

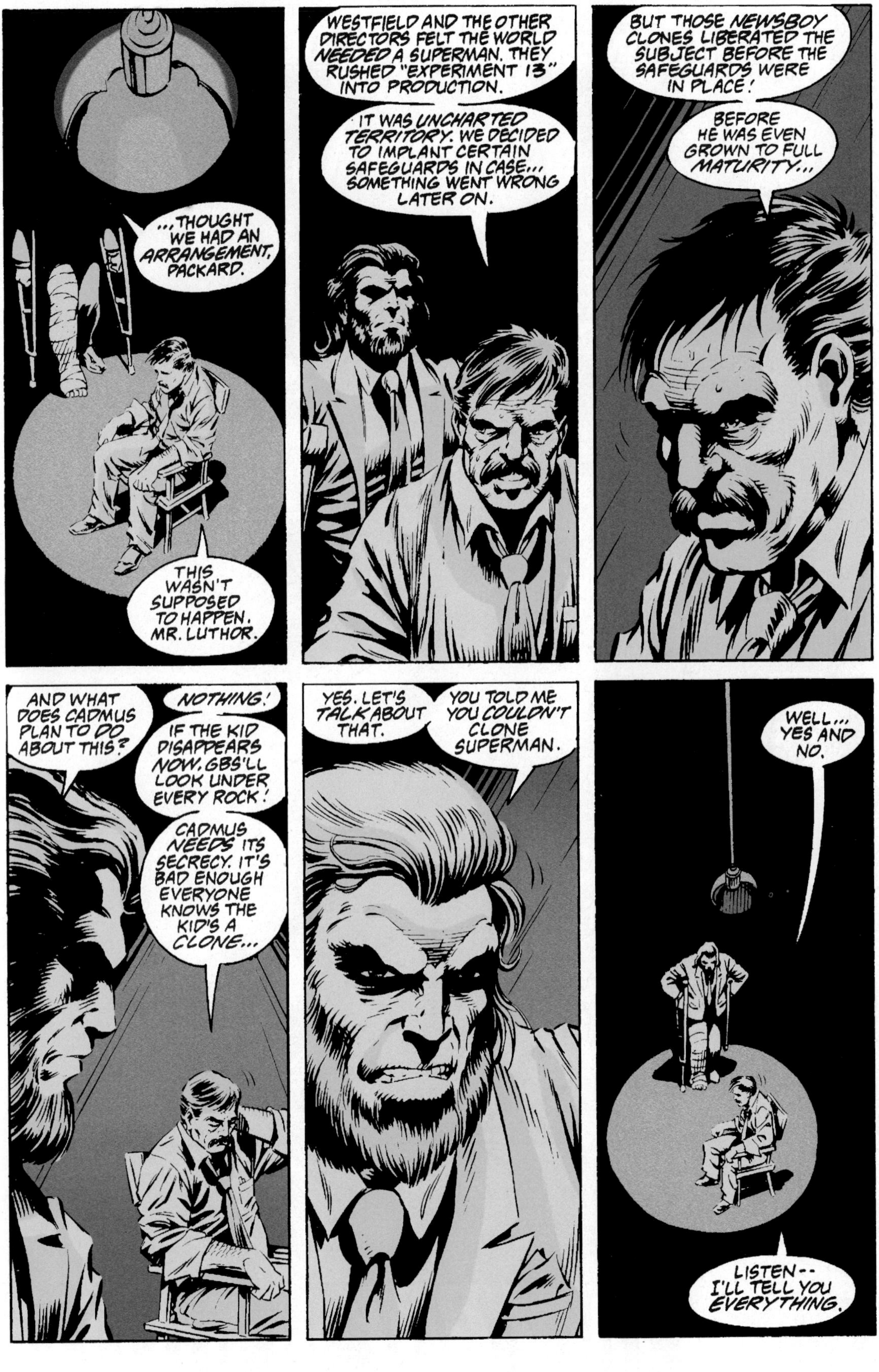
...THOUGHT WE HAD AN ARRANGEMENT, PACKARD.
THIS WASN'T SUPPOSED TO HAPPEN, MR. LUTHOR.
WESTFIELD AND THE OTHER DIRECTORS FELT THE WORLD NEEDED A SUPERMAN. THEY RUSHED "EXPERIMENT 13" INTO PRODUCTION.
IT WAS UNCHARTED TERRITORY. WE DECIDED TO IMPLANT CERTAIN SAFEGUARDS IN CASE... SOMETHING WENT WRONG LATER ON.
BUT THOSE NEWSBOY CLONES LIBERATED THE SUBJECT BEFORE THE SAFEGUARDS WERE IN PLACE!
BEFORE HE WAS EVEN GROWN TO FULL MATURITY...
AND WHAT DOES CADMUS PLAN TO DO ABOUT THIS?
NOTHING!
IF THE KID DISAPPEARS NOW, GBS'LL LOOK UNDER EVERY ROCK!
CADMUS NEEDS ITS SECRECY. IT'S BAD ENOUGH EVERYONE KNOWS THE KID'S A CLONE...
YES. LET'S TALK ABOUT THAT.
YOU TOLD ME YOU COULDN'T CLONE SUPERMAN.
WELL... YES AND NO.
LISTEN-- I'LL TELL YOU EVERYTHING.

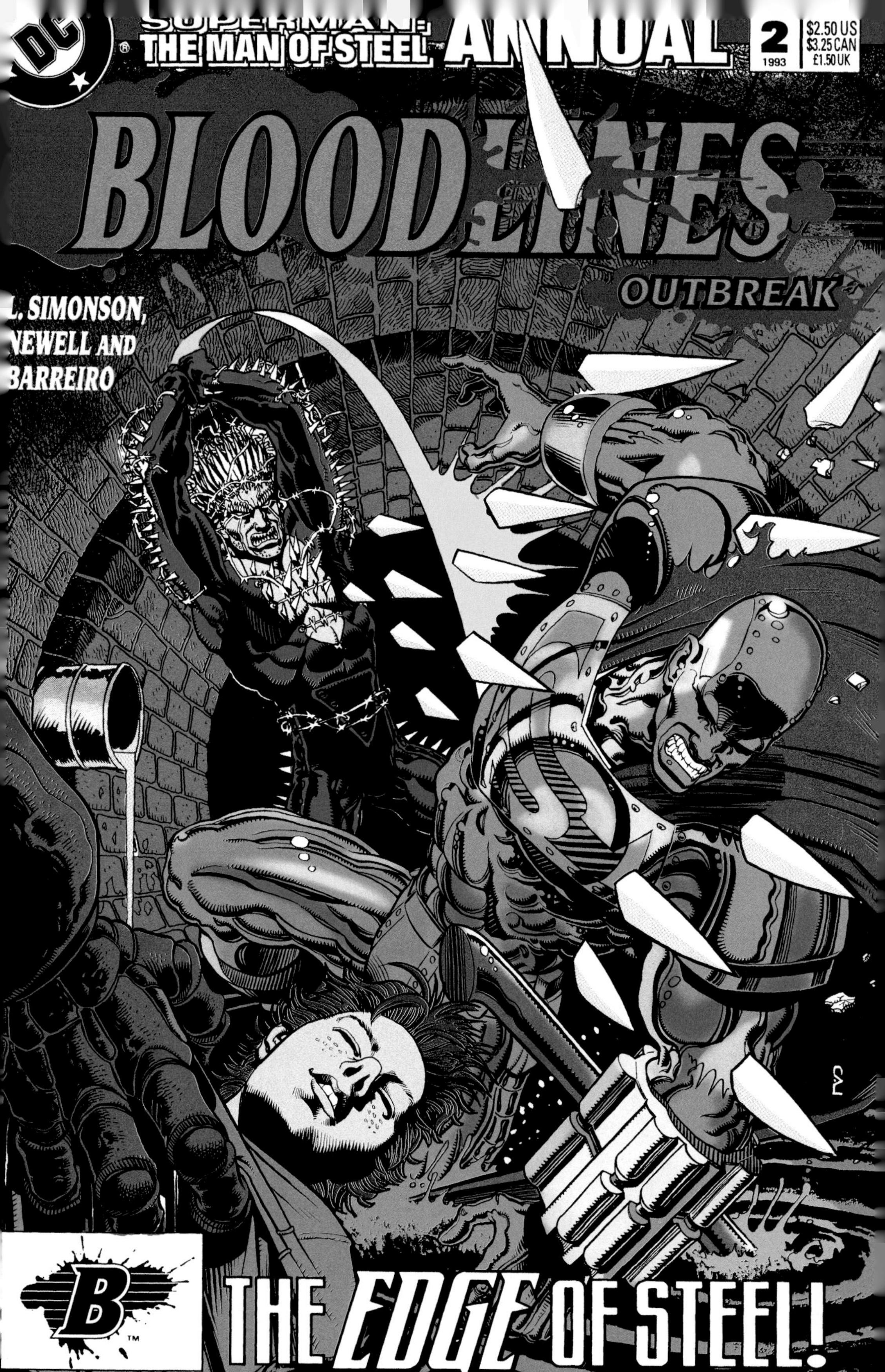

SUPERMAN: THE MAN OF STEEL
ANNUAL
2
1993
$2.50 US
$3.25 CAN
£1.50 UK
BLOODLINES
OUTBREAK
L. SIMONSON,
NEWELL AND
BARREIRO
THE EDGE OF STEEL!

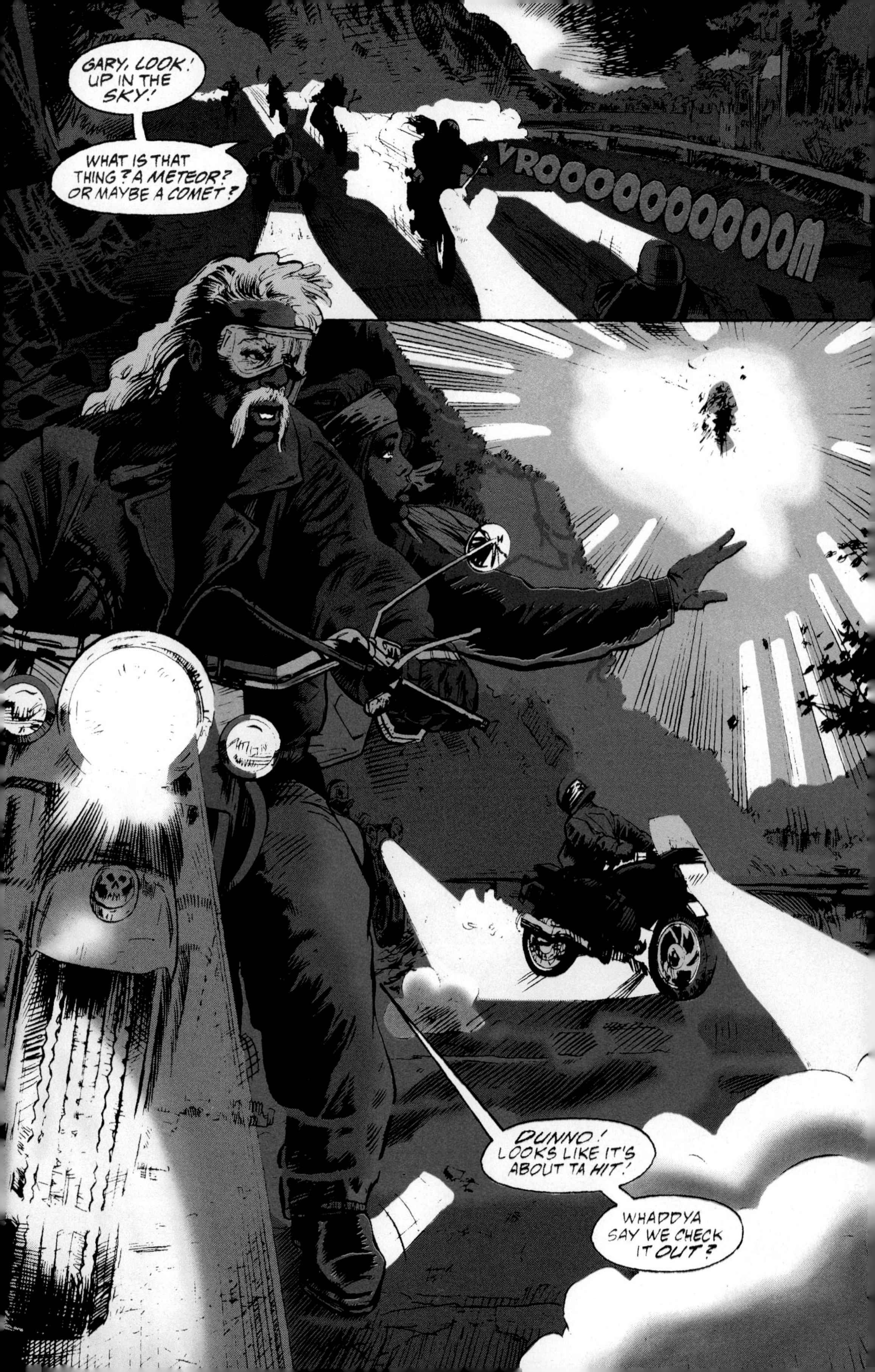
GARY, LOOK! UP IN THE SKY!
WHAT IS THAT THING? A METEOR? OR MAYBE A COMET?
VROOOOOOOOOOOM
DUNNO! LOOKS LIKE IT'S ABOUT TA HIT!
WHADDYA SAY WE CHECK IT OUT?

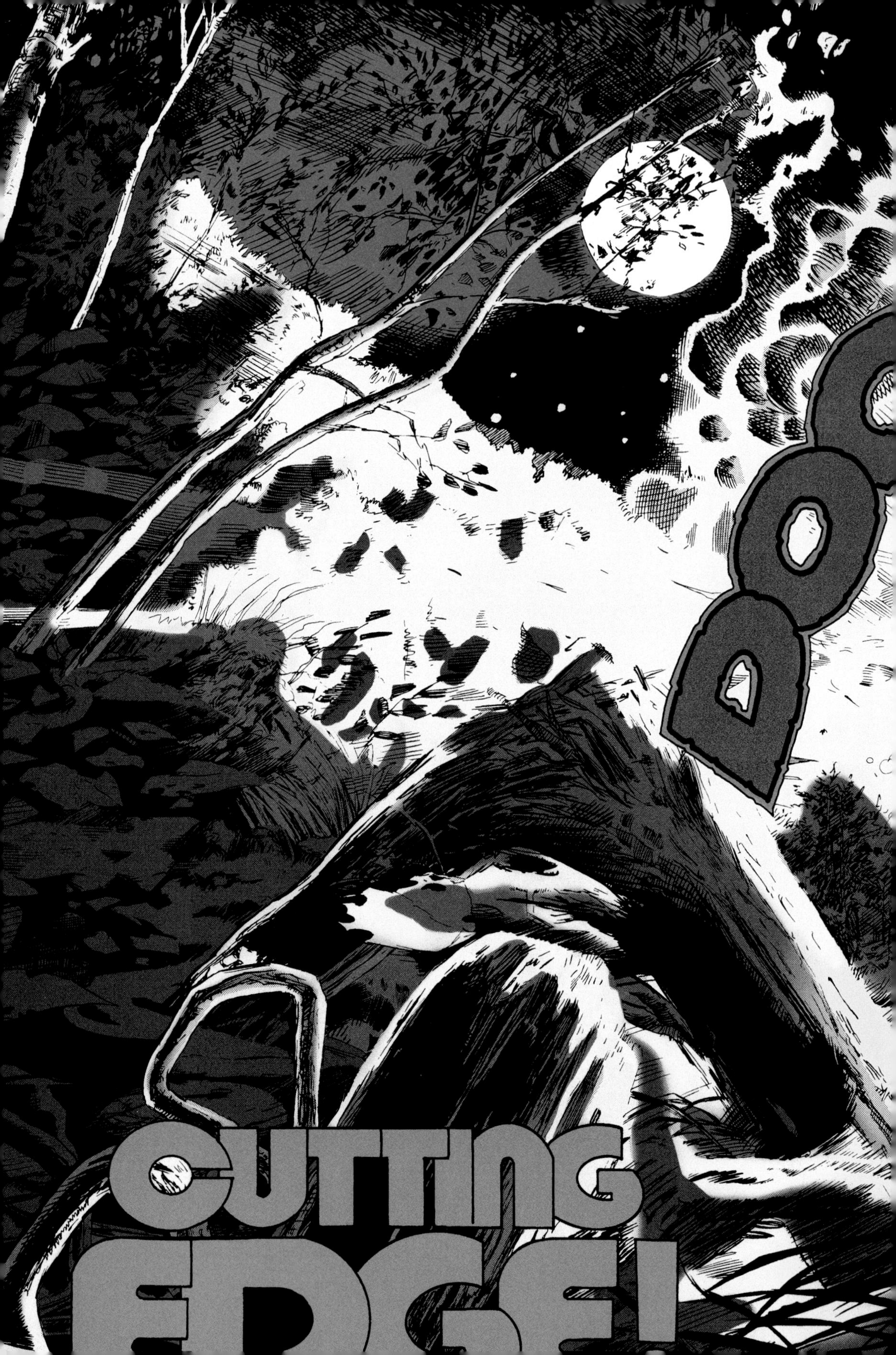
DOO
CUTTING EDGE!

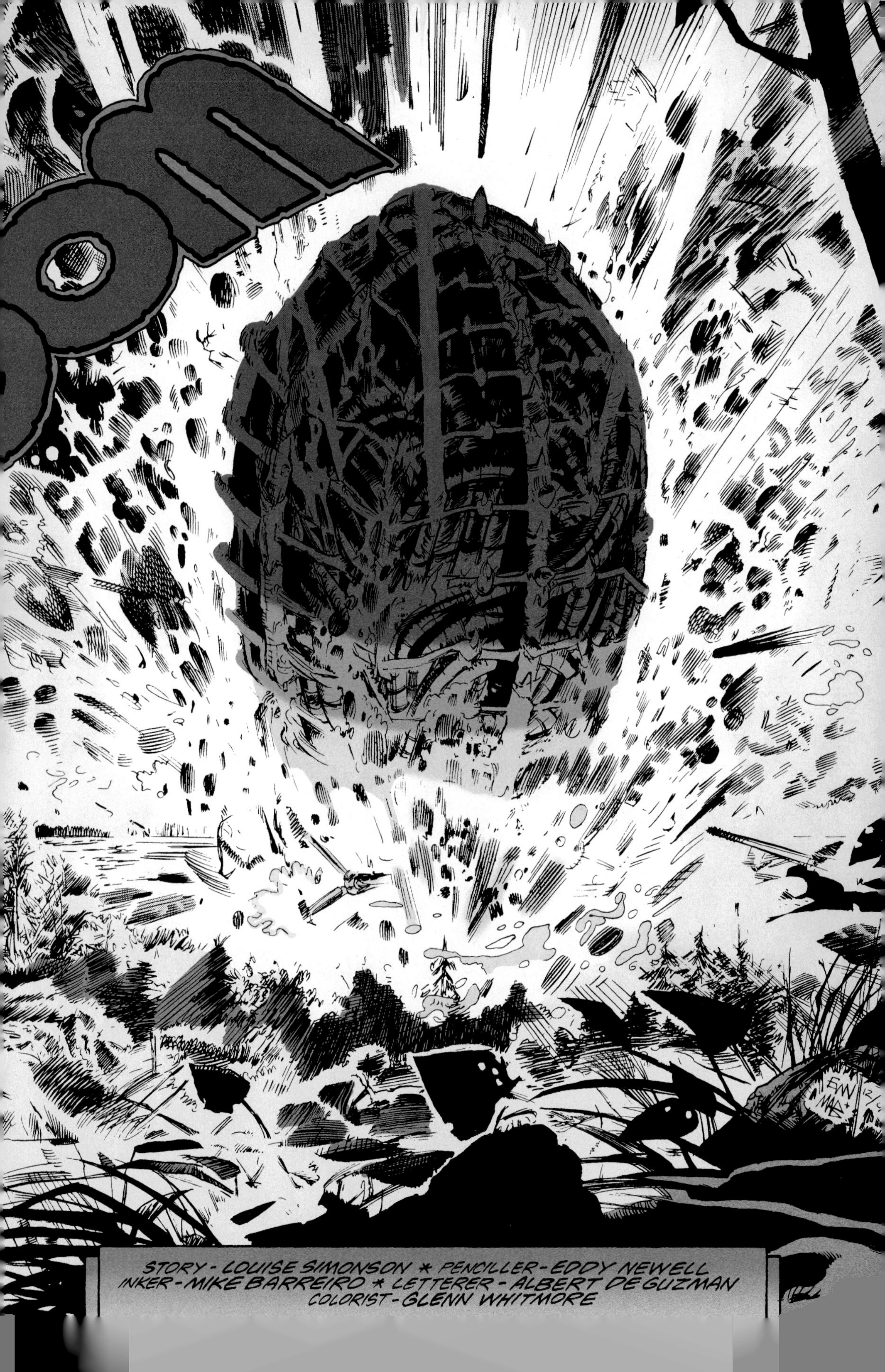
STORY - LOUISE SIMONSON ✶ PENCILLER - EDDY NEWELL
INKER - MIKE BARREIRO ✶ LETTERER - ALBERT DE GUZMAN
COLORIST - GLENN WHITMORE

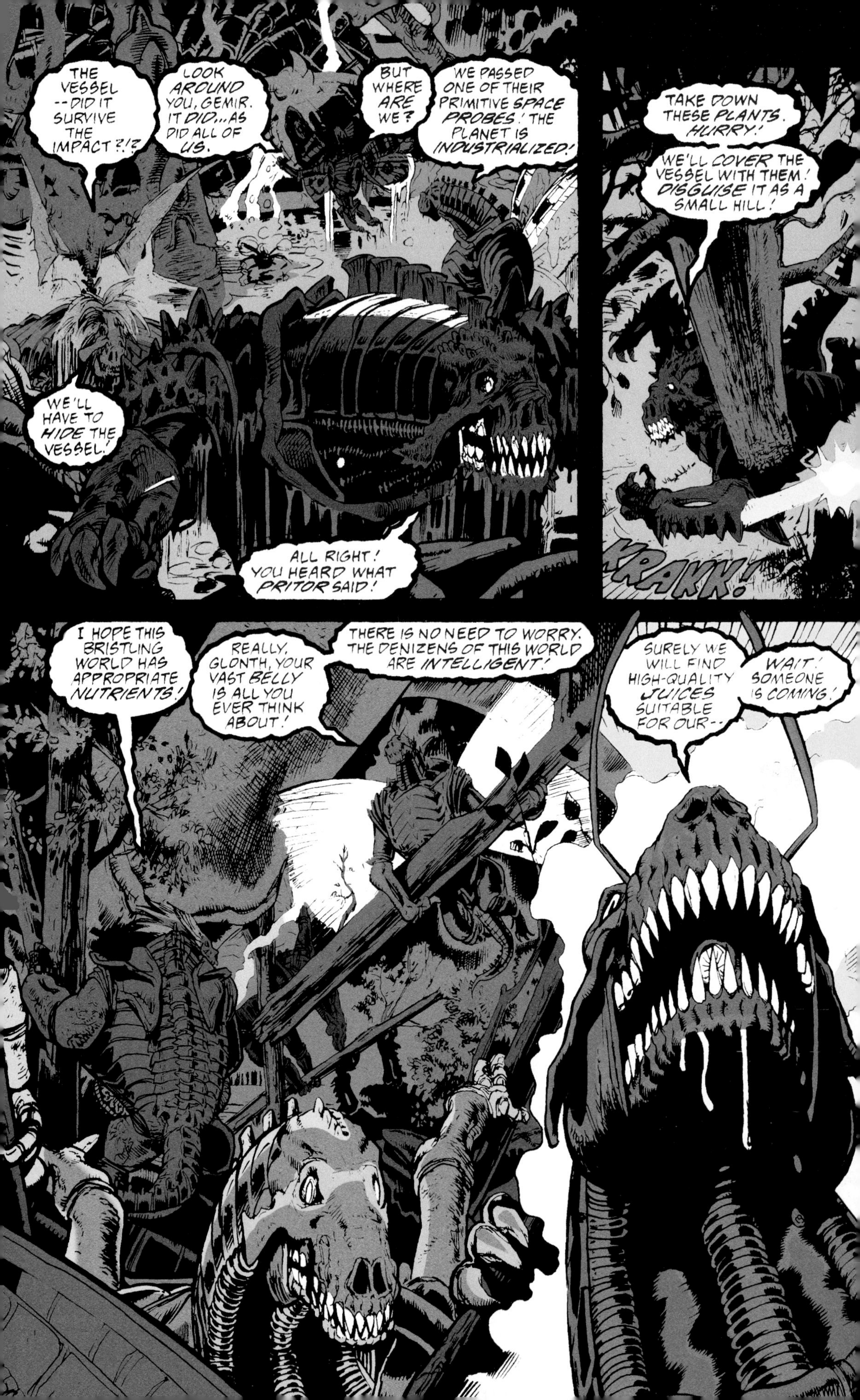
THE VESSEL --DID IT SURVIVE THE IMPACT?!?
LOOK AROUND YOU, GEMIR. IT DID...AS DID ALL OF US.
BUT WHERE ARE WE?
WE PASSED ONE OF THEIR PRIMITIVE SPACE PROBES! THE PLANET IS INDUSTRIALIZED!
WE'LL HAVE TO HIDE THE VESSEL!
ALL RIGHT! YOU HEARD WHAT PRITOR SAID!
TAKE DOWN THESE PLANTS. HURRY!
WE'LL COVER THE VESSEL WITH THEM! DISGUISE IT AS A SMALL HILL!
KRAKK!
I HOPE THIS BRISTLING WORLD HAS APPROPRIATE NUTRIENTS!
REALLY, GLONTH, YOUR VAST BELLY IS ALL YOU EVER THINK ABOUT!
THERE IS NO NEED TO WORRY. THE DENIZENS OF THIS WORLD ARE INTELLIGENT!
SURELY WE WILL FIND HIGH-QUALITY JUICES SUITABLE FOR OUR--
WAIT! SOMEONE IS COMING!

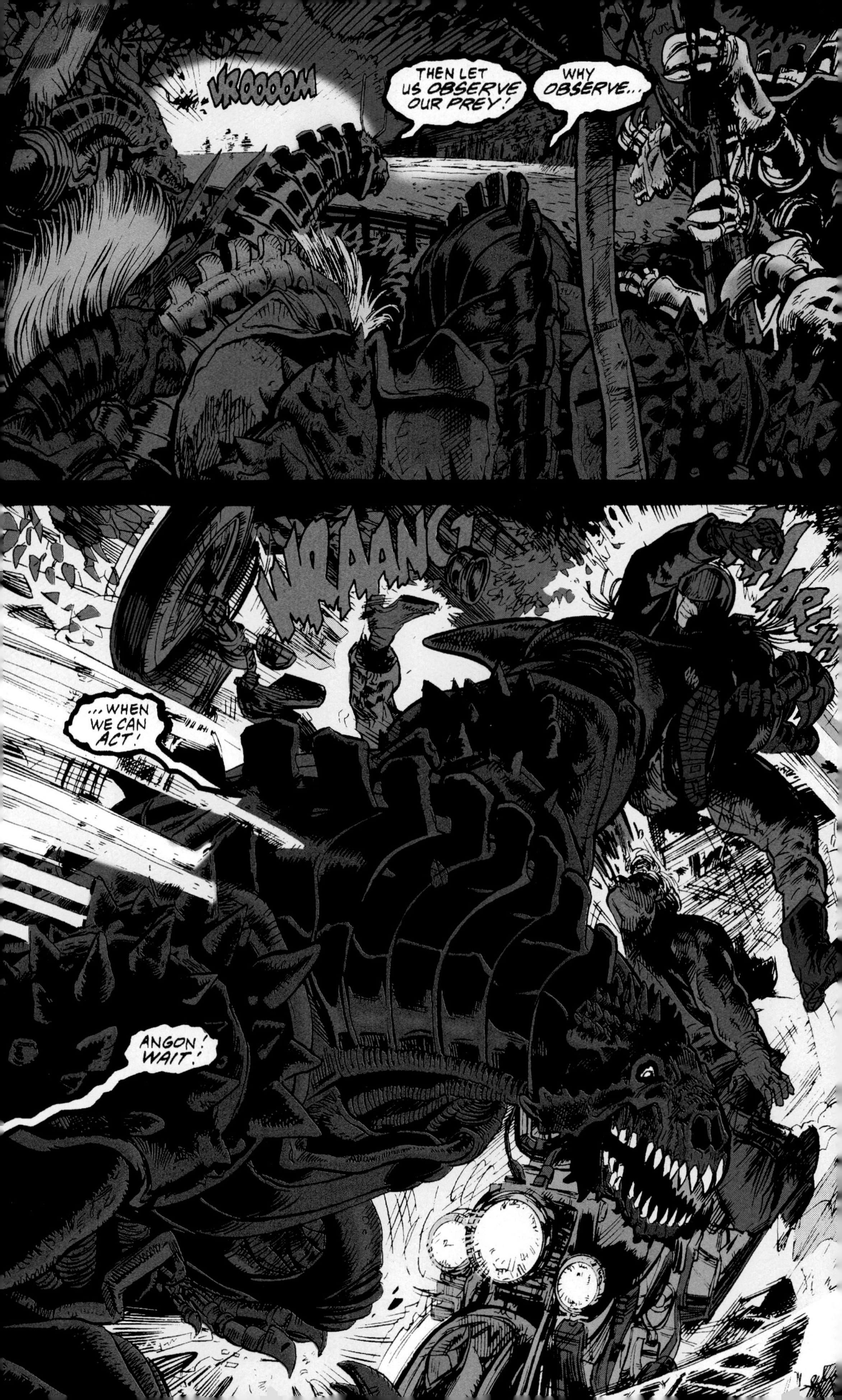
VROOOOOM
THEN LET US OBSERVE OUR PREY!
WHY OBSERVE...
...WHEN WE CAN ACT!
ANGON! WAIT!

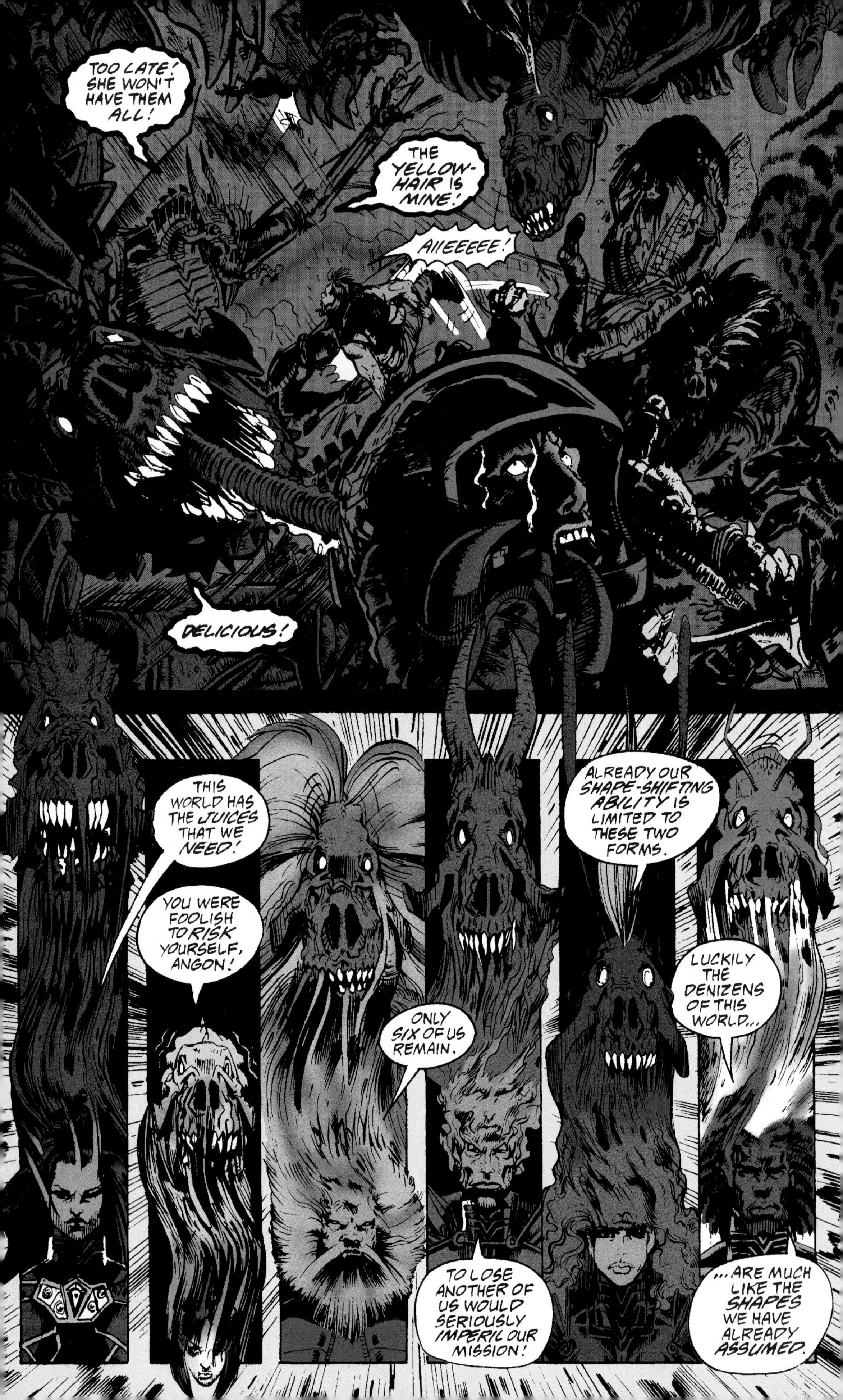
TOO LATE! SHE WON'T HAVE THEM ALL!
THE YELLOW-HAIR IS MINE!
AIIEEEEE!
DELICIOUS!
THIS WORLD HAS THE JUICES THAT WE NEED!
YOU WERE FOOLISH TO RISK YOURSELF, ANGON!
ONLY SIX OF US REMAIN.
TO LOSE ANOTHER OF US WOULD SERIOUSLY IMPERIL OUR MISSION!
ALREADY OUR SHAPE-SHIFTING ABILITY IS LIMITED TO THESE TWO FORMS.
LUCKILY THE DENIZENS OF THIS WORLD...
...ARE MUCH LIKE THE SHAPES WE HAVE ALREADY ASSUMED.

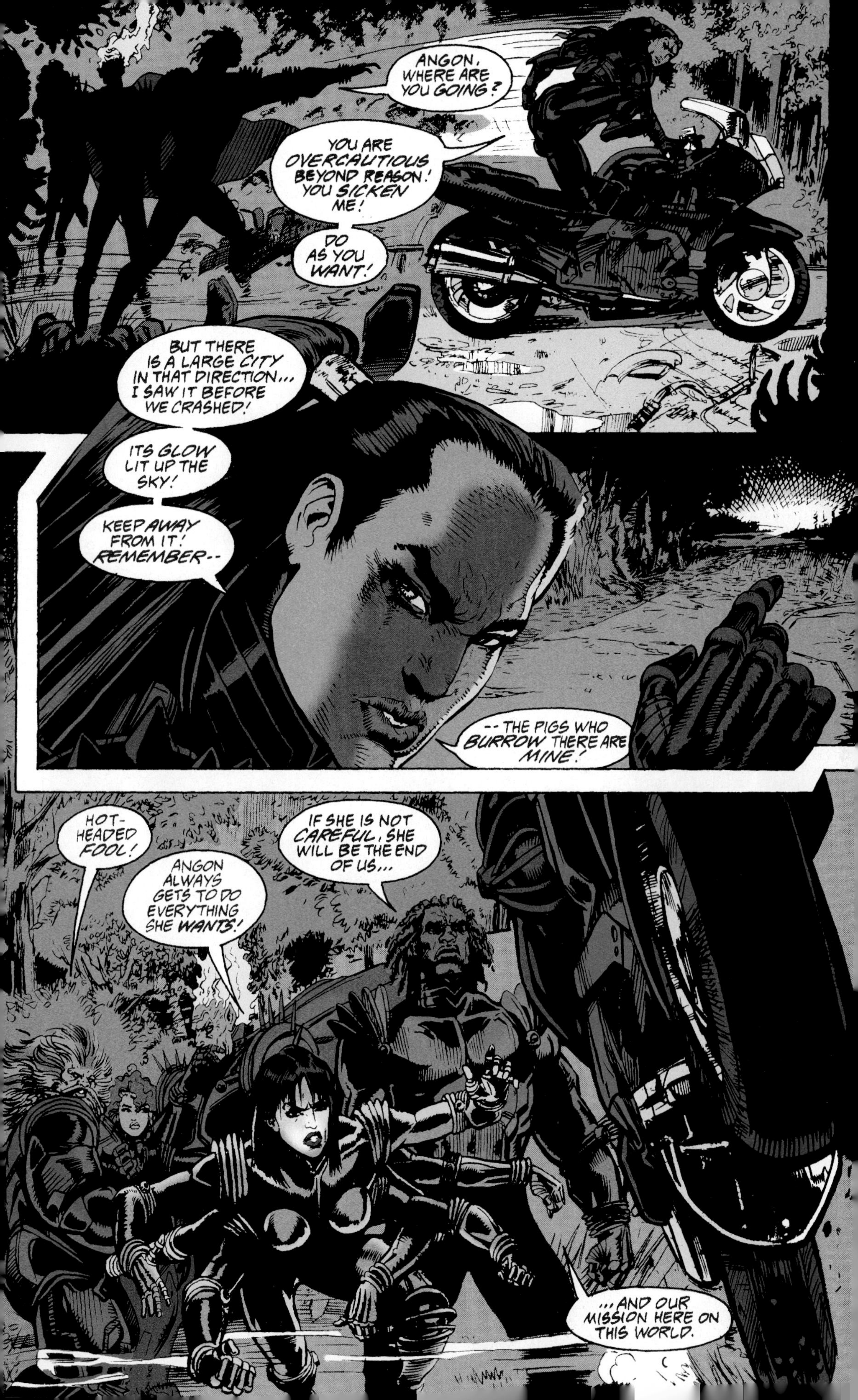
ANGON, WHERE ARE YOU GOING?
YOU ARE OVERCAUTIOUS BEYOND REASON! YOU SICKEN ME!
DO AS YOU WANT!
BUT THERE IS A LARGE CITY IN THAT DIRECTION... I SAW IT BEFORE WE CRASHED!
ITS GLOW LIT UP THE SKY!
KEEP AWAY FROM IT! REMEMBER--
--THE PIGS WHO BURROW THERE ARE MINE!
HOT-HEADED FOOL!
ANGON ALWAYS GETS TO DO EVERYTHING SHE WANTS!
IF SHE IS NOT CAREFUL, SHE WILL BE THE END OF US...
...AND OUR MISSION HERE ON THIS WORLD.

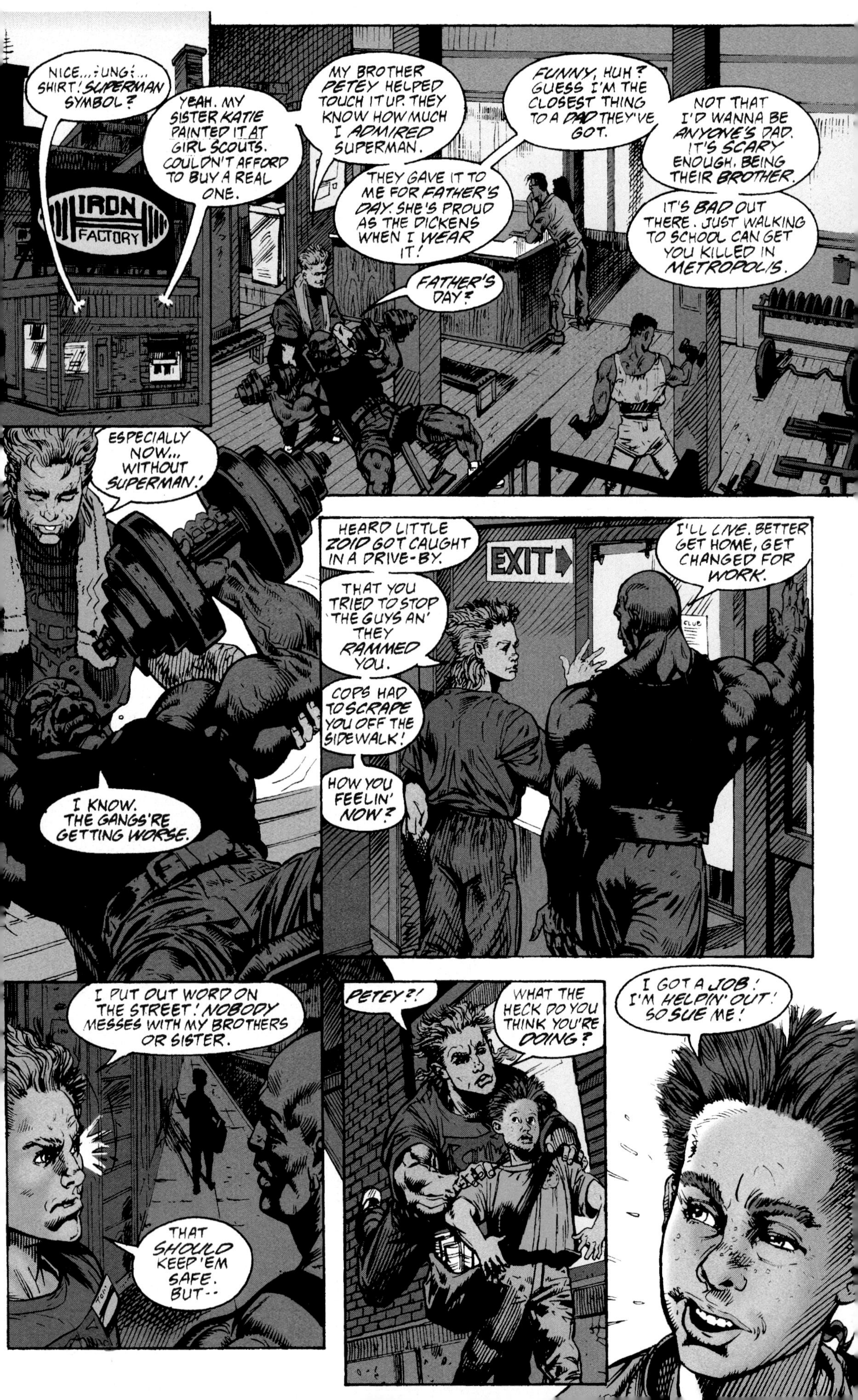
IRON FACTORY
NICE... UNG!... SHIRT! SUPERMAN SYMBOL?
YEAH. MY SISTER KATIE PAINTED IT AT GIRL SCOUTS. COULDN'T AFFORD TO BUY A REAL ONE.
MY BROTHER PETEY HELPED TOUCH IT UP. THEY KNOW HOW MUCH I ADMIRED SUPERMAN.
THEY GAVE IT TO ME FOR FATHER'S DAY. SHE'S PROUD AS THE DICKENS WHEN I WEAR IT!
FATHER'S DAY?
FUNNY, HUH? GUESS I'M THE CLOSEST THING TO A DAD THEY'VE GOT.
NOT THAT I'D WANNA BE ANYONE'S DAD. IT'S SCARY ENOUGH, BEING THEIR BROTHER.
IT'S BAD OUT THERE. JUST WALKING TO SCHOOL CAN GET YOU KILLED IN METROPOLIS.
ESPECIALLY NOW... WITHOUT SUPERMAN!
I KNOW. THE GANGS'RE GETTING WORSE.
HEARD LITTLE ZOID GOT CAUGHT IN A DRIVE-BY.
THAT YOU TRIED TO STOP 'THE GUYS AN' THEY RAMMED YOU.
COPS HAD TO SCRAPE YOU OFF THE SIDEWALK!
HOW YOU FEELIN' NOW?
EXIT
I'LL LIVE. BETTER GET HOME, GET CHANGED FOR WORK.
I PUT OUT WORD ON THE STREET! NOBODY MESSES WITH MY BROTHERS OR SISTER.
THAT SHOULD KEEP 'EM SAFE. BUT--
PETEY?!
WHAT THE HECK DO YOU THINK YOU'RE DOING?
I GOT A JOB! I'M HELPIN' OUT! SO SUE ME!

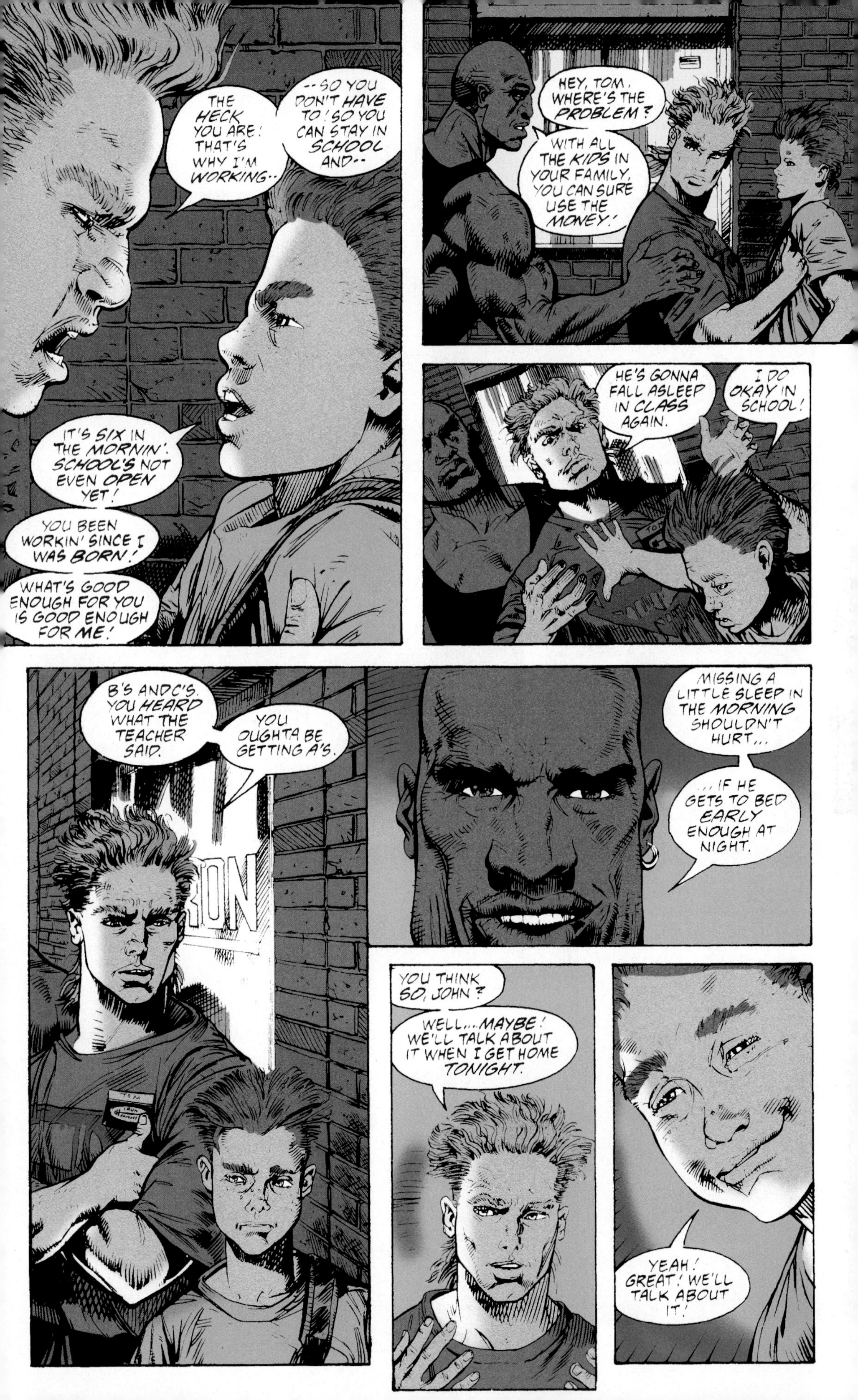
THE HECK YOU ARE! THAT'S WHY I'M WORKING--
--SO YOU DON'T HAVE TO! SO YOU CAN STAY IN SCHOOL AND--
IT'S SIX IN THE MORNIN'. SCHOOL'S NOT EVEN OPEN YET!
YOU BEEN WORKIN' SINCE I WAS BORN!
WHAT'S GOOD ENOUGH FOR YOU IS GOOD ENOUGH FOR ME!
HEY, TOM, WHERE'S THE PROBLEM?
WITH ALL THE KIDS IN YOUR FAMILY, YOU CAN SURE USE THE MONEY!
HE'S GONNA FALL ASLEEP IN CLASS AGAIN.
I DO OKAY IN SCHOOL!
B'S AND C'S. YOU HEARD WHAT THE TEACHER SAID.
YOU OUGHTA BE GETTING A'S.
MISSING A LITTLE SLEEP IN THE MORNING SHOULDN'T HURT...
...IF HE GETS TO BED EARLY ENOUGH AT NIGHT.
YOU THINK SO, JOHN?
WELL... MAYBE! WE'LL TALK ABOUT IT WHEN I GET HOME TONIGHT.
YEAH! GREAT! WE'LL TALK ABOUT IT!

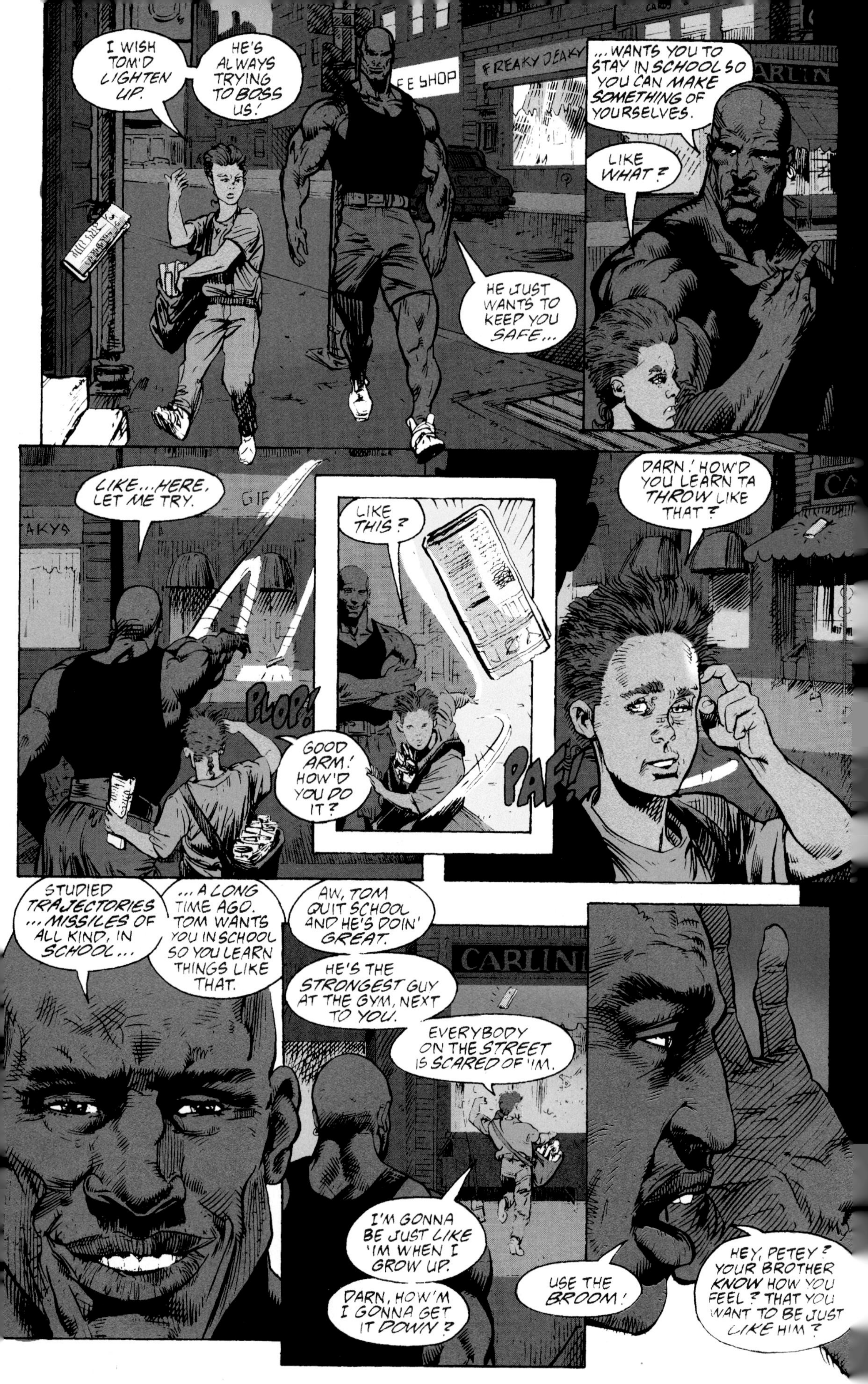
I WISH TOM'D LIGHTEN UP.
HE'S ALWAYS TRYING TO BOSS US!
HE JUST WANTS TO KEEP YOU SAFE...
...WANTS YOU TO STAY IN SCHOOL SO YOU CAN MAKE SOMETHING OF YOURSELVES.
LIKE WHAT?
LIKE... HERE. LET ME TRY.
PLOP!
LIKE THIS?
GOOD ARM! HOW'D YOU DO IT?
PAF!
DARN! HOW'D YOU LEARN TA THROW LIKE THAT?
STUDIED TRAJECTORIES ...MISSILES OF ALL KIND, IN SCHOOL...
...A LONG TIME AGO. TOM WANTS YOU IN SCHOOL SO YOU LEARN THINGS LIKE THAT.
AW, TOM QUIT SCHOOL AND HE'S DOIN' GREAT.
HE'S THE STRONGEST GUY AT THE GYM, NEXT TO YOU.
EVERYBODY ON THE STREET IS SCARED OF 'IM.
I'M GONNA BE JUST LIKE 'IM WHEN I GROW UP.
DARN, HOW'M I GONNA GET IT DOWN?
USE THE BROOM!
HEY, PETEY? YOUR BROTHER KNOW HOW YOU FEEL? THAT YOU WANT TO BE JUST LIKE HIM?

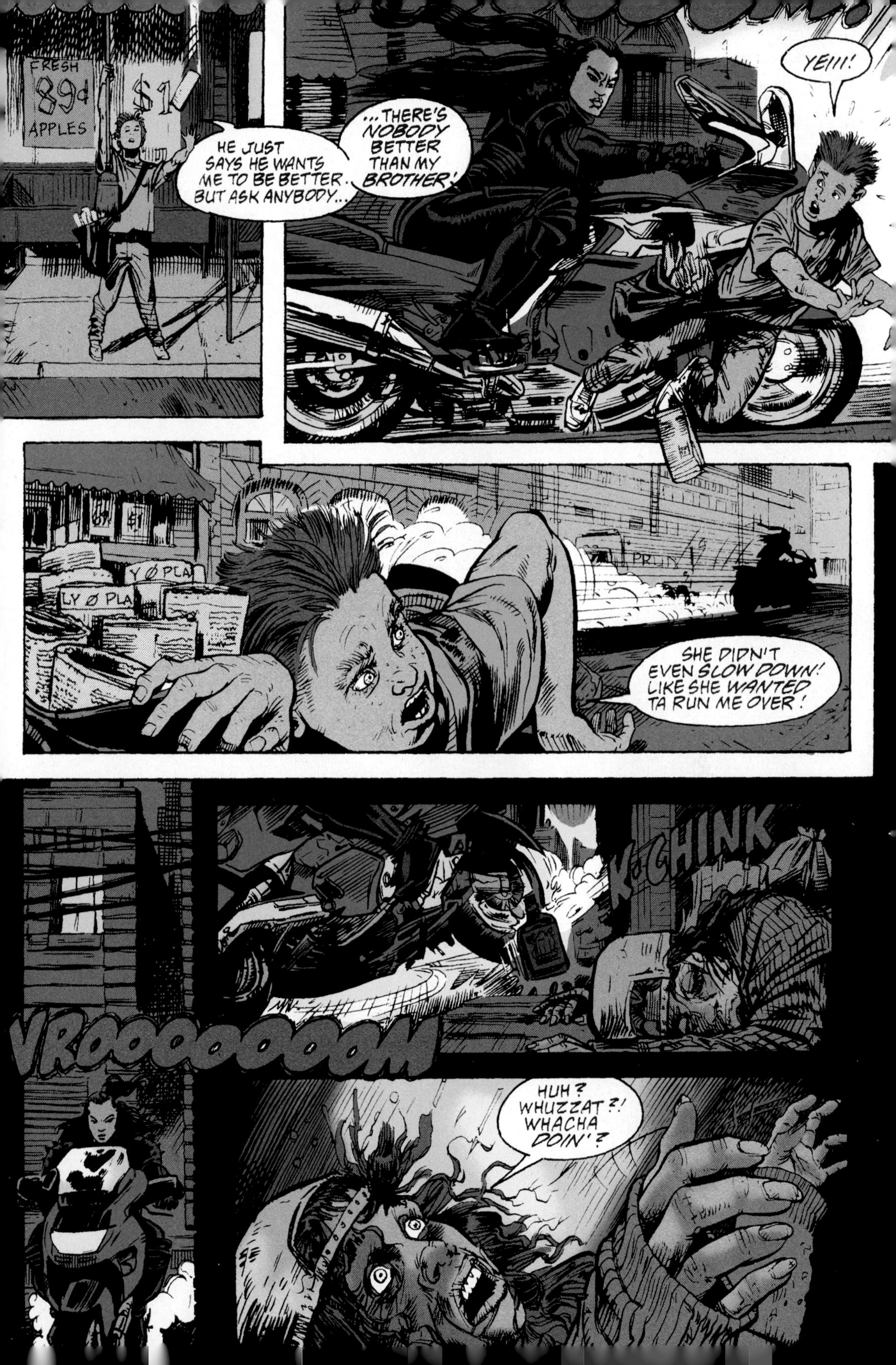
FRESH 89¢ APPLES
$1
HE JUST SAYS HE WANTS ME TO BE BETTER. BUT ASK ANYBODY...
...THERE'S NOBODY BETTER THAN MY BROTHER!
YEIII!
SHE DIDN'T EVEN SLOW DOWN! LIKE SHE WANTED TA RUN ME OVER!
K-CHINK
VROOOOOOOOM
HUH? WHUZZAT?! WHACHA DOIN'?

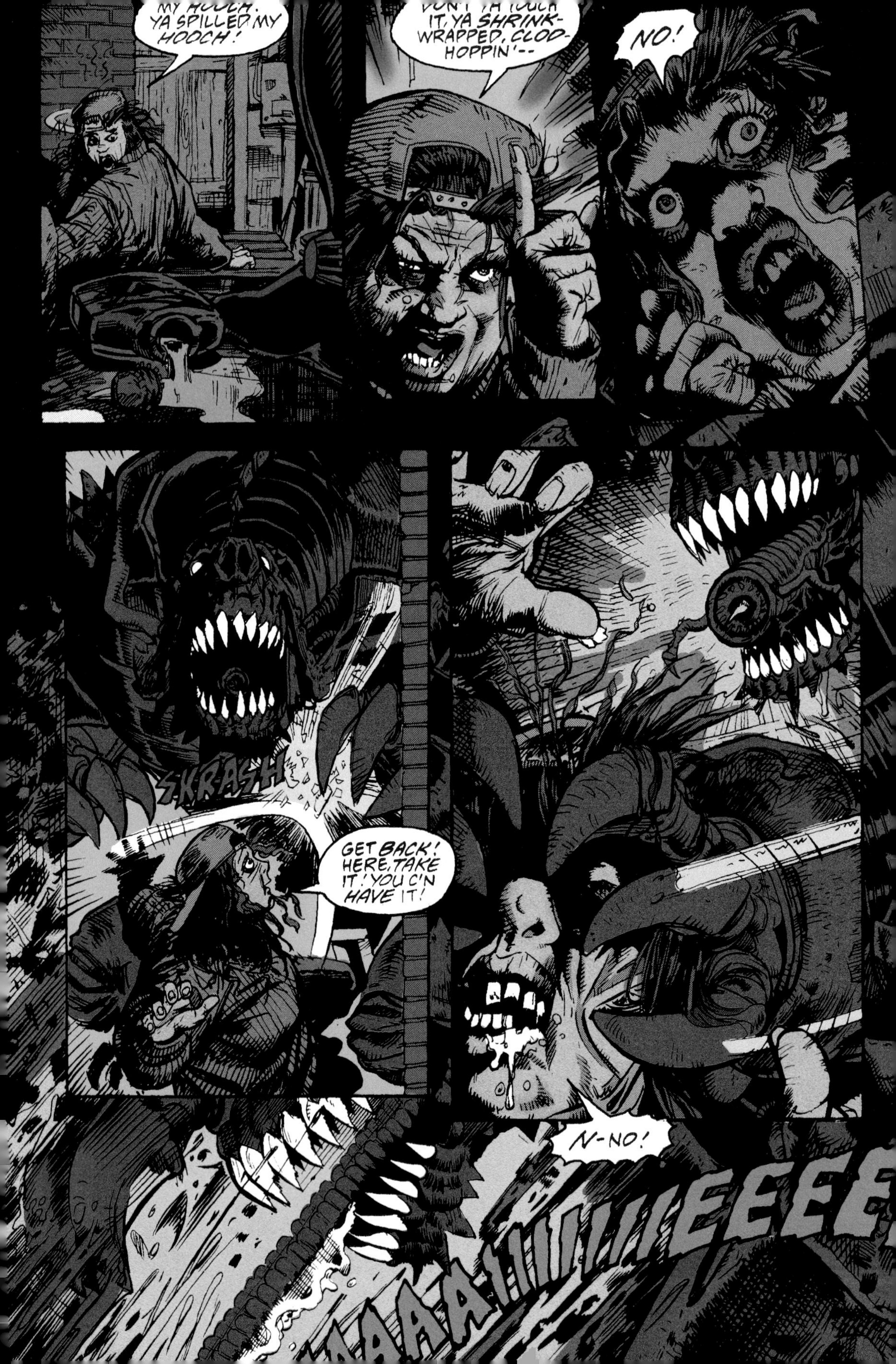
YA SPILLED MY HOOCH!
IT, YA SHRINK-WRAPPED, CLOD-HOPPIN'--
NO!
SKRASH
GET BACK! HERE, TAKE IT! YOU C'N HAVE IT!
N-NO!

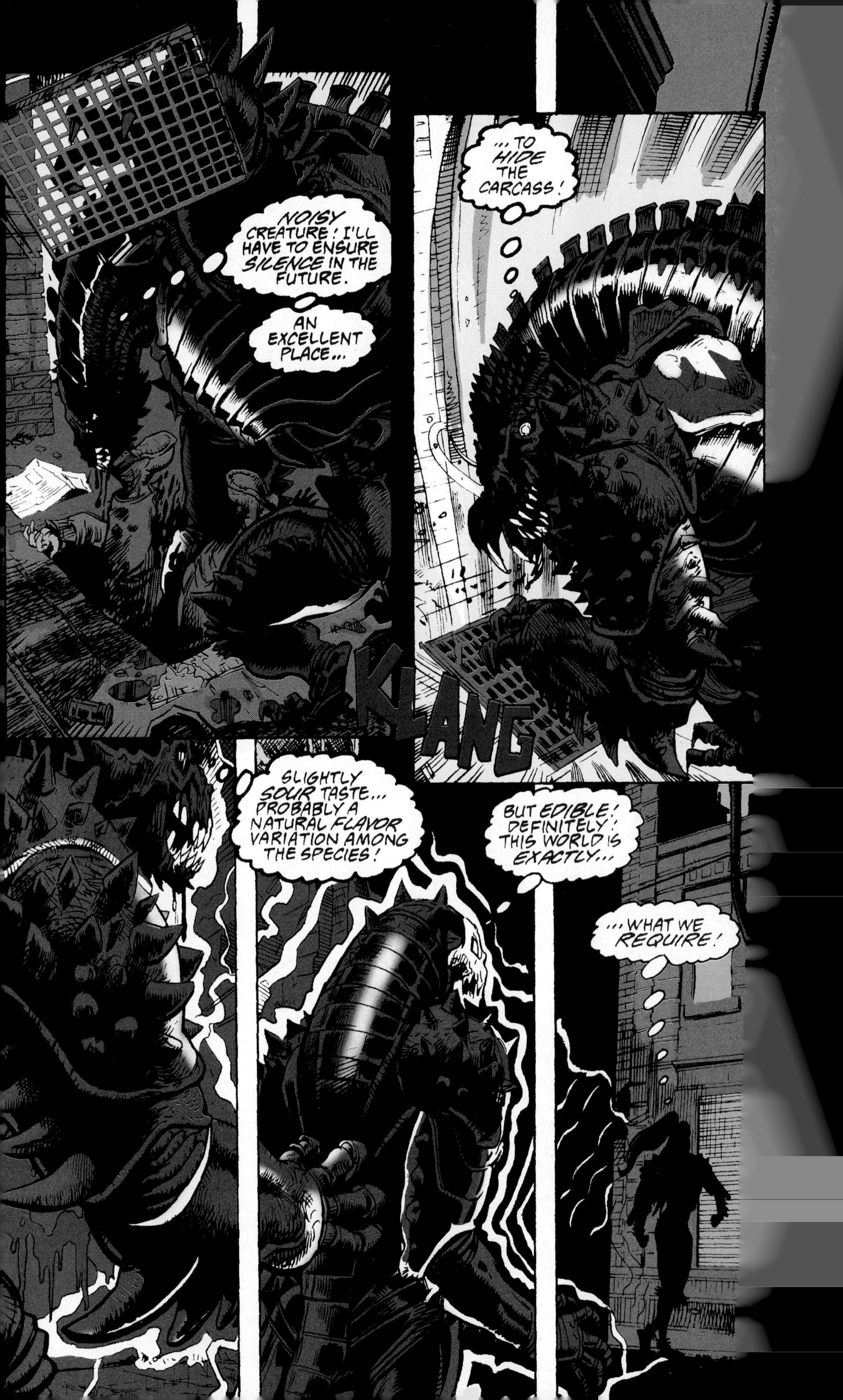
NOISY CREATURE! I'LL HAVE TO ENSURE SILENCE IN THE FUTURE.
AN EXCELLENT PLACE...
...TO HIDE THE CARCASS!
KLANG
SLIGHTLY SOUR TASTE... PROBABLY A NATURAL FLAVOR VARIATION AMONG THE SPECIES!
BUT EDIBLE! DEFINITELY! THIS WORLD IS EXACTLY...
...WHAT WE REQUIRE!

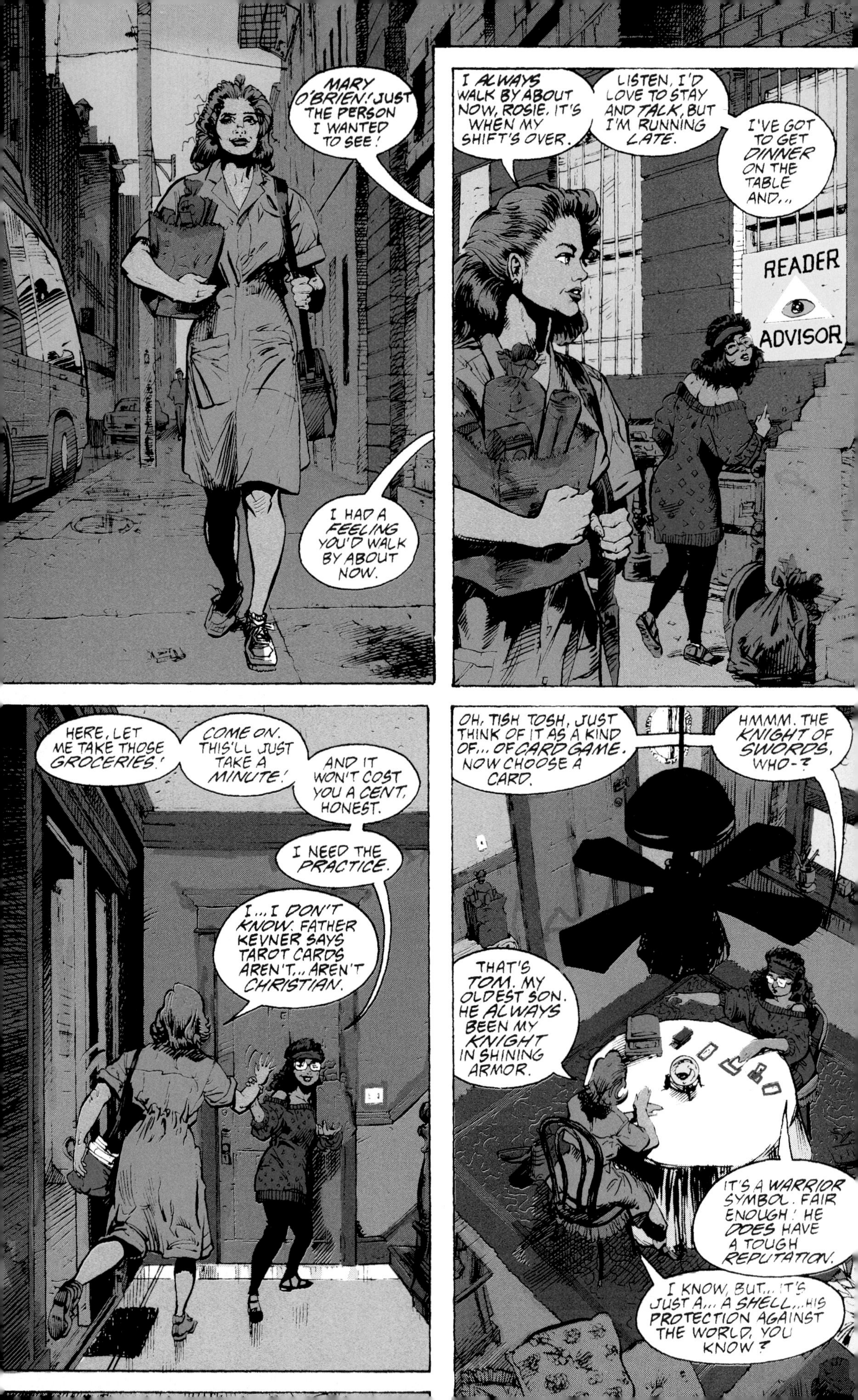
MARY O'BRIEN! JUST THE PERSON I WANTED TO SEE!
I HAD A FEELING YOU'D WALK BY ABOUT NOW.
I ALWAYS WALK BY ABOUT NOW, ROSIE. IT'S WHEN MY SHIFT'S OVER.
LISTEN, I'D LOVE TO STAY AND TALK, BUT I'M RUNNING LATE.
I'VE GOT TO GET DINNER ON THE TABLE AND...
READER ADVISOR
HERE, LET ME TAKE THOSE GROCERIES!
COME ON. THIS'LL JUST TAKE A MINUTE!
AND IT WON'T COST YOU A CENT, HONEST.
I NEED THE PRACTICE.
I... I DON'T KNOW. FATHER KEVNER SAYS TAROT CARDS AREN'T... AREN'T CHRISTIAN.
OH, TISH TOSH, JUST THINK OF IT AS A KIND OF... OF CARD GAME. NOW CHOOSE A CARD.
HMMM. THE KNIGHT OF SWORDS. WHO-?
THAT'S TOM. MY OLDEST SON. HE ALWAYS BEEN MY KNIGHT IN SHINING ARMOR.
IT'S A WARRIOR SYMBOL. FAIR ENOUGH! HE DOES HAVE A TOUGH REPUTATION.
I KNOW, BUT... IT'S JUST A... A SHELL... HIS PROTECTION AGAINST THE WORLD, YOU KNOW?

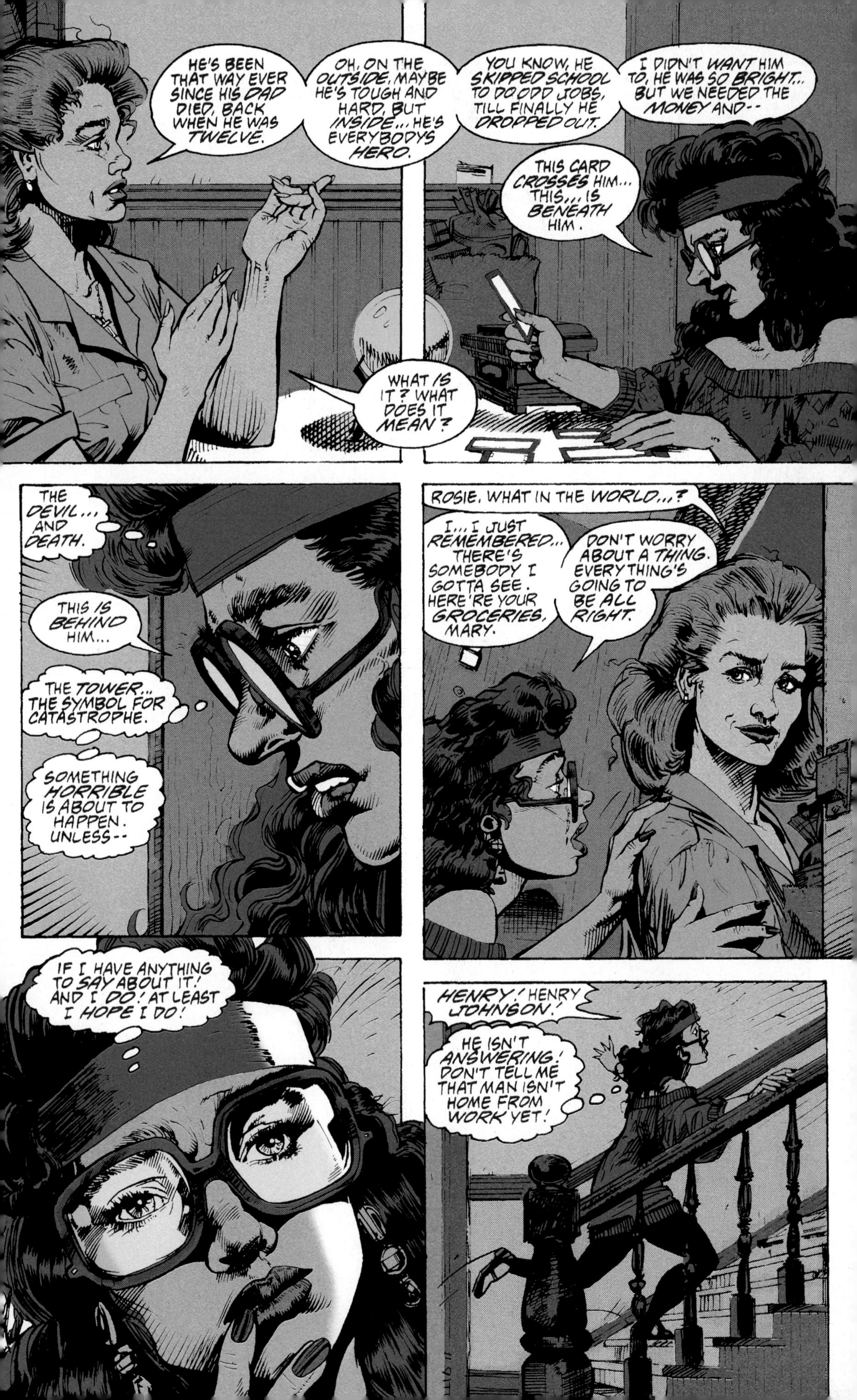
HE'S BEEN THAT WAY EVER SINCE HIS DAD DIED, BACK WHEN HE WAS TWELVE.
OH, ON THE OUTSIDE, MAYBE HE'S TOUGH AND HARD, BUT INSIDE... HE'S EVERYBODY'S HERO.
YOU KNOW, HE SKIPPED SCHOOL TO DO ODD JOBS, TILL FINALLY HE DROPPED OUT.
I DIDN'T WANT HIM TO, HE WAS SO BRIGHT... BUT WE NEEDED THE MONEY AND--
THIS CARD CROSSES HIM... THIS... IS BENEATH HIM.
WHAT IS IT? WHAT DOES IT MEAN?
THE DEVIL... AND DEATH.
THIS IS BEHIND HIM...
THE TOWER... THE SYMBOL FOR CATASTROPHE.
SOMETHING HORRIBLE IS ABOUT TO HAPPEN. UNLESS--
ROSIE. WHAT IN THE WORLD...?
I... I JUST REMEMBERED... THERE'S SOMEBODY I GOTTA SEE. HERE'RE YOUR GROCERIES, MARY.
DON'T WORRY ABOUT A THING. EVERYTHING'S GOING TO BE ALL RIGHT.
IF I HAVE ANYTHING TO SAY ABOUT IT! AND I DO! AT LEAST I HOPE I DO!
HENRY! HENRY JOHNSON!
HE ISN'T ANSWERING! DON'T TELL ME THAT MAN ISN'T HOME FROM WORK YET!

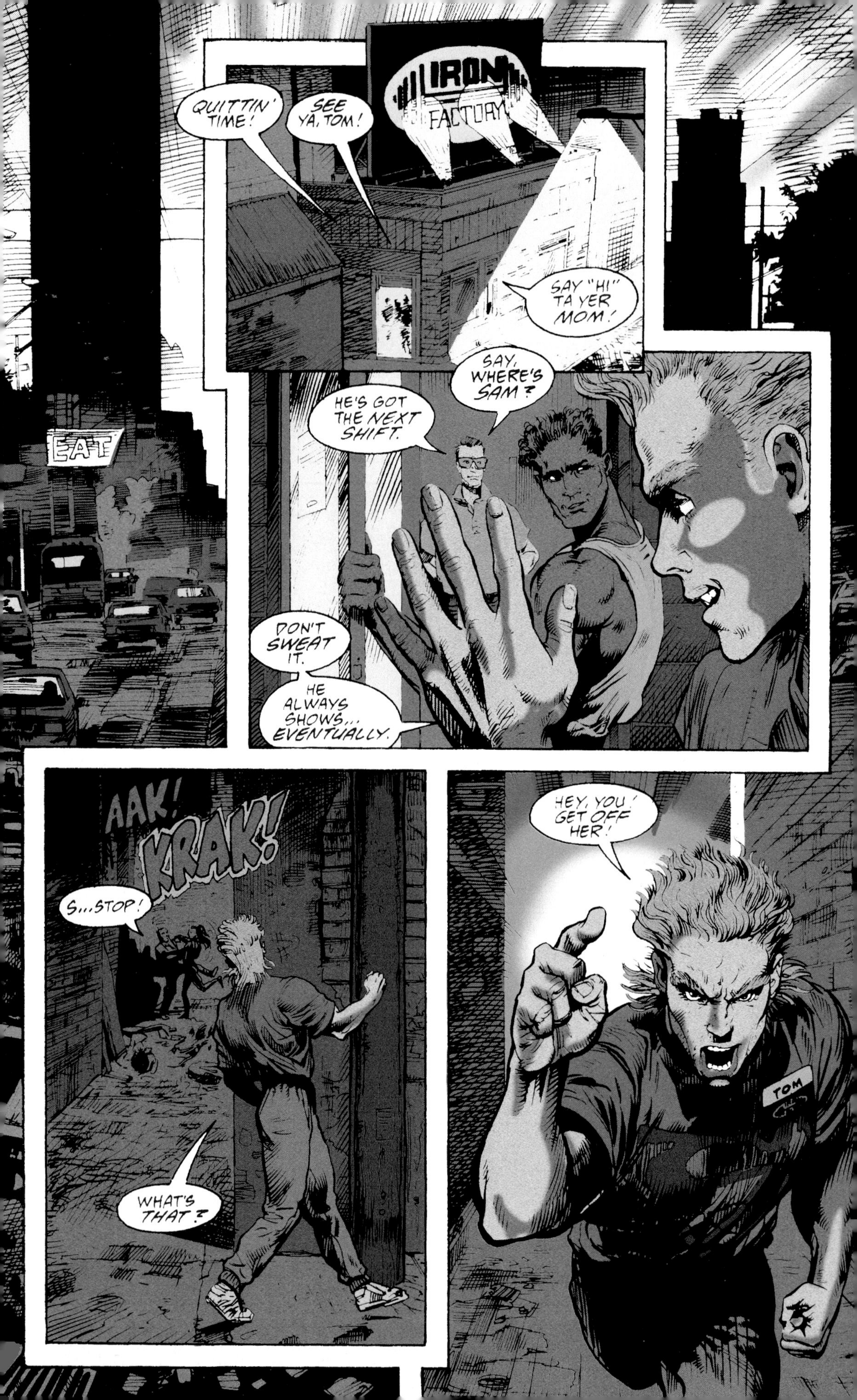
IRON
FACTORY
QUITTIN' TIME!
SEE YA, TOM!
SAY "HI" TA YER MOM!
EAT
SAY, WHERE'S SAM?
HE'S GOT THE NEXT SHIFT.
DON'T SWEAT IT.
HE ALWAYS SHOWS... EVENTUALLY.
AAK!
KRAK!
S...STOP!
WHAT'S THAT?
HEY, YOU! GET OFF HER!
TOM

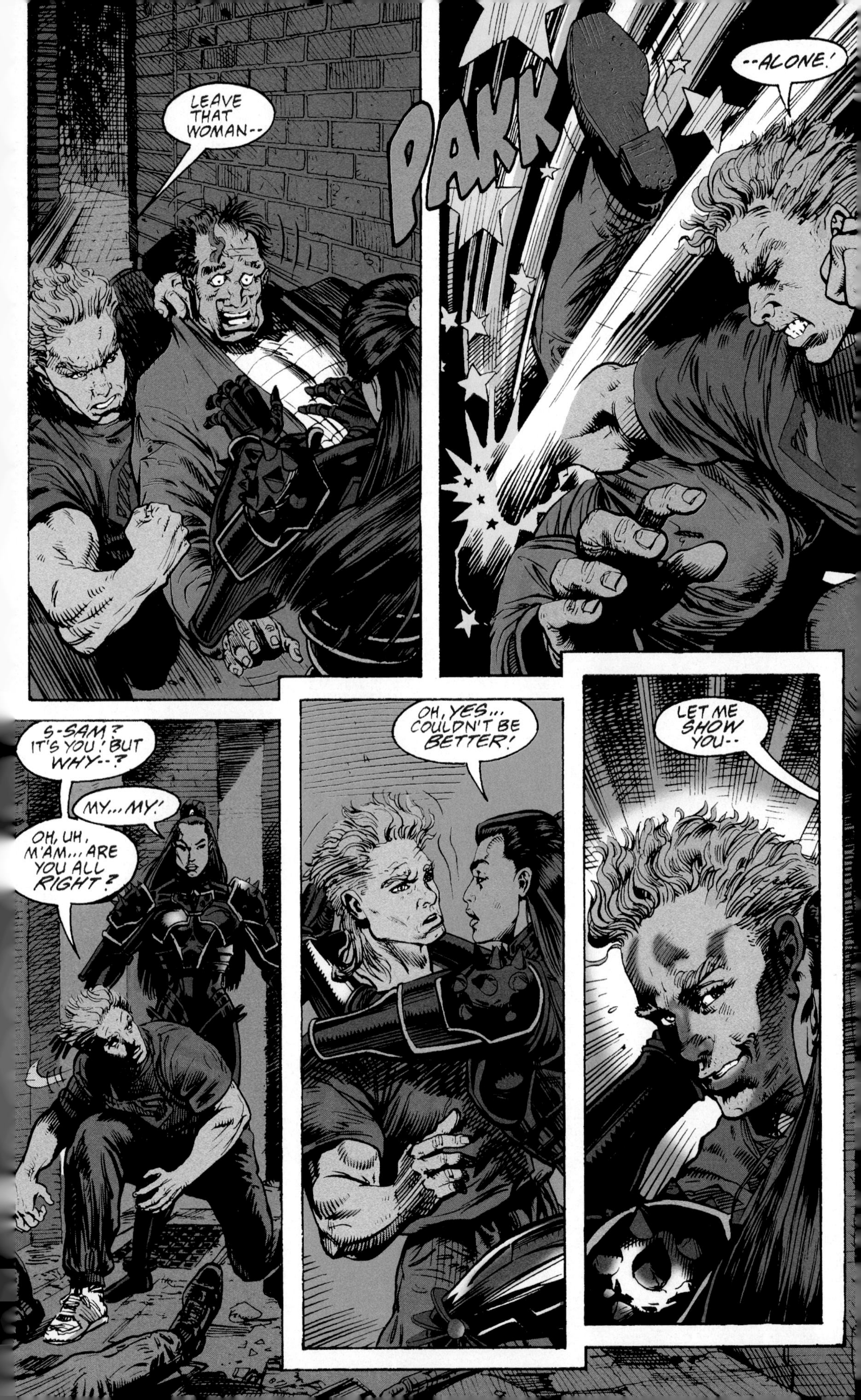
LEAVE THAT WOMAN--
PAKK
--ALONE!
S-SAM? IT'S YOU! BUT WHY--?
MY... MY!
OH, UH, M'AM... ARE YOU ALL RIGHT?
OH, YES... COULDN'T BE BETTER!
LET ME SHOW YOU--

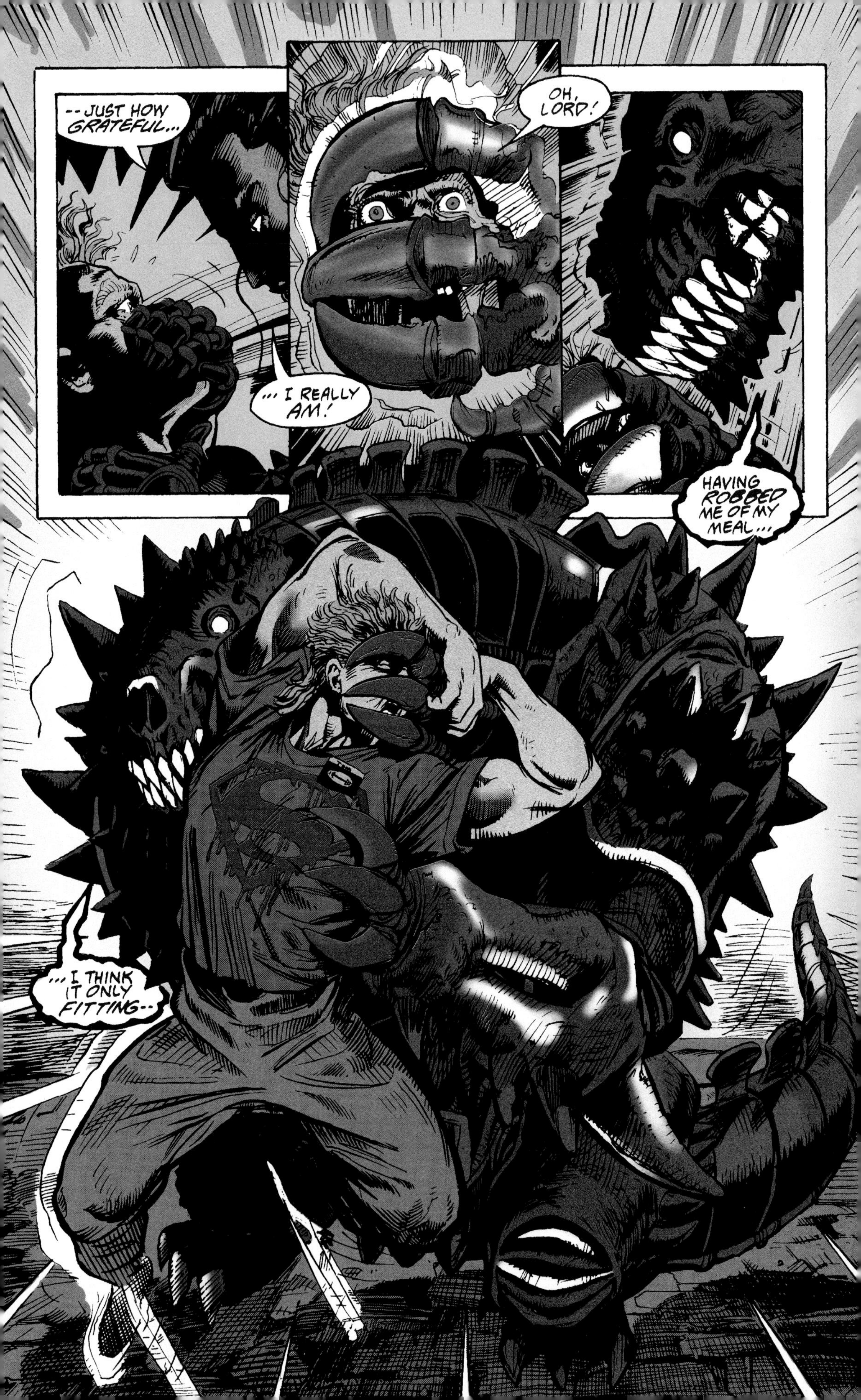
--JUST HOW GRATEFUL...
...I REALLY AM!
OH, LORD!
HAVING ROBBED ME OF MY MEAL...
...I THINK IT ONLY FITTING--

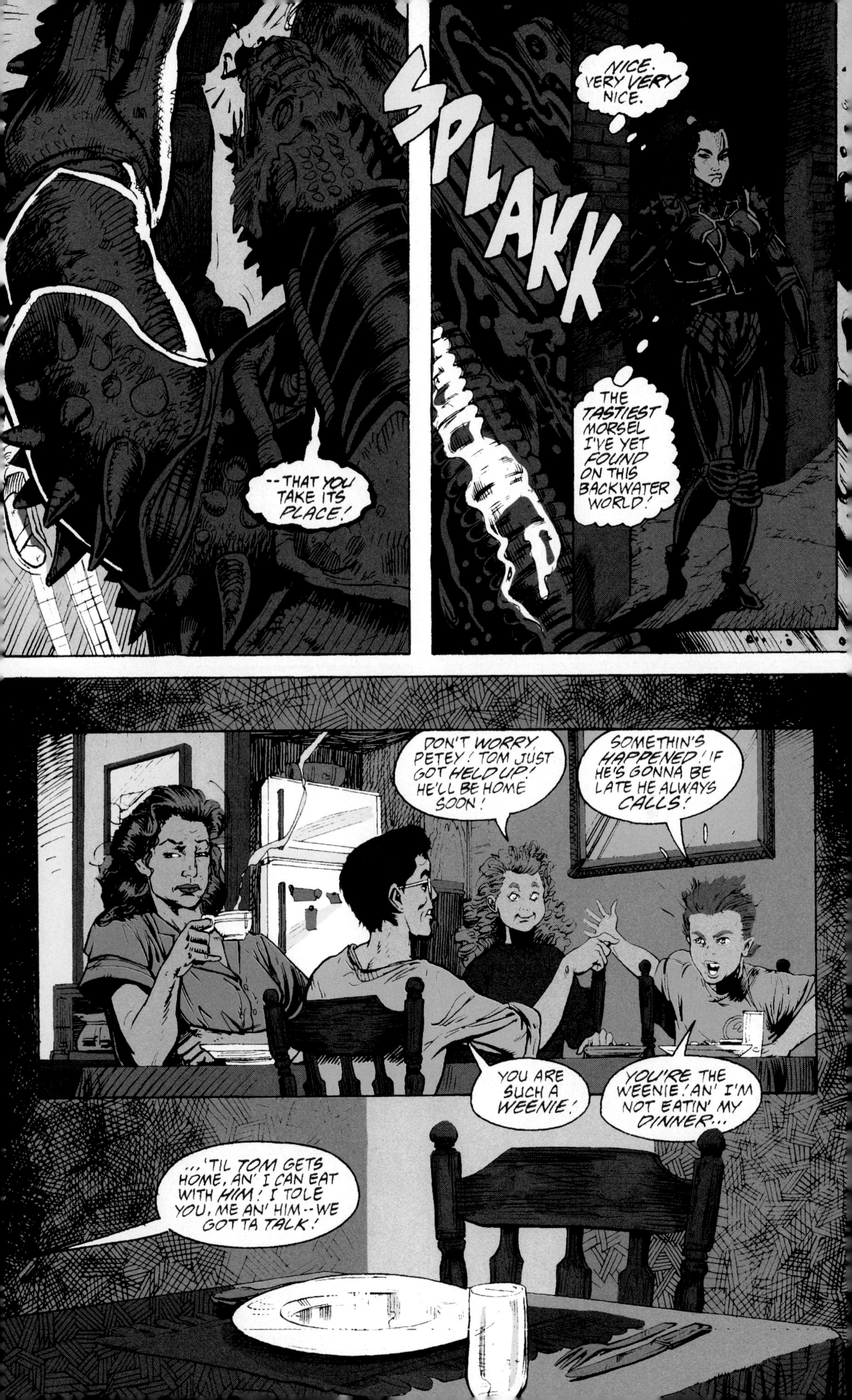

--THAT YOU TAKE ITS PLACE!
SPLAKK
NICE. VERY VERY NICE.
THE TASTIEST MORSEL I'VE YET FOUND ON THIS BACKWATER WORLD!
DON'T WORRY, PETEY! TOM JUST GOT HELD UP! HE'LL BE HOME SOON!
SOMETHIN'S HAPPENED! IF HE'S GONNA BE LATE HE ALWAYS CALLS!
YOU ARE SUCH A WEENIE!
YOU'RE THE WEENIE! AN' I'M NOT EATIN' MY DINNER...
...'TIL TOM GETS HOME, AN' I CAN EAT WITH HIM! I TOLE YOU, ME AN' HIM--WE GOTTA TALK!

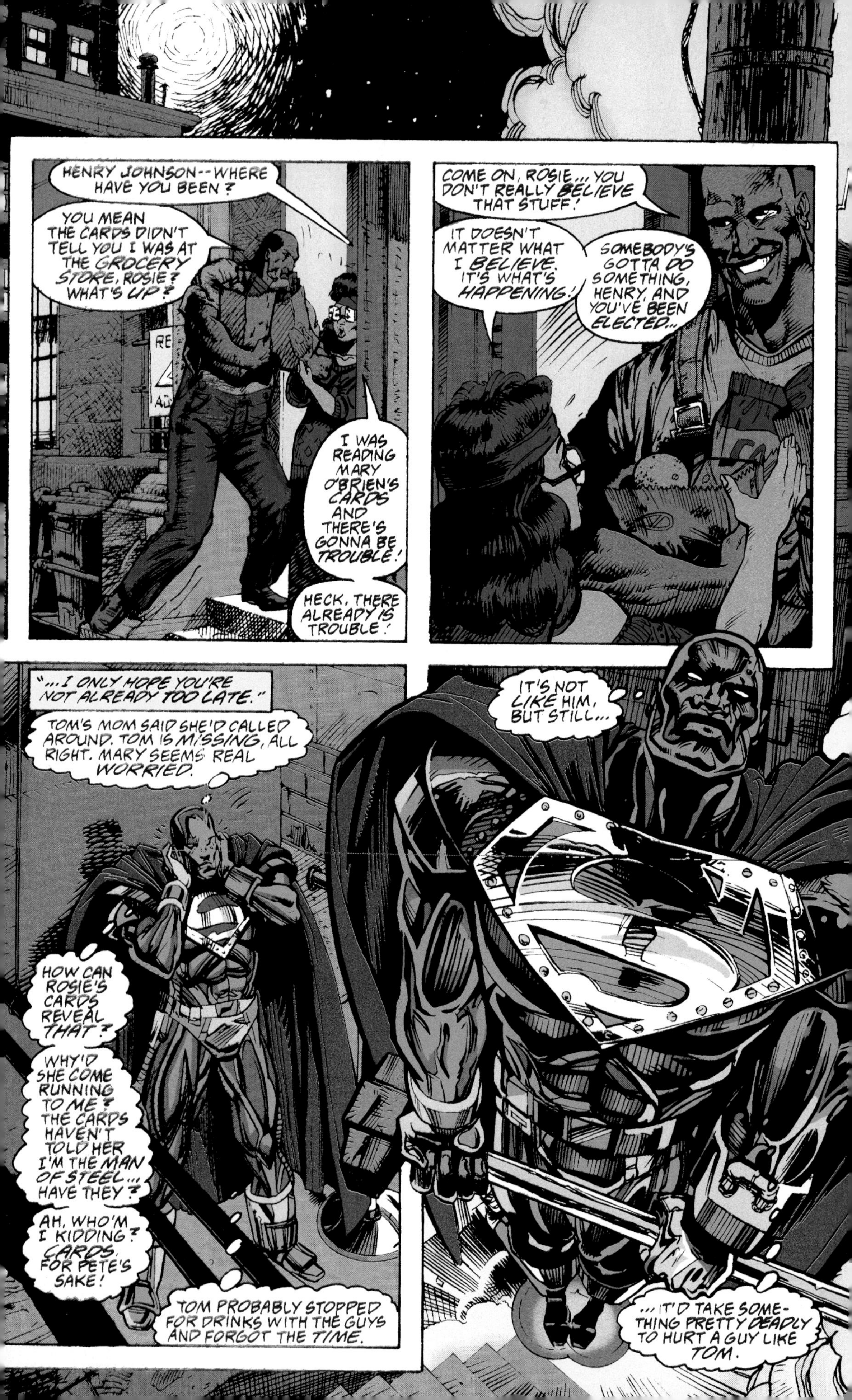
HENRY JOHNSON--WHERE HAVE YOU BEEN?
YOU MEAN THE CARDS DIDN'T TELL YOU I WAS AT THE GROCERY STORE, ROSIE? WHAT'S UP?
I WAS READING MARY O'BRIEN'S CARDS AND THERE'S GONNA BE TROUBLE!
HECK, THERE ALREADY IS TROUBLE!
COME ON, ROSIE... YOU DON'T REALLY BELIEVE THAT STUFF!
IT DOESN'T MATTER WHAT I BELIEVE. IT'S WHAT'S HAPPENING!
SOMEBODY'S GOTTA DO SOMETHING, HENRY, AND YOU'VE BEEN ELECTED...
"...I ONLY HOPE YOU'RE NOT ALREADY TOO LATE."
TOM'S MOM SAID SHE'D CALLED AROUND. TOM IS MISSING, ALL RIGHT. MARY SEEMS REAL WORRIED.
HOW CAN ROSIE'S CARDS REVEAL THAT?
WHY'D SHE COME RUNNING TO ME? THE CARDS HAVEN'T TOLD HER I'M THE MAN OF STEEL... HAVE THEY?
AH, WHO'M I KIDDING? CARDS, FOR PETE'S SAKE!
TOM PROBABLY STOPPED FOR DRINKS WITH THE GUYS AND FORGOT THE TIME.
IT'S NOT LIKE HIM, BUT STILL...
...IT'D TAKE SOMETHING PRETTY DEADLY TO HURT A GUY LIKE TOM.

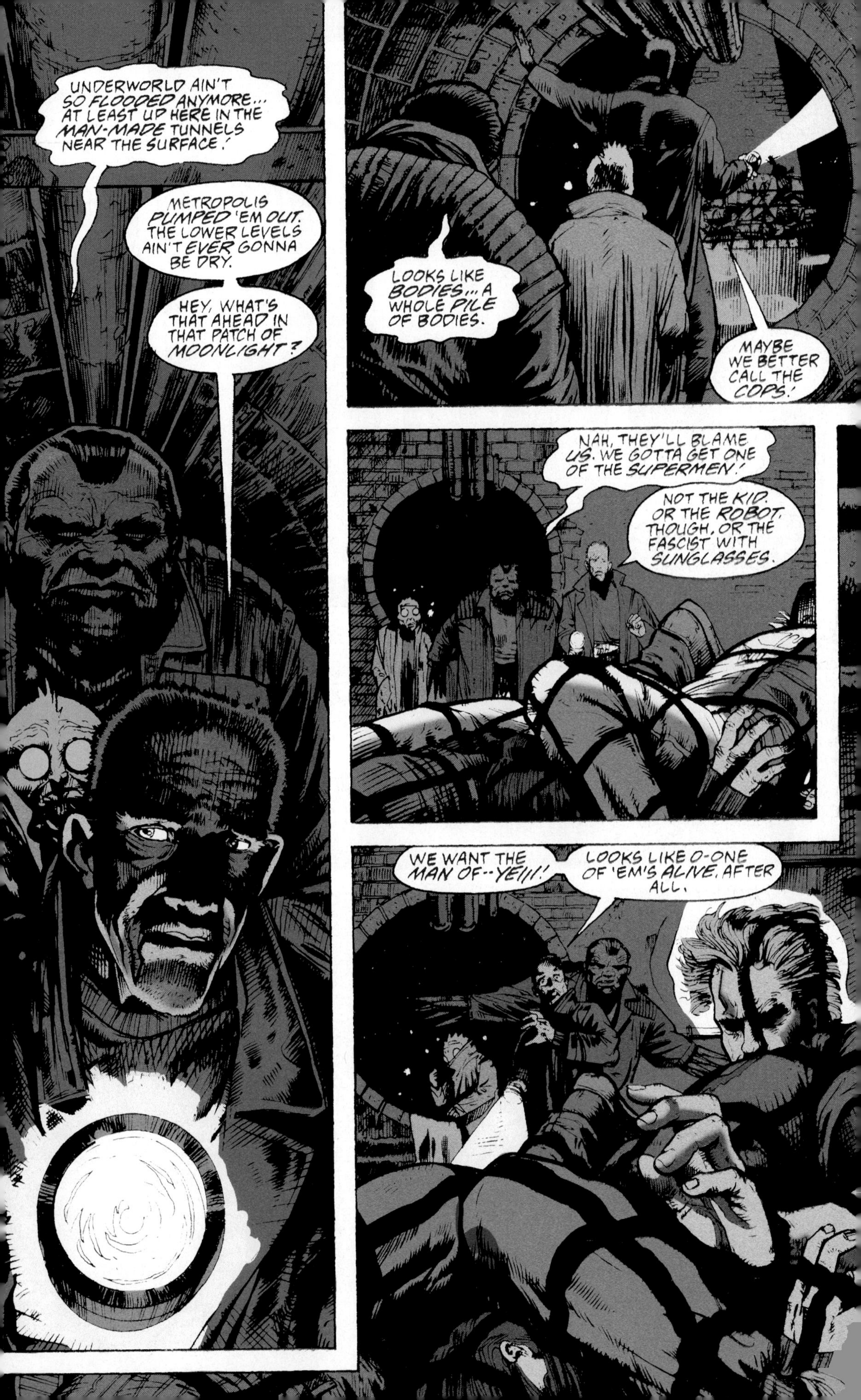
UNDERWORLD AIN'T SO FLOODED ANYMORE... AT LEAST UP HERE IN THE MAN-MADE TUNNELS NEAR THE SURFACE.'
METROPOLIS PUMPED 'EM OUT. THE LOWER LEVELS AIN'T EVER GONNA BE DRY.
HEY, WHAT'S THAT AHEAD IN THAT PATCH OF MOONLIGHT?
LOOKS LIKE BODIES... A WHOLE PILE OF BODIES.
MAYBE WE BETTER CALL THE COPS!
NAH, THEY'LL BLAME US. WE GOTTA GET ONE OF THE SUPERMEN!
NOT THE KID. OR THE ROBOT THOUGH, OR THE FASCIST WITH SUNGLASSES.
WE WANT THE MAN OF--YEIII!
LOOKS LIKE O-ONE OF 'EM'S ALIVE, AFTER ALL.

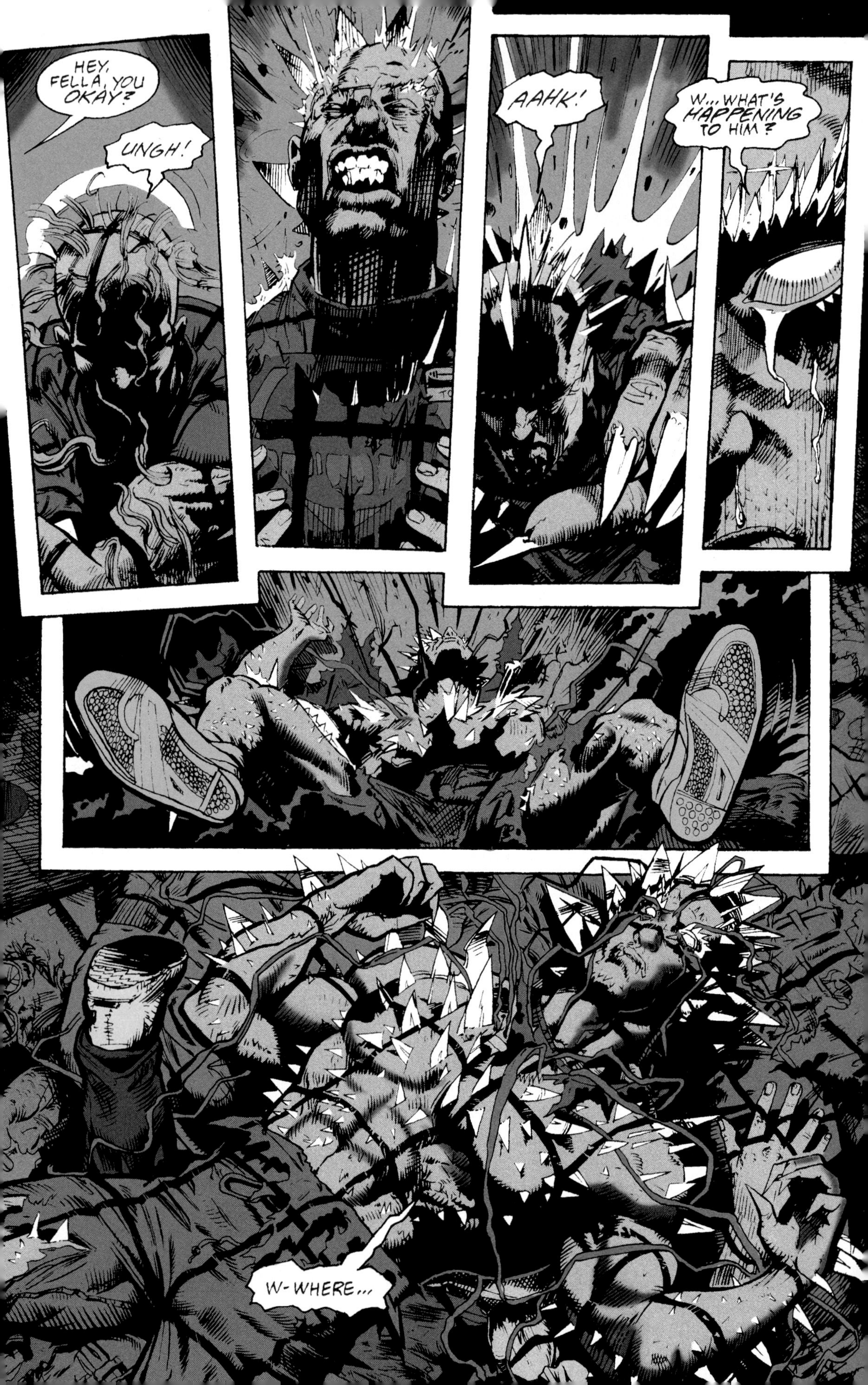
HEY, FELLA, YOU OKAY?
UNGH!
AAHK!
W... WHAT'S HAPPENING TO HIM?
W-WHERE...

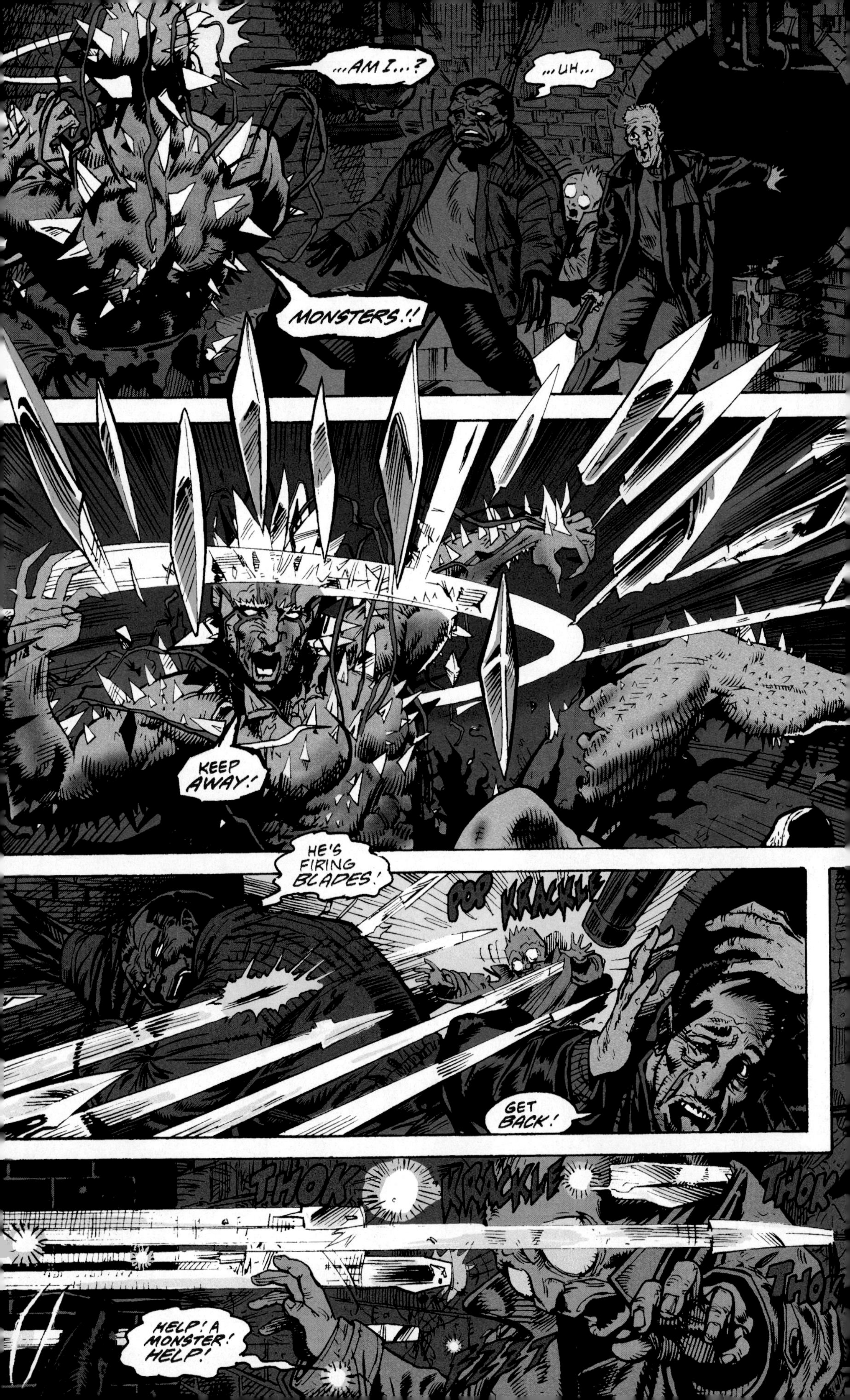
...AM I...?
...UH...
MONSTERS!!
KEEP AWAY!
HE'S FIRING BLADES!
POP
KRACKLE
GET BACK!
THOK
KRACKLE
THOK
THOK
HELP! A MONSTER! HELP!

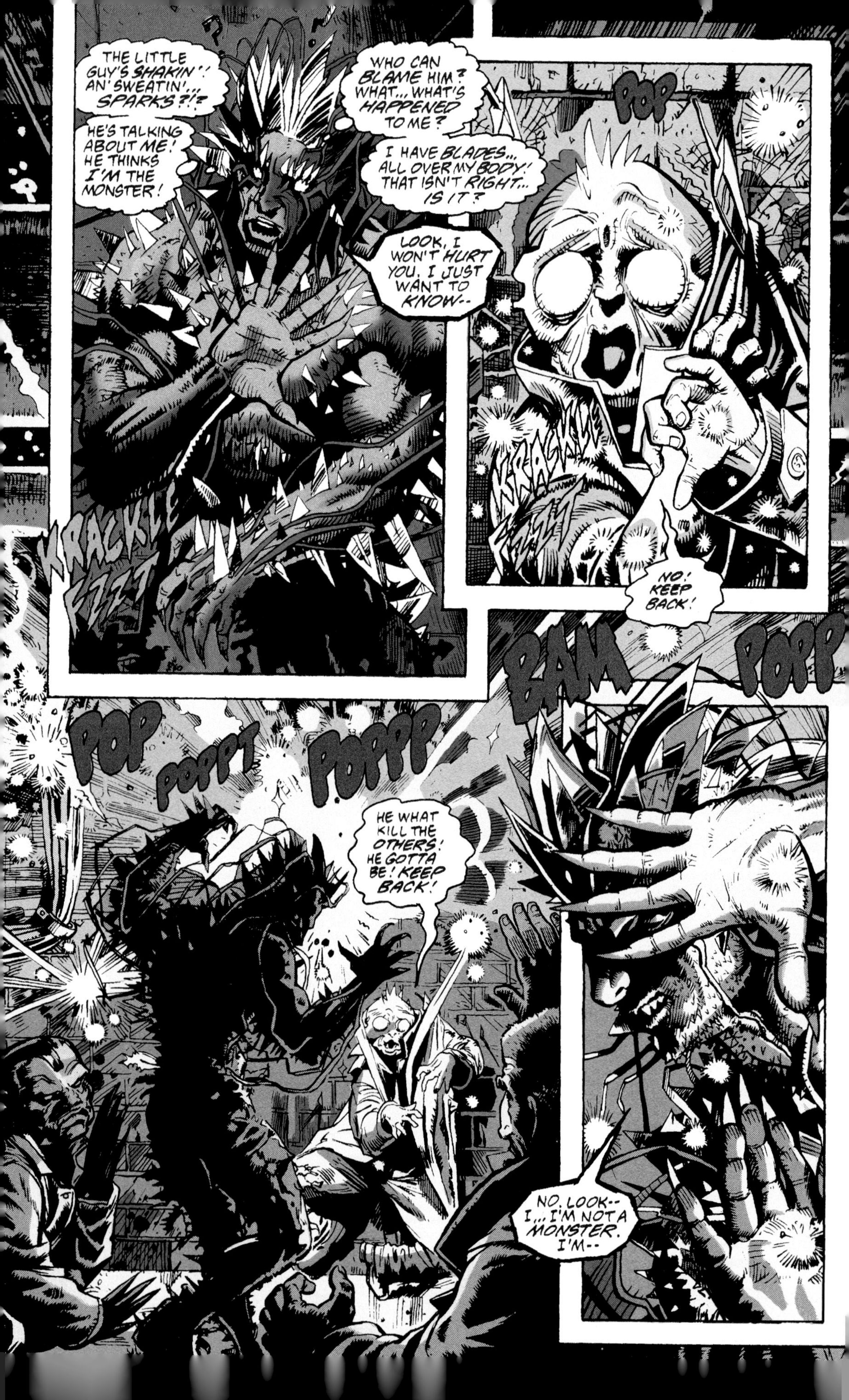
THE LITTLE GUY'S SHAKIN'! AN' SWEATIN'... SPARKS?!?
HE'S TALKING ABOUT ME! HE THINKS I'M THE MONSTER!
WHO CAN BLAME HIM? WHAT... WHAT'S HAPPENED TO ME?
I HAVE BLADES... ALL OVER MY BODY! THAT ISN'T RIGHT... IS IT?
LOOK, I WON'T HURT YOU. I JUST WANT TO KNOW--
KRACKLE
POP
NO! KEEP BACK!
BAM
POPP
POP
POPPT
POPPP
HE WHAT KILL THE OTHERS! HE GOTTA BE! KEEP BACK!
NO. LOOK-- I... I'M NOT A MONSTER. I'M--

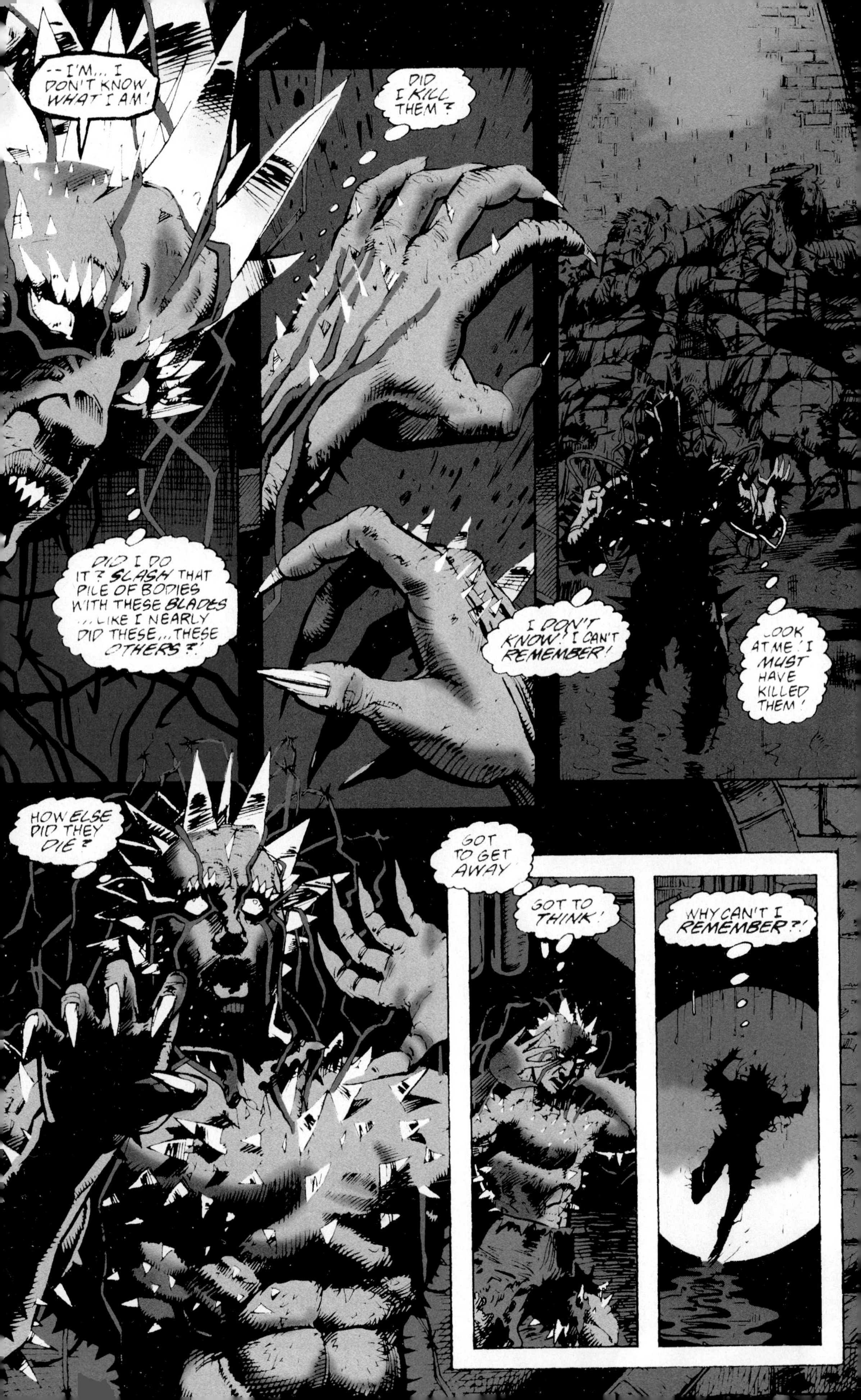
--I'M... I DON'T KNOW WHAT I AM!
DID I KILL THEM?
DID I DO IT? SLASH THAT PILE OF BODIES WITH THESE BLADES ...LIKE I NEARLY DID THESE... THESE OTHERS?!
I DON'T KNOW! I CAN'T REMEMBER!
LOOK AT ME! I MUST HAVE KILLED THEM!
HOW ELSE DID THEY DIE?
GOT TO GET AWAY
GOT TO THINK!
WHY CAN'T I REMEMBER?!

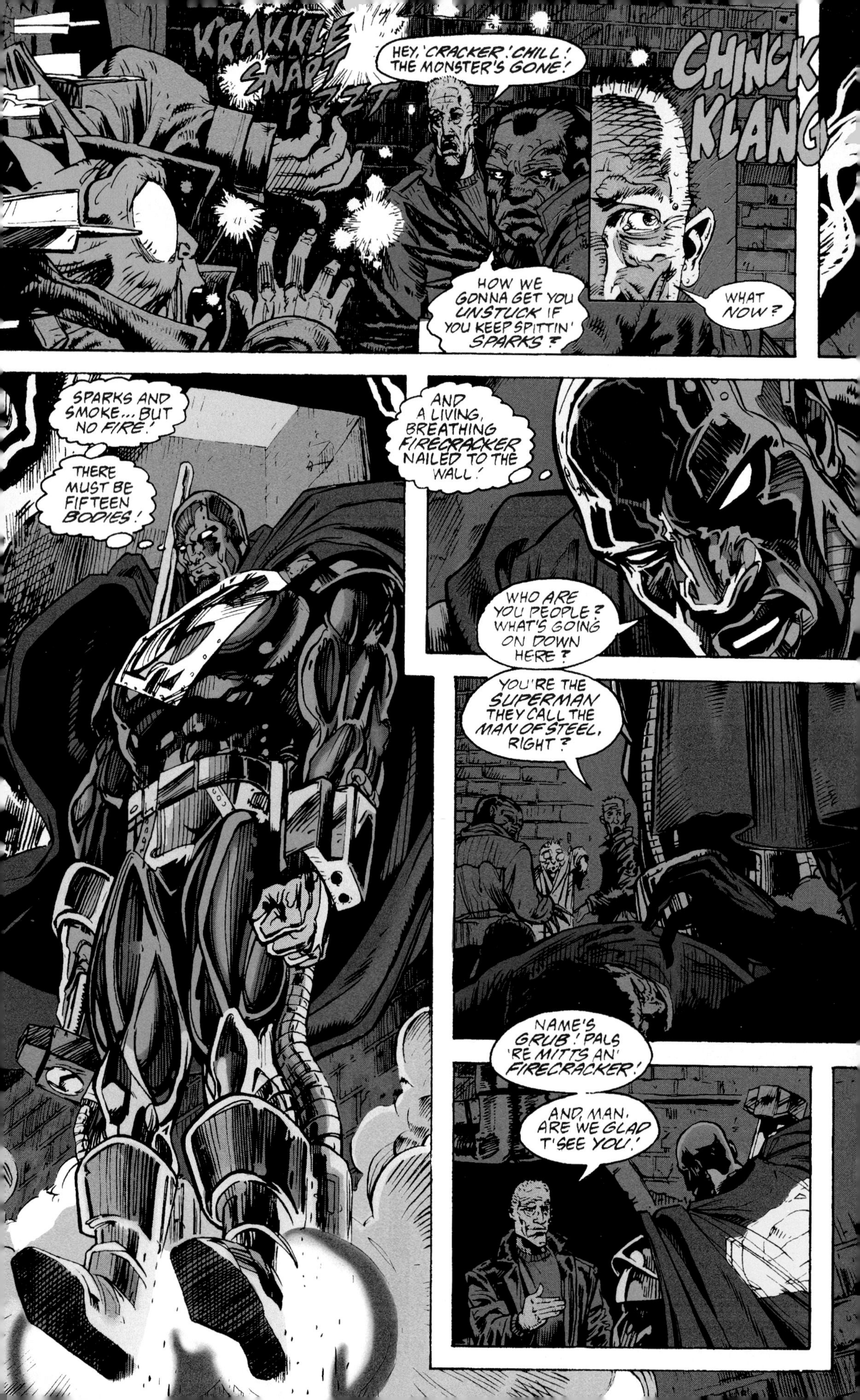
KRAKKLE SNAP FZZT
HEY, 'CRACKER! CHILL! THE MONSTER'S GONE!
HOW WE GONNA GET YOU UNSTUCK IF YOU KEEP SPITTIN' SPARKS?
CHINCK KLANG
WHAT NOW?
SPARKS AND SMOKE... BUT NO FIRE!
THERE MUST BE FIFTEEN BODIES!
AND A LIVING, BREATHING FIRECRACKER NAILED TO THE WALL!
WHO ARE YOU PEOPLE? WHAT'S GOING ON DOWN HERE?
YOU'RE THE SUPERMAN THEY CALL THE MAN OF STEEL, RIGHT?
NAME'S GRUB! PALS 'RE MITTS AN' FIRECRACKER!
AND, MAN, ARE WE GLAD T'SEE YOU!

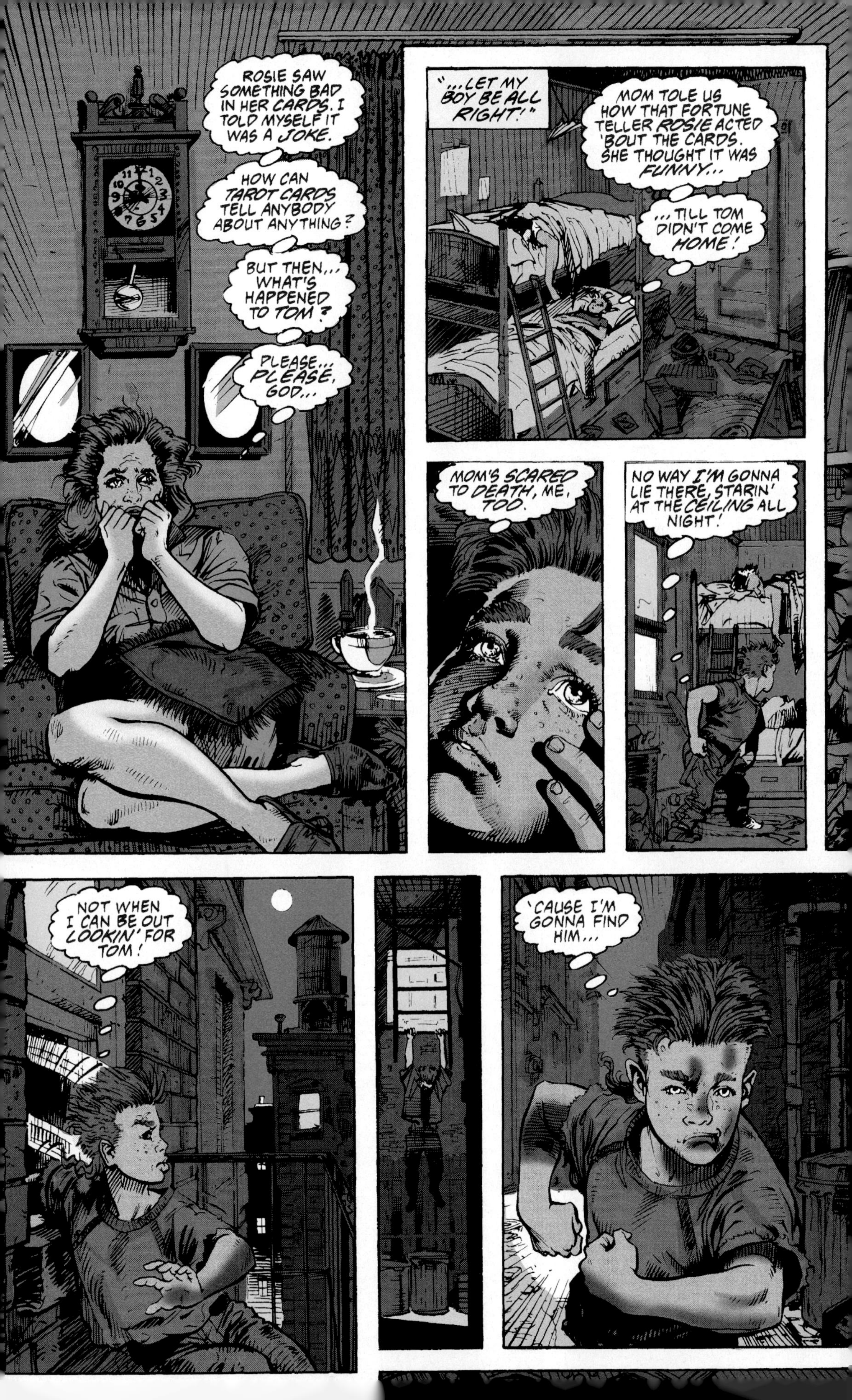
ROSIE SAW SOMETHING BAD IN HER CARDS. I TOLD MYSELF IT WAS A JOKE.
HOW CAN TAROT CARDS TELL ANYBODY ABOUT ANYTHING?
BUT THEN... WHAT'S HAPPENED TO TOM?
PLEASE... PLEASE, GOD...
"...LET MY BOY BE ALL RIGHT!"
MOM TOLE US HOW THAT FORTUNE TELLER ROSIE ACTED 'BOUT THE CARDS. SHE THOUGHT IT WAS FUNNY...
...TILL TOM DIDN'T COME HOME!
MOM'S SCARED TO DEATH. ME, TOO.
NO WAY I'M GONNA LIE THERE, STARIN' AT THE CEILING ALL NIGHT!
NOT WHEN I CAN BE OUT LOOKIN' FOR TOM!
'CAUSE I'M GONNA FIND HIM...

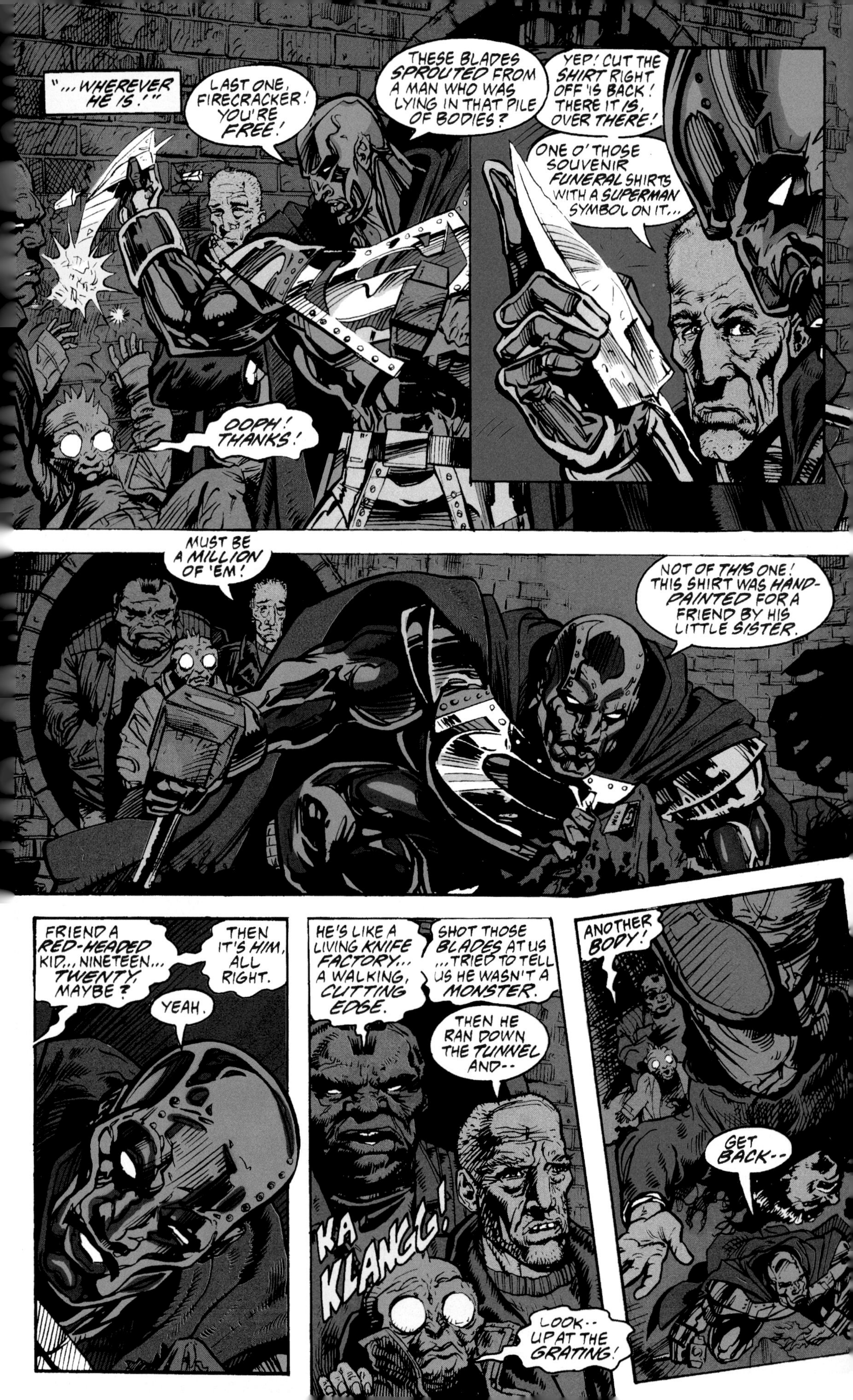
"...WHEREVER HE IS.'"
LAST ONE, FIRECRACKER! YOU'RE FREE!
OOPH! THANKS!
THESE BLADES SPROUTED FROM A MAN WHO WAS LYING IN THAT PILE OF BODIES?
YEP! CUT THE SHIRT RIGHT OFF 'IS BACK! THERE IT IS, OVER THERE!
ONE O' THOSE SOUVENIR FUNERAL SHIRTS WITH A SUPERMAN SYMBOL ON IT...
MUST BE A MILLION OF 'EM!
NOT OF THIS ONE! THIS SHIRT WAS HAND-PAINTED FOR A FRIEND BY HIS LITTLE SISTER.
FRIEND A RED-HEADED KID... NINETEEN... TWENTY, MAYBE?
THEN IT'S HIM, ALL RIGHT.
YEAH.
HE'S LIKE A LIVING KNIFE FACTORY... A WALKING, CUTTING EDGE.
SHOT THOSE BLADES AT US ...TRIED TO TELL US HE WASN'T A MONSTER.
THEN HE RAN DOWN THE TUNNEL AND--
KA KLANGG!
LOOK-- UP AT THE GRATING!
ANOTHER BODY!
GET BACK--

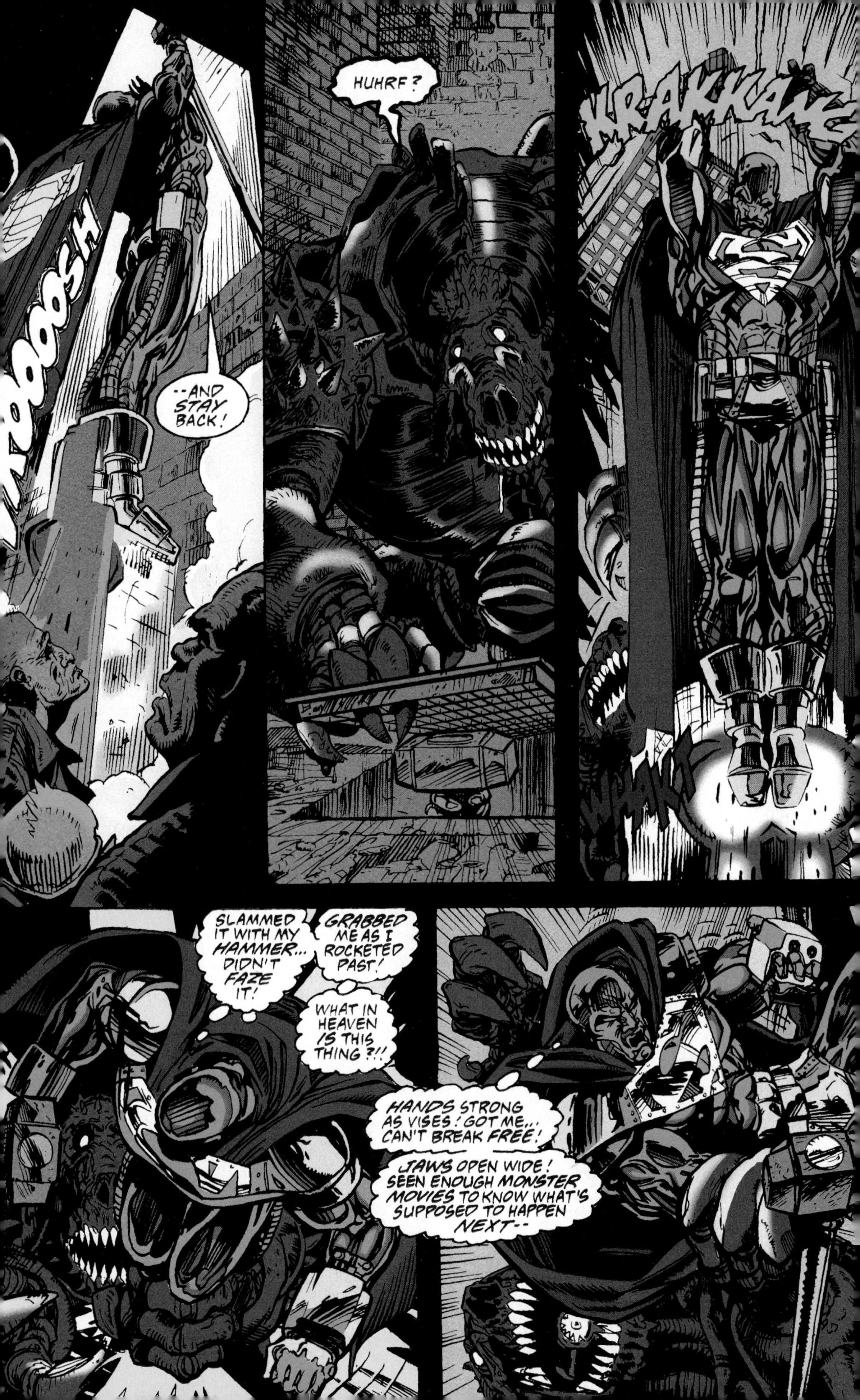
--AND STAY BACK!
HUHRF?
SLAMMED IT WITH MY HAMMER... DIDN'T FAZE IT!
GRABBED ME AS I ROCKETED PAST!
WHAT IN HEAVEN IS THIS THING?!!
HANDS STRONG AS VISES! GOT ME... CAN'T BREAK FREE!
JAWS OPEN WIDE! SEEN ENOUGH MONSTER MOVIES TO KNOW WHAT'S SUPPOSED TO HAPPEN NEXT--

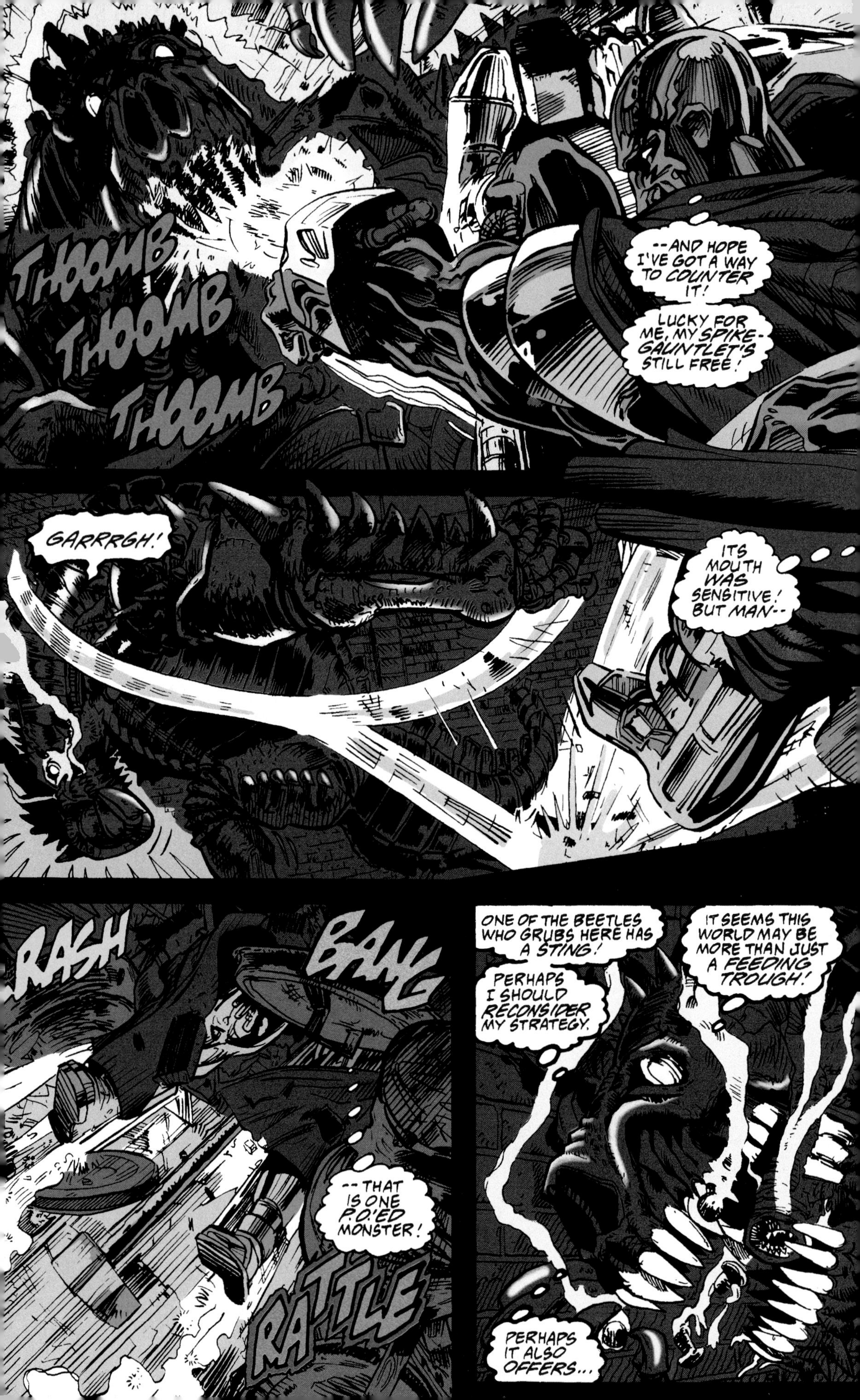
THOOMB
THOOMB
THOOMB
--AND HOPE I'VE GOT A WAY TO COUNTER IT!
LUCKY FOR ME, MY SPIKE-GAUNTLET'S STILL FREE!
GARRRGH!
ITS MOUTH WAS SENSITIVE! BUT MAN--
RASH
BANG
--THAT IS ONE P.O.'ED MONSTER!
RATTLE
ONE OF THE BEETLES WHO GRUBS HERE HAS A STING!
PERHAPS I SHOULD RECONSIDER MY STRATEGY.
IT SEEMS THIS WORLD MAY BE MORE THAN JUST A FEEDING TROUGH!
PERHAPS IT ALSO OFFERS...

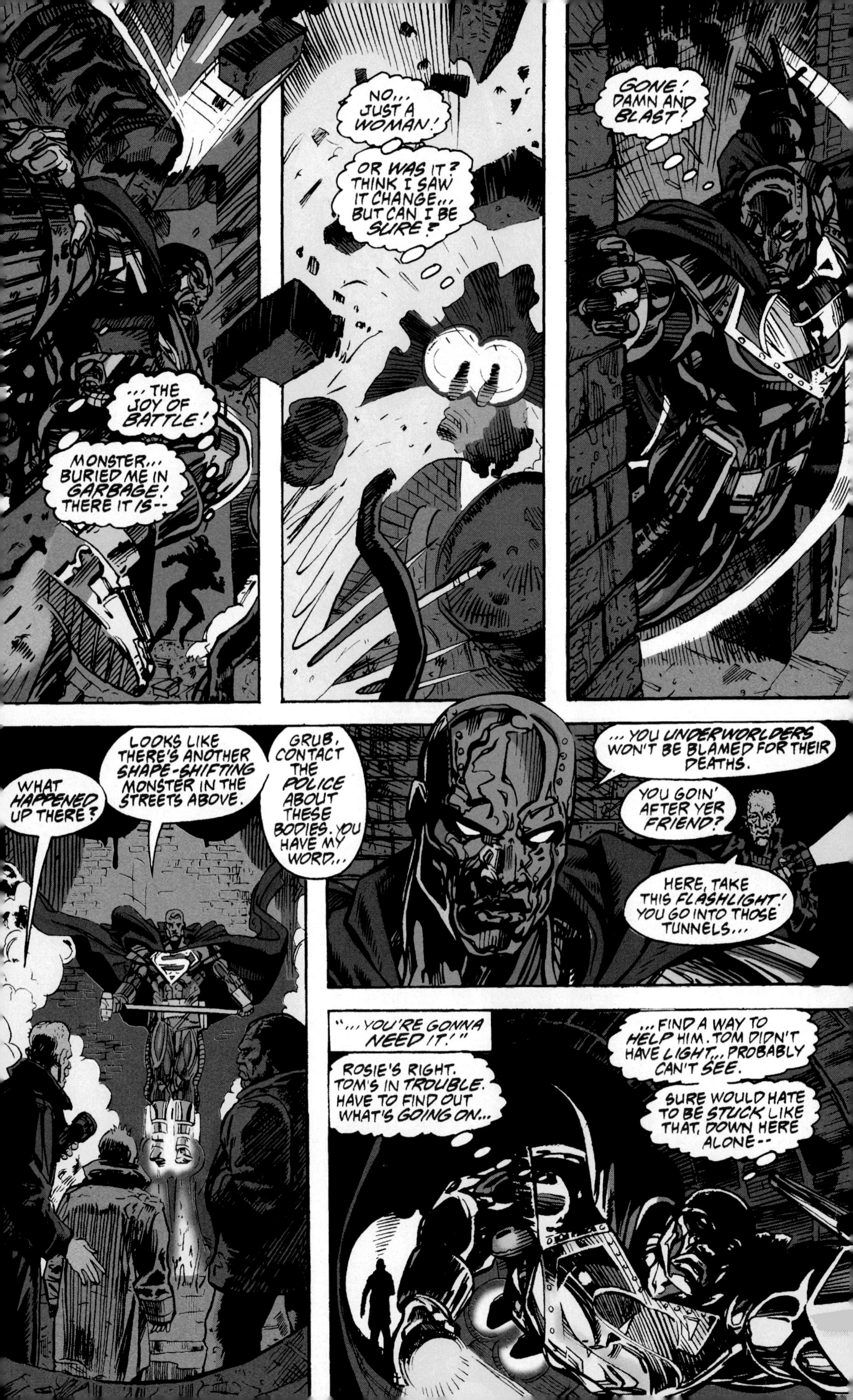
...THE JOY OF BATTLE!
MONSTER... BURIED ME IN GARBAGE! THERE IT IS--
NO... JUST A WOMAN!
OR WAS IT? THINK I SAW IT CHANGE... BUT CAN I BE SURE?
GONE! DAMN AND BLAST!
WHAT HAPPENED UP THERE?
LOOKS LIKE THERE'S ANOTHER SHAPE-SHIFTING MONSTER IN THE STREETS ABOVE.
GRUB, CONTACT THE POLICE ABOUT THESE BODIES. YOU HAVE MY WORD...
...YOU UNDERWORLDERS WON'T BE BLAMED FOR THEIR DEATHS.
YOU GOIN' AFTER YER FRIEND?
HERE, TAKE THIS FLASHLIGHT! YOU GO INTO THOSE TUNNELS...
"...YOU'RE GONNA NEED IT!"
ROSIE'S RIGHT. TOM'S IN TROUBLE. HAVE TO FIND OUT WHAT'S GOING ON...
...FIND A WAY TO HELP HIM. TOM DIDN'T HAVE LIGHT... PROBABLY CAN'T SEE.
SURE WOULD HATE TO BE STUCK LIKE THAT, DOWN HERE ALONE--

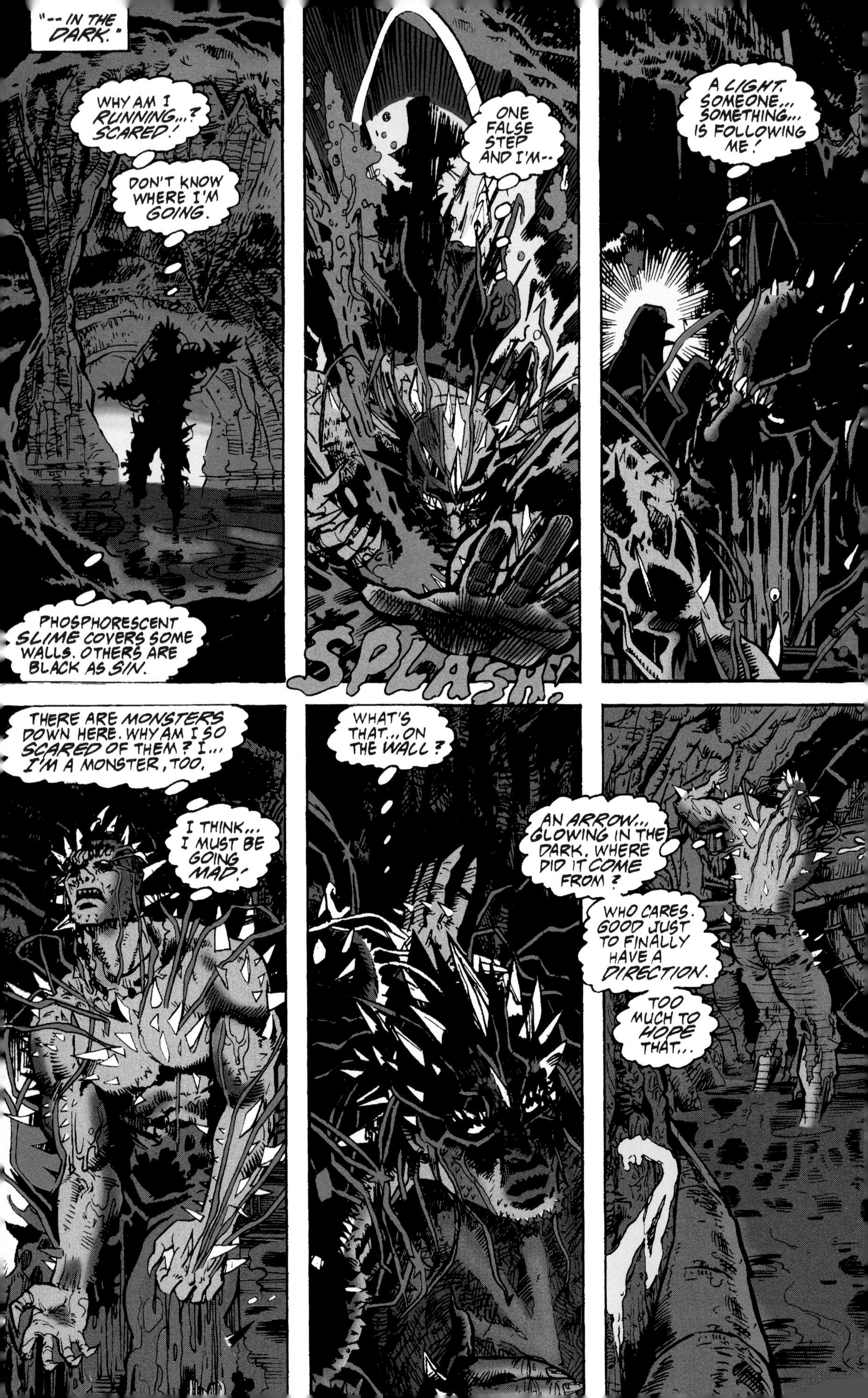
"-- IN THE DARK."
WHY AM I RUNNING...? SCARED!
DON'T KNOW WHERE I'M GOING.
PHOSPHORESCENT SLIME COVERS SOME WALLS. OTHERS ARE BLACK AS SIN.
ONE FALSE STEP AND I'M--
SPLASH!
A LIGHT. SOMEONE... SOMETHING... IS FOLLOWING ME!
THERE ARE MONSTERS DOWN HERE. WHY AM I SO SCARED OF THEM? I... I'M A MONSTER, TOO.
I THINK... I MUST BE GOING MAD!
WHAT'S THAT... ON THE WALL?
AN ARROW... GLOWING IN THE DARK. WHERE DID IT COME FROM?
WHO CARES. GOOD JUST TO FINALLY HAVE A DIRECTION.
TOO MUCH TO HOPE THAT...

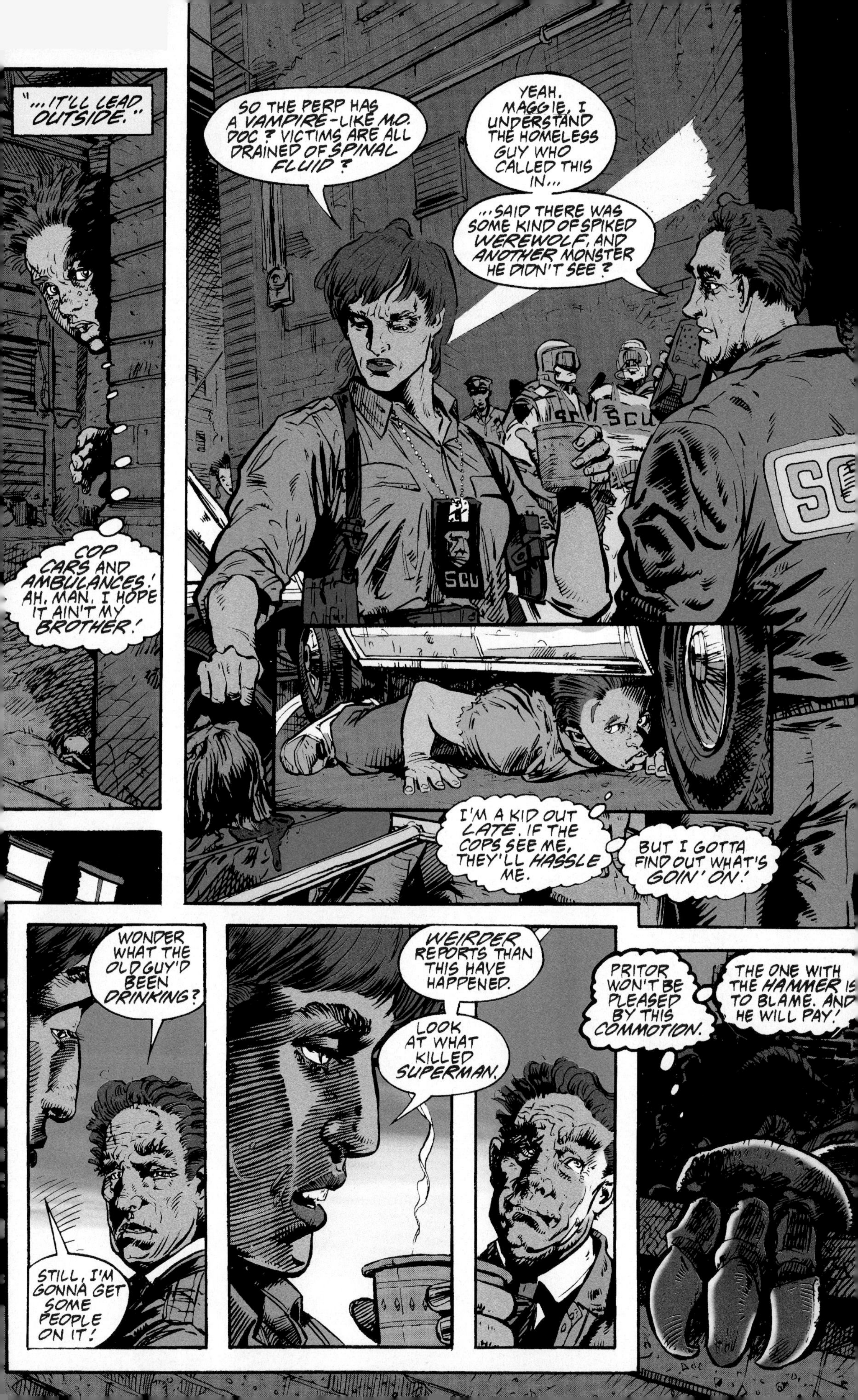
"...IT'LL LEAD OUTSIDE."
SO THE PERP HAS A VAMPIRE-LIKE M.O. DOC? VICTIMS ARE ALL DRAINED OF SPINAL FLUID?
YEAH. MAGGIE, I UNDERSTAND THE HOMELESS GUY WHO CALLED THIS IN...
...SAID THERE WAS SOME KIND OF SPIKED WEREWOLF, AND ANOTHER MONSTER HE DIDN'T SEE?
SCU
COP CARS AND AMBULANCES! AH, MAN, I HOPE IT AIN'T MY BROTHER!
I'M A KID OUT LATE. IF THE COPS SEE ME, THEY'LL HASSLE ME.
BUT I GOTTA FIND OUT WHAT'S GOIN' ON!
WONDER WHAT THE OLD GUY'D BEEN DRINKING?
STILL, I'M GONNA GET SOME PEOPLE ON IT!
WEIRDER REPORTS THAN THIS HAVE HAPPENED.
LOOK AT WHAT KILLED SUPERMAN.
PRITOR WON'T BE PLEASED BY THIS COMMOTION.
THE ONE WITH THE HAMMER IS TO BLAME. AND HE WILL PAY!

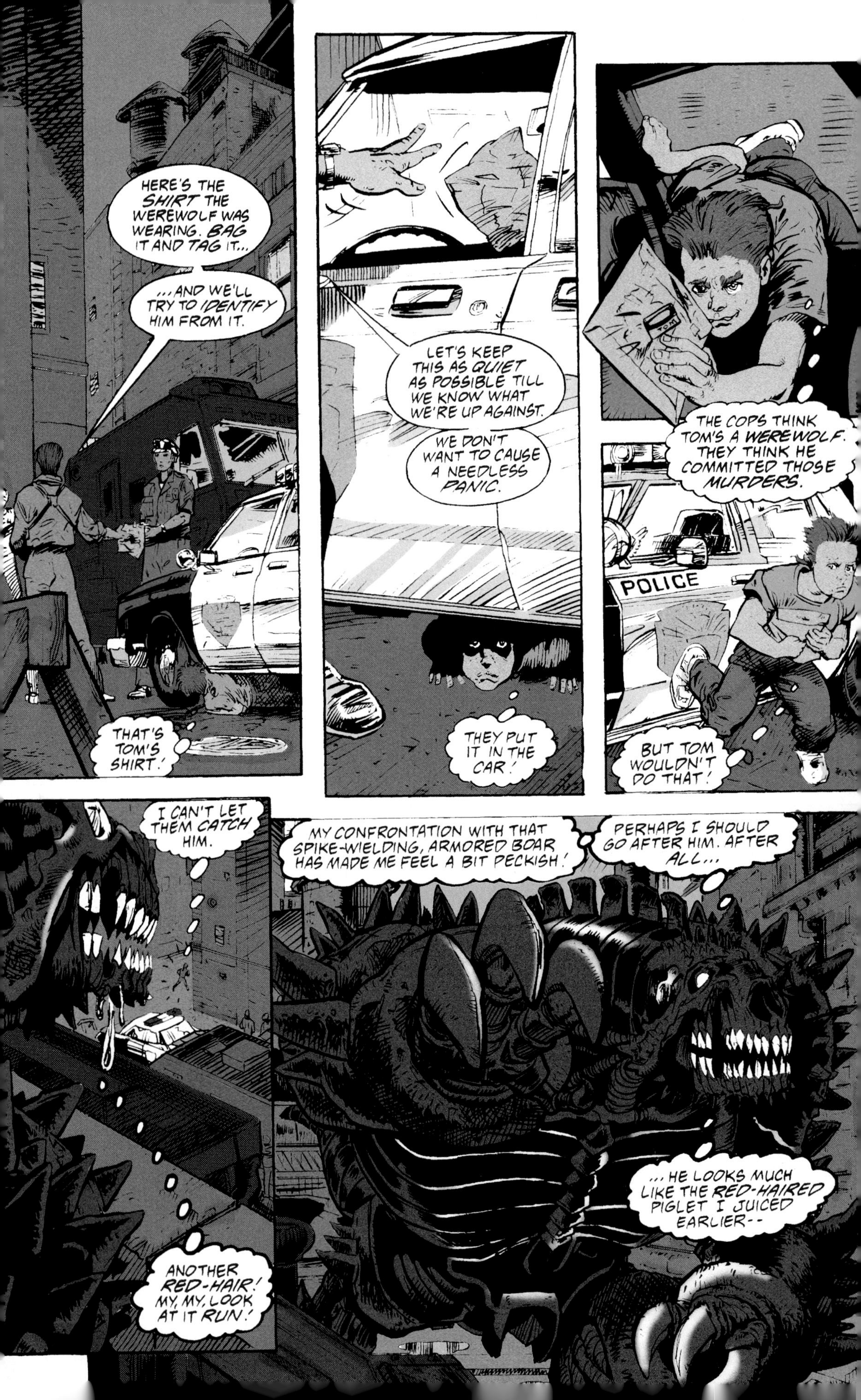
HERE'S THE SHIRT THE WEREWOLF WAS WEARING. BAG IT AND TAG IT...
...AND WE'LL TRY TO IDENTIFY HIM FROM IT.
THAT'S TOM'S SHIRT!
LET'S KEEP THIS AS QUIET AS POSSIBLE TILL WE KNOW WHAT WE'RE UP AGAINST.
WE DON'T WANT TO CAUSE A NEEDLESS PANIC.
THEY PUT IT IN THE CAR!
THE COPS THINK TOM'S A WEREWOLF. THEY THINK HE COMMITTED THOSE MURDERS.
POLICE
BUT TOM WOULDN'T DO THAT!
I CAN'T LET THEM CATCH HIM.
ANOTHER RED-HAIR! MY, MY, LOOK AT IT RUN!
MY CONFRONTATION WITH THAT SPIKE-WIELDING, ARMORED BOAR HAS MADE ME FEEL A BIT PECKISH!
PERHAPS I SHOULD GO AFTER HIM. AFTER ALL...
...HE LOOKS MUCH LIKE THE RED-HAIRED PIGLET I JUICED EARLIER--

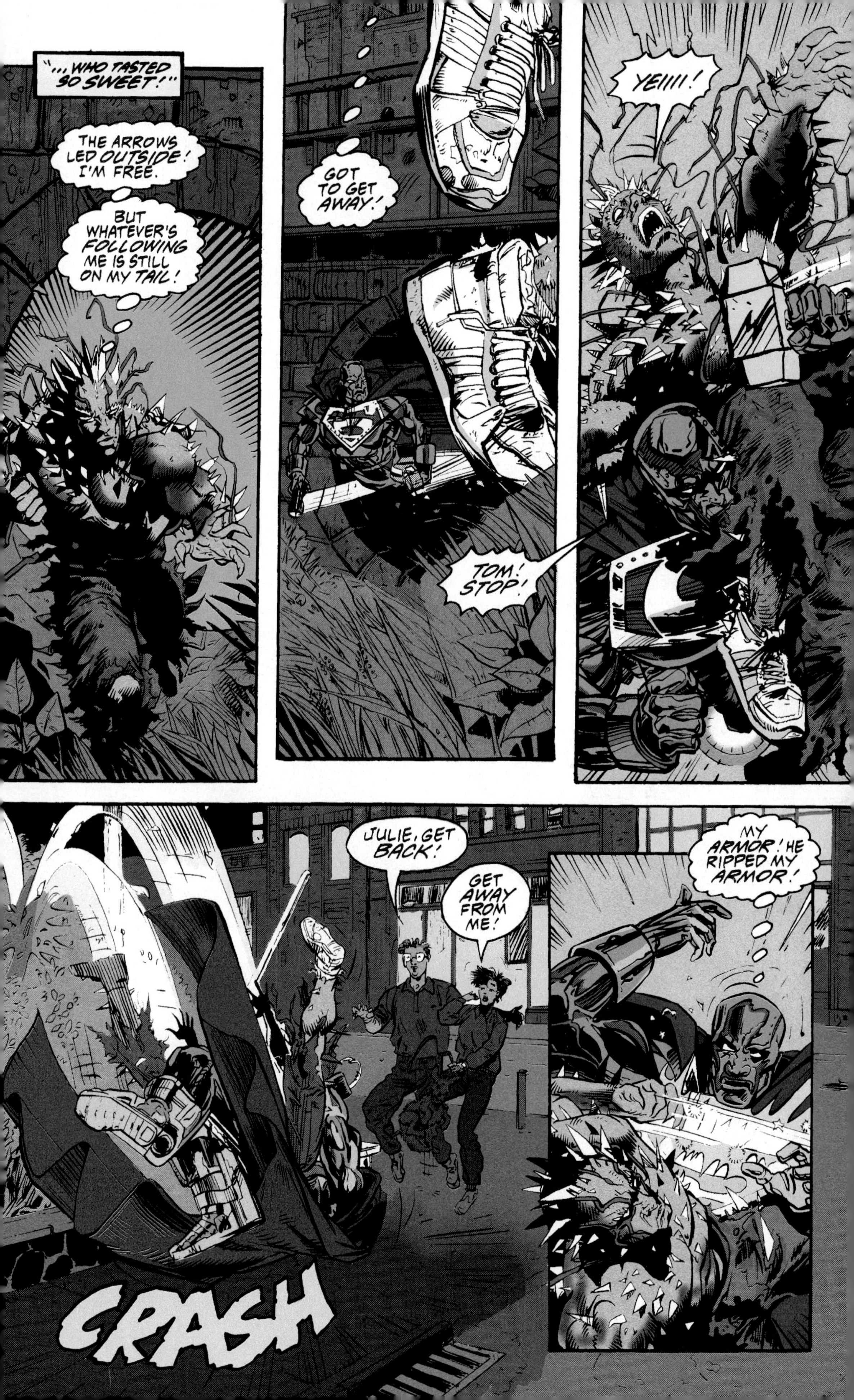
"..., WHO TASTED SO SWEET!"
THE ARROWS LED OUTSIDE! I'M FREE.
BUT WHATEVER'S FOLLOWING ME IS STILL ON MY TAIL!
GOT TO GET AWAY!
YEIIII!
TOM! STOP!
JULIE, GET BACK!
GET AWAY FROM ME!
MY ARMOR! HE RIPPED MY ARMOR!
CRASH

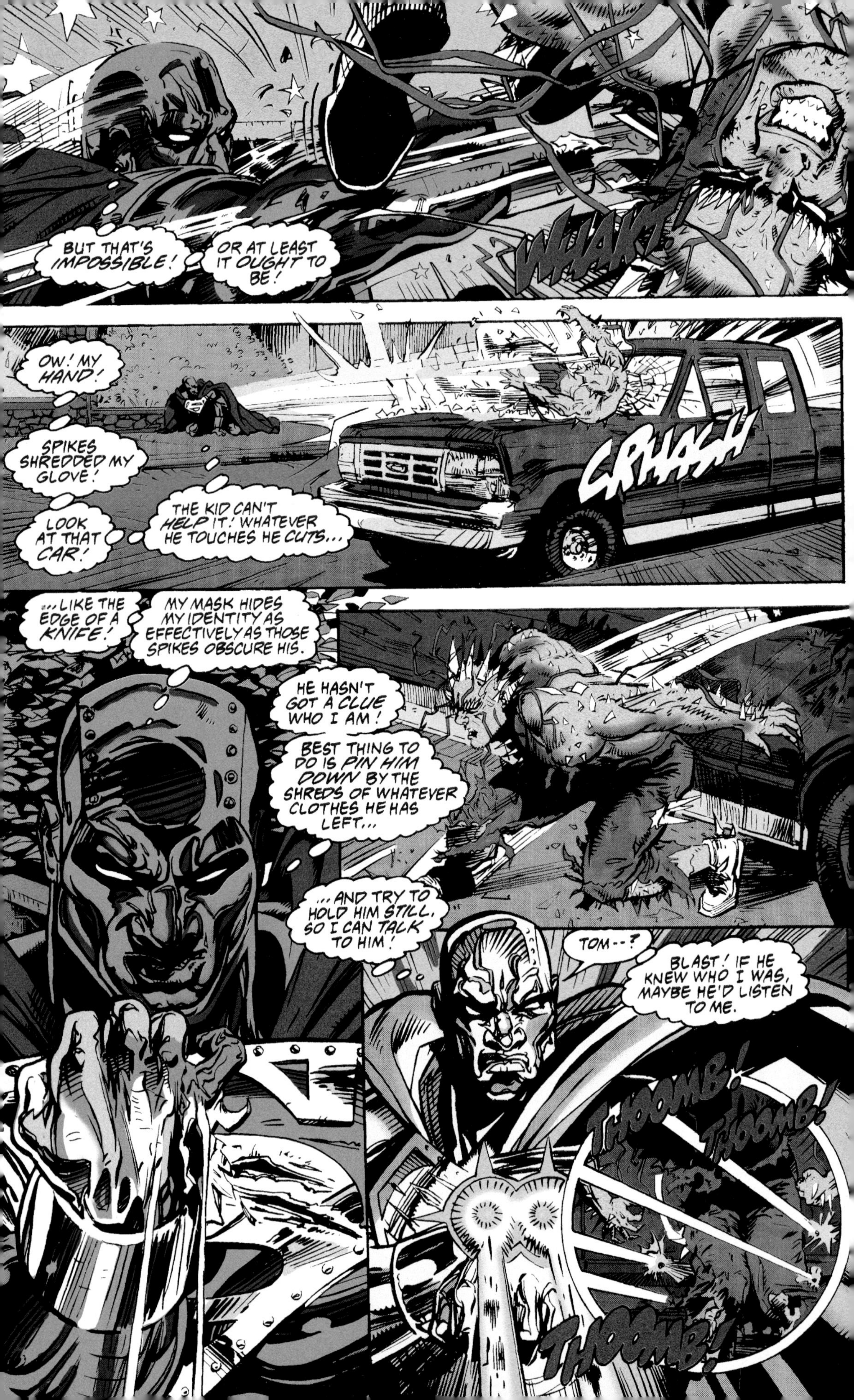
BUT THAT'S IMPOSSIBLE!
OR AT LEAST IT OUGHT TO BE!
WHAM!
OW! MY HAND!
SPIKES SHREDDED MY GLOVE!
LOOK AT THAT CAR!
THE KID CAN'T HELP IT! WHATEVER HE TOUCHES HE CUTS...
CRASH
...LIKE THE EDGE OF A KNIFE!
MY MASK HIDES MY IDENTITY AS EFFECTIVELY AS THOSE SPIKES OBSCURE HIS.
HE HASN'T GOT A CLUE WHO I AM!
BEST THING TO DO IS PIN HIM DOWN BY THE SHREDS OF WHATEVER CLOTHES HE HAS LEFT...
...AND TRY TO HOLD HIM STILL, SO I CAN TALK TO HIM!
TOM--?
BLAST! IF HE KNEW WHO I WAS, MAYBE HE'D LISTEN TO ME.
THOOMB! THOOMB!
THOOMB!

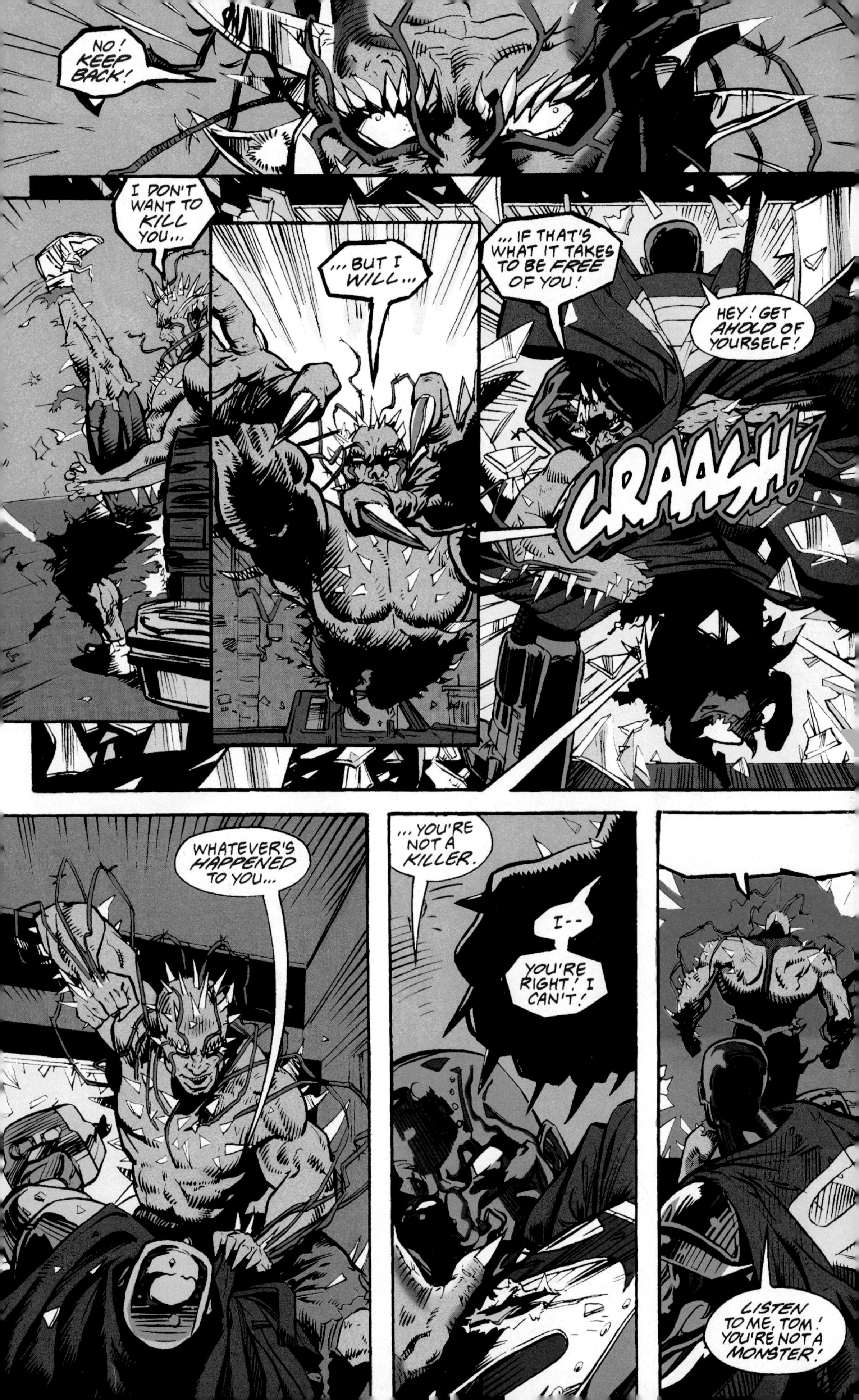

NO! KEEP BACK!
I DON'T WANT TO KILL YOU...
...BUT I WILL...
...IF THAT'S WHAT IT TAKES TO BE FREE OF YOU!
HEY! GET AHOLD OF YOURSELF!
CRAASH!
WHATEVER'S HAPPENED TO YOU...
...YOU'RE NOT A KILLER.
I--
YOU'RE RIGHT! I CAN'T!
LISTEN TO ME, TOM! YOU'RE NOT A MONSTER!

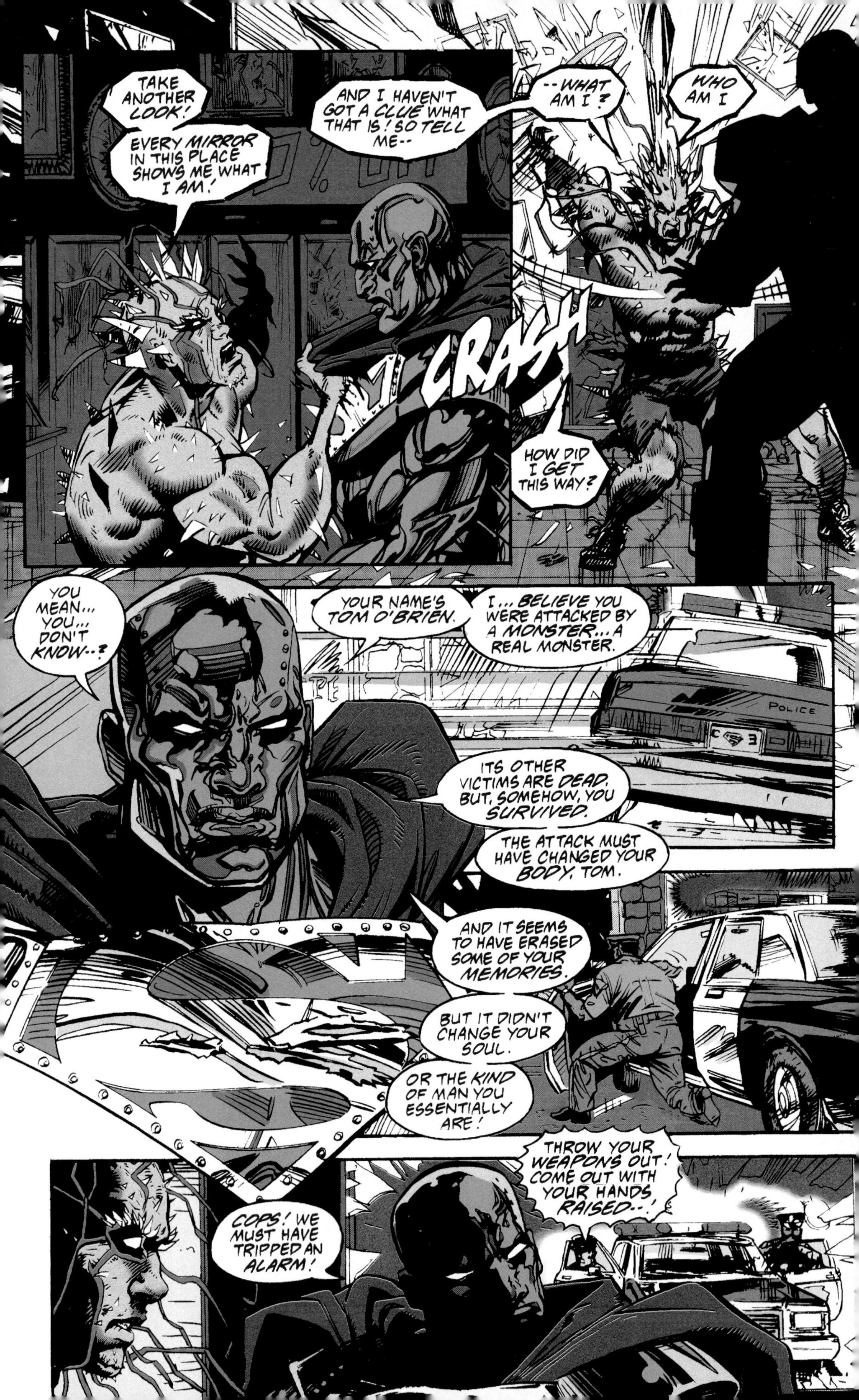
TAKE ANOTHER LOOK!
EVERY MIRROR IN THIS PLACE SHOWS ME WHAT I AM!
AND I HAVEN'T GOT A CLUE WHAT THAT IS! SO TELL ME--
--WHAT AM I?
WHO AM I
CRASH
HOW DID I GET THIS WAY?
YOU MEAN... YOU... DON'T KNOW--?
YOUR NAME'S TOM O'BRIEN.
I... BELIEVE YOU WERE ATTACKED BY A MONSTER... A REAL MONSTER.
POLICE
ITS OTHER VICTIMS ARE DEAD. BUT, SOMEHOW, YOU SURVIVED.
THE ATTACK MUST HAVE CHANGED YOUR BODY, TOM.
AND IT SEEMS TO HAVE ERASED SOME OF YOUR MEMORIES.
BUT IT DIDN'T CHANGE YOUR SOUL.
OR THE KIND OF MAN YOU ESSENTIALLY ARE!
THROW YOUR WEAPONS OUT! COME OUT WITH YOUR HANDS RAISED--!
COPS! WE MUST HAVE TRIPPED AN ALARM!

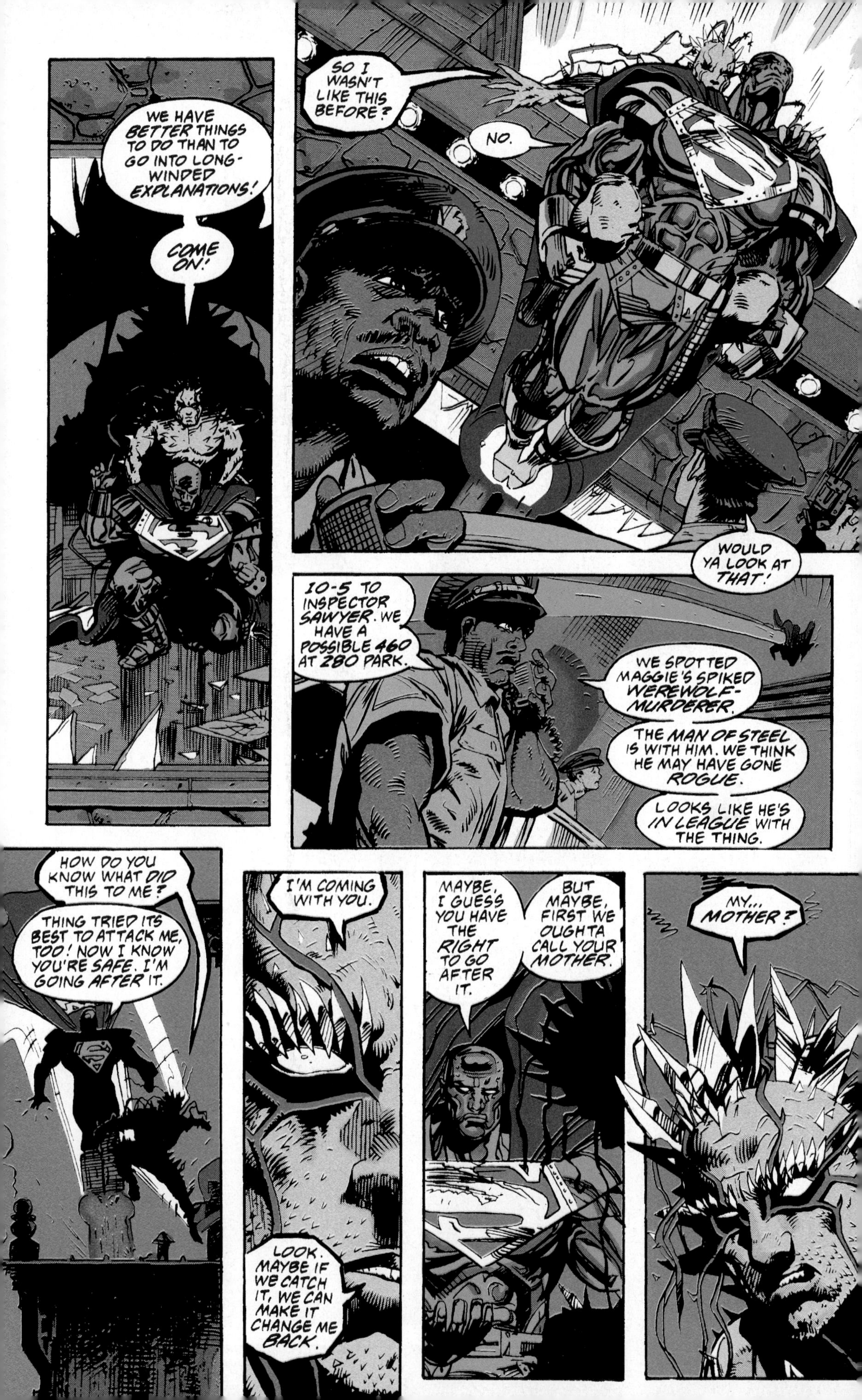

WE HAVE BETTER THINGS TO DO THAN TO GO INTO LONG-WINDED EXPLANATIONS!
COME ON!
SO I WASN'T LIKE THIS BEFORE?
NO.
WOULD YA LOOK AT THAT!
10-5 TO INSPECTOR SAWYER. WE HAVE A POSSIBLE 460 AT 280 PARK.
WE SPOTTED MAGGIE'S SPIKED WEREWOLF-MURDERER.
THE MAN OF STEEL IS WITH HIM. WE THINK HE MAY HAVE GONE ROGUE.
LOOKS LIKE HE'S IN LEAGUE WITH THE THING.
HOW DO YOU KNOW WHAT DID THIS TO ME?
THING TRIED ITS BEST TO ATTACK ME, TOO! NOW I KNOW YOU'RE SAFE. I'M GOING AFTER IT.
I'M COMING WITH YOU.
LOOK. MAYBE IF WE CATCH IT, WE CAN MAKE IT CHANGE ME BACK.
MAYBE, I GUESS YOU HAVE THE RIGHT TO GO AFTER IT.
BUT MAYBE, FIRST WE OUGHTA CALL YOUR MOTHER.
MY... MOTHER?

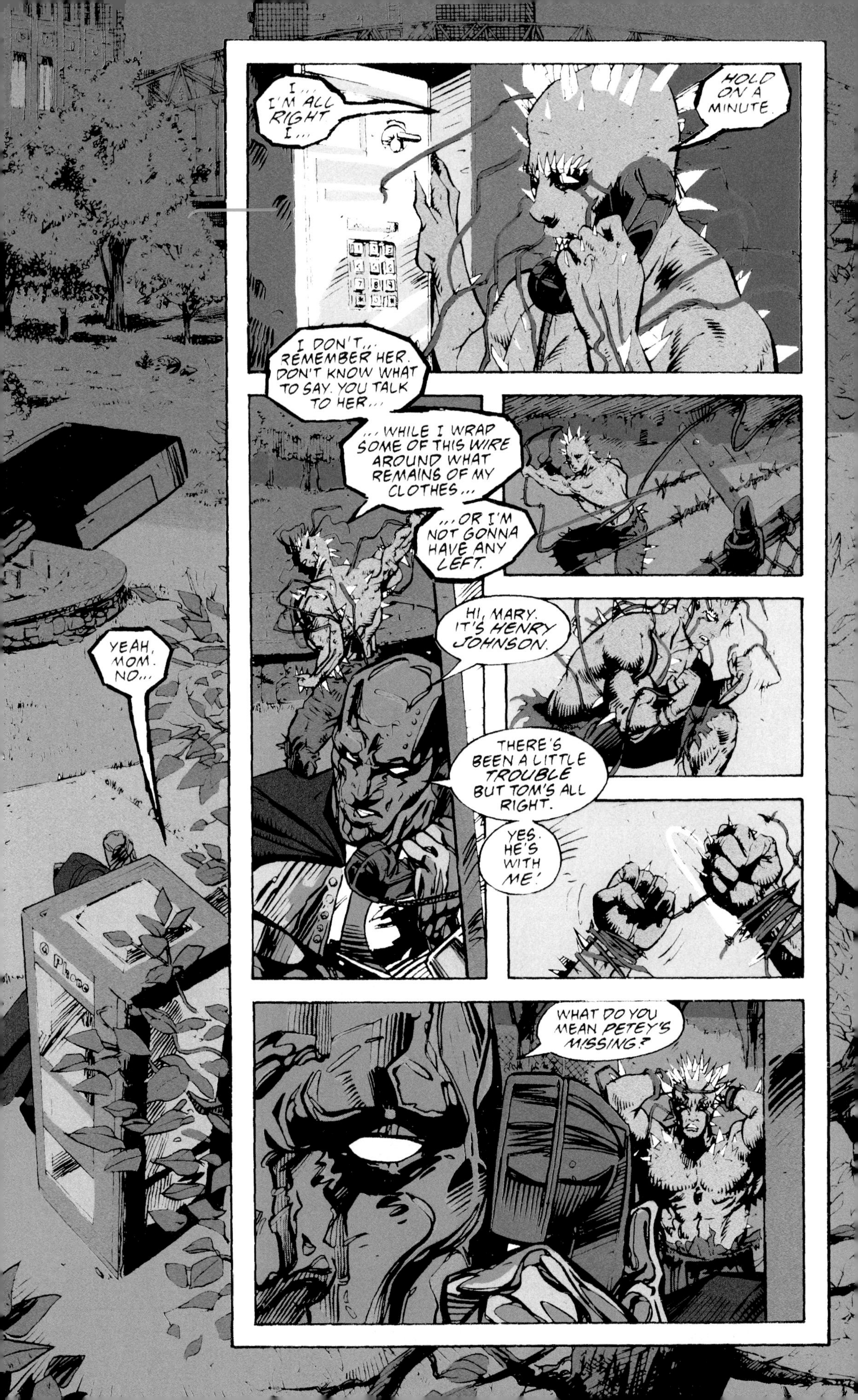
I... I'M ALL RIGHT I...
HOLD ON A MINUTE.
I DON'T... REMEMBER HER. DON'T KNOW WHAT TO SAY. YOU TALK TO HER...
...WHILE I WRAP SOME OF THIS WIRE AROUND WHAT REMAINS OF MY CLOTHES...
...OR I'M NOT GONNA HAVE ANY LEFT.
HI, MARY. IT'S HENRY JOHNSON.
THERE'S BEEN A LITTLE TROUBLE BUT TOM'S ALL RIGHT.
YES. HE'S WITH ME!
YEAH, MOM. NO...
WHAT DO YOU MEAN PETEY'S MISSING?

WHO'S PETEY?

YOUR LITTLE BROTHER, TWELVE OR SO, SPITTING *IMAGE* OF YOU...

I DON'T *REMEMBER* HIM. I DON'T EVEN REMEMBER MY OWN *MOTHER*.

...AT LEAST THE WAY YOU *USED* TO BE.

YOUR MOM SAID PETEY WAS *WORRIED* WHEN YOU DIDN'T COME HOME.

SHE THINKS HE WENT *LOOKING* FOR YOU.

BUT... WHERE WOULD HE GO? WHERE WOULD HE THINK *I'D* GO?

MAYBE THE *GYM* WHERE YOU WORK.

THAT KID MUST BE *CRAZY!* WE'VE GOTTA FIND HIM, *FAST--*

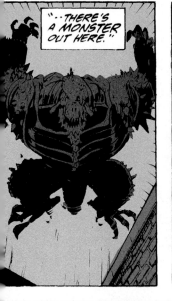

"--THERE'S A *MONSTER* OUT HERE."

GYM'S THE ONLY PLACE I HAVEN'T CHECKED. AND THE *DOOR'S* LOCKED.

WHAT IF TOM'S IN THERE AND HE *NEEDS* ME?

I COULD TAKE THIS *ROCK!*

OR MAYBE THAT OLD *BAR* BREAK THE WINDOW...

KEEP OUT

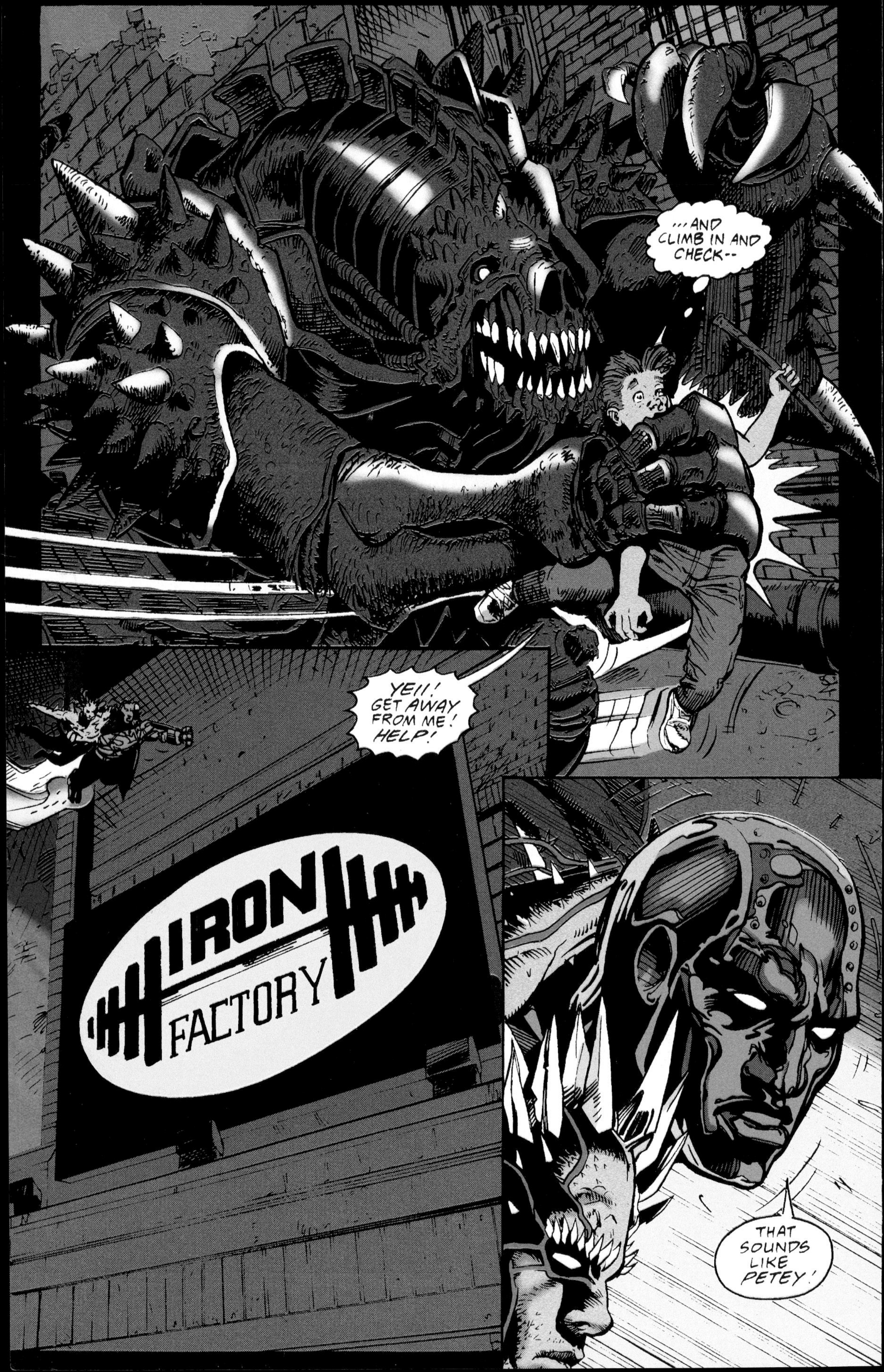
...AND CLIMB IN AND CHECK--
YEII! GET AWAY FROM ME! HELP!
IRON FACTORY
THAT SOUNDS LIKE PETEY!

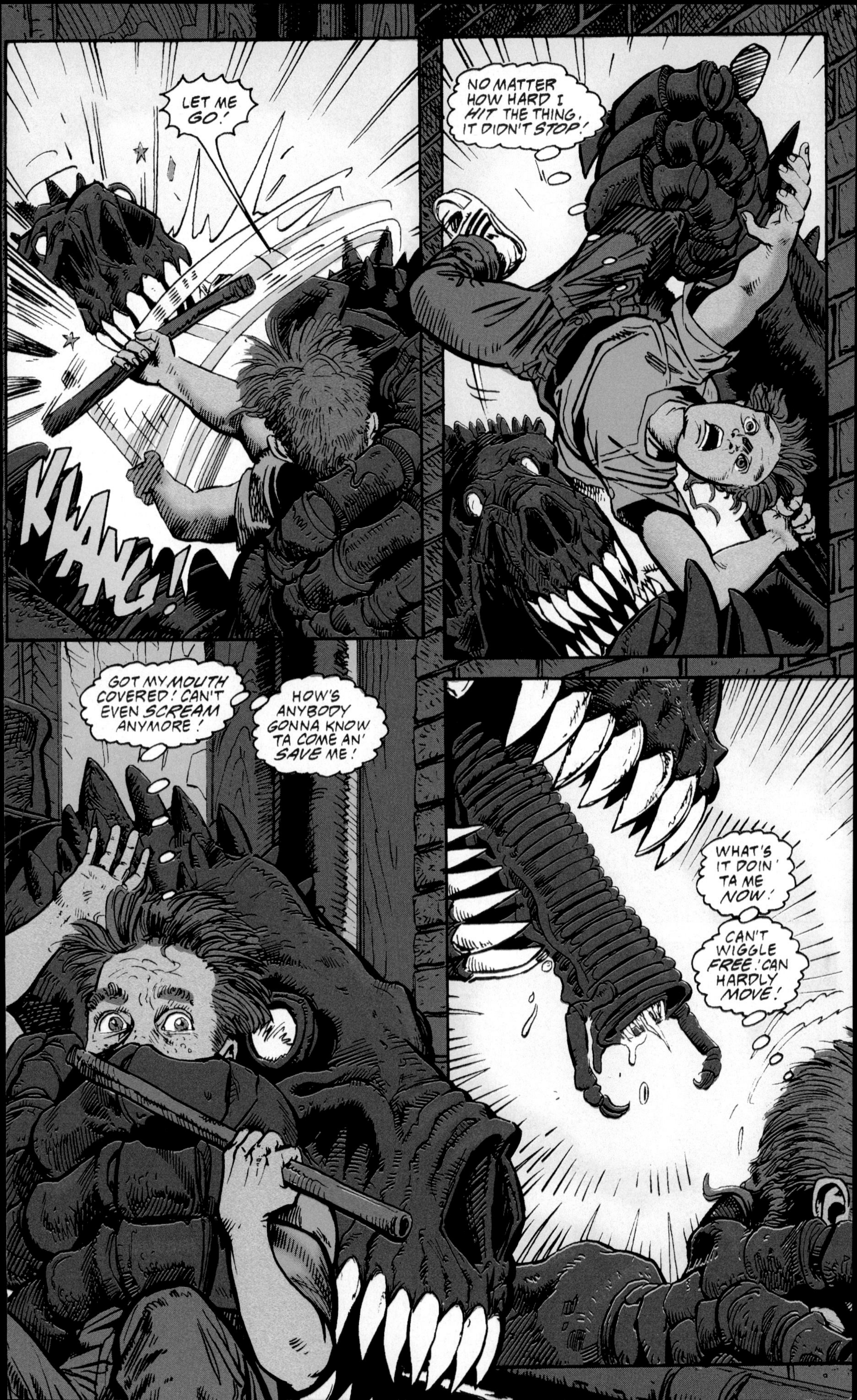
LET ME GO!
KHANG!
NO MATTER HOW HARD I HIT THE THING, IT DIDN'T STOP!
GOT MY MOUTH COVERED! CAN'T EVEN SCREAM ANYMORE!
HOW'S ANYBODY GONNA KNOW TA COME AN' SAVE ME!
WHAT'S IT DOIN' TA ME NOW!
CAN'T WIGGLE FREE! CAN HARDLY MOVE!

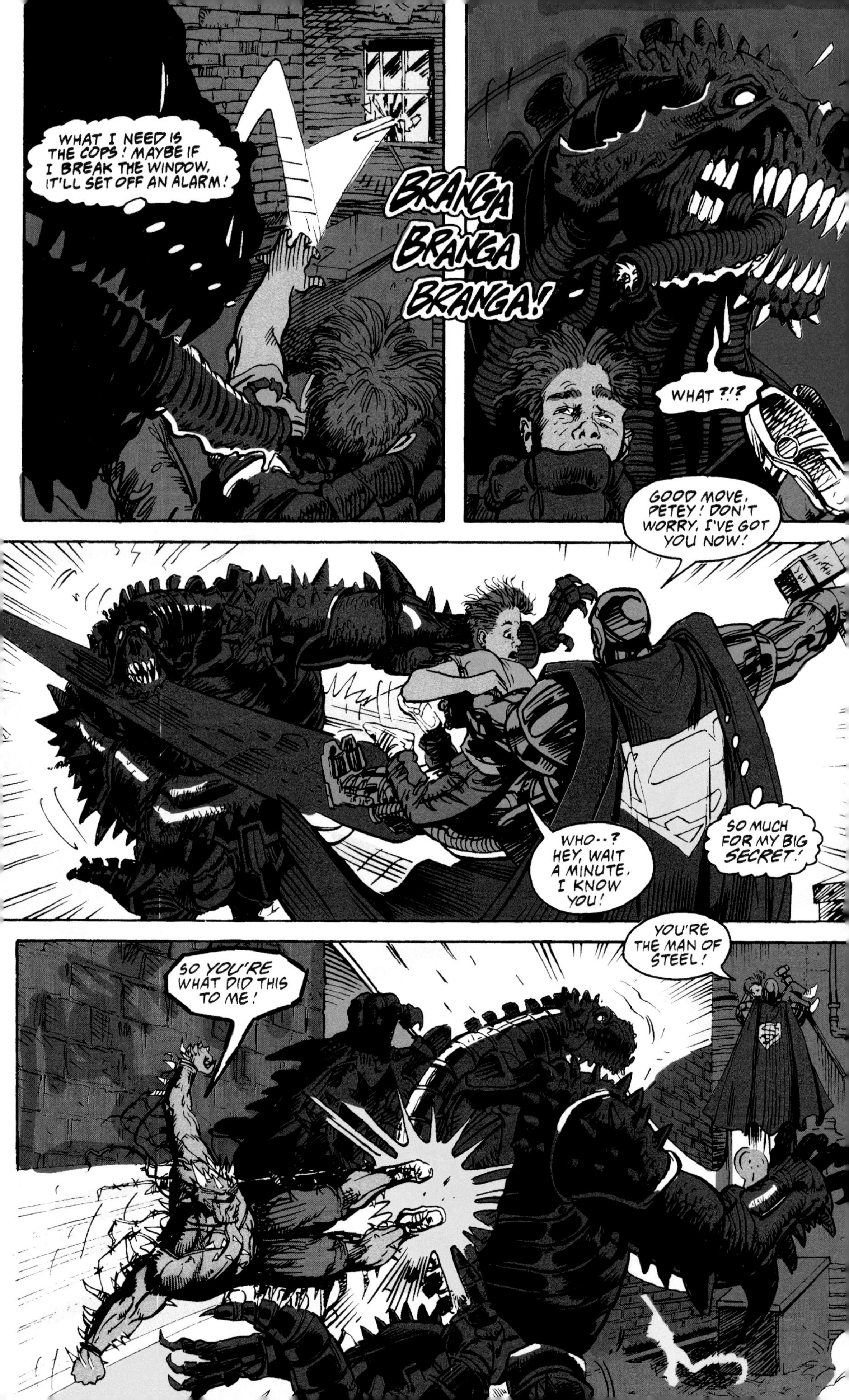
WHAT I NEED IS THE COPS! MAYBE IF I BREAK THE WINDOW, IT'LL SET OFF AN ALARM!
BRANGA BRANGA BRANGA!
WHAT?!?
GOOD MOVE, PETEY! DON'T WORRY, I'VE GOT YOU NOW!
WHO..? HEY, WAIT A MINUTE, I KNOW YOU!
SO MUCH FOR MY BIG SECRET!
YOU'RE THE MAN OF STEEL!
SO YOU'RE WHAT DID THIS TO ME!

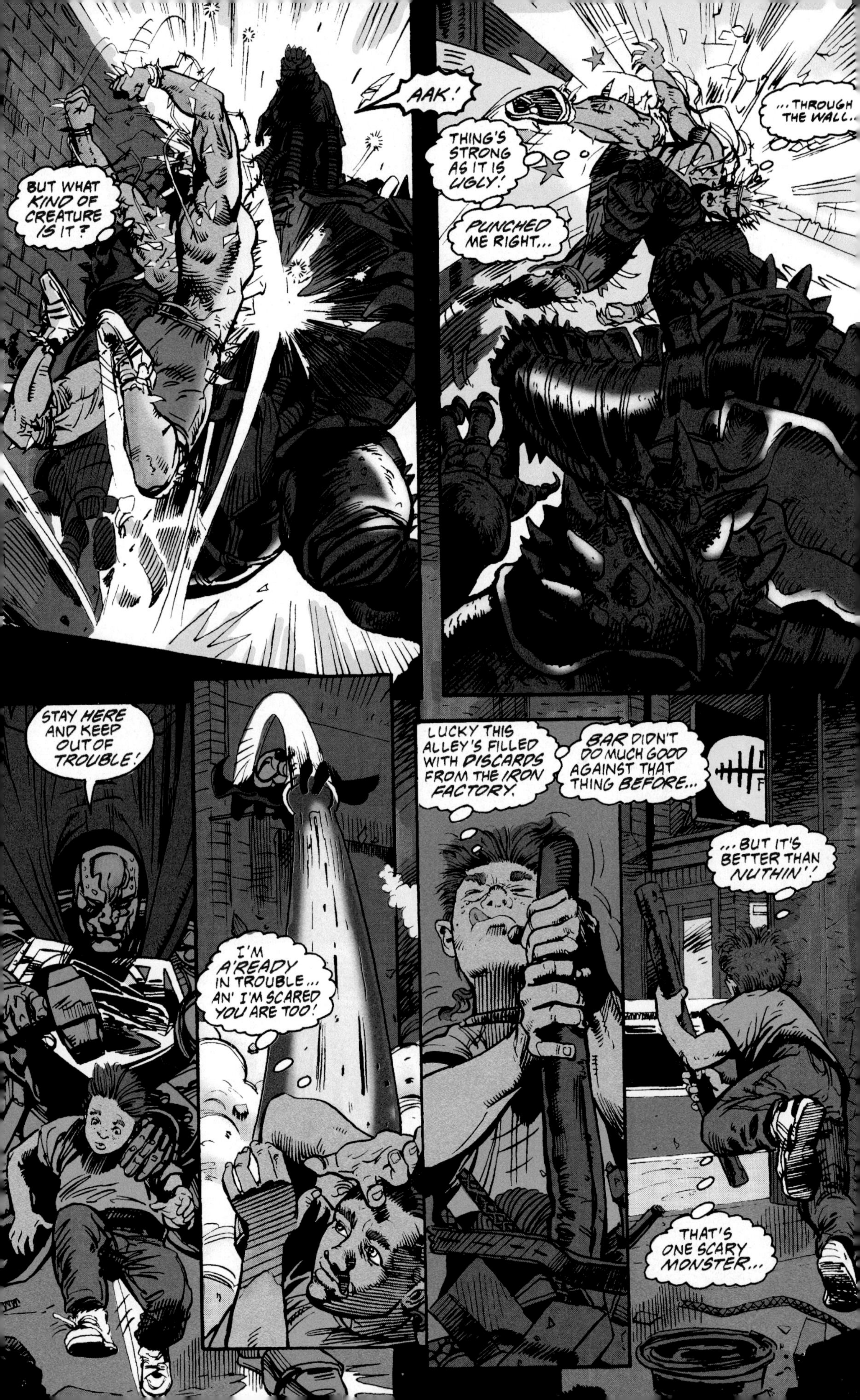
BUT WHAT KIND OF CREATURE IS IT?
AAK!
THING'S STRONG AS IT IS UGLY!
PUNCHED ME RIGHT...
...THROUGH THE WALL...
STAY HERE AND KEEP OUT OF TROUBLE!
I'M A'READY IN TROUBLE... AN' I'M SCARED YOU ARE TOO!
LUCKY THIS ALLEY'S FILLED WITH DISCARDS FROM THE IRON FACTORY.
BAR DIDN'T DO MUCH GOOD AGAINST THAT THING BEFORE...
...BUT IT'S BETTER THAN NUTHIN'!
THAT'S ONE SCARY MONSTER...

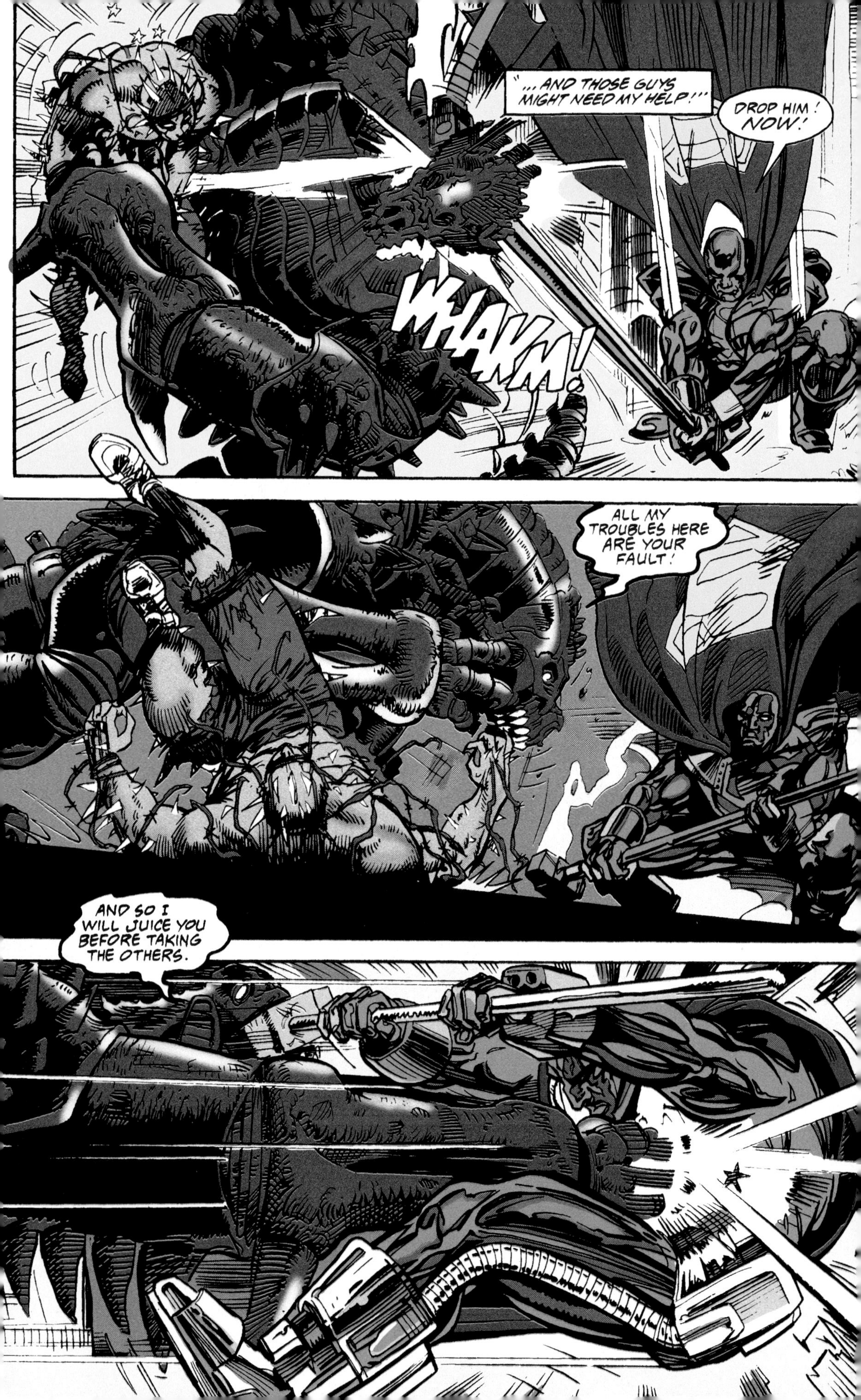
"...AND THOSE GUYS MIGHT NEED MY HELP!"
DROP HIM! NOW!
WHAKM!
ALL MY TROUBLES HERE ARE YOUR FAULT!
AND SO I WILL JUICE YOU BEFORE TAKING THE OTHERS.

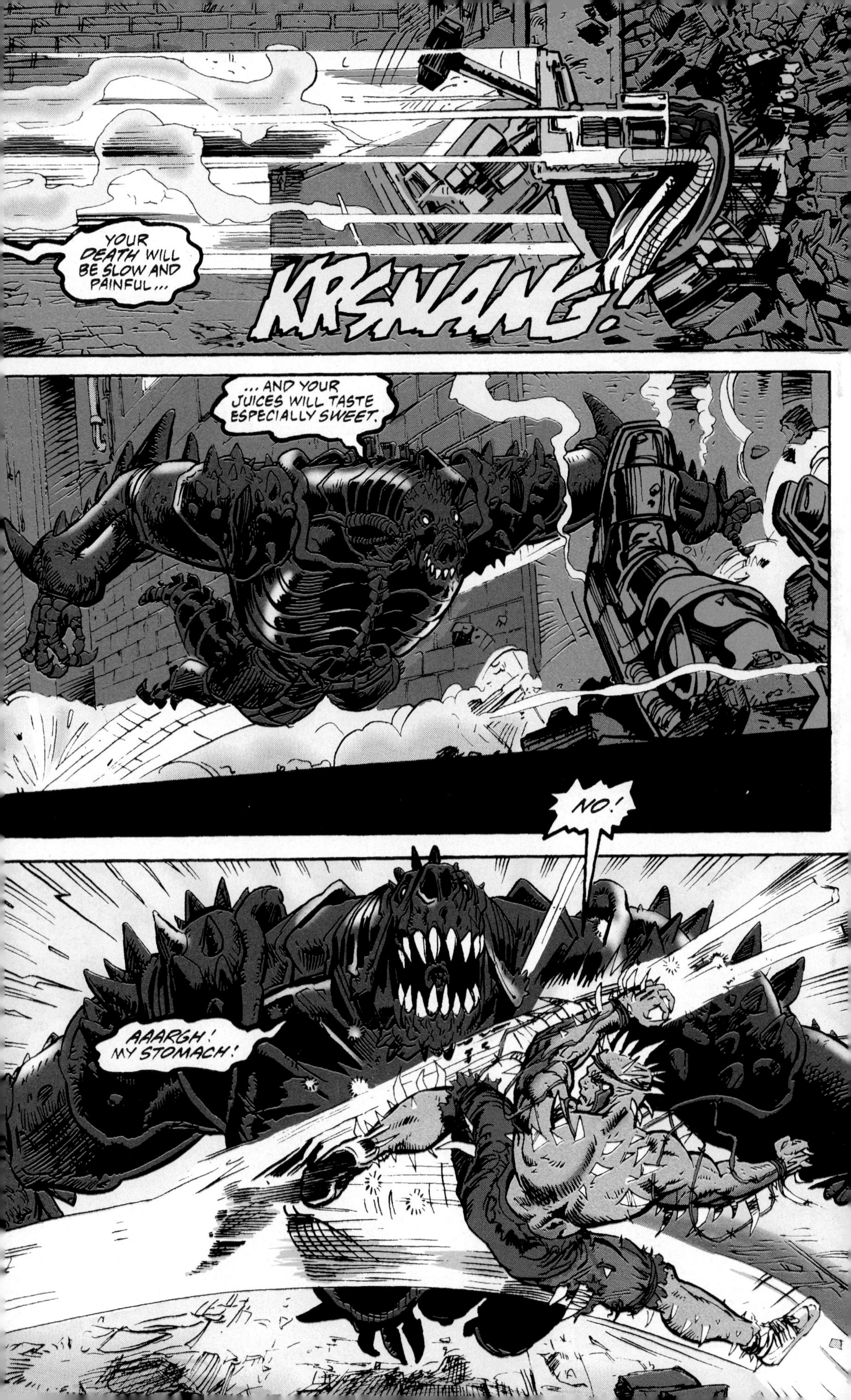
YOUR DEATH WILL BE SLOW AND PAINFUL...
KRSNANG!
...AND YOUR JUICES WILL TASTE ESPECIALLY SWEET.
NO!
AAARGH! MY STOMACH!

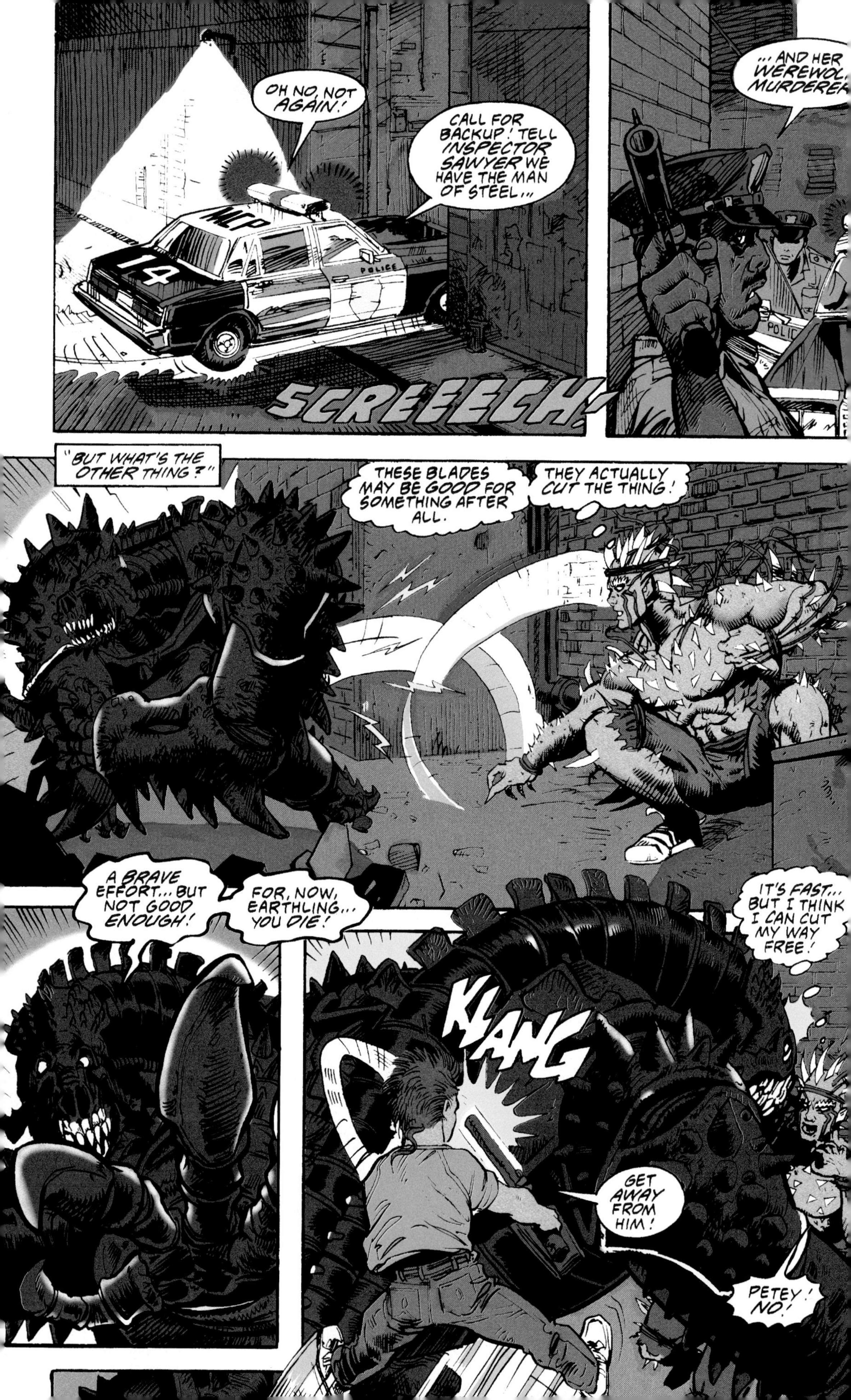
OH NO, NOT AGAIN!
CALL FOR BACKUP! TELL INSPECTOR SAWYER WE HAVE THE MAN OF STEEL...
SCREEEECH!
...AND HER WEREWOL MURDERER
"BUT WHAT'S THE OTHER THING?"
THESE BLADES MAY BE GOOD FOR SOMETHING AFTER ALL.
THEY ACTUALLY CUT THE THING!
A BRAVE EFFORT... BUT NOT GOOD ENOUGH!
FOR, NOW, EARTHLING... YOU DIE!
IT'S FAST... BUT I THINK I CAN CUT MY WAY FREE!
KLANG
GET AWAY FROM HIM!
PETEY! NO!

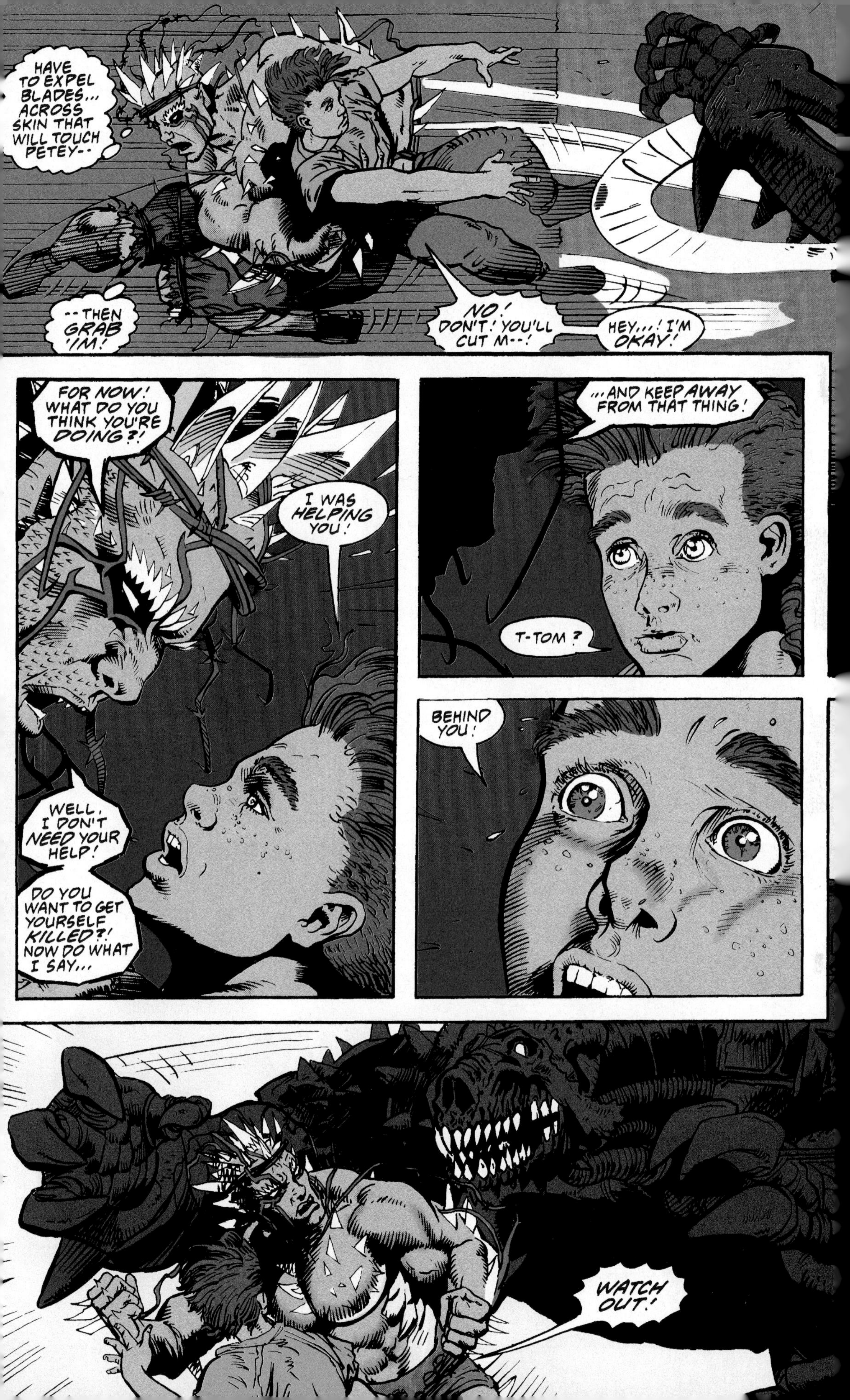
HAVE TO EXPEL BLADES... ACROSS SKIN THAT WILL TOUCH PETEY--
--THEN GRAB 'IM!
NO! DON'T! YOU'LL CUT M--!
HEY...! I'M OKAY!
FOR NOW! WHAT DO YOU THINK YOU'RE DOING?!
I WAS HELPING YOU!
WELL, I DON'T NEED YOUR HELP!
DO YOU WANT TO GET YOURSELF KILLED?! NOW DO WHAT I SAY...
...AND KEEP AWAY FROM THAT THING!
T-TOM?
BEHIND YOU!
WATCH OUT!

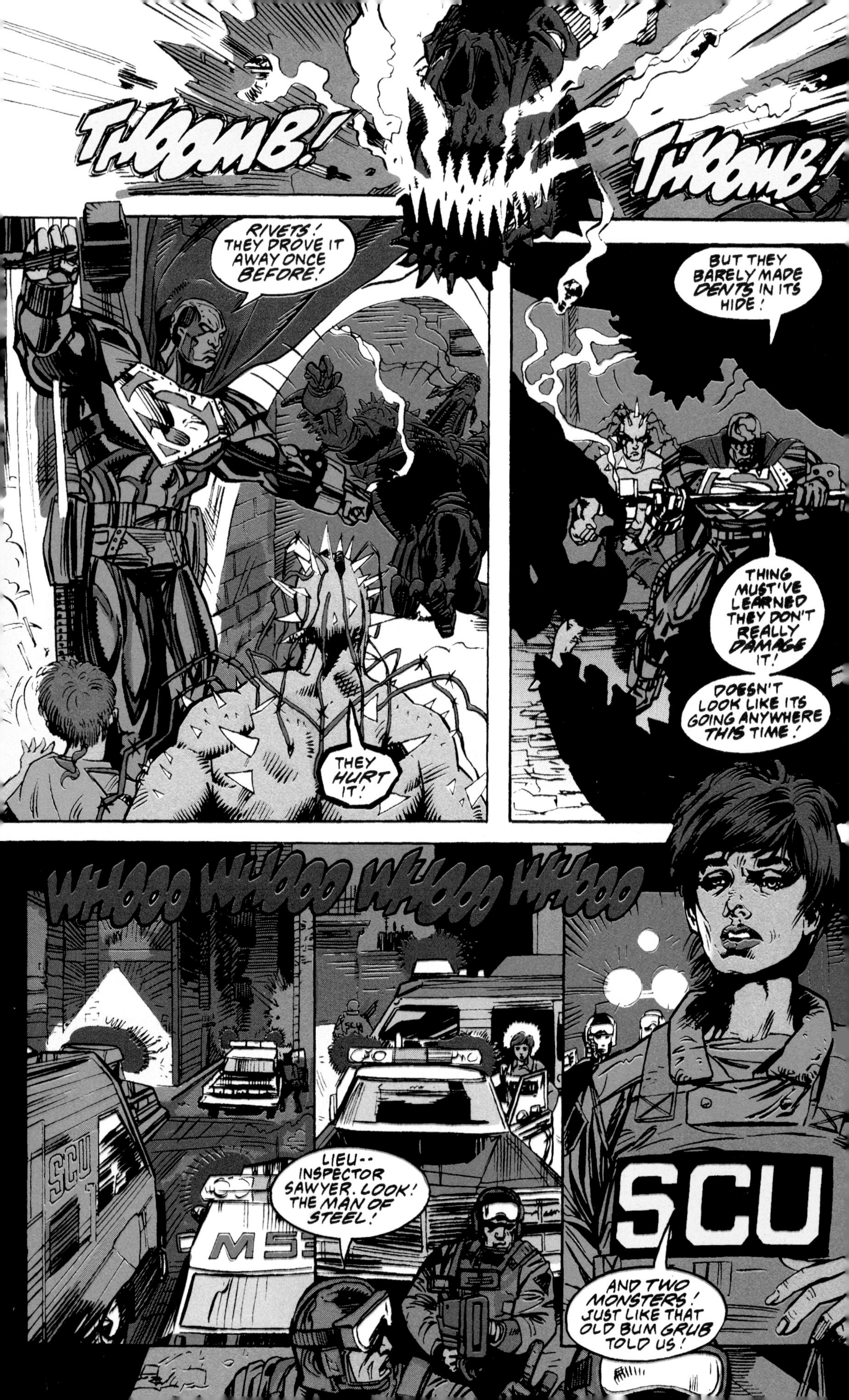
THOOMB!
THOOMB!
RIVETS! THEY DROVE IT AWAY ONCE BEFORE!
THEY HURT IT!
BUT THEY BARELY MADE DENTS IN ITS HIDE!
THING MUST'VE LEARNED THEY DON'T REALLY DAMAGE IT!
DOESN'T LOOK LIKE ITS GOING ANYWHERE THIS TIME!
WHOOO WHOOO WHOOO WHOOO
LIEU-- INSPECTOR SAWYER. LOOK! THE MAN OF STEEL!
AND TWO MONSTERS! JUST LIKE THAT OLD BUM GRUB TOLD US!

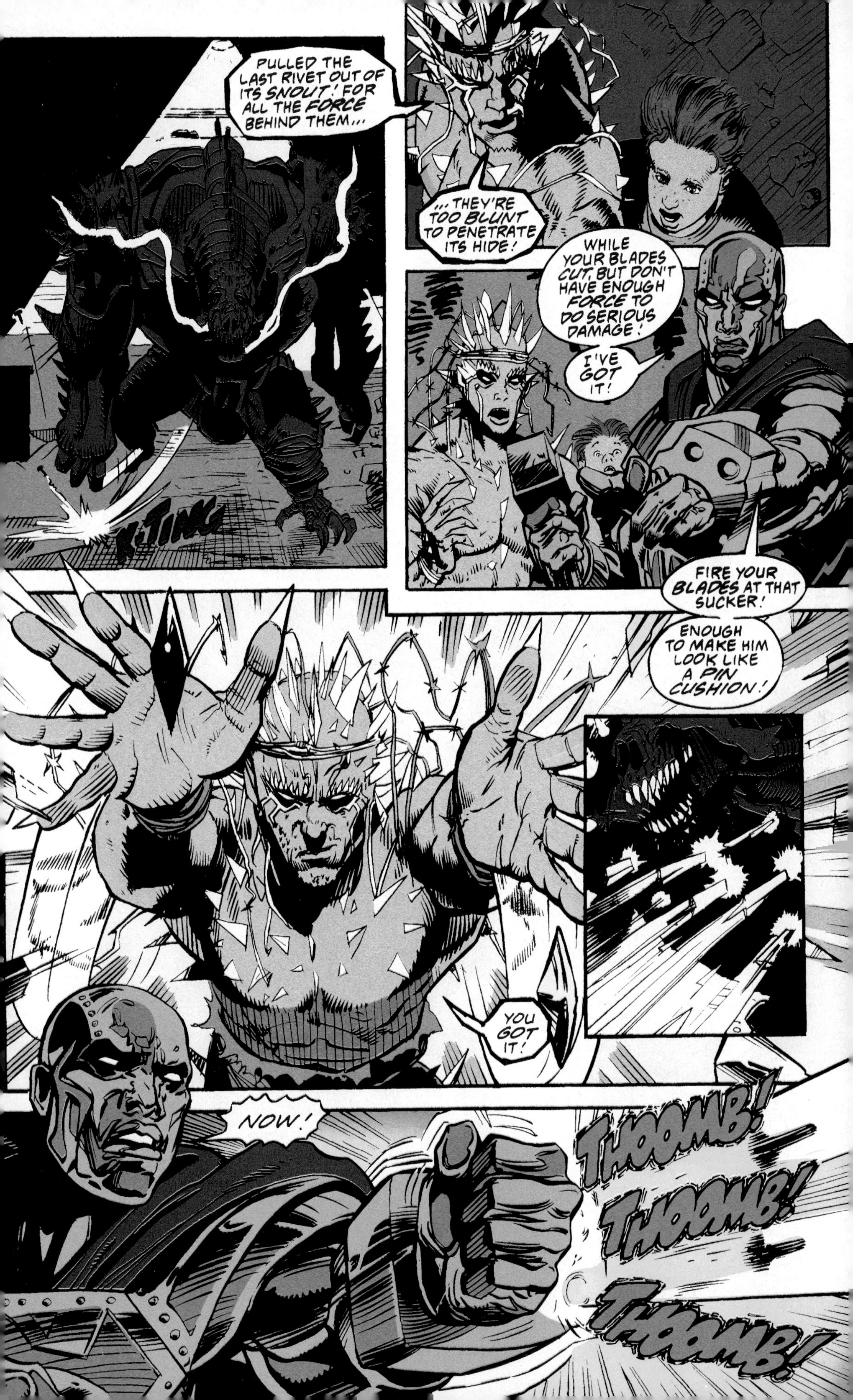
PULLED THE LAST RIVET OUT OF ITS SNOUT! FOR ALL THE FORCE BEHIND THEM...
...THEY'RE TOO BLUNT TO PENETRATE ITS HIDE!
K-TING
WHILE YOUR BLADES CUT, BUT DON'T HAVE ENOUGH FORCE TO DO SERIOUS DAMAGE!
I'VE GOT IT!
FIRE YOUR BLADES AT THAT SUCKER!
ENOUGH TO MAKE HIM LOOK LIKE A PIN CUSHION!
YOU GOT IT!
NOW!
THOOMB!
THOOMB!
THOOMB!

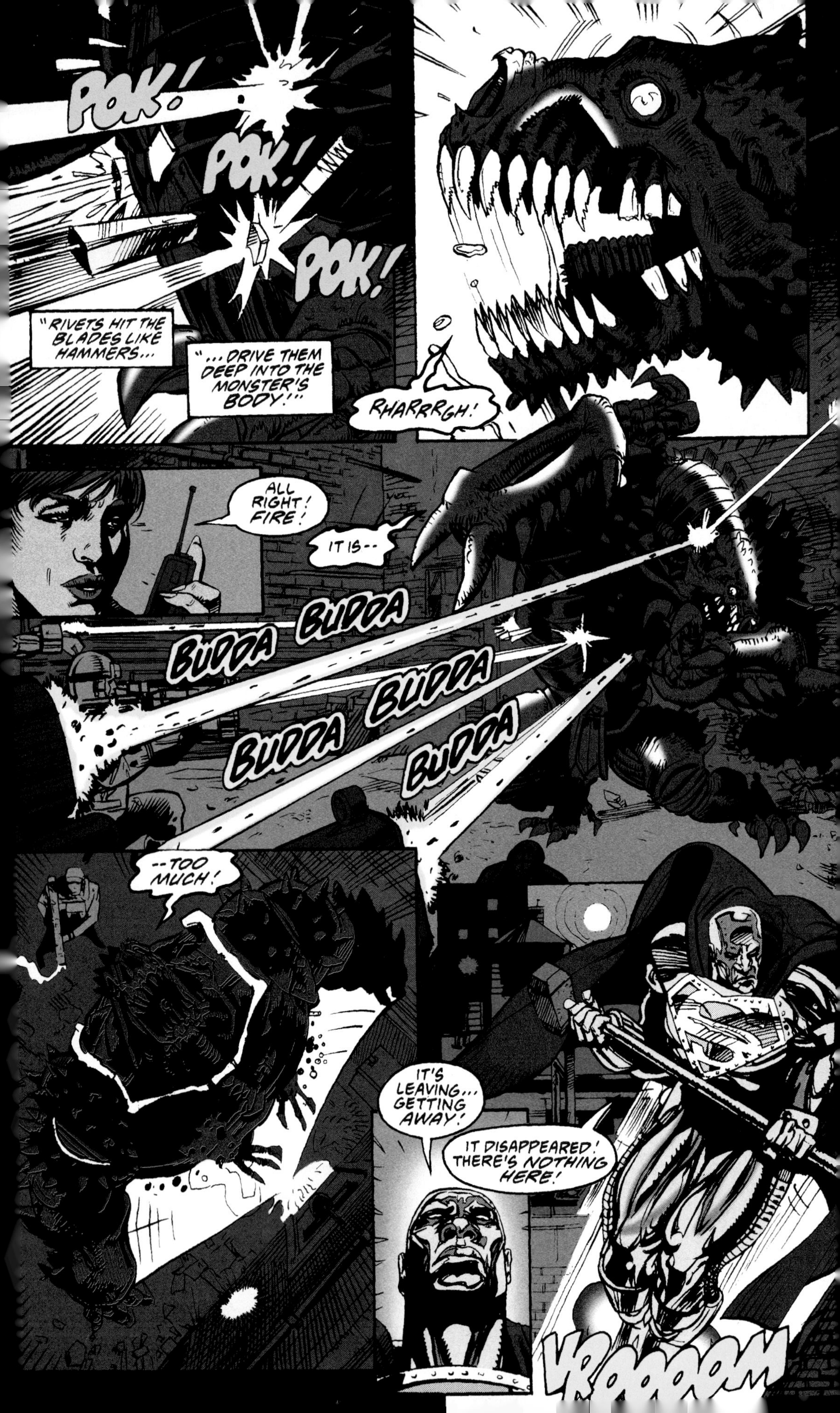
POK!
POK!
POK!
"RIVETS HIT THE BLADES LIKE HAMMERS...
"...DRIVE THEM DEEP INTO THE MONSTER'S BODY!"
RHARRRGH!
ALL RIGHT! FIRE!
IT IS--
BUDDA BUDDA
BUDDA BUDDA
BUDDA
--TOO MUCH!
IT'S LEAVING... GETTING AWAY!
IT DISAPPEARED! THERE'S NOTHING HERE!
VROOOOOM

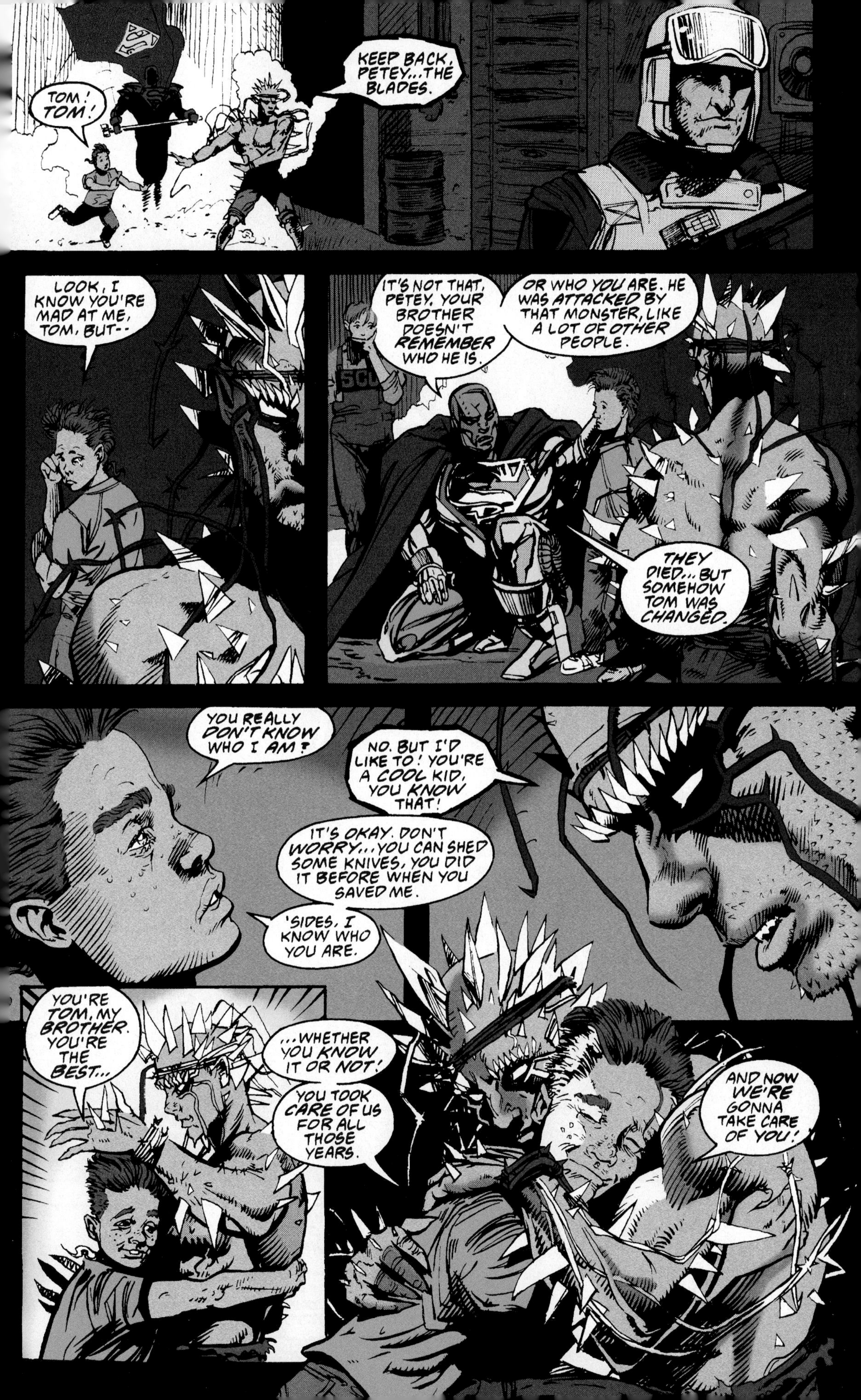
TOM! TOM!
KEEP BACK, PETEY... THE BLADES.
LOOK, I KNOW YOU'RE MAD AT ME, TOM, BUT--
IT'S NOT THAT, PETEY. YOUR BROTHER DOESN'T REMEMBER WHO HE IS.
OR WHO YOU ARE. HE WAS ATTACKED BY THAT MONSTER, LIKE A LOT OF OTHER PEOPLE.
THEY DIED... BUT SOMEHOW TOM WAS CHANGED.
YOU REALLY DON'T KNOW WHO I AM?
NO. BUT I'D LIKE TO! YOU'RE A COOL KID, YOU KNOW THAT!
IT'S OKAY. DON'T WORRY... YOU CAN SHED SOME KNIVES, YOU DID IT BEFORE WHEN YOU SAVED ME.
'SIDES, I KNOW WHO YOU ARE.
YOU'RE TOM, MY BROTHER. YOU'RE THE BEST...
...WHETHER YOU KNOW IT OR NOT!
YOU TOOK CARE OF US FOR ALL THOSE YEARS.
AND NOW WE'RE GONNA TAKE CARE OF YOU!

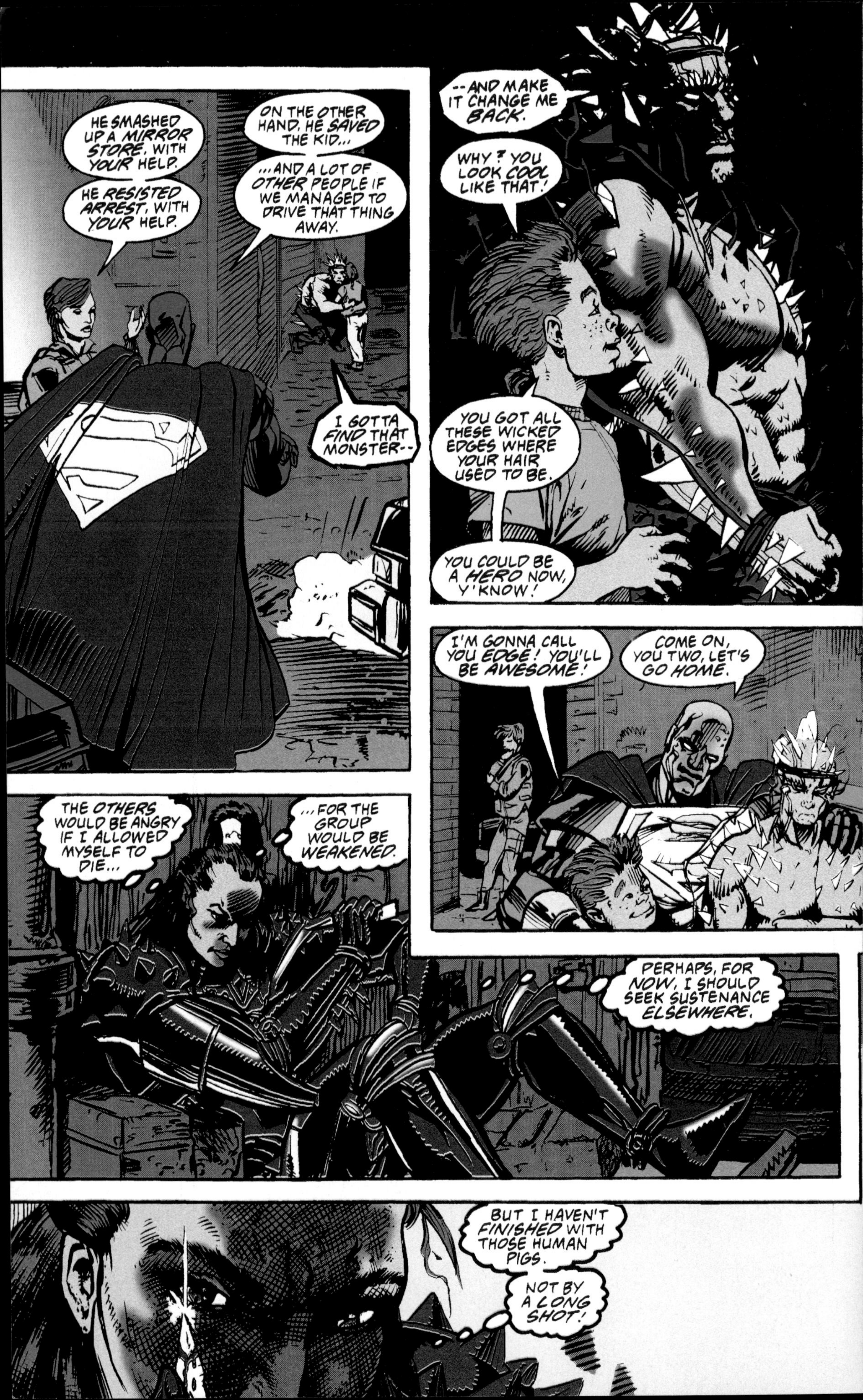
HE SMASHED UP A MIRROR STORE, WITH YOUR HELP.
HE RESISTED ARREST, WITH YOUR HELP.
ON THE OTHER HAND, HE SAVED THE KID...
...AND A LOT OF OTHER PEOPLE IF WE MANAGED TO DRIVE THAT THING AWAY.
I GOTTA FIND THAT MONSTER--
--AND MAKE IT CHANGE ME BACK.
WHY? YOU LOOK COOL LIKE THAT!
YOU GOT ALL THESE WICKED EDGES WHERE YOUR HAIR USED TO BE.
YOU COULD BE A HERO NOW, Y'KNOW!
I'M GONNA CALL YOU EDGE! YOU'LL BE AWESOME!
COME ON, YOU TWO, LET'S GO HOME.
THE OTHERS WOULD BE ANGRY IF I ALLOWED MYSELF TO DIE...
...FOR THE GROUP WOULD BE WEAKENED.
PERHAPS, FOR NOW, I SHOULD SEEK SUSTENANCE ELSEWHERE.
BUT I HAVEN'T FINISHED WITH THOSE HUMAN PIGS.
NOT BY A LONG SHOT!

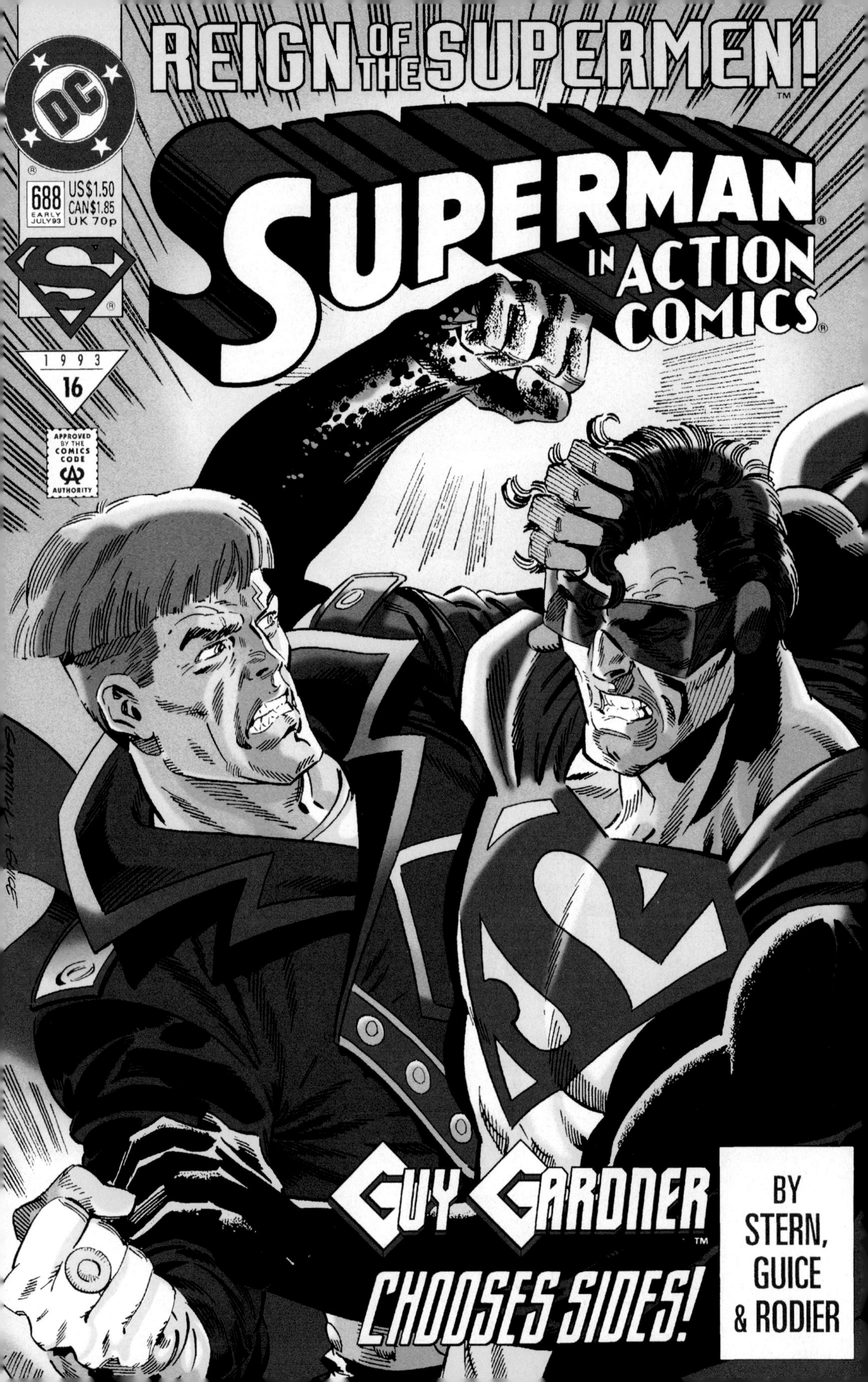

REIGN OF THE SUPERMEN!™
DC
688 EARLY JULY 93
US$1.50 CAN$1.85 UK 70p
1993 16
APPROVED BY THE COMICS CODE CA AUTHORITY
SUPERMAN® IN ACTION COMICS®
GUY GARDNER™
CHOOSES SIDES!
BY STERN, GUICE & RODIER

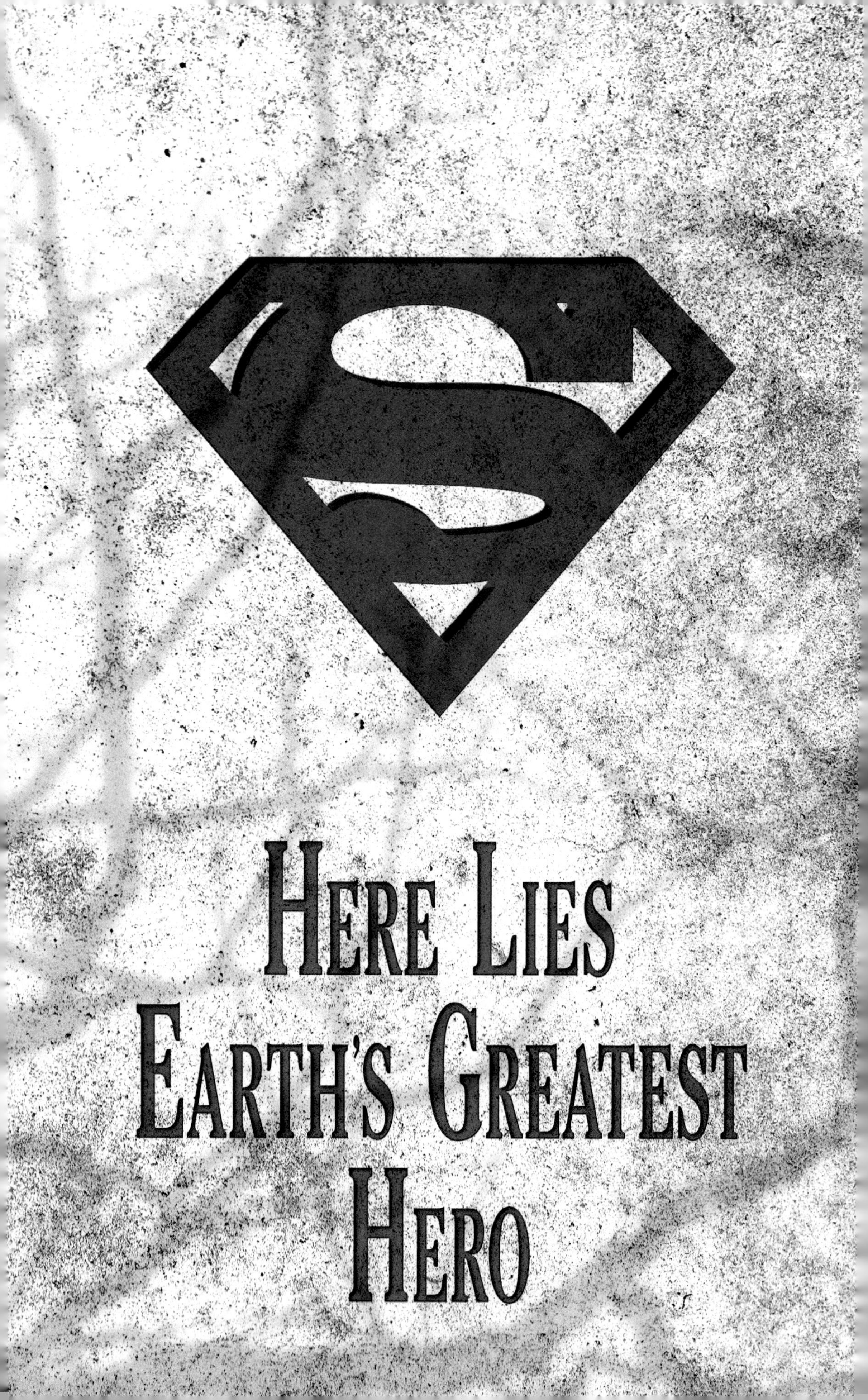
HERE LIES
EARTH'S GREATEST
HERO

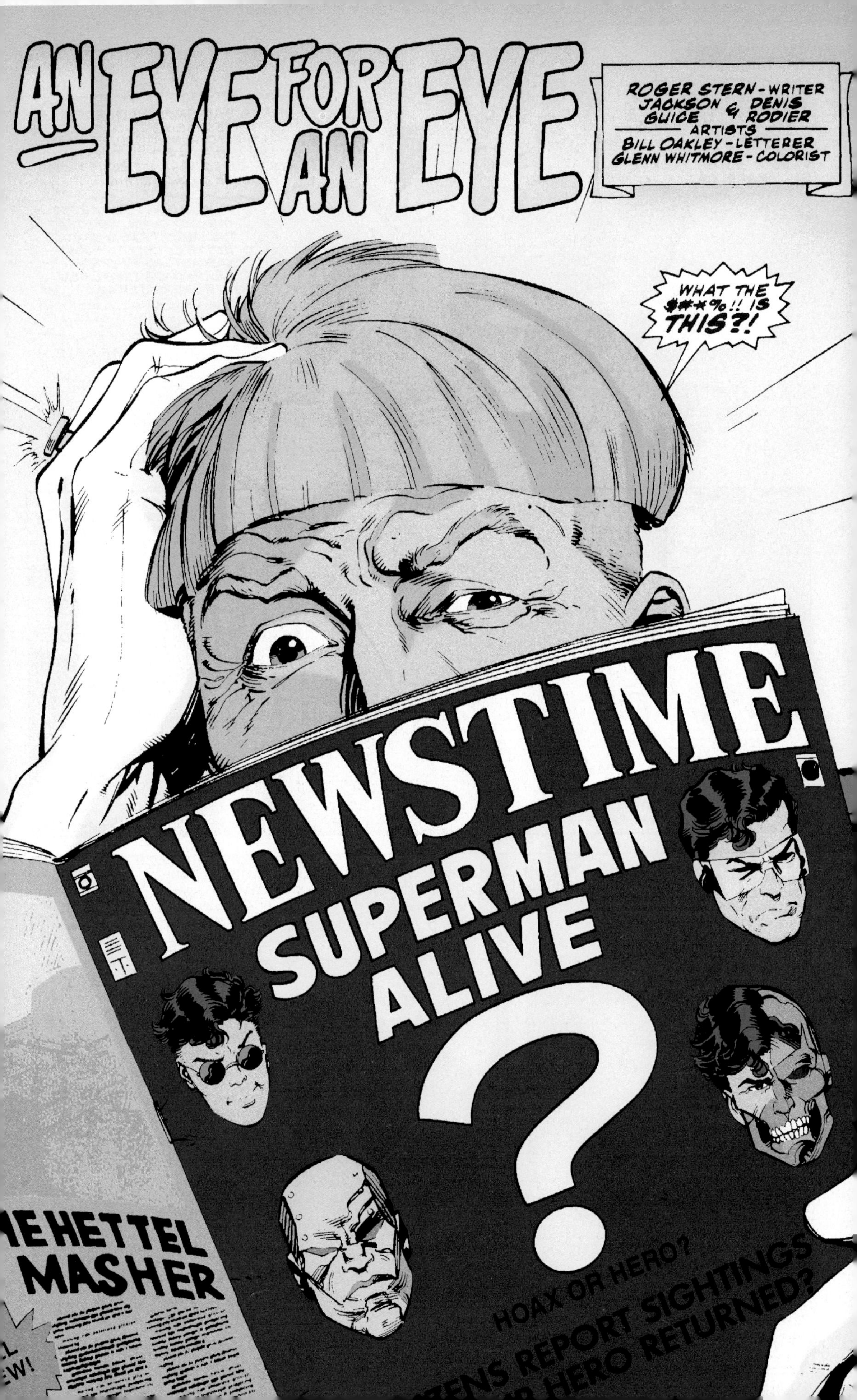
AN EYE FOR AN EYE
ROGER STERN - WRITER
JACKSON GUICE & DENIS RODIER
ARTISTS
BILL OAKLEY - LETTERER
GLENN WHITMORE - COLORIST
WHAT THE $#*%!! IS THIS?!
NEWSTIME
SUPERMAN ALIVE ?
HOAX OR HERO?
REPORT SIGHTINGS
HERO RETURNED?
MASHER

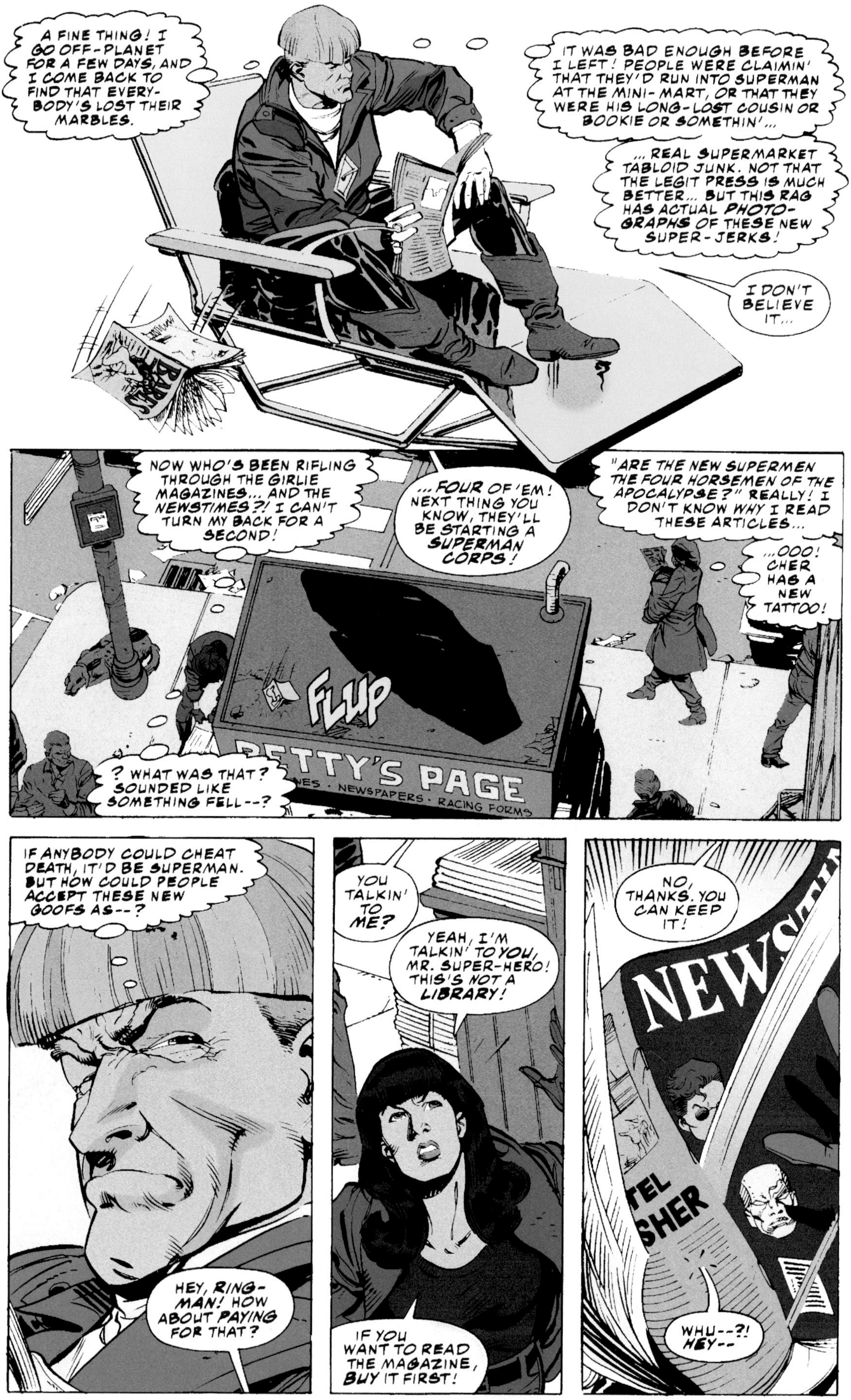

A FINE THING! I GO OFF-PLANET FOR A FEW DAYS, AND I COME BACK TO FIND THAT EVERYBODY'S LOST THEIR MARBLES.
IT WAS BAD ENOUGH BEFORE I LEFT! PEOPLE WERE CLAIMIN' THAT THEY'D RUN INTO SUPERMAN AT THE MINI-MART, OR THAT THEY WERE HIS LONG-LOST COUSIN OR BOOKIE OR SOMETHIN'...
... REAL SUPERMARKET TABLOID JUNK. NOT THAT THE LEGIT PRESS IS MUCH BETTER... BUT THIS RAG HAS ACTUAL PHOTOGRAPHS OF THESE NEW SUPER-JERKS!
I DON'T BELIEVE IT...
NOW WHO'S BEEN RIFLING THROUGH THE GIRLIE MAGAZINES... AND THE NEWSTIMES?! I CAN'T TURN MY BACK FOR A SECOND!
...FOUR OF 'EM! NEXT THING YOU KNOW, THEY'LL BE STARTING A SUPERMAN CORPS!
"ARE THE NEW SUPERMEN THE FOUR HORSEMEN OF THE APOCALYPSE?" REALLY! I DON'T KNOW WHY I READ THESE ARTICLES...
...OOO! CHER HAS A NEW TATTOO!
FLUP
BETTY'S PAGE
NEWSPAPERS · RACING FORMS
? WHAT WAS THAT? SOUNDED LIKE SOMETHING FELL--?
IF ANYBODY COULD CHEAT DEATH, IT'D BE SUPERMAN. BUT HOW COULD PEOPLE ACCEPT THESE NEW GOOFS AS--?
HEY, RING-MAN! HOW ABOUT PAYING FOR THAT?
YOU TALKIN' TO ME?
YEAH, I'M TALKIN' TO YOU, MR. SUPER-HERO! THIS'S NOT A LIBRARY!
IF YOU WANT TO READ THE MAGAZINE, BUY IT FIRST!
NO, THANKS. YOU CAN KEEP IT!
NEWS
WHU--?! HEY--

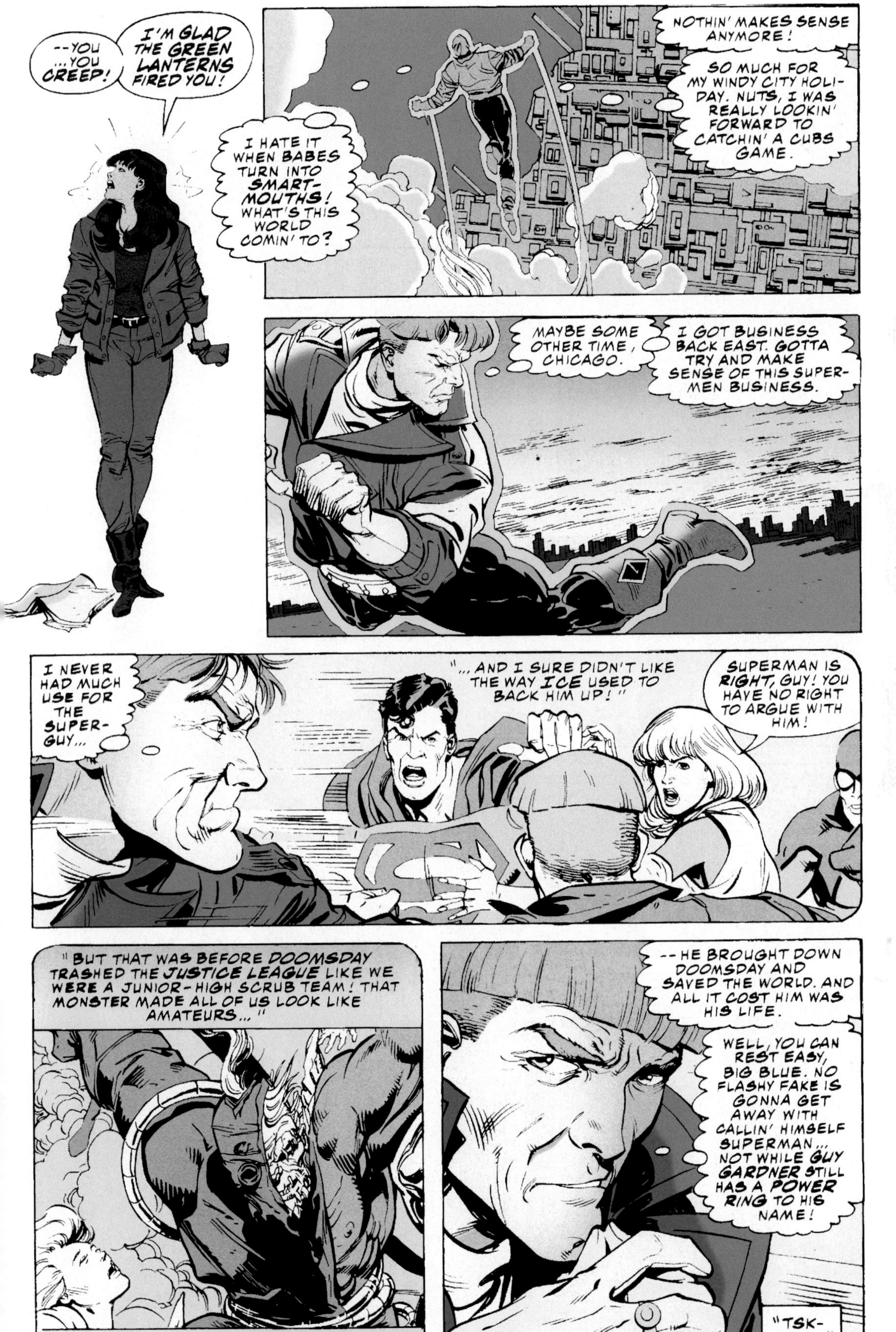
--YOU ...YOU CREEP!
I'M GLAD THE GREEN LANTERNS FIRED YOU!
I HATE IT WHEN BABES TURN INTO SMART-MOUTHS! WHAT'S THIS WORLD COMIN' TO?
NOTHIN' MAKES SENSE ANYMORE!
SO MUCH FOR MY WINDY CITY HOLIDAY. NUTS, I WAS REALLY LOOKIN' FORWARD TO CATCHIN' A CUBS GAME.
MAYBE SOME OTHER TIME, CHICAGO.
I GOT BUSINESS BACK EAST. GOTTA TRY AND MAKE SENSE OF THIS SUPERMEN BUSINESS.
I NEVER HAD MUCH USE FOR THE SUPER-GUY...
"...AND I SURE DIDN'T LIKE THE WAY ICE USED TO BACK HIM UP!"
SUPERMAN IS RIGHT, GUY! YOU HAVE NO RIGHT TO ARGUE WITH HIM!
"BUT THAT WAS BEFORE DOOMSDAY TRASHED THE JUSTICE LEAGUE LIKE WE WERE A JUNIOR-HIGH SCRUB TEAM! THAT MONSTER MADE ALL OF US LOOK LIKE AMATEURS..."
"...ALL OF US, EXCEPT SUPERMAN! HE DID WHAT NOBODY ELSE COULD DO--"
--HE BROUGHT DOWN DOOMSDAY AND SAVED THE WORLD. AND ALL IT COST HIM WAS HIS LIFE.
WELL, YOU CAN REST EASY, BIG BLUE. NO FLASHY FAKE IS GONNA GET AWAY WITH CALLIN' HIMSELF SUPERMAN... NOT WHILE GUY GARDNER STILL HAS A POWER RING TO HIS NAME!
"TSK-TSK..."

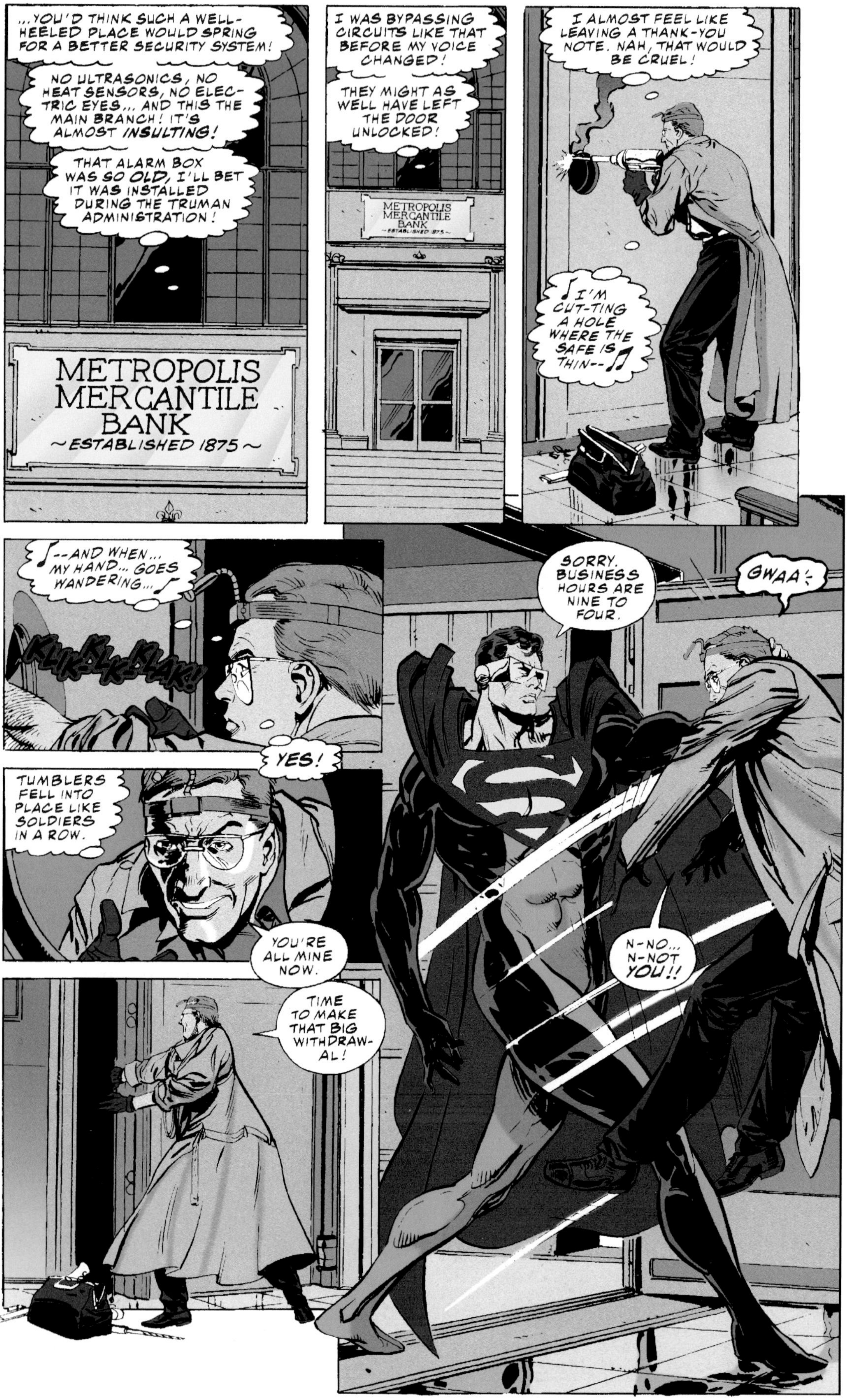
...YOU'D THINK SUCH A WELL-HEELED PLACE WOULD SPRING FOR A BETTER SECURITY SYSTEM!
NO ULTRASONICS, NO HEAT SENSORS, NO ELECTRIC EYES... AND THIS THE MAIN BRANCH! IT'S ALMOST INSULTING!
THAT ALARM BOX WAS SO OLD, I'LL BET IT WAS INSTALLED DURING THE TRUMAN ADMINISTRATION!
METROPOLIS MERCANTILE BANK
~ESTABLISHED 1875~
I WAS BYPASSING CIRCUITS LIKE THAT BEFORE MY VOICE CHANGED!
THEY MIGHT AS WELL HAVE LEFT THE DOOR UNLOCKED!
METROPOLIS MERCANTILE BANK
~ESTABLISHED 1875~
I ALMOST FEEL LIKE LEAVING A THANK-YOU NOTE. NAH, THAT WOULD BE CRUEL!
♪I'M CUT-TING A HOLE WHERE THE SAFE IS THIN--♪
♪--AND WHEN... MY HAND... GOES WANDERING...♪
KLIK-KLIK-KLAK!
YES!
TUMBLERS FELL INTO PLACE LIKE SOLDIERS IN A ROW.
YOU'RE ALL MINE NOW.
TIME TO MAKE THAT BIG WITHDRAWAL!
SORRY. BUSINESS HOURS ARE NINE TO FOUR.
GWAA!-
N-NO... N-NOT YOU!!

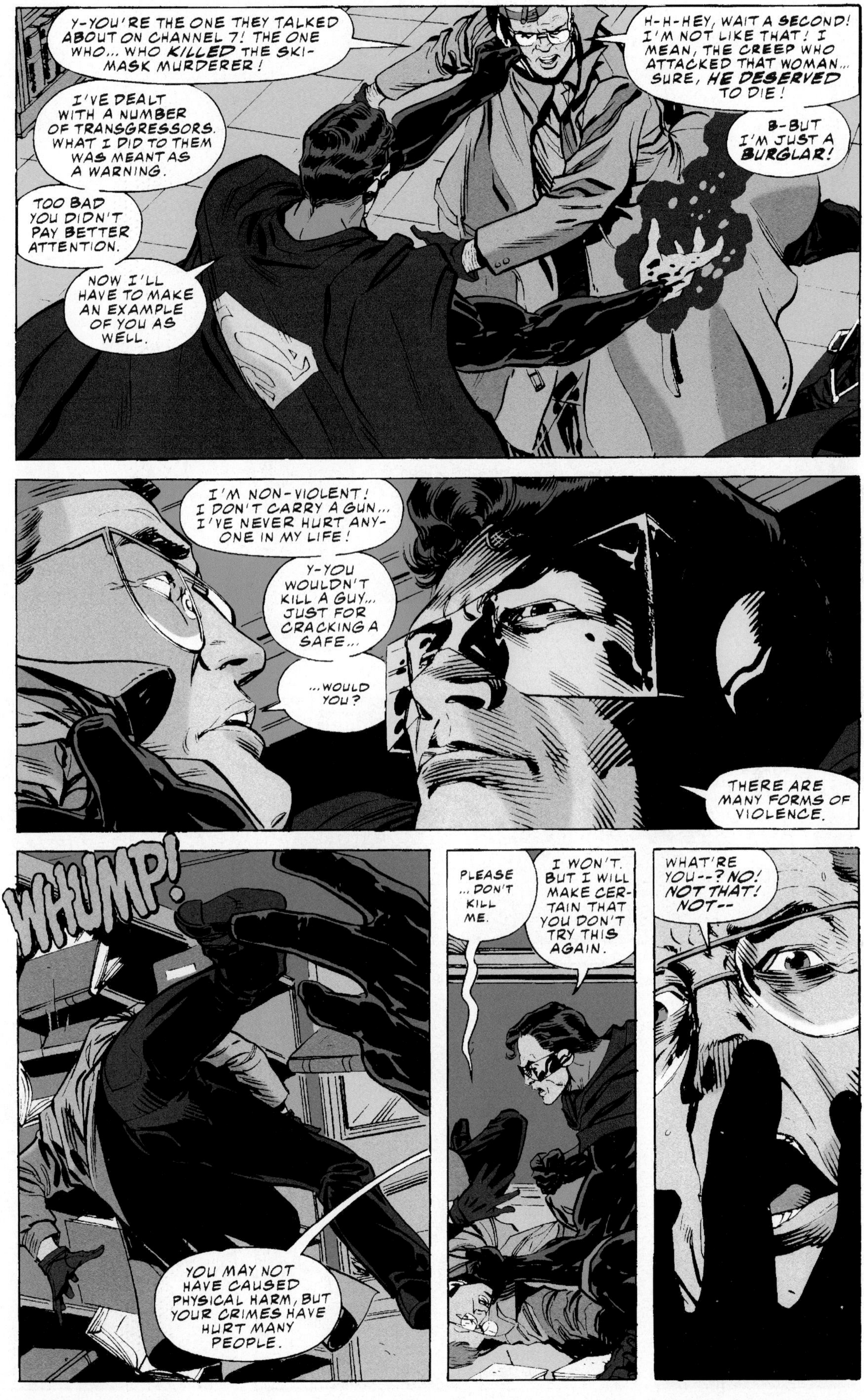
Y-YOU'RE THE ONE THEY TALKED ABOUT ON CHANNEL 7! THE ONE WHO... WHO KILLED THE SKI-MASK MURDERER!
I'VE DEALT WITH A NUMBER OF TRANSGRESSORS. WHAT I DID TO THEM WAS MEANT AS A WARNING.
H-H-HEY, WAIT A SECOND! I'M NOT LIKE THAT! I MEAN, THE CREEP WHO ATTACKED THAT WOMAN... SURE, HE DESERVED TO DIE!
B-BUT I'M JUST A BURGLAR!
TOO BAD YOU DIDN'T PAY BETTER ATTENTION.
NOW I'LL HAVE TO MAKE AN EXAMPLE OF YOU AS WELL.
I'M NON-VIOLENT! I DON'T CARRY A GUN... I'VE NEVER HURT ANY-ONE IN MY LIFE!
Y-YOU WOULDN'T KILL A GUY... JUST FOR CRACKING A SAFE...
...WOULD YOU?
THERE ARE MANY FORMS OF VIOLENCE.
WHUMP!
YOU MAY NOT HAVE CAUSED PHYSICAL HARM, BUT YOUR CRIMES HAVE HURT MANY PEOPLE.
PLEASE ...DON'T KILL ME.
I WON'T. BUT I WILL MAKE CER-TAIN THAT YOU DON'T TRY THIS AGAIN.
WHAT'RE YOU--? NO! NOT THAT! NOT--

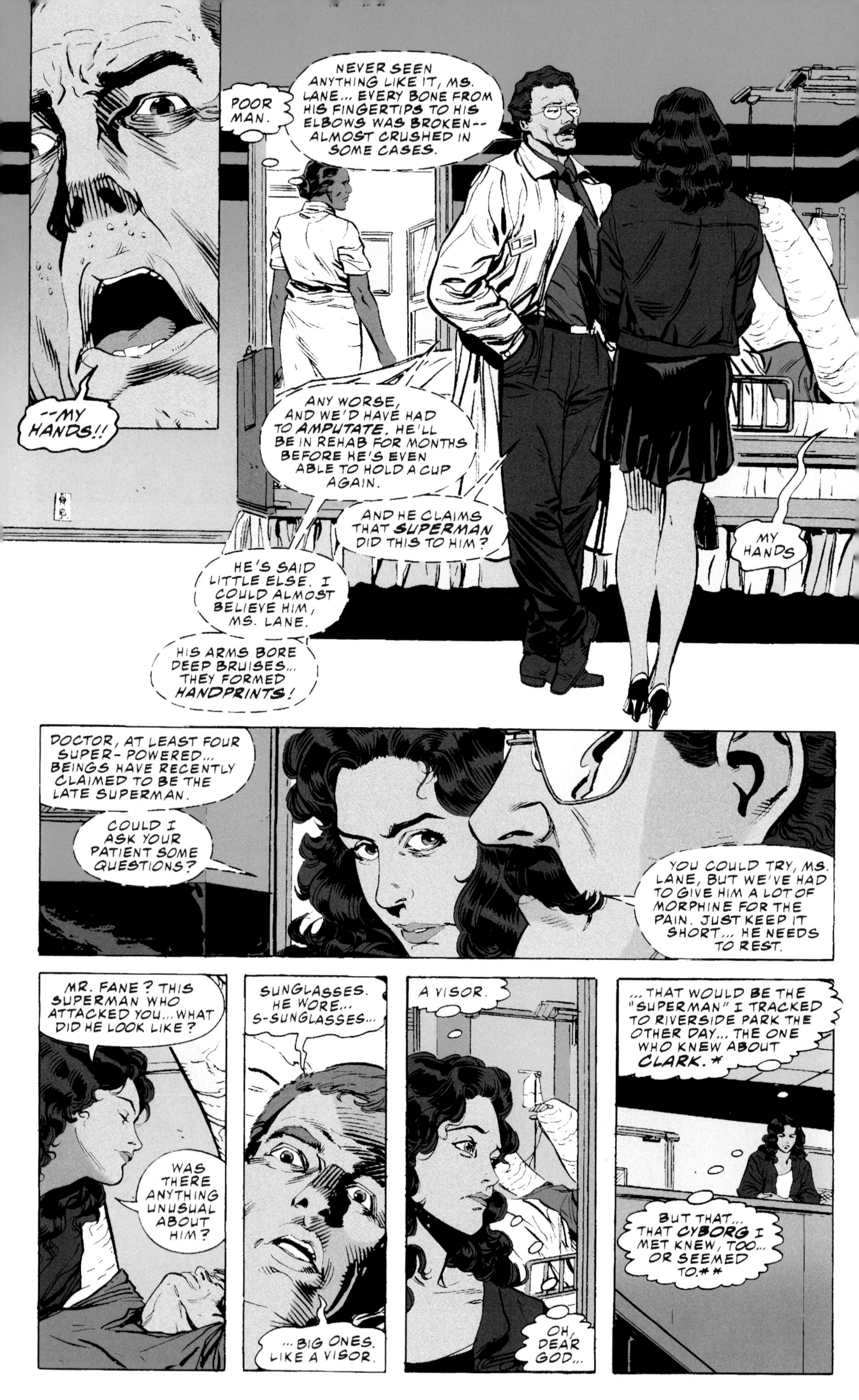
--MY HANDS!!
POOR MAN.
NEVER SEEN ANYTHING LIKE IT, MS. LANE... EVERY BONE FROM HIS FINGERTIPS TO HIS ELBOWS WAS BROKEN-- ALMOST CRUSHED IN SOME CASES.
ANY WORSE, AND WE'D HAVE HAD TO AMPUTATE. HE'LL BE IN REHAB FOR MONTHS BEFORE HE'S EVEN ABLE TO HOLD A CUP AGAIN.
AND HE CLAIMS THAT SUPERMAN DID THIS TO HIM?
MY HANDS
HE'S SAID LITTLE ELSE. I COULD ALMOST BELIEVE HIM, MS. LANE.
HIS ARMS BORE DEEP BRUISES... THEY FORMED HANDPRINTS!
DOCTOR, AT LEAST FOUR SUPER-POWERED... BEINGS HAVE RECENTLY CLAIMED TO BE THE LATE SUPERMAN.
COULD I ASK YOUR PATIENT SOME QUESTIONS?
YOU COULD TRY, MS. LANE, BUT WE'VE HAD TO GIVE HIM A LOT OF MORPHINE FOR THE PAIN. JUST KEEP IT SHORT... HE NEEDS TO REST.
MR. FANE? THIS SUPERMAN WHO ATTACKED YOU... WHAT DID HE LOOK LIKE?
WAS THERE ANYTHING UNUSUAL ABOUT HIM?
SUNGLASSES. HE WORE... S-SUNGLASSES...
...BIG ONES. LIKE A VISOR.
A VISOR.
OH, DEAR GOD...
...THAT WOULD BE THE "SUPERMAN" I TRACKED TO RIVERSIDE PARK THE OTHER DAY... THE ONE WHO KNEW ABOUT CLARK.*
BUT THAT... THAT CYBORG I MET KNEW, TOO... OR SEEMED TO.**

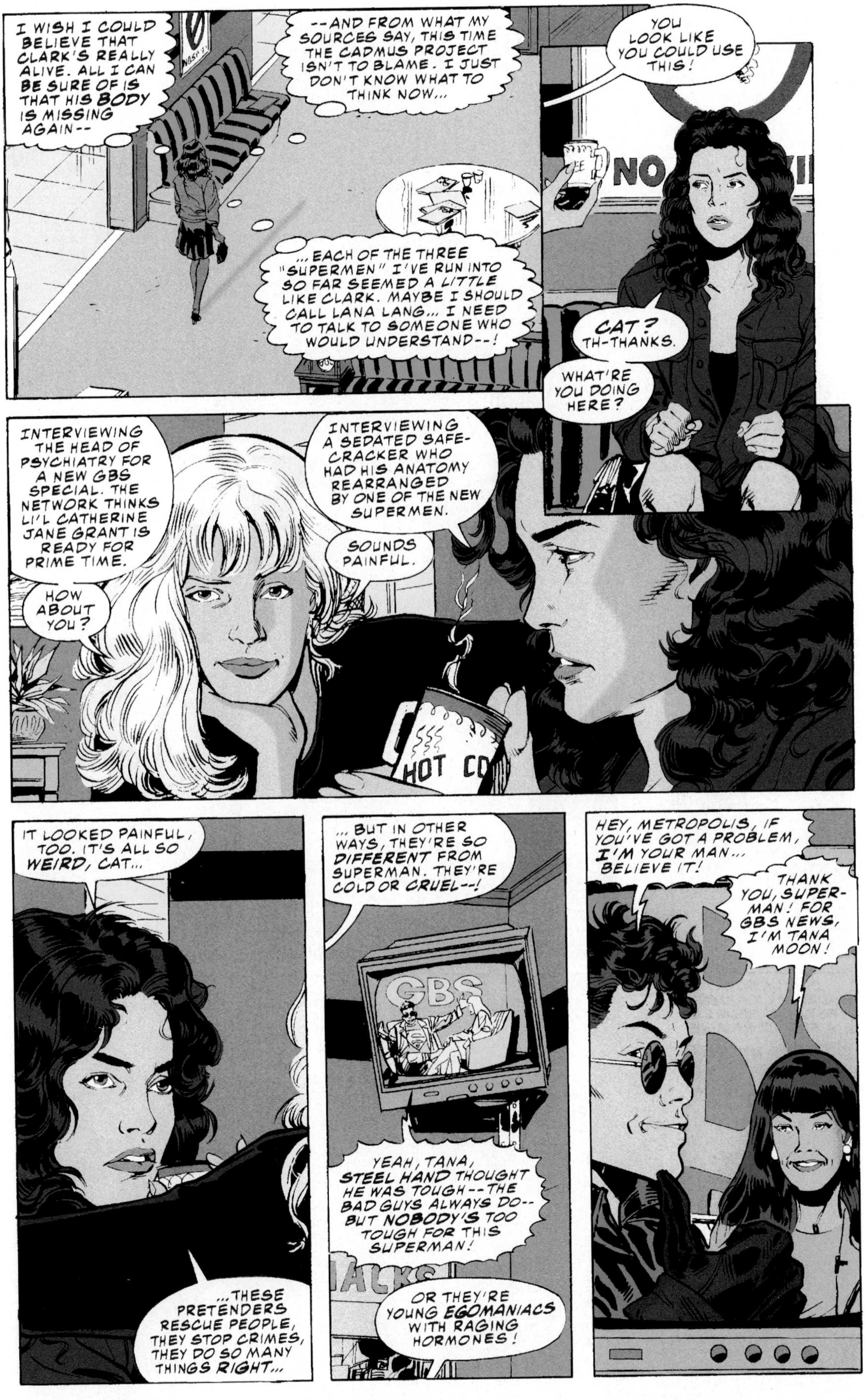
I WISH I COULD BELIEVE THAT CLARK'S REALLY ALIVE. ALL I CAN BE SURE OF IS THAT HIS BODY IS MISSING AGAIN--
--AND FROM WHAT MY SOURCES SAY, THIS TIME THE CADMUS PROJECT ISN'T TO BLAME. I JUST DON'T KNOW WHAT TO THINK NOW...
...EACH OF THE THREE "SUPERMEN" I'VE RUN INTO SO FAR SEEMED A LITTLE LIKE CLARK. MAYBE I SHOULD CALL LANA LANG... I NEED TO TALK TO SOMEONE WHO WOULD UNDERSTAND--!
YOU LOOK LIKE YOU COULD USE THIS!
CAT? TH-THANKS.
WHAT'RE YOU DOING HERE?
INTERVIEWING THE HEAD OF PSYCHIATRY FOR A NEW GBS SPECIAL. THE NETWORK THINKS LI'L CATHERINE JANE GRANT IS READY FOR PRIME TIME.
HOW ABOUT YOU?
INTERVIEWING A SEDATED SAFE-CRACKER WHO HAD HIS ANATOMY REARRANGED BY ONE OF THE NEW SUPERMEN.
SOUNDS PAINFUL.
HOT CO
IT LOOKED PAINFUL, TOO. IT'S ALL SO WEIRD, CAT...
...THESE PRETENDERS RESCUE PEOPLE, THEY STOP CRIMES, THEY DO SO MANY THINGS RIGHT...
...BUT IN OTHER WAYS, THEY'RE SO DIFFERENT FROM SUPERMAN. THEY'RE COLD OR CRUEL--!
GBS
YEAH, TANA, STEEL HAND THOUGHT HE WAS TOUGH--THE BAD GUYS ALWAYS DO-- BUT NOBODY'S TOO TOUGH FOR THIS SUPERMAN!
OR THEY'RE YOUNG EGOMANIACS WITH RAGING HORMONES!
HEY, METROPOLIS, IF YOU'VE GOT A PROBLEM, I'M YOUR MAN... BELIEVE IT!
THANK YOU, SUPER-MAN! FOR GBS NEWS, I'M TANA MOON!

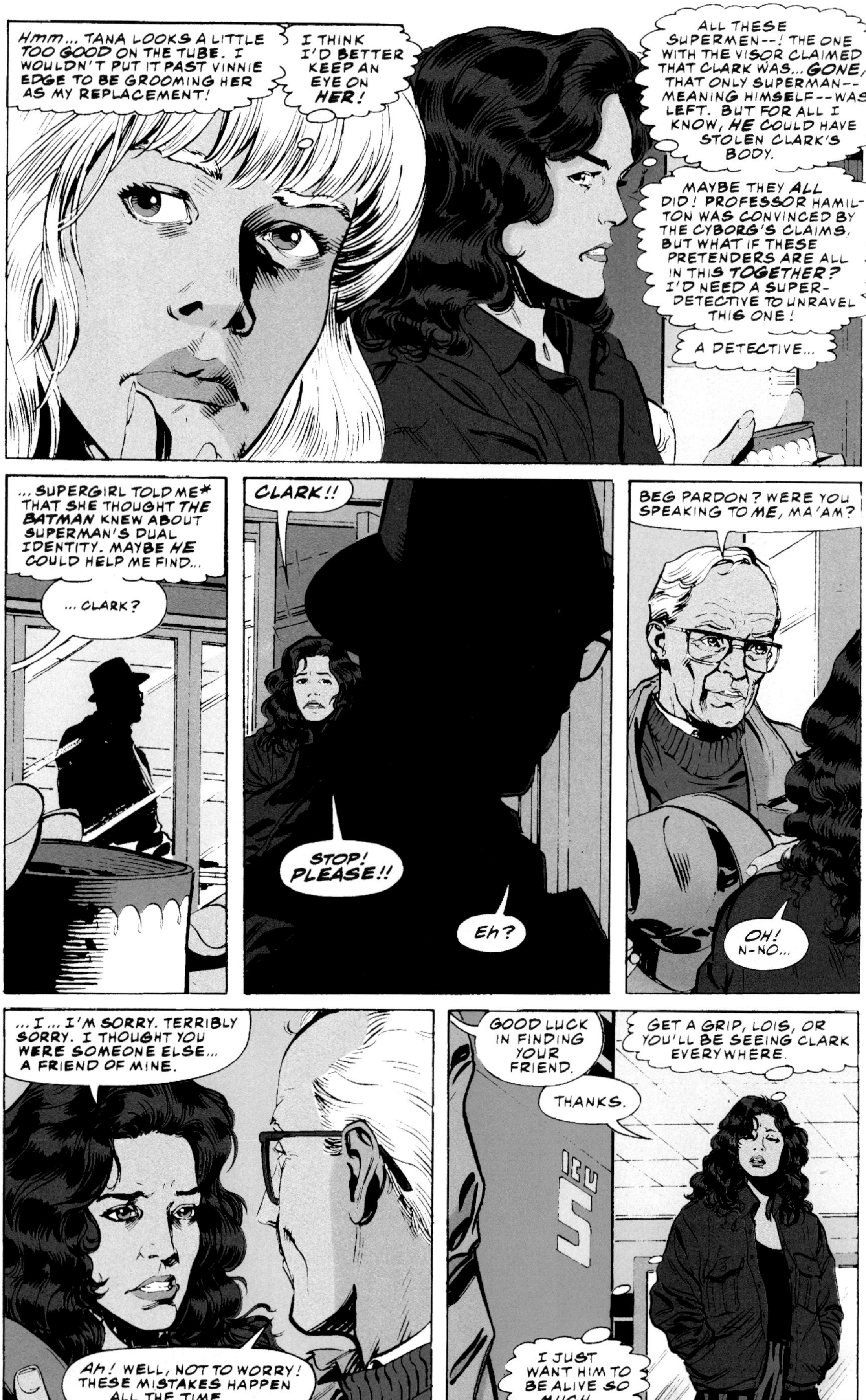
Hmm... TANA LOOKS A LITTLE TOO GOOD ON THE TUBE. I WOULDN'T PUT IT PAST VINNIE EDGE TO BE GROOMING HER AS MY REPLACEMENT!
I THINK I'D BETTER KEEP AN EYE ON HER!
ALL THESE SUPERMEN--! THE ONE WITH THE VISOR CLAIMED THAT CLARK WAS... GONE, THAT ONLY SUPERMAN--MEANING HIMSELF--WAS LEFT. BUT FOR ALL I KNOW, HE COULD HAVE STOLEN CLARK'S BODY.
MAYBE THEY ALL DID! PROFESSOR HAMILTON WAS CONVINCED BY THE CYBORG'S CLAIMS, BUT WHAT IF THESE PRETENDERS ARE ALL IN THIS TOGETHER? I'D NEED A SUPER-DETECTIVE TO UNRAVEL THIS ONE!
A DETECTIVE...
...SUPERGIRL TOLD ME* THAT SHE THOUGHT THE BATMAN KNEW ABOUT SUPERMAN'S DUAL IDENTITY. MAYBE HE COULD HELP ME FIND...
...CLARK?
CLARK!!
STOP! PLEASE!!
Eh?
BEG PARDON? WERE YOU SPEAKING TO ME, MA'AM?
OH! N-NO...
...I... I'M SORRY. TERRIBLY SORRY. I THOUGHT YOU WERE SOMEONE ELSE... A FRIEND OF MINE.
Ah! WELL, NOT TO WORRY! THESE MISTAKES HAPPEN ALL THE TIME.
GOOD LUCK IN FINDING YOUR FRIEND.
THANKS.
GET A GRIP, LOIS, OR YOU'LL BE SEEING CLARK EVERYWHERE.
I JUST WANT HIM TO BE ALIVE SO MUCH...

ANTARCTICA...

I FEEL... *EXHILARATED!* LIVES HAVE BEEN SAVED, EVIL HAS BEEN PUNISHED.

BY NOW, THE PEOPLE MUST KNOW THAT THEY AGAIN HAVE A SUPER-MAN ON WHOM THEY CAN DEPEND. IT HAS BEEN A GOOD BEGINNING...

...IN SPITE OF MY ENCOUNTER WITH LOIS. THAT WAS... TROUBLING. I FELT A DISTURBING EMPTI-NESS UPON LEAVING HER. ECHOES, NO DOUBT, OF EXPERI-ENCES FROM MY PRE-VIOUS LIFE.

I MUST NOT LET SUCH EVENTS DETER ME. THERE IS TOO MUCH YET TO BE DONE.

THANK THE CREATOR, I CAN RETIRE TO THIS FINE FORTRESS AND PLAN MY NEXT MOVE.

UNITS-- ATTEND ME!

YES, SIR.

AS YOU WISH.

PARDON, SIR, DO YOU WISH TO CHANGE?

NOT AS YET, UNIT 3.

WHAT IS THE STATUS OF THE NEW MONITOR ARRAY?

ON-LINE AND RECEIV-ING, SIR.

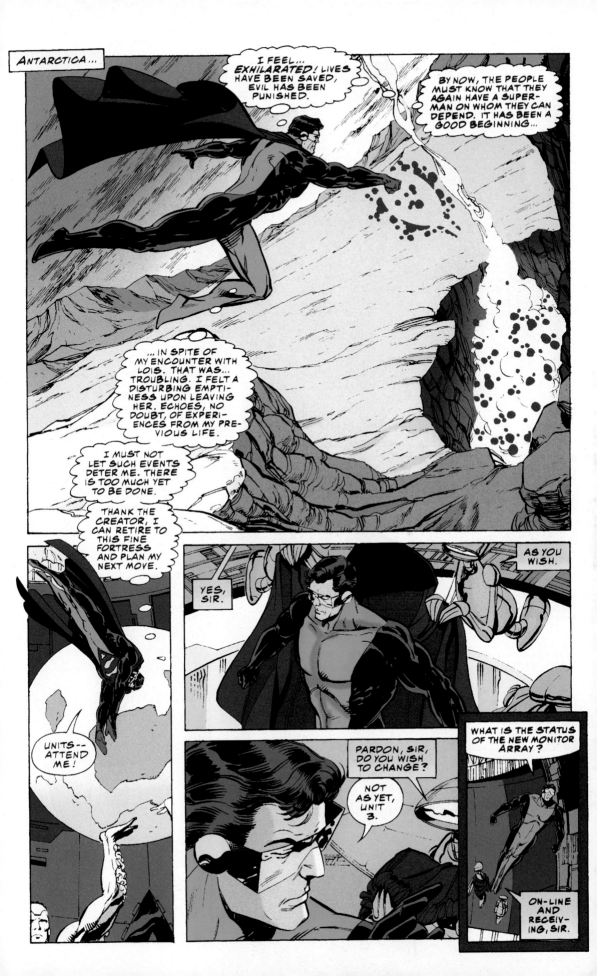

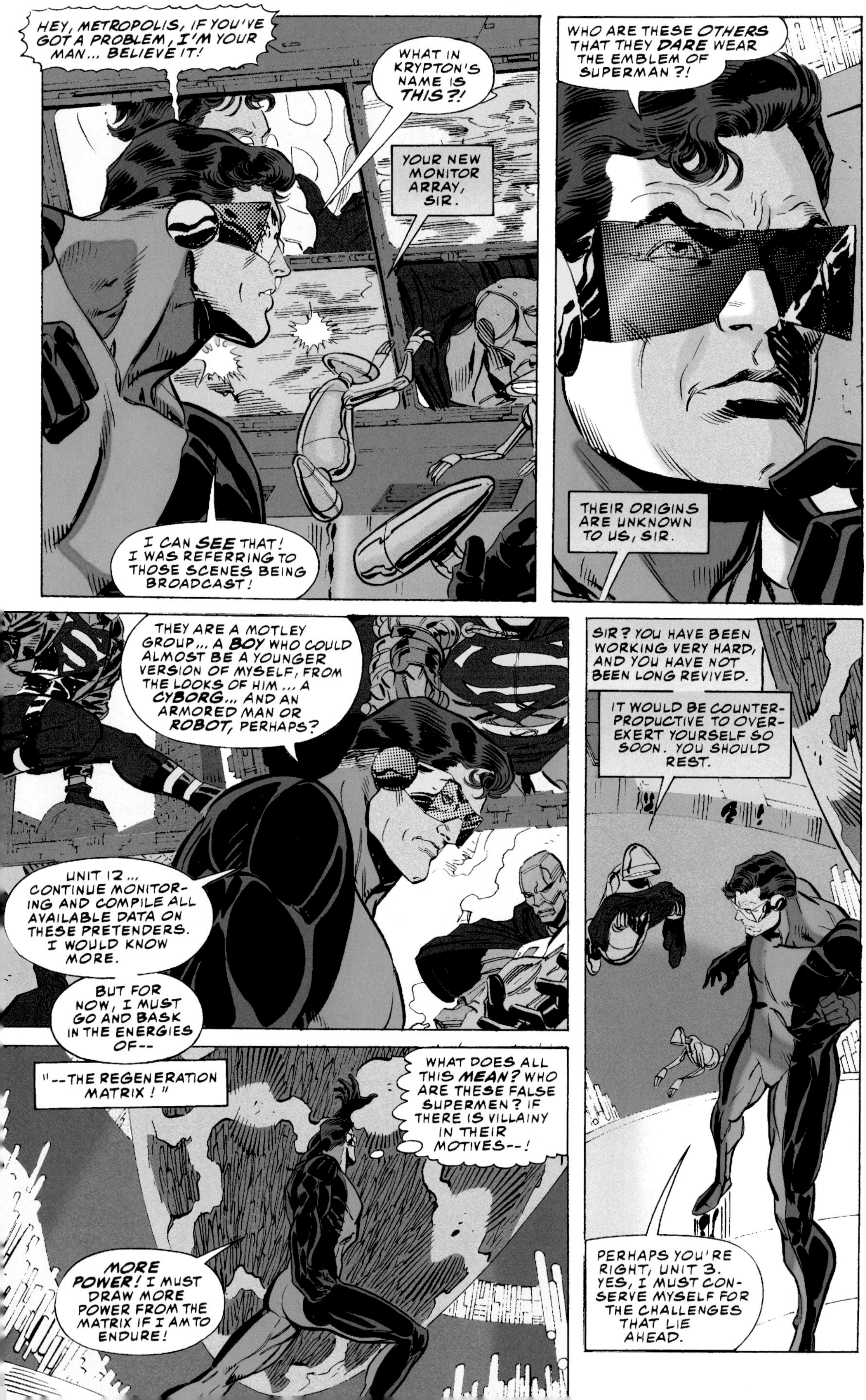
HEY, METROPOLIS, IF YOU'VE GOT A PROBLEM, I'M YOUR MAN... BELIEVE IT!
WHAT IN KRYPTON'S NAME IS THIS?!
YOUR NEW MONITOR ARRAY, SIR.
I CAN SEE THAT! I WAS REFERRING TO THOSE SCENES BEING BROADCAST!
WHO ARE THESE OTHERS THAT THEY DARE WEAR THE EMBLEM OF SUPERMAN?!
THEIR ORIGINS ARE UNKNOWN TO US, SIR.
THEY ARE A MOTLEY GROUP... A BOY WHO COULD ALMOST BE A YOUNGER VERSION OF MYSELF, FROM THE LOOKS OF HIM... A CYBORG... AND AN ARMORED MAN OR ROBOT, PERHAPS?
UNIT 12... CONTINUE MONITORING AND COMPILE ALL AVAILABLE DATA ON THESE PRETENDERS. I WOULD KNOW MORE.
BUT FOR NOW, I MUST GO AND BASK IN THE ENERGIES OF--
"--THE REGENERATION MATRIX!"
WHAT DOES ALL THIS MEAN? WHO ARE THESE FALSE SUPERMEN? IF THERE IS VILLAINY IN THEIR MOTIVES--!
MORE POWER! I MUST DRAW MORE POWER FROM THE MATRIX IF I AM TO ENDURE!
SIR? YOU HAVE BEEN WORKING VERY HARD, AND YOU HAVE NOT BEEN LONG REVIVED.
IT WOULD BE COUNTER-PRODUCTIVE TO OVER-EXERT YOURSELF SO SOON. YOU SHOULD REST.
PERHAPS YOU'RE RIGHT, UNIT 3. YES, I MUST CONSERVE MYSELF FOR THE CHALLENGES THAT LIE AHEAD.

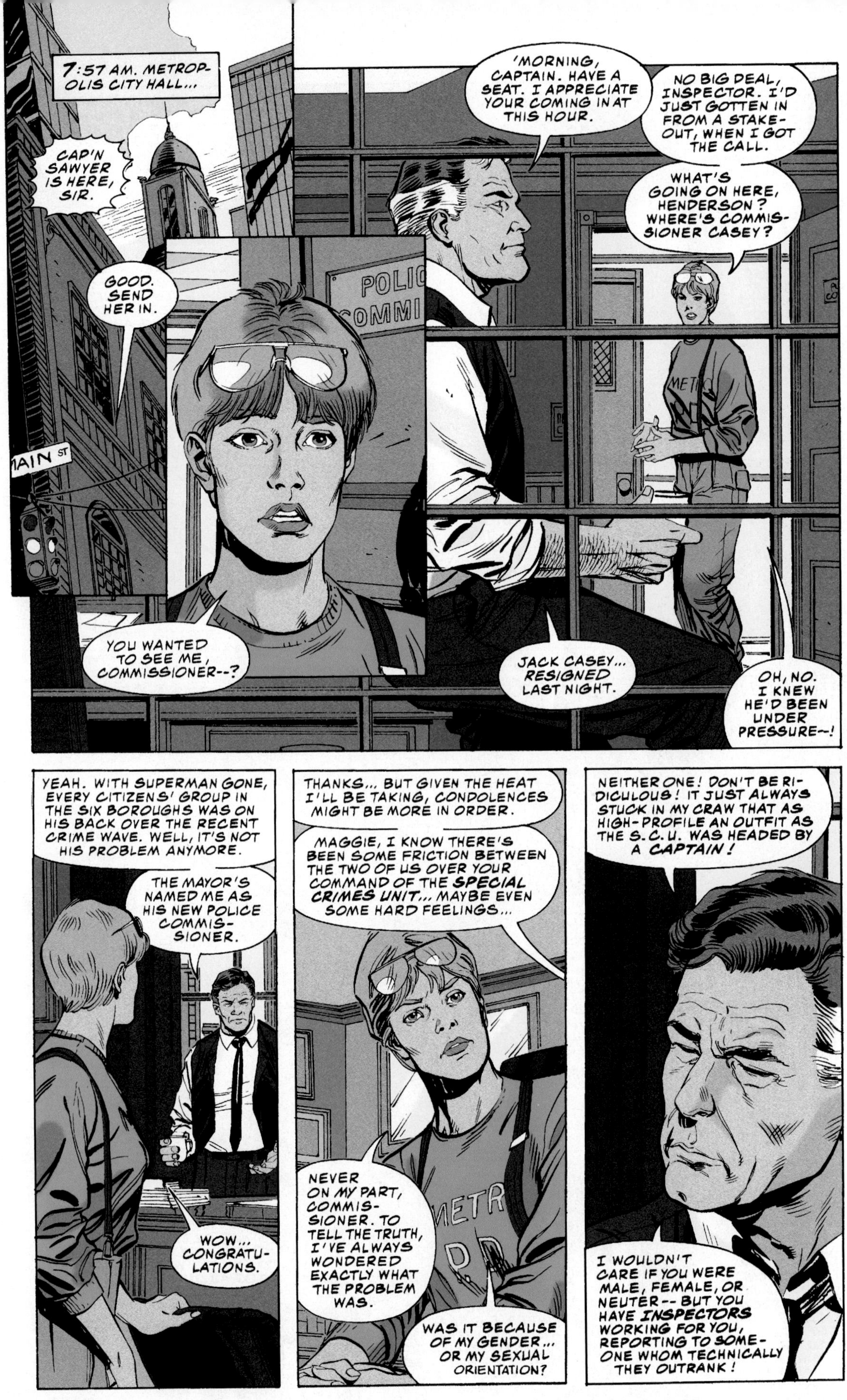
7:57 AM. METROPOLIS CITY HALL...
CAP'N SAWYER IS HERE, SIR.
GOOD. SEND HER IN.
MAIN ST
POLIC
COMMI
YOU WANTED TO SEE ME, COMMISSIONER--?
'MORNING, CAPTAIN. HAVE A SEAT. I APPRECIATE YOUR COMING IN AT THIS HOUR.
NO BIG DEAL, INSPECTOR. I'D JUST GOTTEN IN FROM A STAKE-OUT, WHEN I GOT THE CALL.
WHAT'S GOING ON HERE, HENDERSON? WHERE'S COMMISSIONER CASEY?
JACK CASEY... RESIGNED LAST NIGHT.
OH, NO. I KNEW HE'D BEEN UNDER PRESSURE--!
YEAH. WITH SUPERMAN GONE, EVERY CITIZENS' GROUP IN THE SIX BOROUGHS WAS ON HIS BACK OVER THE RECENT CRIME WAVE. WELL, IT'S NOT HIS PROBLEM ANYMORE.
THE MAYOR'S NAMED ME AS HIS NEW POLICE COMMISSIONER.
WOW... CONGRATULATIONS.
THANKS... BUT GIVEN THE HEAT I'LL BE TAKING, CONDOLENCES MIGHT BE MORE IN ORDER.
MAGGIE, I KNOW THERE'S BEEN SOME FRICTION BETWEEN THE TWO OF US OVER YOUR COMMAND OF THE SPECIAL CRIMES UNIT... MAYBE EVEN SOME HARD FEELINGS...
NEVER ON MY PART, COMMISSIONER. TO TELL THE TRUTH, I'VE ALWAYS WONDERED EXACTLY WHAT THE PROBLEM WAS.
WAS IT BECAUSE OF MY GENDER... OR MY SEXUAL ORIENTATION?
NEITHER ONE! DON'T BE RIDICULOUS! IT JUST ALWAYS STUCK IN MY CRAW THAT AS HIGH-PROFILE AN OUTFIT AS THE S.C.U. WAS HEADED BY A CAPTAIN!
I WOULDN'T CARE IF YOU WERE MALE, FEMALE, OR NEUTER -- BUT YOU HAVE INSPECTORS WORKING FOR YOU, REPORTING TO SOMEONE WHOM TECHNICALLY THEY OUTRANK!

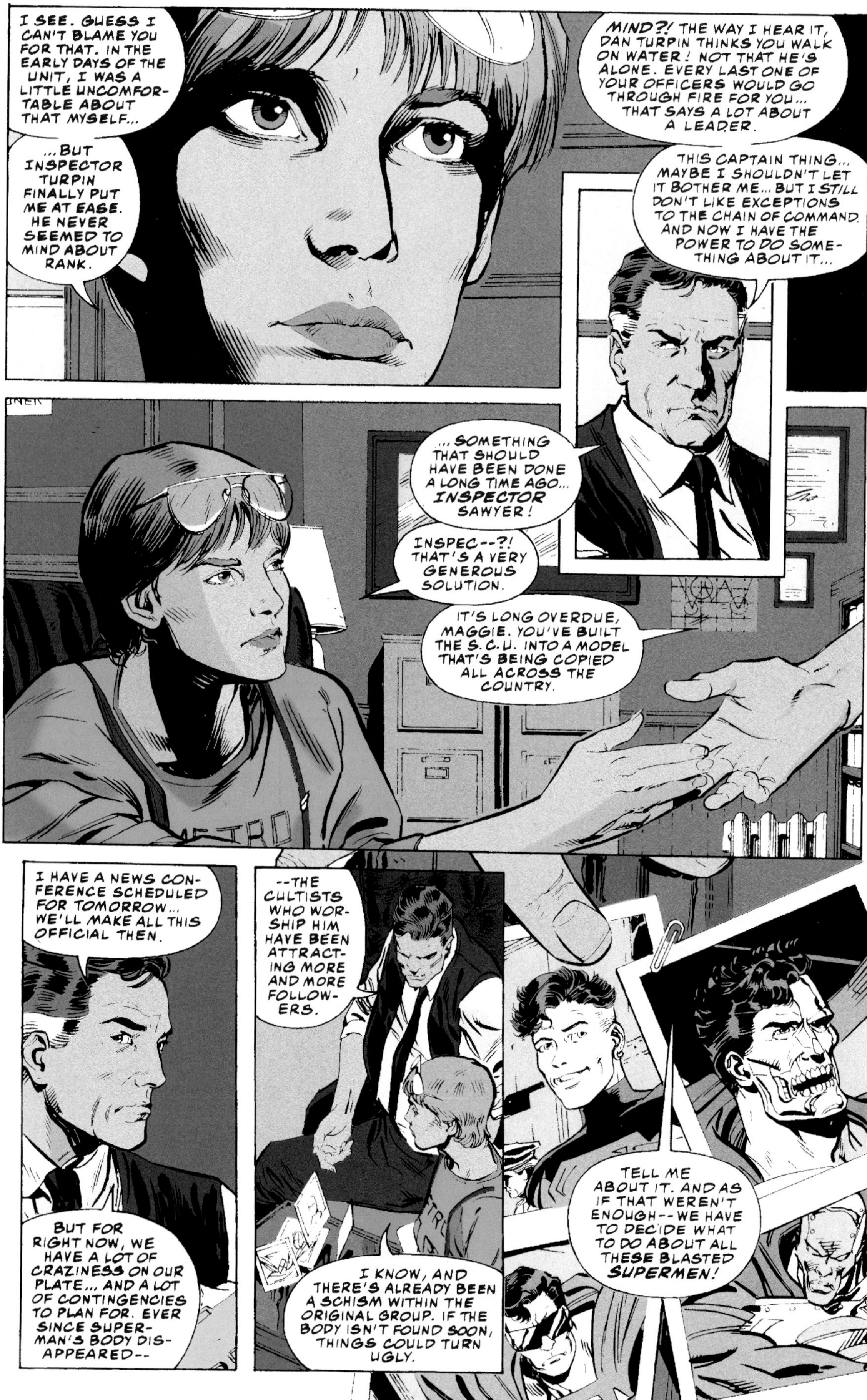
I SEE. GUESS I CAN'T BLAME YOU FOR THAT. IN THE EARLY DAYS OF THE UNIT, I WAS A LITTLE UNCOMFORTABLE ABOUT THAT MYSELF...
...BUT INSPECTOR TURPIN FINALLY PUT ME AT EASE. HE NEVER SEEMED TO MIND ABOUT RANK.
MIND?! THE WAY I HEAR IT, DAN TURPIN THINKS YOU WALK ON WATER! NOT THAT HE'S ALONE. EVERY LAST ONE OF YOUR OFFICERS WOULD GO THROUGH FIRE FOR YOU... THAT SAYS A LOT ABOUT A LEADER.
THIS CAPTAIN THING... MAYBE I SHOULDN'T LET IT BOTHER ME... BUT I STILL DON'T LIKE EXCEPTIONS TO THE CHAIN OF COMMAND. AND NOW I HAVE THE POWER TO DO SOMETHING ABOUT IT...
...SOMETHING THAT SHOULD HAVE BEEN DONE A LONG TIME AGO... INSPECTOR SAWYER!
INSPEC--?! THAT'S A VERY GENEROUS SOLUTION.
IT'S LONG OVERDUE, MAGGIE. YOU'VE BUILT THE S.C.U. INTO A MODEL THAT'S BEING COPIED ALL ACROSS THE COUNTRY.
I HAVE A NEWS CONFERENCE SCHEDULED FOR TOMORROW... WE'LL MAKE ALL THIS OFFICIAL THEN.
BUT FOR RIGHT NOW, WE HAVE A LOT OF CRAZINESS ON OUR PLATE... AND A LOT OF CONTINGENCIES TO PLAN FOR. EVER SINCE SUPERMAN'S BODY DISAPPEARED--
--THE CULTISTS WHO WORSHIP HIM HAVE BEEN ATTRACTING MORE AND MORE FOLLOWERS.
I KNOW, AND THERE'S ALREADY BEEN A SCHISM WITHIN THE ORIGINAL GROUP. IF THE BODY ISN'T FOUND SOON, THINGS COULD TURN UGLY.
TELL ME ABOUT IT. AND AS IF THAT WEREN'T ENOUGH-- WE HAVE TO DECIDE WHAT TO DO ABOUT ALL THESE BLASTED SUPERMEN!

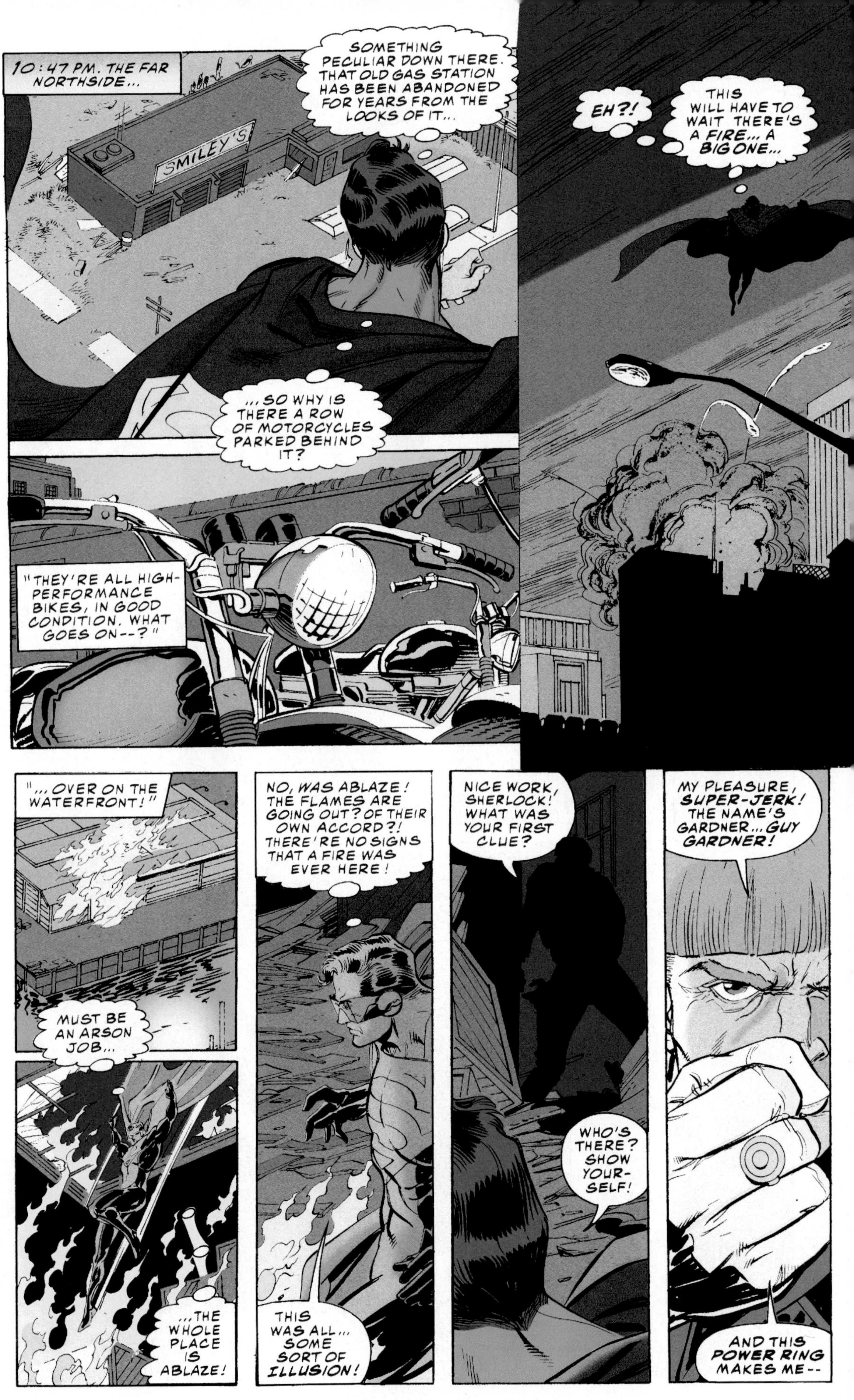
10:47 PM. THE FAR NORTHSIDE...
SOMETHING PECULIAR DOWN THERE. THAT OLD GAS STATION HAS BEEN ABANDONED FOR YEARS FROM THE LOOKS OF IT...
SMILEY'S
...SO WHY IS THERE A ROW OF MOTORCYCLES PARKED BEHIND IT?
"THEY'RE ALL HIGH-PERFORMANCE BIKES, IN GOOD CONDITION. WHAT GOES ON--?"
EH?!
THIS WILL HAVE TO WAIT THERE'S A FIRE... A BIG ONE...
"...OVER ON THE WATERFRONT!"
MUST BE AN ARSON JOB...
...THE WHOLE PLACE IS ABLAZE!
NO, WAS ABLAZE! THE FLAMES ARE GOING OUT? OF THEIR OWN ACCORD?! THERE'RE NO SIGNS THAT A FIRE WAS EVER HERE!
THIS WAS ALL... SOME SORT OF ILLUSION!
NICE WORK, SHERLOCK! WHAT WAS YOUR FIRST CLUE?
WHO'S THERE? SHOW YOUR-SELF!
MY PLEASURE, SUPER-JERK! THE NAME'S GARDNER... GUY GARDNER!
AND THIS POWER RING MAKES ME--

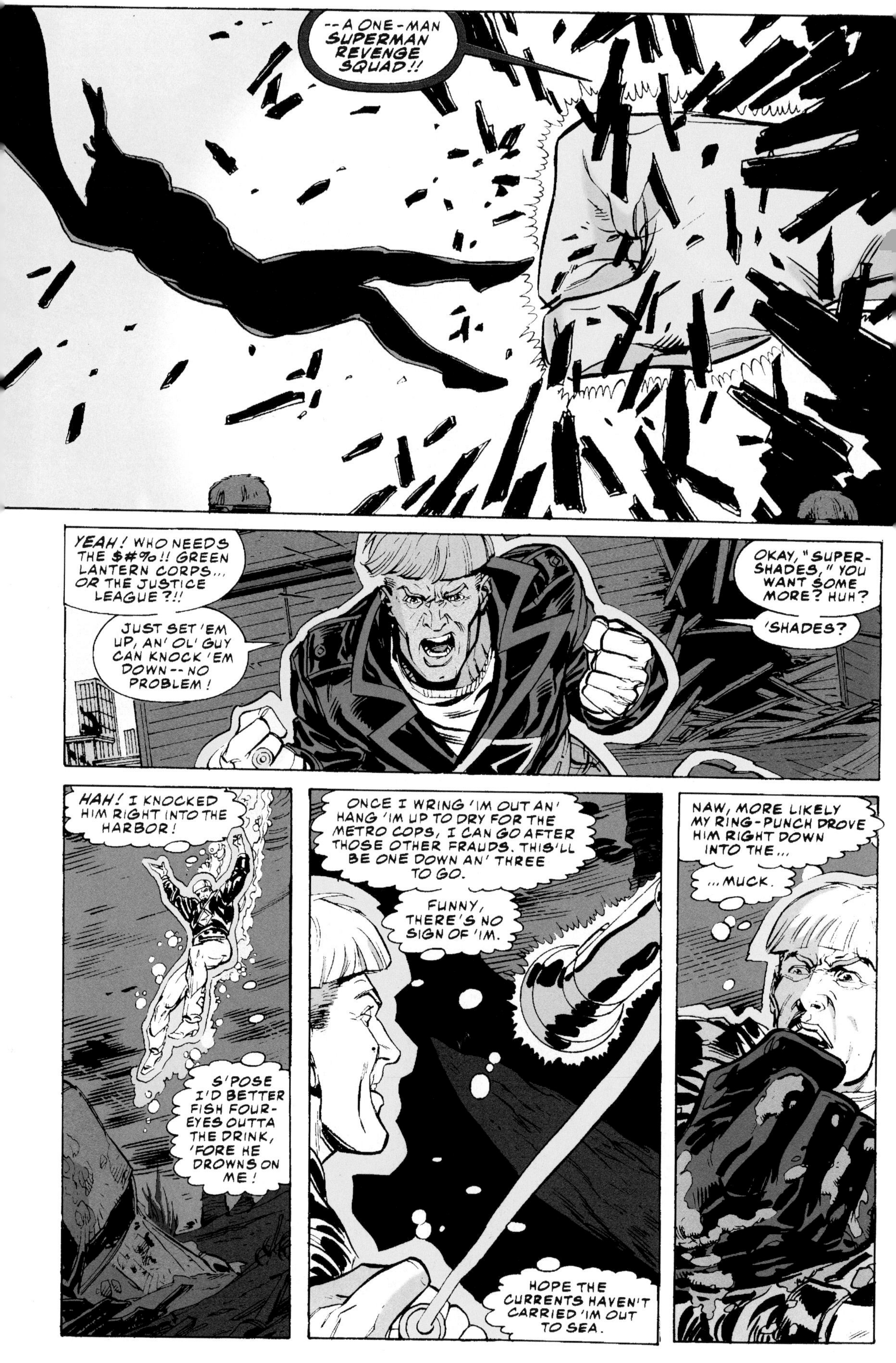
--A ONE-MAN SUPERMAN REVENGE SQUAD!!
YEAH! WHO NEEDS THE $#%!! GREEN LANTERN CORPS... OR THE JUSTICE LEAGUE?!!
JUST SET 'EM UP, AN' OL' GUY CAN KNOCK 'EM DOWN--NO PROBLEM!
OKAY, "SUPER-SHADES," YOU WANT SOME MORE? HUH?
'SHADES?
HAH! I KNOCKED HIM RIGHT INTO THE HARBOR!
S'POSE I'D BETTER FISH FOUR-EYES OUTTA THE DRINK, 'FORE HE DROWNS ON ME!
ONCE I WRING 'IM OUT AN' HANG 'IM UP TO DRY FOR THE METRO COPS, I CAN GO AFTER THOSE OTHER FRAUDS. THIS'LL BE ONE DOWN AN' THREE TO GO.
FUNNY, THERE'S NO SIGN OF 'IM.
HOPE THE CURRENTS HAVEN'T CARRIED 'IM OUT TO SEA.
NAW, MORE LIKELY MY RING-PUNCH DROVE HIM RIGHT DOWN INTO THE...
...MUCK.

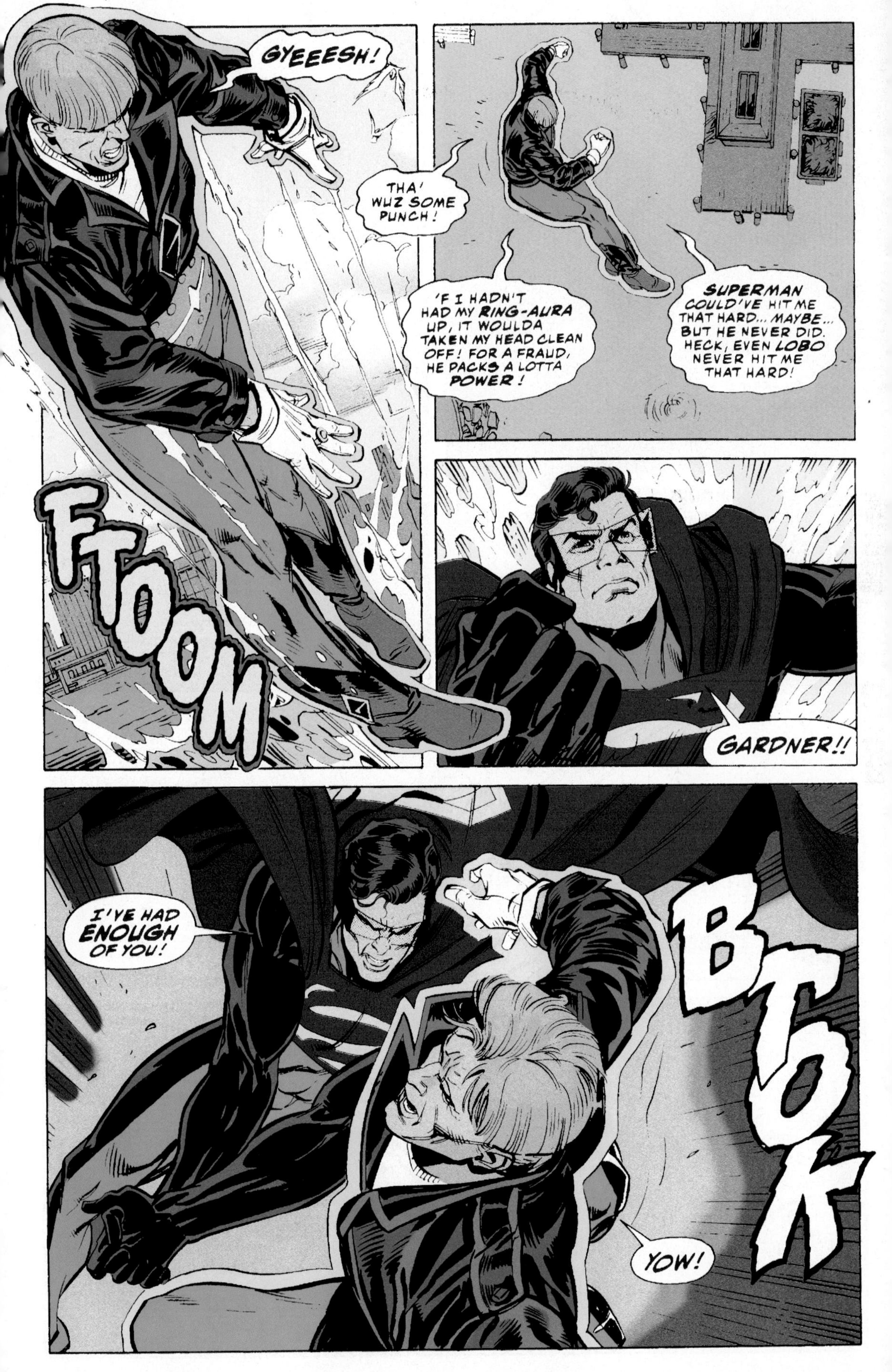
GYEEESH!
THA' WUZ SOME PUNCH!
FTOOM
'F I HADN'T HAD MY RING-AURA UP, IT WOULDA TAKEN MY HEAD CLEAN OFF! FOR A FRAUD, HE PACKS A LOTTA POWER!
SUPERMAN COULD'VE HIT ME THAT HARD... MAYBE... BUT HE NEVER DID. HECK, EVEN LOBO NEVER HIT ME THAT HARD!
GARDNER!!
I'VE HAD ENOUGH OF YOU!
BTOK
YOW!

KER-RACK!

WHOA!

THIS SUCKER'S--

--TOUGH!

THE REST OF THIS WORLD MAY HAVE TO PUT UP WITH YOU-- BUT *SUPERMAN* DOES NOT!

AND I *WILL NOT!*

GOT A SHORT FUSE, TOO... THIS COULD GET *INTERESTIN'*...

...BUT I CAN'T LET 'IM KEEP ME ON THE DEFENSIVE.

YOU TALK A GOOD FIGHT, SHADES--

--BUT I'M *BETTIN'* THAT THIS SHINING *KNIGHT* CAN PIN YOU TO THE WALL!

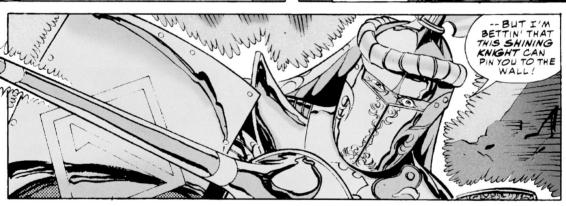

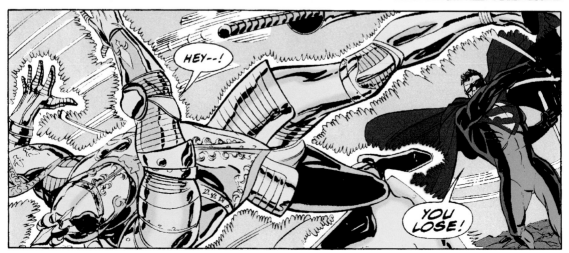

HEY--!

YOU *LOSE!*

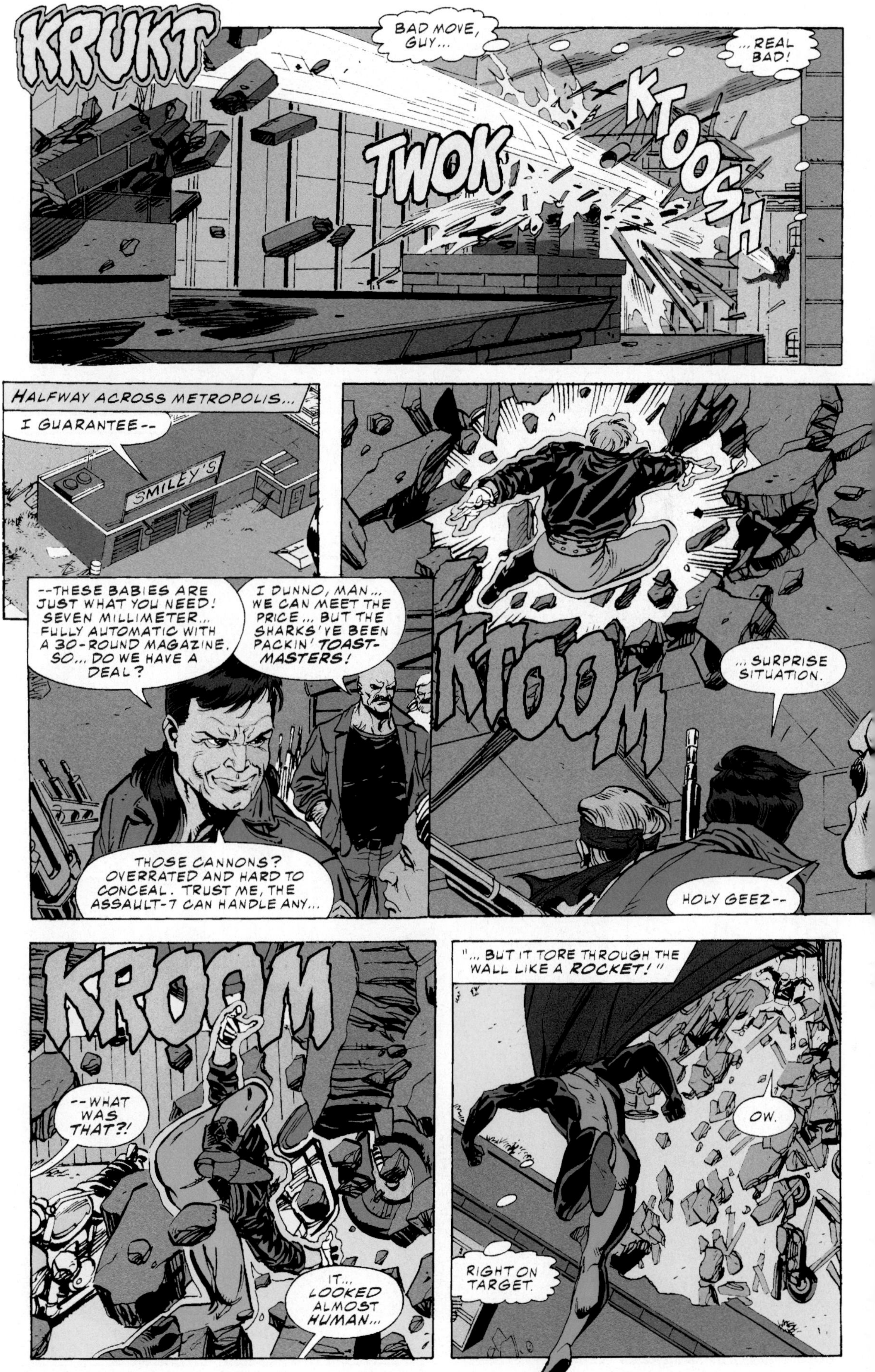
KRUKT
BAD MOVE, GUY...
...REAL BAD!
TWOK
KTOOSH
HALFWAY ACROSS METROPOLIS...
I GUARANTEE--
SMILEY'S
--THESE BABIES ARE JUST WHAT YOU NEED! SEVEN MILLIMETER... FULLY AUTOMATIC WITH A 30-ROUND MAGAZINE. SO... DO WE HAVE A DEAL?
I DUNNO, MAN... WE CAN MEET THE PRICE... BUT THE SHARKS'VE BEEN PACKIN' TOAST-MASTERS!
THOSE CANNONS? OVERRATED AND HARD TO CONCEAL. TRUST ME, THE ASSAULT-7 CAN HANDLE ANY...
KTOOM
...SURPRISE SITUATION.
HOLY GEEZ--
KROOM
--WHAT WAS THAT?!
IT... LOOKED ALMOST HUMAN...
"...BUT IT TORE THROUGH THE WALL LIKE A ROCKET!"
OW.
RIGHT ON TARGET.

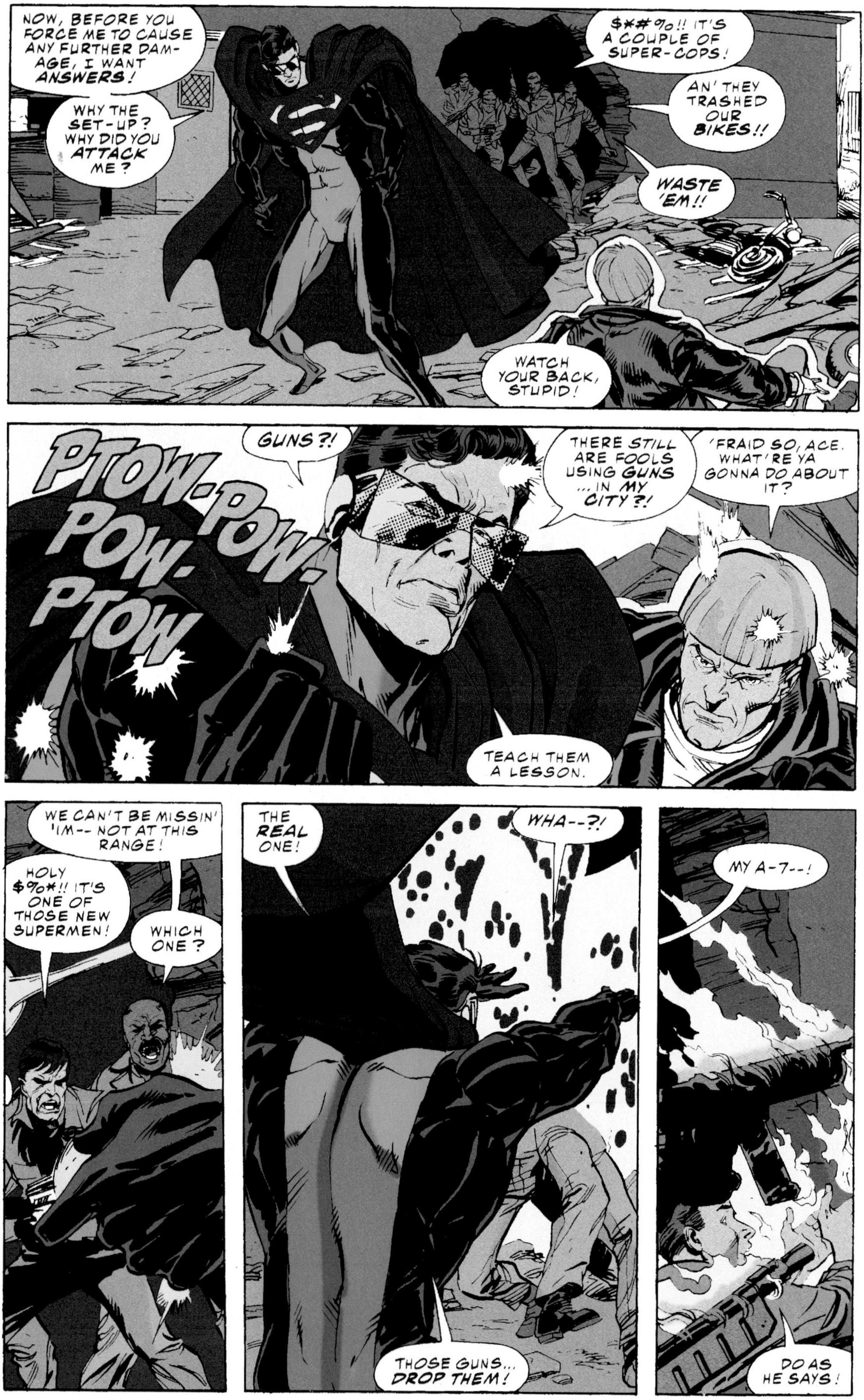
NOW, BEFORE YOU FORCE ME TO CAUSE ANY FURTHER DAM-AGE, I WANT ANSWERS!
WHY THE SET-UP? WHY DID YOU ATTACK ME?
$*#%!! IT'S A COUPLE OF SUPER-COPS!
AN' THEY TRASHED OUR BIKES!!
WASTE 'EM!!
WATCH YOUR BACK, STUPID!
PTOW-POW-POW-PTOW
GUNS?!
THERE STILL ARE FOOLS USING GUNS ...IN MY CITY?!
'FRAID SO, ACE. WHAT'RE YA GONNA DO ABOUT IT?
TEACH THEM A LESSON.
WE CAN'T BE MISSIN' 'IM-- NOT AT THIS RANGE!
HOLY $%*!! IT'S ONE OF THOSE NEW SUPERMEN!
WHICH ONE?
THE REAL ONE!
WHA--?!
THOSE GUNS... DROP THEM!
MY A-7--!
DO AS HE SAYS!

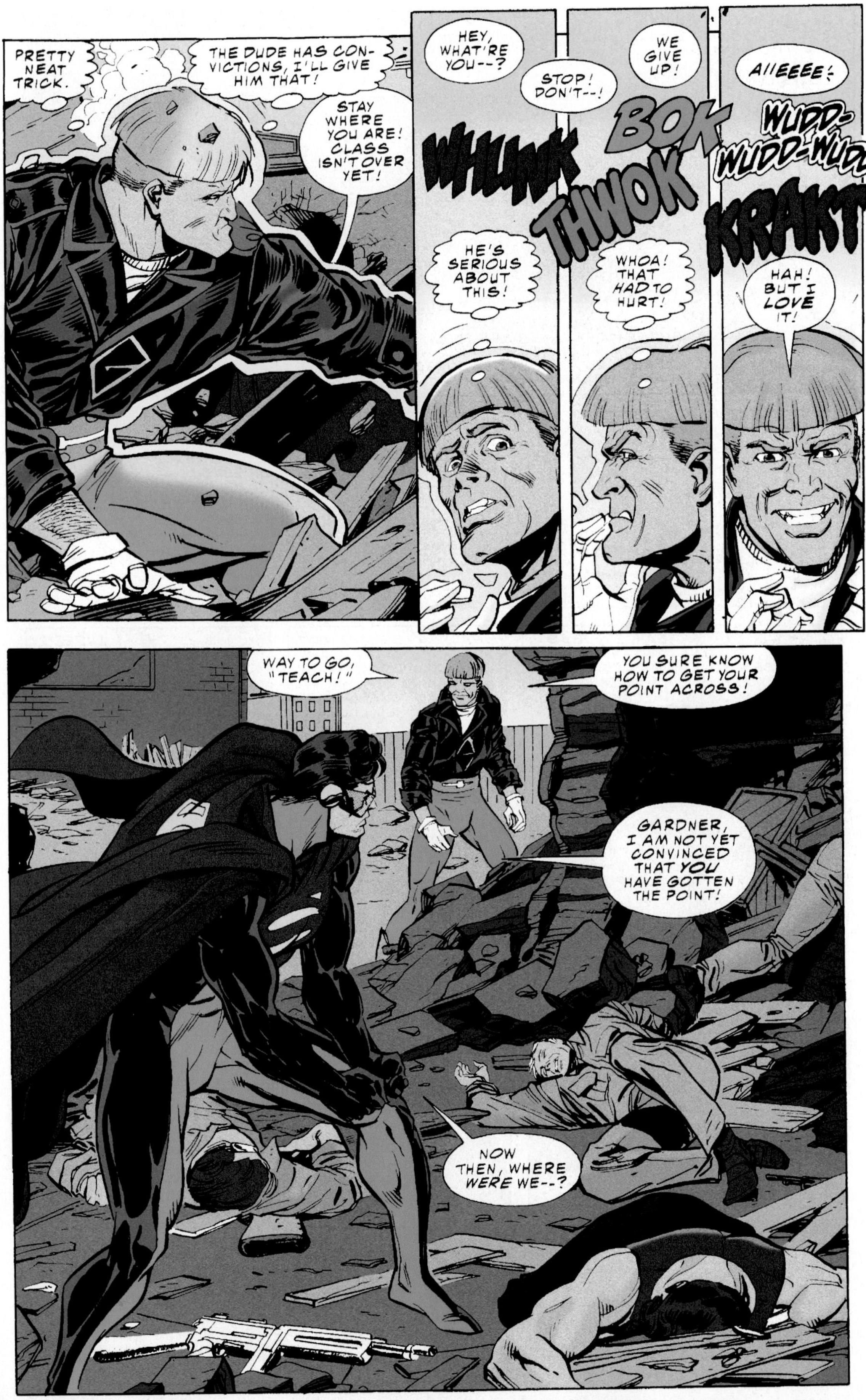

PRETTY NEAT TRICK.
THE DUDE HAS CONVICTIONS, I'LL GIVE HIM THAT!
STAY WHERE YOU ARE! CLASS ISN'T OVER YET!
HEY, WHAT'RE YOU--?
WHUNK
HE'S SERIOUS ABOUT THIS!
STOP! DON'T--!
WE GIVE UP!
BOK
THWOK
WHOA! THAT HAD TO HURT!
AIIEEEE!
WUDD-WUDD-WUDD
KRAKT
HAH! BUT I LOVE IT!
WAY TO GO, "TEACH!"
YOU SURE KNOW HOW TO GET YOUR POINT ACROSS!
GARDNER, I AM NOT YET CONVINCED THAT YOU HAVE GOTTEN THE POINT!
NOW THEN, WHERE WERE WE--?

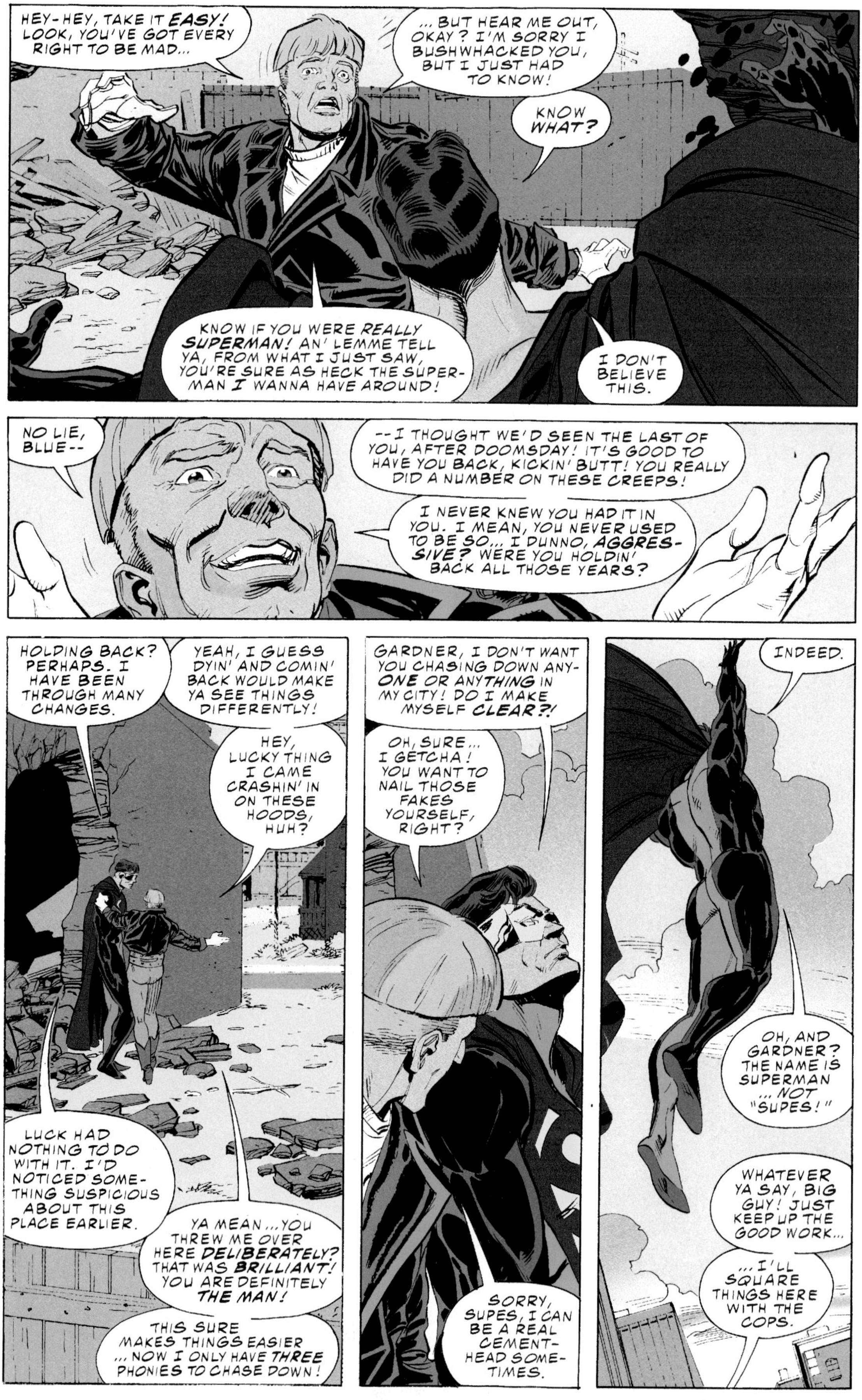
HEY-HEY, TAKE IT EASY! LOOK, YOU'VE GOT EVERY RIGHT TO BE MAD...
...BUT HEAR ME OUT, OKAY? I'M SORRY I BUSHWHACKED YOU, BUT I JUST HAD TO KNOW!
KNOW WHAT?
KNOW IF YOU WERE REALLY SUPERMAN! AN' LEMME TELL YA, FROM WHAT I JUST SAW, YOU'RE SURE AS HECK THE SUPERMAN I WANNA HAVE AROUND!
I DON'T BELIEVE THIS.
NO LIE, BLUE--
--I THOUGHT WE'D SEEN THE LAST OF YOU, AFTER DOOMSDAY! IT'S GOOD TO HAVE YOU BACK, KICKIN' BUTT! YOU REALLY DID A NUMBER ON THESE CREEPS!
I NEVER KNEW YOU HAD IT IN YOU. I MEAN, YOU NEVER USED TO BE SO... I DUNNO, AGGRESSIVE? WERE YOU HOLDIN' BACK ALL THOSE YEARS?
HOLDING BACK? PERHAPS. I HAVE BEEN THROUGH MANY CHANGES.
YEAH, I GUESS DYIN' AND COMIN' BACK WOULD MAKE YA SEE THINGS DIFFERENTLY!
HEY, LUCKY THING I CAME CRASHIN' IN ON THESE HOODS, HUH?
LUCK HAD NOTHING TO DO WITH IT. I'D NOTICED SOMETHING SUSPICIOUS ABOUT THIS PLACE EARLIER.
YA MEAN...YOU THREW ME OVER HERE DELIBERATELY? THAT WAS BRILLIANT! YOU ARE DEFINITELY THE MAN!
THIS SURE MAKES THINGS EASIER ...NOW I ONLY HAVE THREE PHONIES TO CHASE DOWN!
GARDNER, I DON'T WANT YOU CHASING DOWN ANYONE OR ANYTHING IN MY CITY! DO I MAKE MYSELF CLEAR?!
OH, SURE... I GETCHA! YOU WANT TO NAIL THOSE FAKES YOURSELF, RIGHT?
SORRY, SUPES, I CAN BE A REAL CEMENT-HEAD SOMETIMES.
INDEED.
OH, AND GARDNER? THE NAME IS SUPERMAN ...NOT "SUPES!"
WHATEVER YA SAY, BIG GUY! JUST KEEP UP THE GOOD WORK...
...I'LL SQUARE THINGS HERE WITH THE COPS.

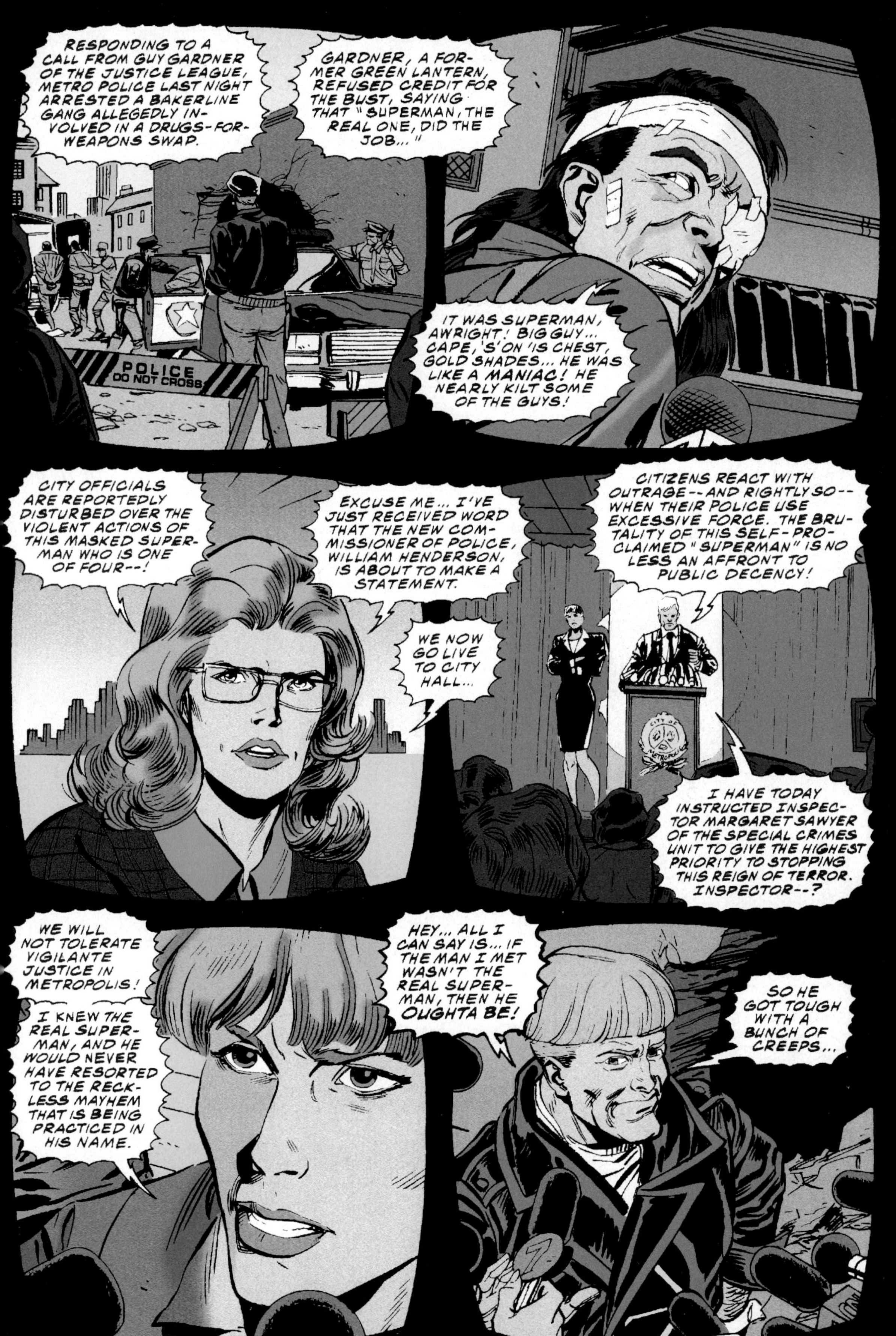
RESPONDING TO A CALL FROM GUY GARDNER OF THE JUSTICE LEAGUE, METRO POLICE LAST NIGHT ARRESTED A BAKERLINE GANG ALLEGEDLY INVOLVED IN A DRUGS-FOR-WEAPONS SWAP.
GARDNER, A FORMER GREEN LANTERN, REFUSED CREDIT FOR THE BUST, SAYING THAT "SUPERMAN, THE REAL ONE, DID THE JOB..."
POLICE DO NOT CROSS
IT WAS SUPERMAN, AWRIGHT! BIG GUY... CAPE, 'S' ON 'IS CHEST, GOLD SHADES... HE WAS LIKE A MANIAC! HE NEARLY KILT SOME OF THE GUYS!
CITY OFFICIALS ARE REPORTEDLY DISTURBED OVER THE VIOLENT ACTIONS OF THIS MASKED SUPERMAN WHO IS ONE OF FOUR--!
EXCUSE ME... I'VE JUST RECEIVED WORD THAT THE NEW COMMISSIONER OF POLICE, WILLIAM HENDERSON, IS ABOUT TO MAKE A STATEMENT.
WE NOW GO LIVE TO CITY HALL...
CITIZENS REACT WITH OUTRAGE--AND RIGHTLY SO--WHEN THEIR POLICE USE EXCESSIVE FORCE. THE BRUTALITY OF THIS SELF-PROCLAIMED "SUPERMAN" IS NO LESS AN AFFRONT TO PUBLIC DECENCY!
I HAVE TODAY INSTRUCTED INSPECTOR MARGARET SAWYER OF THE SPECIAL CRIMES UNIT TO GIVE THE HIGHEST PRIORITY TO STOPPING THIS REIGN OF TERROR. INSPECTOR--?
WE WILL NOT TOLERATE VIGILANTE JUSTICE IN METROPOLIS!
I KNEW THE REAL SUPERMAN, AND HE WOULD NEVER HAVE RESORTED TO THE RECKLESS MAYHEM THAT IS BEING PRACTICED IN HIS NAME.
HEY... ALL I CAN SAY IS... IF THE MAN I MET WASN'T THE REAL SUPERMAN, THEN HE OUGHTA BE!
SO HE GOT TOUGH WITH A BUNCH OF CREEPS...

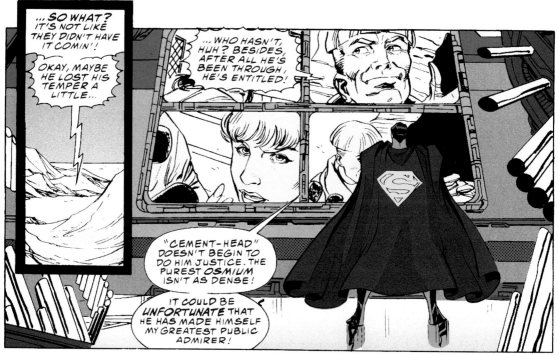

...SO WHAT? IT'S NOT LIKE THEY DIDN'T HAVE IT COMIN'!

OKAY, MAYBE HE LOST HIS TEMPER A LITTLE...

...WHO HASN'T, HUH? BESIDES, AFTER ALL HE'S BEEN THROUGH, HE'S ENTITLED!

"CEMENT-HEAD" DOESN'T BEGIN TO DO HIM JUSTICE. THE PUREST OSMIUM ISN'T AS DENSE!

IT COULD BE UNFORTUNATE THAT HE HAS MADE HIMSELF MY GREATEST PUBLIC ADMIRER!

SIR, DO YOU WISH TO CHANGE?

WHAT?! OH, YOU MEAN--!

YES, I BELIEVE I SHALL.

THIS SHIELD HAS LONG STOOD FOR JUSTICE. IF TOO MANY CLAIM IT...

...MISUSE IT... WHAT WILL IT STAND FOR THEN?

UNTIL THIS MOMENT, MY ACTIONS FELT ABSOLUTELY RIGHT. BUT... I DID LET MY ANGER AT GARDNER GET THE BETTER OF ME.

I TOOK IT OUT ON THOSE LESS CAPABLE OF DEFENDING THEMSELVES. AND NOW GARDNER CHEERS ME ON.

THAT ALONE IS REASON TO REFLECT, TO QUESTION WHAT I HAVE DONE.

PERHAPS THERE IS A BETTER WAY...

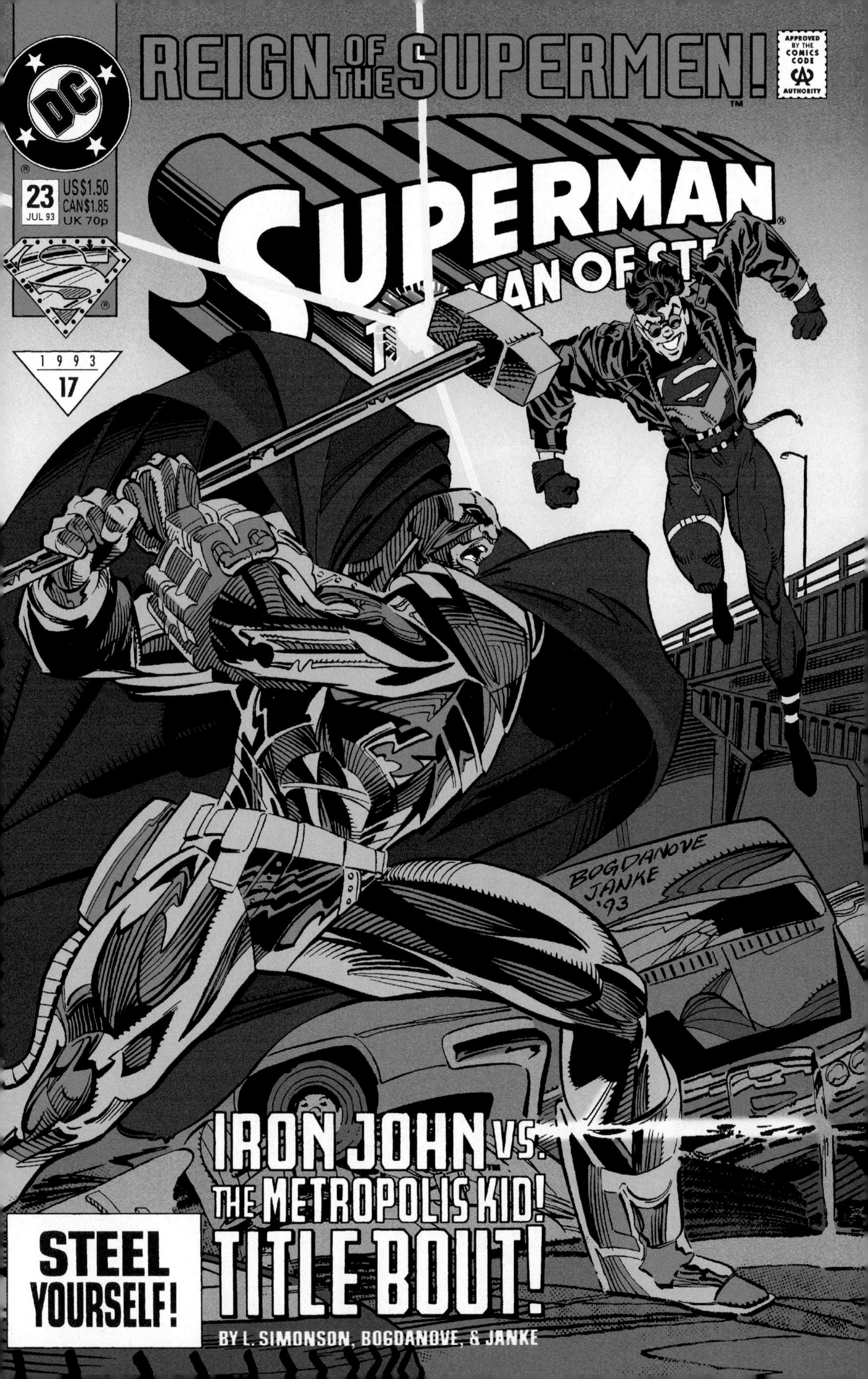
REIGN OF THE SUPERMEN!
APPROVED BY THE COMICS CODE AUTHORITY
DC
23 US$1.50 CAN$1.85 JUL 93 UK 70p
SUPERMAN THE MAN OF STEEL
1993 17
BOGDANOVE JANKE '93
IRON JOHN VS. THE METROPOLIS KID! TITLE BOUT!
STEEL YOURSELF!
BY L. SIMONSON, BOGDANOVE, & JANKE

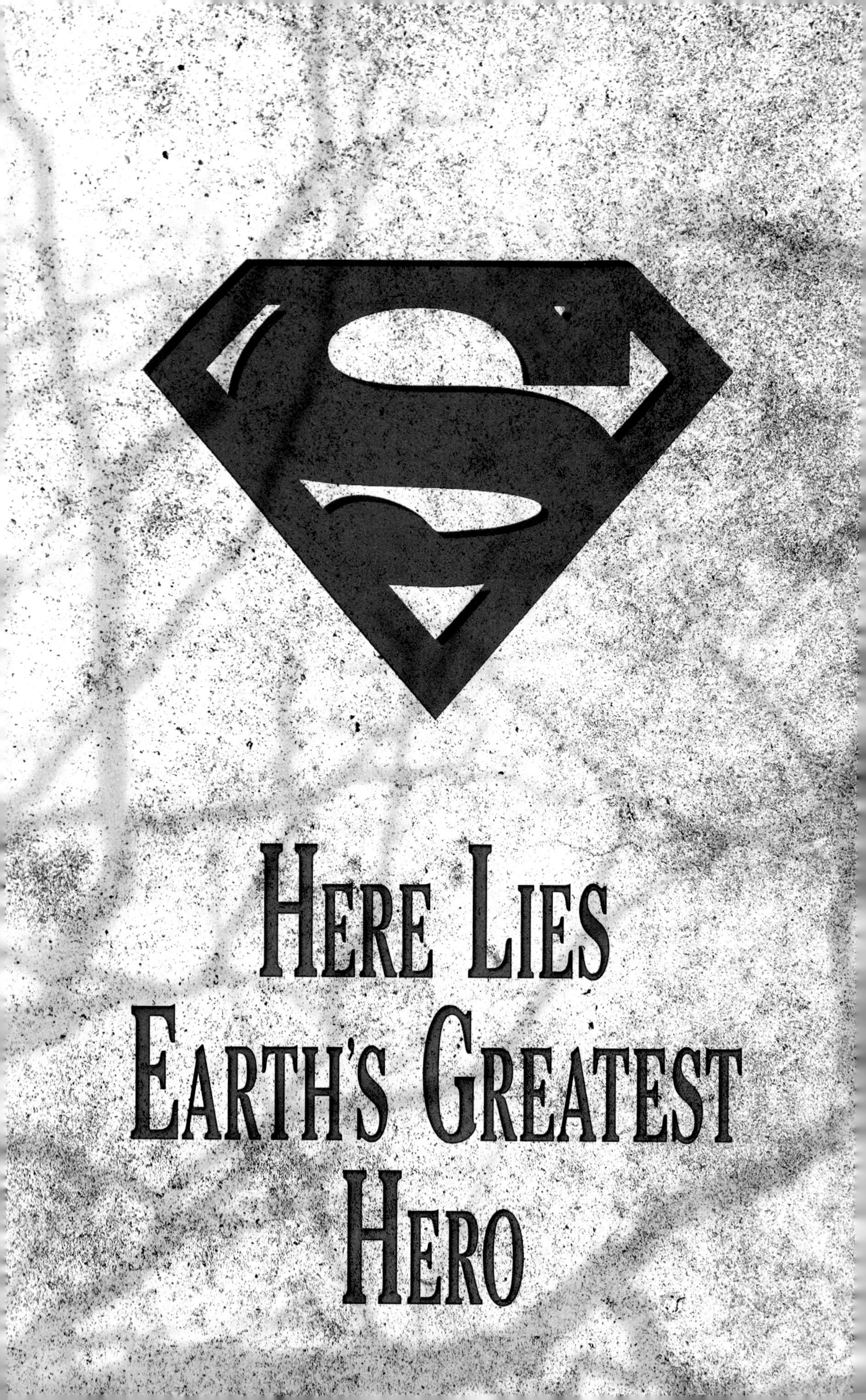
HERE LIES
EARTH'S GREATEST
HERO

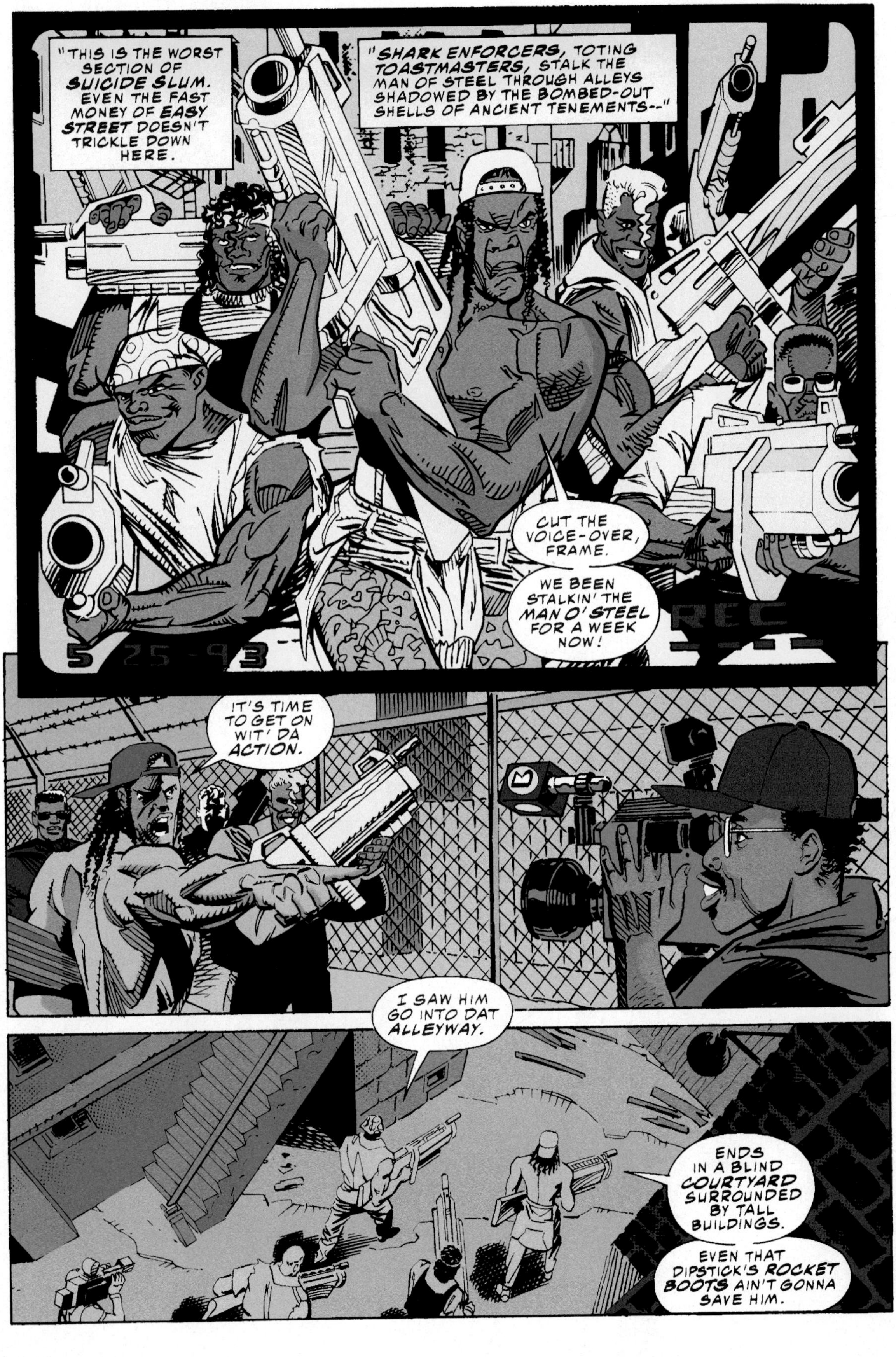
"THIS IS THE WORST SECTION OF SUICIDE SLUM. EVEN THE FAST MONEY OF EASY STREET DOESN'T TRICKLE DOWN HERE.
"SHARK ENFORCERS, TOTING TOASTMASTERS, STALK THE MAN OF STEEL THROUGH ALLEYS SHADOWED BY THE BOMBED-OUT SHELLS OF ANCIENT TENEMENTS--"
CUT THE VOICE-OVER, FRAME.
WE BEEN STALKIN' THE MAN O' STEEL FOR A WEEK NOW!
REC
5 25 93
IT'S TIME TO GET ON WIT' DA ACTION.
I SAW HIM GO INTO DAT ALLEYWAY.
ENDS IN A BLIND COURTYARD SURROUNDED BY TALL BUILDINGS.
EVEN THAT DIPSTICK'S ROCKET BOOTS AIN'T GONNA SAVE HIM.

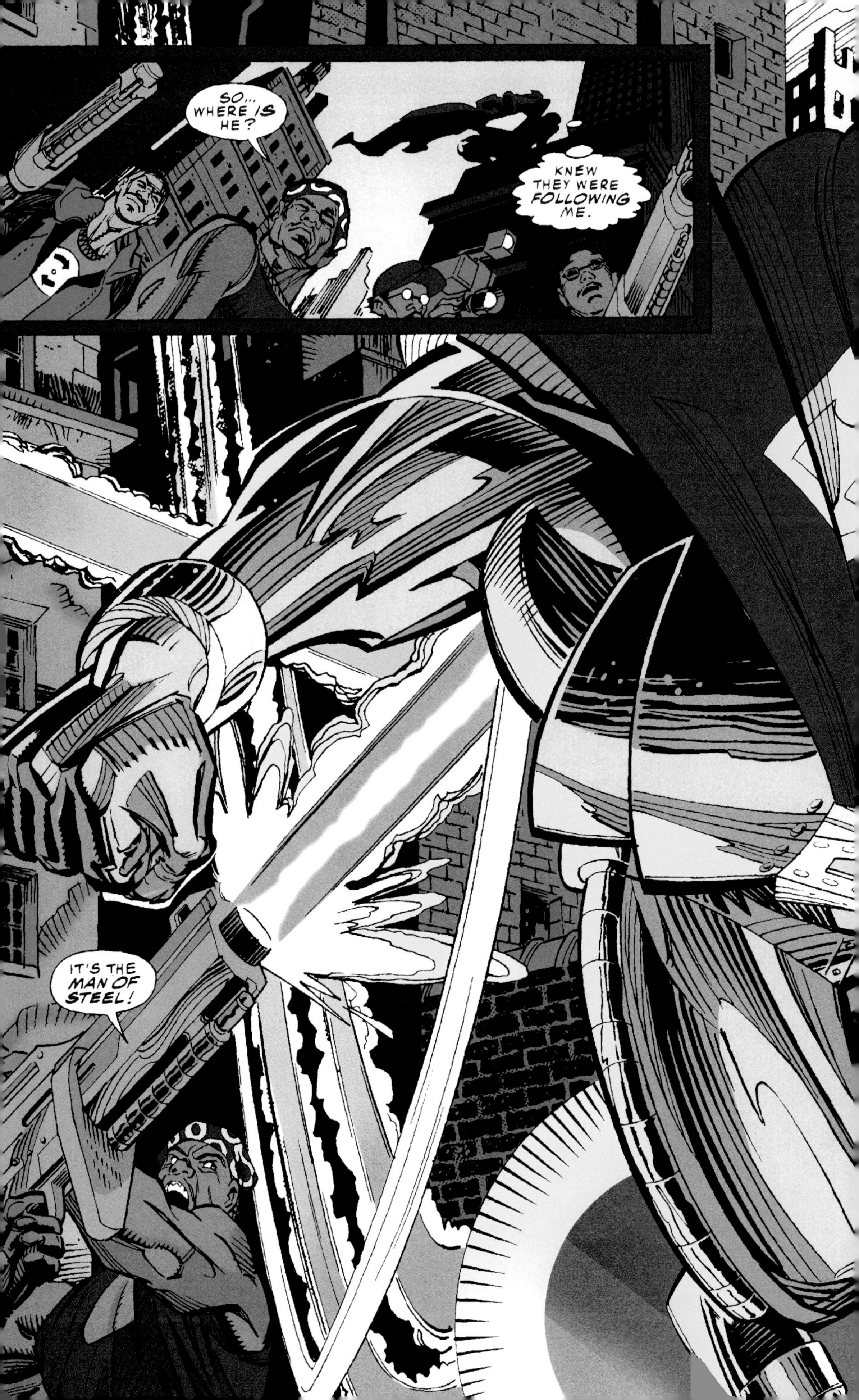
SO... WHERE IS HE?
KNEW THEY WERE FOLLOWING ME.
IT'S THE MAN OF STEEL!

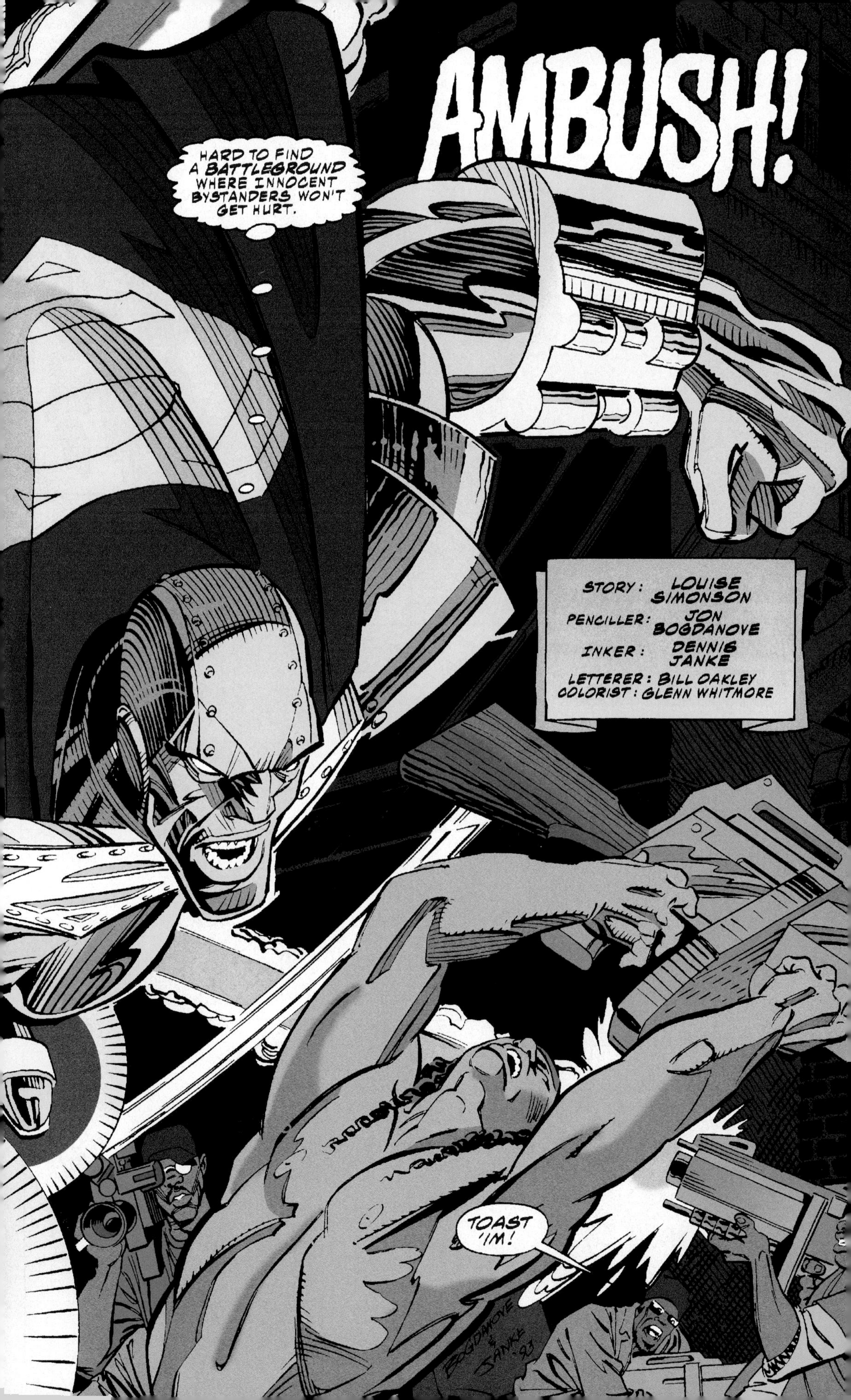
AMBUSH!
HARD TO FIND A BATTLEGROUND WHERE INNOCENT BYSTANDERS WON'T GET HURT.
STORY: LOUISE SIMONSON
PENCILLER: JON BOGDANOVE
INKER: DENNIS JANKE
LETTERER: BILL OAKLEY
COLORIST: GLENN WHITMORE
TOAST 'IM!
BOGDANOVE & JANKE -93

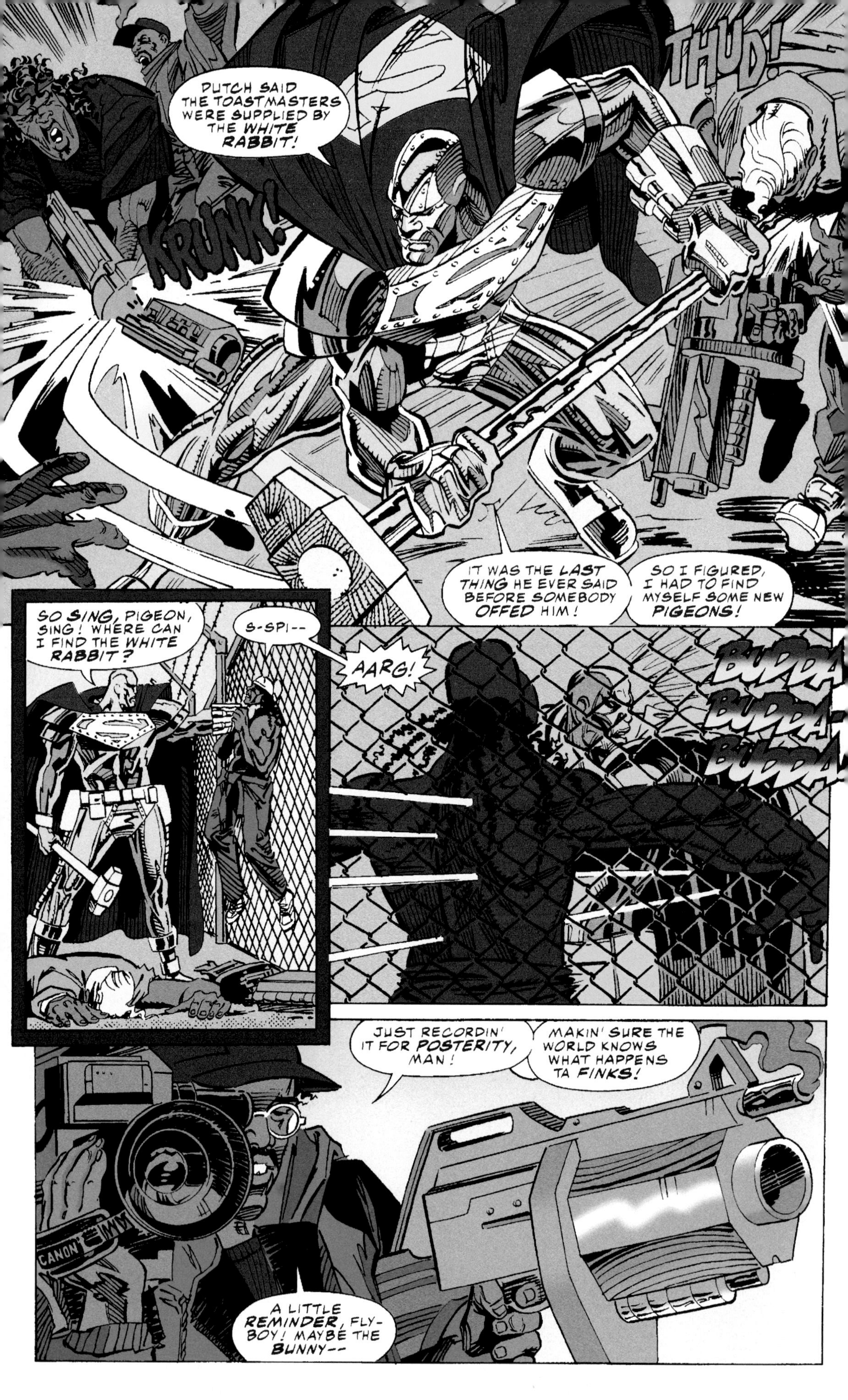
DUTCH SAID THE TOASTMASTERS WERE SUPPLIED BY THE WHITE RABBIT!
THUD!
KRUNK!
IT WAS THE LAST THING HE EVER SAID BEFORE SOMEBODY OFFED HIM!
SO I FIGURED, I HAD TO FIND MYSELF SOME NEW PIGEONS!
SO SING, PIGEON, SING! WHERE CAN I FIND THE WHITE RABBIT?
S-SPI--
AARG!
BUDDA BUDDA-BUDDA!
JUST RECORDIN' IT FOR POSTERITY, MAN!
MAKIN' SURE THE WORLD KNOWS WHAT HAPPENS TA FINKS!
CANON
A LITTLE REMINDER, FLY-BOY! MAYBE THE BUNNY--

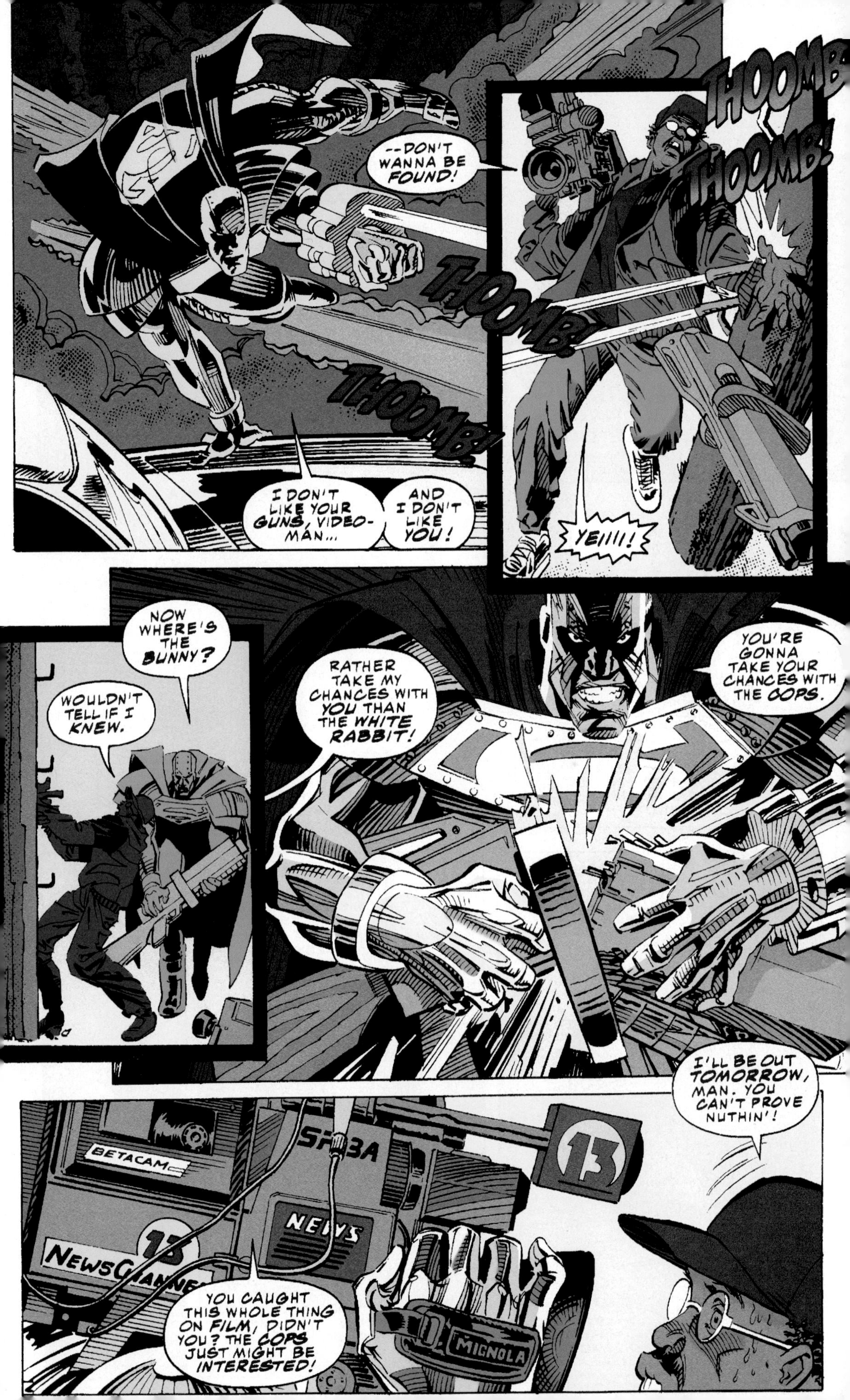

--DON'T WANNA BE FOUND!
THOOMB
THOOMB!
THOOMB
THOOMB
THOOMB!
I DON'T LIKE YOUR GUNS, VIDEO-MAN...
AND I DON'T LIKE YOU!
YEIIII!
NOW WHERE'S THE BUNNY?
WOULDN'T TELL IF I KNEW.
RATHER TAKE MY CHANCES WITH YOU THAN THE WHITE RABBIT!
YOU'RE GONNA TAKE YOUR CHANCES WITH THE COPS.
I'LL BE OUT TOMORROW, MAN. YOU CAN'T PROVE NUTHIN'!
BETACAM
SHIBA
13
NEWS
NEWSCHANNEL
YOU CAUGHT THIS WHOLE THING ON FILM, DIDN'T YOU? THE COPS JUST MIGHT BE INTERESTED!
MIGNOLA

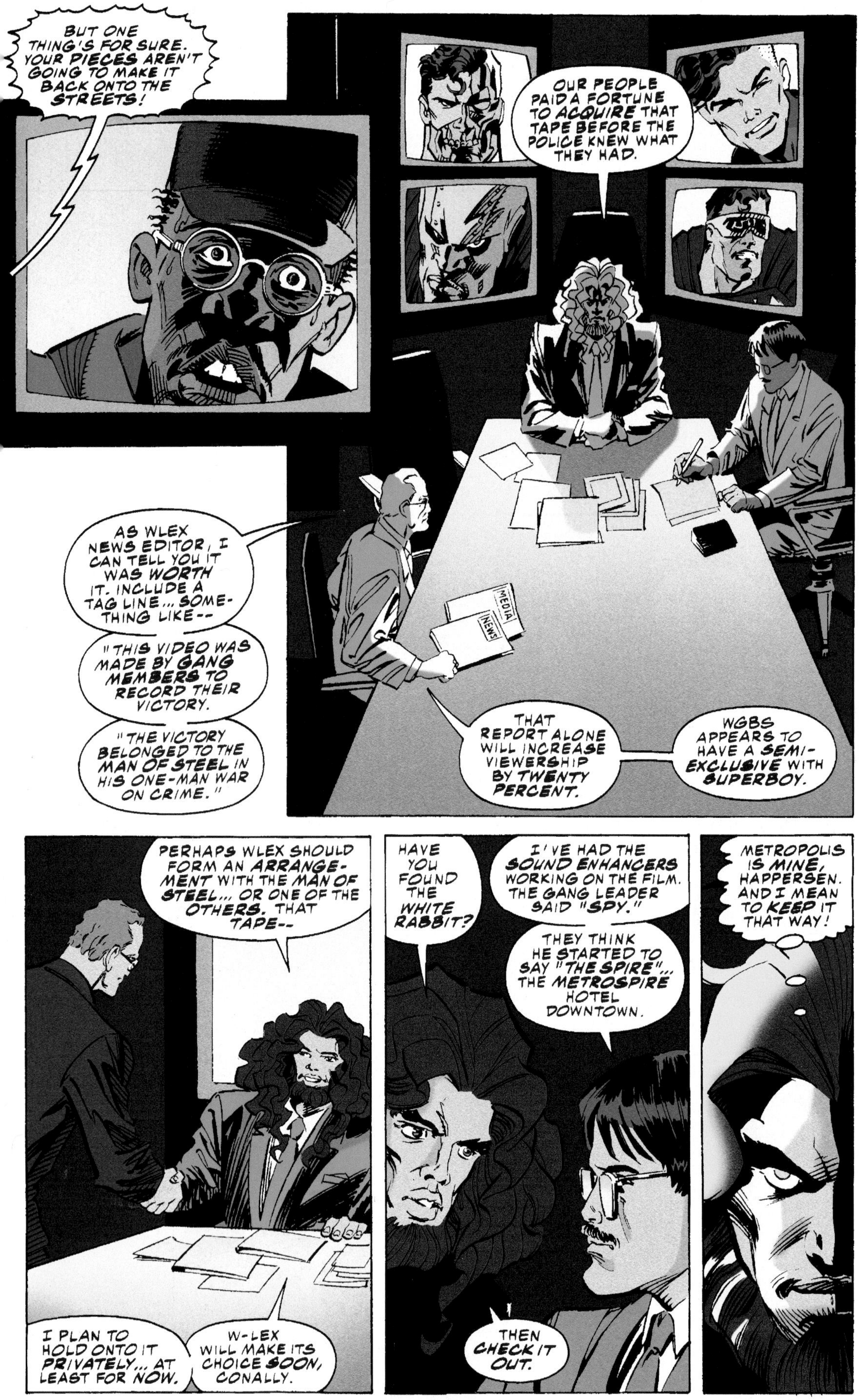
BUT ONE THING'S FOR SURE. YOUR PIECES AREN'T GOING TO MAKE IT BACK ONTO THE STREETS!
OUR PEOPLE PAID A FORTUNE TO ACQUIRE THAT TAPE BEFORE THE POLICE KNEW WHAT THEY HAD.
AS WLEX NEWS EDITOR, I CAN TELL YOU IT WAS WORTH IT. INCLUDE A TAG LINE... SOMETHING LIKE--
"THIS VIDEO WAS MADE BY GANG MEMBERS TO RECORD THEIR VICTORY.
"THE VICTORY BELONGED TO THE MAN OF STEEL IN HIS ONE-MAN WAR ON CRIME."
MEDIA
NEWS
THAT REPORT ALONE WILL INCREASE VIEWERSHIP BY TWENTY PERCENT.
WGBS APPEARS TO HAVE A SEMI-EXCLUSIVE WITH SUPERBOY.
PERHAPS WLEX SHOULD FORM AN ARRANGEMENT WITH THE MAN OF STEEL... OR ONE OF THE OTHERS. THAT TAPE--
I PLAN TO HOLD ONTO IT PRIVATELY... AT LEAST FOR NOW.
W-LEX WILL MAKE ITS CHOICE SOON, CONALLY.
HAVE YOU FOUND THE WHITE RABBIT?
I'VE HAD THE SOUND ENHANCERS WORKING ON THE FILM. THE GANG LEADER SAID "SPY."
THEY THINK HE STARTED TO SAY "THE SPIRE"... THE METROSPIRE HOTEL DOWNTOWN.
THEN CHECK IT OUT.
METROPOLIS IS MINE, HAPPERSEN. AND I MEAN TO KEEP IT THAT WAY!

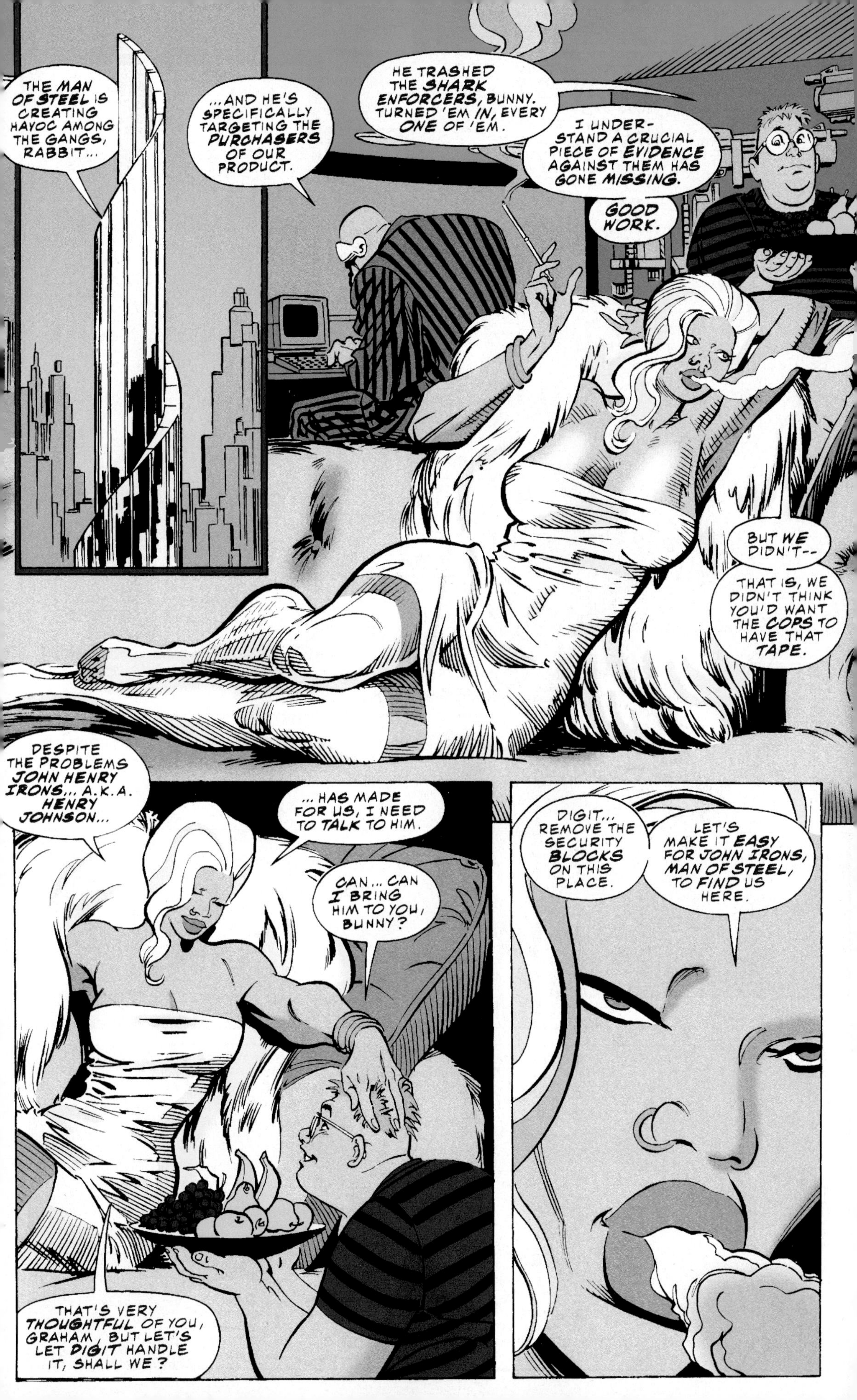
THE MAN OF STEEL IS CREATING HAVOC AMONG THE GANGS, RABBIT...
...AND HE'S SPECIFICALLY TARGETING THE PURCHASERS OF OUR PRODUCT.
HE TRASHED THE SHARK ENFORCERS, BUNNY. TURNED 'EM IN, EVERY ONE OF 'EM.
I UNDERSTAND A CRUCIAL PIECE OF EVIDENCE AGAINST THEM HAS GONE MISSING.
GOOD WORK.
BUT WE DIDN'T--
THAT IS, WE DIDN'T THINK YOU'D WANT THE COPS TO HAVE THAT TAPE.
DESPITE THE PROBLEMS JOHN HENRY IRONS... A.K.A. HENRY JOHNSON...
...HAS MADE FOR US, I NEED TO TALK TO HIM.
CAN... CAN I BRING HIM TO YOU, BUNNY?
THAT'S VERY THOUGHTFUL OF YOU, GRAHAM, BUT LET'S LET DIGIT HANDLE IT, SHALL WE?
DIGIT... REMOVE THE SECURITY BLOCKS ON THIS PLACE.
LET'S MAKE IT EASY FOR JOHN IRONS, MAN OF STEEL, TO FIND US HERE.

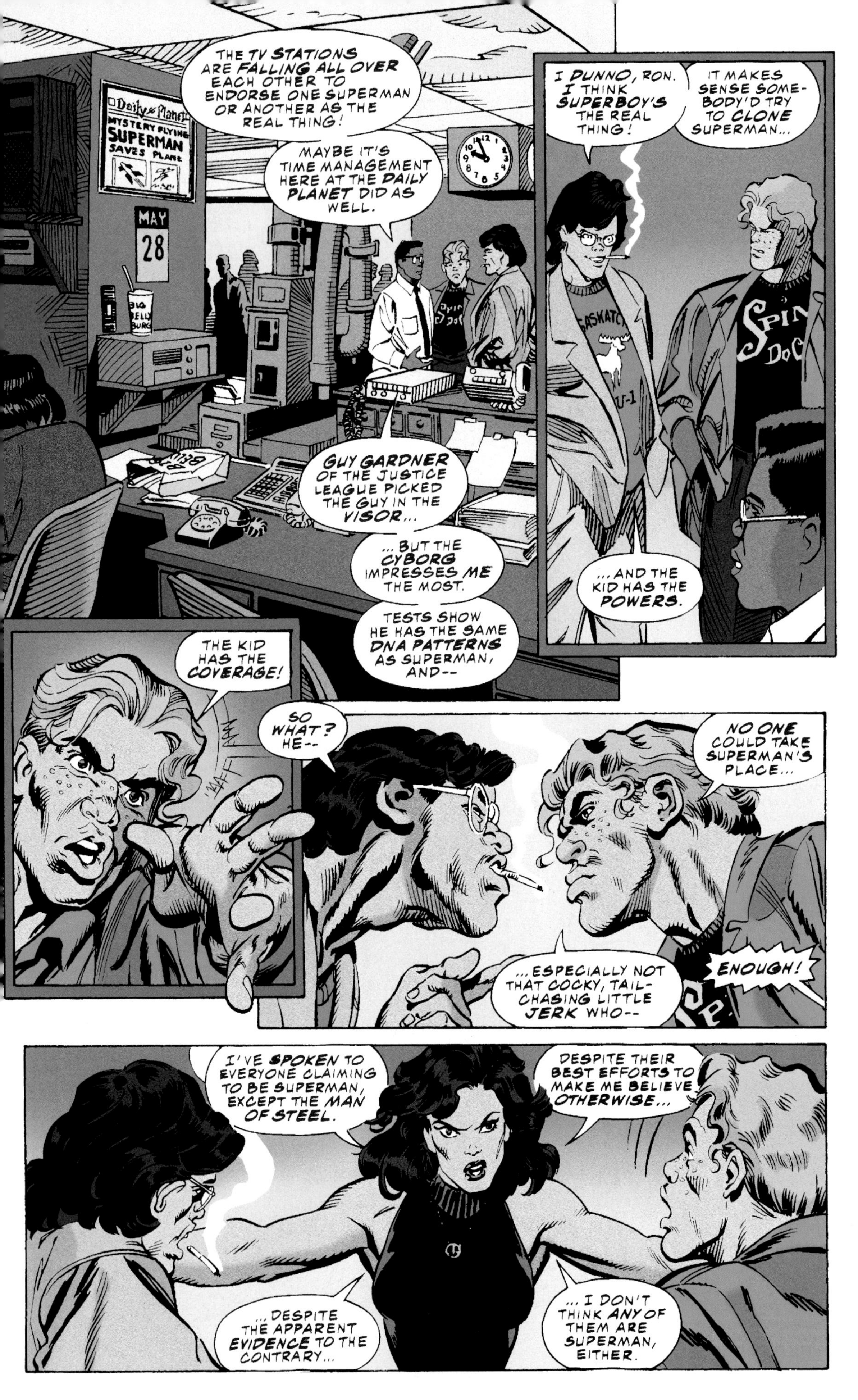
THE TV STATIONS ARE FALLING ALL OVER EACH OTHER TO ENDORSE ONE SUPERMAN OR ANOTHER AS THE REAL THING!
MAYBE IT'S TIME MANAGEMENT HERE AT THE DAILY PLANET DID AS WELL.
Daily Planet
MYSTERY FLYING SUPERMAN SAVES PLANE
MAY
28
GUY GARDNER OF THE JUSTICE LEAGUE PICKED THE GUY IN THE VISOR...
...BUT THE CYBORG IMPRESSES ME THE MOST.
TESTS SHOW HE HAS THE SAME DNA PATTERNS AS SUPERMAN, AND--
I DUNNO, RON. I THINK SUPERBOY'S THE REAL THING!
IT MAKES SENSE SOMEBODY'D TRY TO CLONE SUPERMAN...
...AND THE KID HAS THE POWERS.
THE KID HAS THE COVERAGE!
SO WHAT? HE--
NO ONE COULD TAKE SUPERMAN'S PLACE...
...ESPECIALLY NOT THAT COCKY, TAIL-CHASING LITTLE JERK WHO--
ENOUGH!
I'VE SPOKEN TO EVERYONE CLAIMING TO BE SUPERMAN, EXCEPT THE MAN OF STEEL.
...DESPITE THE APPARENT EVIDENCE TO THE CONTRARY...
DESPITE THEIR BEST EFFORTS TO MAKE ME BELIEVE OTHERWISE...
...I DON'T THINK ANY OF THEM ARE SUPERMAN, EITHER.

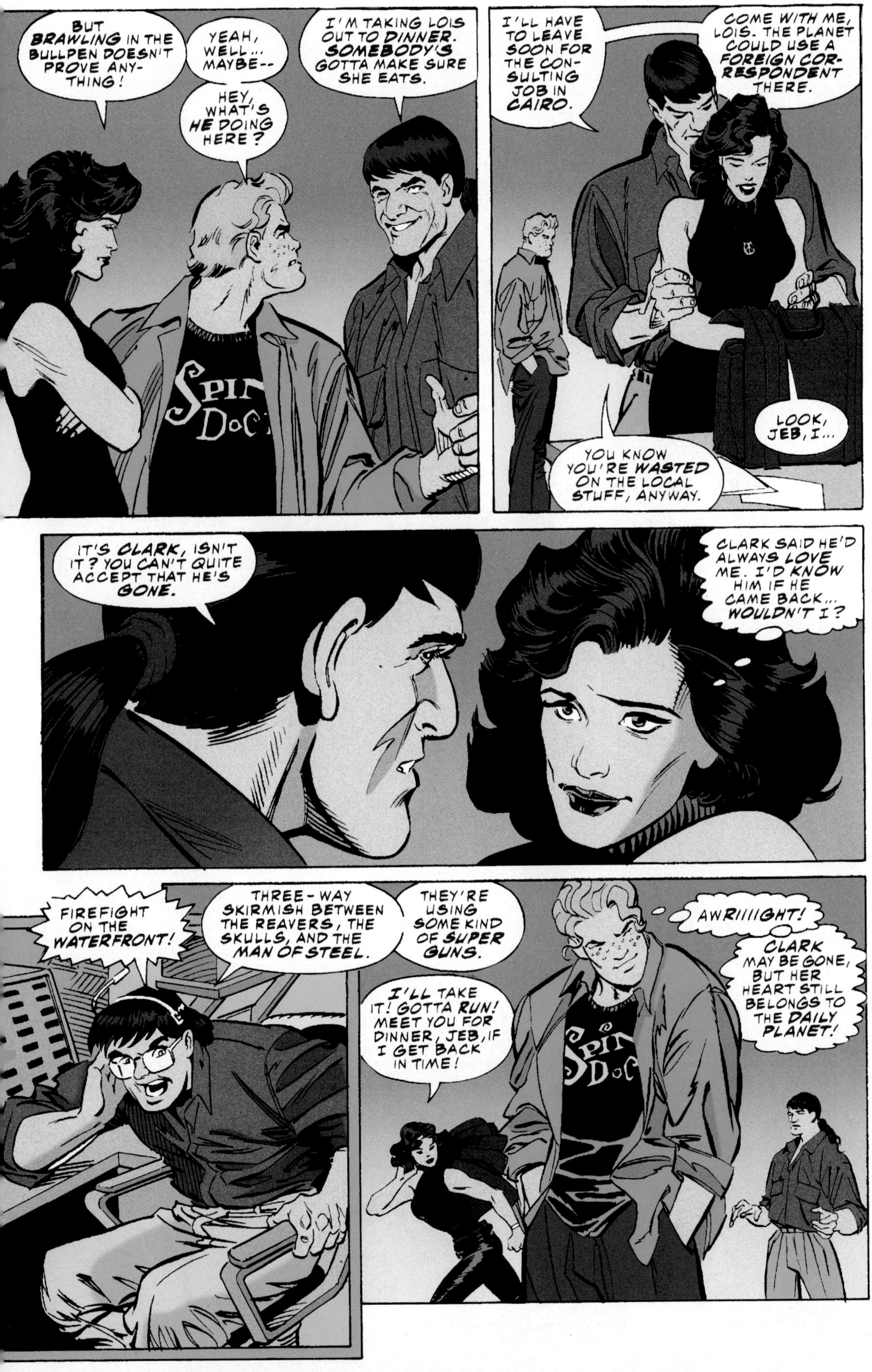
BUT BRAWLING IN THE BULLPEN DOESN'T PROVE ANY-THING!
YEAH, WELL... MAYBE--
HEY, WHAT'S HE DOING HERE?
I'M TAKING LOIS OUT TO DINNER. SOMEBODY'S GOTTA MAKE SURE SHE EATS.
I'LL HAVE TO LEAVE SOON FOR THE CON-SULTING JOB IN CAIRO.
COME WITH ME, LOIS. THE PLANET COULD USE A FOREIGN COR-RESPONDENT THERE.
YOU KNOW YOU'RE WASTED ON THE LOCAL STUFF, ANYWAY.
LOOK, JEB, I...
IT'S CLARK, ISN'T IT? YOU CAN'T QUITE ACCEPT THAT HE'S GONE.
CLARK SAID HE'D ALWAYS LOVE ME. I'D KNOW HIM IF HE CAME BACK... WOULDN'T I?
FIREFIGHT ON THE WATERFRONT!
THREE-WAY SKIRMISH BETWEEN THE REAVERS, THE SKULLS, AND THE MAN OF STEEL.
THEY'RE USING SOME KIND OF SUPER GUNS.
I'LL TAKE IT! GOTTA RUN! MEET YOU FOR DINNER, JEB, IF I GET BACK IN TIME!
AWRIIIIGHT!
CLARK MAY BE GONE, BUT HER HEART STILL BELONGS TO THE DAILY PLANET!

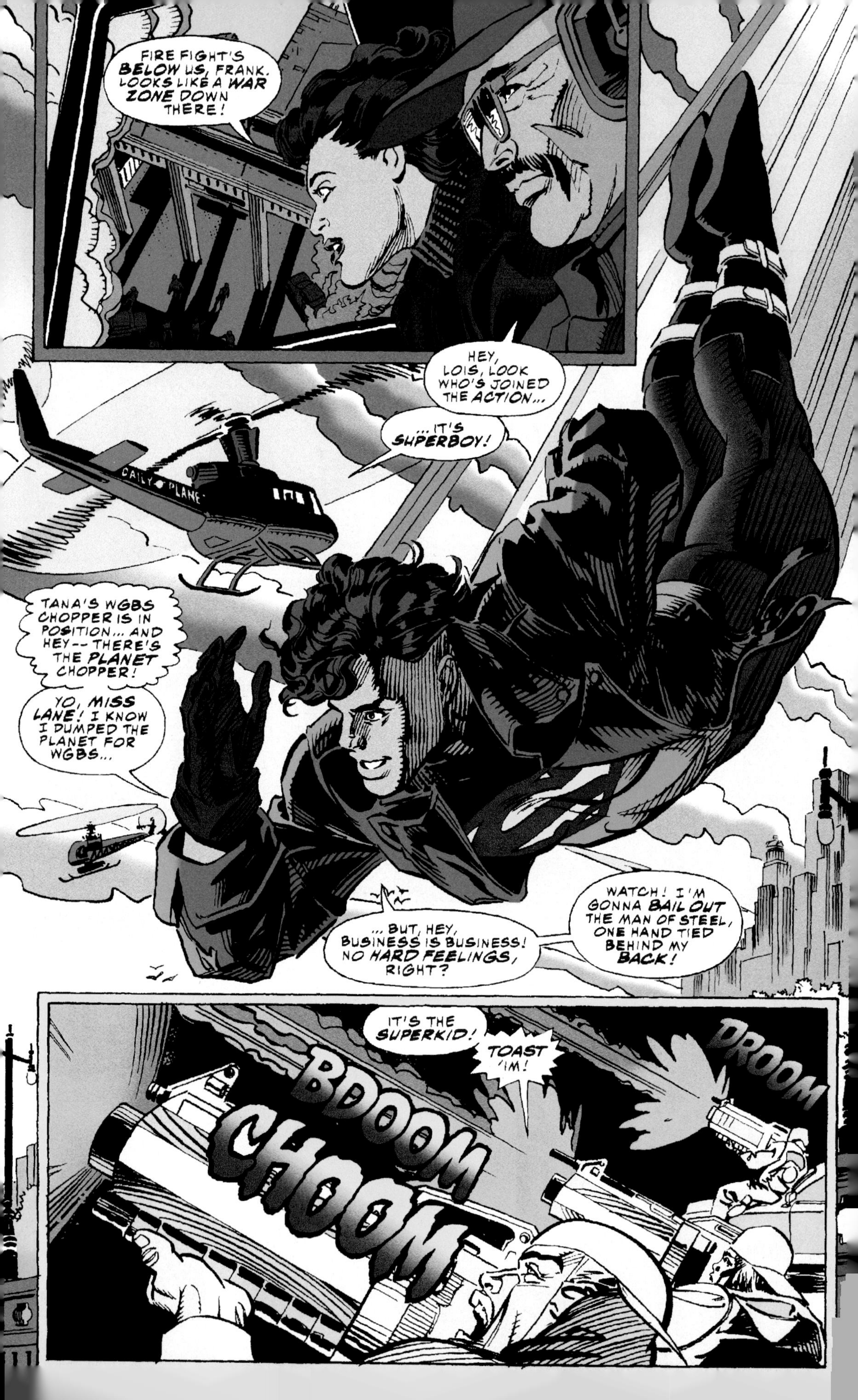
FIRE FIGHT'S BELOW US, FRANK. LOOKS LIKE A WAR ZONE DOWN THERE!
HEY, LOIS, LOOK WHO'S JOINED THE ACTION...
...IT'S SUPERBOY!
DAILY PLANET
TANA'S WGBS CHOPPER IS IN POSITION... AND HEY -- THERE'S THE PLANET CHOPPER!
YO, MISS LANE! I KNOW I DUMPED THE PLANET FOR WGBS...
...BUT, HEY, BUSINESS IS BUSINESS! NO HARD FEELINGS, RIGHT?
WATCH! I'M GONNA BAIL OUT THE MAN OF STEEL, ONE HAND TIED BEHIND MY BACK!
IT'S THE SUPERKID!
TOAST 'IM!
BDOOM
CHOOM
DROOM

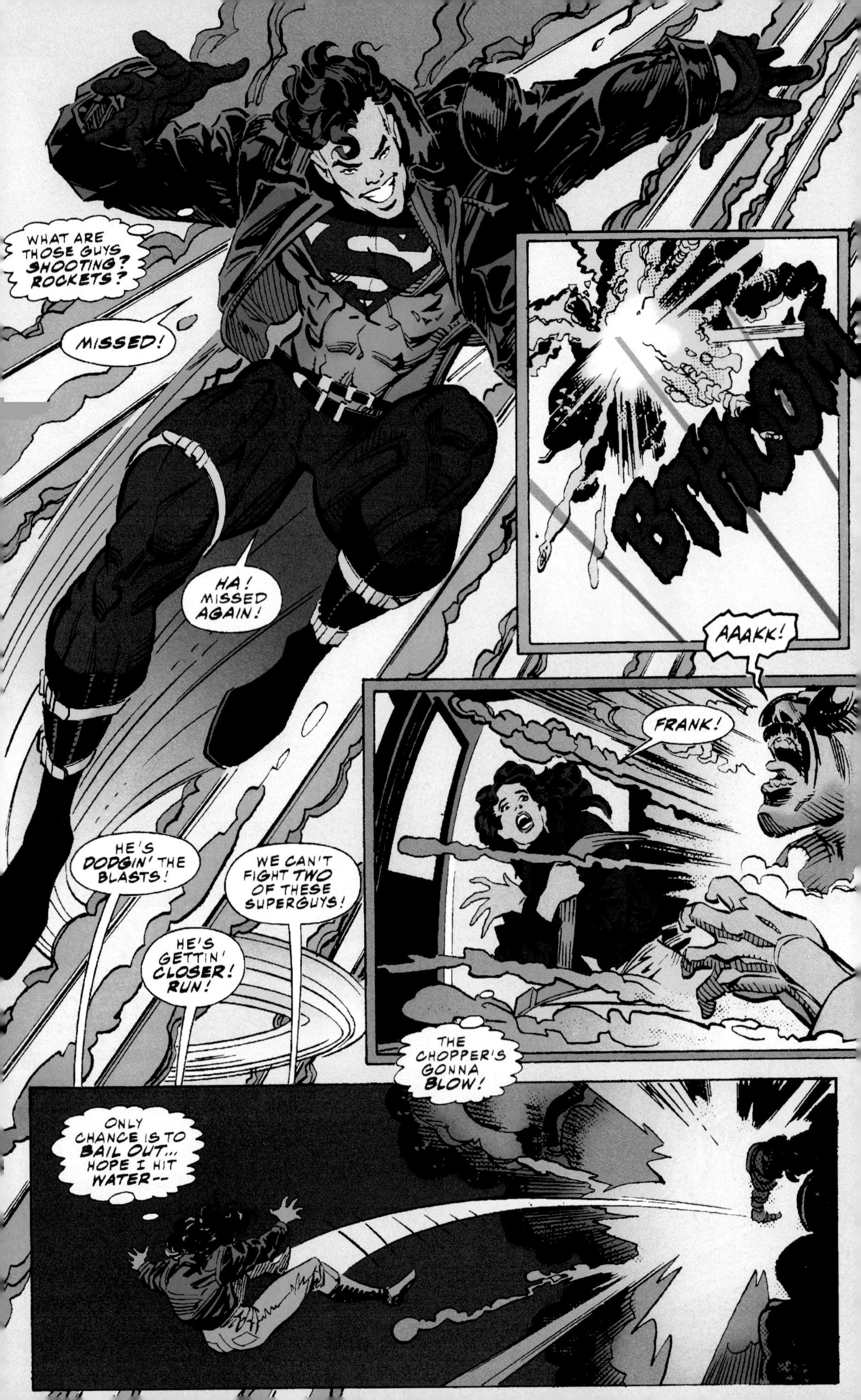
WHAT ARE THOSE GUYS SHOOTING? ROCKETS?
MISSED!
HA! MISSED AGAIN!
BTHOOM
AAAKK!
FRANK!
HE'S DODGIN' THE BLASTS!
HE'S GETTIN' CLOSER! RUN!
WE CAN'T FIGHT TWO OF THESE SUPERGUYS!
THE CHOPPER'S GONNA BLOW!
ONLY CHANCE IS TO BAIL OUT... HOPE I HIT WATER--

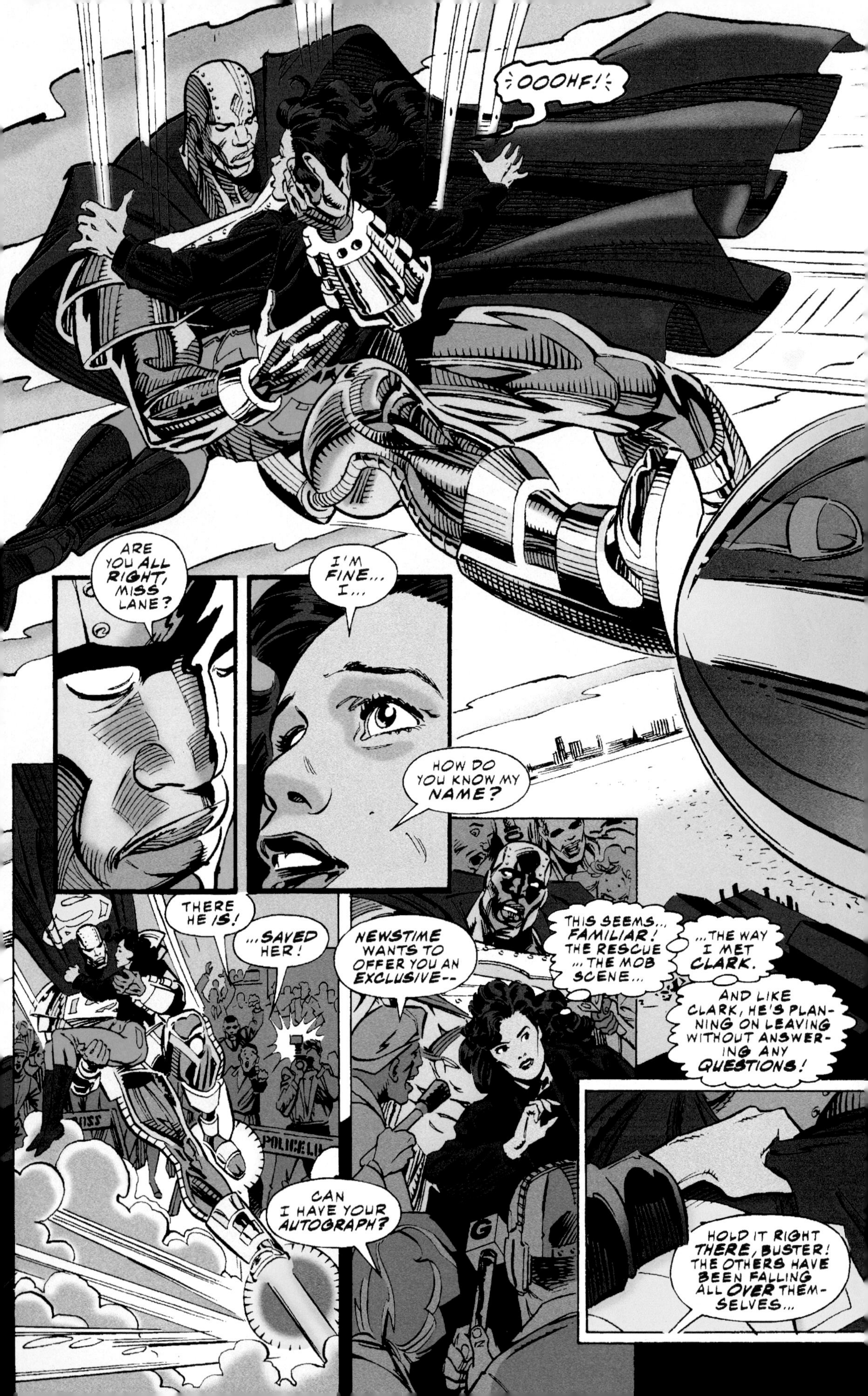
OOOHF!
ARE YOU ALL RIGHT, MISS LANE?
I'M FINE... I...
HOW DO YOU KNOW MY NAME?
THERE HE IS!
...SAVED HER!
NEWSTIME WANTS TO OFFER YOU AN EXCLUSIVE--
THIS SEEMS... FAMILIAR! THE RESCUE ...THE MOB SCENE...
...THE WAY I MET CLARK.
AND LIKE CLARK, HE'S PLANNING ON LEAVING WITHOUT ANSWERING ANY QUESTIONS!
CAN I HAVE YOUR AUTOGRAPH?
HOLD IT RIGHT THERE, BUSTER! THE OTHERS HAVE BEEN FALLING ALL OVER THEMSELVES...

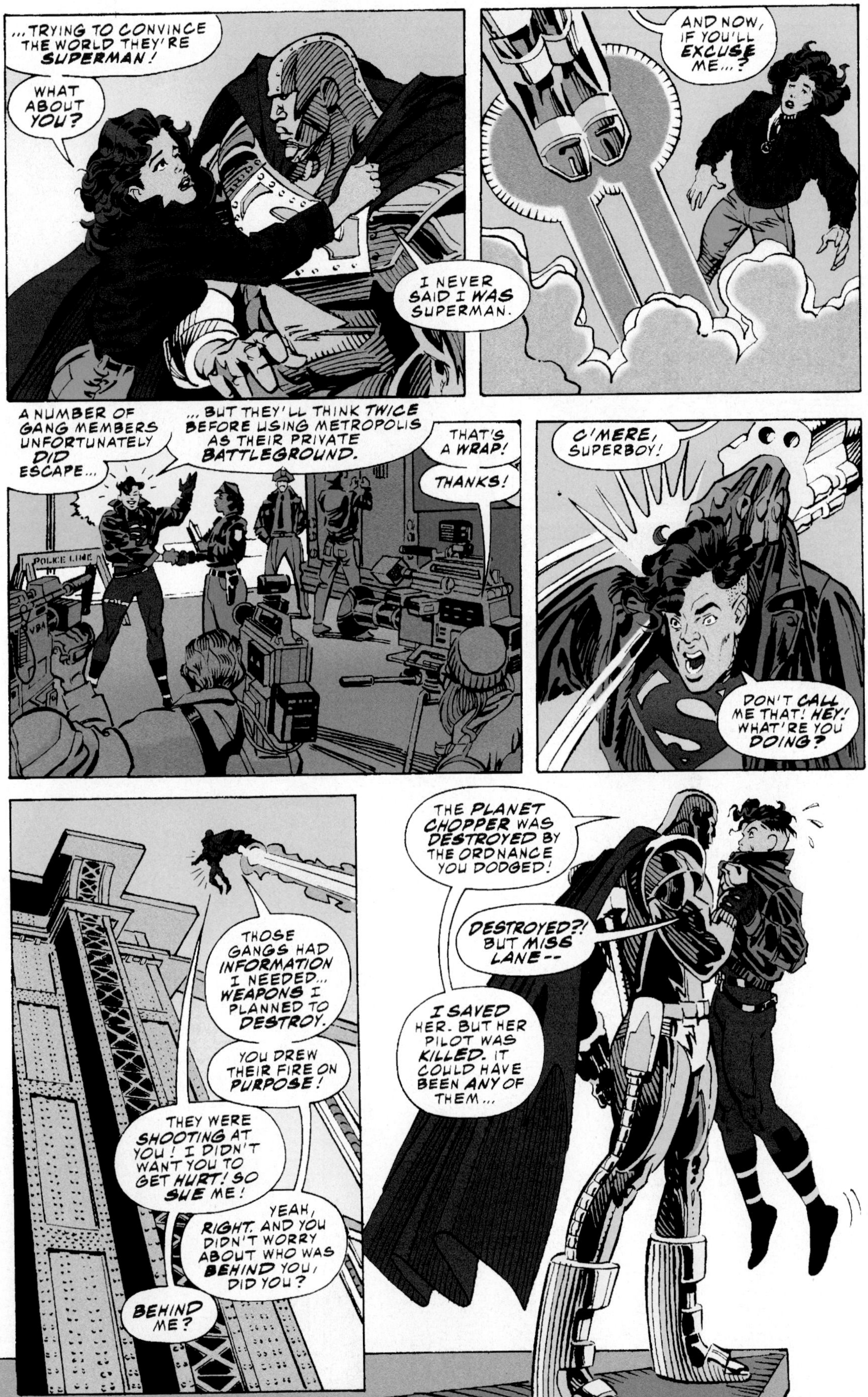

...TRYING TO CONVINCE THE WORLD THEY'RE SUPERMAN!
WHAT ABOUT YOU?
I NEVER SAID I WAS SUPERMAN.
AND NOW, IF YOU'LL EXCUSE ME...?
A NUMBER OF GANG MEMBERS UNFORTUNATELY DID ESCAPE...
...BUT THEY'LL THINK TWICE BEFORE USING METROPOLIS AS THEIR PRIVATE BATTLEGROUND.
THAT'S A WRAP!
THANKS!
POLICE LINE
C'MERE, SUPERBOY!
DON'T CALL ME THAT! HEY! WHAT'RE YOU DOING?
THOSE GANGS HAD INFORMATION I NEEDED... WEAPONS I PLANNED TO DESTROY.
YOU DREW THEIR FIRE ON PURPOSE!
THEY WERE SHOOTING AT YOU! I DIDN'T WANT YOU TO GET HURT! SO SUE ME!
YEAH, RIGHT. AND YOU DIDN'T WORRY ABOUT WHO WAS BEHIND YOU, DID YOU?
BEHIND ME?
THE PLANET CHOPPER WAS DESTROYED BY THE ORDNANCE YOU DODGED!
DESTROYED?! BUT MISS LANE--
I SAVED HER. BUT HER PILOT WAS KILLED. IT COULD HAVE BEEN ANY OF THEM...

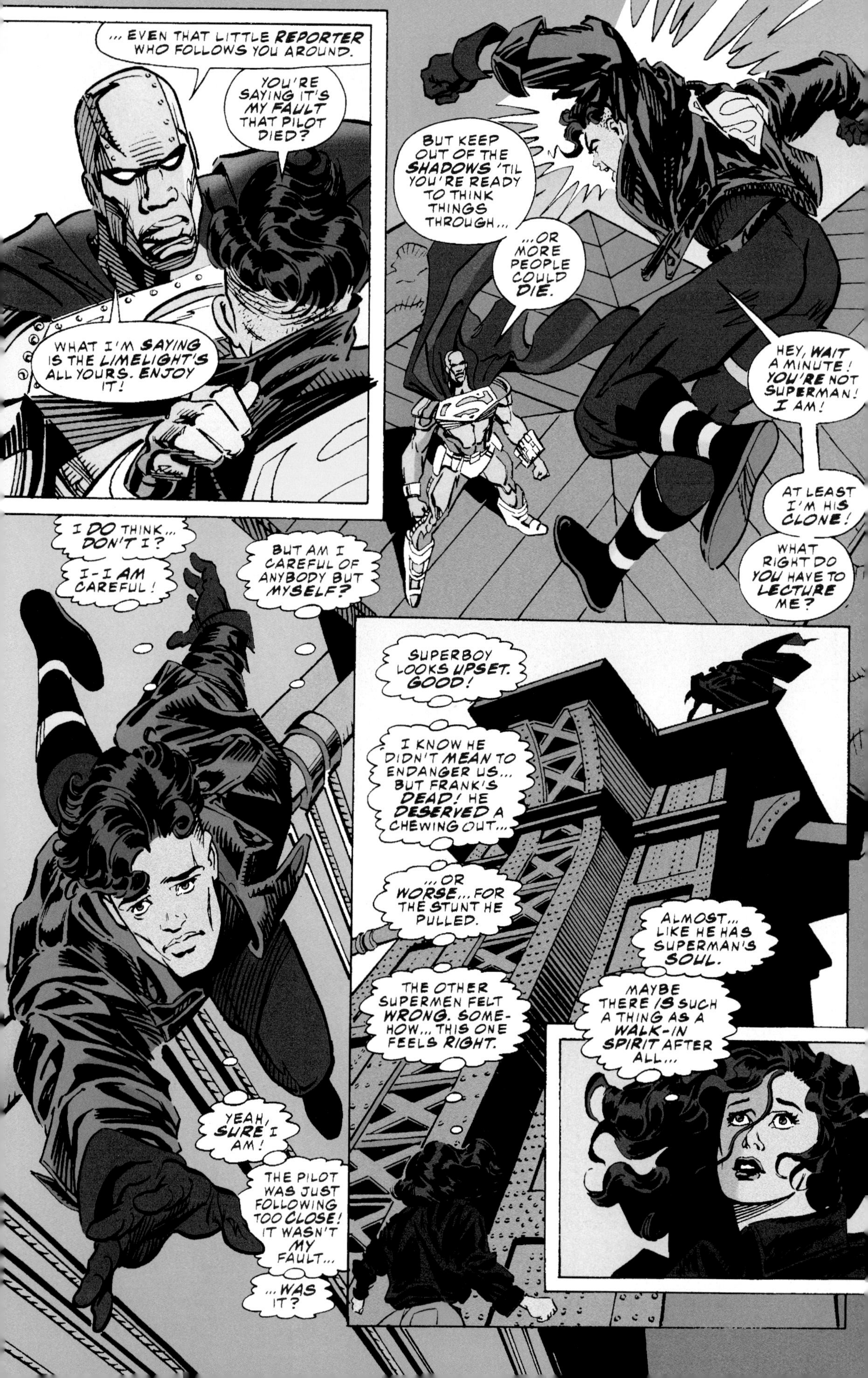
... EVEN THAT LITTLE REPORTER WHO FOLLOWS YOU AROUND.
YOU'RE SAYING IT'S MY FAULT THAT PILOT DIED?
WHAT I'M SAYING IS THE LIMELIGHT'S ALL YOURS. ENJOY IT!
BUT KEEP OUT OF THE SHADOWS 'TIL YOU'RE READY TO THINK THINGS THROUGH...
...OR MORE PEOPLE COULD DIE.
HEY, WAIT A MINUTE! YOU'RE NOT SUPERMAN! I AM!
AT LEAST I'M HIS CLONE!
WHAT RIGHT DO YOU HAVE TO LECTURE ME?
I DO THINK... DON'T I?
I-I AM CAREFUL!
BUT AM I CAREFUL OF ANYBODY BUT MYSELF?
YEAH, SURE I AM!
THE PILOT WAS JUST FOLLOWING TOO CLOSE! IT WASN'T MY FAULT...
...WAS IT?
SUPERBOY LOOKS UPSET. GOOD!
I KNOW HE DIDN'T MEAN TO ENDANGER US... BUT FRANK'S DEAD! HE DESERVED A CHEWING OUT...
...OR WORSE... FOR THE STUNT HE PULLED.
THE OTHER SUPERMEN FELT WRONG. SOME-HOW... THIS ONE FEELS RIGHT.
ALMOST... LIKE HE HAS SUPERMAN'S SOUL.
MAYBE THERE IS SUCH A THING AS A WALK-IN SPIRIT AFTER ALL...

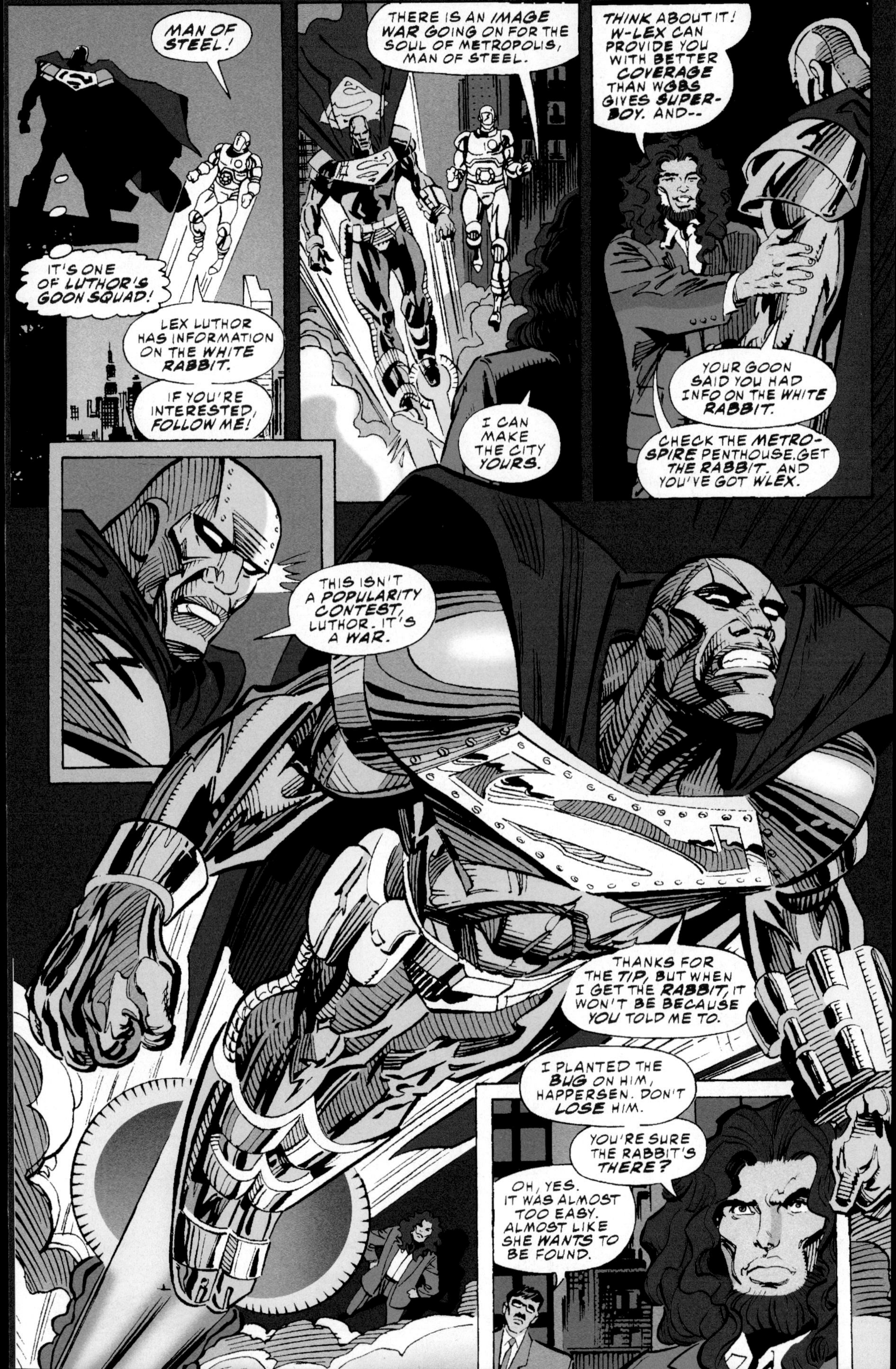
MAN OF STEEL!
IT'S ONE OF LUTHOR'S GOON SQUAD!
LEX LUTHOR HAS INFORMATION ON THE WHITE RABBIT.
IF YOU'RE INTERESTED, FOLLOW ME!
THERE IS AN IMAGE WAR GOING ON FOR THE SOUL OF METROPOLIS, MAN OF STEEL.
I CAN MAKE THE CITY YOURS.
THINK ABOUT IT! W-LEX CAN PROVIDE YOU WITH BETTER COVERAGE THAN WGBS GIVES SUPERBOY. AND--
YOUR GOON SAID YOU HAD INFO ON THE WHITE RABBIT.
CHECK THE METROSPIRE PENTHOUSE. GET THE RABBIT. AND YOU'VE GOT WLEX.
THIS ISN'T A POPULARITY CONTEST, LUTHOR. IT'S A WAR.
THANKS FOR THE TIP, BUT WHEN I GET THE RABBIT, IT WON'T BE BECAUSE YOU TOLD ME TO.
I PLANTED THE BUG ON HIM, HAPPERSEN. DON'T LOSE HIM.
YOU'RE SURE THE RABBIT'S THERE?
OH, YES. IT WAS ALMOST TOO EASY. ALMOST LIKE SHE WANTS TO BE FOUND.

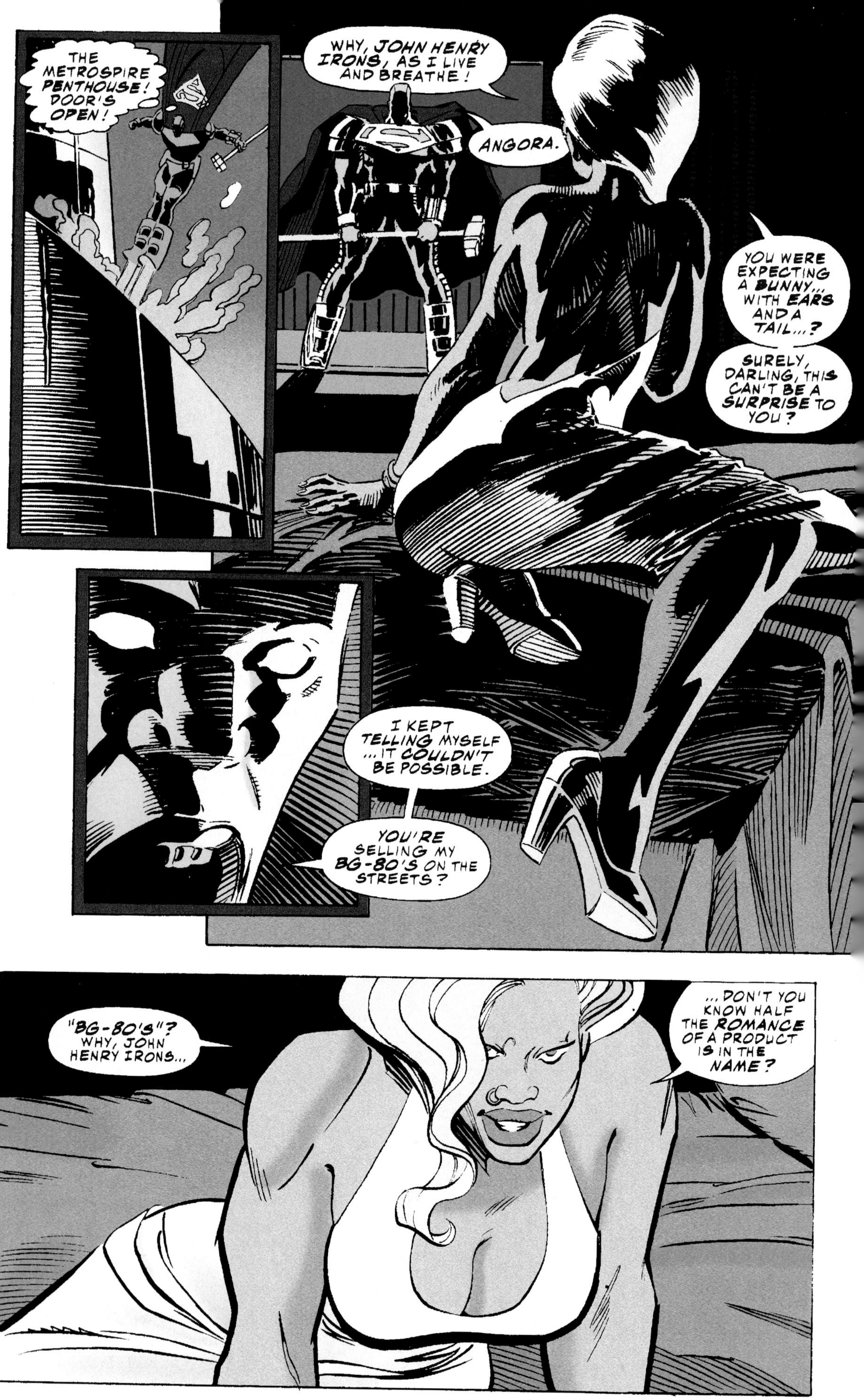
THE METROSPIRE PENTHOUSE! DOOR'S OPEN!
WHY, JOHN HENRY IRONS, AS I LIVE AND BREATHE!
ANGORA.
YOU WERE EXPECTING A BUNNY... WITH EARS AND A TAIL...?
SURELY, DARLING, THIS CAN'T BE A SURPRISE TO YOU?
I KEPT TELLING MYSELF ...IT COULDN'T BE POSSIBLE.
YOU'RE SELLING MY BG-80'S ON THE STREETS?
"BG-80'S"? WHY, JOHN HENRY IRONS...
...DON'T YOU KNOW HALF THE ROMANCE OF A PRODUCT IS IN THE NAME?

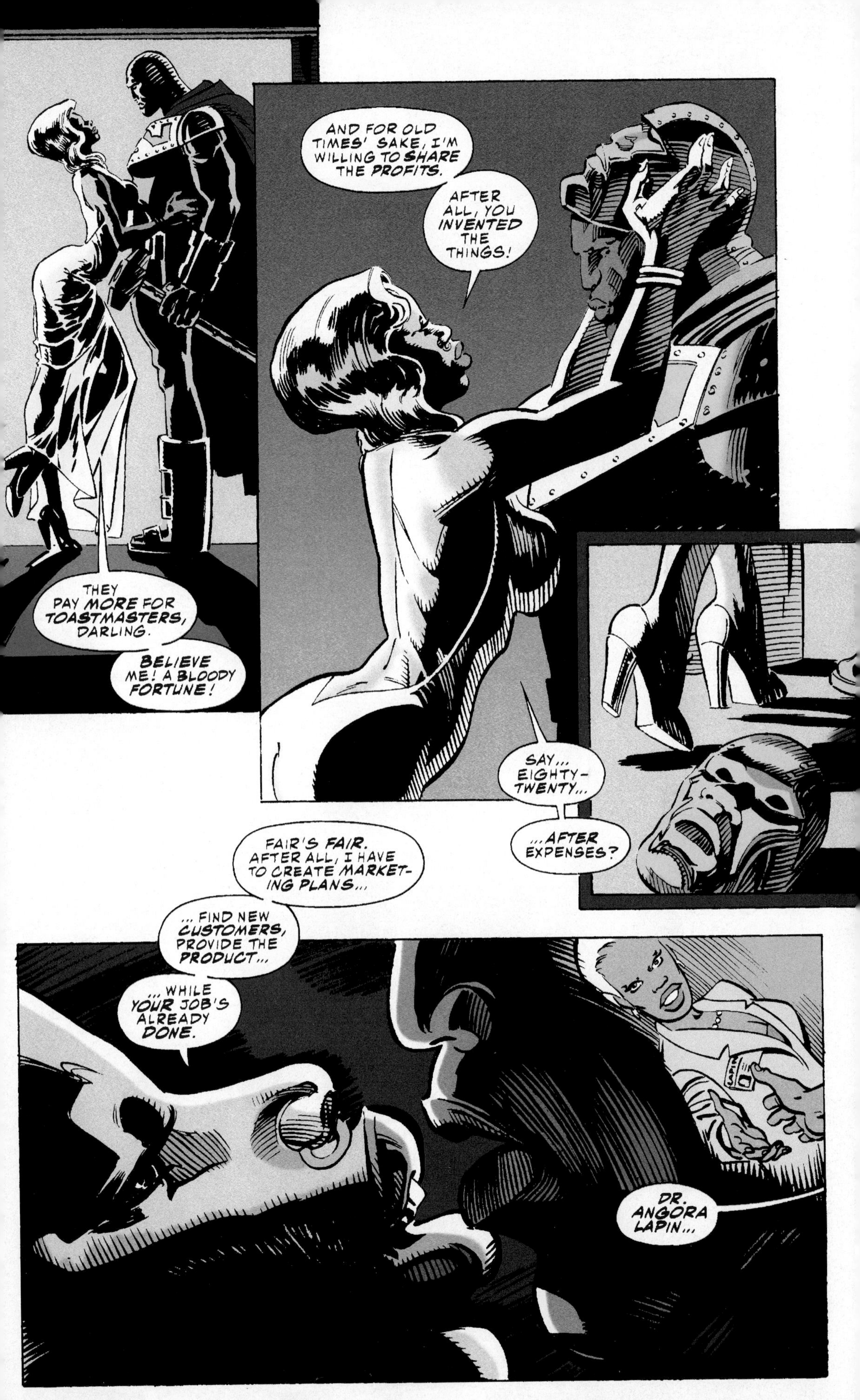
AND FOR OLD TIMES' SAKE, I'M WILLING TO SHARE THE PROFITS.
AFTER ALL, YOU INVENTED THE THINGS!
THEY PAY MORE FOR TOASTMASTERS, DARLING.
BELIEVE ME! A BLOODY FORTUNE!
SAY... EIGHTY-TWENTY...
...AFTER EXPENSES?
FAIR'S FAIR. AFTER ALL, I HAVE TO CREATE MARKET-ING PLANS...
... FIND NEW CUSTOMERS, PROVIDE THE PRODUCT...
... WHILE YOUR JOB'S ALREADY DONE.
DR. ANGORA LAPIN...

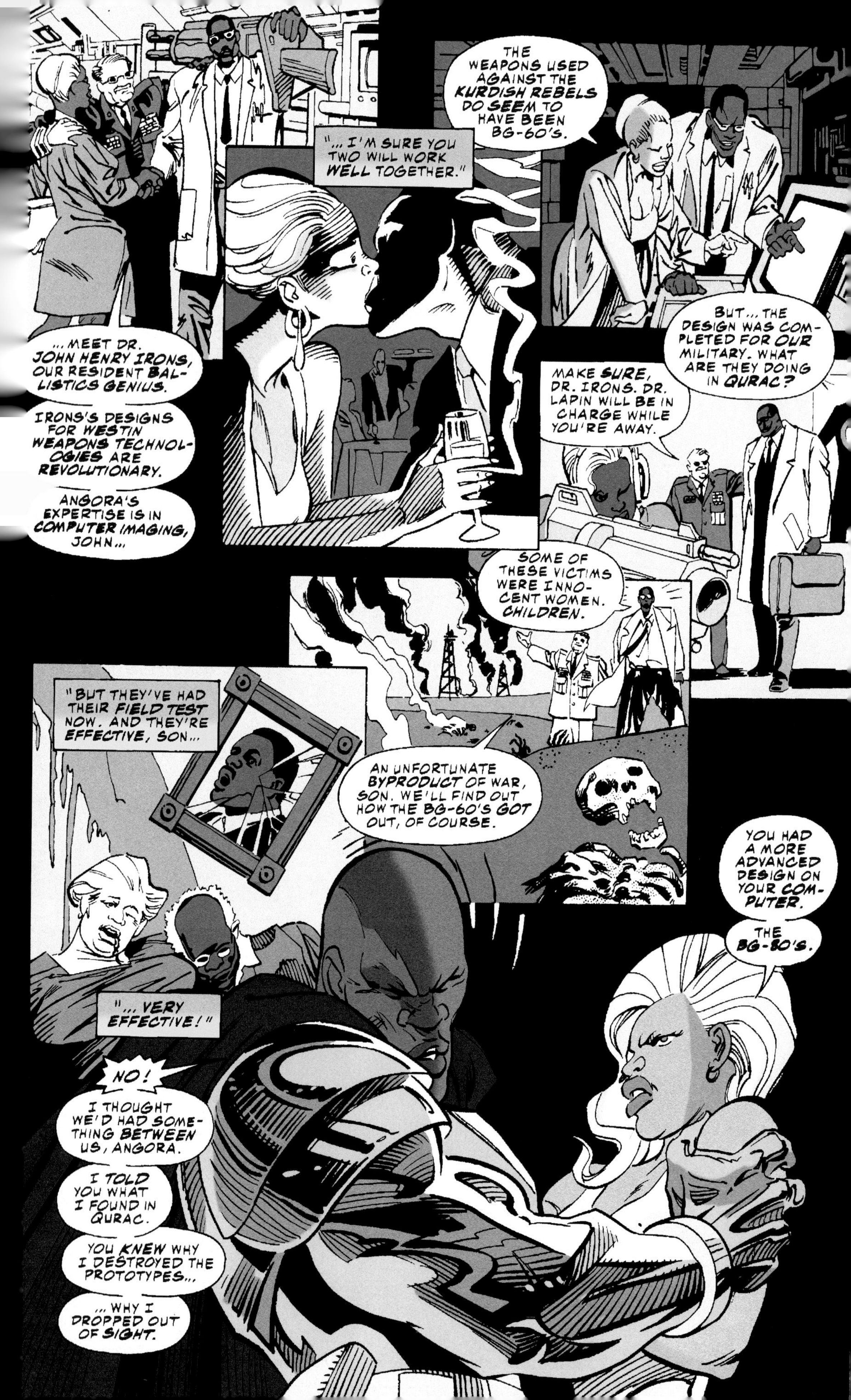
...MEET DR. JOHN HENRY IRONS, OUR RESIDENT BALLISTICS GENIUS.
IRONS'S DESIGNS FOR WESTIN WEAPONS TECHNOLOGIES ARE REVOLUTIONARY.
ANGORA'S EXPERTISE IS IN COMPUTER IMAGING, JOHN...
"...I'M SURE YOU TWO WILL WORK WELL TOGETHER."
THE WEAPONS USED AGAINST THE KURDISH REBELS DO SEEM TO HAVE BEEN BG-60'S.
BUT... THE DESIGN WAS COMPLETED FOR OUR MILITARY. WHAT ARE THEY DOING IN QURAC?
MAKE SURE, DR. IRONS. DR. LAPIN WILL BE IN CHARGE WHILE YOU'RE AWAY.
SOME OF THESE VICTIMS WERE INNOCENT WOMEN. CHILDREN.
AN UNFORTUNATE BYPRODUCT OF WAR, SON. WE'LL FIND OUT HOW THE BG-60'S GOT OUT, OF COURSE.
"BUT THEY'VE HAD THEIR FIELD TEST NOW. AND THEY'RE EFFECTIVE, SON...
"...VERY EFFECTIVE!"
YOU HAD A MORE ADVANCED DESIGN ON YOUR COMPUTER.
THE BG-80'S.
NO!
I THOUGHT WE'D HAD SOMETHING BETWEEN US, ANGORA.
I TOLD YOU WHAT I FOUND IN QURAC.
YOU KNEW WHY I DESTROYED THE PROTOTYPES...
...WHY I DROPPED OUT OF SIGHT.

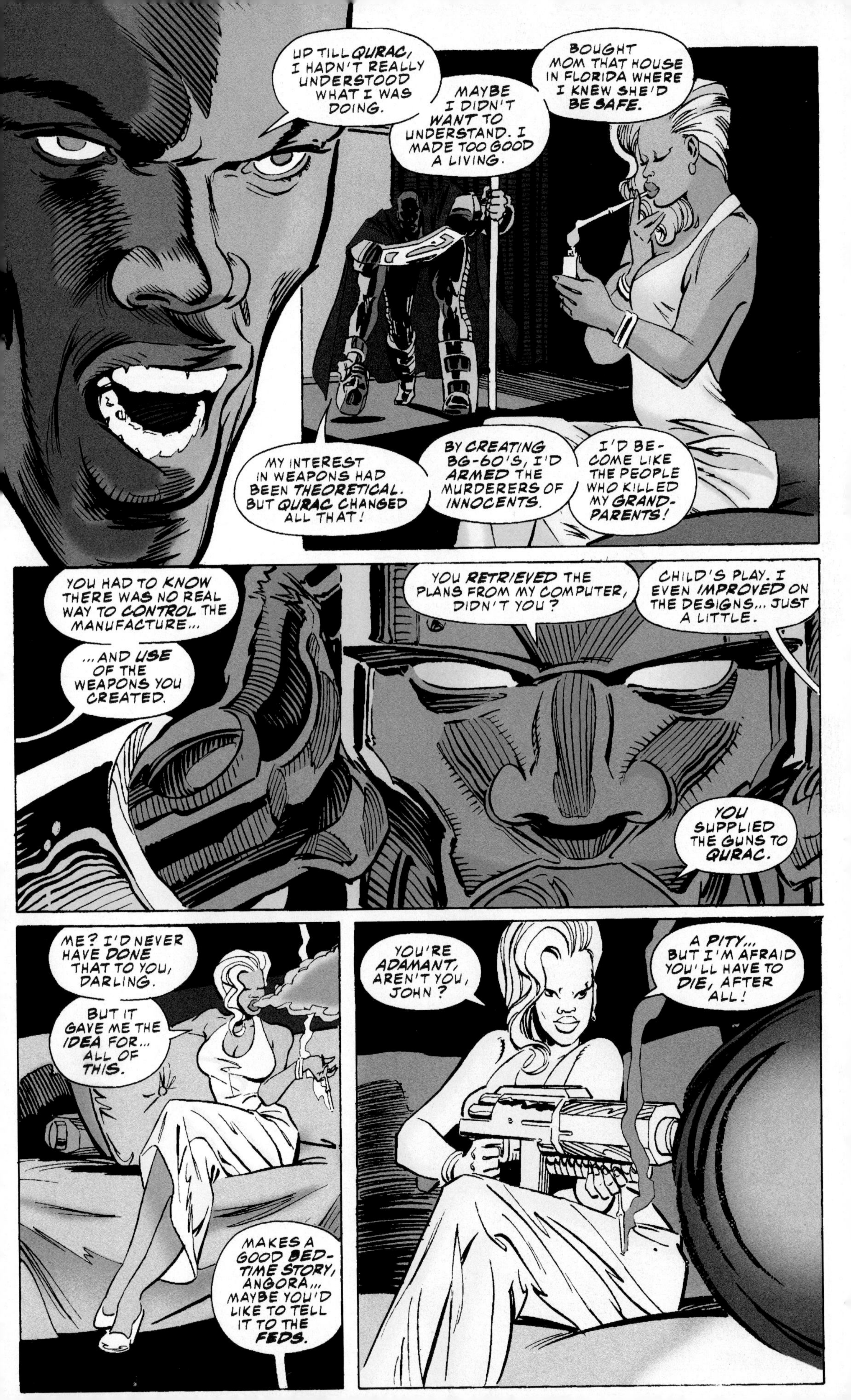
UP TILL QURAC, I HADN'T REALLY UNDERSTOOD WHAT I WAS DOING.
MAYBE I DIDN'T WANT TO UNDERSTAND. I MADE TOO GOOD A LIVING.
BOUGHT MOM THAT HOUSE IN FLORIDA WHERE I KNEW SHE'D BE SAFE.
MY INTEREST IN WEAPONS HAD BEEN THEORETICAL. BUT QURAC CHANGED ALL THAT!
BY CREATING BG-60'S, I'D ARMED THE MURDERERS OF INNOCENTS.
I'D BE-COME LIKE THE PEOPLE WHO KILLED MY GRAND-PARENTS!
YOU HAD TO KNOW THERE WAS NO REAL WAY TO CONTROL THE MANUFACTURE...
...AND USE OF THE WEAPONS YOU CREATED.
YOU RETRIEVED THE PLANS FROM MY COMPUTER, DIDN'T YOU?
CHILD'S PLAY. I EVEN IMPROVED ON THE DESIGNS... JUST A LITTLE.
YOU SUPPLIED THE GUNS TO QURAC.
ME? I'D NEVER HAVE DONE THAT TO YOU, DARLING.
BUT IT GAVE ME THE IDEA FOR... ALL OF THIS.
MAKES A GOOD BED-TIME STORY, ANGORA... MAYBE YOU'D LIKE TO TELL IT TO THE FEDS.
YOU'RE ADAMANT, AREN'T YOU, JOHN?
A PITY... BUT I'M AFRAID YOU'LL HAVE TO DIE, AFTER ALL!

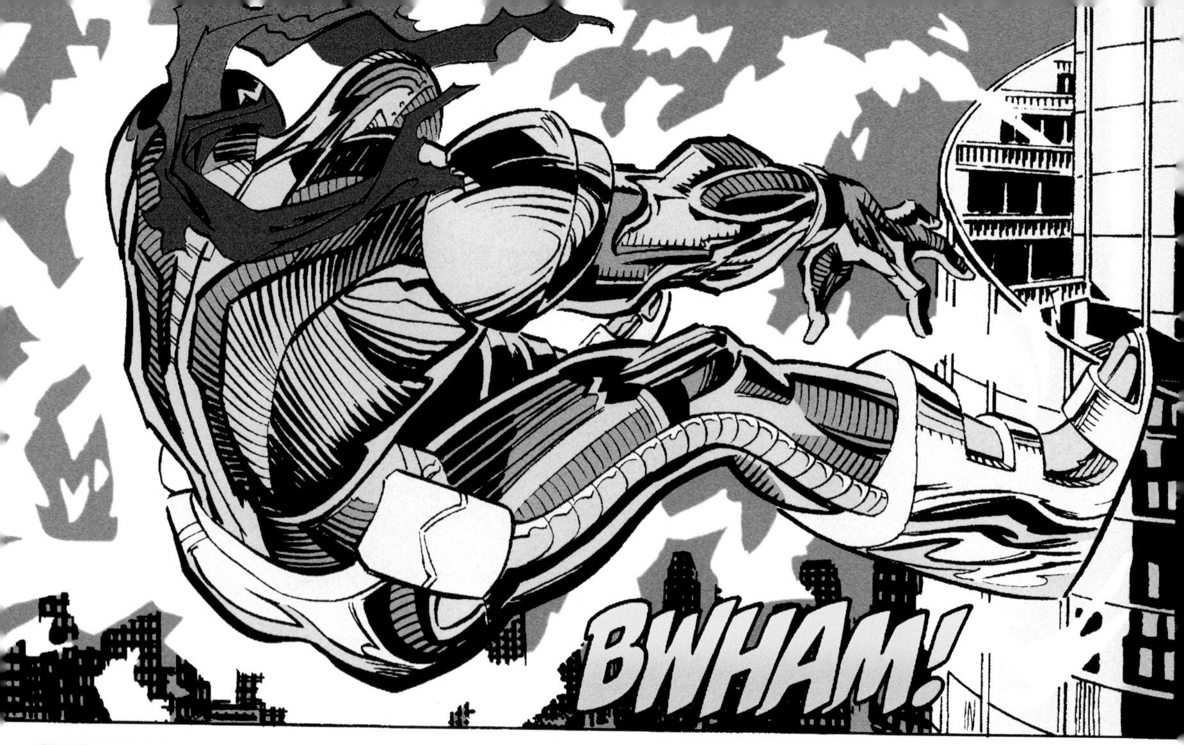
BWHAM!

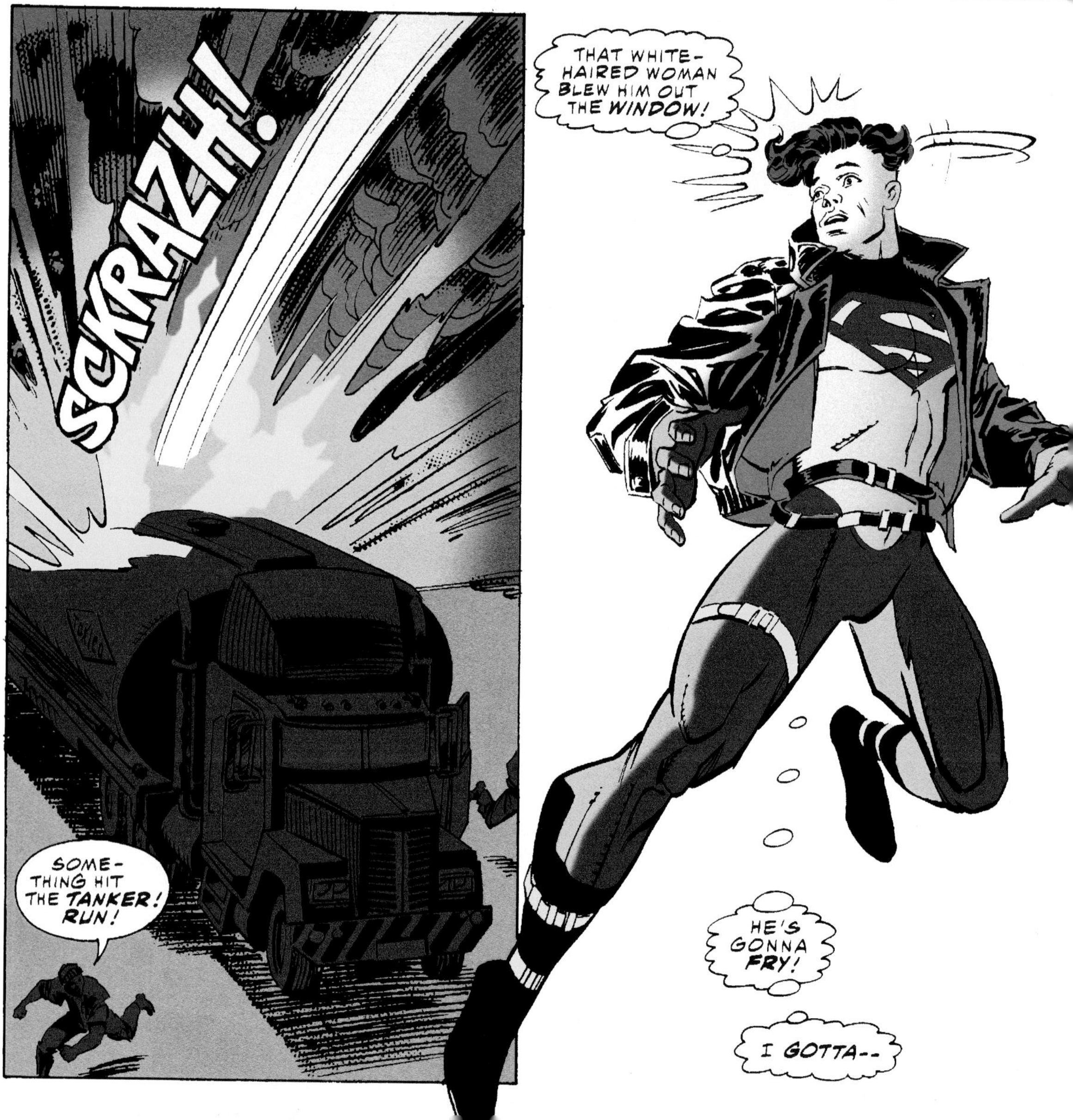
SCKRAZH!
THAT WHITE-HAIRED WOMAN BLEW HIM OUT THE WINDOW!
SOME-THING HIT THE TANKER! RUN!
HE'S GONNA FRY!
I GOTTA--

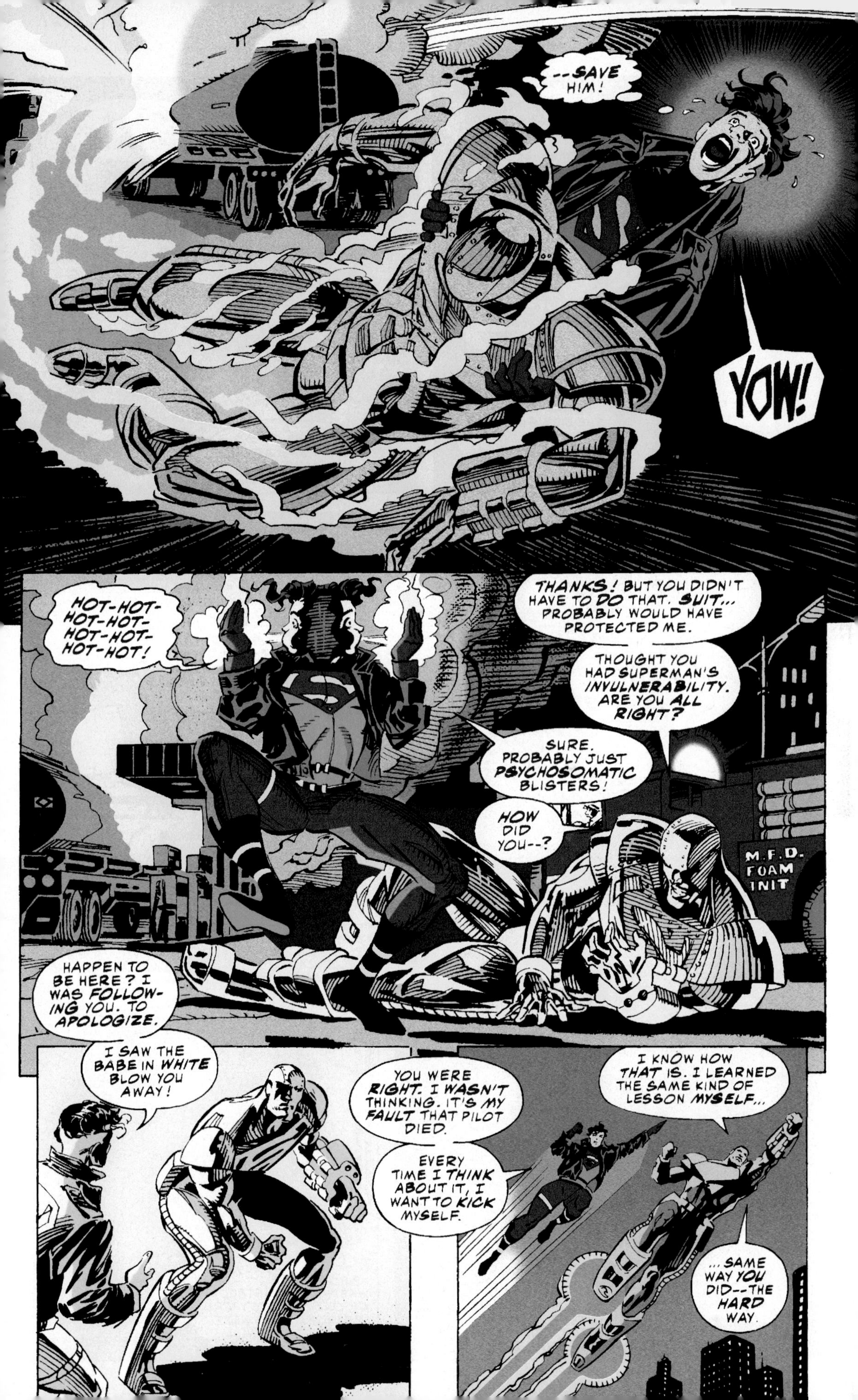
--SAVE HIM!
YOW!
HOT-HOT-HOT-HOT-HOT-HOT-HOT-HOT!
THANKS! BUT YOU DIDN'T HAVE TO DO THAT. SUIT... PROBABLY WOULD HAVE PROTECTED ME.
THOUGHT YOU HAD SUPERMAN'S INVULNERABILITY. ARE YOU ALL RIGHT?
SURE. PROBABLY JUST PSYCHOSOMATIC BLISTERS!
HOW DID YOU--?
M.F.D. FOAM UNIT
HAPPEN TO BE HERE? I WAS FOLLOWING YOU. TO APOLOGIZE.
I SAW THE BABE IN WHITE BLOW YOU AWAY!
YOU WERE RIGHT. I WASN'T THINKING. IT'S MY FAULT THAT PILOT DIED.
EVERY TIME I THINK ABOUT IT, I WANT TO KICK MYSELF.
I KNOW HOW THAT IS. I LEARNED THE SAME KIND OF LESSON MYSELF...
...SAME WAY YOU DID--THE HARD WAY.

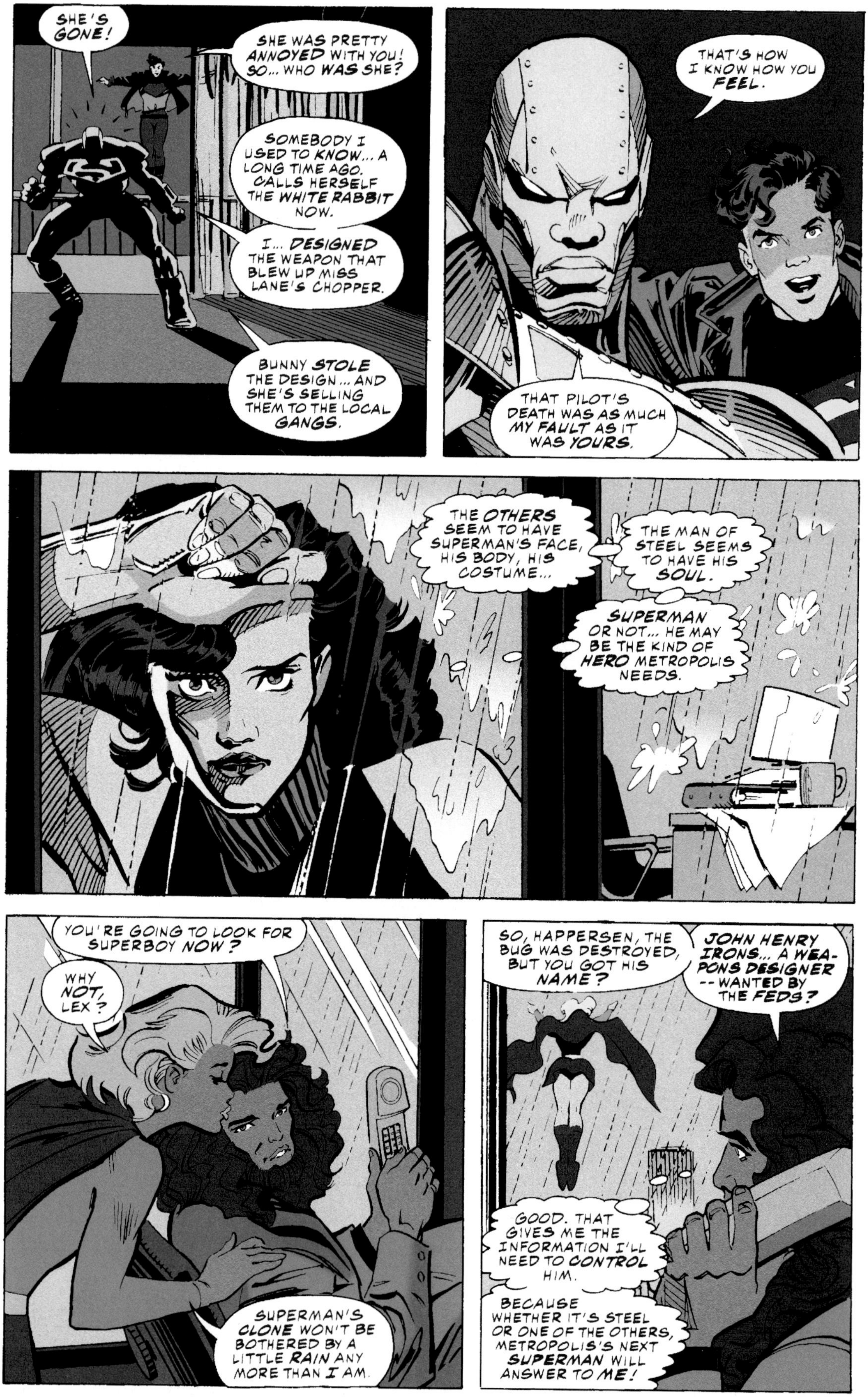

SHE'S GONE!
SHE WAS PRETTY ANNOYED WITH YOU! SO... WHO WAS SHE?
SOMEBODY I USED TO KNOW... A LONG TIME AGO. CALLS HERSELF THE WHITE RABBIT NOW.
I... DESIGNED THE WEAPON THAT BLEW UP MISS LANE'S CHOPPER.
BUNNY STOLE THE DESIGN... AND SHE'S SELLING THEM TO THE LOCAL GANGS.
THAT'S HOW I KNOW HOW YOU FEEL.
THAT PILOT'S DEATH WAS AS MUCH MY FAULT AS IT WAS YOURS.
THE OTHERS SEEM TO HAVE SUPERMAN'S FACE, HIS BODY, HIS COSTUME...
THE MAN OF STEEL SEEMS TO HAVE HIS SOUL.
SUPERMAN OR NOT... HE MAY BE THE KIND OF HERO METROPOLIS NEEDS.
YOU'RE GOING TO LOOK FOR SUPERBOY NOW?
WHY NOT, LEX?
SUPERMAN'S CLONE WON'T BE BOTHERED BY A LITTLE RAIN ANY MORE THAN I AM.
SO, HAPPERSEN, THE BUG WAS DESTROYED, BUT YOU GOT HIS NAME?
JOHN HENRY IRONS... A WEAPONS DESIGNER --WANTED BY THE FEDS?
GOOD. THAT GIVES ME THE INFORMATION I'LL NEED TO CONTROL HIM.
BECAUSE WHETHER IT'S STEEL OR ONE OF THE OTHERS, METROPOLIS'S NEXT SUPERMAN WILL ANSWER TO ME!

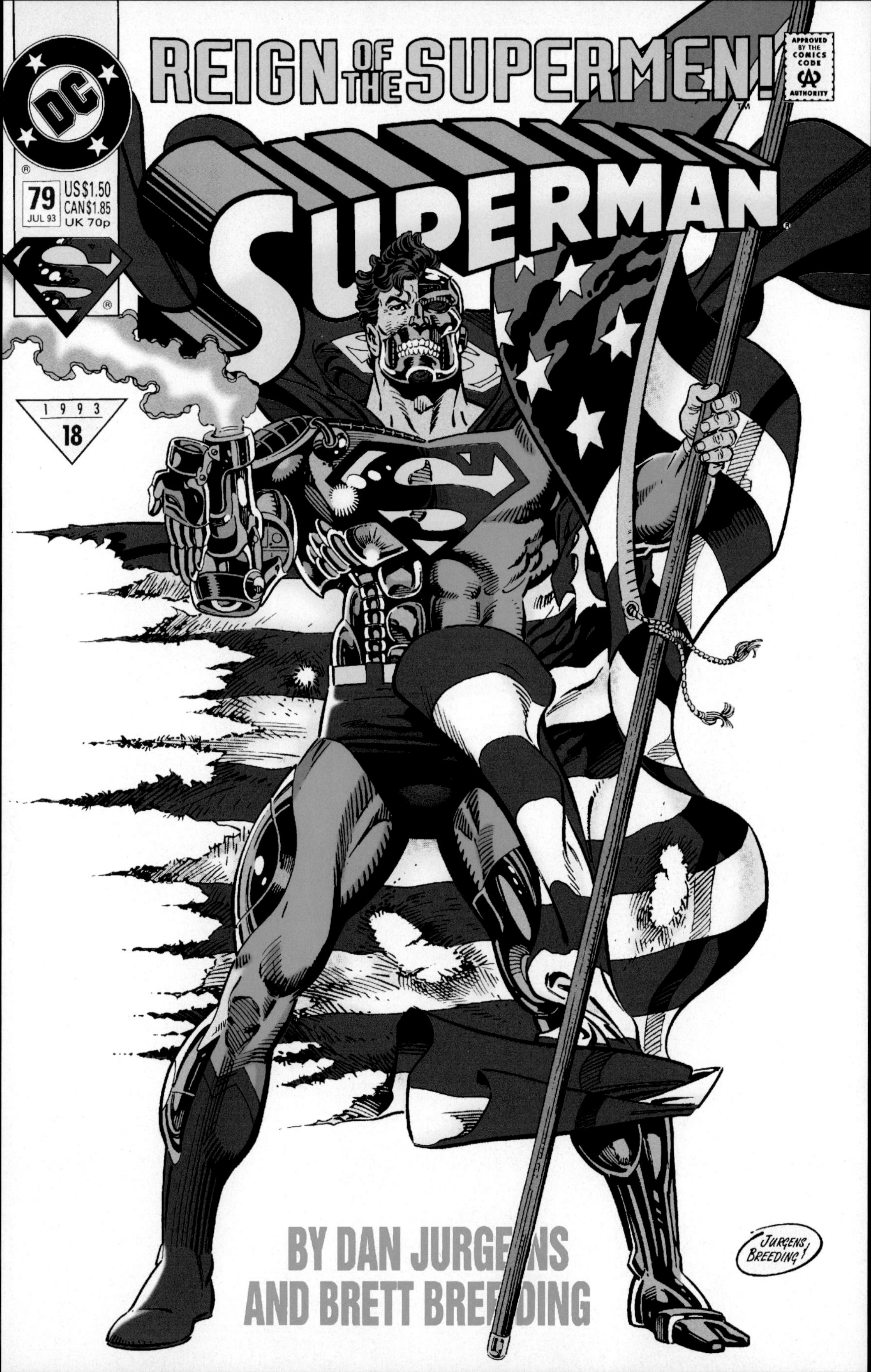

REIGN OF THE SUPERMEN!
APPROVED BY THE COMICS CODE AUTHORITY
DC
79
JUL 93
US$1.50
CAN$1.85
UK 70p
SUPERMAN
1993
18
BY DAN JURGENS
AND BRETT BREEDING
JURGENS BREEDING

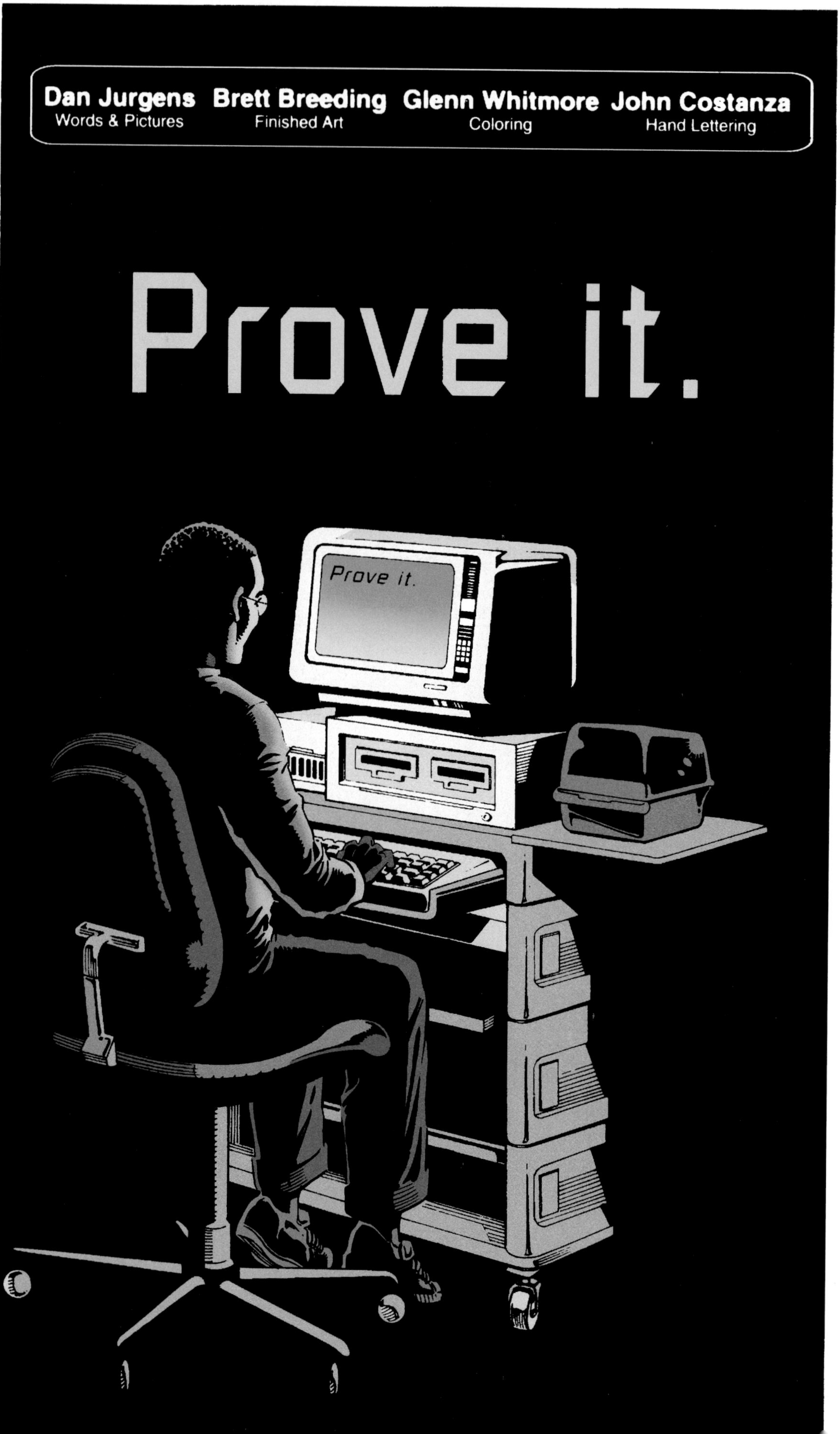
Dan Jurgens
Words & Pictures
Brett Breeding
Finished Art
Glenn Whitmore
Coloring
John Costanza
Hand Lettering
Prove it.
Prove it.

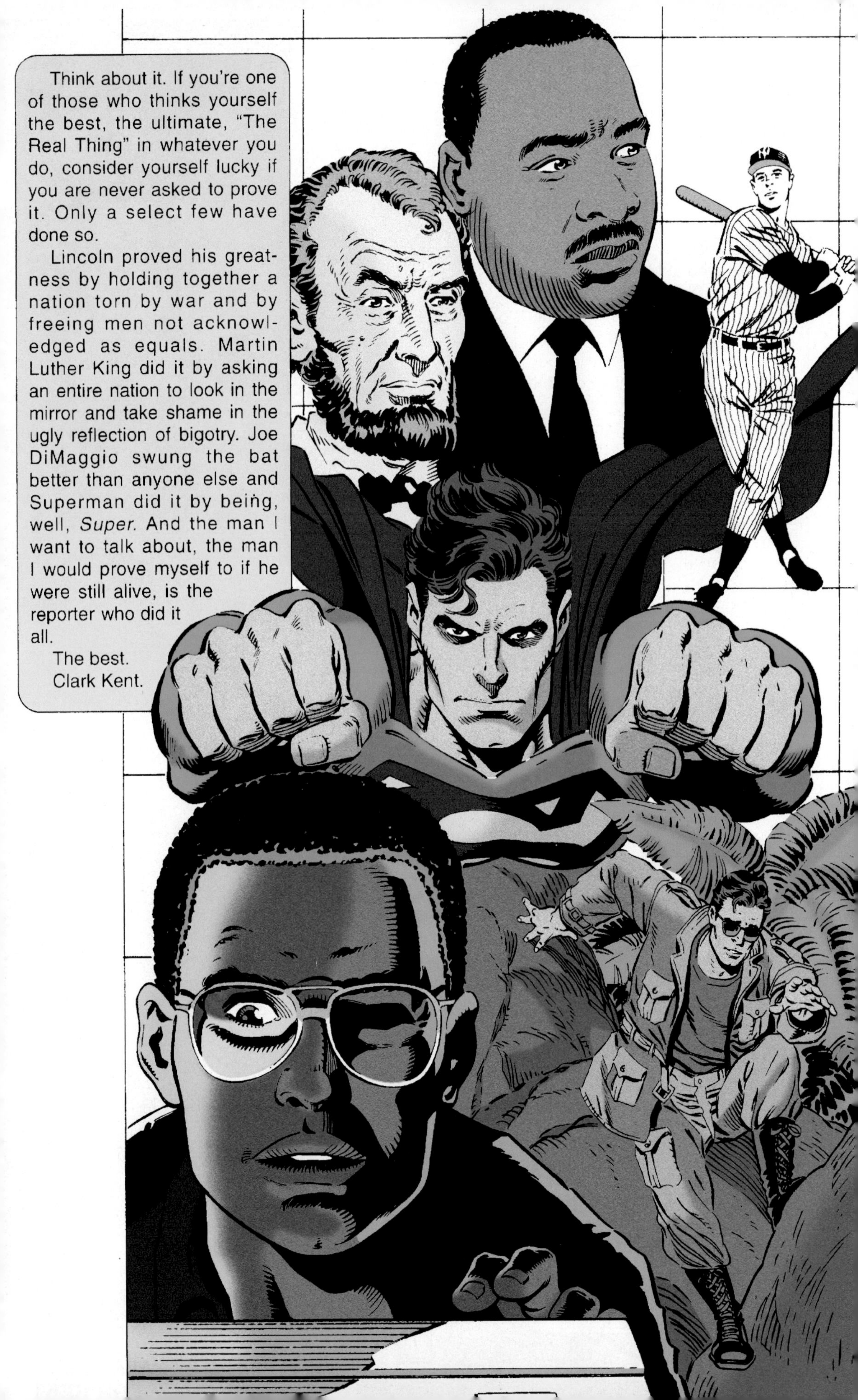
Think about it. If you're one of those who thinks yourself the best, the ultimate, "The Real Thing" in whatever you do, consider yourself lucky if you are never asked to prove it. Only a select few have done so.
Lincoln proved his greatness by holding together a nation torn by war and by freeing men not acknowledged as equals. Martin Luther King did it by asking an entire nation to look in the mirror and take shame in the ugly reflection of bigotry. Joe DiMaggio swung the bat better than anyone else and Superman did it by being, well, *Super.* And the man I want to talk about, the man I would prove myself to if he were still alive, is the reporter who did it all.
The best.
Clark Kent.

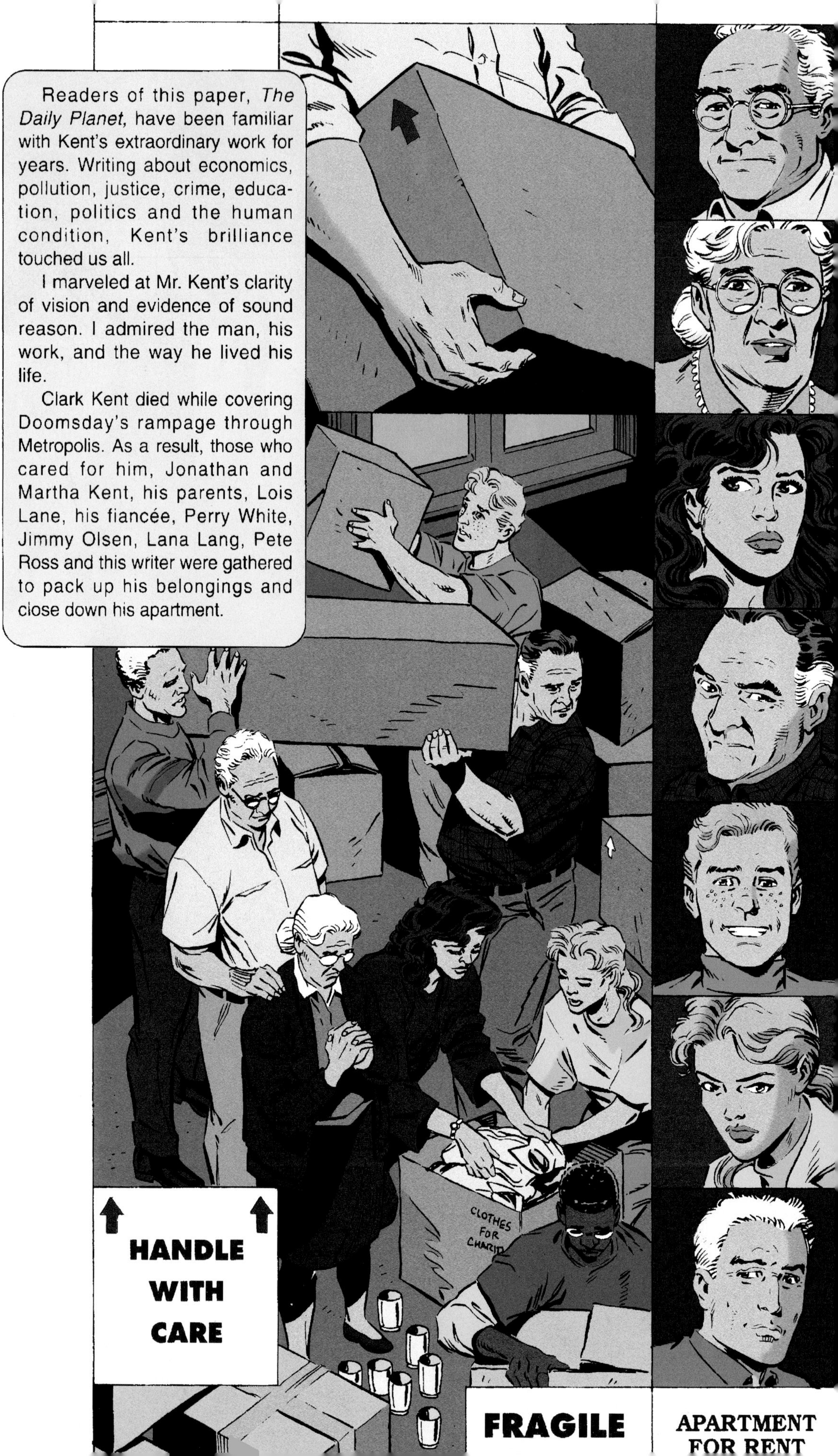
Readers of this paper, *The Daily Planet,* have been familiar with Kent's extraordinary work for years. Writing about economics, pollution, justice, crime, education, politics and the human condition, Kent's brilliance touched us all.
I marveled at Mr. Kent's clarity of vision and evidence of sound reason. I admired the man, his work, and the way he lived his life.
Clark Kent died while covering Doomsday's rampage through Metropolis. As a result, those who cared for him, Jonathan and Martha Kent, his parents, Lois Lane, his fiancée, Perry White, Jimmy Olsen, Lana Lang, Pete Ross and this writer were gathered to pack up his belongings and close down his apartment.
HANDLE WITH CARE
CLOTHES FOR CHARITY
FRAGILE
APARTMENT FOR RENT

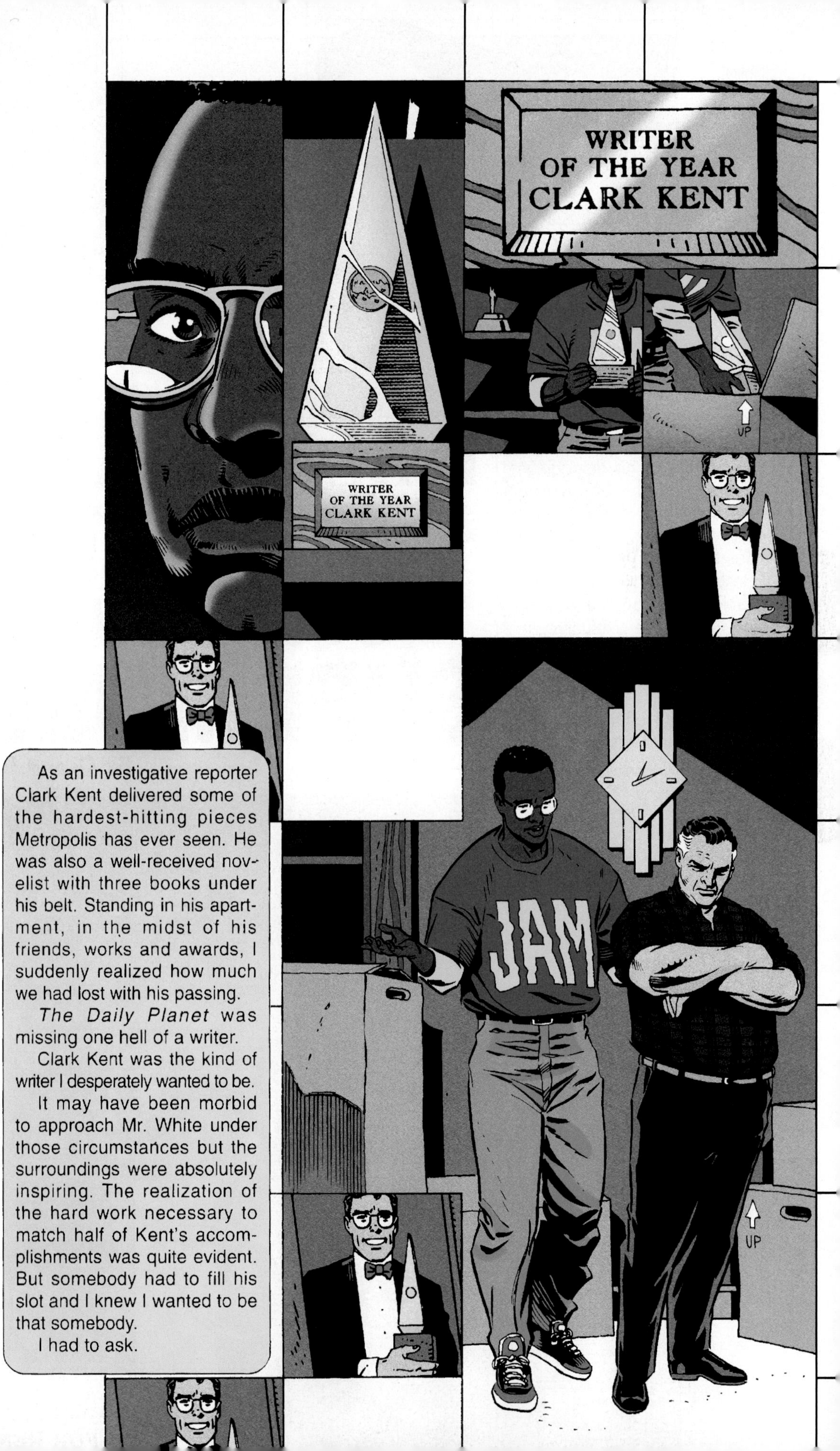
WRITER
OF THE YEAR
CLARK KENT
WRITER
OF THE YEAR
CLARK KENT
UP
As an investigative reporter Clark Kent delivered some of the hardest-hitting pieces Metropolis has ever seen. He was also a well-received novelist with three books under his belt. Standing in his apartment, in the midst of his friends, works and awards, I suddenly realized how much we had lost with his passing.
The Daily Planet was missing one hell of a writer.
Clark Kent was the kind of writer I desperately wanted to be.
It may have been morbid to approach Mr. White under those circumstances but the surroundings were absolutely inspiring. The realization of the hard work necessary to match half of Kent's accomplishments was quite evident. But somebody had to fill his slot and I knew I wanted to be that somebody.
I had to ask.
JAM
UP

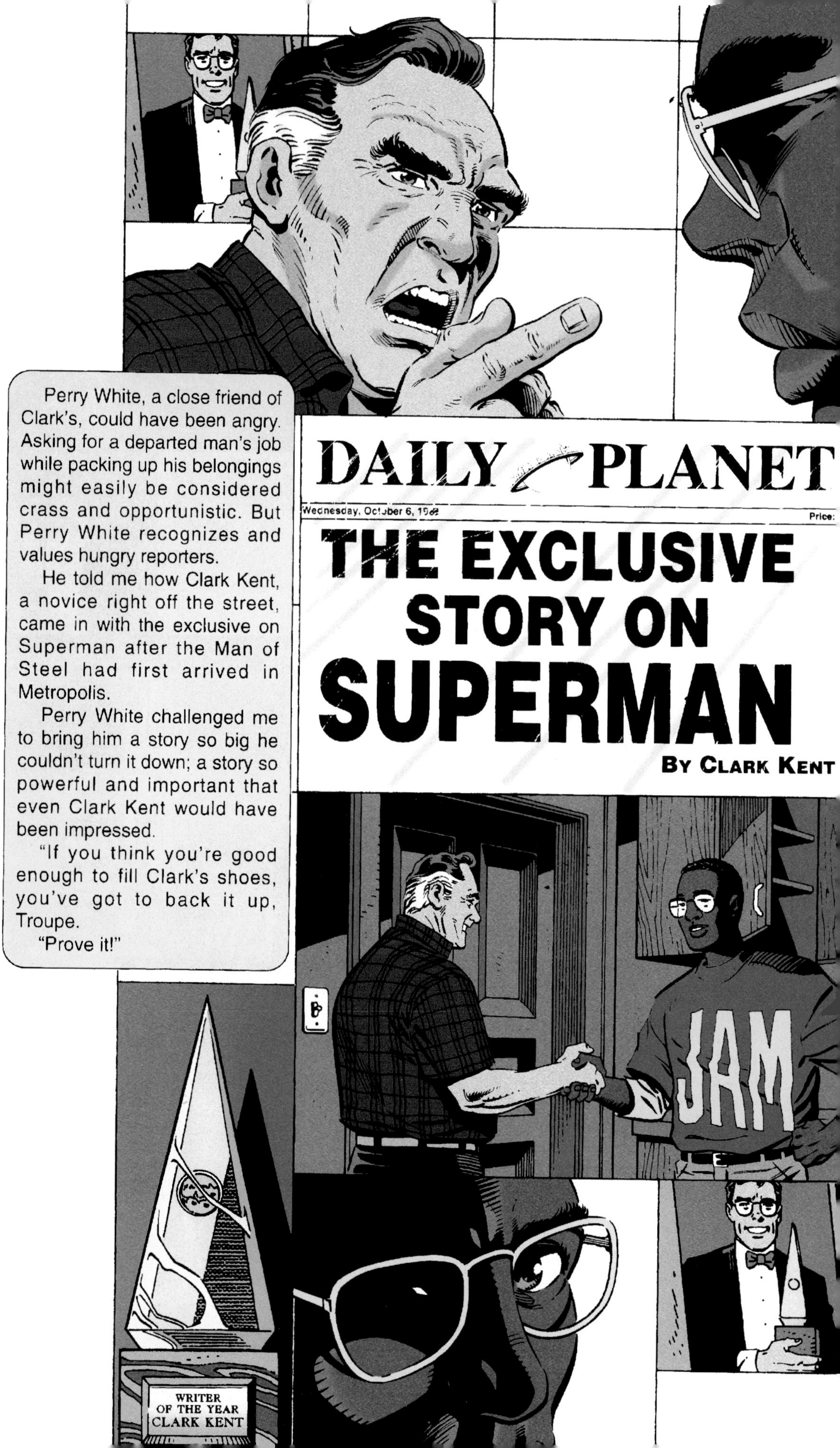

Perry White, a close friend of Clark's, could have been angry. Asking for a departed man's job while packing up his belongings might easily be considered crass and opportunistic. But Perry White recognizes and values hungry reporters.
He told me how Clark Kent, a novice right off the street, came in with the exclusive on Superman after the Man of Steel had first arrived in Metropolis.
Perry White challenged me to bring him a story so big he couldn't turn it down; a story so powerful and important that even Clark Kent would have been impressed.
"If you think you're good enough to fill Clark's shoes, you've got to back it up, Troupe.
"Prove it!"
DAILY PLANET
Wednesday, October 6, 19
Price:
THE EXCLUSIVE STORY ON SUPERMAN
BY CLARK KENT
JAM
WRITER OF THE YEAR CLARK KENT

Leaving, I felt like a five-year-old marching off to the first day of school.

I had no idea where to begin but Kent's Superman exclusive was constantly on my mind. Back then Superman was a great mystery to Metropolis until that story appeared.

We had our own mystery to solve. Three men and a boy, all claiming to be Superman to one degree or another, were trying to replace him much as I was trying to replace Clark Kent.

Doubt cast a shadow over all of them, but one in particular, the half-man, half-machine character, offered compelling evidence of being Superman brought back to life.

I knew what my story had to be. Now all I had to do was find a way to get it.

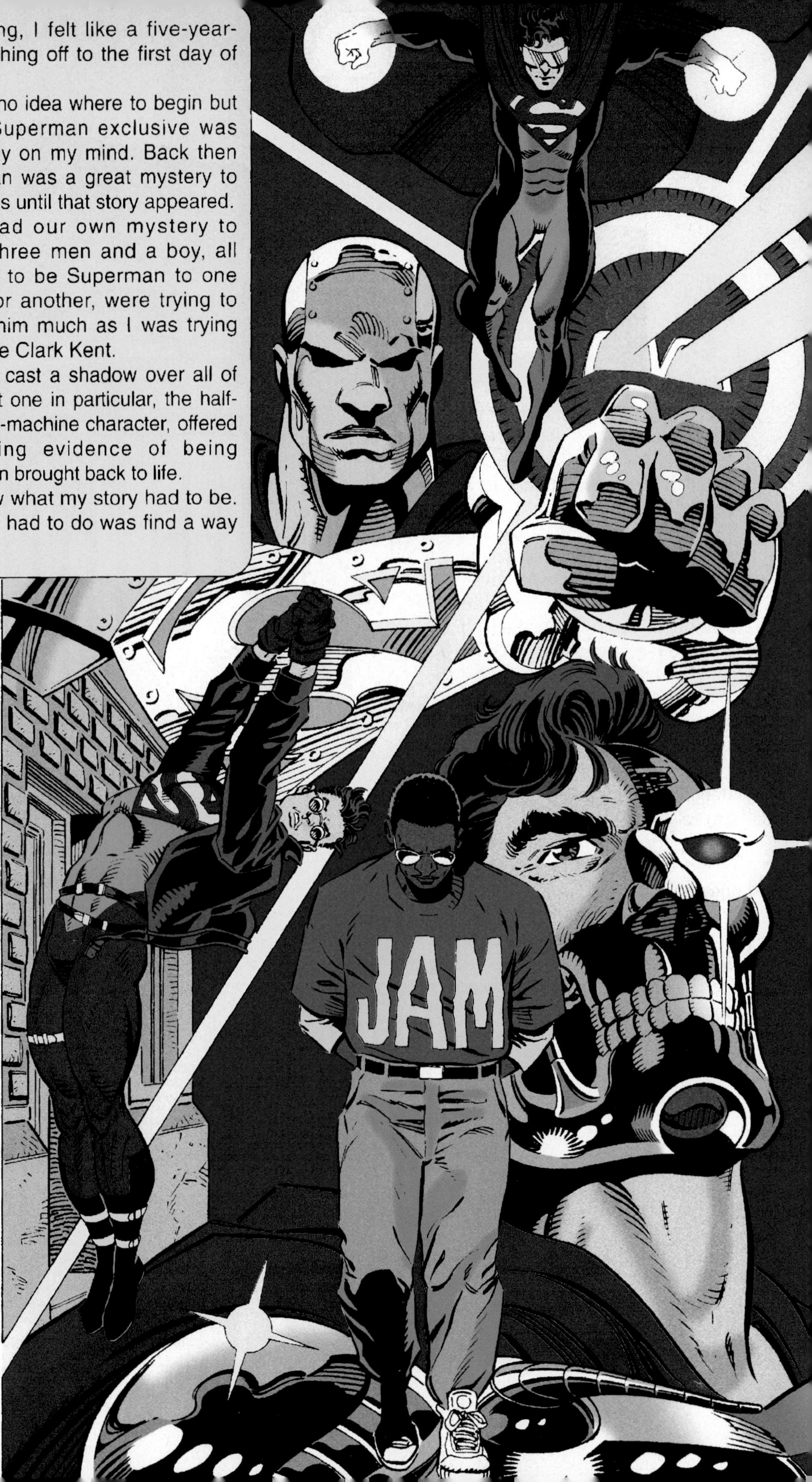
JAM

I made my initial inquiries by calling The Justice League Compound, thinking that if anyone had some answers it might be their civilian liaison, Max Lord. Another civilian, the obsequious Oberon, told me Lord was traveling to Washington to brief the President. If Lord had something to tell our Commander-in-Chief he might be able to tell me something as well, so I hopped the first train to D.C.

Expecting Lord might want to avoid reporters, I planned to stand outside the White House gates all day and night if necessary. When his limousine pulled up, I coaxed him out of the car for a few questions.

Hoping he wouldn't detect my nervousness, I asked Lord about these Supermen. Even then I had no idea of what was about to happen.

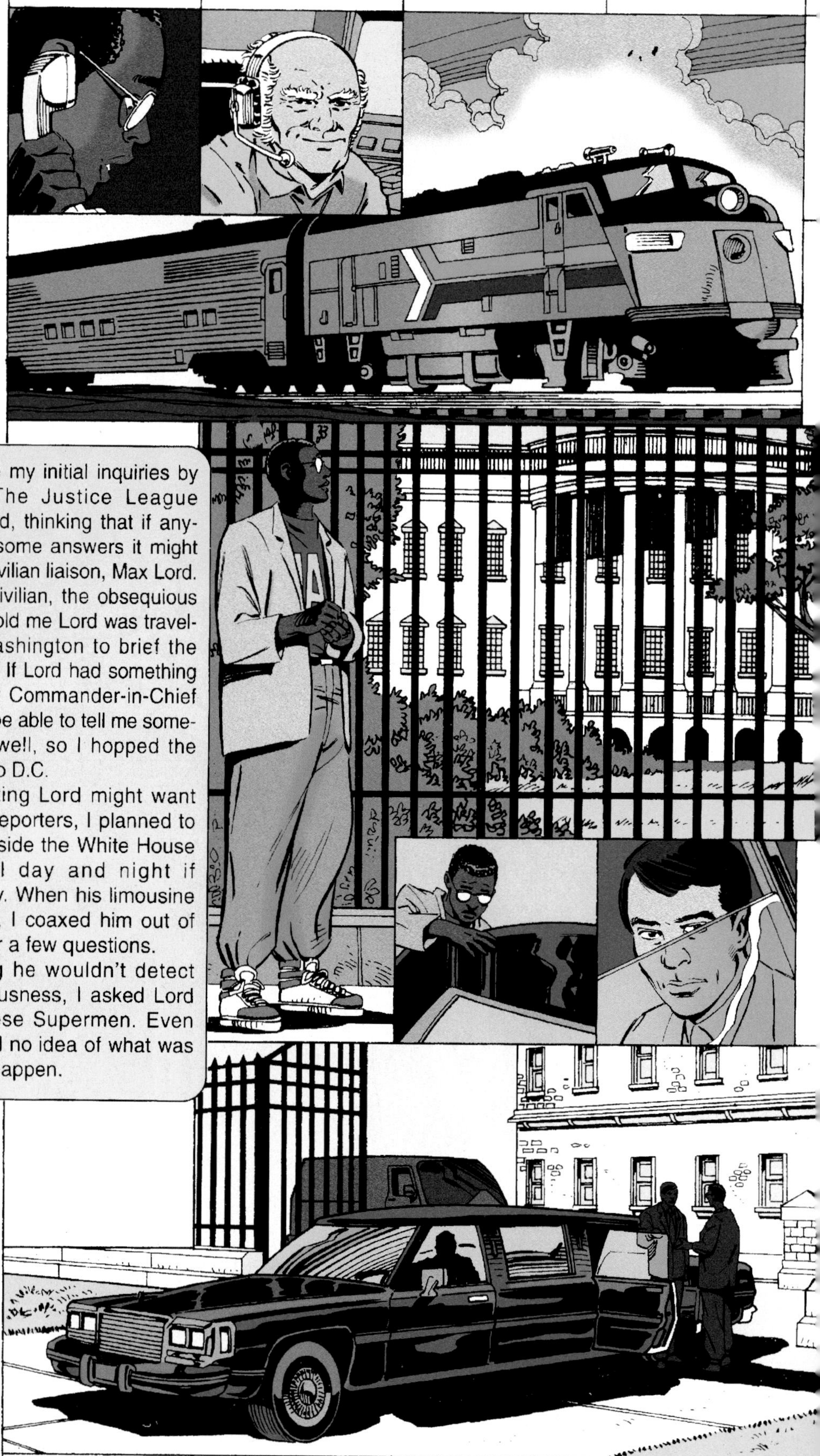

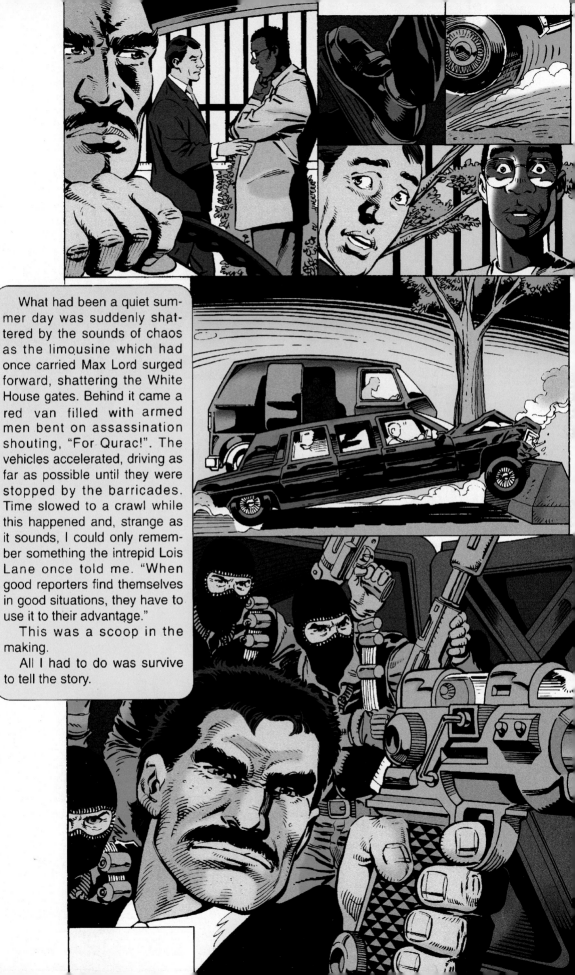

What had been a quiet summer day was suddenly shattered by the sounds of chaos as the limousine which had once carried Max Lord surged forward, shattering the White House gates. Behind it came a red van filled with armed men bent on assassination shouting, "For Qurac!". The vehicles accelerated, driving as far as possible until they were stopped by the barricades. Time slowed to a crawl while this happened and, strange as it sounds, I could only remember something the intrepid Lois Lane once told me. "When good reporters find themselves in good situations, they have to use it to their advantage."

This was a scoop in the making.

All I had to do was survive to tell the story.

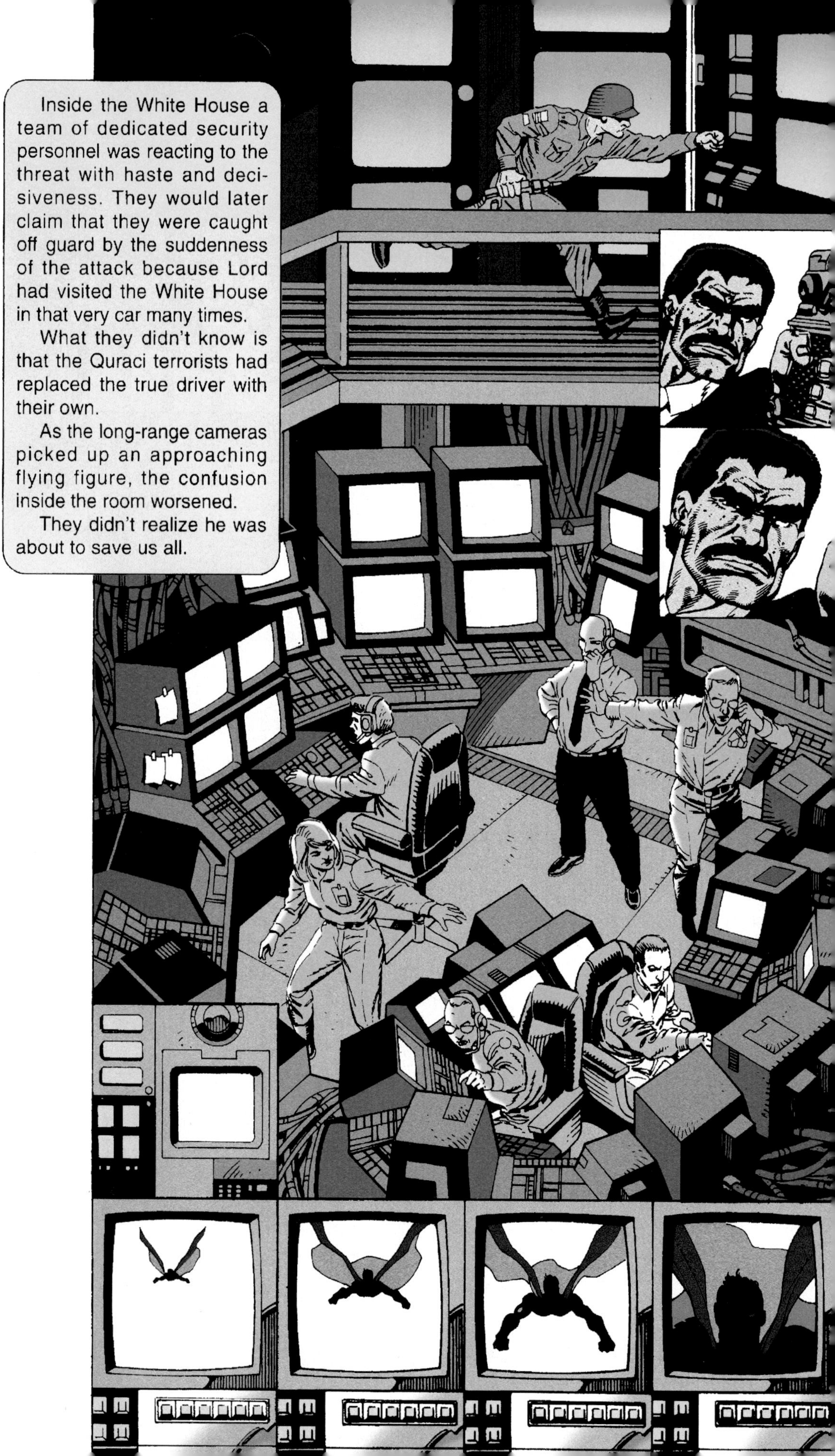
Inside the White House a team of dedicated security personnel was reacting to the threat with haste and decisiveness. They would later claim that they were caught off guard by the suddenness of the attack because Lord had visited the White House in that very car many times.
What they didn't know is that the Quraci terrorists had replaced the true driver with their own.
As the long-range cameras picked up an approaching flying figure, the confusion inside the room worsened.
They didn't realize he was about to save us all.

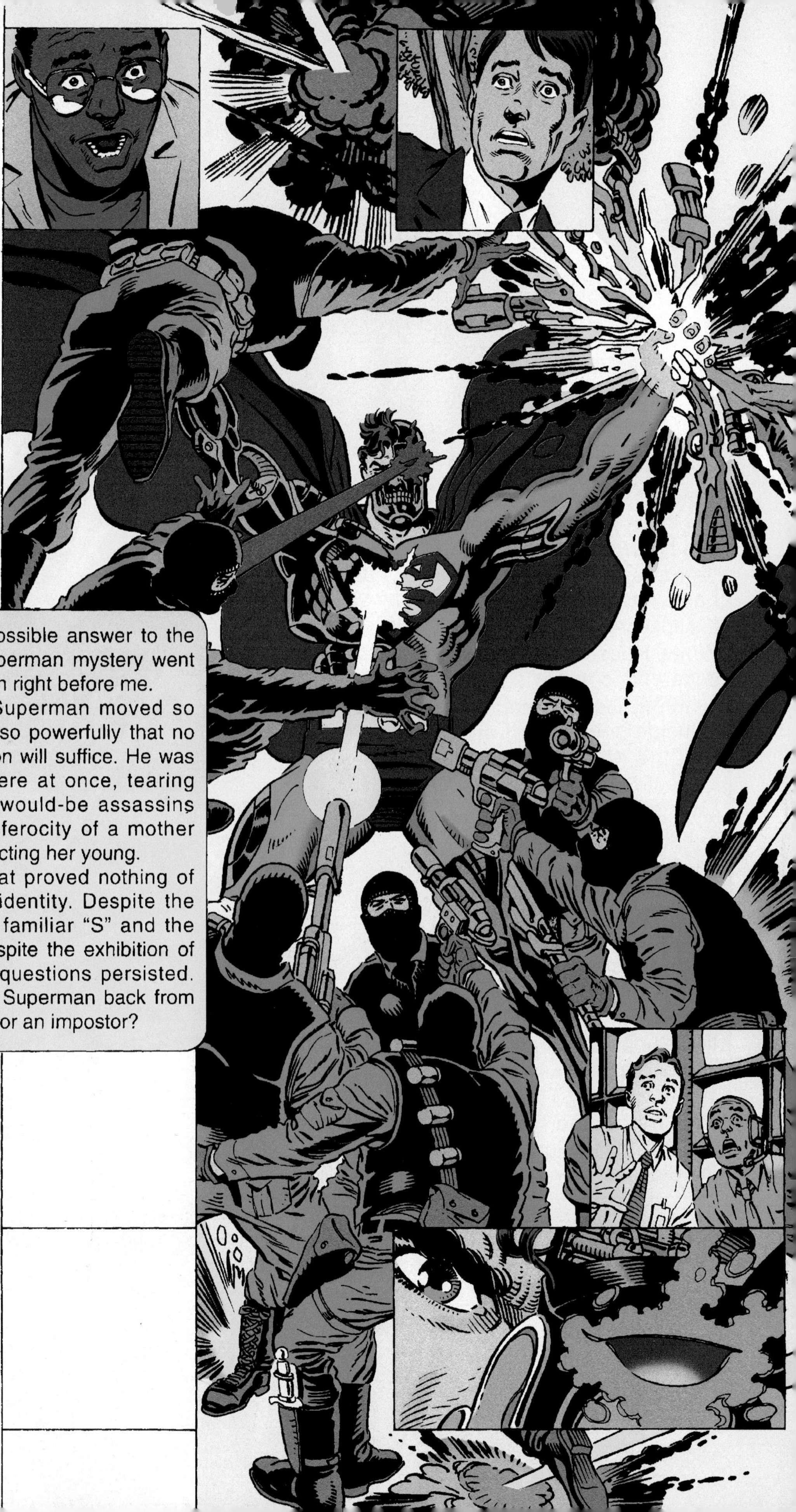

The possible answer to the great Superman mystery went into action right before me.

This Superman moved so fast and so powerfully that no description will suffice. He was everywhere at once, tearing into the would-be assassins with the ferocity of a mother lion protecting her young.

But that proved nothing of his true identity. Despite the suit, the familiar "S" and the cape; despite the exhibition of powers, questions persisted. Was this Superman back from the dead or an impostor?

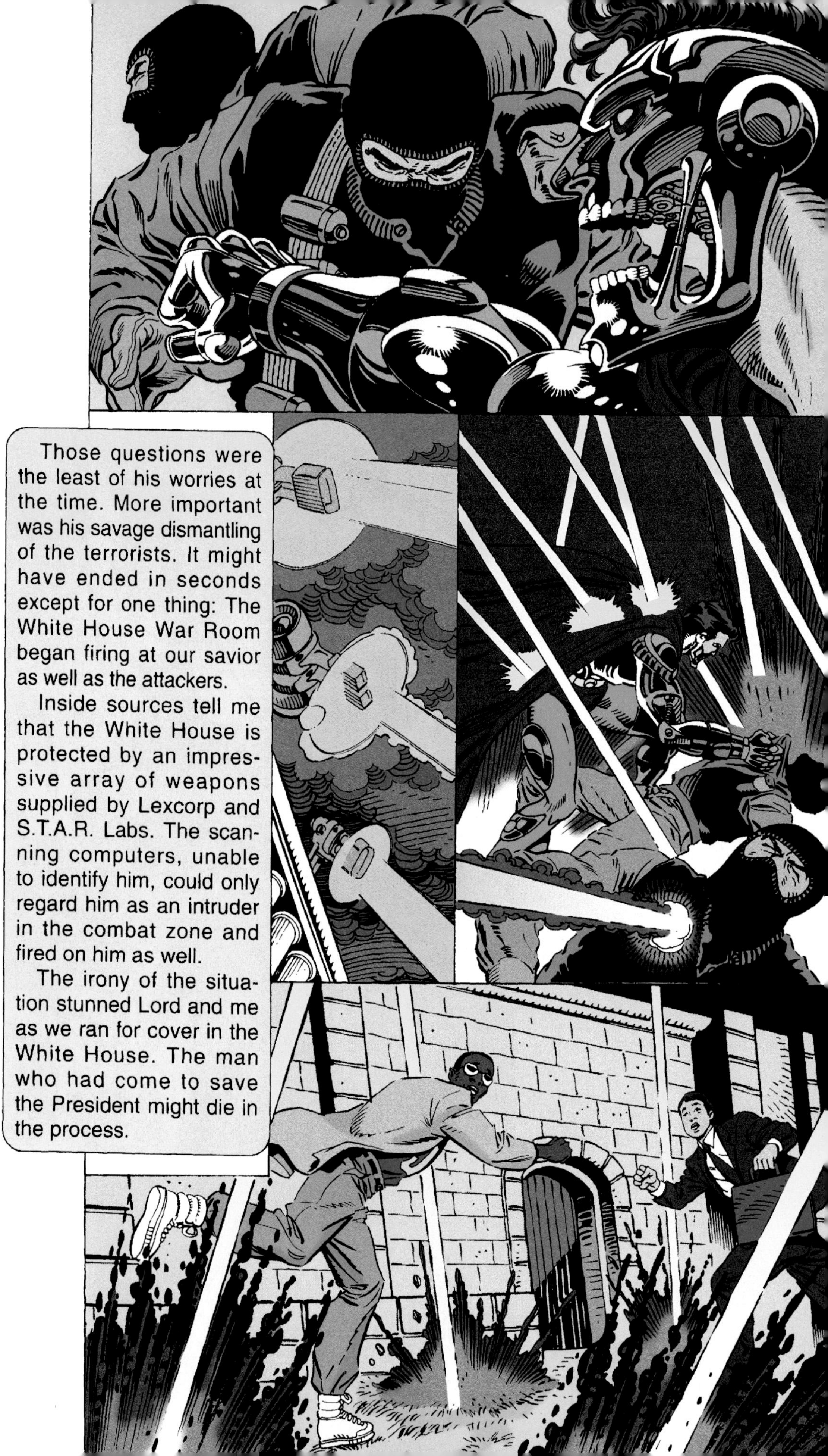
Those questions were the least of his worries at the time. More important was his savage dismantling of the terrorists. It might have ended in seconds except for one thing: The White House War Room began firing at our savior as well as the attackers.
Inside sources tell me that the White House is protected by an impressive array of weapons supplied by Lexcorp and S.T.A.R. Labs. The scanning computers, unable to identify him, could only regard him as an intruder in the combat zone and fired on him as well.
The irony of the situation stunned Lord and me as we ran for cover in the White House. The man who had come to save the President might die in the process.

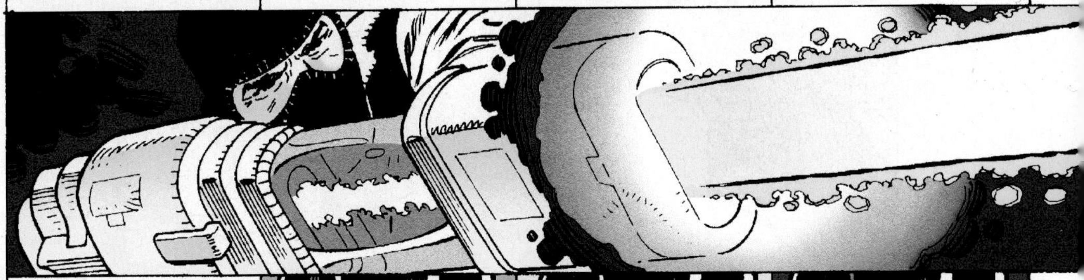

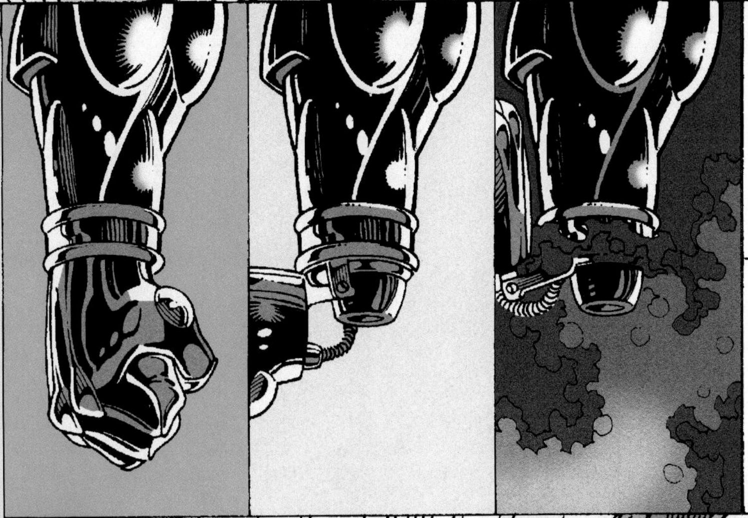

The White House was not alone in having impressive weapons. The Quraci terrorists obviously knew they'd face formidable odds and brought the fire power to match it.

As one of them fired a futuristic bazooka, this neo-Superman began to change. One arm, seemingly constructed of metal, twisted and re-formed into a cannon-like apparatus.

Superman fired a blinding burst of energy before the assassin could concentrate his bazooka on the White House, and the matter was resolved.

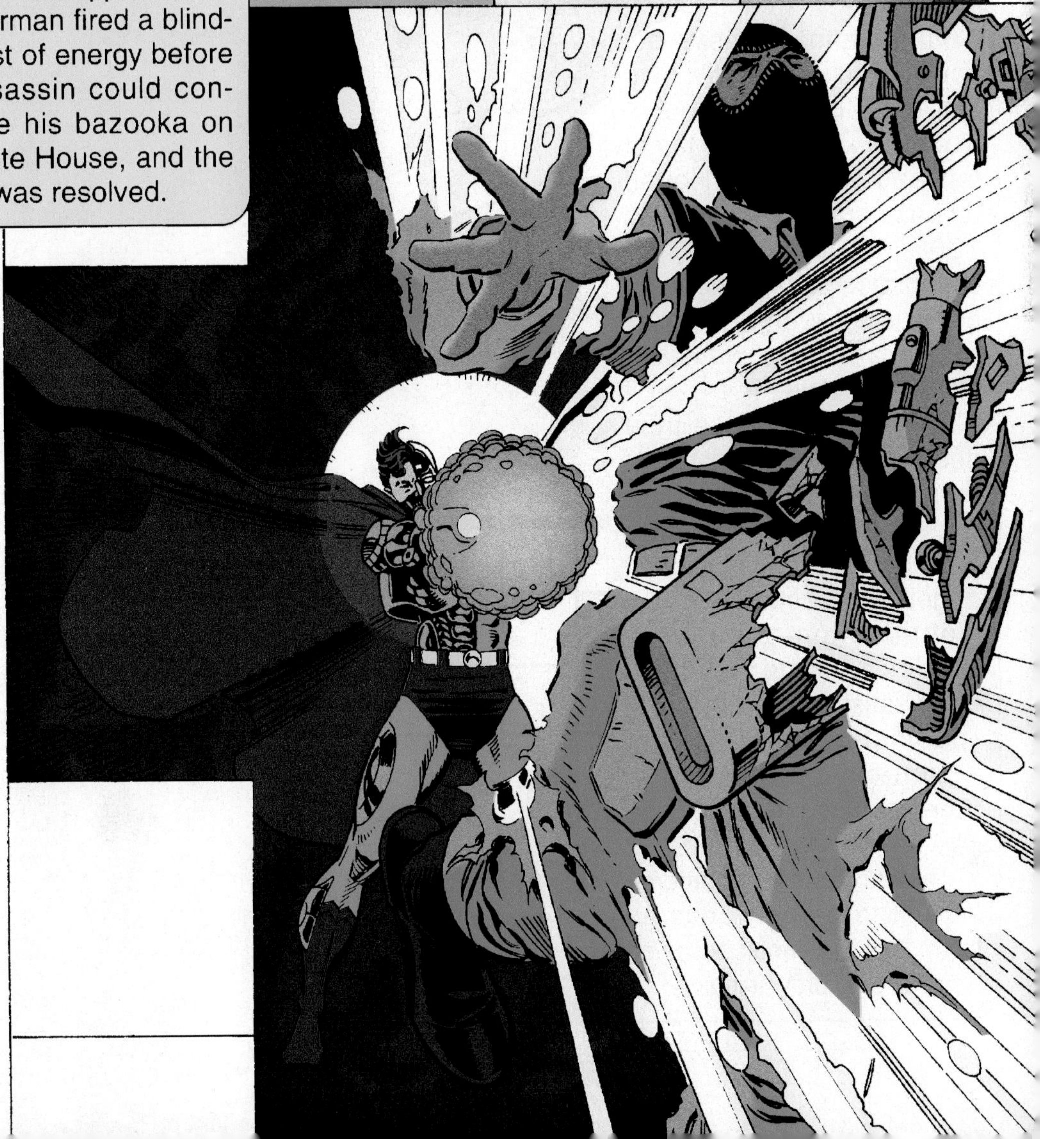

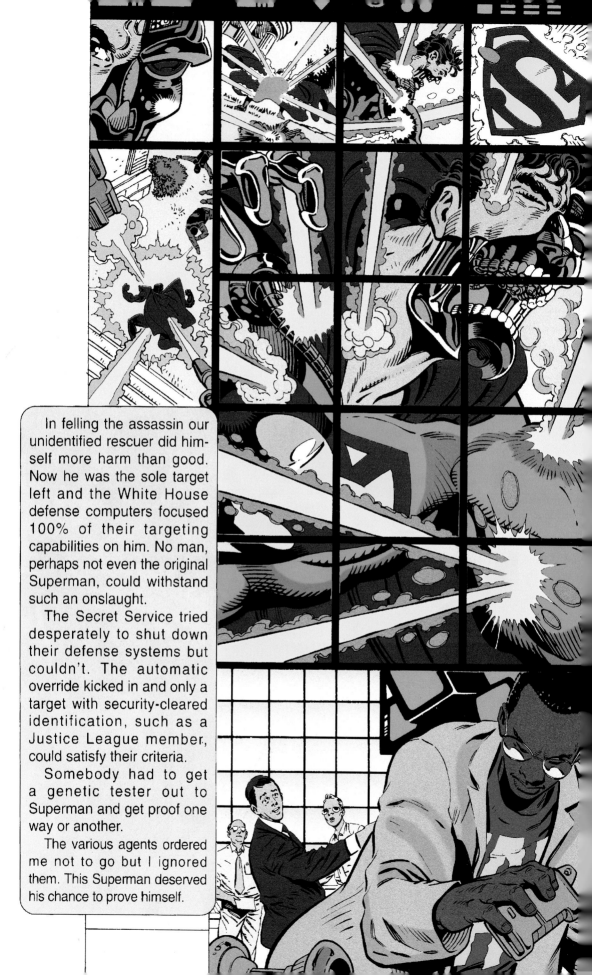

In felling the assassin our unidentified rescuer did himself more harm than good. Now he was the sole target left and the White House defense computers focused 100% of their targeting capabilities on him. No man, perhaps not even the original Superman, could withstand such an onslaught.

The Secret Service tried desperately to shut down their defense systems but couldn't. The automatic override kicked in and only a target with security-cleared identification, such as a Justice League member, could satisfy their criteria.

Somebody had to get a genetic tester out to Superman and get proof one way or another.

The various agents ordered me not to go but I ignored them. This Superman deserved his chance to prove himself.

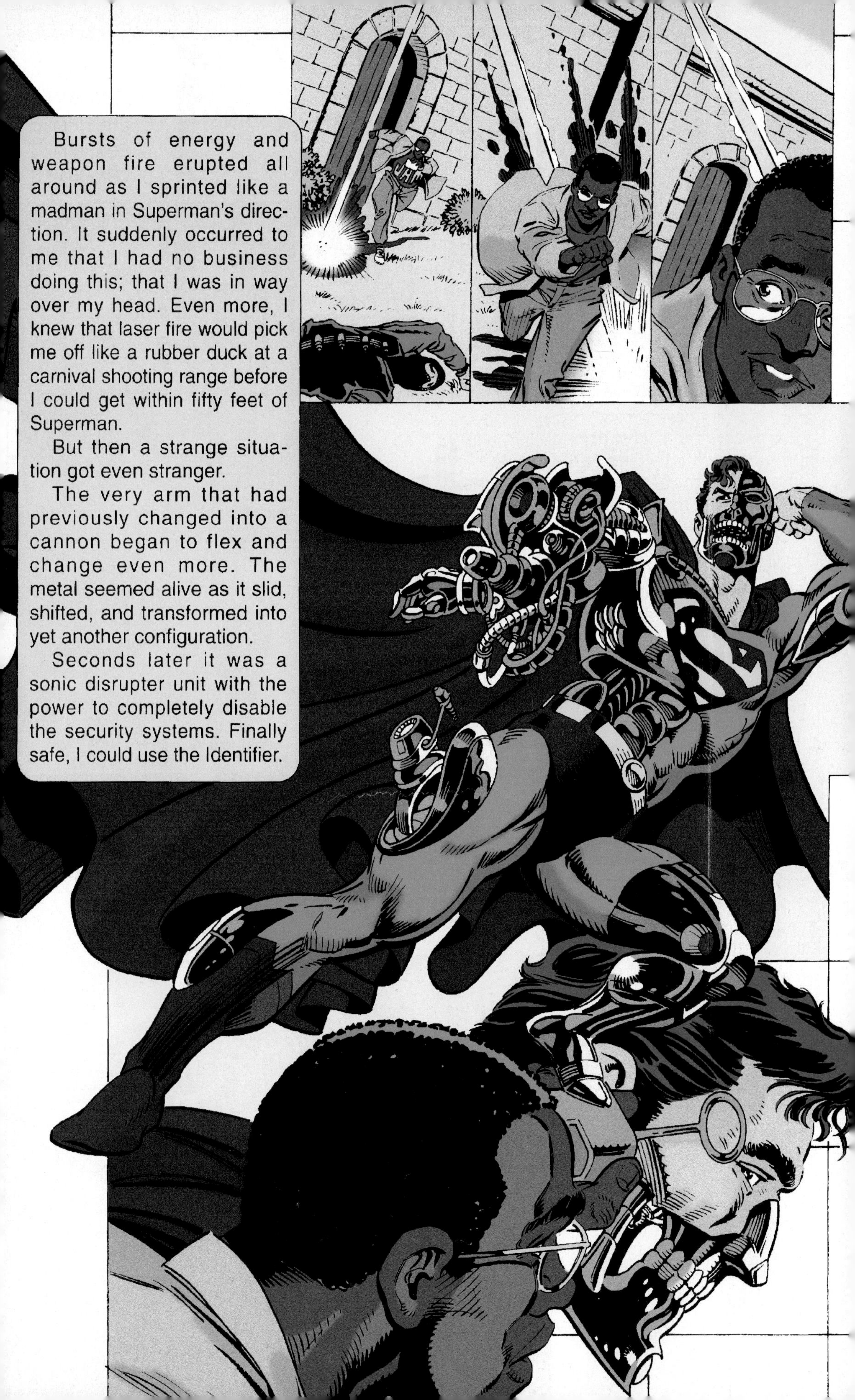

Bursts of energy and weapon fire erupted all around as I sprinted like a madman in Superman's direction. It suddenly occurred to me that I had no business doing this; that I was in way over my head. Even more, I knew that laser fire would pick me off like a rubber duck at a carnival shooting range before I could get within fifty feet of Superman.

But then a strange situation got even stranger.

The very arm that had previously changed into a cannon began to flex and change even more. The metal seemed alive as it slid, shifted, and transformed into yet another configuration.

Seconds later it was a sonic disrupter unit with the power to completely disable the security systems. Finally safe, I could use the Identifier.

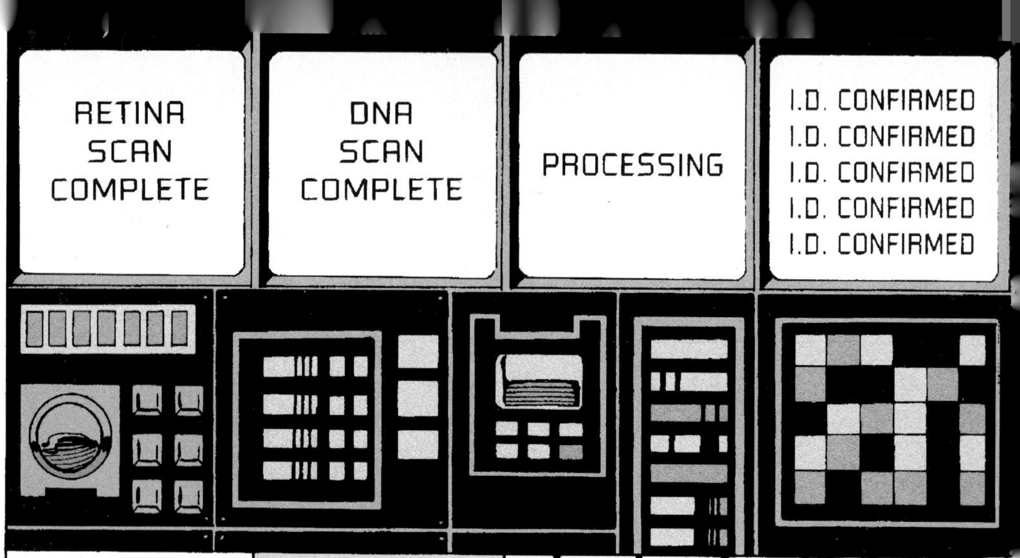
RETINA SCAN COMPLETE
DNA SCAN COMPLETE
PROCESSING
I.D. CONFIRMED
I.D. CONFIRMED
I.D. CONFIRMED
I.D. CONFIRMED
I.D. CONFIRMED

Every single identifying process available indicated this half-man, half-machine standing in front of me was undoubtedly Superman.

The greatest of them all, the man who paid the ultimate price protecting Metropolis, Superman, was rebuilt, alive and well.

He strode toward the White House with the determination, confidence and aura only a true hero could muster.

His commanding presence left them in awe. Even Max Lord, who lives in the midst of heroes, was speechless.

But Superman was all business, telling us the terrorist attack might not be over and a thorough security check was needed. He wanted to access the White House computers which, in turn, could tap into virtually every computer system in the world.

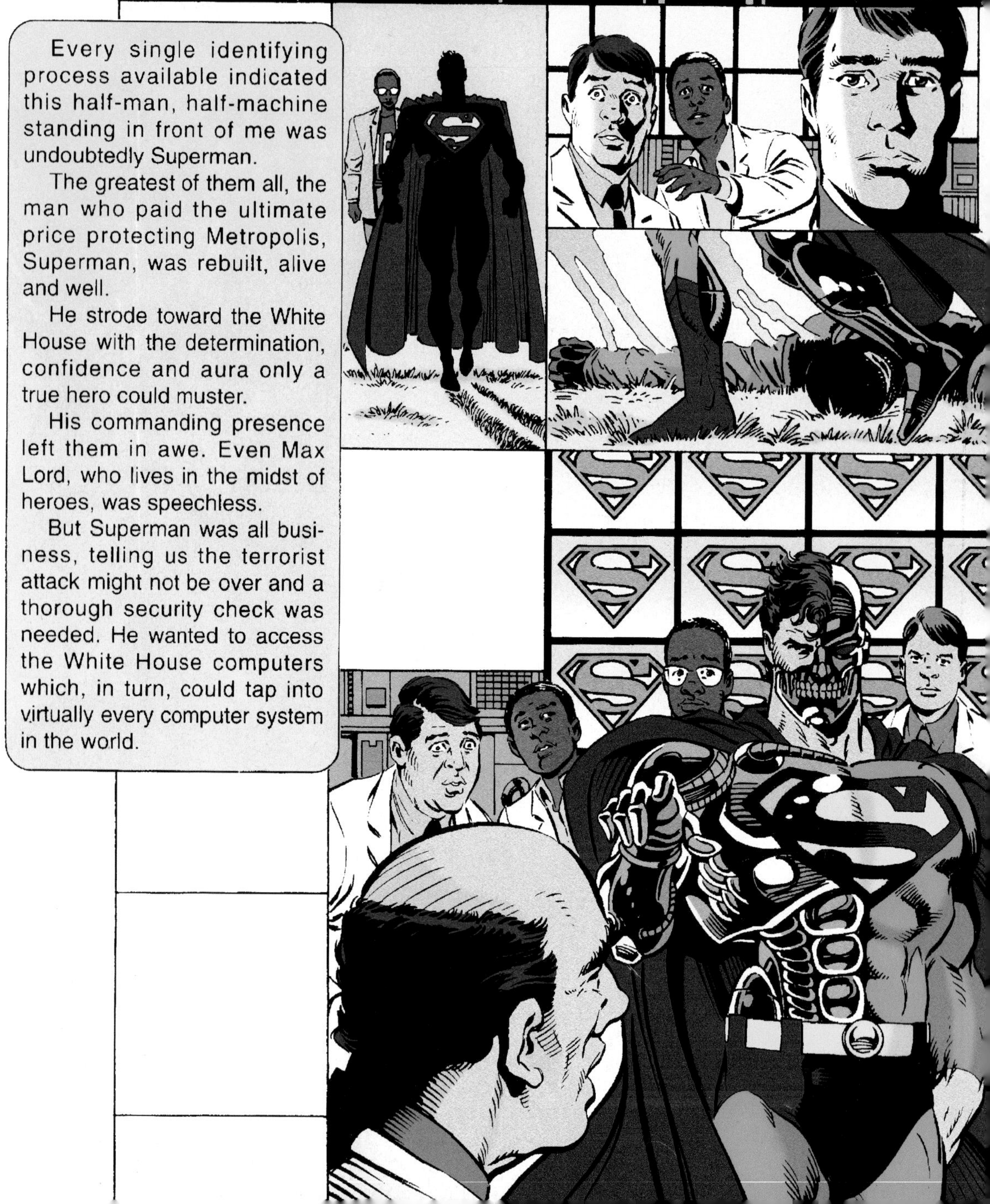

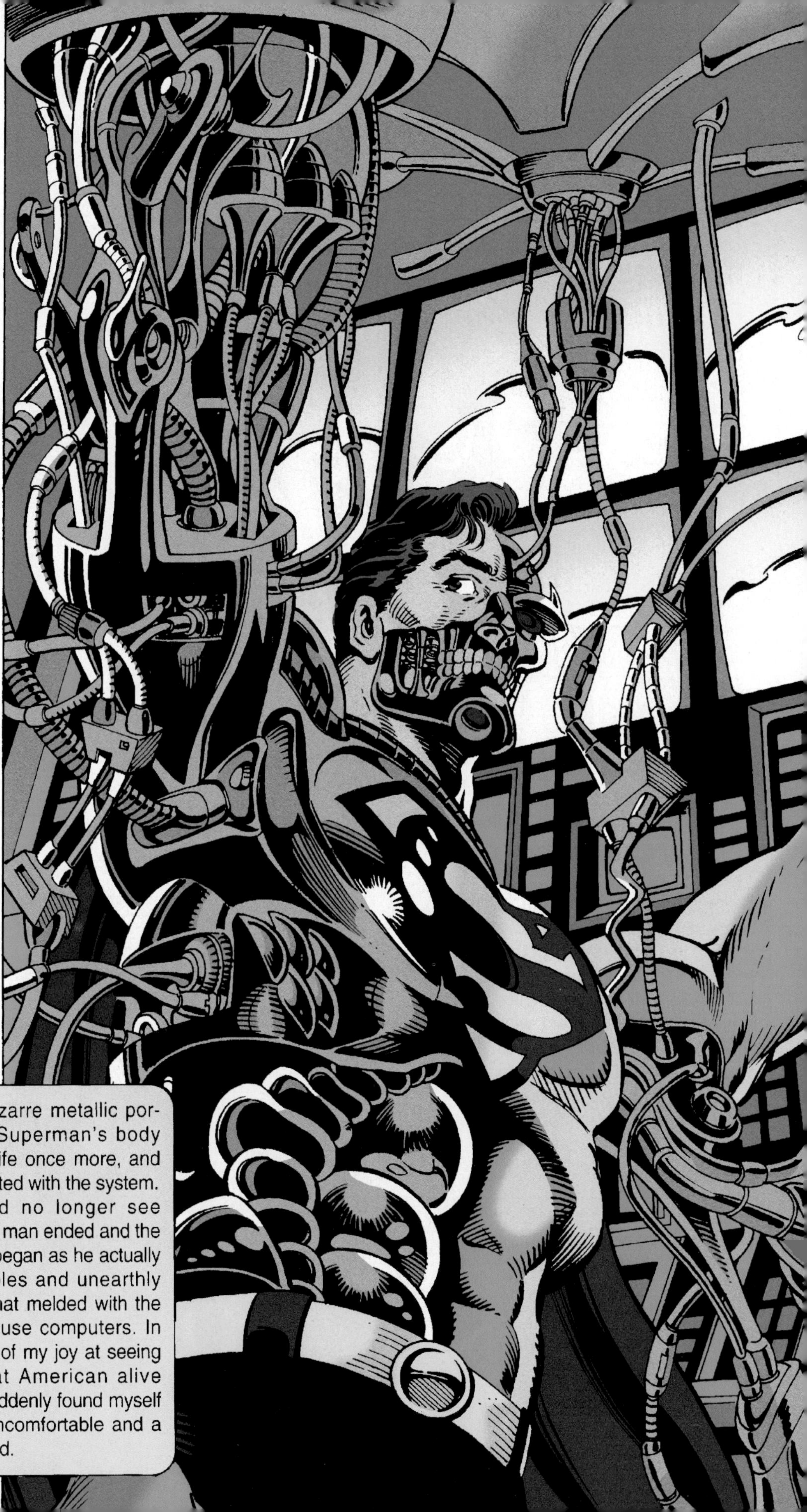

The bizarre metallic portions of Superman's body came to life once more, and he integrated with the system.

I could no longer see where the man ended and the machine began as he actually grew cables and unearthly devices that melded with the White House computers. In the midst of my joy at seeing this great American alive again I suddenly found myself slightly uncomfortable and a little scared.

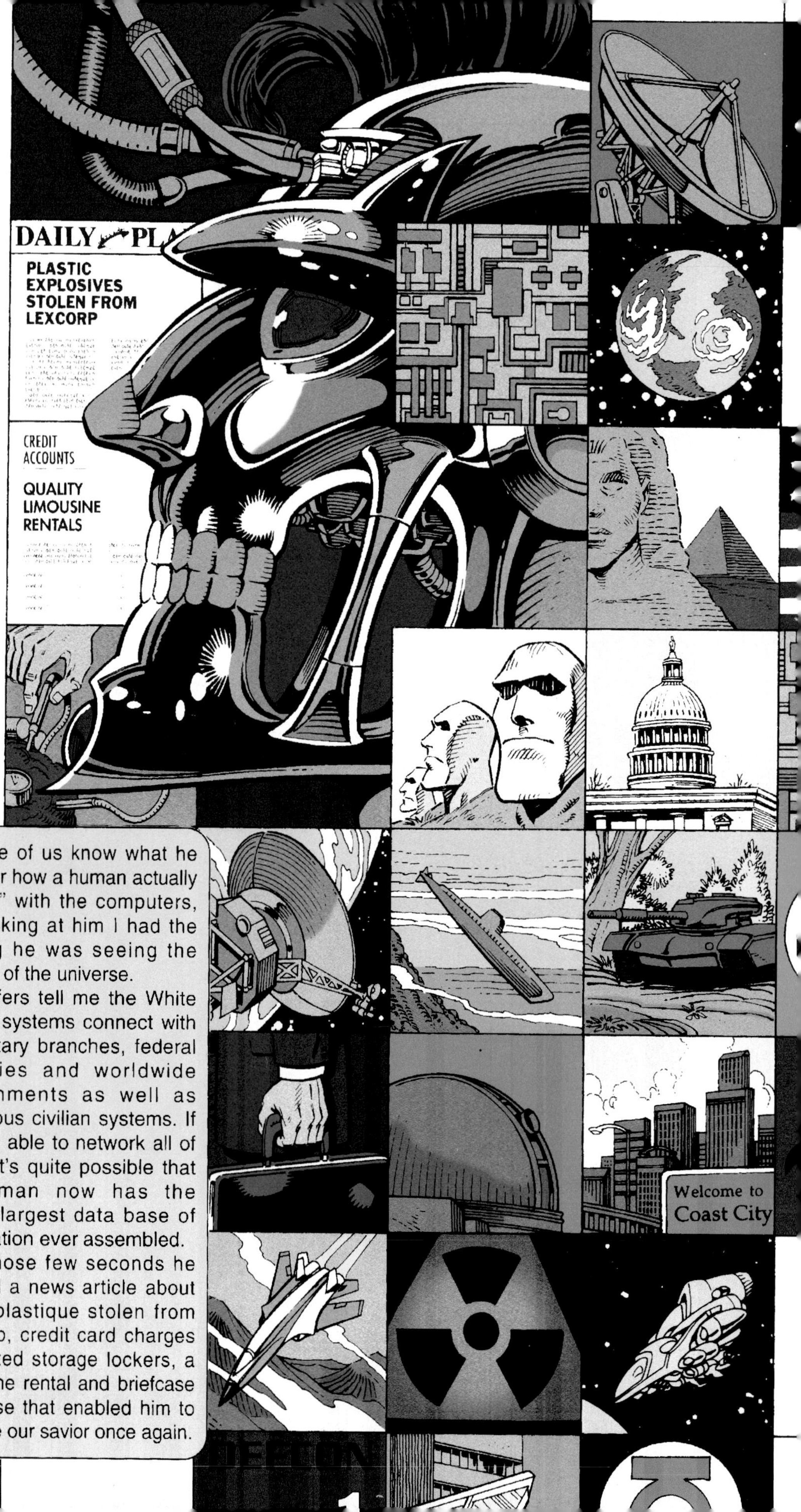
DAILY PLA
PLASTIC EXPLOSIVES STOLEN FROM LEXCORP
CREDIT ACCOUNTS
QUALITY LIMOUSINE RENTALS
Welcome to Coast City

None of us know what he "saw" or how a human actually "talked" with the computers, but looking at him I had the feeling he was seeing the secrets of the universe.

Staffers tell me the White House systems connect with all military branches, federal agencies and worldwide governments as well as numerous civilian systems. If he was able to network all of them, it's quite possible that Superman now has the single largest data base of information ever assembled.

In those few seconds he tracked a news article about some plastique stolen from Lexcorp, credit card charges for rented storage lockers, a limousine rental and briefcase purchase that enabled him to become our savior once again.

As this new Superman disconnected from the security system, he looked over in Max Lord's direction with a cold, hard expression.

He stared at Lord's briefcase as though he was looking right through it, and then that unique jeweled eye of his began glowing. Before Lord could object, Superman's scarlet burst of heat-vision melted his entire briefcase on the spot.

Superman, speaking in a metallic-sounding monotone voice, told us that the terrorists bought a briefcase identical to Lord's, put a bomb inside it and switched it while Lord got in the limousine at the airport. They knew their brazen attack might not succeed and also knew Lord would eventually get close to the President. Even though they would die, Lord would still become their assassin.

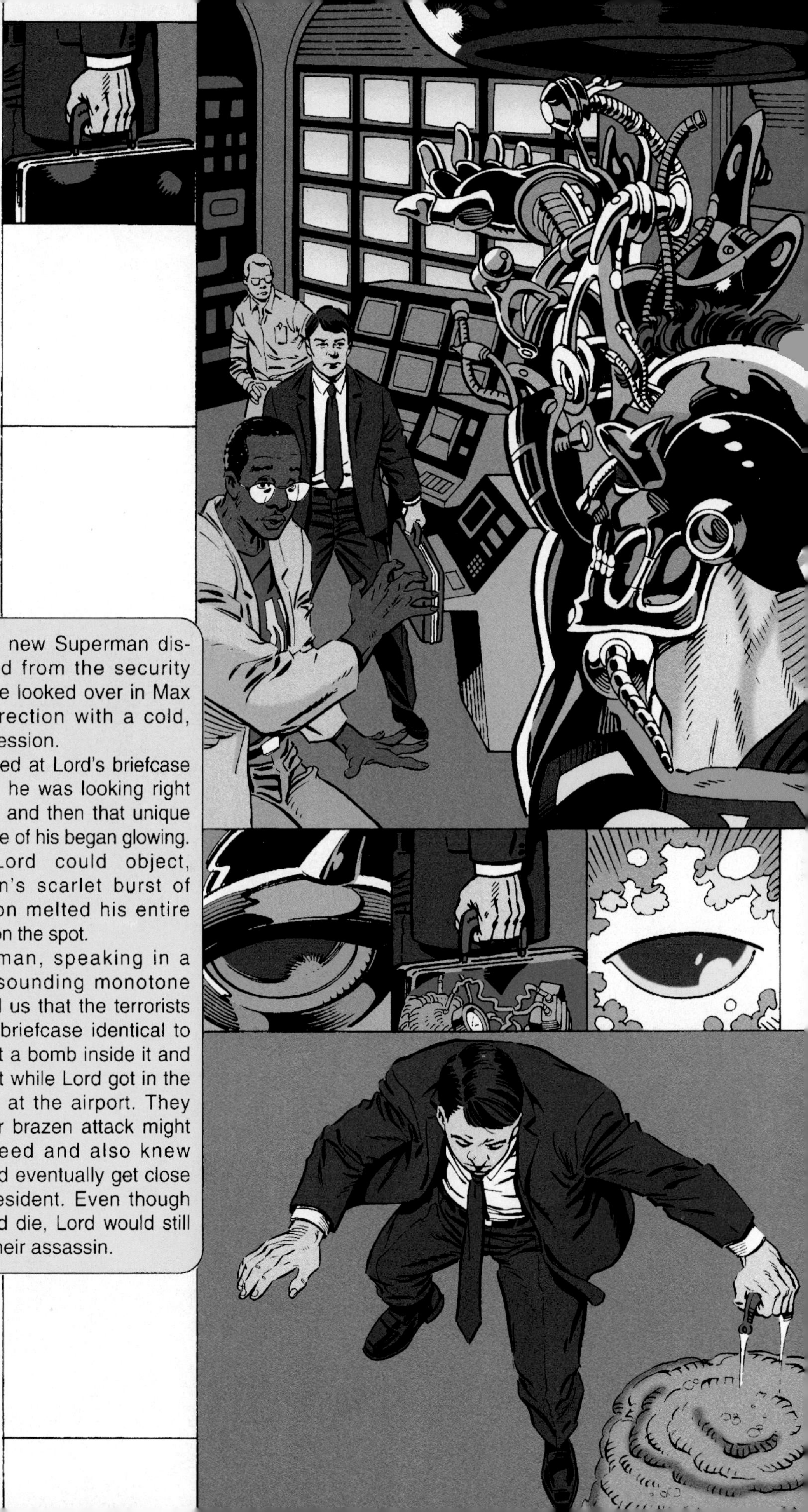

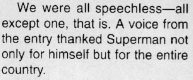

We were all speechless—all except one, that is. A voice from the entry thanked Superman not only for himself but for the entire country.

It was an historic meeting between two powerful men of the free world. Superman accepted this man's thanks and told him that should he ever need his services, he merely had to contact him on a special device. Superman actually seemed to construct it, even grow it, on the spot.

He handed it over saying it was a personal communications device, something he'd never given any President in the past.

With that, the President accepted the device and acknowledged this Man of Steel as the one, true Superman.

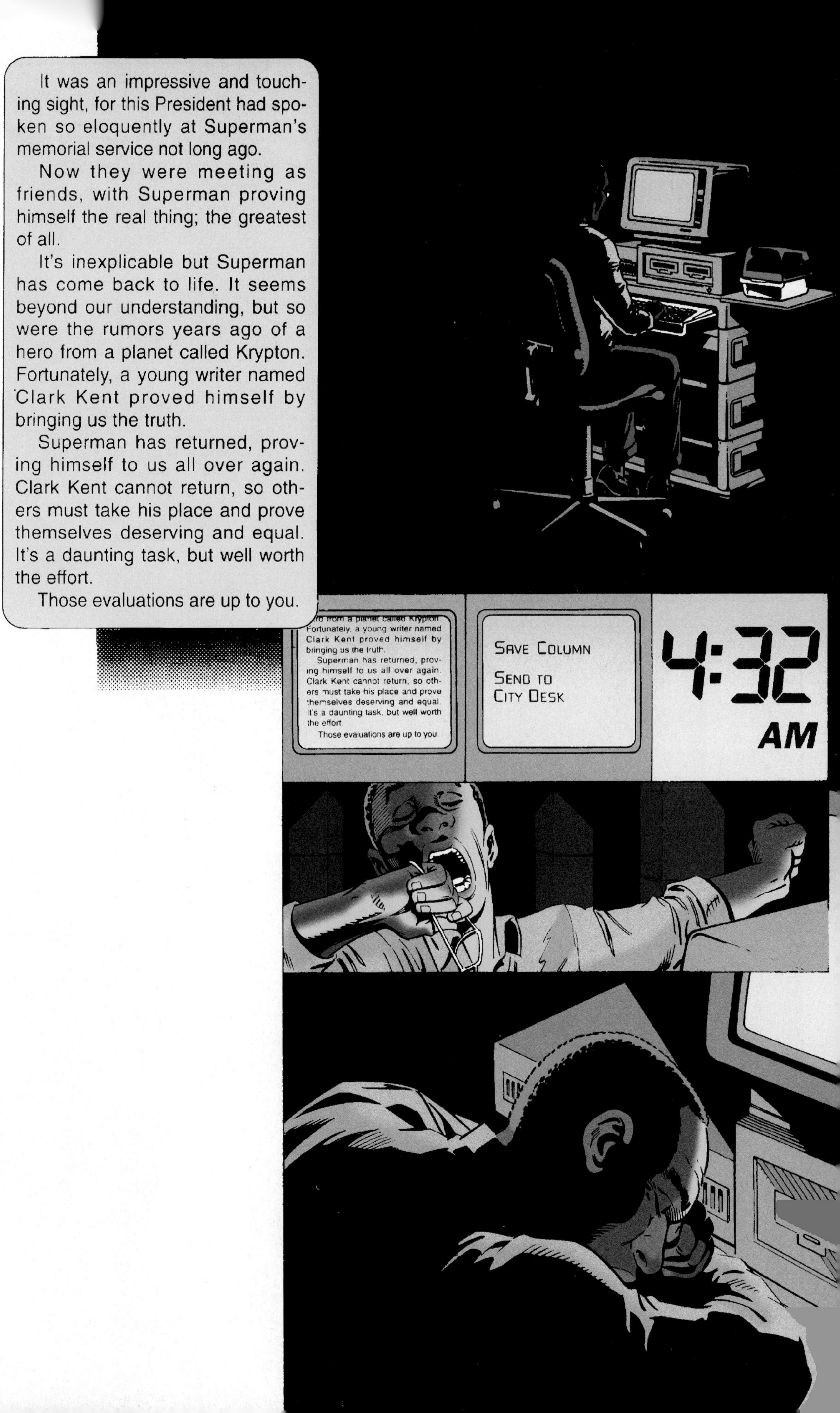
It was an impressive and touching sight, for this President had spoken so eloquently at Superman's memorial service not long ago.
Now they were meeting as friends, with Superman proving himself the real thing; the greatest of all.
It's inexplicable but Superman has come back to life. It seems beyond our understanding, but so were the rumors years ago of a hero from a planet called Krypton. Fortunately, a young writer named Clark Kent proved himself by bringing us the truth.
Superman has returned, proving himself to us all over again. Clark Kent cannot return, so others must take his place and prove themselves deserving and equal. It's a daunting task, but well worth the effort.
Those evaluations are up to you.
Fortunately, a young writer named Clark Kent proved himself by bringing us the truth.
Superman has returned, proving himself to us all over again. Clark Kent cannot return, so others must take his place and prove themselves deserving and equal. It's a daunting task, but well worth the effort.
Those evaluations are up to you.
SAVE COLUMN
SEND TO CITY DESK
4:32 AM

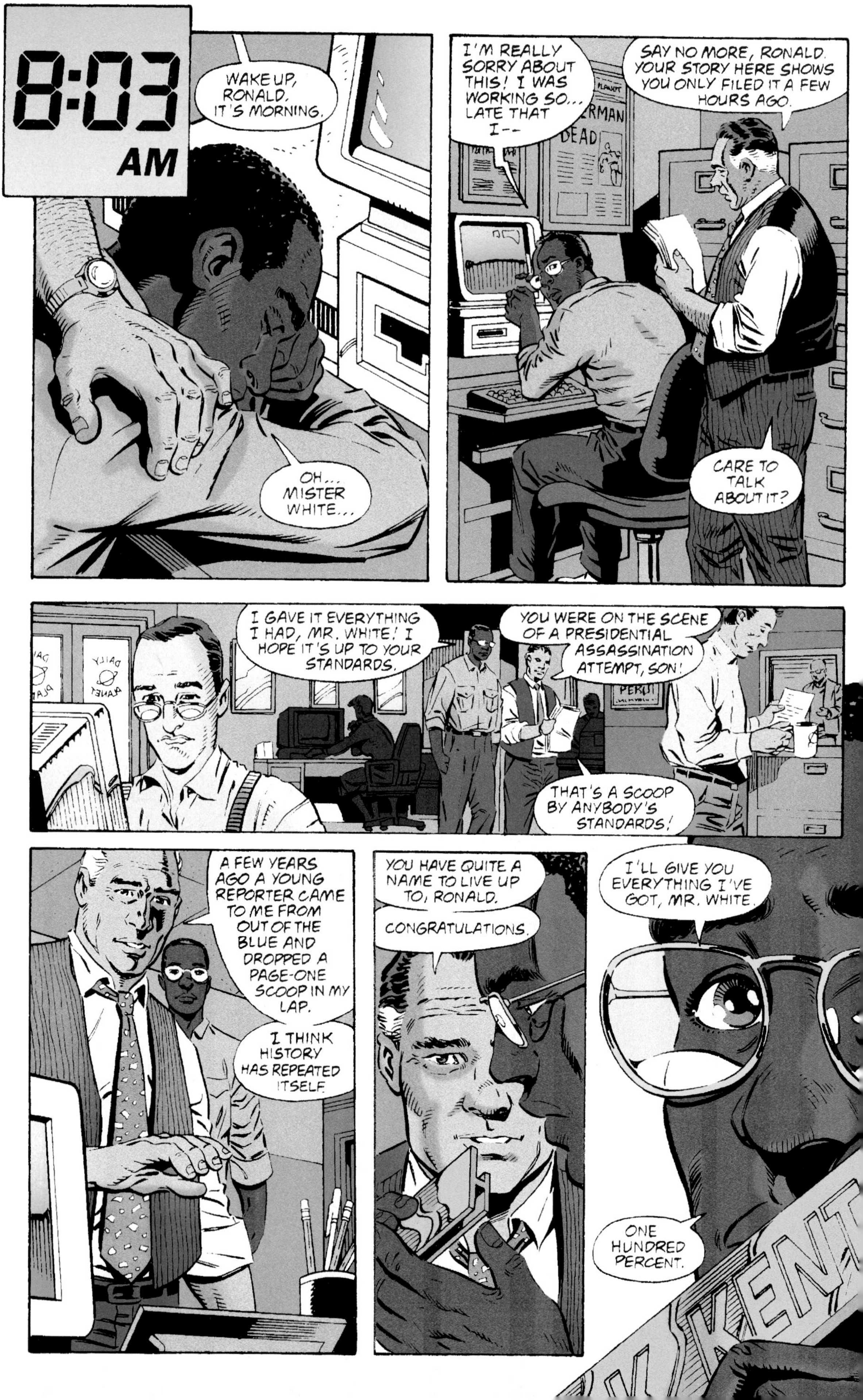
8:03 AM
WAKE UP, RONALD. IT'S MORNING.
OH... MISTER WHITE...
I'M REALLY SORRY ABOUT THIS! I WAS WORKING SO... LATE THAT I--
SAY NO MORE, RONALD. YOUR STORY HERE SHOWS YOU ONLY FILED IT A FEW HOURS AGO.
CARE TO TALK ABOUT IT?
I GAVE IT EVERYTHING I HAD, MR. WHITE! I HOPE IT'S UP TO YOUR STANDARDS.
YOU WERE ON THE SCENE OF A PRESIDENTIAL ASSASSINATION ATTEMPT, SON!
THAT'S A SCOOP BY ANYBODY'S STANDARDS!
A FEW YEARS AGO A YOUNG REPORTER CAME TO ME FROM OUT OF THE BLUE AND DROPPED A PAGE-ONE SCOOP IN MY LAP.
I THINK HISTORY HAS REPEATED ITSELF.
YOU HAVE QUITE A NAME TO LIVE UP TO, RONALD.
CONGRATULATIONS.
I'LL GIVE YOU EVERYTHING I'VE GOT, MR. WHITE.
ONE HUNDRED PERCENT.
KENT

DAILY PLANET

Friday, May 28, 1993

Price: 40¢

SUPERMAN IS BACK!

Story by RONALD TROUPE

"Prove it!"

Think about it. If you're one of those who thinks yourself the best, the ultimate, "The Real Thing" in whatever you do, consider yourself lucky if you are never asked to prove it. Only a select few have done so.

Lincoln proved his greatness by holding together a nation torn by war and by freeing men not acknowledged as equals. Martin Luther King did it by asking an entire nation to look in the mirror and take shame in the ugly reflection of bigotry. Joe DiMaggio swung the bat better than anyone else and Superman did it by being, well, *Super*. And the man I want to talk about, the man I would prove myself to if he were still alive, is the reporter who did it all.

The best.

Clark Kent.

Readers of this paper, *The Daily Planet,* have been familiar with Kent's extraordinary work for years. Writing about economics, pollution, justice, crime, education, politics and the human condition, Kent's brilliance touched us all.

I marveled at Mr. Kent's clarity of vision and evidence of sound reason. I admired the man, his work, and the way he lived his life.

—story continued on page A3

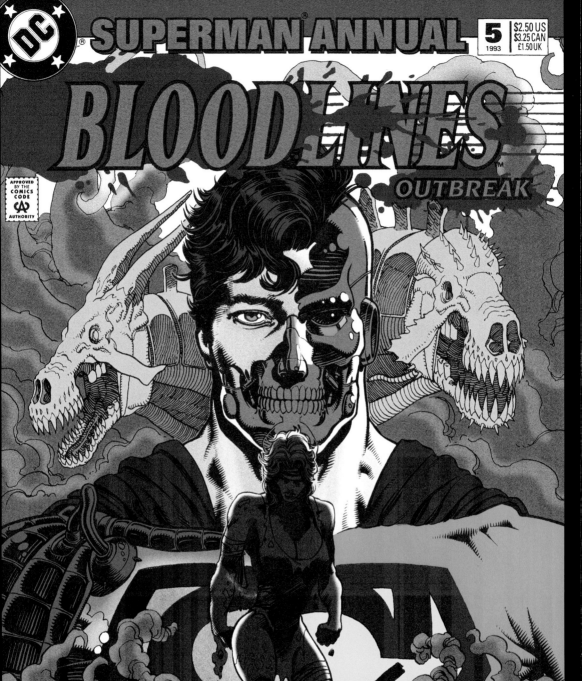

SUPERMAN ANNUAL

5
1993

$2.50 US
$3.25 CAN
£1.50 UK

APPROVED
BY THE
COMICS
CODE
CAD
AUTHORITY

BLOODLINES

OUTBREAK

MYRIAD!

JURGENS · **LAPHAM** ✦ **MACHLAN**

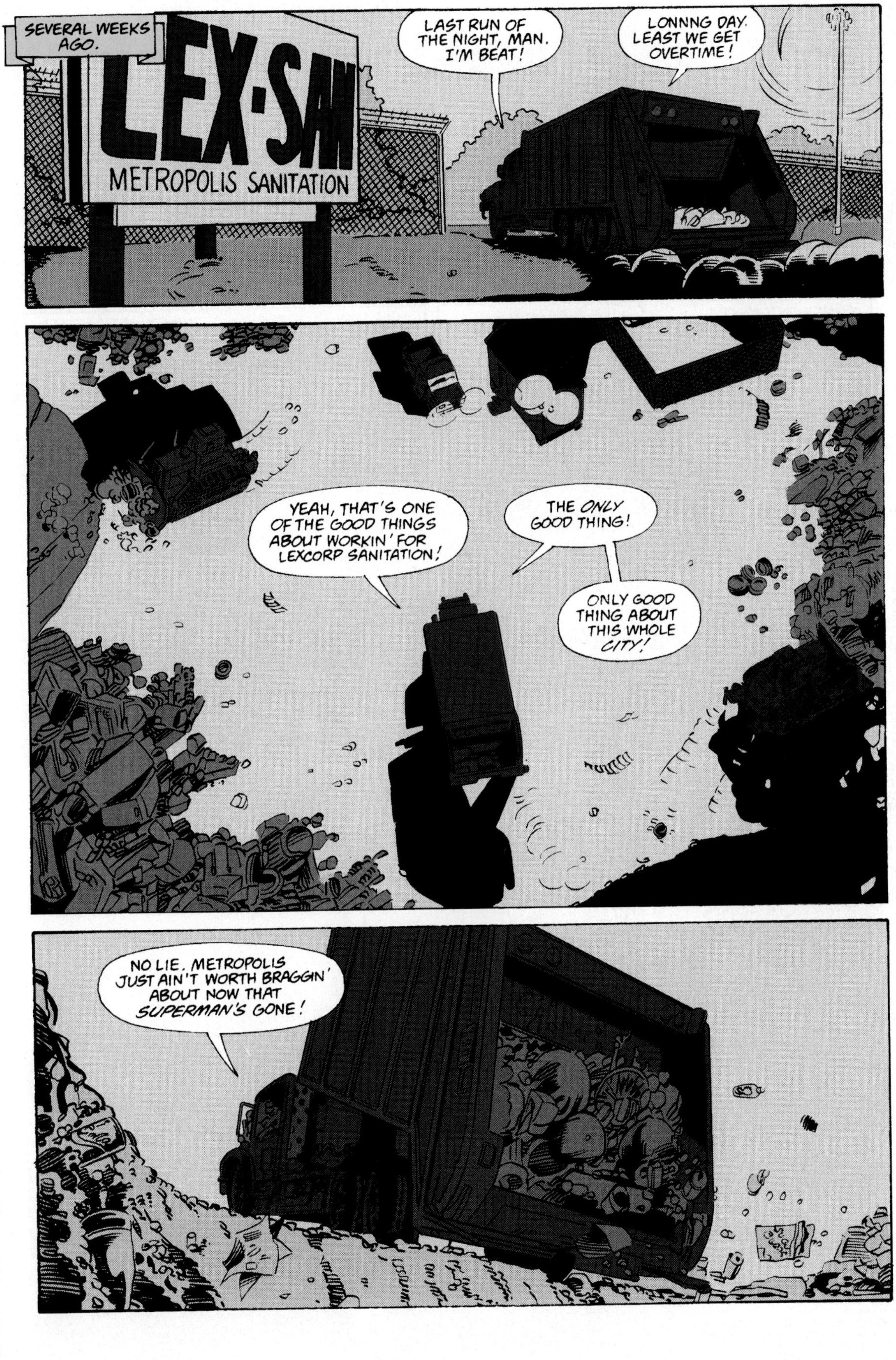
SEVERAL WEEKS AGO.
LEX-SAN
METROPOLIS SANITATION
LAST RUN OF THE NIGHT, MAN. I'M BEAT!
LONNNG DAY. LEAST WE GET OVERTIME!
YEAH, THAT'S ONE OF THE GOOD THINGS ABOUT WORKIN' FOR LEXCORP SANITATION!
THE ONLY GOOD THING!
ONLY GOOD THING ABOUT THIS WHOLE CITY!
NO LIE. METROPOLIS JUST AIN'T WORTH BRAGGIN' ABOUT NOW THAT SUPERMAN'S GONE!

I DON'T EVEN WANNA TELL THE FOLKS BACK HOME I LIVE HERE!

I HEAR YA! PEOPLE JUST REMEMBER METROPOLIS FOR SUPERMAN DYIN' HERE SAME AS THEY REMEMBER DALLAS AND JFK!

LIKE WE ACTUALLY SENT *DOOMSDAY* AFTER HIM OR SOMETHING!

I HEAR YOU BUMS MENTION *DOOMSDAY?*

SURE DON'T KNOW WHERE THAT SUCKER CAME FROM BUT HE SHOULDA GOT *THIS!*

BLAM

LIKE THAT LITTLE PEA-SHOOTER WOULD ACE HIM WHEN SUPES COULDN'T!

THIS MAY BE A PEA-SHOOTER BUT IT'S STILL GOOD ENOUGH FOR SNUFFIN' THESE GARBAGE RATS!

THEY MIGHT AS WELL BE PAYIN' YOU FOR SOMETHING, RODRIGUEZ!

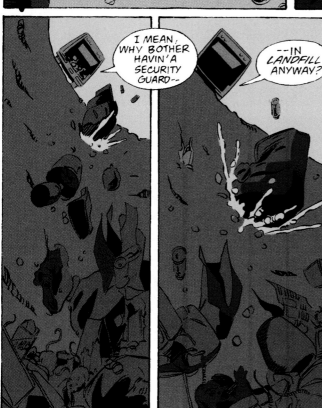

I MEAN, WHY BOTHER HAVIN' A SECURITY GUARD--

--IN *LANDFILL* ANYWAY?

THEY AFRAID SOMEBODY'S GONNA COME IN AND STEAL SOME BIG BELLY LEFTOVERS?

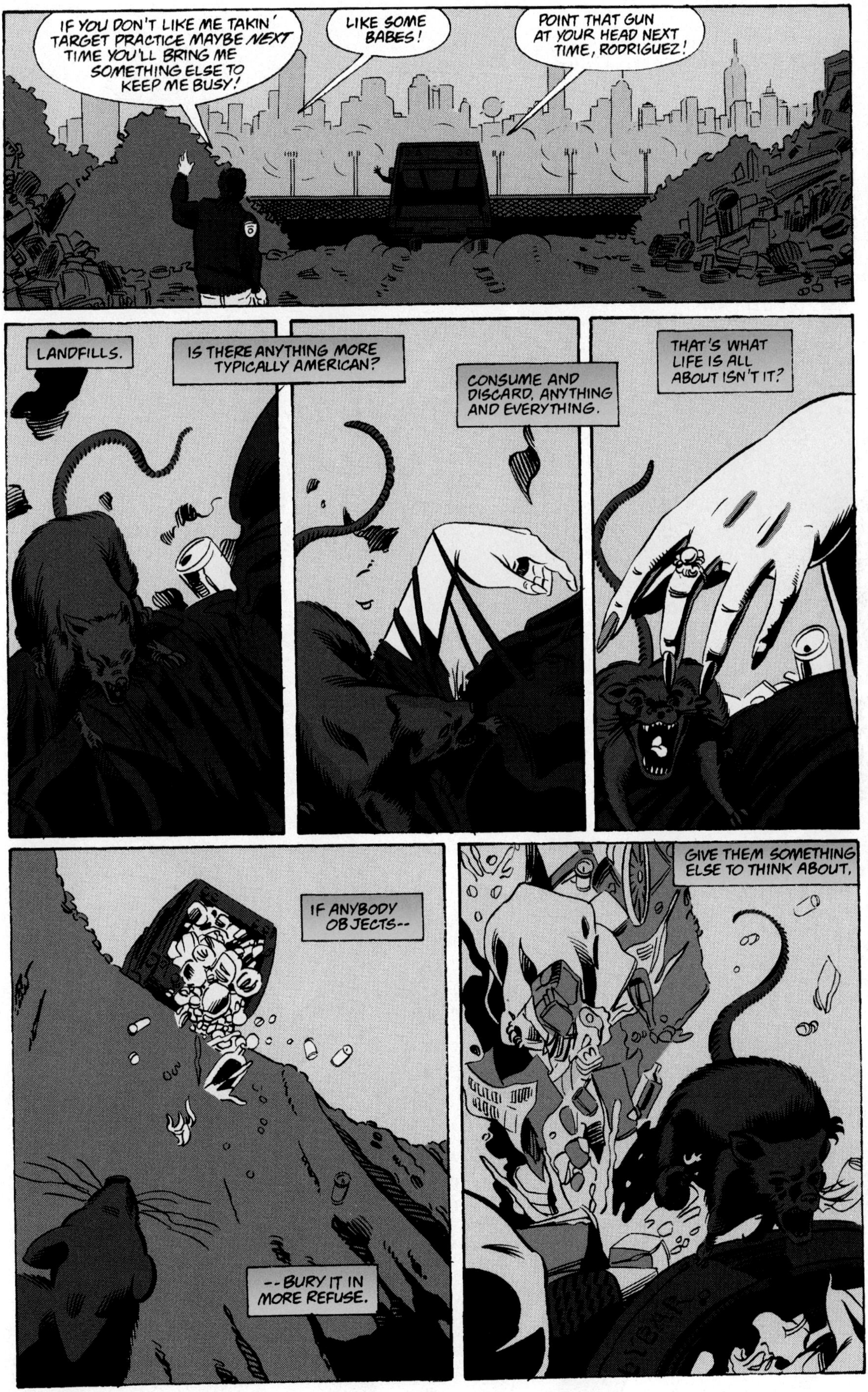
IF YOU DON'T LIKE ME TAKIN' TARGET PRACTICE MAYBE NEXT TIME YOU'LL BRING ME SOMETHING ELSE TO KEEP ME BUSY!
LIKE SOME BABES!
POINT THAT GUN AT YOUR HEAD NEXT TIME, RODRIGUEZ!
LANDFILLS.
IS THERE ANYTHING MORE TYPICALLY AMERICAN?
CONSUME AND DISCARD, ANYTHING AND EVERYTHING.
THAT'S WHAT LIFE IS ALL ABOUT ISN'T IT?
IF ANYBODY OBJECTS--
--BURY IT IN MORE REFUSE.
GIVE THEM SOMETHING ELSE TO THINK ABOUT.

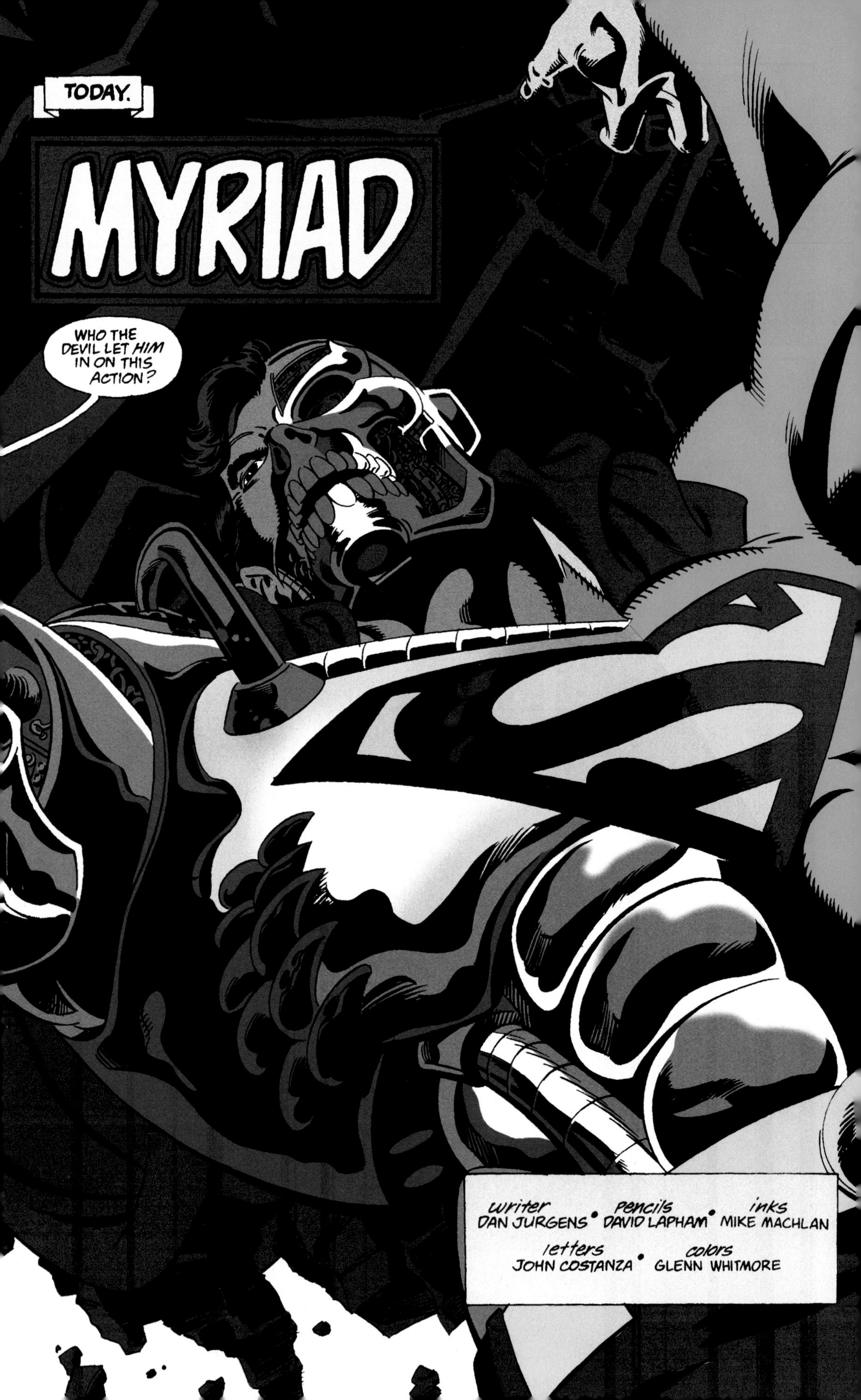
TODAY.
MYRIAD
WHO THE DEVIL LET HIM IN ON THIS ACTION?
writer DAN JURGENS • pencils DAVID LAPHAM • inks MIKE MACHLAN
letters JOHN COSTANZA • colors GLENN WHITMORE

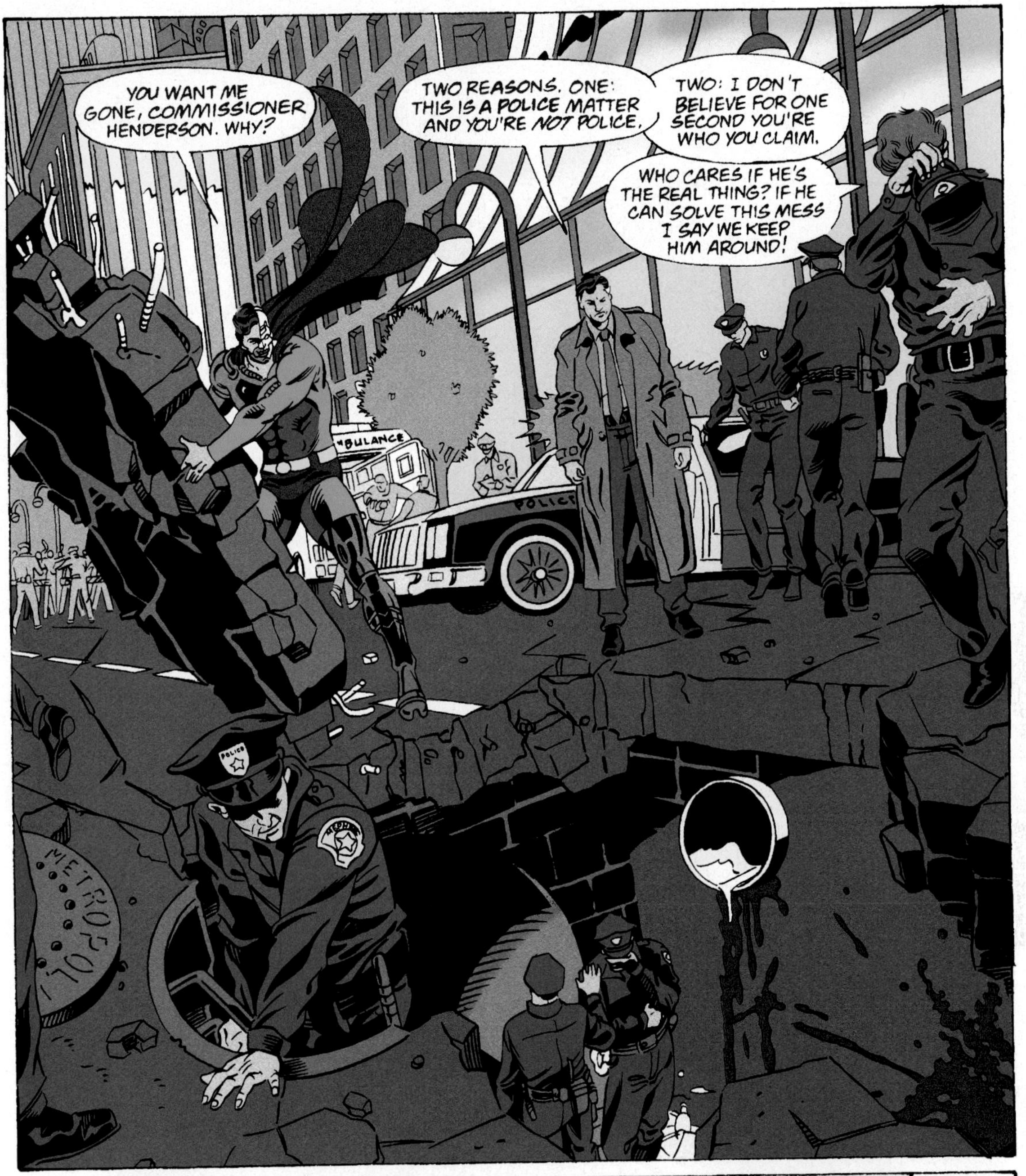
YOU WANT ME GONE, COMMISSIONER HENDERSON. WHY?
TWO REASONS. ONE: THIS IS A POLICE MATTER AND YOU'RE NOT POLICE.
TWO: I DON'T BELIEVE FOR ONE SECOND YOU'RE WHO YOU CLAIM.
WHO CARES IF HE'S THE REAL THING? IF HE CAN SOLVE THIS MESS I SAY WE KEEP HIM AROUND!
AMBULANCE
POLICE
POLICE
METROPOL

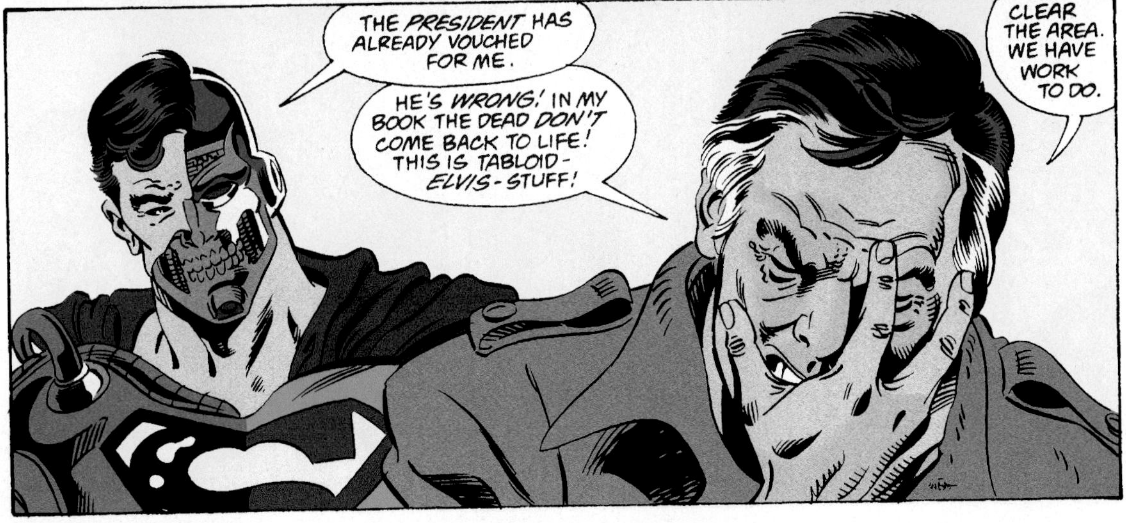
THE PRESIDENT HAS ALREADY VOUCHED FOR ME.
HE'S WRONG! IN MY BOOK THE DEAD DON'T COME BACK TO LIFE! THIS IS TABLOID-ELVIS-STUFF!
CLEAR THE AREA. WE HAVE WORK TO DO.

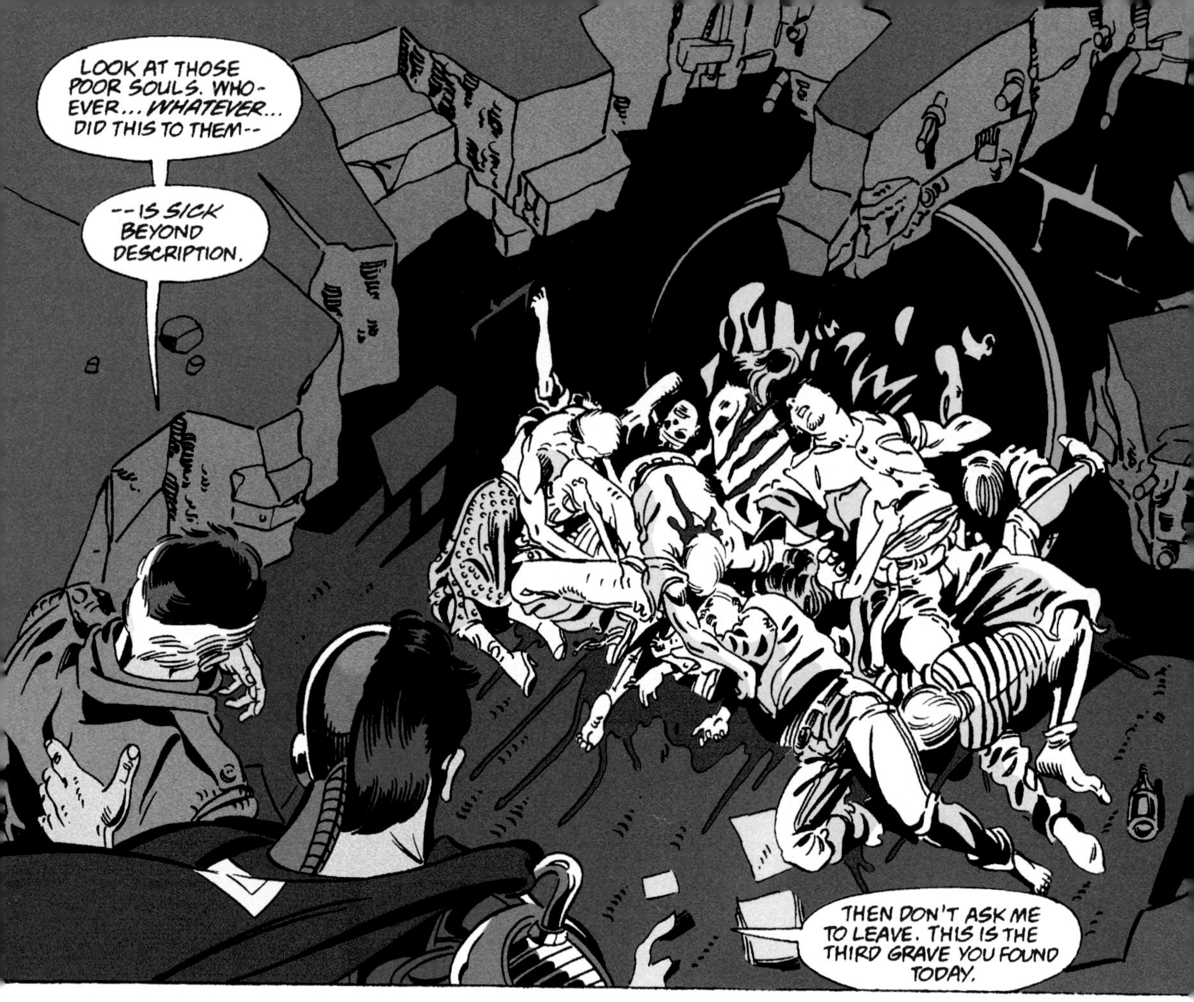
LOOK AT THOSE POOR SOULS. WHO-EVER... WHATEVER... DID THIS TO THEM--
--IS SICK BEYOND DESCRIPTION.
THEN DON'T ASK ME TO LEAVE. THIS IS THE THIRD GRAVE YOU FOUND TODAY.

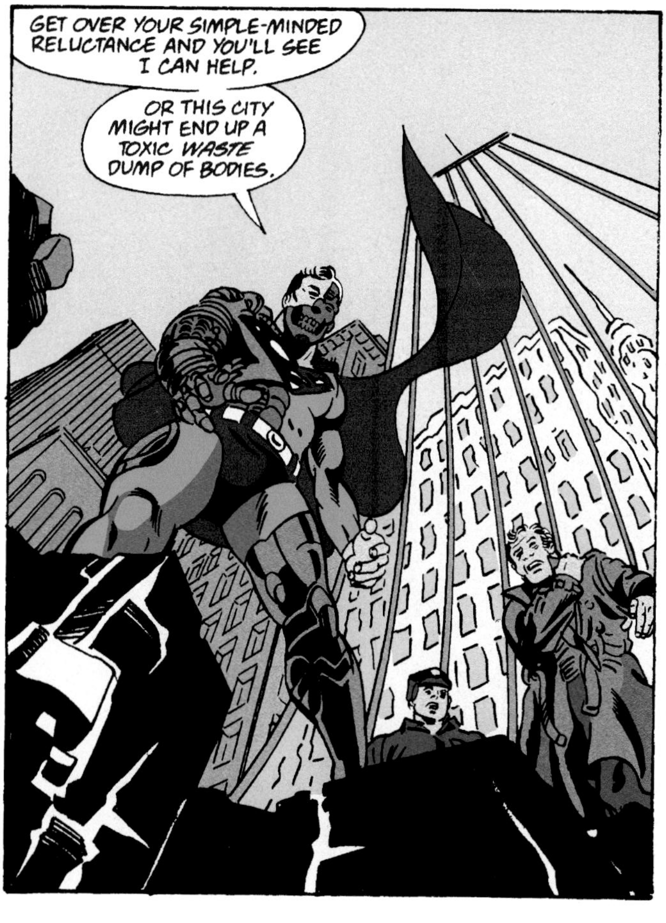
GET OVER YOUR SIMPLE-MINDED RELUCTANCE AND YOU'LL SEE I CAN HELP.
OR THIS CITY MIGHT END UP A TOXIC WASTE DUMP OF BODIES.

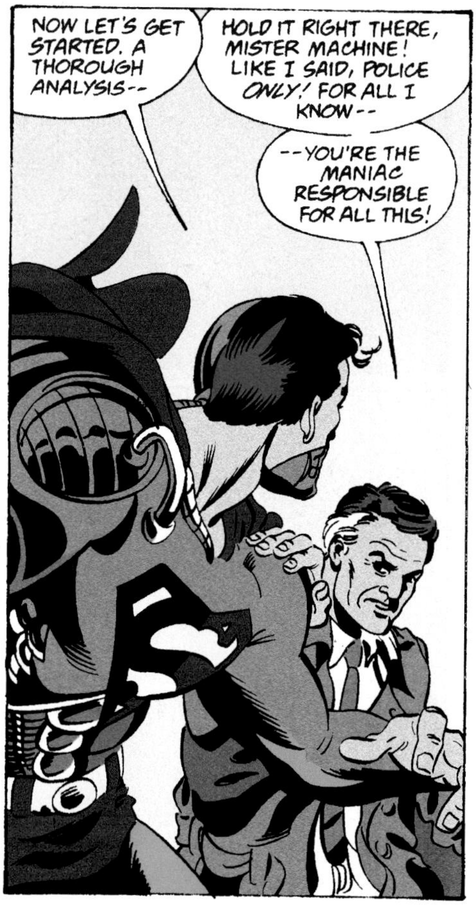
NOW LET'S GET STARTED. A THOROUGH ANALYSIS--
HOLD IT RIGHT THERE, MISTER MACHINE! LIKE I SAID, POLICE ONLY! FOR ALL I KNOW--
--YOU'RE THE MANIAC RESPONSIBLE FOR ALL THIS!

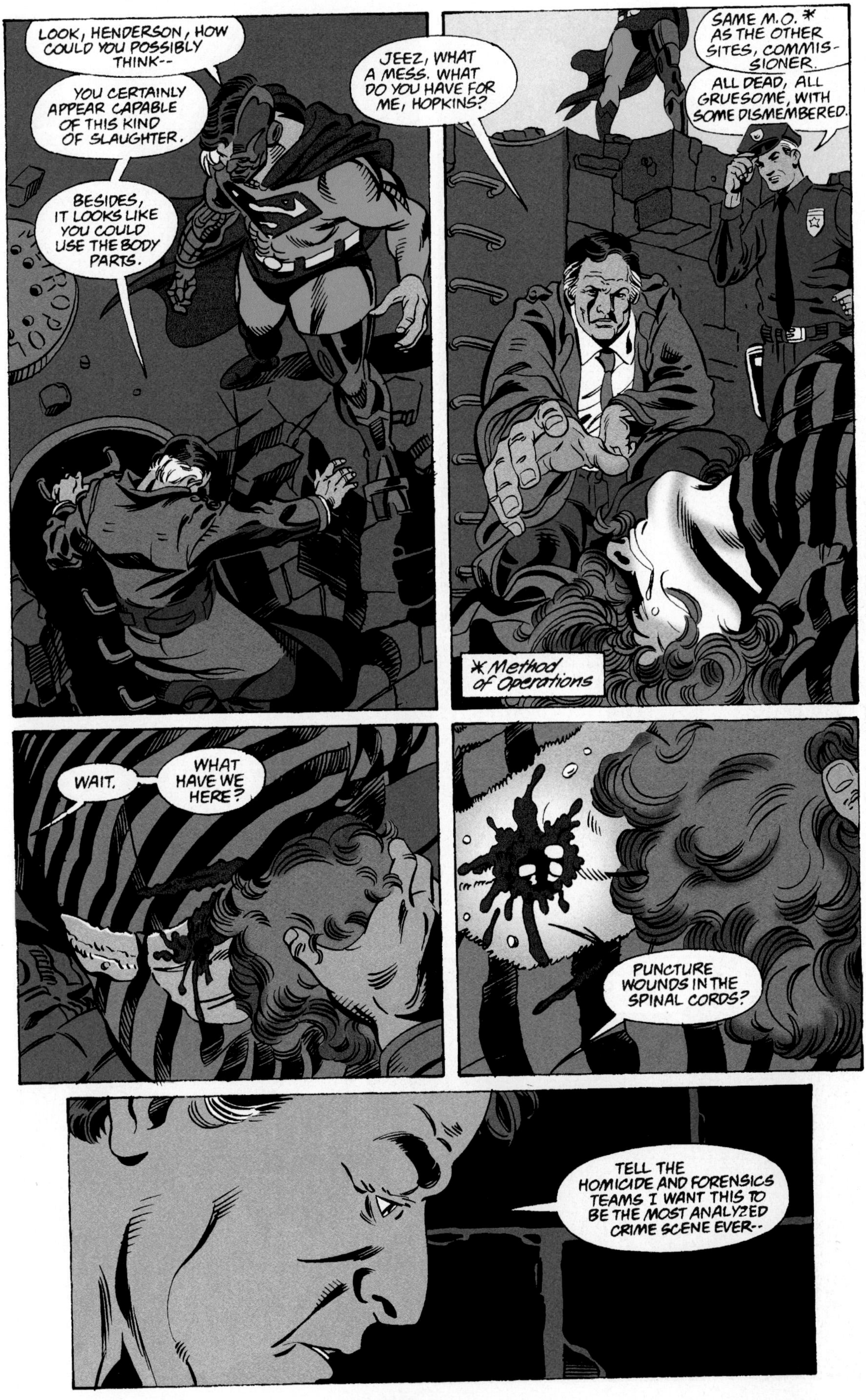
LOOK, HENDERSON, HOW COULD YOU POSSIBLY THINK--
YOU CERTAINLY APPEAR CAPABLE OF THIS KIND OF SLAUGHTER.
BESIDES, IT LOOKS LIKE YOU COULD USE THE BODY PARTS.
JEEZ, WHAT A MESS. WHAT DO YOU HAVE FOR ME, HOPKINS?
SAME M.O.* AS THE OTHER SITES, COMMISSIONER.
ALL DEAD, ALL GRUESOME, WITH SOME DISMEMBERED.
*Method of Operations
WAIT.
WHAT HAVE WE HERE?
PUNCTURE WOUNDS IN THE SPINAL CORDS?
TELL THE HOMICIDE AND FORENSICS TEAMS I WANT THIS TO BE THE MOST ANALYZED CRIME SCENE EVER--

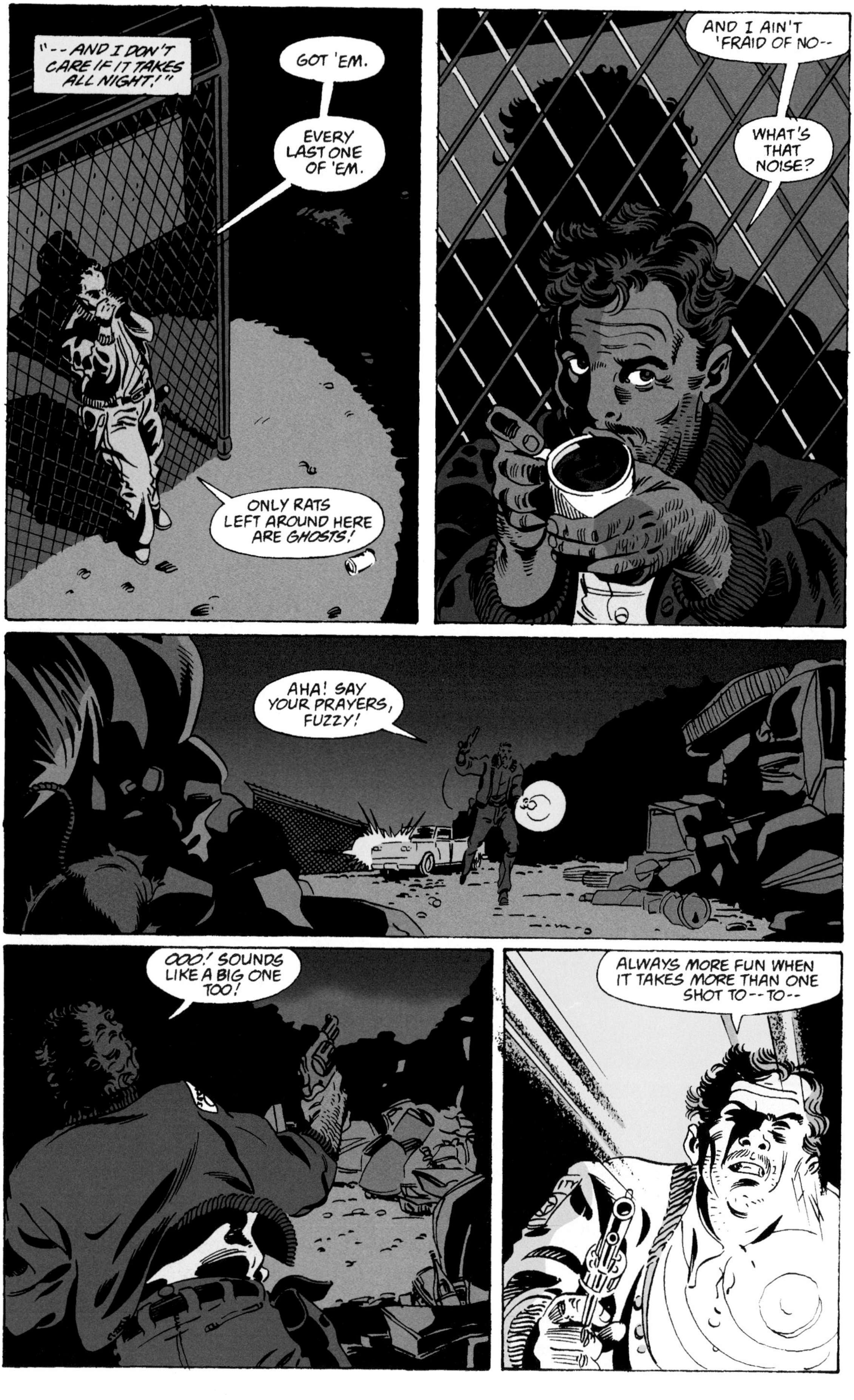
"--AND I DON'T CARE IF IT TAKES ALL NIGHT!"
GOT 'EM.
EVERY LAST ONE OF 'EM.
ONLY RATS LEFT AROUND HERE ARE GHOSTS!
AND I AIN'T 'FRAID OF NO--
WHAT'S THAT NOISE?
AHA! SAY YOUR PRAYERS, FUZZY!
OOO! SOUNDS LIKE A BIG ONE TOO!
ALWAYS MORE FUN WHEN IT TAKES MORE THAN ONE SHOT TO--TO--

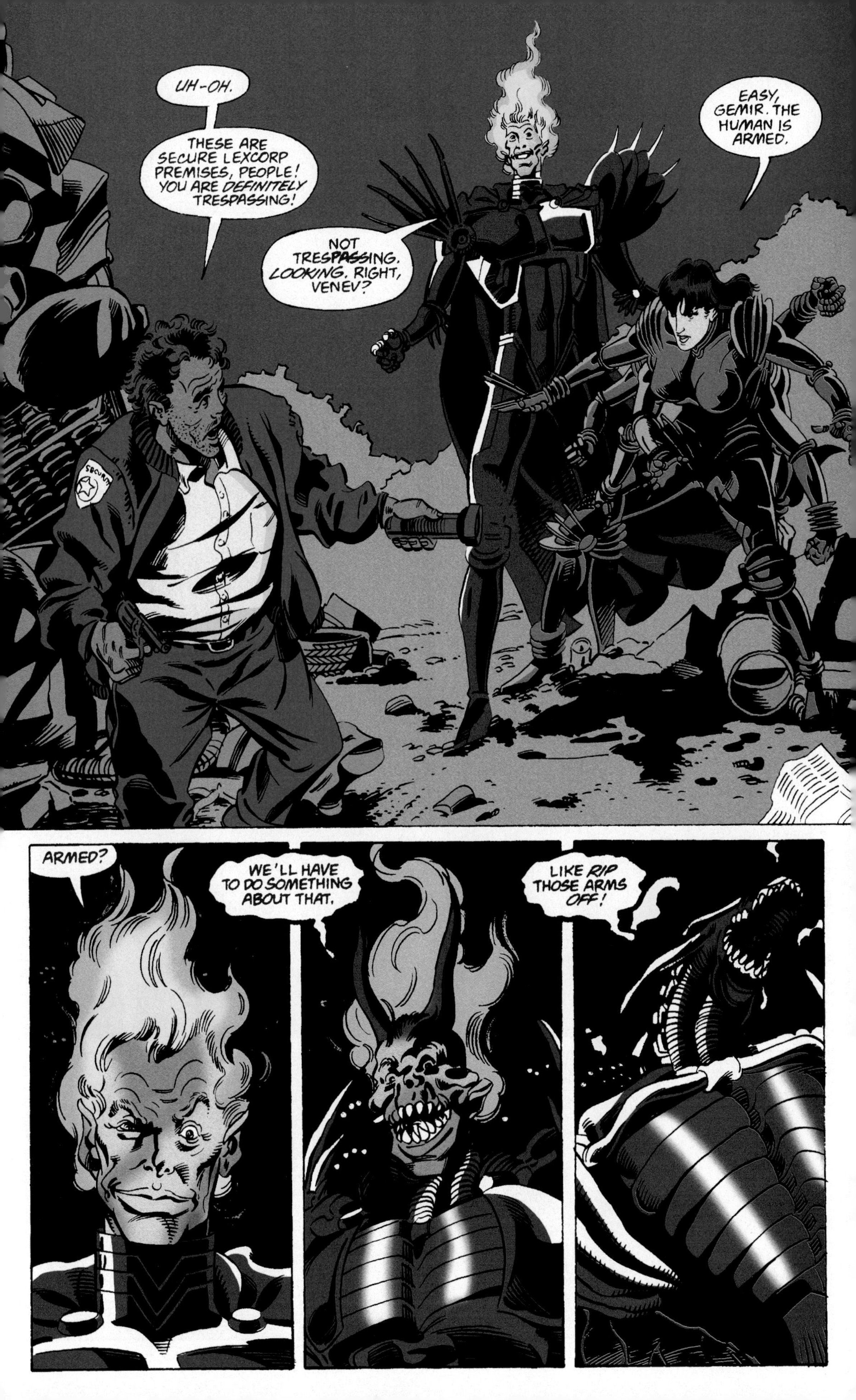
UH-OH.
THESE ARE SECURE LEXCORP PREMISES, PEOPLE! YOU ARE DEFINITELY TRESPASSING!
NOT TRESPASSING. LOOKING. RIGHT, VENEV?
EASY, GEMIR. THE HUMAN IS ARMED.
ARMED?
WE'LL HAVE TO DO SOMETHING ABOUT THAT.
LIKE RIP THOSE ARMS OFF!

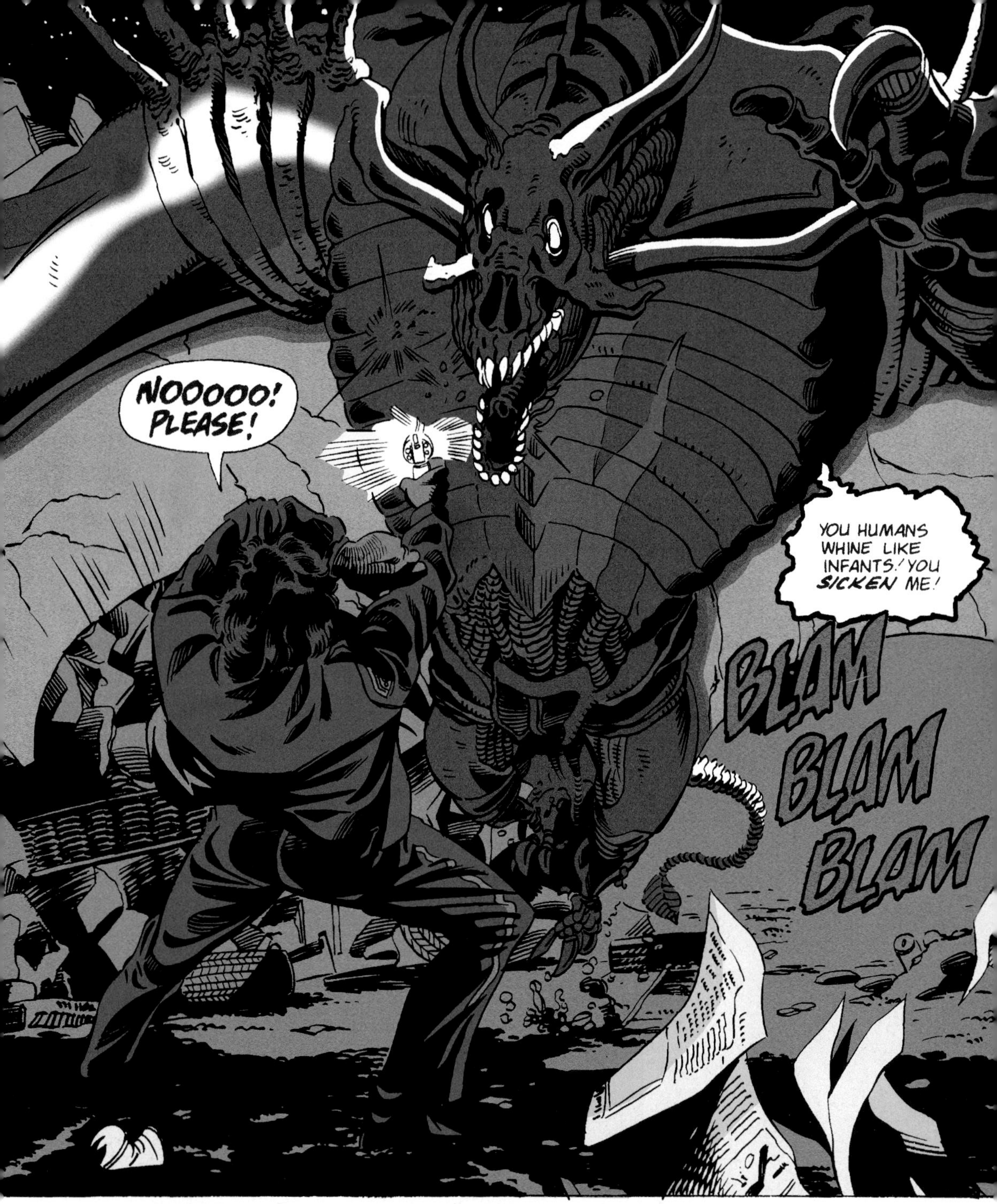
NOOOOO! PLEASE!
YOU HUMANS WHINE LIKE INFANTS! YOU SICKEN ME!
BLAM
BLAM
BLAM

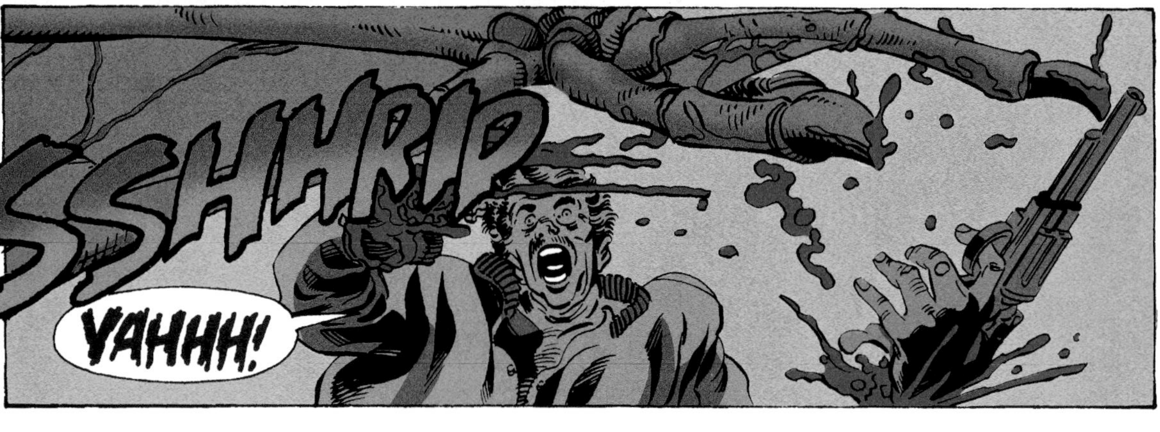
SSHHRIP
YAHHH!

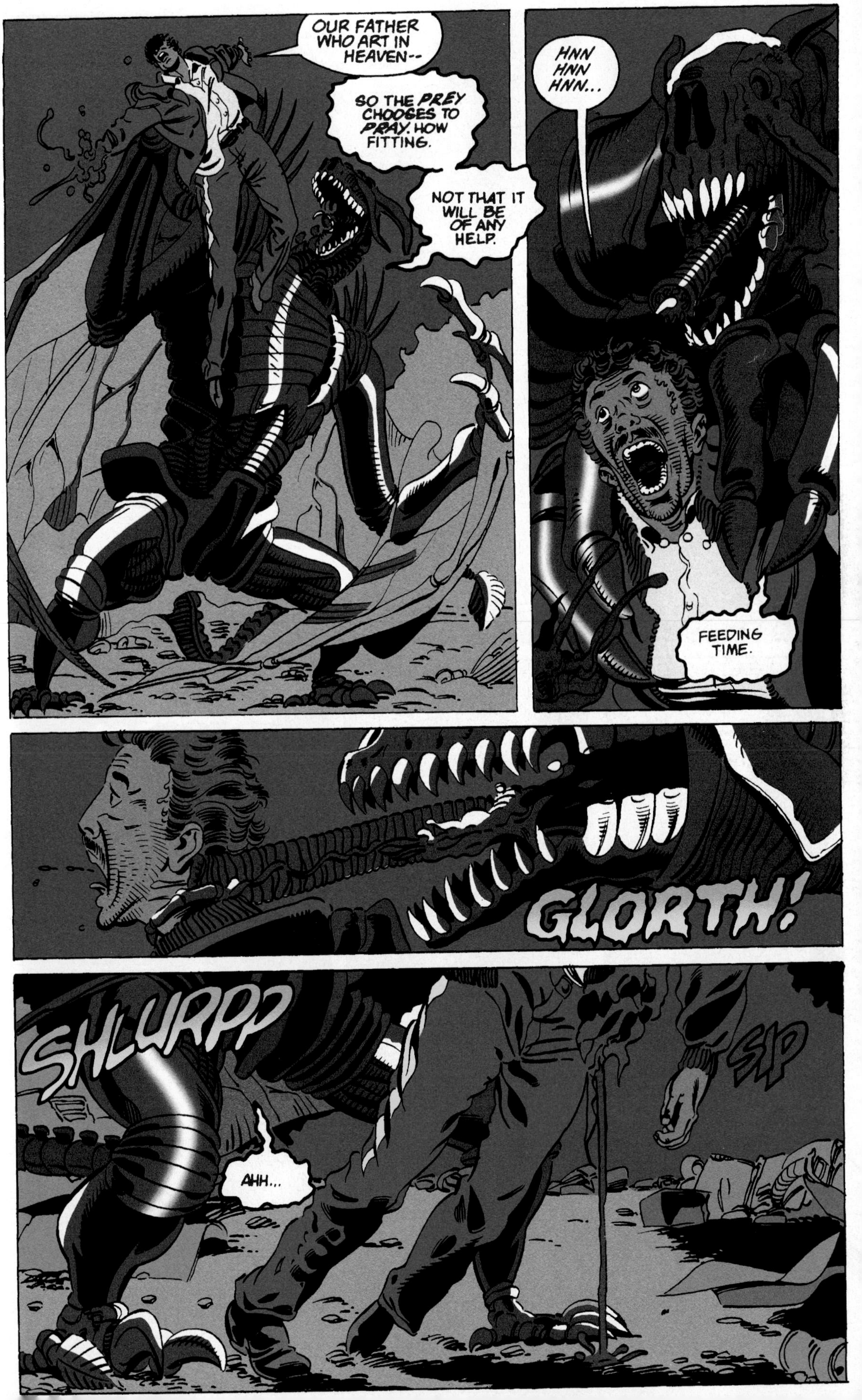
OUR FATHER WHO ART IN HEAVEN--
SO THE PREY CHOOSES TO PRAY. HOW FITTING.
NOT THAT IT WILL BE OF ANY HELP.
HNN HNN HNN...
FEEDING TIME.
GLORTH!
SHLURPP
SIP
AHH...

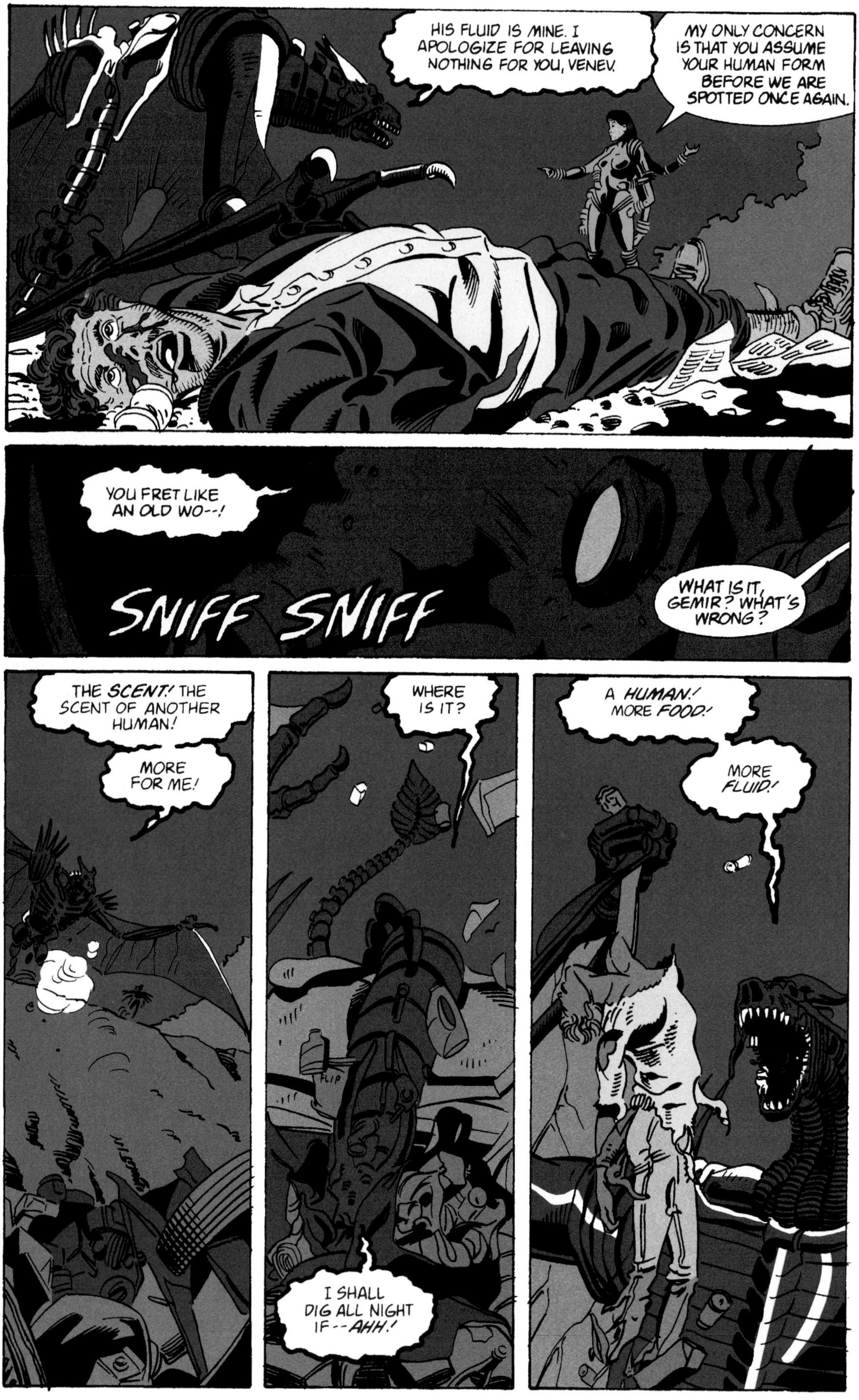
HIS FLUID IS MINE. I APOLOGIZE FOR LEAVING NOTHING FOR YOU, VENEV.
MY ONLY CONCERN IS THAT YOU ASSUME YOUR HUMAN FORM BEFORE WE ARE SPOTTED ONCE AGAIN.
YOU FRET LIKE AN OLD WO--!
SNIFF SNIFF
WHAT IS IT, GEMIR? WHAT'S WRONG?
THE SCENT! THE SCENT OF ANOTHER HUMAN!
MORE FOR ME!
WHERE IS IT?
FLIP
I SHALL DIG ALL NIGHT IF--AHH!
A HUMAN! MORE FOOD!
MORE FLUID!

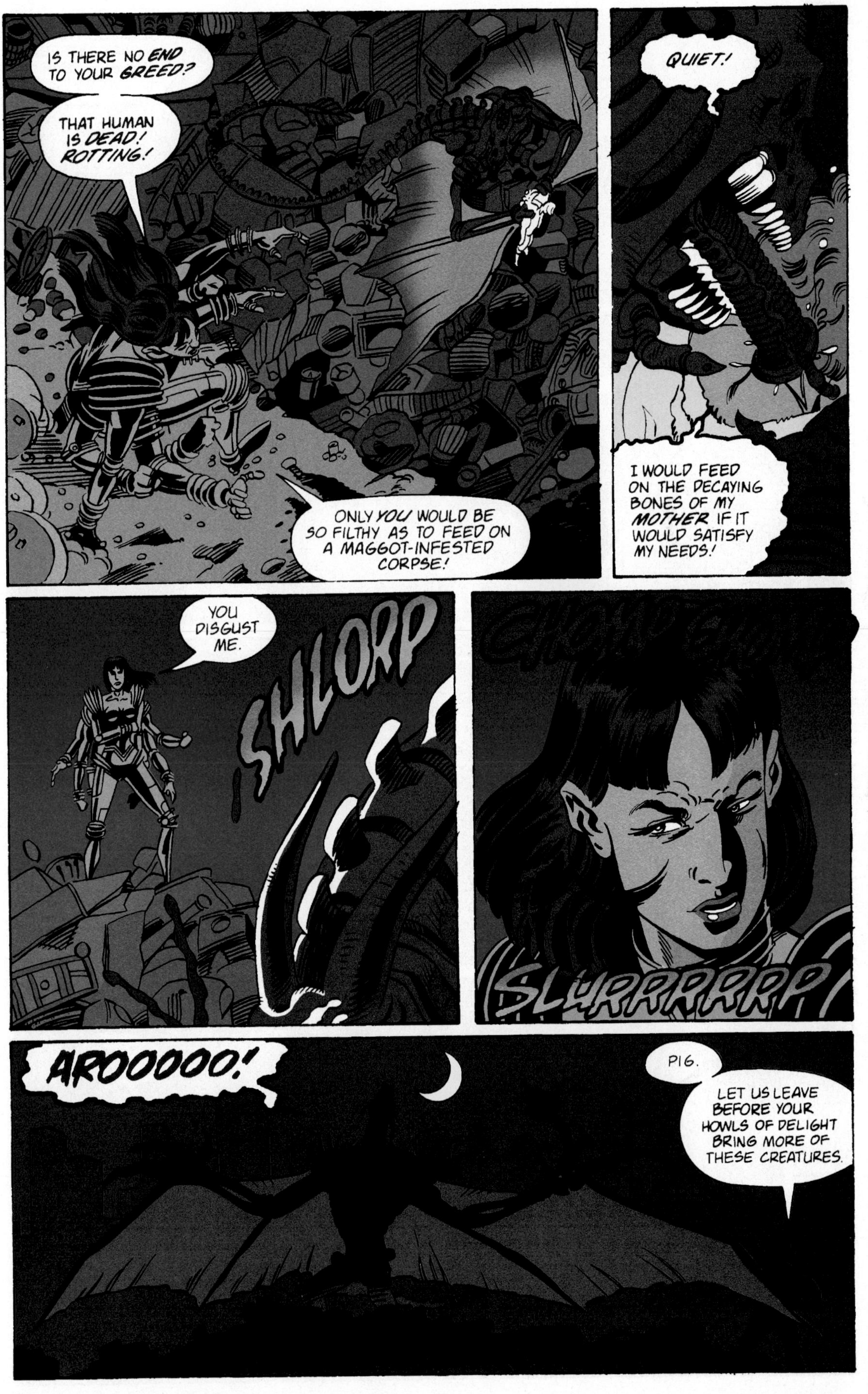
IS THERE NO END TO YOUR GREED?
THAT HUMAN IS DEAD! ROTTING!
ONLY YOU WOULD BE SO FILTHY AS TO FEED ON A MAGGOT-INFESTED CORPSE!
QUIET!
I WOULD FEED ON THE DECAYING BONES OF MY MOTHER IF IT WOULD SATISFY MY NEEDS!
YOU DISGUST ME.
SHLORP
SLURRRRRRP
AROOOOO!
PIG.
LET US LEAVE BEFORE YOUR HOWLS OF DELIGHT BRING MORE OF THESE CREATURES.

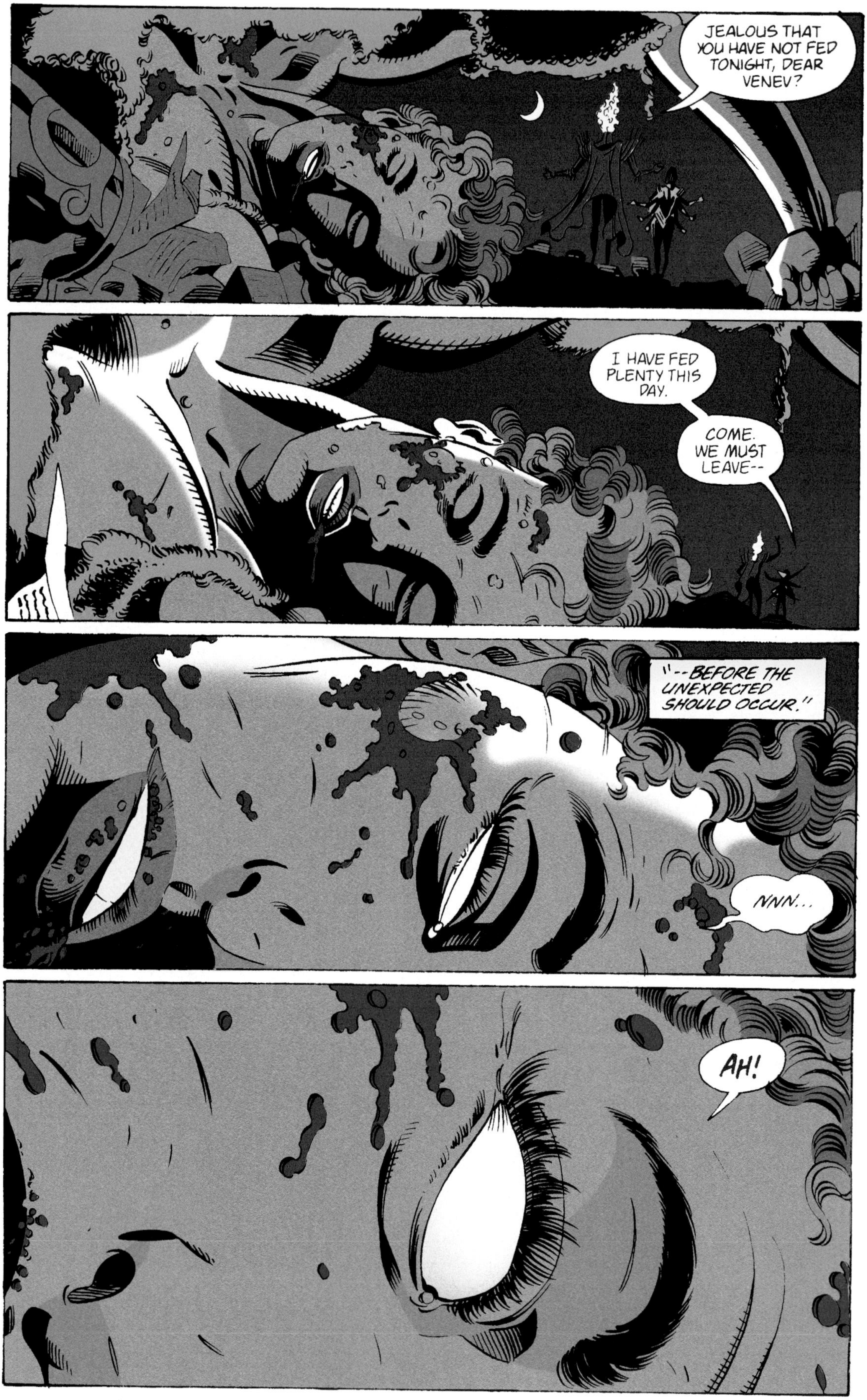
JEALOUS THAT YOU HAVE NOT FED TONIGHT, DEAR VENEV?
I HAVE FED PLENTY THIS DAY.
COME. WE MUST LEAVE--
"--BEFORE THE UNEXPECTED SHOULD OCCUR."
NNN...
AH!

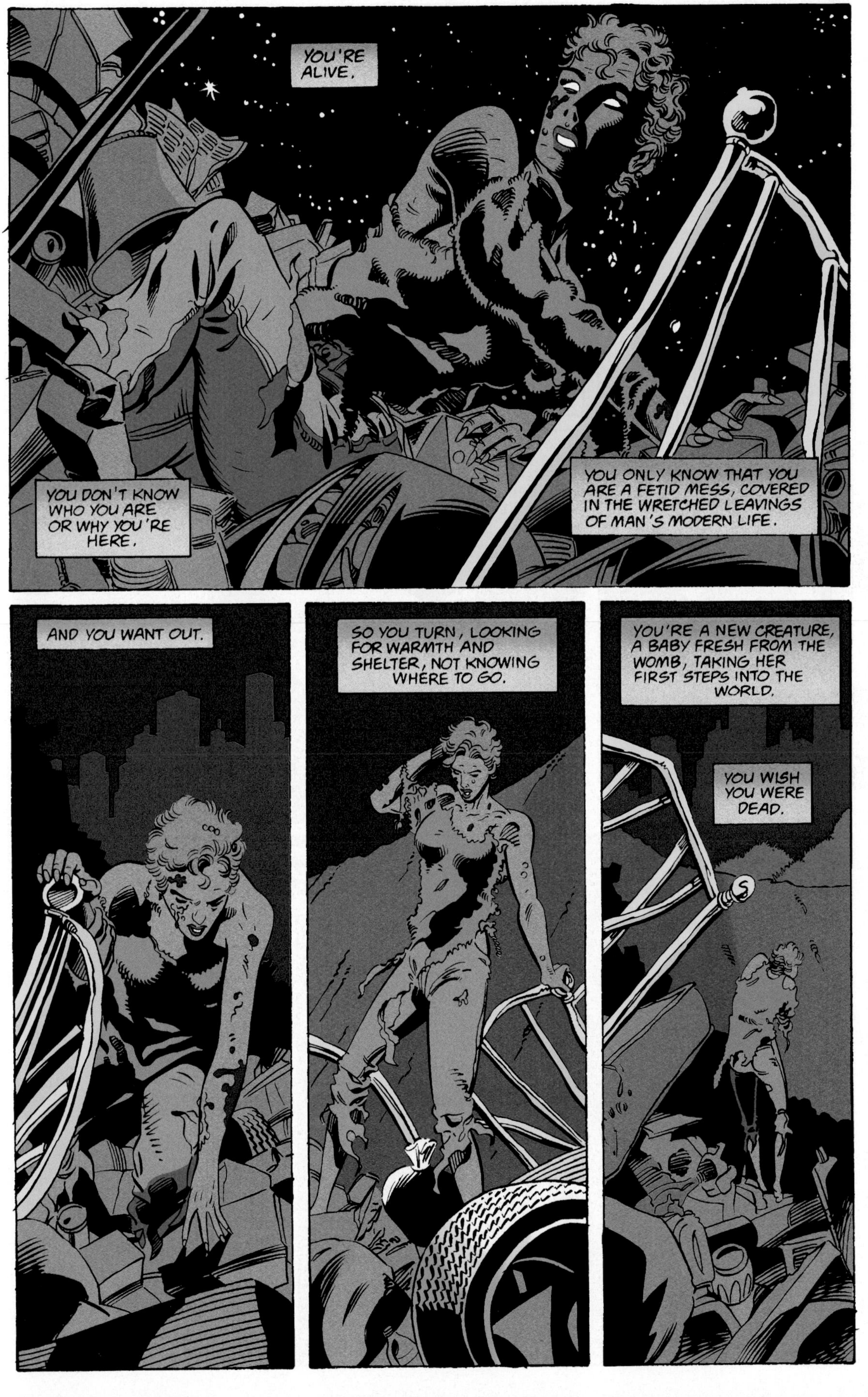
YOU'RE ALIVE.
YOU DON'T KNOW WHO YOU ARE OR WHY YOU'RE HERE.
YOU ONLY KNOW THAT YOU ARE A FETID MESS, COVERED IN THE WRETCHED LEAVINGS OF MAN'S MODERN LIFE.
AND YOU WANT OUT.
SO YOU TURN, LOOKING FOR WARMTH AND SHELTER, NOT KNOWING WHERE TO GO.
YOU'RE A NEW CREATURE, A BABY FRESH FROM THE WOMB, TAKING HER FIRST STEPS INTO THE WORLD.
YOU WISH YOU WERE DEAD.

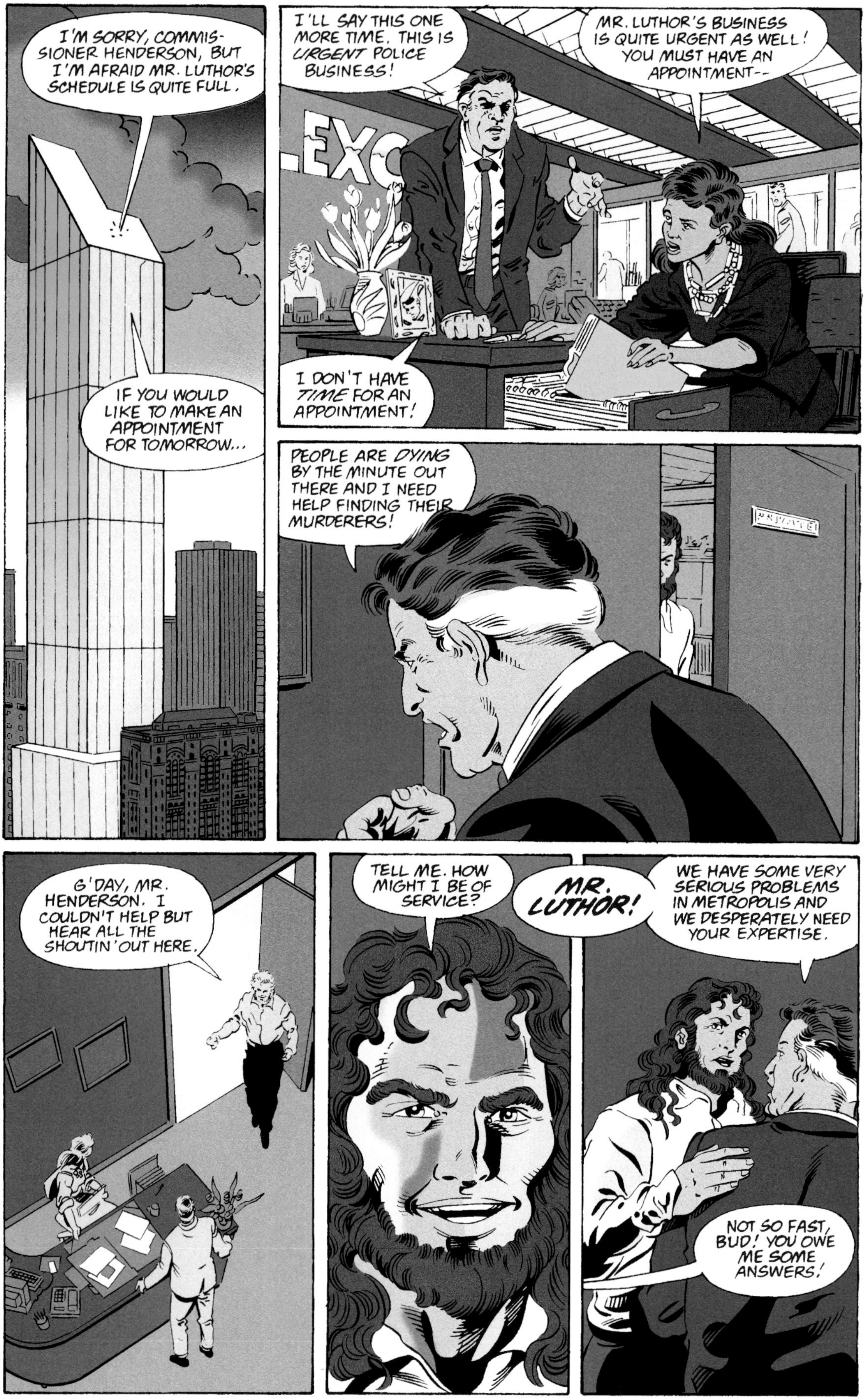
I'M SORRY, COMMISSIONER HENDERSON, BUT I'M AFRAID MR. LUTHOR'S SCHEDULE IS QUITE FULL.
IF YOU WOULD LIKE TO MAKE AN APPOINTMENT FOR TOMORROW...
I'LL SAY THIS ONE MORE TIME. THIS IS URGENT POLICE BUSINESS!
MR. LUTHOR'S BUSINESS IS QUITE URGENT AS WELL! YOU MUST HAVE AN APPOINTMENT--
I DON'T HAVE TIME FOR AN APPOINTMENT!
PEOPLE ARE DYING BY THE MINUTE OUT THERE AND I NEED HELP FINDING THEIR MURDERERS!
G'DAY, MR. HENDERSON. I COULDN'T HELP BUT HEAR ALL THE SHOUTIN' OUT HERE.
TELL ME. HOW MIGHT I BE OF SERVICE?
MR. LUTHOR!
WE HAVE SOME VERY SERIOUS PROBLEMS IN METROPOLIS AND WE DESPERATELY NEED YOUR EXPERTISE.
NOT SO FAST, BUD! YOU OWE ME SOME ANSWERS!

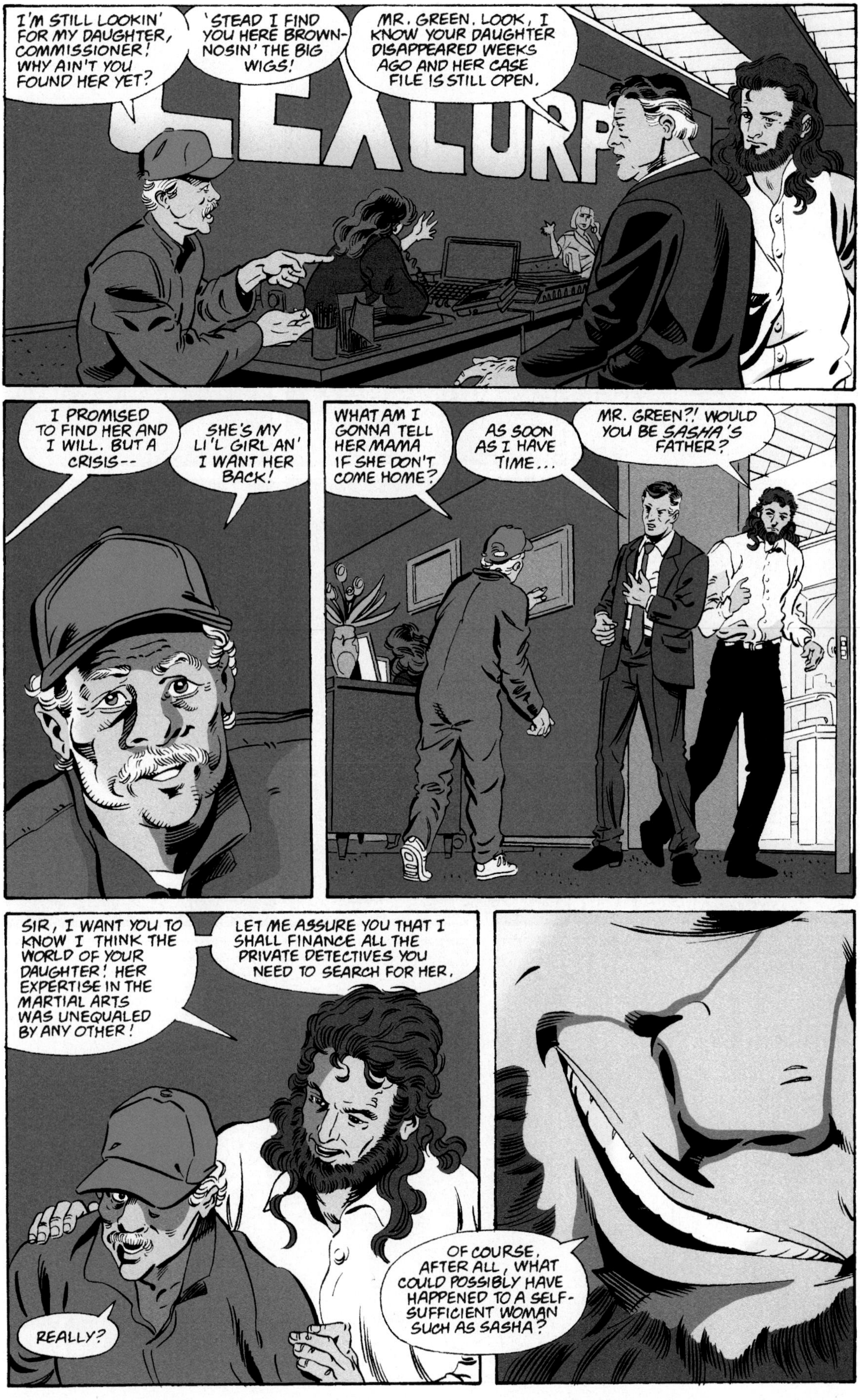
I'M STILL LOOKIN' FOR MY DAUGHTER, COMMISSIONER! WHY AIN'T YOU FOUND HER YET?
'STEAD I FIND YOU HERE BROWN-NOSIN' THE BIG WIGS!
MR. GREEN. LOOK, I KNOW YOUR DAUGHTER DISAPPEARED WEEKS AGO AND HER CASE FILE IS STILL OPEN.
I PROMISED TO FIND HER AND I WILL. BUT A CRISIS--
SHE'S MY LI'L GIRL AN' I WANT HER BACK!
WHAT AM I GONNA TELL HER MAMA IF SHE DON'T COME HOME?
AS SOON AS I HAVE TIME...
MR. GREEN?! WOULD YOU BE SASHA'S FATHER?
SIR, I WANT YOU TO KNOW I THINK THE WORLD OF YOUR DAUGHTER! HER EXPERTISE IN THE MARTIAL ARTS WAS UNEQUALED BY ANY OTHER!
LET ME ASSURE YOU THAT I SHALL FINANCE ALL THE PRIVATE DETECTIVES YOU NEED TO SEARCH FOR HER.
REALLY?
OF COURSE. AFTER ALL, WHAT COULD POSSIBLY HAVE HAPPENED TO A SELF-SUFFICIENT WOMAN SUCH AS SASHA?

MEMORIES.

AMAZING HOW A PERIOD OF HOURS CAN BE PACKED INTO FLASHES AND IMAGES THAT CAN BE REPLAYED IN THE BLINK OF AN EYE.

IMAGES OF THE YOUNG WOMAN, SASHA GREEN, DOWNING ME WITH A KICK.

SUPERGIRL AND LOIS LANE LAUGHING. *LAUGHING!*

SHE SHOWED *ME* UP--*LEX LUTHOR!* --NO...WOMAN... CAN DO THAT!

LATER...

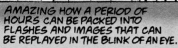

ATTACK.

REVENGE.

AND *MURDER.*

IT'S ALL A GAME. A GAME TO BE WON AND A CRIME TO BE GOTTEN AWAY WITH.

JUST LIKE ALWAYS.

Y'MEAN IT? YOU'LL REALLY HELP ME LOOK FOR MY GIRL?

OF COURSE I WILL! YOU HAVE MY WORD AND SOLEMN PLEDGE! WHER- EVER YOUNG SASHA HAS GOTTEN OFF TOO--

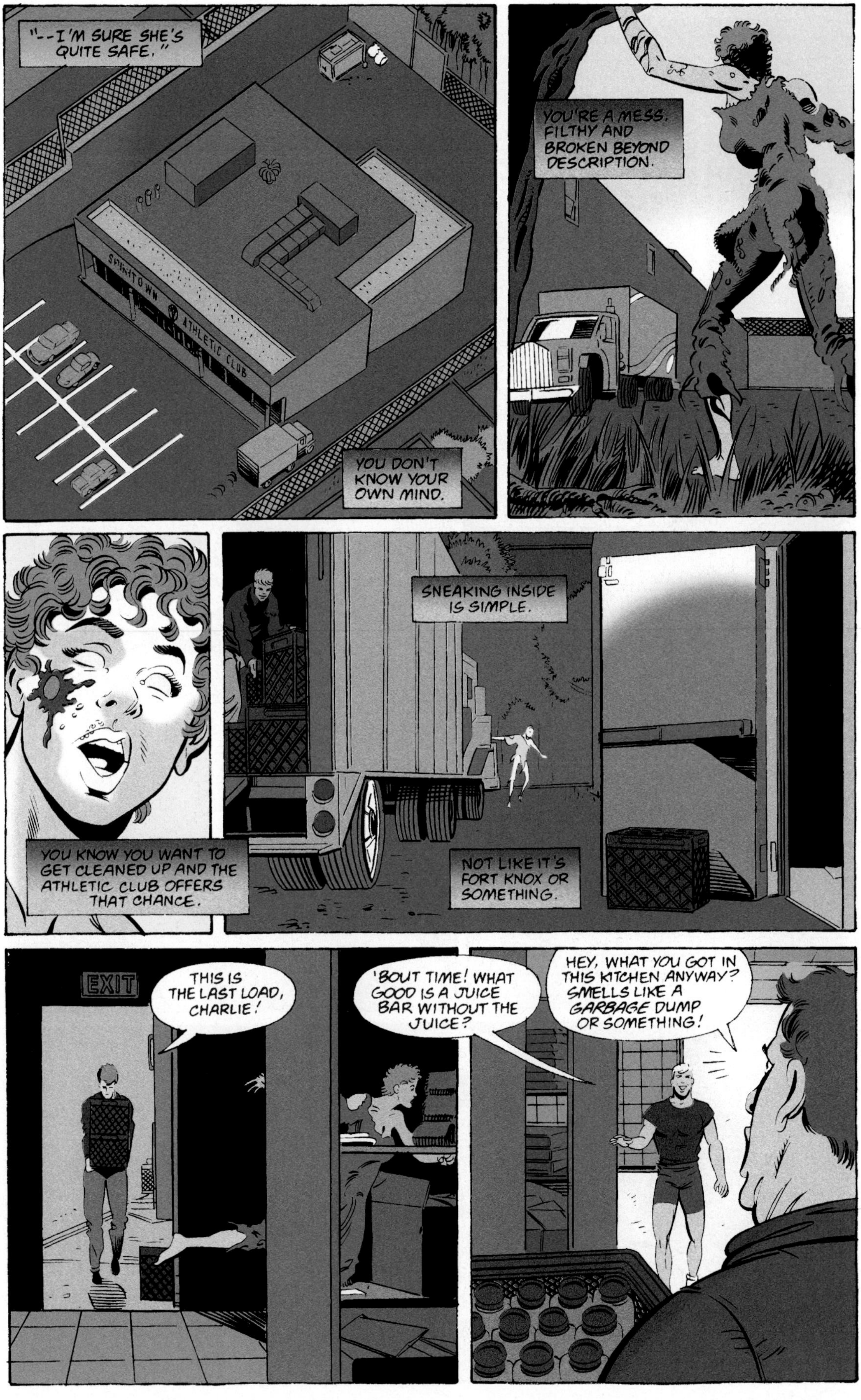
"--I'M SURE SHE'S QUITE SAFE."
SPIRITOWN ATHLETIC CLUB
YOU DON'T KNOW YOUR OWN MIND.
YOU'RE A MESS. FILTHY AND BROKEN BEYOND DESCRIPTION.
YOU KNOW YOU WANT TO GET CLEANED UP AND THE ATHLETIC CLUB OFFERS THAT CHANCE.
SNEAKING INSIDE IS SIMPLE.
NOT LIKE IT'S FORT KNOX OR SOMETHING.
EXIT
THIS IS THE LAST LOAD, CHARLIE!
'BOUT TIME! WHAT GOOD IS A JUICE BAR WITHOUT THE JUICE?
HEY, WHAT YOU GOT IN THIS KITCHEN ANYWAY? SMELLS LIKE A GARBAGE DUMP OR SOMETHING!

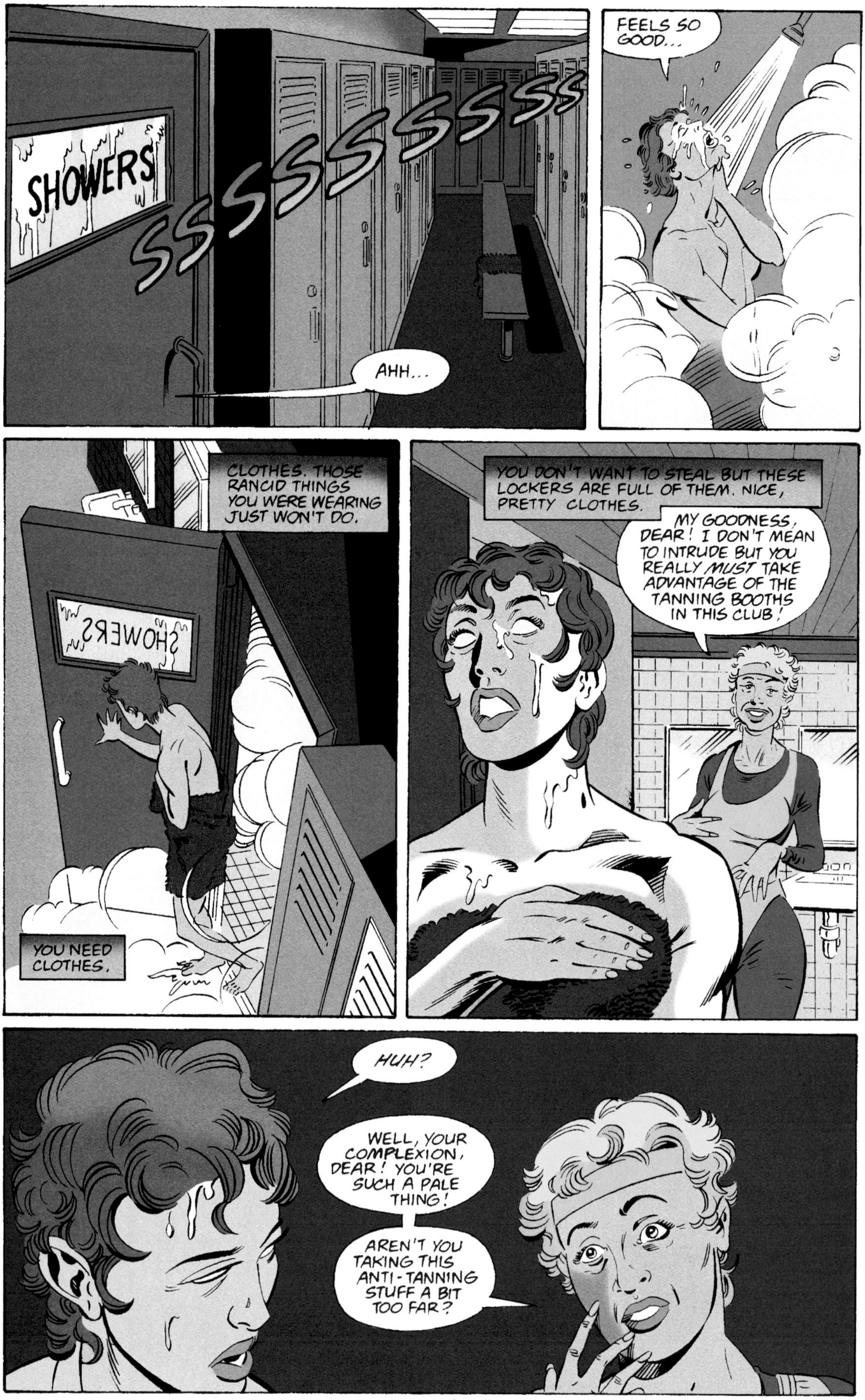
SHOWERS
SSSSSSSSSSSS
AHH...
FEELS SO GOOD...
CLOTHES. THOSE RANCID THINGS YOU WERE WEARING JUST WON'T DO.
SHOWERS
YOU NEED CLOTHES.
YOU DON'T WANT TO STEAL BUT THESE LOCKERS ARE FULL OF THEM. NICE, PRETTY CLOTHES.
MY GOODNESS, DEAR! I DON'T MEAN TO INTRUDE BUT YOU REALLY MUST TAKE ADVANTAGE OF THE TANNING BOOTHS IN THIS CLUB!
HUH?
WELL, YOUR COMPLEXION, DEAR! YOU'RE SUCH A PALE THING!
AREN'T YOU TAKING THIS ANTI-TANNING STUFF A BIT TOO FAR?

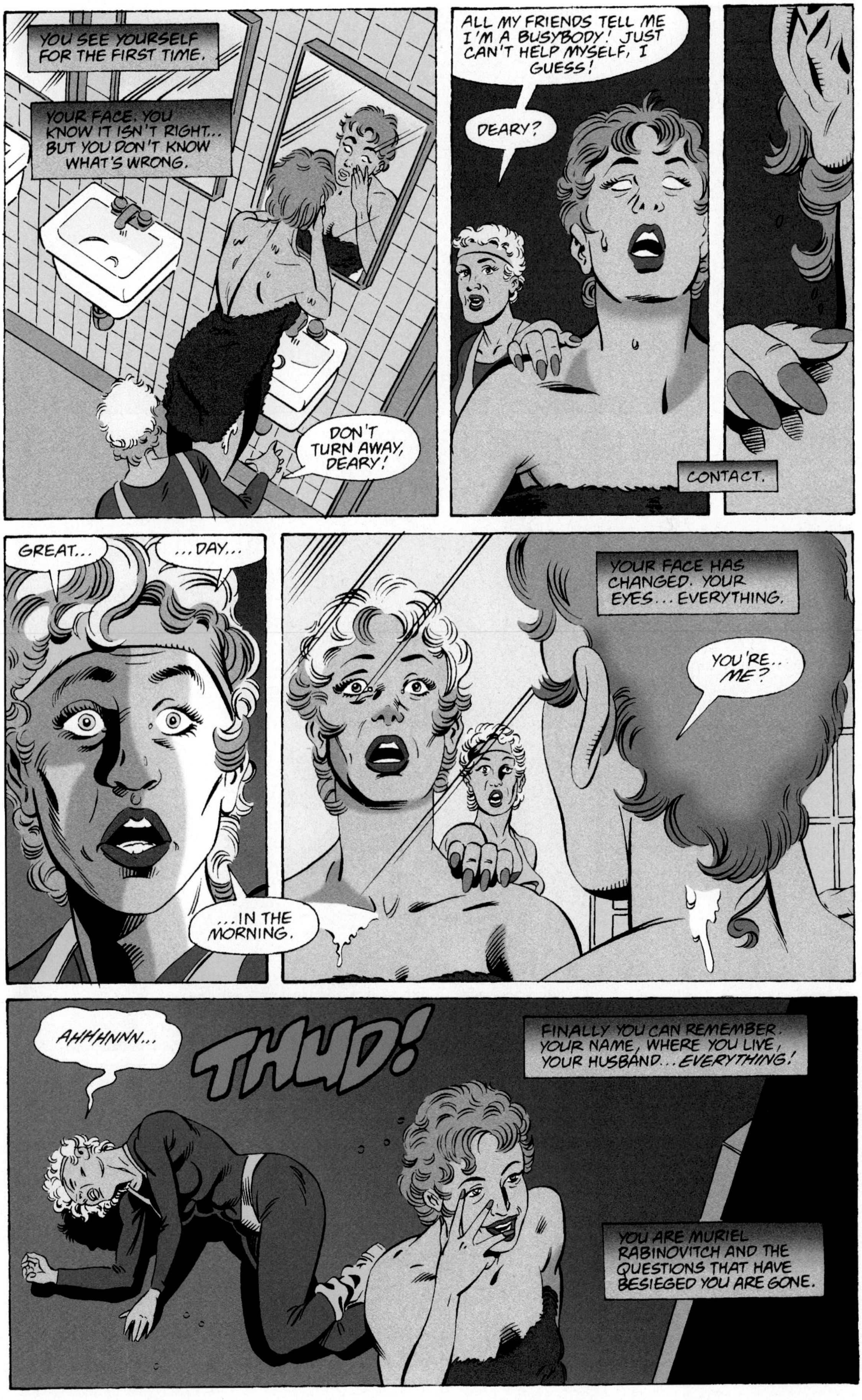
YOU SEE YOURSELF FOR THE FIRST TIME.
YOUR FACE. YOU KNOW IT ISN'T RIGHT... BUT YOU DON'T KNOW WHAT'S WRONG.
DON'T TURN AWAY, DEARY!
ALL MY FRIENDS TELL ME I'M A BUSYBODY! JUST CAN'T HELP MYSELF, I GUESS!
DEARY?
CONTACT.
GREAT...
...DAY...
...IN THE MORNING.
YOUR FACE HAS CHANGED. YOUR EYES... EVERYTHING.
YOU'RE... ME?
AHHHNNN...
THUD!
FINALLY YOU CAN REMEMBER. YOUR NAME, WHERE YOU LIVE, YOUR HUSBAND... EVERYTHING!
YOU ARE MURIEL RABINOVITCH AND THE QUESTIONS THAT HAVE BESIEGED YOU ARE GONE.

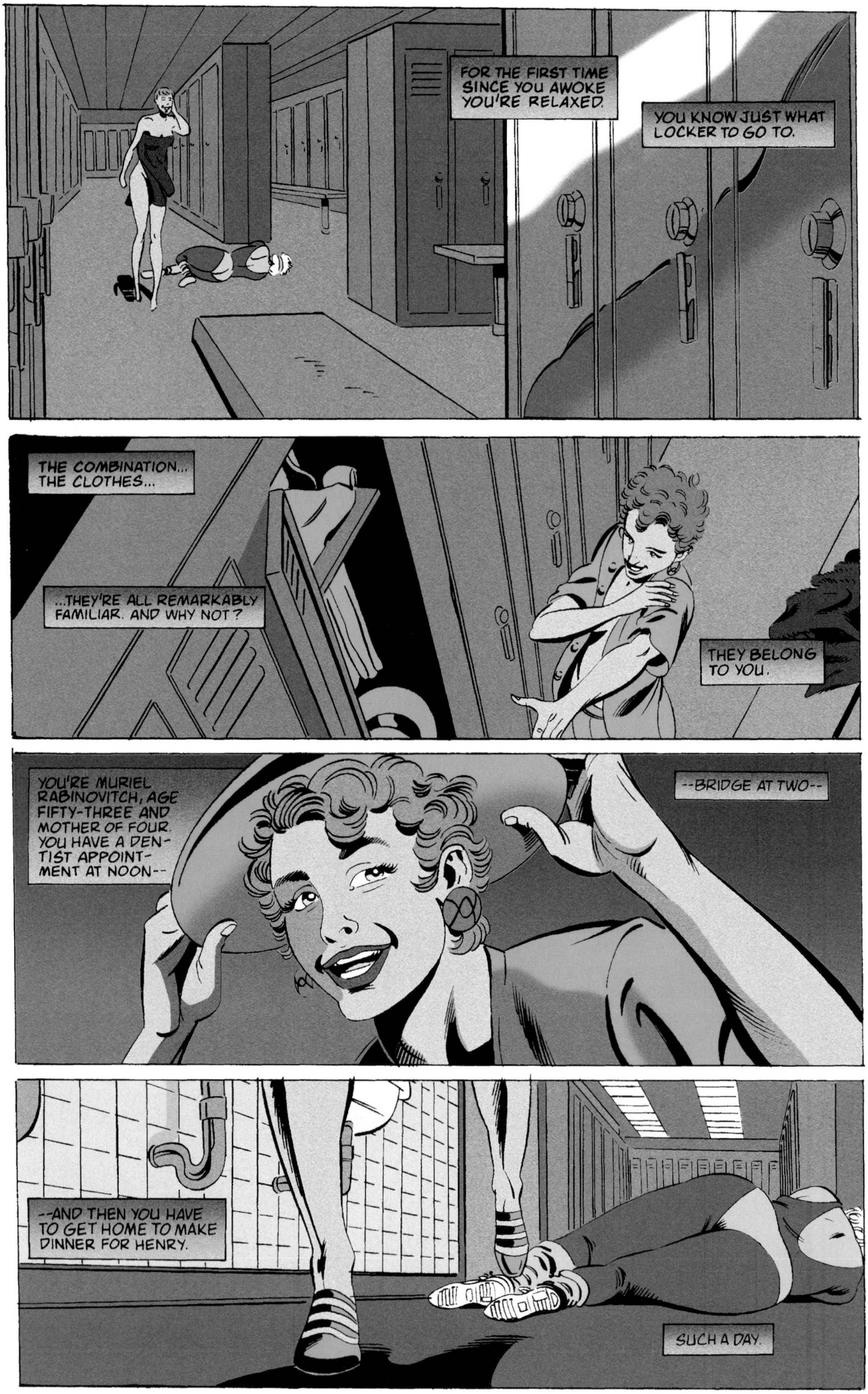
FOR THE FIRST TIME SINCE YOU AWOKE YOU'RE RELAXED.
YOU KNOW JUST WHAT LOCKER TO GO TO.
THE COMBINATION... THE CLOTHES...
...THEY'RE ALL REMARKABLY FAMILIAR. AND WHY NOT?
THEY BELONG TO YOU.
YOU'RE MURIEL RABINOVITCH, AGE FIFTY-THREE AND MOTHER OF FOUR. YOU HAVE A DENTIST APPOINTMENT AT NOON--
--BRIDGE AT TWO--
--AND THEN YOU HAVE TO GET HOME TO MAKE DINNER FOR HENRY.
SUCH A DAY.

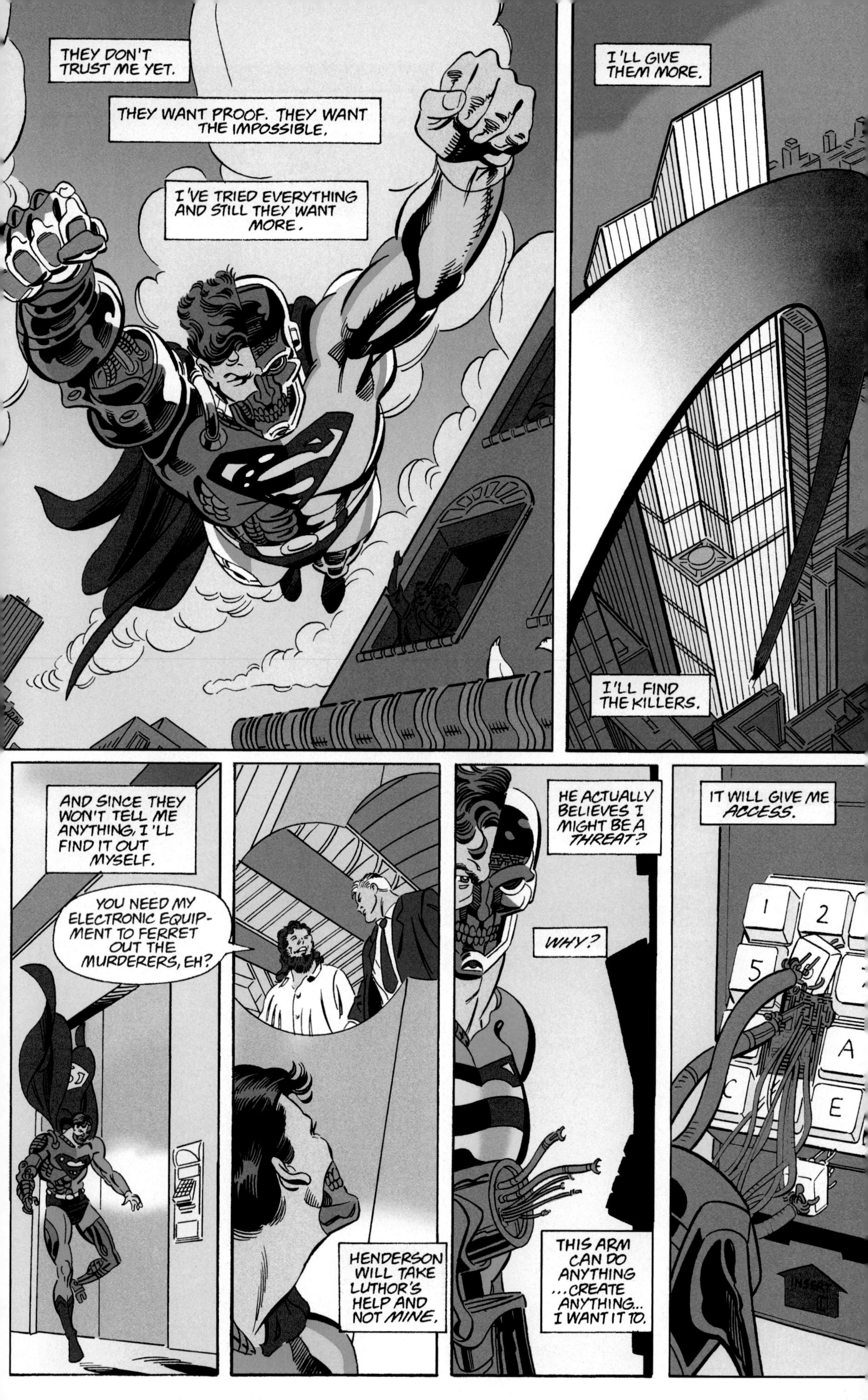
THEY DON'T TRUST ME YET.
THEY WANT PROOF. THEY WANT THE IMPOSSIBLE.
I'VE TRIED EVERYTHING AND STILL THEY WANT MORE.
I'LL GIVE THEM MORE.
I'LL FIND THE KILLERS.
AND SINCE THEY WON'T TELL ME ANYTHING, I'LL FIND IT OUT MYSELF.
YOU NEED MY ELECTRONIC EQUIPMENT TO FERRET OUT THE MURDERERS, EH?
HENDERSON WILL TAKE LUTHOR'S HELP AND NOT MINE.
HE ACTUALLY BELIEVES I MIGHT BE A THREAT?
WHY?
THIS ARM CAN DO ANYTHING ...CREATE ANYTHING... I WANT IT TO.
IT WILL GIVE ME ACCESS.

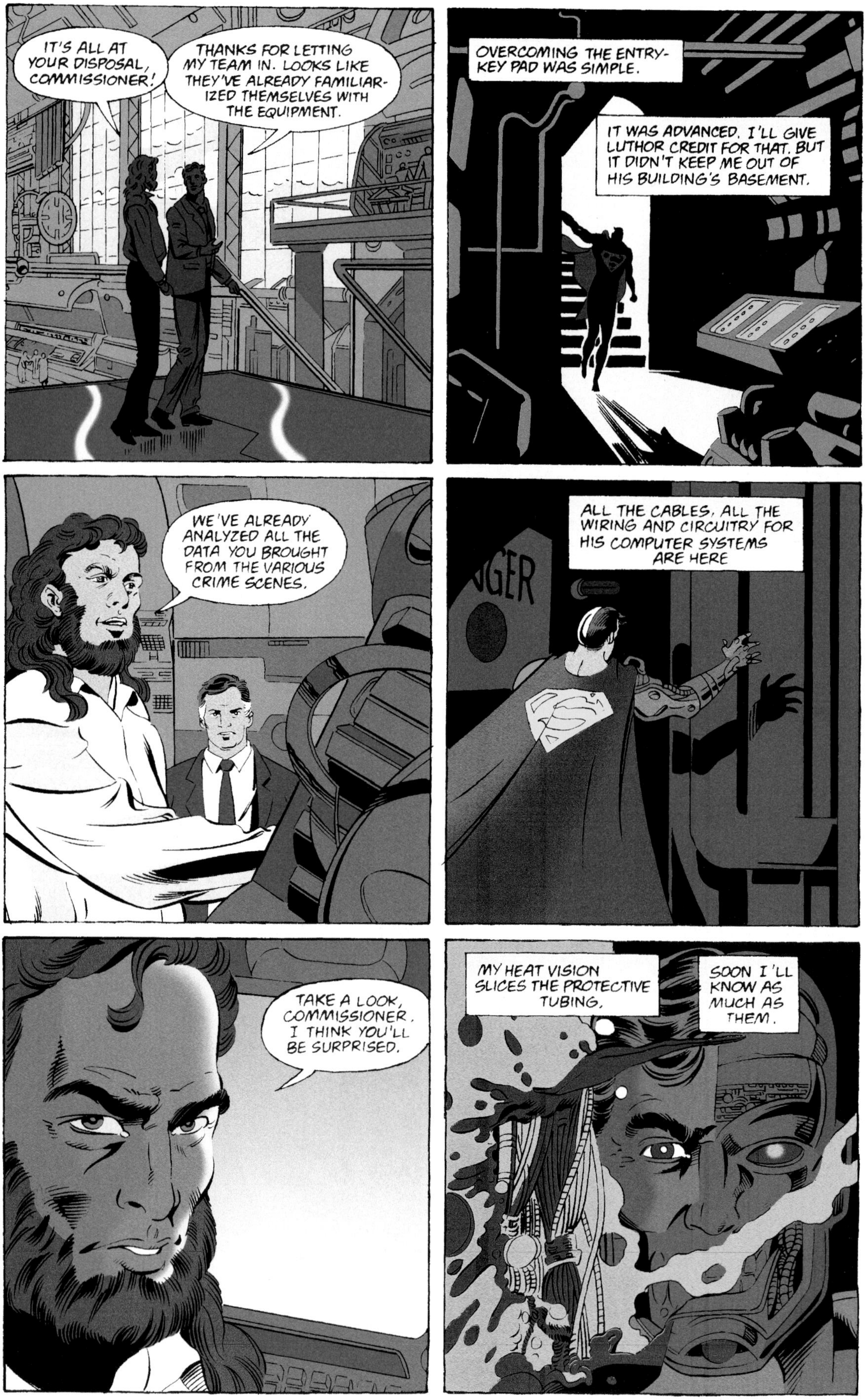
IT'S ALL AT YOUR DISPOSAL, COMMISSIONER!
THANKS FOR LETTING MY TEAM IN. LOOKS LIKE THEY'VE ALREADY FAMILIARIZED THEMSELVES WITH THE EQUIPMENT.
OVERCOMING THE ENTRY-KEY PAD WAS SIMPLE.
IT WAS ADVANCED. I'LL GIVE LUTHOR CREDIT FOR THAT. BUT IT DIDN'T KEEP ME OUT OF HIS BUILDING'S BASEMENT.
WE'VE ALREADY ANALYZED ALL THE DATA YOU BROUGHT FROM THE VARIOUS CRIME SCENES.
ALL THE CABLES, ALL THE WIRING AND CIRCUITRY FOR HIS COMPUTER SYSTEMS ARE HERE
TAKE A LOOK, COMMISSIONER. I THINK YOU'LL BE SURPRISED.
MY HEAT VISION SLICES THE PROTECTIVE TUBING.
SOON I'LL KNOW AS MUCH AS THEM.

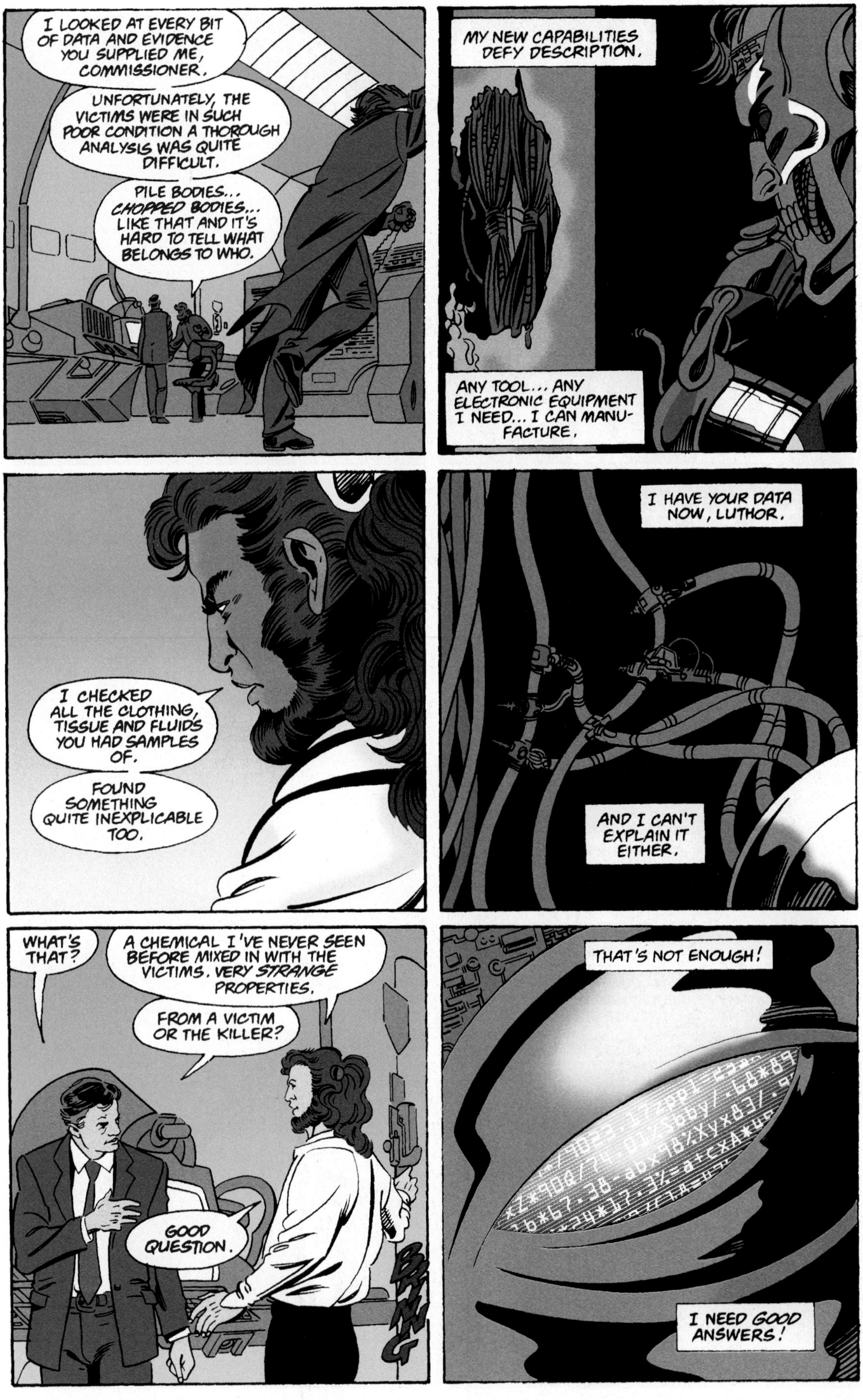
I LOOKED AT EVERY BIT OF DATA AND EVIDENCE YOU SUPPLIED ME, COMMISSIONER.
UNFORTUNATELY, THE VICTIMS WERE IN SUCH POOR CONDITION A THOROUGH ANALYSIS WAS QUITE DIFFICULT.
PILE BODIES... *CHOPPED* BODIES... LIKE THAT AND IT'S HARD TO TELL WHAT BELONGS TO WHO.
MY NEW CAPABILITIES DEFY DESCRIPTION.
ANY TOOL... ANY ELECTRONIC EQUIPMENT I NEED... I CAN MANUFACTURE.
I CHECKED ALL THE CLOTHING, TISSUE AND FLUIDS YOU HAD SAMPLES OF.
FOUND SOMETHING QUITE INEXPLICABLE TOO.
I HAVE YOUR DATA NOW, LUTHOR.
AND I CAN'T EXPLAIN IT EITHER.
WHAT'S THAT?
A CHEMICAL I'VE NEVER SEEN BEFORE MIXED IN WITH THE VICTIMS. VERY *STRANGE* PROPERTIES.
FROM A VICTIM OR THE KILLER?
GOOD QUESTION.
THAT'S NOT ENOUGH!
I NEED *GOOD* ANSWERS!

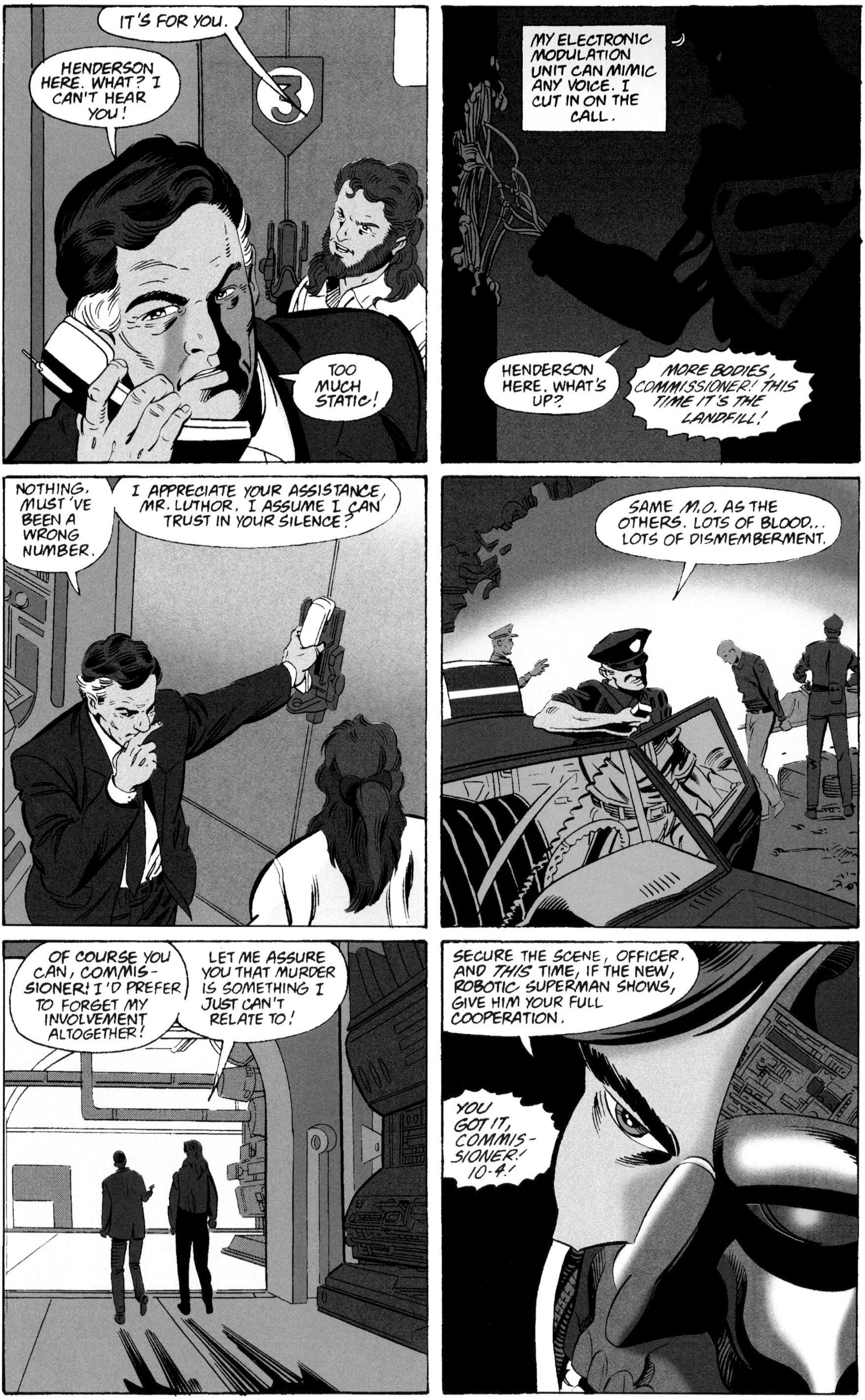
IT'S FOR YOU.
HENDERSON HERE. WHAT? I CAN'T HEAR YOU!
TOO MUCH STATIC!
MY ELECTRONIC MODULATION UNIT CAN MIMIC ANY VOICE. I CUT IN ON THE CALL.
HENDERSON HERE. WHAT'S UP?
MORE BODIES, COMMISSIONER! THIS TIME IT'S THE LANDFILL!
NOTHING. MUST'VE BEEN A WRONG NUMBER.
I APPRECIATE YOUR ASSISTANCE, MR. LUTHOR. I ASSUME I CAN TRUST IN YOUR SILENCE?
SAME M.O. AS THE OTHERS. LOTS OF BLOOD... LOTS OF DISMEMBERMENT.
OF COURSE YOU CAN, COMMISSIONER! I'D PREFER TO FORGET MY INVOLVEMENT ALTOGETHER!
LET ME ASSURE YOU THAT MURDER IS SOMETHING I JUST CAN'T RELATE TO!
SECURE THE SCENE, OFFICER. AND THIS TIME, IF THE NEW, ROBOTIC SUPERMAN SHOWS, GIVE HIM YOUR FULL COOPERATION.
YOU GOT IT, COMMISSIONER! 10-4!

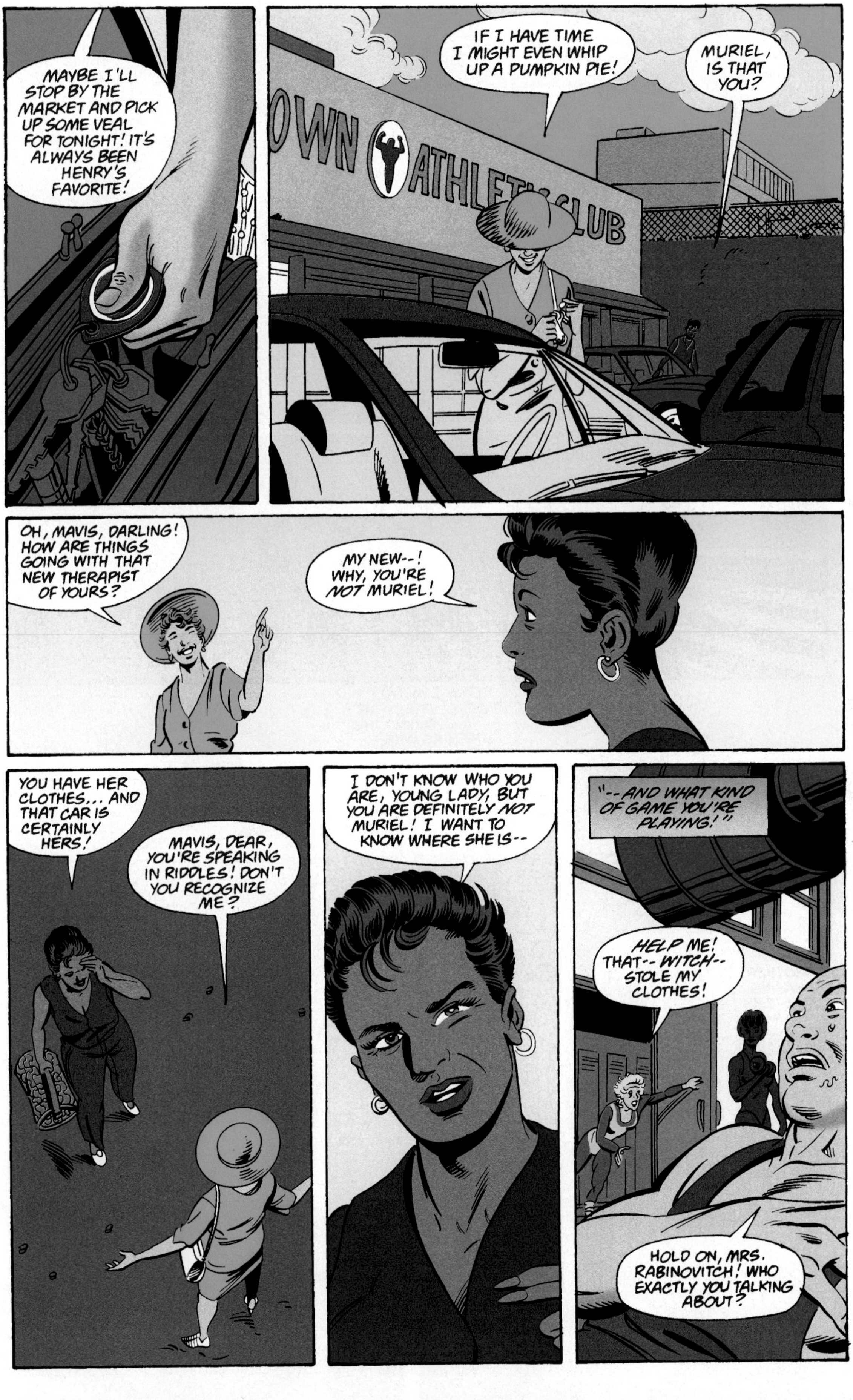
MAYBE I'LL STOP BY THE MARKET AND PICK UP SOME VEAL FOR TONIGHT! IT'S ALWAYS BEEN HENRY'S FAVORITE!
IF I HAVE TIME I MIGHT EVEN WHIP UP A PUMPKIN PIE!
MURIEL, IS THAT YOU?
OWN ATHLETIC CLUB
OH, MAVIS, DARLING! HOW ARE THINGS GOING WITH THAT NEW THERAPIST OF YOURS?
MY NEW--! WHY, YOU'RE NOT MURIEL!
YOU HAVE HER CLOTHES... AND THAT CAR IS CERTAINLY HERS!
MAVIS, DEAR, YOU'RE SPEAKING IN RIDDLES! DON'T YOU RECOGNIZE ME?
I DON'T KNOW WHO YOU ARE, YOUNG LADY, BUT YOU ARE DEFINITELY NOT MURIEL! I WANT TO KNOW WHERE SHE IS--
"--AND WHAT KIND OF GAME YOU'RE PLAYING!"
HELP ME! THAT--WITCH--STOLE MY CLOTHES!
HOLD ON, MRS. RABINOVITCH! WHO EXACTLY YOU TALKING ABOUT?

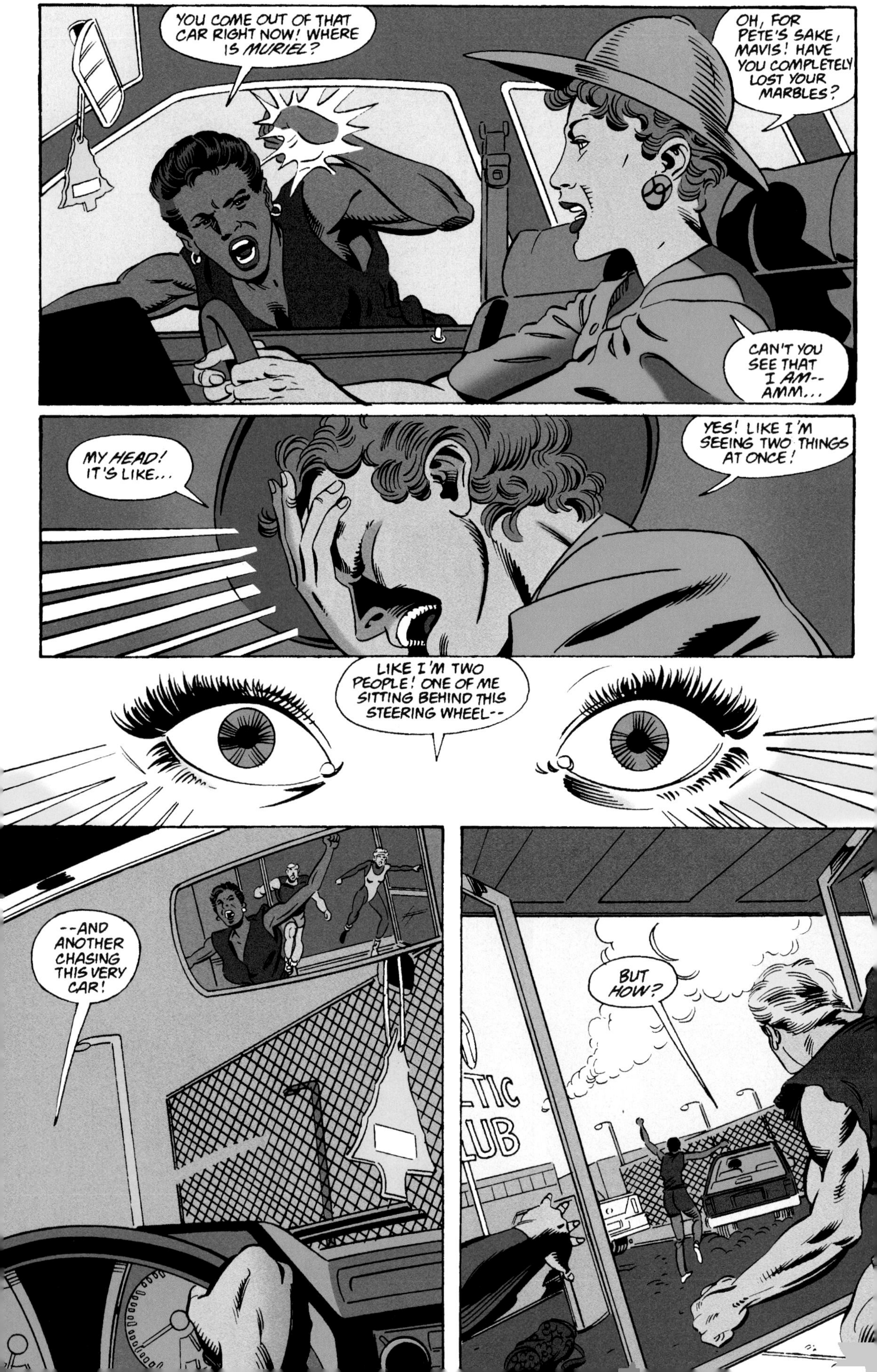
YOU COME OUT OF THAT CAR RIGHT NOW! WHERE IS MURIEL?
OH, FOR PETE'S SAKE, MAVIS! HAVE YOU COMPLETELY LOST YOUR MARBLES?
CAN'T YOU SEE THAT I AM-- AMM...
MY HEAD! IT'S LIKE...
YES! LIKE I'M SEEING TWO THINGS AT ONCE!
LIKE I'M TWO PEOPLE! ONE OF ME SITTING BEHIND THIS STEERING WHEEL--
--AND ANOTHER CHASING THIS VERY CAR!
BUT HOW?

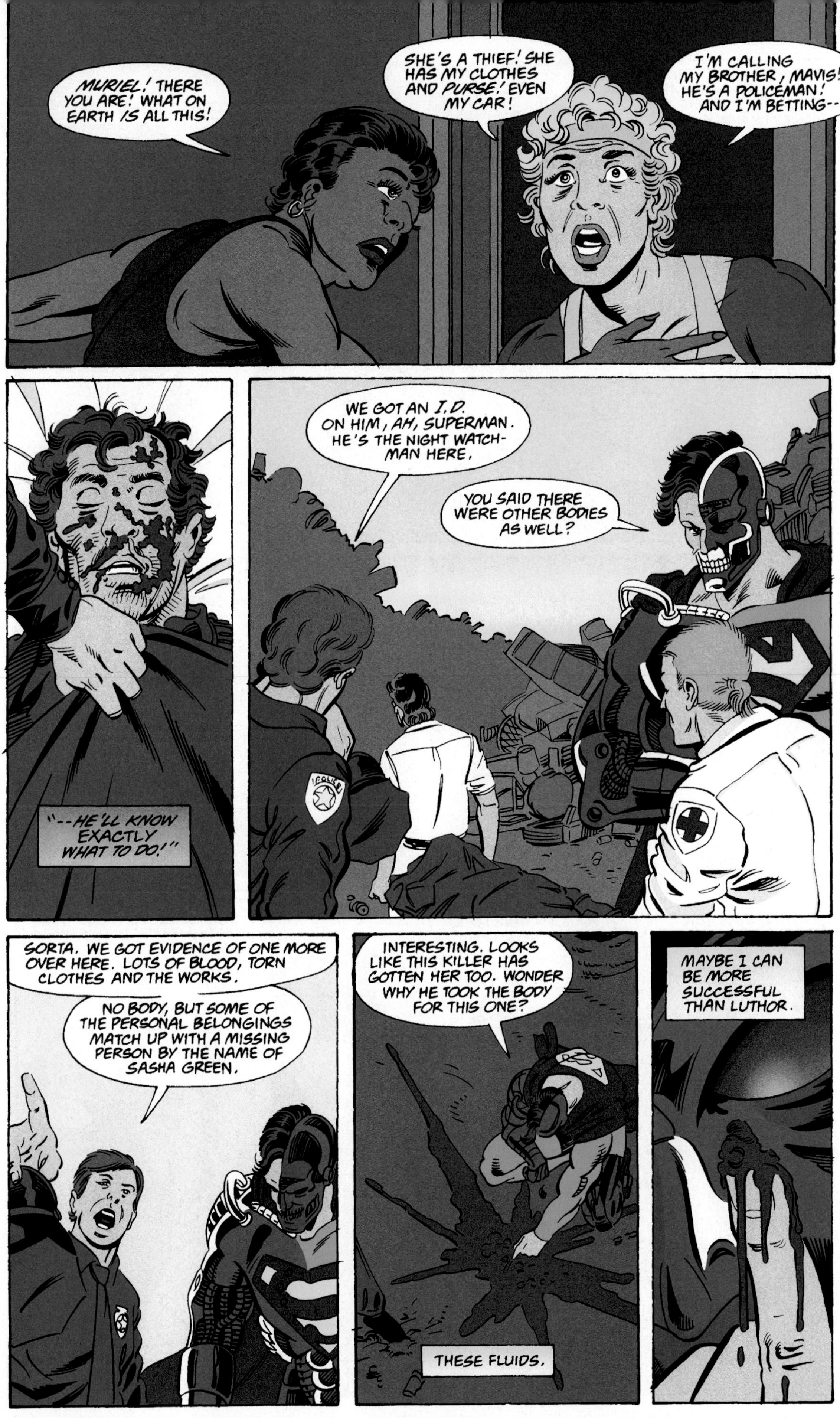
MURIEL! THERE YOU ARE! WHAT ON EARTH IS ALL THIS!
SHE'S A THIEF! SHE HAS MY CLOTHES AND PURSE! EVEN MY CAR!
I'M CALLING MY BROTHER, MAVIS! HE'S A POLICEMAN! AND I'M BETTING--
"--HE'LL KNOW EXACTLY WHAT TO DO!"
WE GOT AN I.D. ON HIM, AH, SUPERMAN. HE'S THE NIGHT WATCH-MAN HERE.
YOU SAID THERE WERE OTHER BODIES AS WELL?
POLICE
SORTA. WE GOT EVIDENCE OF ONE MORE OVER HERE. LOTS OF BLOOD, TORN CLOTHES AND THE WORKS.
NO BODY, BUT SOME OF THE PERSONAL BELONGINGS MATCH UP WITH A MISSING PERSON BY THE NAME OF SASHA GREEN.
INTERESTING. LOOKS LIKE THIS KILLER HAS GOTTEN HER TOO. WONDER WHY HE TOOK THE BODY FOR THIS ONE?
THESE FLUIDS.
MAYBE I CAN BE MORE SUCCESSFUL THAN LUTHOR.

THE BODY MIGHT STILL BE HERE. LOTS OF TRASH GOT MOVED AROUND BEFORE THEY FOUND THE WATCHMAN'S BODY.

THAT'S ONE WAY OF PUTTING IT.

UM... WHAT ARE YOU DOING?

ANALYZING THESE BODILY FLUIDS.

YOU CAN GROW WIRES AND STUFF?

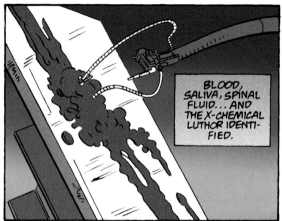

BLOOD, SALIVA, SPINAL FLUID... AND THE X-CHEMICAL LUTHOR IDENTIFIED.

RUN A COMPLETE BREAKDOWN OF THE CHEMICAL'S COMPOSITION AND...

INTERESTING.

WE HAVE A NEW LEAD, OFFICER. SOMETHING I HADN'T ANTICIPATED.

ARE YOU SAYING YOU CAN TAKE US TO JACK THE RIPPER?

NO, BUT I CAN TELL YOU THIS. I'VE IDENTIFIED ONE OF THE FLUIDS IN THIS MESS AND FOUND QUITE A SURPRISE.

WE'RE DEALING WITH AN EXTRA-TERRESTRIAL HERE.

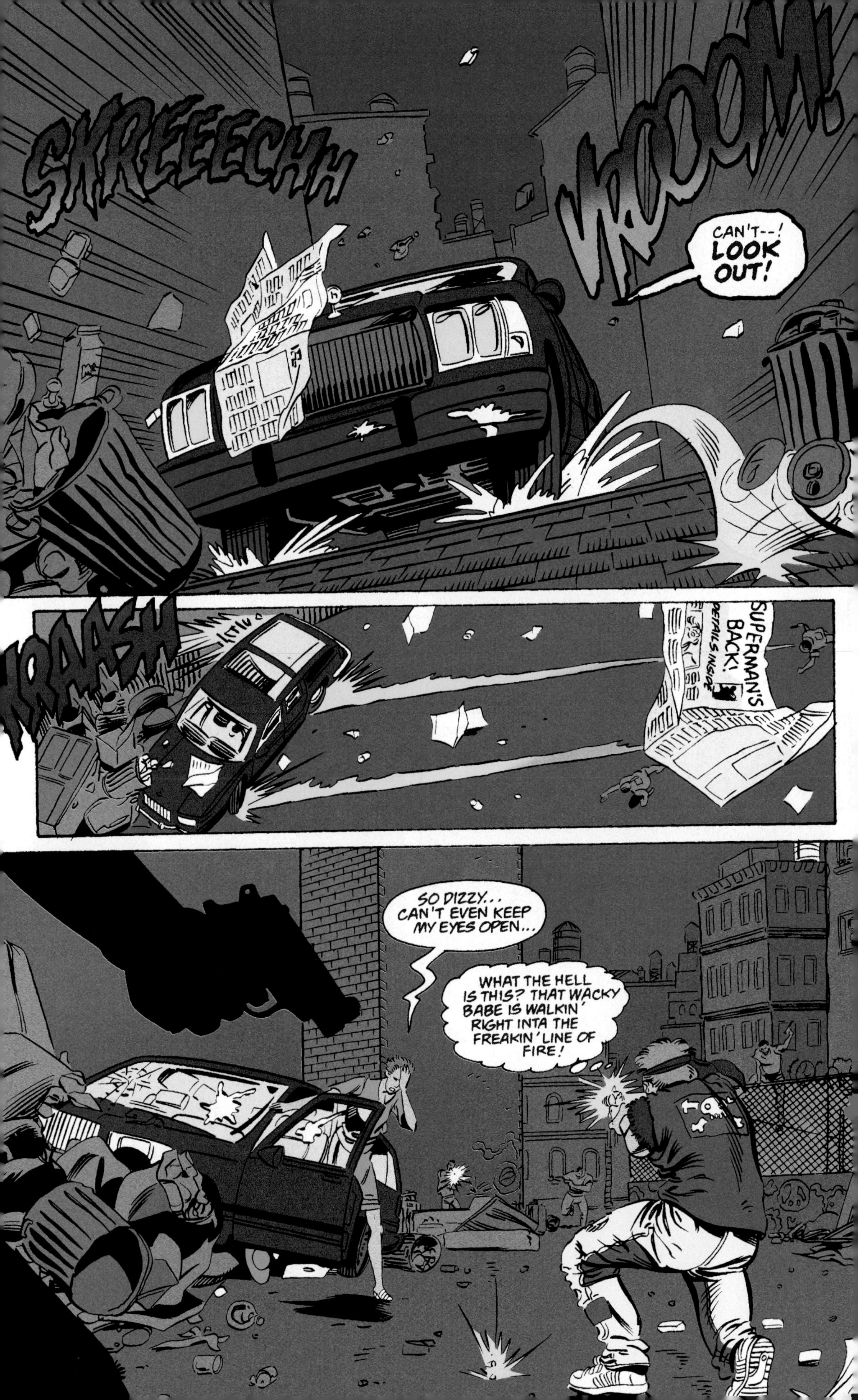
SKREEECHH
VROOOOM!
CAN'T--! LOOK OUT!
KRAASH
SUPERMAN'S BACK! DETAILS INSIDE
SO DIZZY... CAN'T EVEN KEEP MY EYES OPEN...
WHAT THE HELL IS THIS? THAT WACKY BABE IS WALKIN' RIGHT INTA THE FREAKIN' LINE OF FIRE!

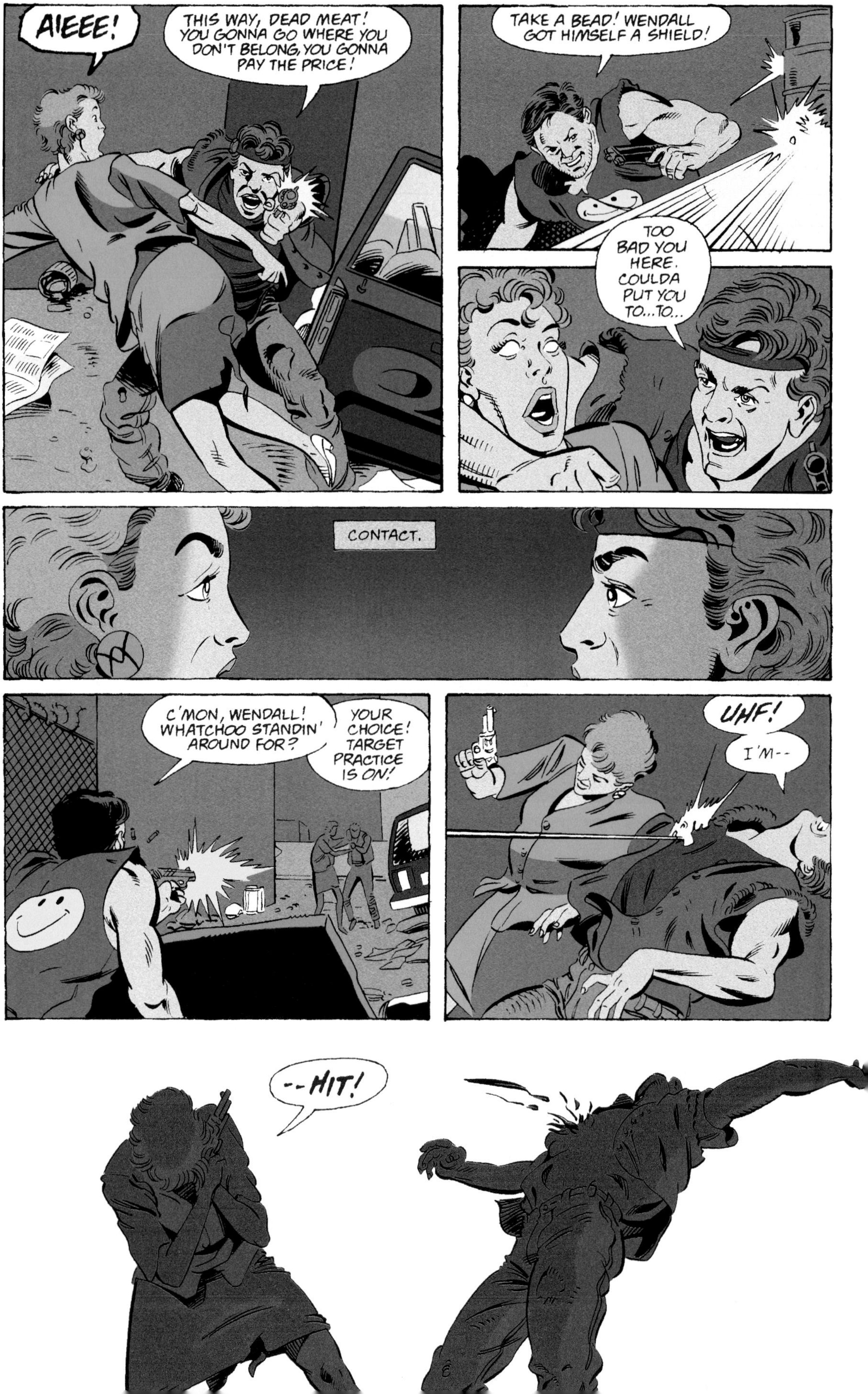
AIEEE!
THIS WAY, DEAD MEAT! YOU GONNA GO WHERE YOU DON'T BELONG, YOU GONNA PAY THE PRICE!
TAKE A BEAD! WENDALL GOT HIMSELF A SHIELD!
TOO BAD YOU HERE. COULDA PUT YOU TO...TO...
CONTACT.
C'MON, WENDALL! WHATCHOO STANDIN' AROUND FOR?
YOUR CHOICE! TARGET PRACTICE IS ON!
UHF!
I'M--
--HIT!

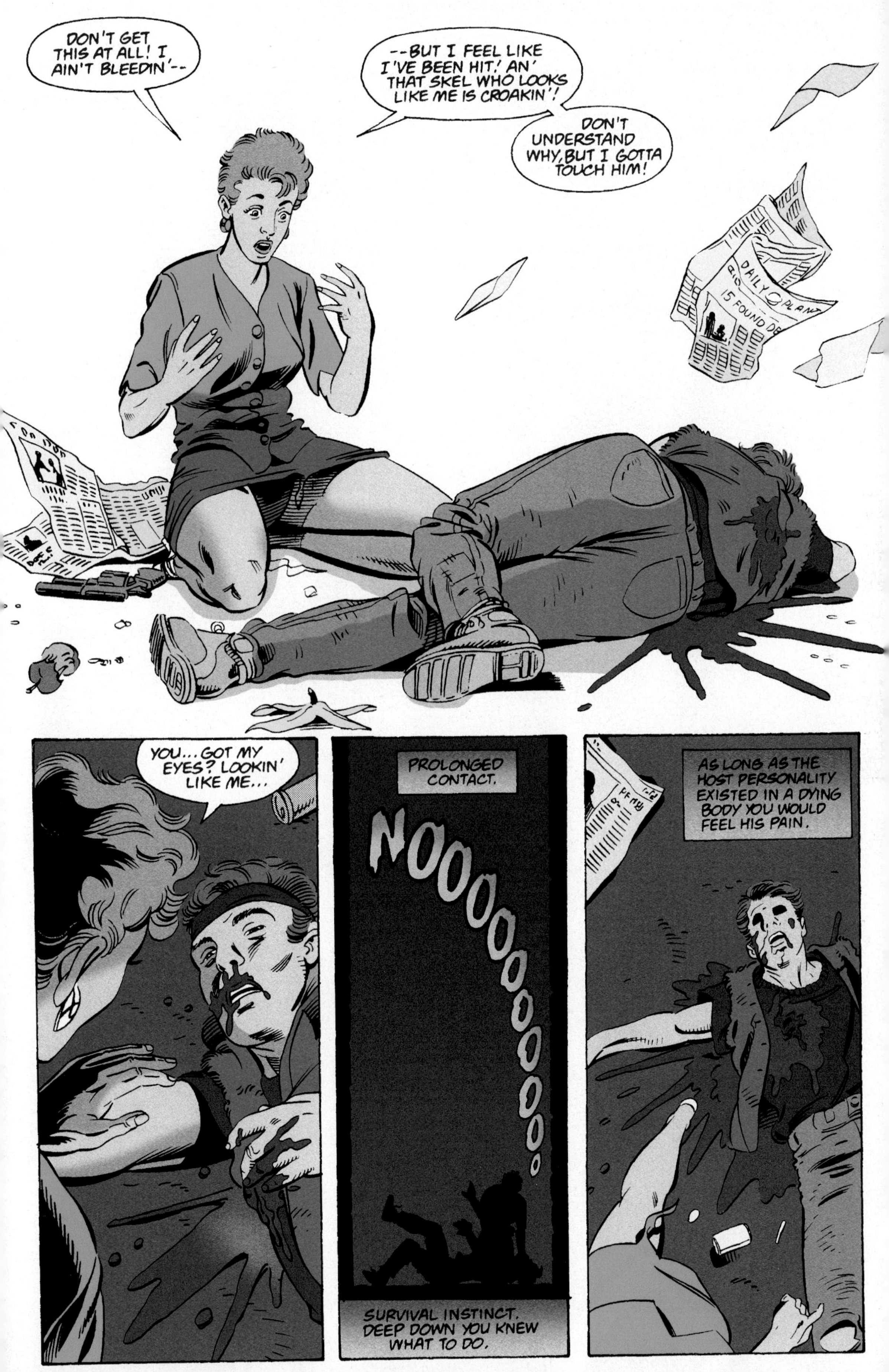
DON'T GET THIS AT ALL! I AIN'T BLEEDIN'--
--BUT I FEEL LIKE I'VE BEEN HIT! AN' THAT SKEL WHO LOOKS LIKE ME IS CROAKIN'!
DON'T UNDERSTAND WHY, BUT I GOTTA TOUCH HIM!
YOU...GOT MY EYES? LOOKIN' LIKE ME...
PROLONGED CONTACT.
NOOOOOOOOOOOOOO
SURVIVAL INSTINCT. DEEP DOWN YOU KNEW WHAT TO DO.
AS LONG AS THE HOST PERSONALITY EXISTED IN A DYING BODY YOU WOULD FEEL HIS PAIN.

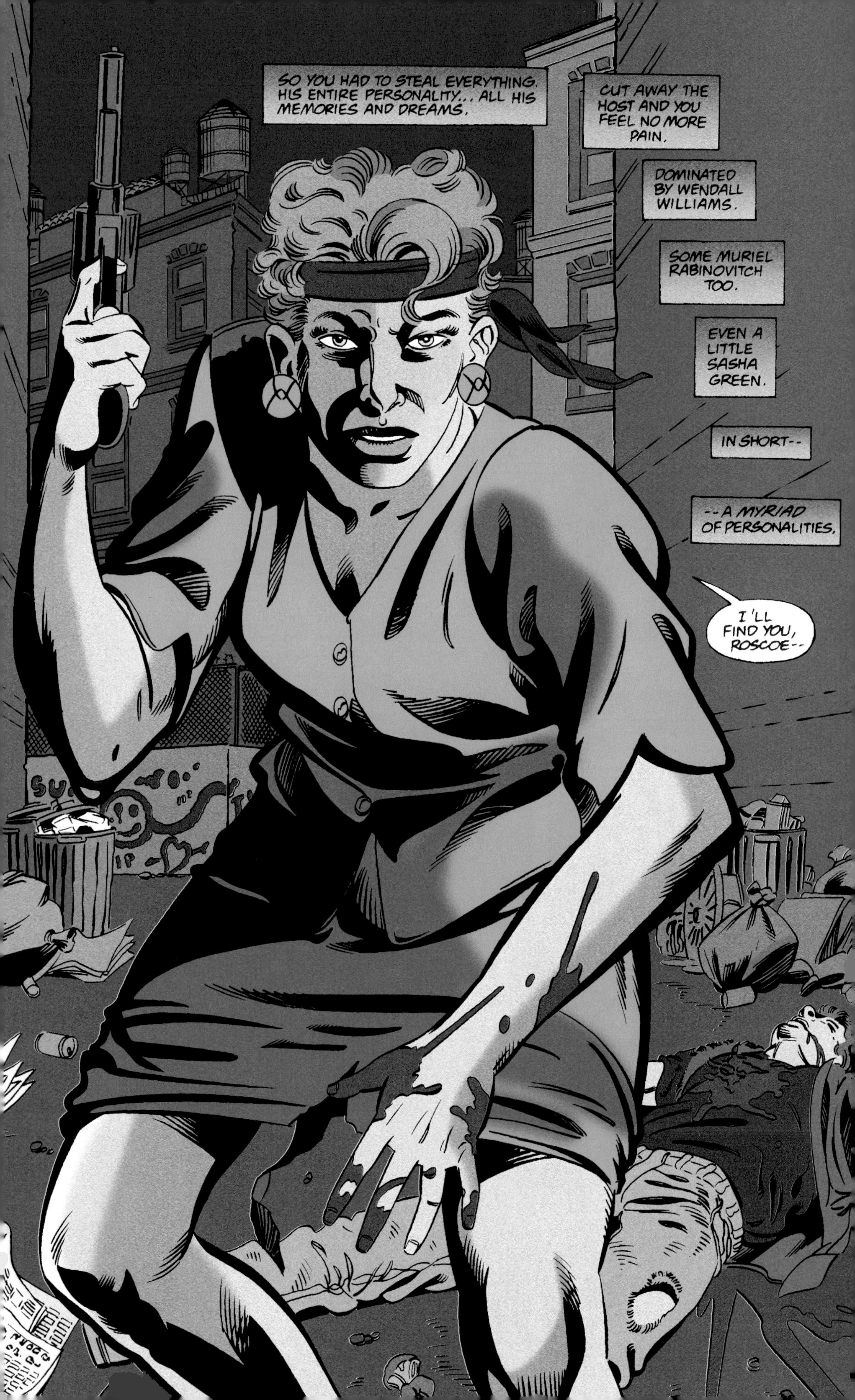
SO YOU HAD TO STEAL EVERYTHING. HIS ENTIRE PERSONALITY... ALL HIS MEMORIES AND DREAMS.
CUT AWAY THE HOST AND YOU FEEL NO MORE PAIN.
DOMINATED BY WENDALL WILLIAMS.
SOME MURIEL RABINOVITCH TOO.
EVEN A LITTLE SASHA GREEN.
IN SHORT--
--A MYRIAD OF PERSONALITIES.
I'LL FIND YOU, ROSCOE--

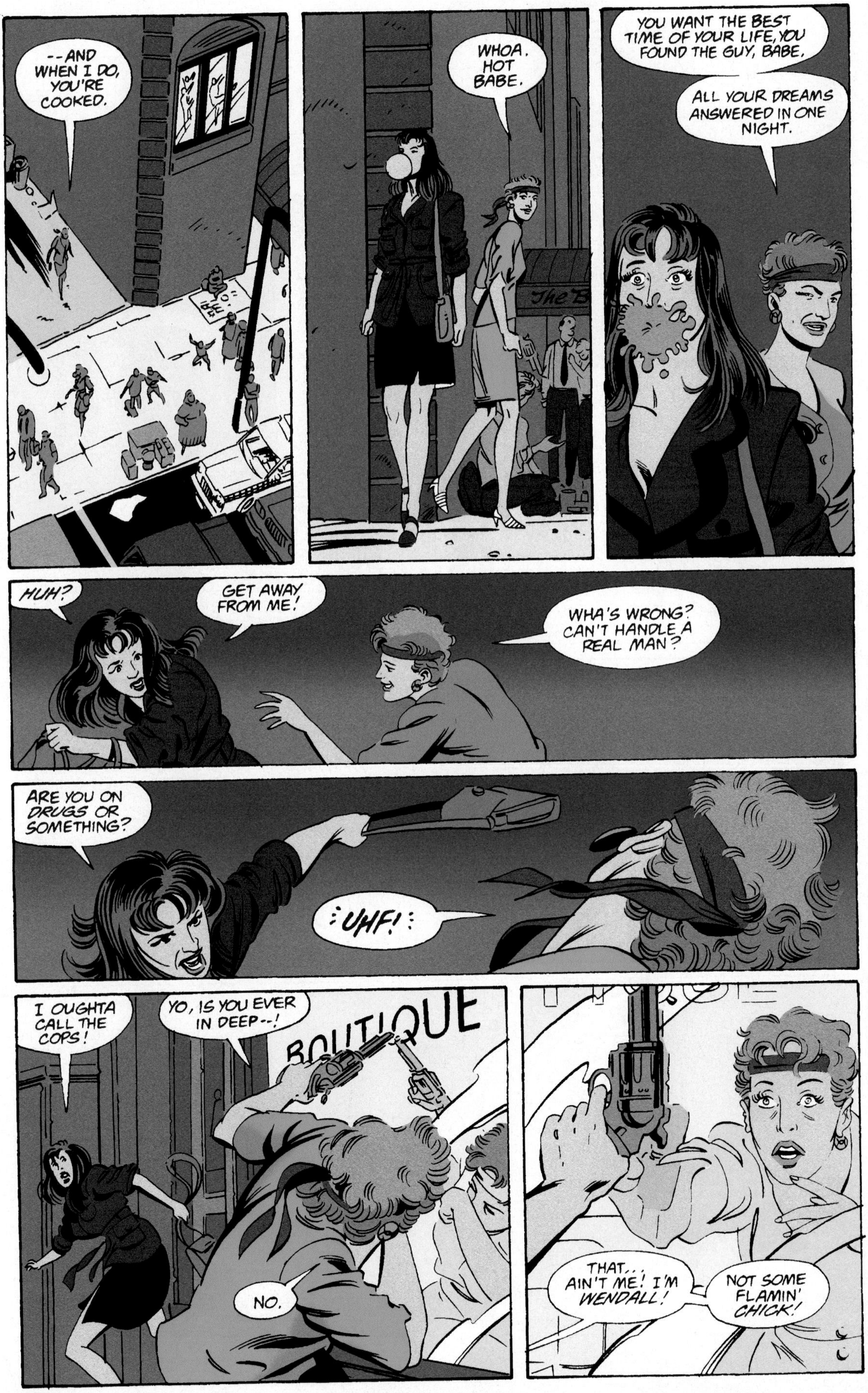
--AND WHEN I DO, YOU'RE COOKED.
WHOA. HOT BABE.
YOU WANT THE BEST TIME OF YOUR LIFE, YOU FOUND THE GUY, BABE.
ALL YOUR DREAMS ANSWERED IN ONE NIGHT.
HUH?
GET AWAY FROM ME!
WHA'S WRONG? CAN'T HANDLE A REAL MAN?
ARE YOU ON DRUGS OR SOMETHING?
UHF!
I OUGHTA CALL THE COPS!
YO, IS YOU EVER IN DEEP--!
BOUTIQUE
NO.
THAT... AIN'T ME! I'M WENDALL!
NOT SOME FLAMIN' CHICK!

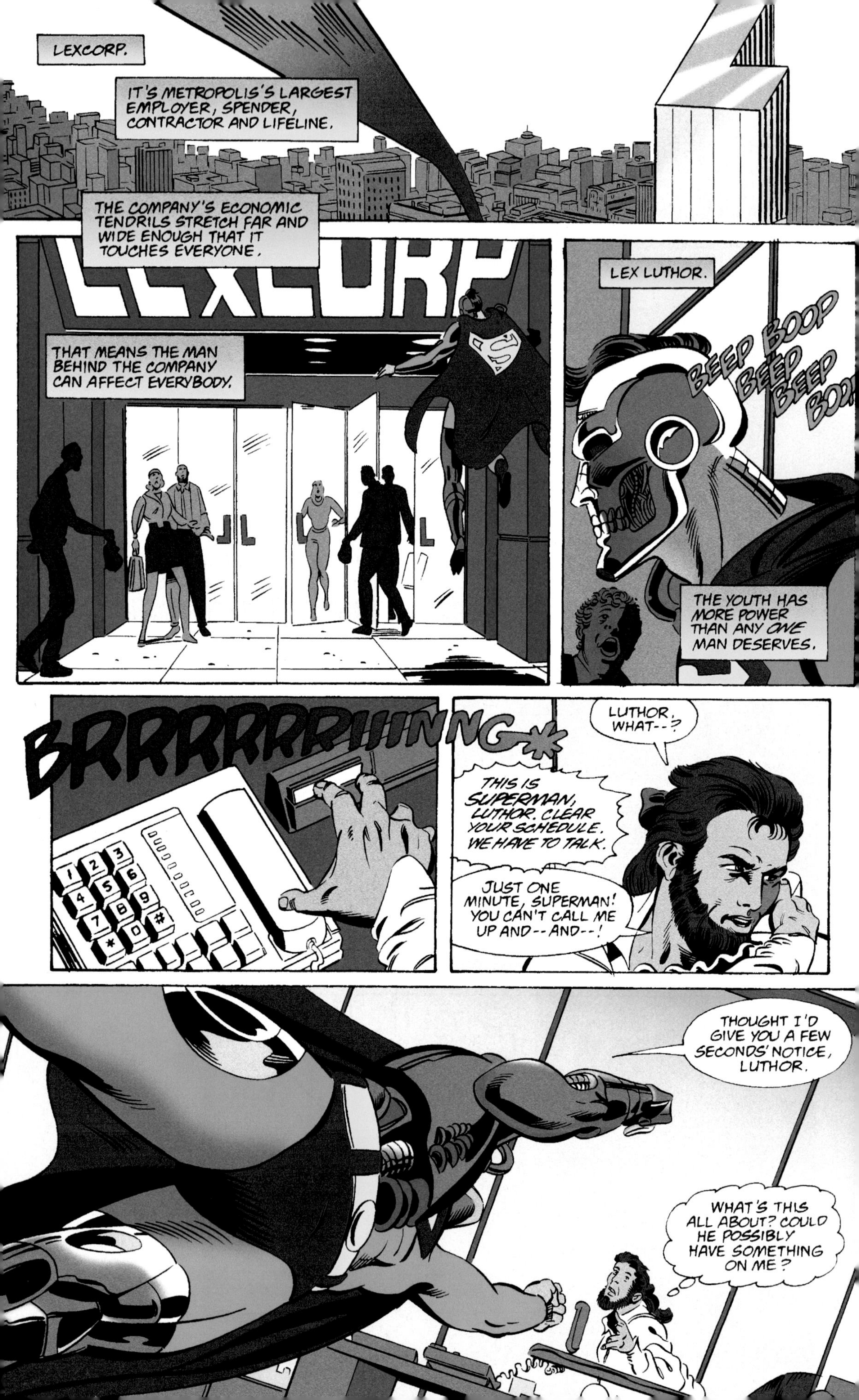

LEXCORP.
IT'S METROPOLIS'S LARGEST EMPLOYER, SPENDER, CONTRACTOR AND LIFELINE.
THE COMPANY'S ECONOMIC TENDRILS STRETCH FAR AND WIDE ENOUGH THAT IT TOUCHES EVERYONE.
THAT MEANS THE MAN BEHIND THE COMPANY CAN AFFECT EVERYBODY.
LEX LUTHOR.
BEEP BOOP BEEP BEEP
THE YOUTH HAS MORE POWER THAN ANY ONE MAN DESERVES.
BRRRRRRIIINNG
LUTHOR, WHAT--?
THIS IS SUPERMAN, LUTHOR. CLEAR YOUR SCHEDULE. WE HAVE TO TALK.
JUST ONE MINUTE, SUPERMAN! YOU CAN'T CALL ME UP AND--AND--!
THOUGHT I'D GIVE YOU A FEW SECONDS' NOTICE, LUTHOR.
WHAT'S THIS ALL ABOUT? COULD HE POSSIBLY HAVE SOMETHING ON ME?

I'M HERE TO ASK YOU ABOUT SASHA GREEN, LUTHOR.

SHE'S BEEN MURDERED AND I THINK YOU HAVE SOME ANSWERS.

H-HOW MAY I BE OF SERVICE?

HE KNOWS! BETTER PREPARE FOR ESCAPE CONTINGENCY!

I'VE SPENT MONTHS BUILDING THIS INSIPID "GOOD GUY" IMAGE AND THIS WALKING ERECTOR SET IS ABOUT TO DESTROY EVERY-THING!

SASHA... WAS A GOOD WOMAN, SUPERMAN. MY PERSONAL MARTIAL ARTS INSTRUCTOR. I SEE YOU'VE FOUND HER RING.

I FOUND IT IN YOUR GARBAGE DUMP, LEX, ALONG WITH THE FEW REMAINS LEFT OF THE POOR GIRL.

THE POLICE TELL ME YOU WERE ONE OF THE LAST PEOPLE TO SEE HER ALIVE. CARE TO TALK ABOUT HER LAST MINUTES?

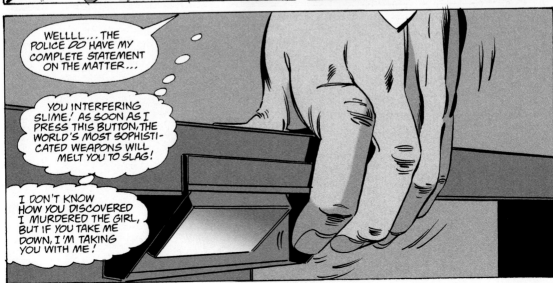

WELLLL... THE POLICE DO HAVE MY COMPLETE STATEMENT ON THE MATTER...

YOU INTERFERING SLIME! AS SOON AS I PRESS THIS BUTTON, THE WORLD'S MOST SOPHISTI-CATED WEAPONS WILL MELT YOU TO SLAG!

I DON'T KNOW HOW YOU DISCOVERED I MURDERED THE GIRL, BUT IF YOU TAKE ME DOWN, I'M TAKING YOU WITH ME!

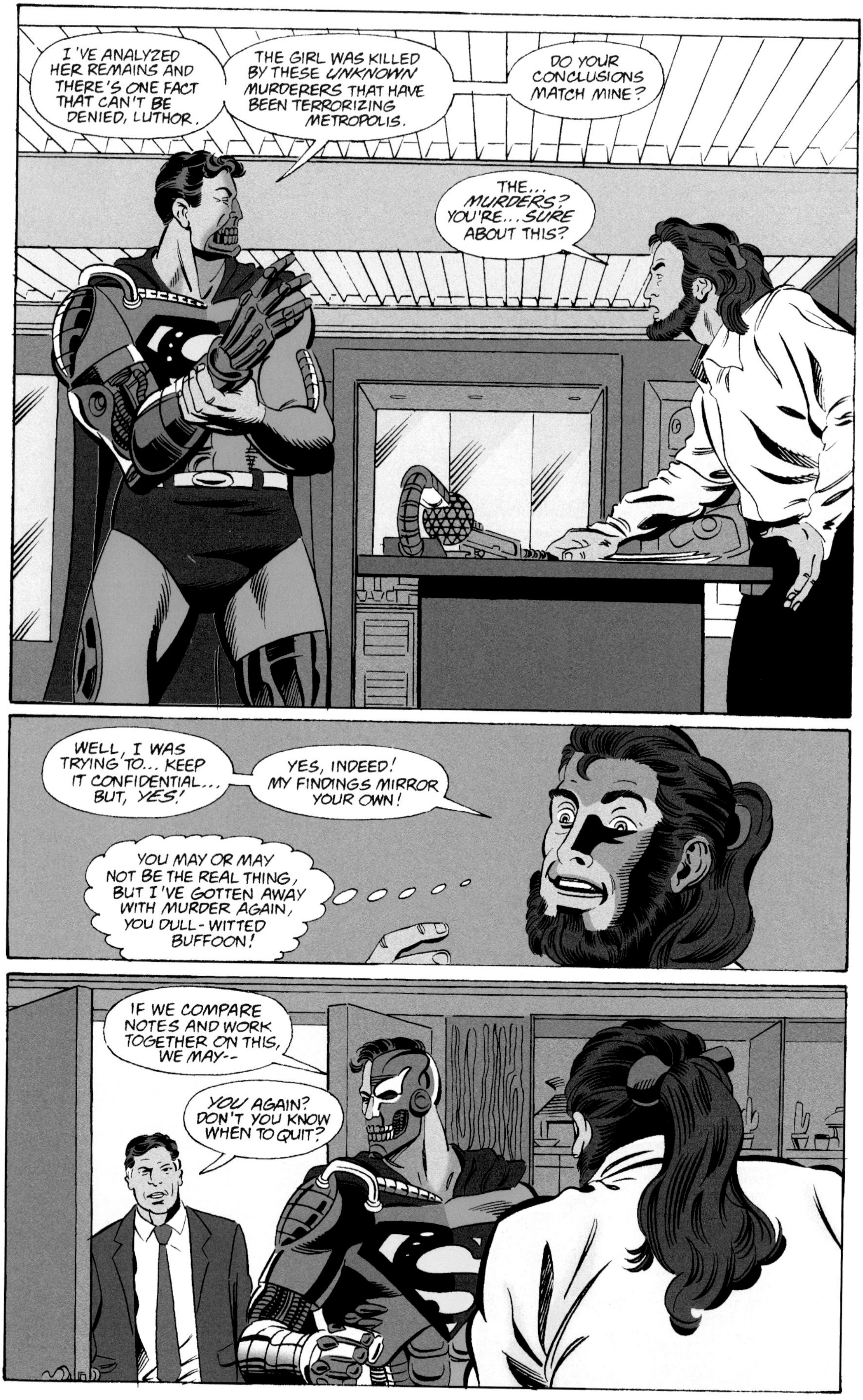
I'VE ANALYZED HER REMAINS AND THERE'S ONE FACT THAT CAN'T BE DENIED, LUTHOR.
THE GIRL WAS KILLED BY THESE UNKNOWN MURDERERS THAT HAVE BEEN TERRORIZING METROPOLIS.
DO YOUR CONCLUSIONS MATCH MINE?
THE... MURDERS? YOU'RE... SURE ABOUT THIS?
WELL, I WAS TRYING TO... KEEP IT CONFIDENTIAL... BUT, YES!
YES, INDEED! MY FINDINGS MIRROR YOUR OWN!
YOU MAY OR MAY NOT BE THE REAL THING, BUT I'VE GOTTEN AWAY WITH MURDER AGAIN, YOU DULL-WITTED BUFFOON!
IF WE COMPARE NOTES AND WORK TOGETHER ON THIS, WE MAY--
YOU AGAIN? DON'T YOU KNOW WHEN TO QUIT?

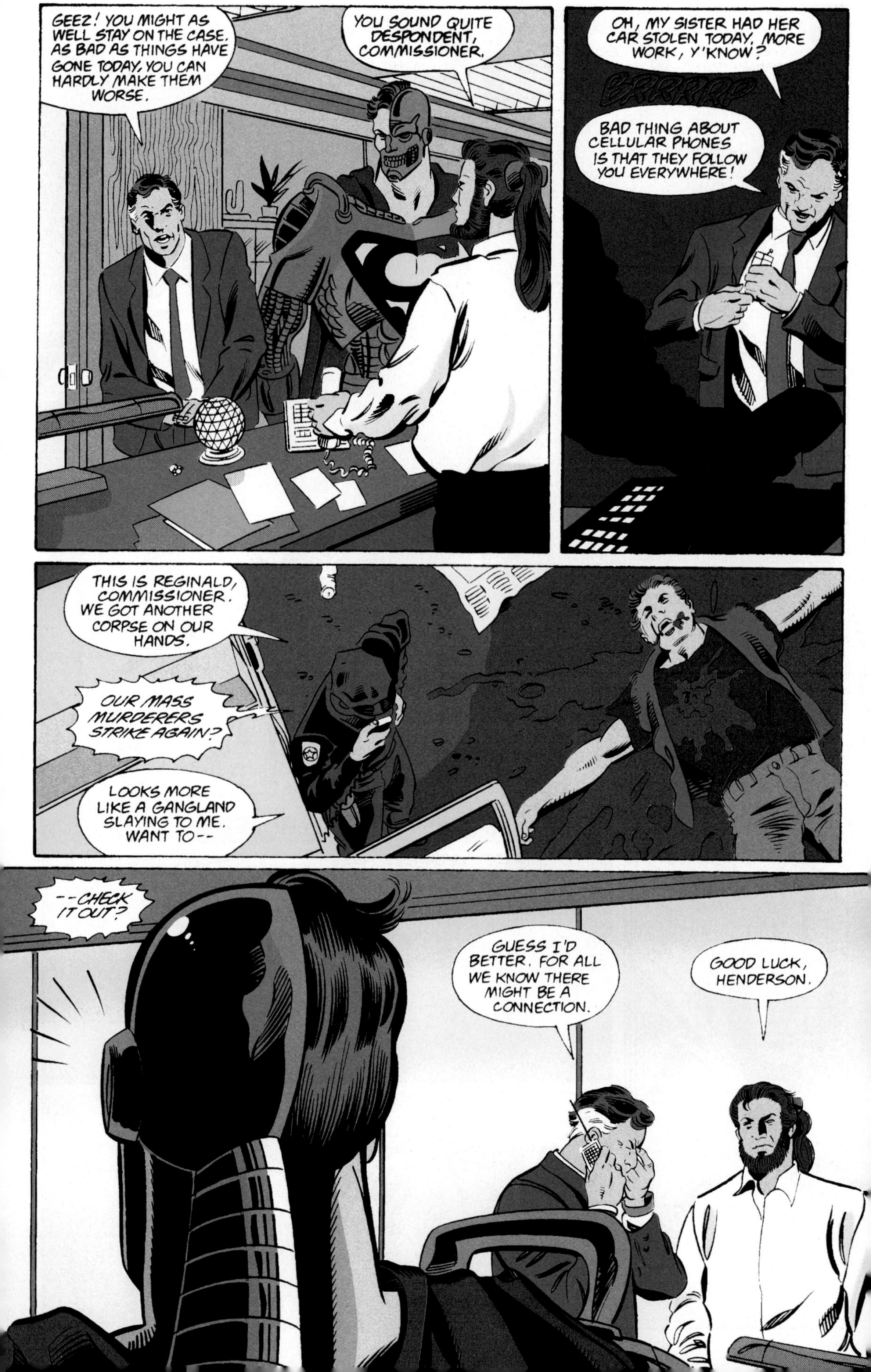
GEEZ! YOU MIGHT AS WELL STAY ON THE CASE. AS BAD AS THINGS HAVE GONE TODAY, YOU CAN HARDLY MAKE THEM WORSE.
YOU SOUND QUITE DESPONDENT, COMMISSIONER.
OH, MY SISTER HAD HER CAR STOLEN TODAY. MORE WORK, Y'KNOW?
BRRRRP
BAD THING ABOUT CELLULAR PHONES IS THAT THEY FOLLOW YOU EVERYWHERE!
THIS IS REGINALD, COMMISSIONER. WE GOT ANOTHER CORPSE ON OUR HANDS.
OUR MASS MURDERERS STRIKE AGAIN?
LOOKS MORE LIKE A GANGLAND SLAYING TO ME. WANT TO--
--CHECK IT OUT?
GUESS I'D BETTER. FOR ALL WE KNOW THERE MIGHT BE A CONNECTION.
GOOD LUCK, HENDERSON.

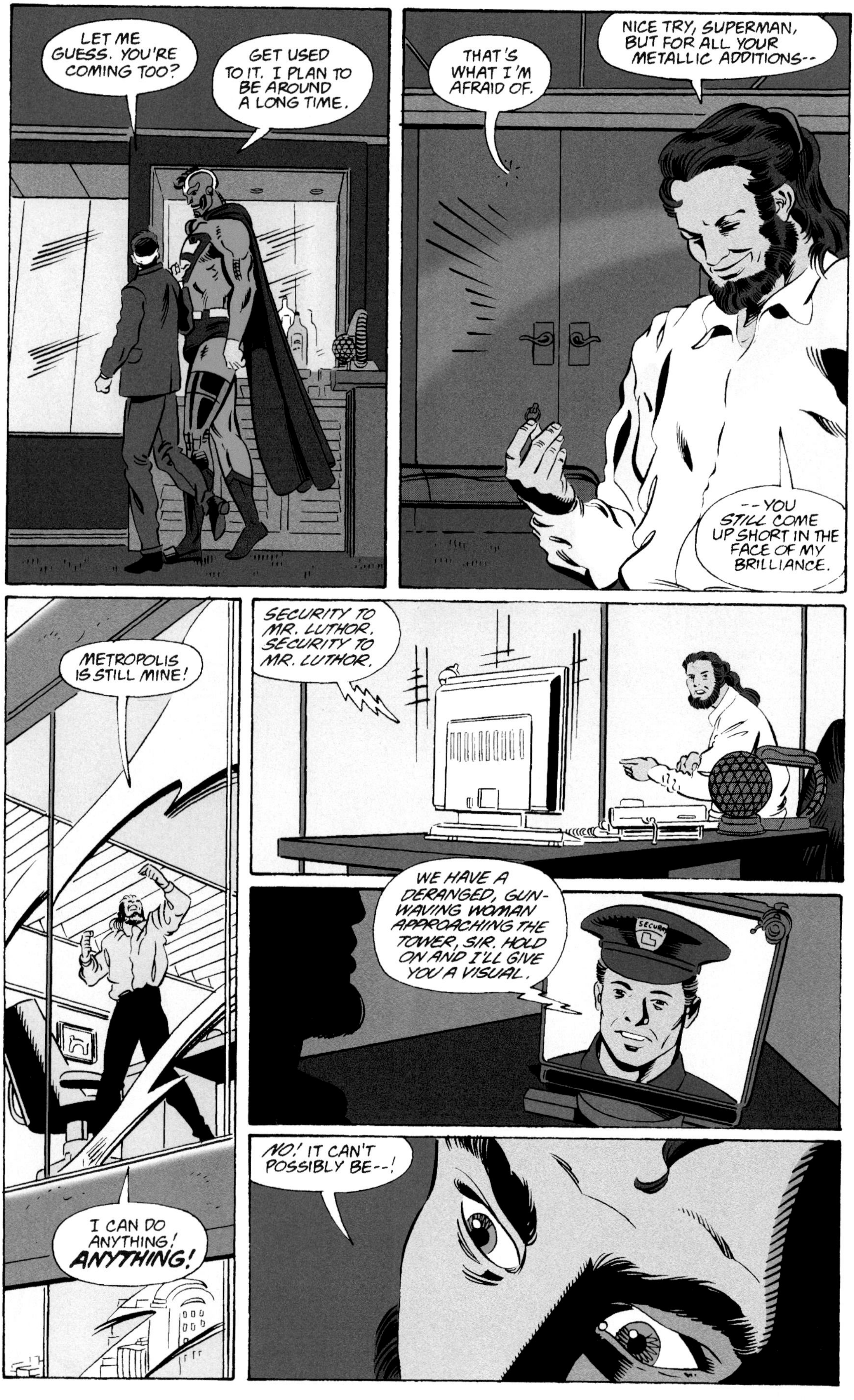
LET ME GUESS. YOU'RE COMING TOO?
GET USED TO IT. I PLAN TO BE AROUND A LONG TIME.
THAT'S WHAT I'M AFRAID OF.
NICE TRY, SUPERMAN, BUT FOR ALL YOUR METALLIC ADDITIONS--
--YOU STILL COME UP SHORT IN THE FACE OF MY BRILLIANCE.
METROPOLIS IS STILL MINE!
I CAN DO ANYTHING! ANYTHING!
SECURITY TO MR. LUTHOR. SECURITY TO MR. LUTHOR.
WE HAVE A DERANGED, GUN-WAVING WOMAN APPROACHING THE TOWER, SIR. HOLD ON AND I'LL GIVE YOU A VISUAL.
NO! IT CAN'T POSSIBLY BE--!

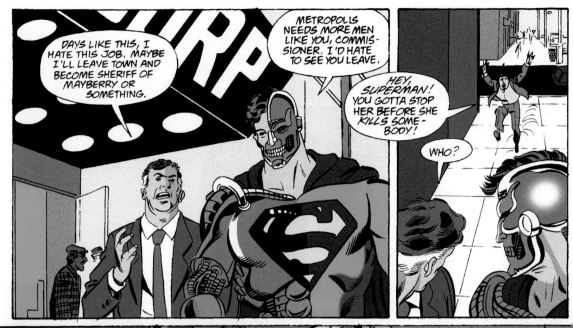

DAYS LIKE THIS, I HATE THIS JOB. MAYBE I'LL LEAVE TOWN AND BECOME SHERIFF OF MAYBERRY OR SOMETHING.

METROPOLIS NEEDS MORE MEN LIKE YOU, COMMISSIONER. I'D HATE TO SEE YOU LEAVE.

HEY, SUPERMAN! YOU GOTTA STOP HER BEFORE SHE KILLS SOMEBODY!

WHO?

"SOME WILD CHICK WITH A GUN, THAT'S WHO."

OH, MY GOD!

WHAT YOU PEOPLE STARIN' AT?

WHAT IN THE WORLD...

THERE SHE IS!

I'LL HANDLE THIS! THE POLICE ARE STILL GOOD FOR SOMETHING, YOU KNOW.

EVERYTHING WILL BE ALL RIGHT, MISS. I WANT YOU TO TAKE A DEEP BREATH, CALM YOURSELF--

--AND GIVE ME THAT GUN.

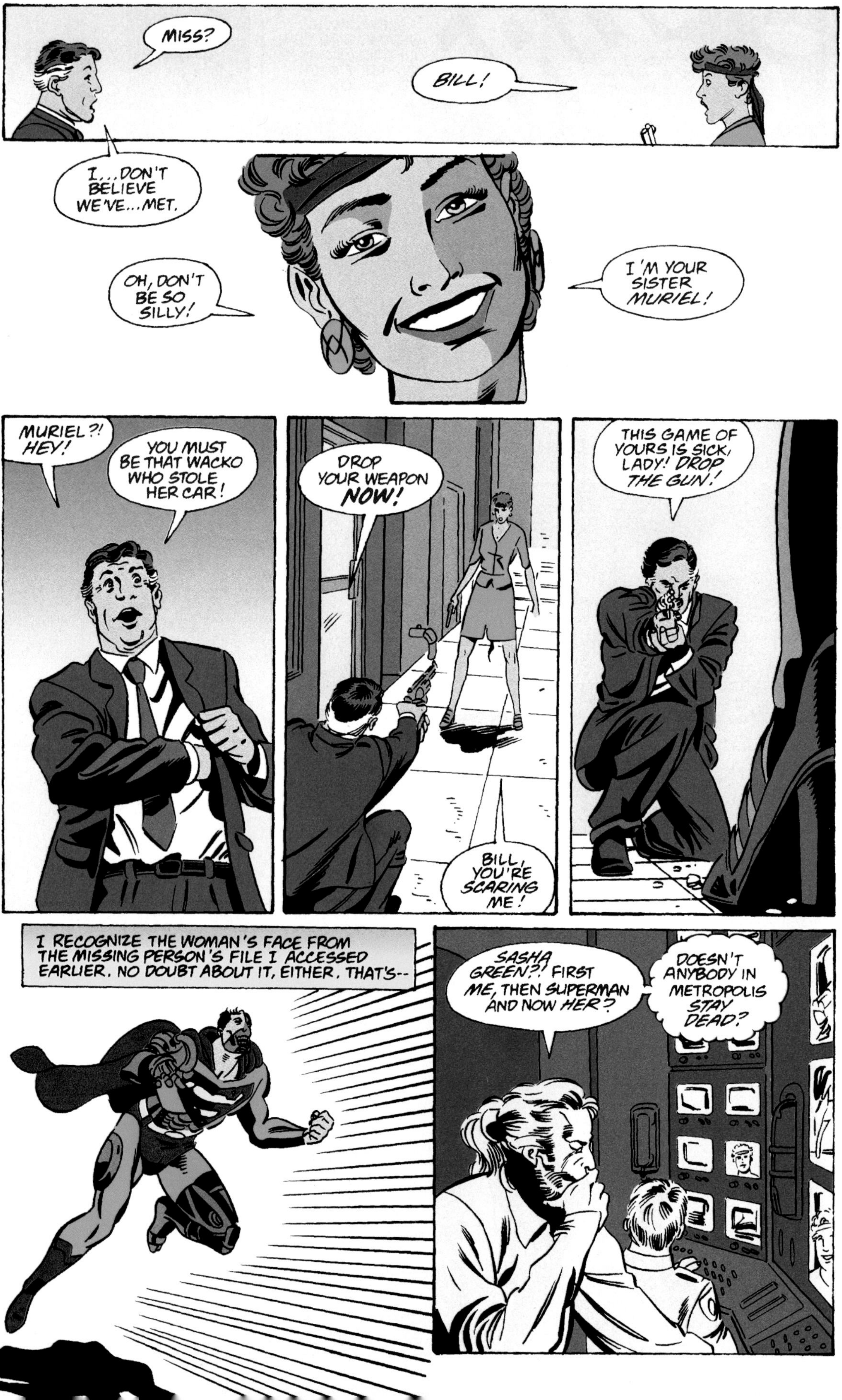
MISS?
BILL!
I...DON'T BELIEVE WE'VE...MET.
OH, DON'T BE SO SILLY!
I'M YOUR SISTER MURIEL!
MURIEL?! HEY!
YOU MUST BE THAT WACKO WHO STOLE HER CAR!
DROP YOUR WEAPON NOW!
BILL, YOU'RE SCARING ME!
THIS GAME OF YOURS IS SICK, LADY! DROP THE GUN!
I RECOGNIZE THE WOMAN'S FACE FROM THE MISSING PERSON'S FILE I ACCESSED EARLIER. NO DOUBT ABOUT IT, EITHER. THAT'S--
SASHA GREEN?! FIRST ME, THEN SUPERMAN AND NOW HER?
DOESN'T ANYBODY IN METROPOLIS STAY DEAD?

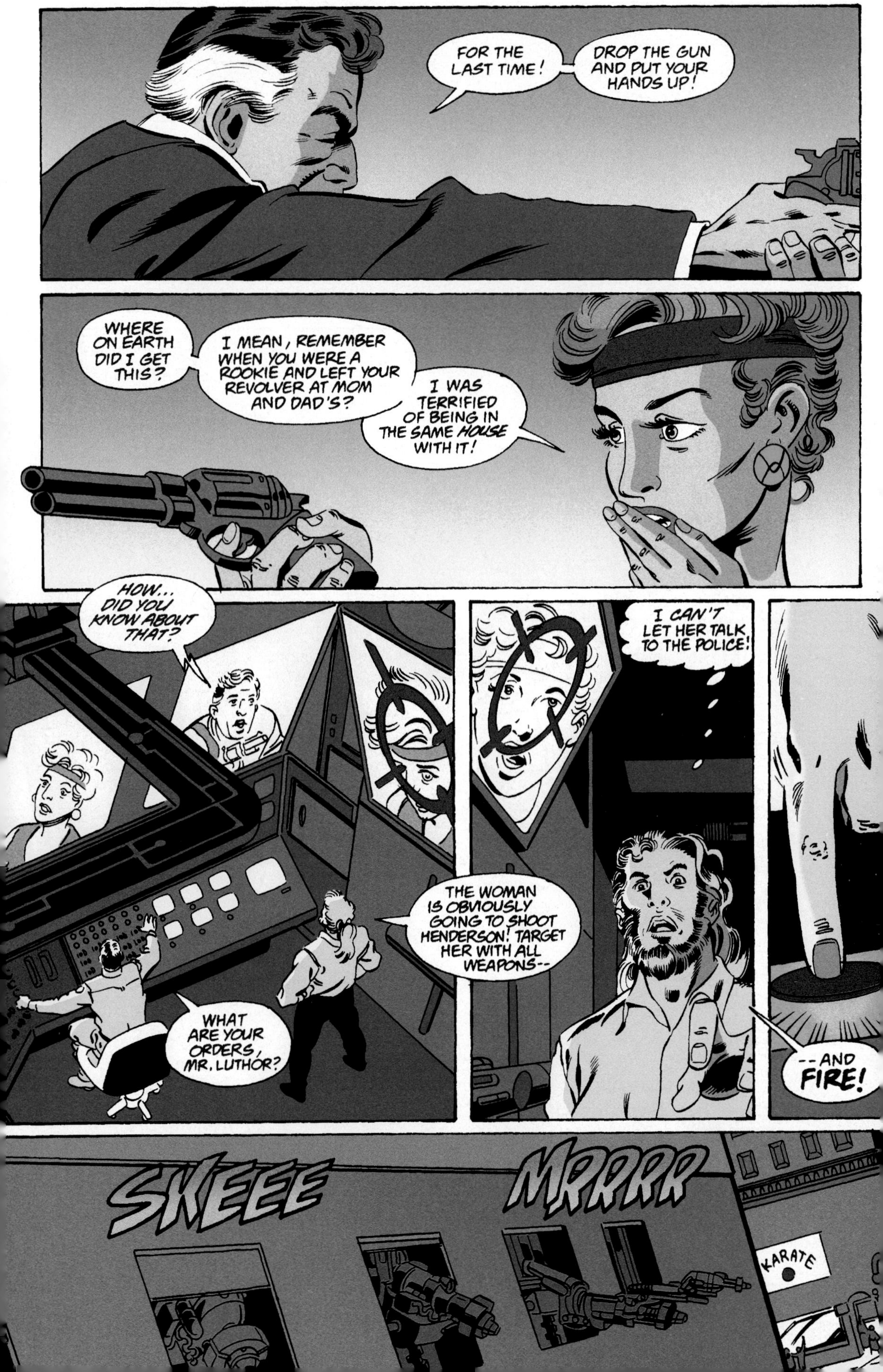

FOR THE LAST TIME!
DROP THE GUN AND PUT YOUR HANDS UP!
WHERE ON EARTH DID I GET THIS?
I MEAN, REMEMBER WHEN YOU WERE A ROOKIE AND LEFT YOUR REVOLVER AT MOM AND DAD'S?
I WAS TERRIFIED OF BEING IN THE SAME *HOUSE* WITH IT!
HOW... DID YOU KNOW ABOUT THAT?
WHAT ARE YOUR ORDERS, MR. LUTHOR?
THE WOMAN IS OBVIOUSLY GOING TO SHOOT HENDERSON! TARGET HER WITH ALL WEAPONS--
I *CAN'T* LET HER TALK TO THE POLICE!
--AND **FIRE!**
SKEEE
MRRRR
KARATE

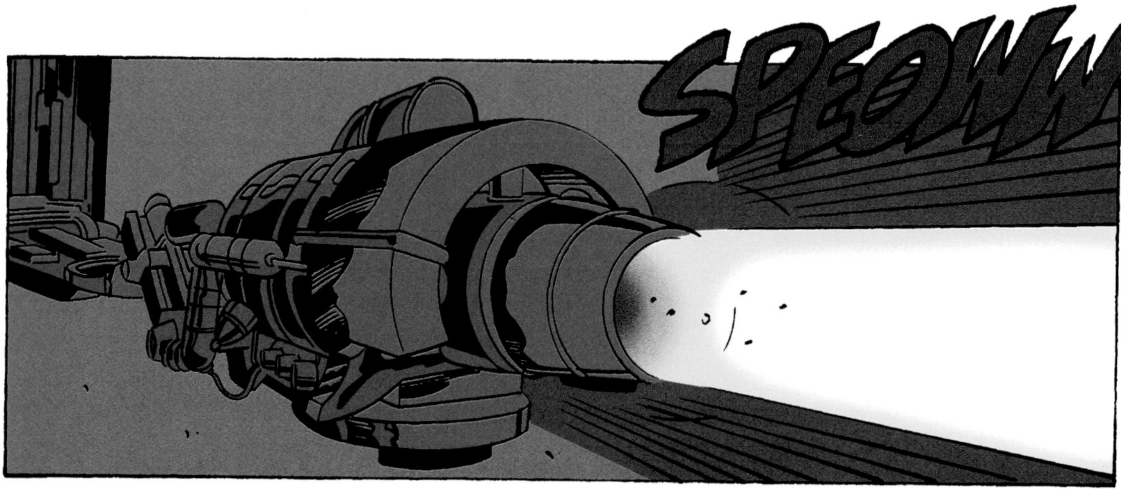
SPEOWW

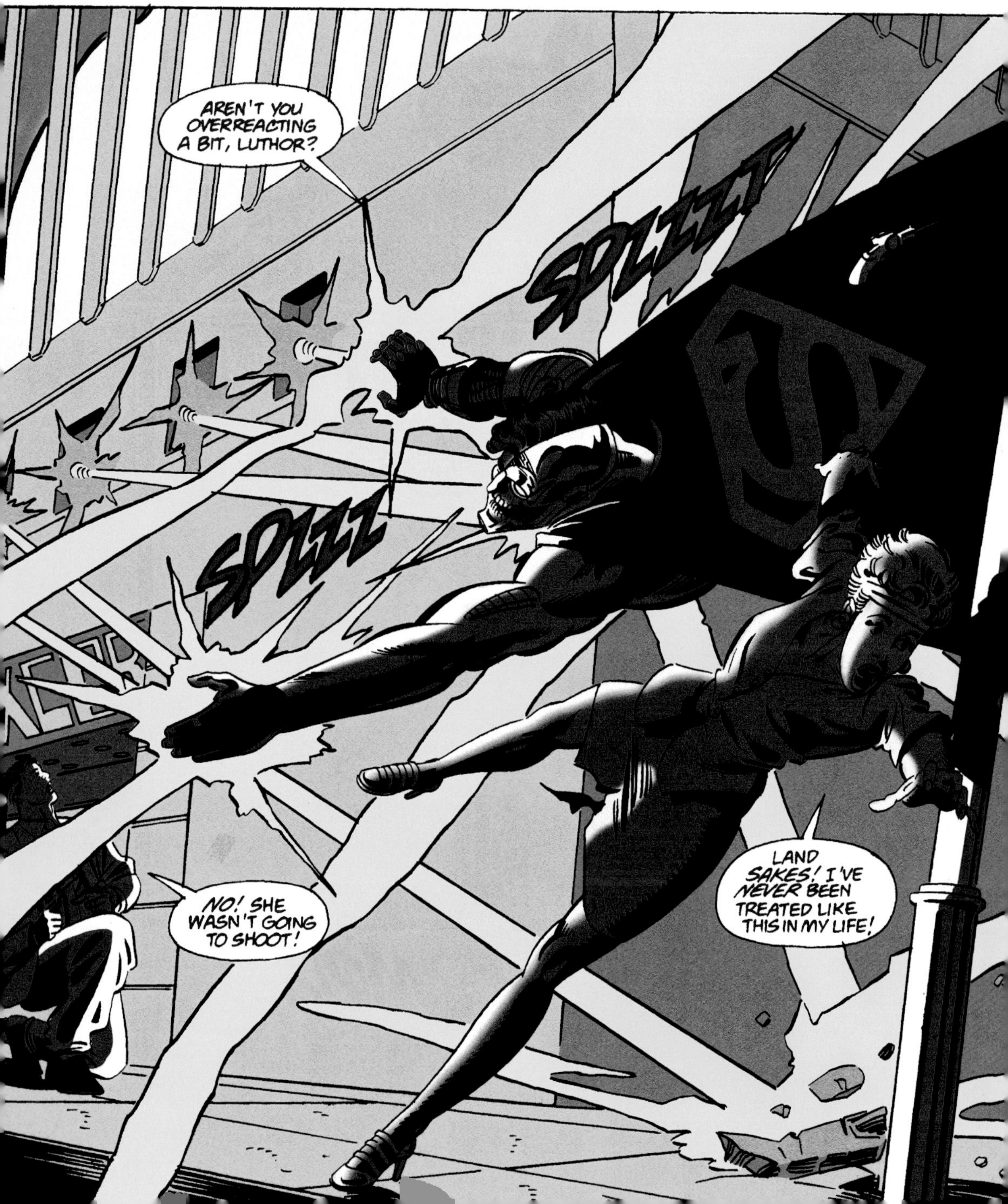
AREN'T YOU OVERREACTING A BIT, LUTHOR?
SPZZZT
SPZZZ
NO! SHE WASN'T GOING TO SHOOT!
LAND SAKES! I'VE NEVER BEEN TREATED LIKE THIS IN MY LIFE!

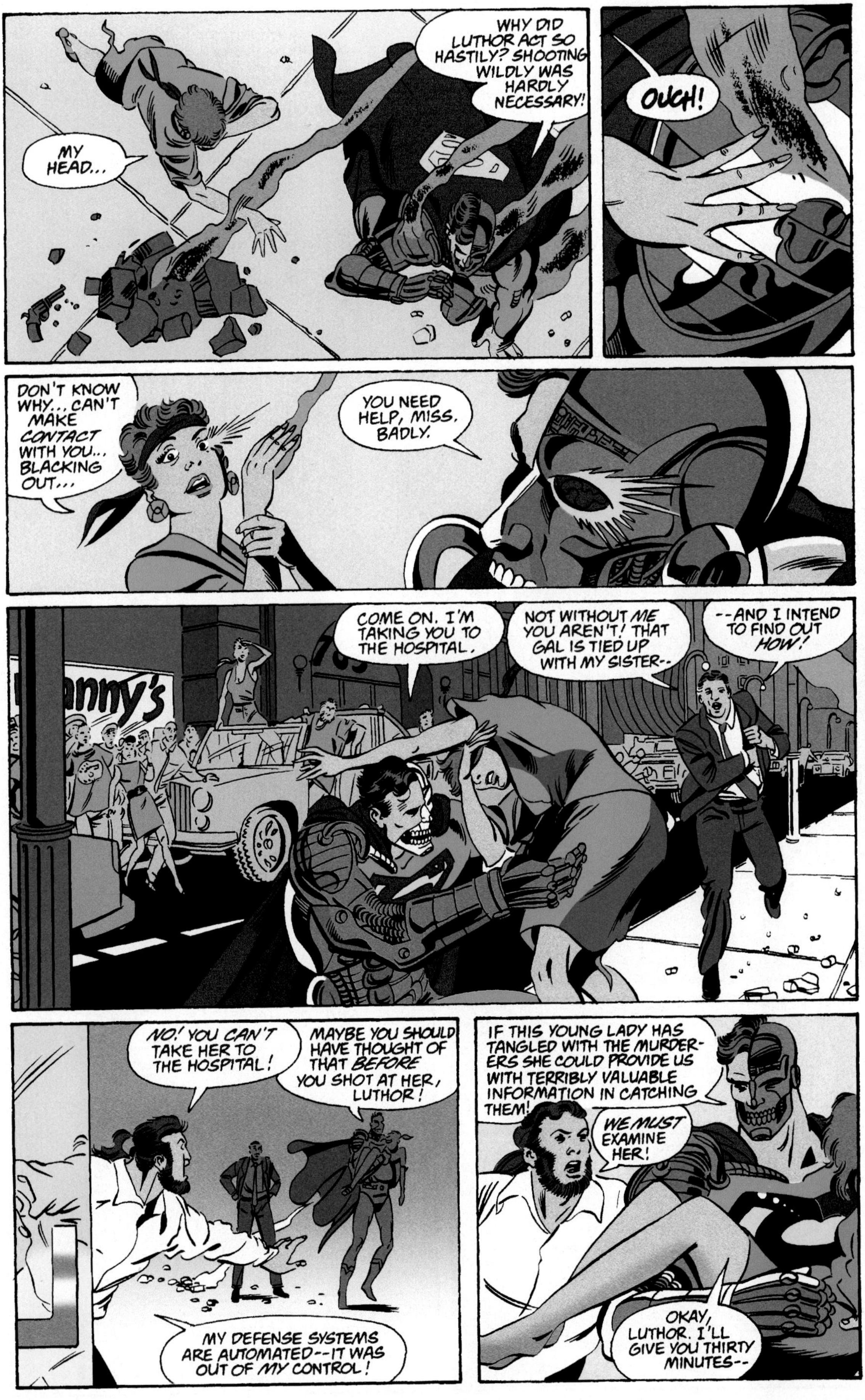
WHY DID LUTHOR ACT SO HASTILY? SHOOTING WILDLY WAS HARDLY NECESSARY!
MY HEAD...
OUCH!
DON'T KNOW WHY... CAN'T MAKE CONTACT WITH YOU... BLACKING OUT...
YOU NEED HELP, MISS. BADLY.
COME ON. I'M TAKING YOU TO THE HOSPITAL.
NOT WITHOUT ME YOU AREN'T! THAT GAL IS TIED UP WITH MY SISTER--
--AND I INTEND TO FIND OUT HOW!
NO! YOU CAN'T TAKE HER TO THE HOSPITAL!
MAYBE YOU SHOULD HAVE THOUGHT OF THAT BEFORE YOU SHOT AT HER, LUTHOR!
MY DEFENSE SYSTEMS ARE AUTOMATED--IT WAS OUT OF MY CONTROL!
IF THIS YOUNG LADY HAS TANGLED WITH THE MURDERERS SHE COULD PROVIDE US WITH TERRIBLY VALUABLE INFORMATION IN CATCHING THEM!
WE MUST EXAMINE HER!
OKAY, LUTHOR. I'LL GIVE YOU THIRTY MINUTES--

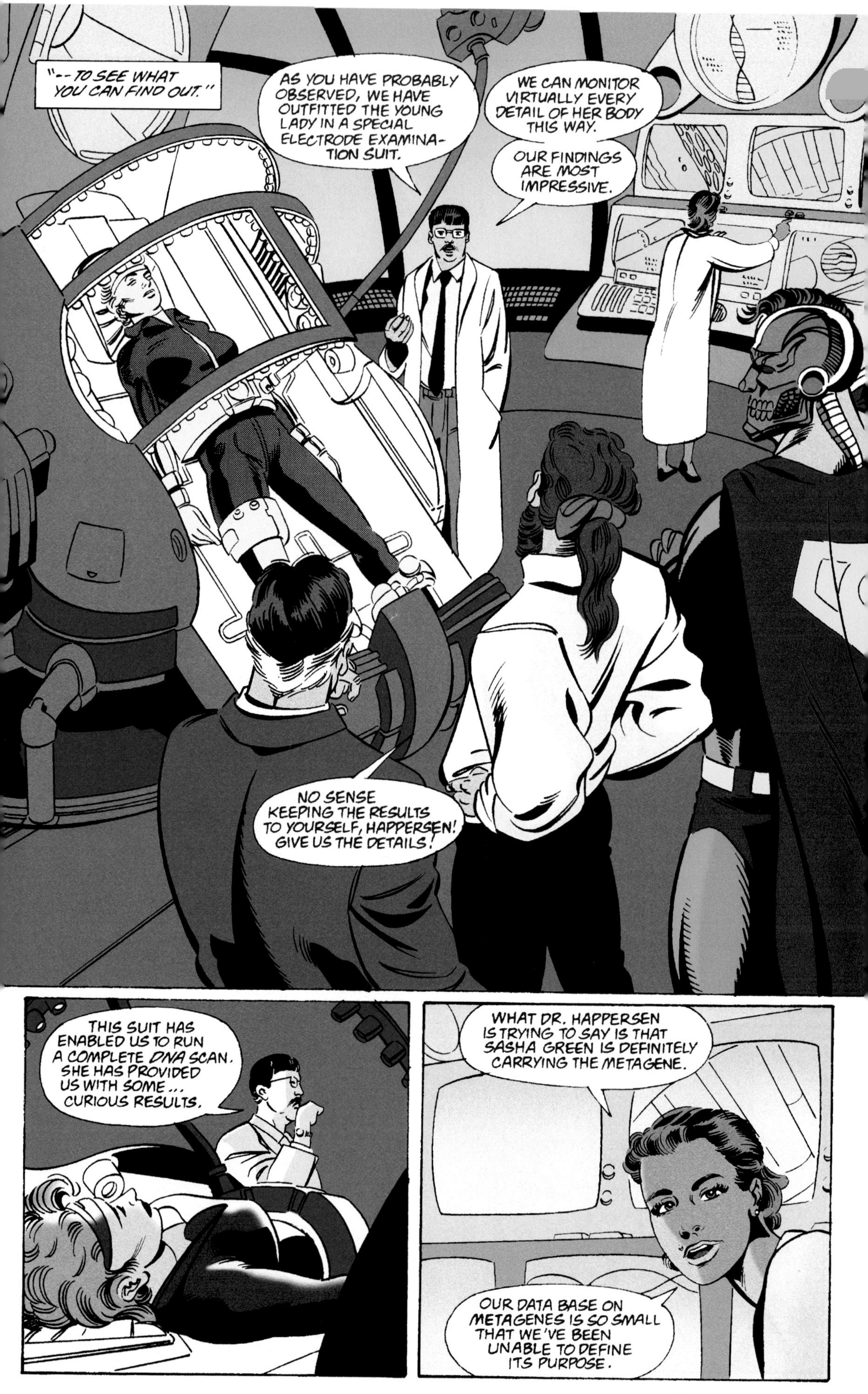
"--TO SEE WHAT YOU CAN FIND OUT."
AS YOU HAVE PROBABLY OBSERVED, WE HAVE OUTFITTED THE YOUNG LADY IN A SPECIAL ELECTRODE EXAMINATION SUIT.
WE CAN MONITOR VIRTUALLY EVERY DETAIL OF HER BODY THIS WAY.
OUR FINDINGS ARE MOST IMPRESSIVE.
NO SENSE KEEPING THE RESULTS TO YOURSELF, HAPPERSEN! GIVE US THE DETAILS!
THIS SUIT HAS ENABLED US TO RUN A COMPLETE DNA SCAN. SHE HAS PROVIDED US WITH SOME... CURIOUS RESULTS.
WHAT DR. HAPPERSEN IS TRYING TO SAY IS THAT SASHA GREEN IS DEFINITELY CARRYING THE METAGENE.
OUR DATA BASE ON METAGENES IS SO SMALL THAT WE'VE BEEN UNABLE TO DEFINE ITS PURPOSE.

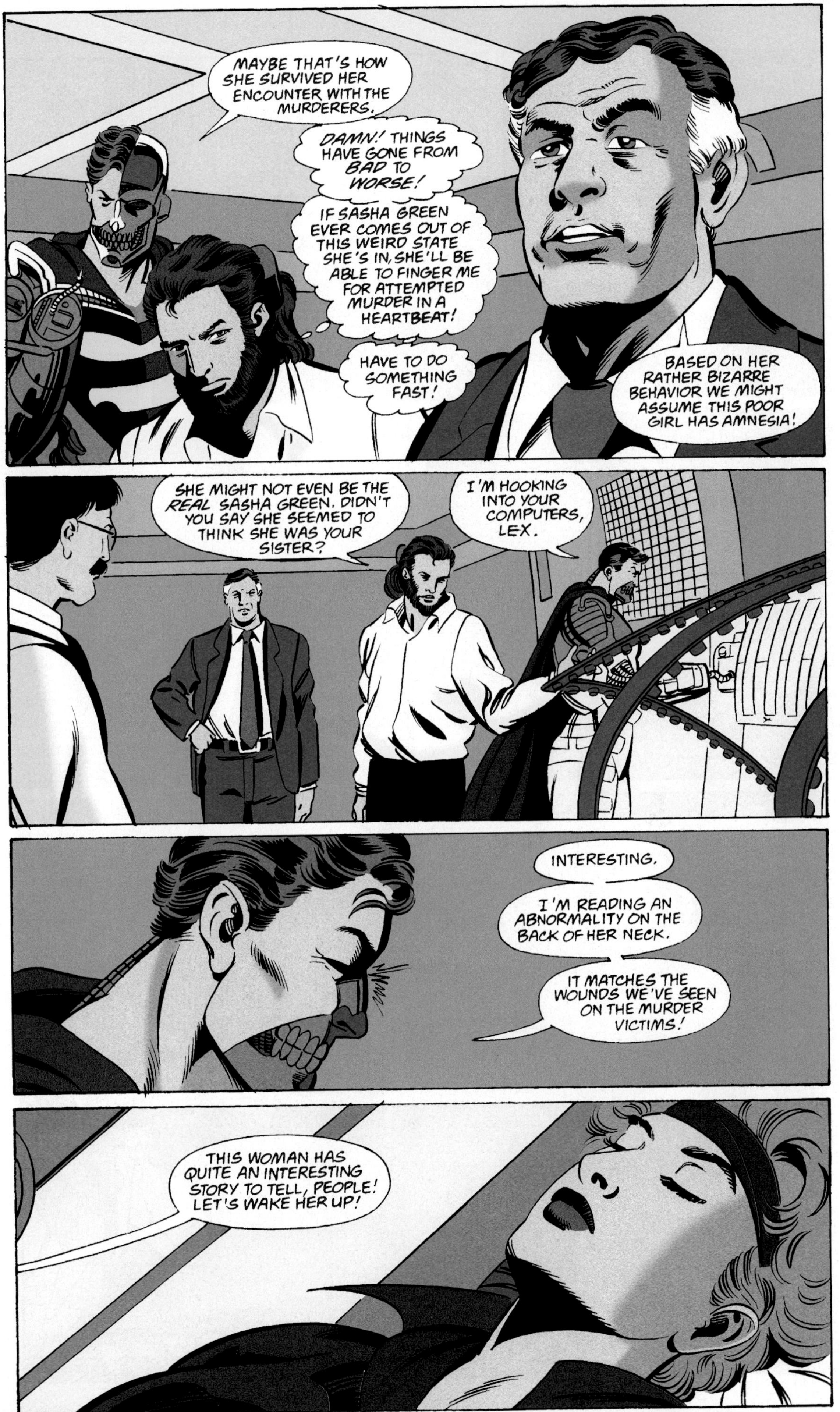
MAYBE THAT'S HOW SHE SURVIVED HER ENCOUNTER WITH THE MURDERERS.
DAMN! THINGS HAVE GONE FROM BAD TO WORSE!
IF SASHA GREEN EVER COMES OUT OF THIS WEIRD STATE SHE'S IN, SHE'LL BE ABLE TO FINGER ME FOR ATTEMPTED MURDER IN A HEARTBEAT!
HAVE TO DO SOMETHING FAST!
BASED ON HER RATHER BIZARRE BEHAVIOR WE MIGHT ASSUME THIS POOR GIRL HAS AMNESIA!
SHE MIGHT NOT EVEN BE THE REAL SASHA GREEN. DIDN'T YOU SAY SHE SEEMED TO THINK SHE WAS YOUR SISTER?
I'M HOOKING INTO YOUR COMPUTERS, LEX.
INTERESTING.
I'M READING AN ABNORMALITY ON THE BACK OF HER NECK.
IT MATCHES THE WOUNDS WE'VE SEEN ON THE MURDER VICTIMS!
THIS WOMAN HAS QUITE AN INTERESTING STORY TO TELL, PEOPLE! LET'S WAKE HER UP!

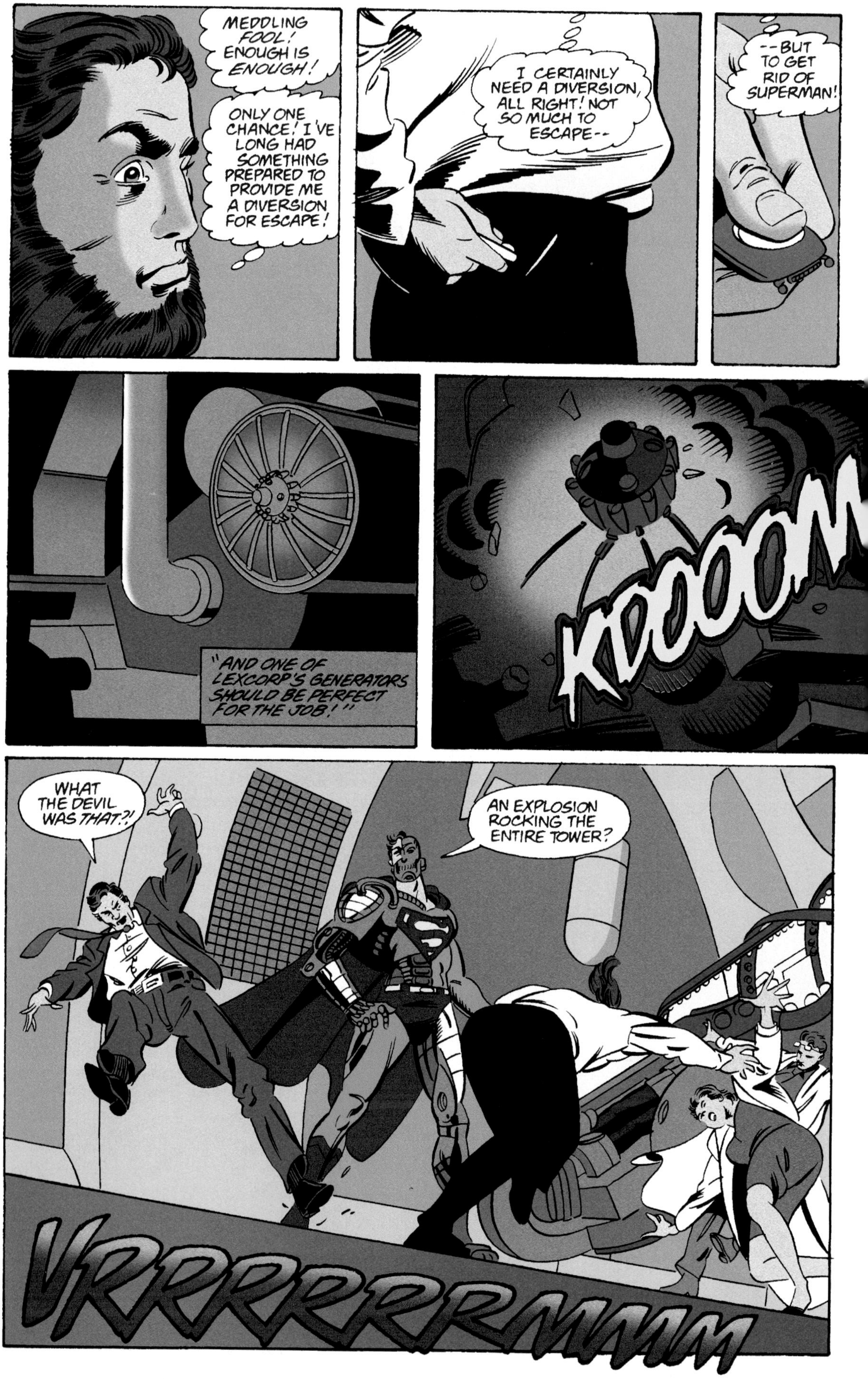
MEDDLING FOOL! ENOUGH IS ENOUGH!
ONLY ONE CHANCE! I'VE LONG HAD SOMETHING PREPARED TO PROVIDE ME A DIVERSION FOR ESCAPE!
I CERTAINLY NEED A DIVERSION, ALL RIGHT! NOT SO MUCH TO ESCAPE--
--BUT TO GET RID OF SUPERMAN!
"AND ONE OF LEXCORP'S GENERATORS SHOULD BE PERFECT FOR THE JOB!"
KDOOOM
WHAT THE DEVIL WAS THAT?!
AN EXPLOSION ROCKING THE ENTIRE TOWER?
VRRRRRRMMM

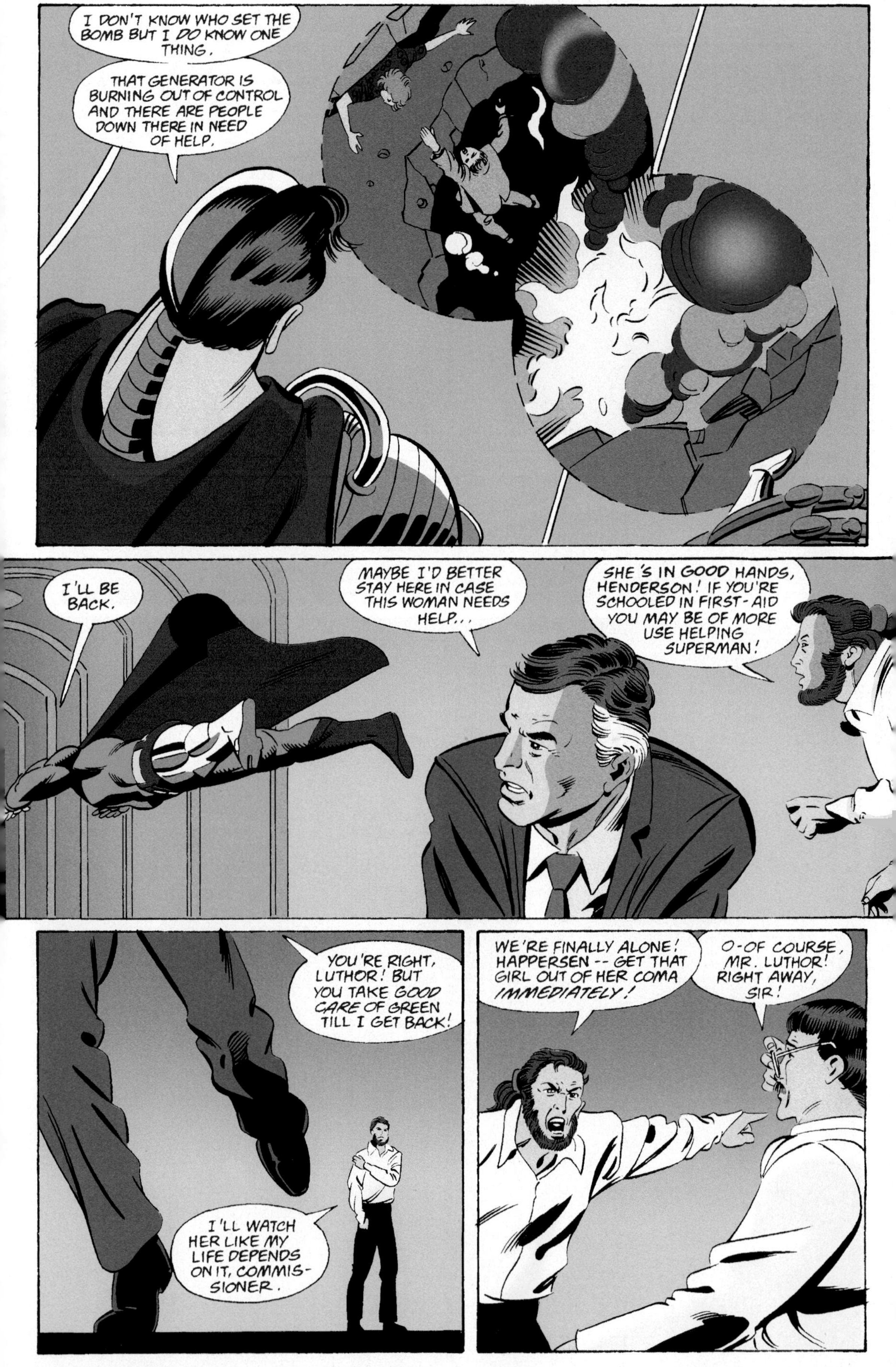
I DON'T KNOW WHO SET THE BOMB BUT I DO KNOW ONE THING.
THAT GENERATOR IS BURNING OUT OF CONTROL AND THERE ARE PEOPLE DOWN THERE IN NEED OF HELP.
I'LL BE BACK.
MAYBE I'D BETTER STAY HERE IN CASE THIS WOMAN NEEDS HELP...
SHE'S IN GOOD HANDS, HENDERSON! IF YOU'RE SCHOOLED IN FIRST-AID YOU MAY BE OF MORE USE HELPING SUPERMAN!
YOU'RE RIGHT, LUTHOR! BUT YOU TAKE GOOD CARE OF GREEN TILL I GET BACK!
I'LL WATCH HER LIKE MY LIFE DEPENDS ON IT, COMMISSIONER.
WE'RE FINALLY ALONE! HAPPERSEN -- GET THAT GIRL OUT OF HER COMA IMMEDIATELY!
O-OF COURSE, MR. LUTHOR! RIGHT AWAY, SIR!

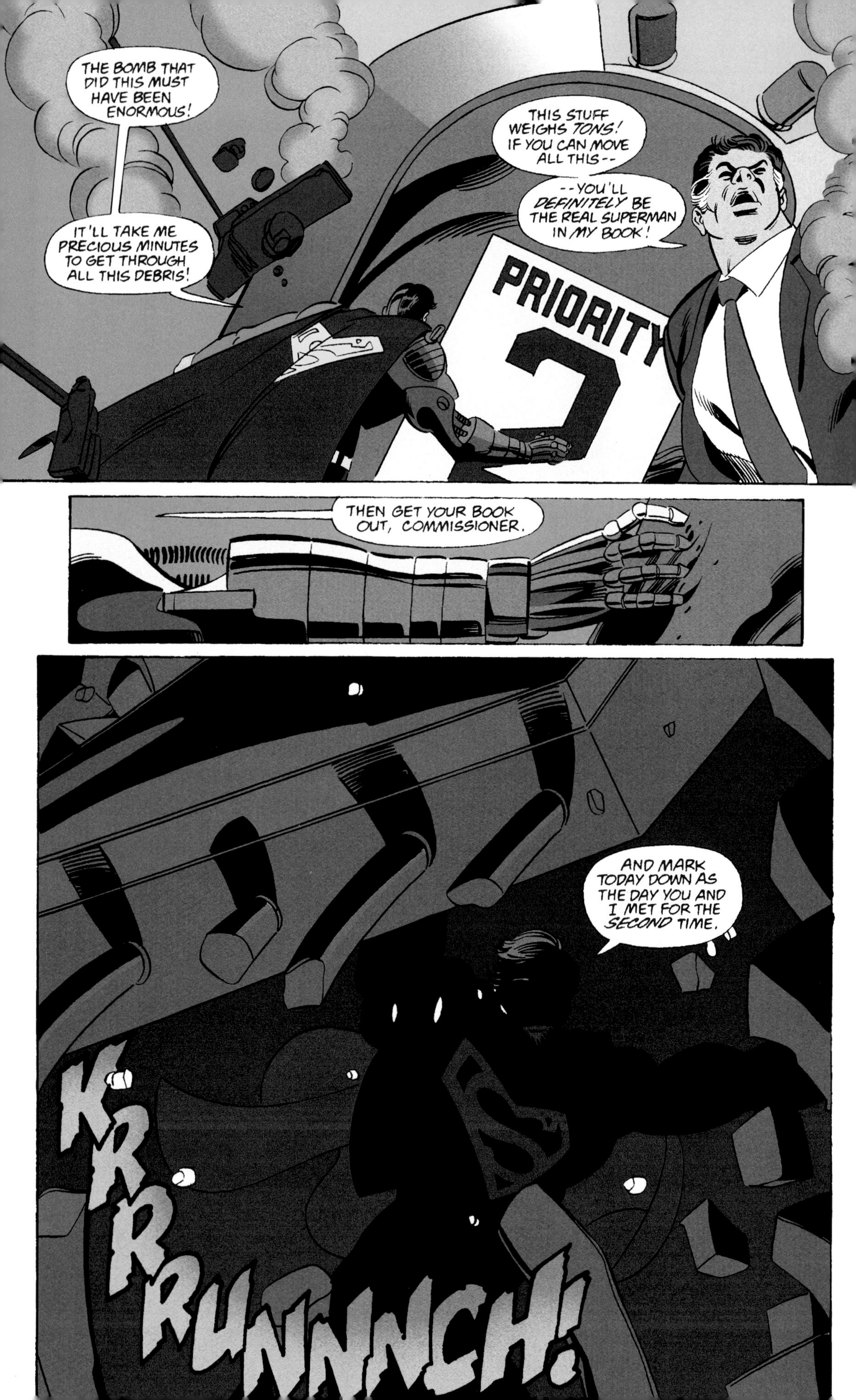
THE BOMB THAT DID THIS MUST HAVE BEEN ENORMOUS!
IT'LL TAKE ME PRECIOUS MINUTES TO GET THROUGH ALL THIS DEBRIS!
THIS STUFF WEIGHS TONS! IF YOU CAN MOVE ALL THIS--
--YOU'LL DEFINITELY BE THE REAL SUPERMAN IN MY BOOK!
PRIORITY
THEN GET YOUR BOOK OUT, COMMISSIONER.
AND MARK TODAY DOWN AS THE DAY YOU AND I MET FOR THE SECOND TIME.
KRRRUNNNCH!

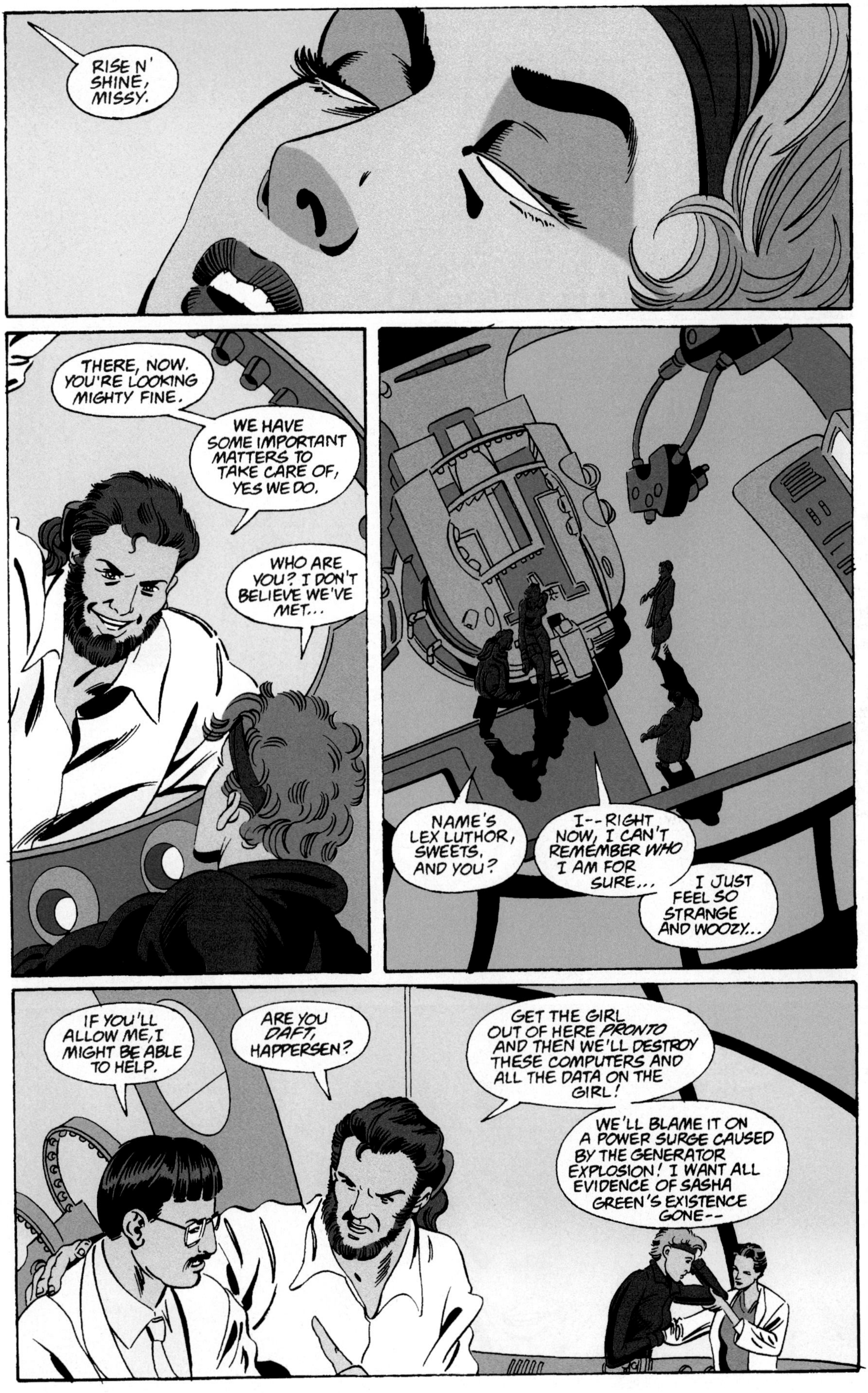
RISE N' SHINE, MISSY.
THERE, NOW. YOU'RE LOOKING MIGHTY FINE.
WE HAVE SOME IMPORTANT MATTERS TO TAKE CARE OF, YES WE DO.
WHO ARE YOU? I DON'T BELIEVE WE'VE MET...
NAME'S LEX LUTHOR, SWEETS. AND YOU?
I--RIGHT NOW, I CAN'T REMEMBER WHO I AM FOR SURE...
I JUST FEEL SO STRANGE AND WOOZY...
IF YOU'LL ALLOW ME, I MIGHT BE ABLE TO HELP.
ARE YOU DAFT, HAPPERSEN?
GET THE GIRL OUT OF HERE PRONTO AND THEN WE'LL DESTROY THESE COMPUTERS AND ALL THE DATA ON THE GIRL!
WE'LL BLAME IT ON A POWER SURGE CAUSED BY THE GENERATOR EXPLOSION! I WANT ALL EVIDENCE OF SASHA GREEN'S EXISTENCE GONE--

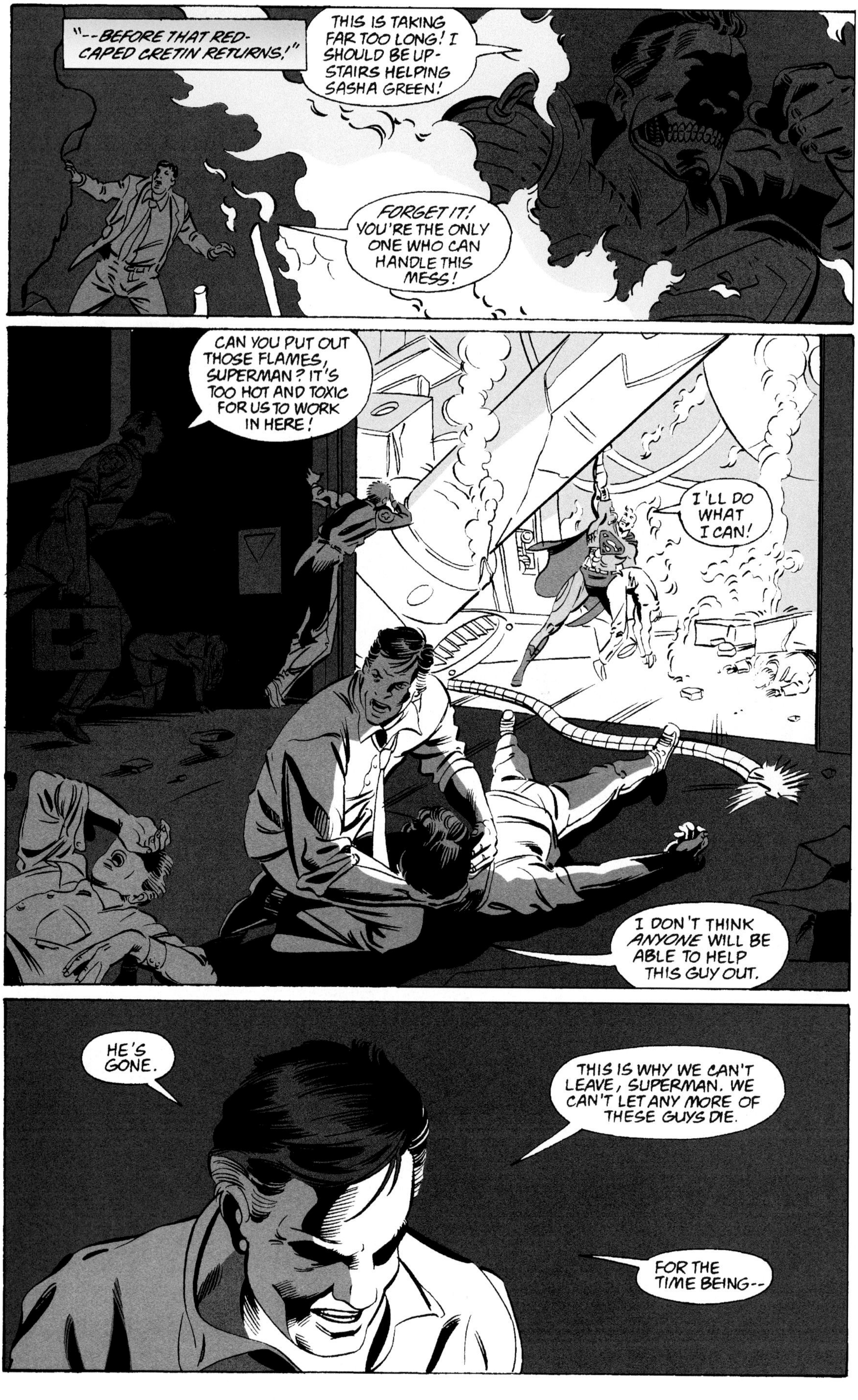
"--BEFORE THAT RED-CAPED CRETIN RETURNS!"
THIS IS TAKING FAR TOO LONG! I SHOULD BE UP-STAIRS HELPING SASHA GREEN!
FORGET IT! YOU'RE THE ONLY ONE WHO CAN HANDLE THIS MESS!
CAN YOU PUT OUT THOSE FLAMES, SUPERMAN? IT'S TOO HOT AND TOXIC FOR US TO WORK IN HERE!
I'LL DO WHAT I CAN!
I DON'T THINK ANYONE WILL BE ABLE TO HELP THIS GUY OUT.
HE'S GONE.
THIS IS WHY WE CAN'T LEAVE, SUPERMAN. WE CAN'T LET ANY MORE OF THESE GUYS DIE.
FOR THE TIME BEING--

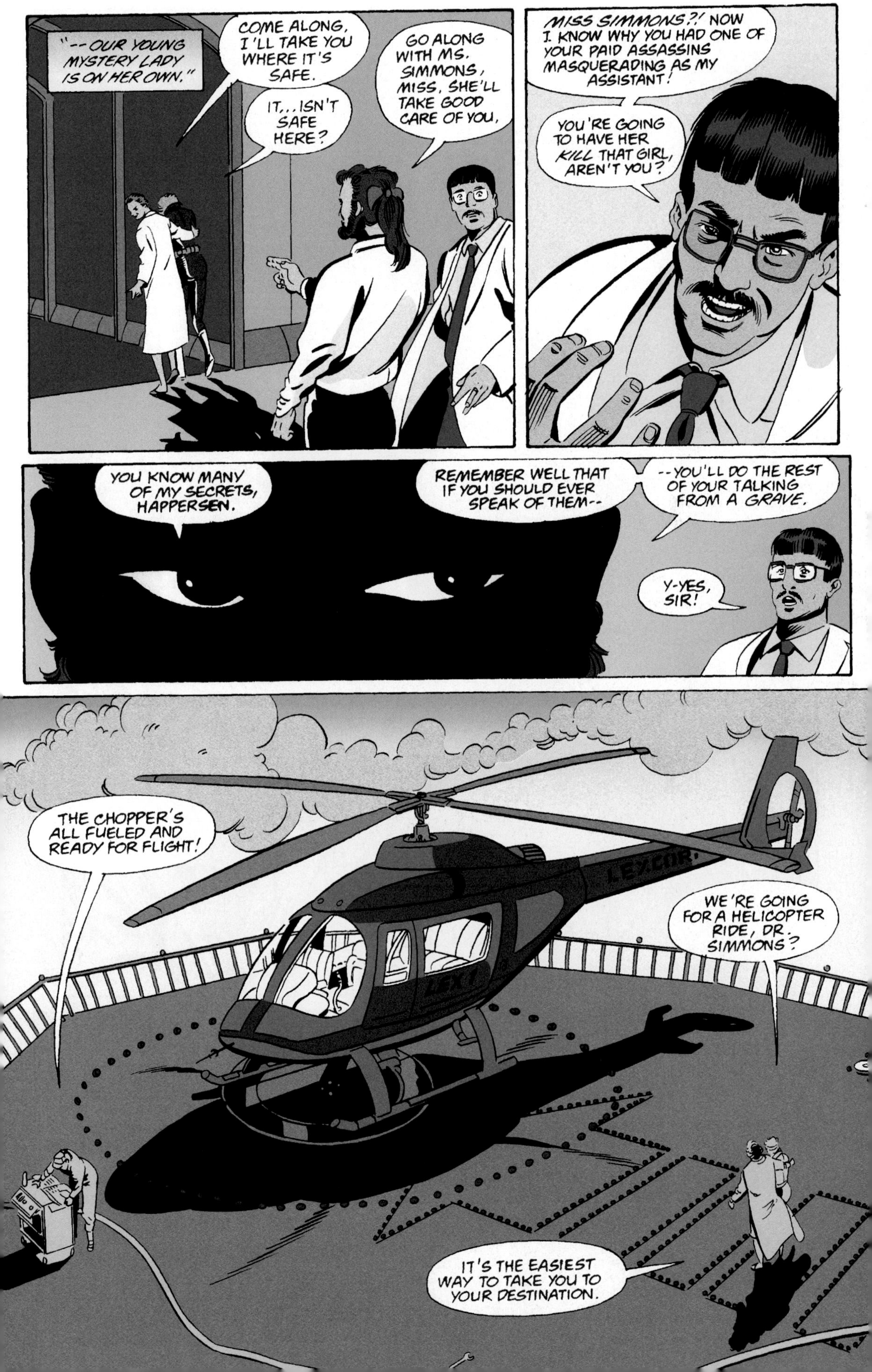
"--OUR YOUNG MYSTERY LADY IS ON HER OWN."
COME ALONG, I'LL TAKE YOU WHERE IT'S SAFE.
IT... ISN'T SAFE HERE?
GO ALONG WITH MS. SIMMONS, MISS. SHE'LL TAKE GOOD CARE OF YOU.
MISS SIMMONS?! NOW I KNOW WHY YOU HAD ONE OF YOUR PAID ASSASSINS MASQUERADING AS MY ASSISTANT!
YOU'RE GOING TO HAVE HER KILL THAT GIRL, AREN'T YOU?
YOU KNOW MANY OF MY SECRETS, HAPPERSEN.
REMEMBER WELL THAT IF YOU SHOULD EVER SPEAK OF THEM--
--YOU'LL DO THE REST OF YOUR TALKING FROM A GRAVE.
Y-YES, SIR!
THE CHOPPER'S ALL FUELED AND READY FOR FLIGHT!
LEXCOR
LEX 1
WE'RE GOING FOR A HELICOPTER RIDE, DR. SIMMONS?
IT'S THE EASIEST WAY TO TAKE YOU TO YOUR DESTINATION.

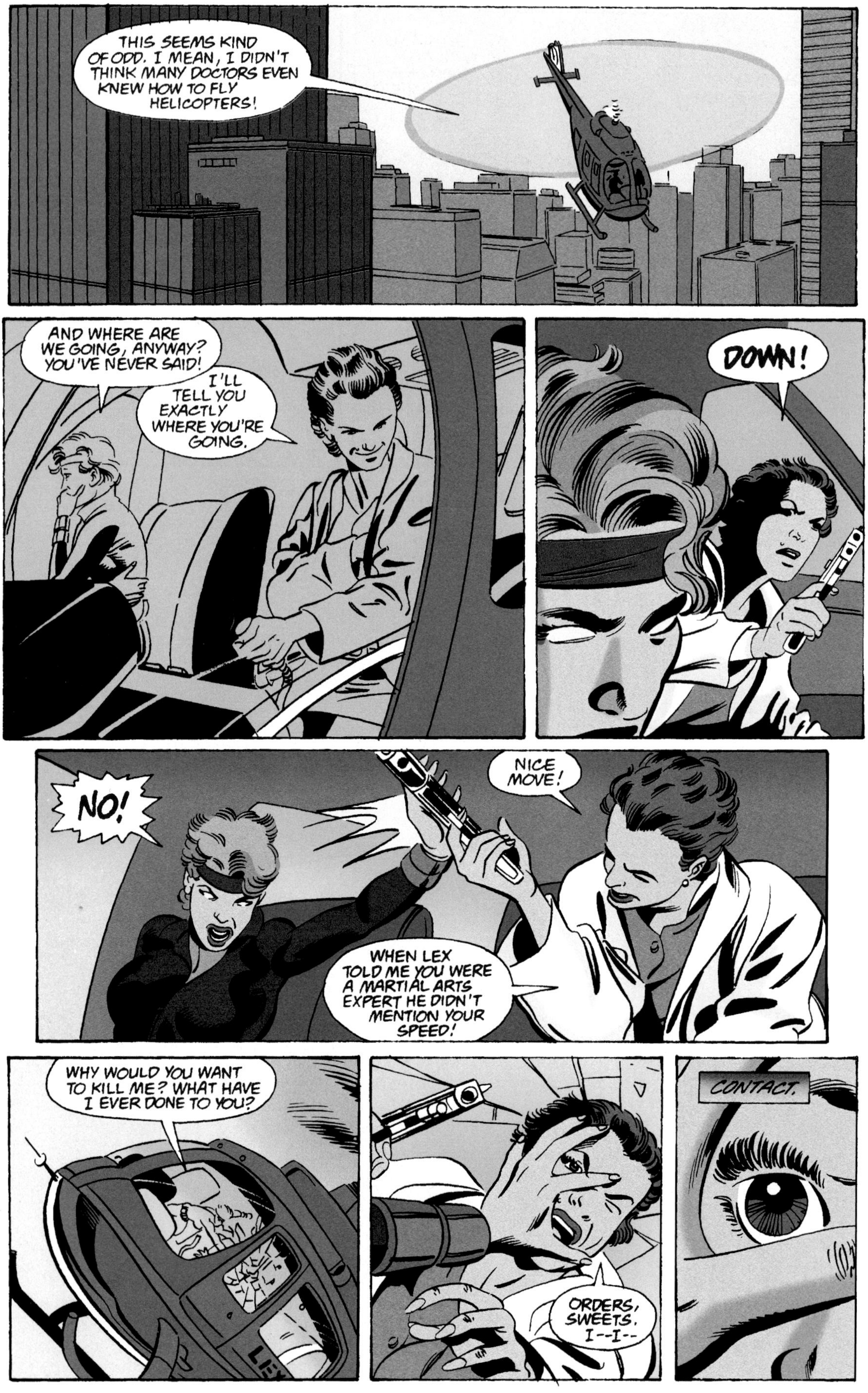

THIS SEEMS KIND OF ODD. I MEAN, I DIDN'T THINK MANY DOCTORS EVEN KNEW HOW TO FLY HELICOPTERS!
AND WHERE ARE WE GOING, ANYWAY? YOU'VE NEVER SAID!
I'LL TELL YOU EXACTLY WHERE YOU'RE GOING.
DOWN!
NO!
NICE MOVE!
WHEN LEX TOLD ME YOU WERE A MARTIAL ARTS EXPERT HE DIDN'T MENTION YOUR SPEED!
WHY WOULD YOU WANT TO KILL ME? WHAT HAVE I EVER DONE TO YOU?
ORDERS, SWEETS. I--I--
CONTACT.

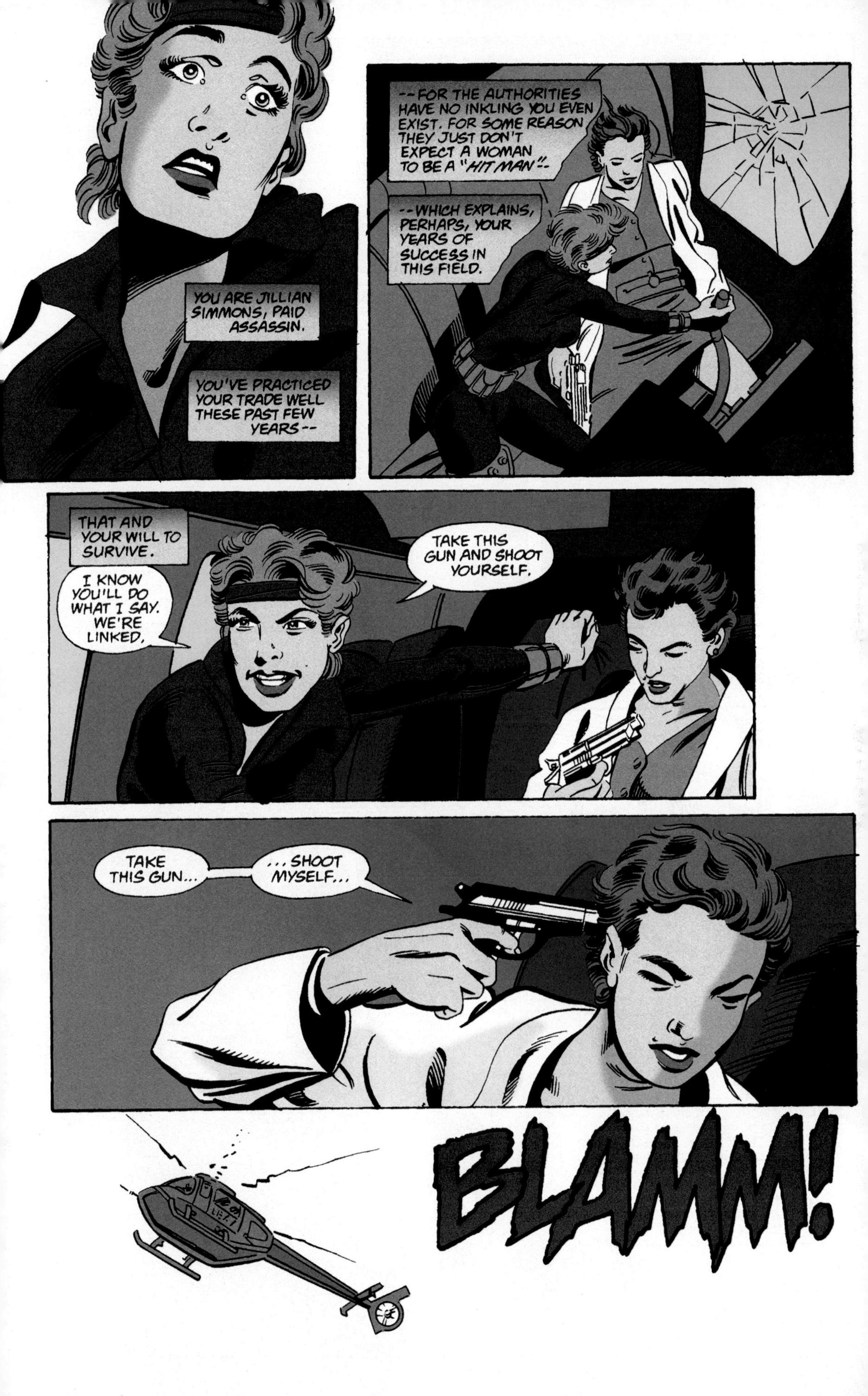
YOU ARE JILLIAN SIMMONS, PAID ASSASSIN.
YOU'VE PRACTICED YOUR TRADE WELL THESE PAST FEW YEARS --
-- FOR THE AUTHORITIES HAVE NO INKLING YOU EVEN EXIST. FOR SOME REASON THEY JUST DON'T EXPECT A WOMAN TO BE A "HIT MAN"!--
--WHICH EXPLAINS, PERHAPS, YOUR YEARS OF SUCCESS IN THIS FIELD.
THAT AND YOUR WILL TO SURVIVE.
I KNOW YOU'LL DO WHAT I SAY. WE'RE LINKED.
TAKE THIS GUN AND SHOOT YOURSELF.
TAKE THIS GUN...
...SHOOT MYSELF...
BLAMM!

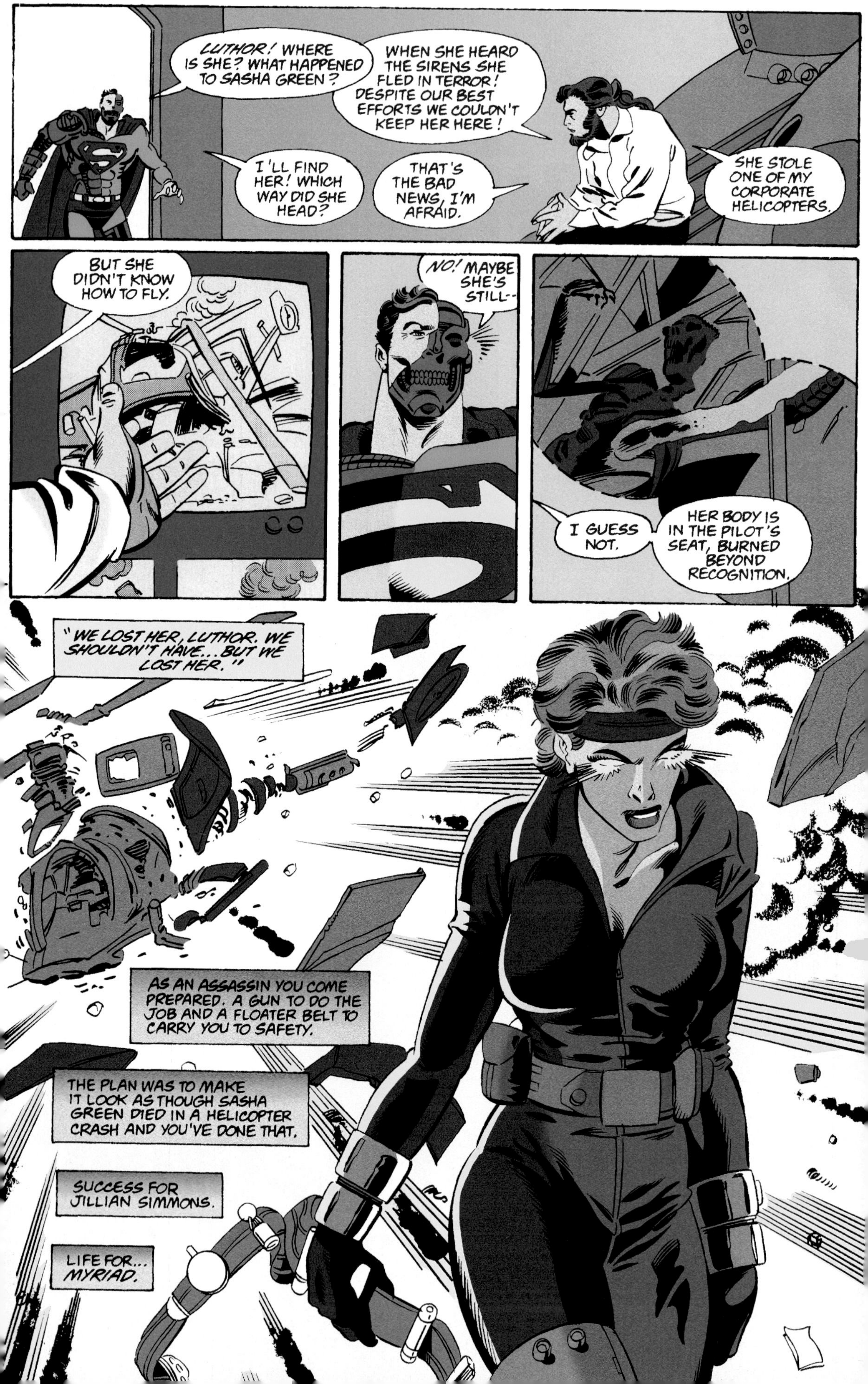
LUTHOR! WHERE IS SHE? WHAT HAPPENED TO SASHA GREEN?
WHEN SHE HEARD THE SIRENS SHE FLED IN TERROR! DESPITE OUR BEST EFFORTS WE COULDN'T KEEP HER HERE!
I'LL FIND HER! WHICH WAY DID SHE HEAD?
THAT'S THE BAD NEWS, I'M AFRAID.
SHE STOLE ONE OF MY CORPORATE HELICOPTERS.
BUT SHE DIDN'T KNOW HOW TO FLY.
NO! MAYBE SHE'S STILL--
I GUESS NOT.
HER BODY IS IN THE PILOT'S SEAT, BURNED BEYOND RECOGNITION.
"WE LOST HER, LUTHOR. WE SHOULDN'T HAVE... BUT WE LOST HER."
AS AN ASSASSIN YOU COME PREPARED. A GUN TO DO THE JOB AND A FLOATER BELT TO CARRY YOU TO SAFETY.
THE PLAN WAS TO MAKE IT LOOK AS THOUGH SASHA GREEN DIED IN A HELICOPTER CRASH AND YOU'VE DONE THAT.
SUCCESS FOR JILLIAN SIMMONS.
LIFE FOR... MYRIAD.

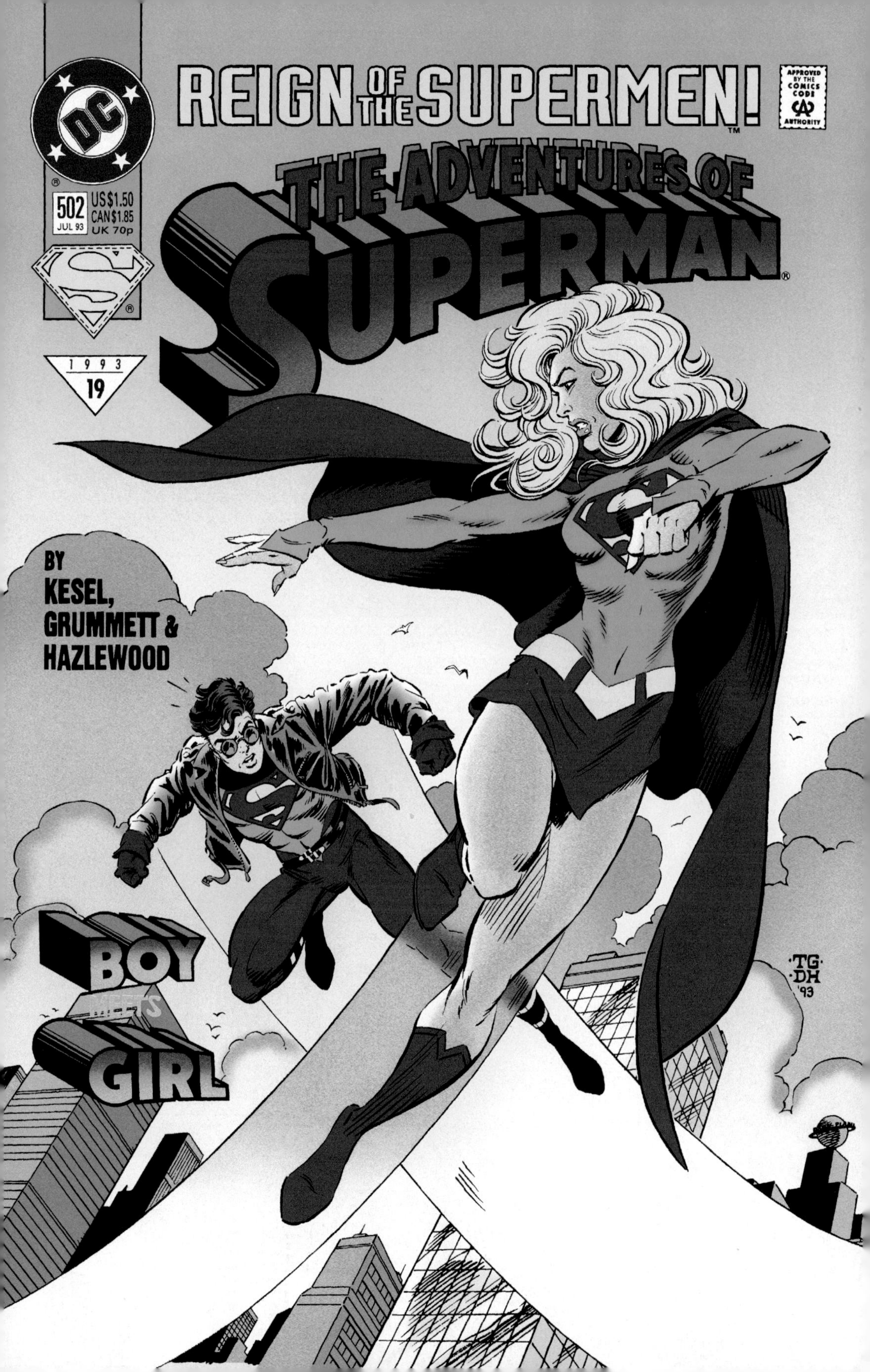
REIGN OF THE SUPERMEN!
APPROVED BY THE COMICS CODE AUTHORITY
DC
502 JUL 93 US$1.50 CAN$1.85 UK 70p
THE ADVENTURES OF SUPERMAN
1993 19
BY KESEL, GRUMMETT & HAZLEWOOD
BOY MEETS GIRL
TG DH '93

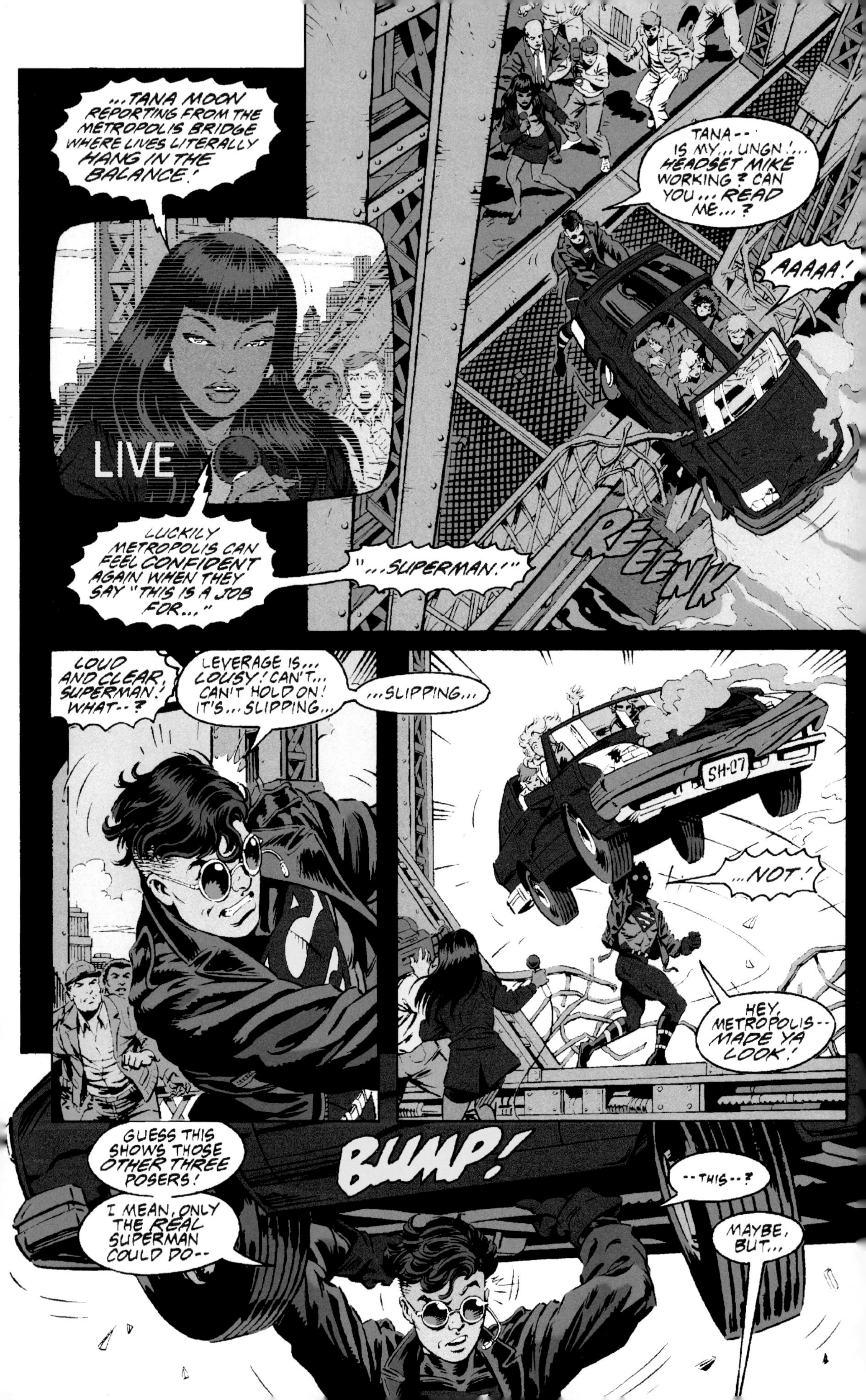
...TANA MOON REPORTING FROM THE METROPOLIS BRIDGE WHERE LIVES LITERALLY HANG IN THE BALANCE!
LIVE
LUCKILY METROPOLIS CAN FEEL CONFIDENT AGAIN WHEN THEY SAY "THIS IS A JOB FOR..."
"...SUPERMAN!"
TANA-- IS MY...UNGN!... HEADSET MIKE WORKING? CAN YOU...READ ME...?
AAAAA!
REEENK
LOUD AND CLEAR, SUPERMAN! WHAT--?
LEVERAGE IS... LOUSY! CAN'T... CAN'T HOLD ON! IT'S...SLIPPING...
...SLIPPING...
SH-07
...NOT!
HEY, METROPOLIS-- MADE YA LOOK!
BUMP!
GUESS THIS SHOWS THOSE OTHER THREE POSERS!
I MEAN, ONLY THE REAL SUPERMAN COULD DO--
--THIS--?
MAYBE, BUT...

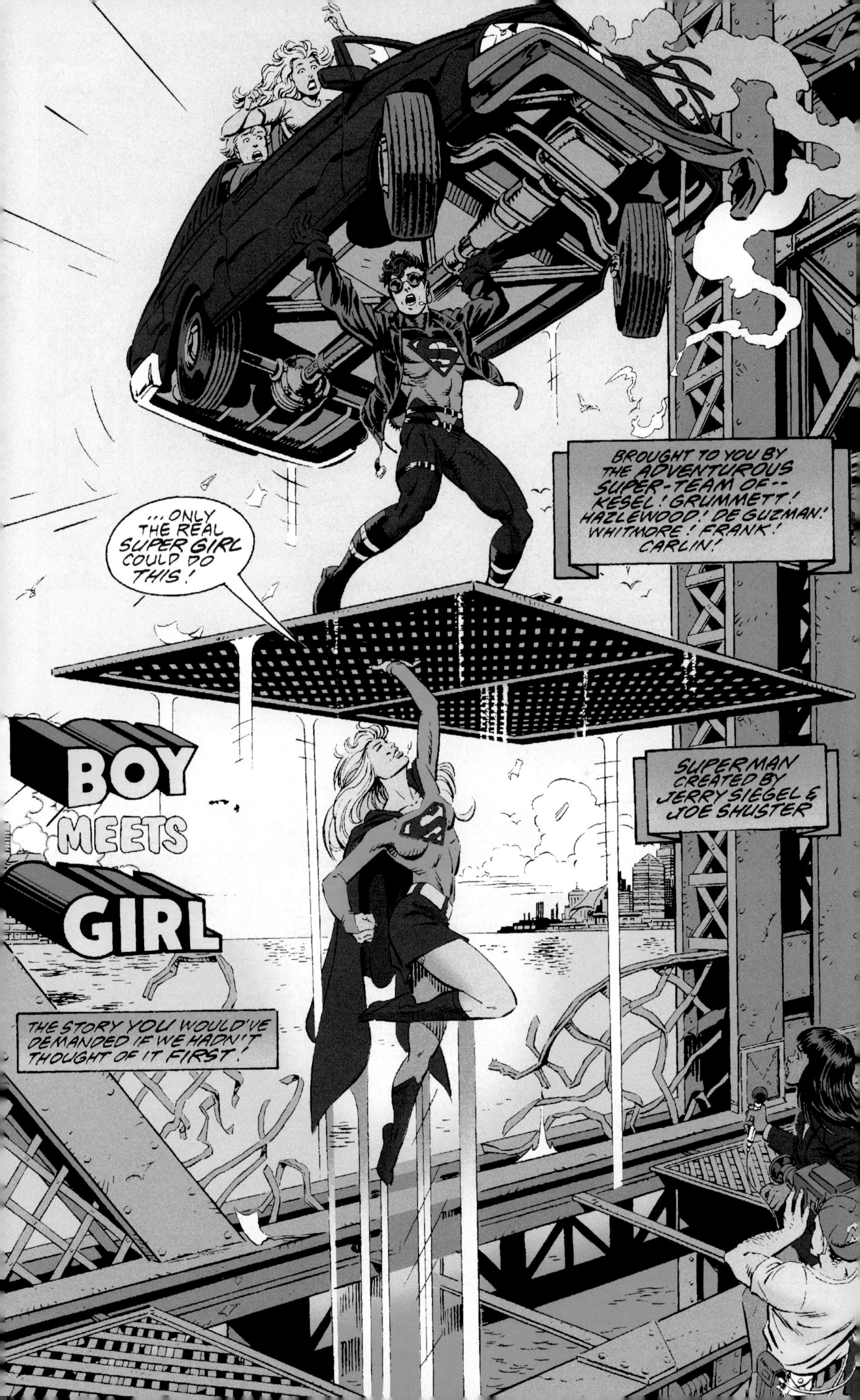
...ONLY THE REAL SUPER GIRL COULD DO THIS!
BROUGHT TO YOU BY THE ADVENTUROUS SUPER-TEAM OF-- KESEL! GRUMMETT! HAZLEWOOD! DE GUZMAN! WHITMORE! FRANK! CARLIN!
BOY MEETS GIRL
SUPERMAN CREATED BY JERRY SIEGEL & JOE SHUSTER
THE STORY YOU WOULD'VE DEMANDED IF WE HADN'T THOUGHT OF IT FIRST!

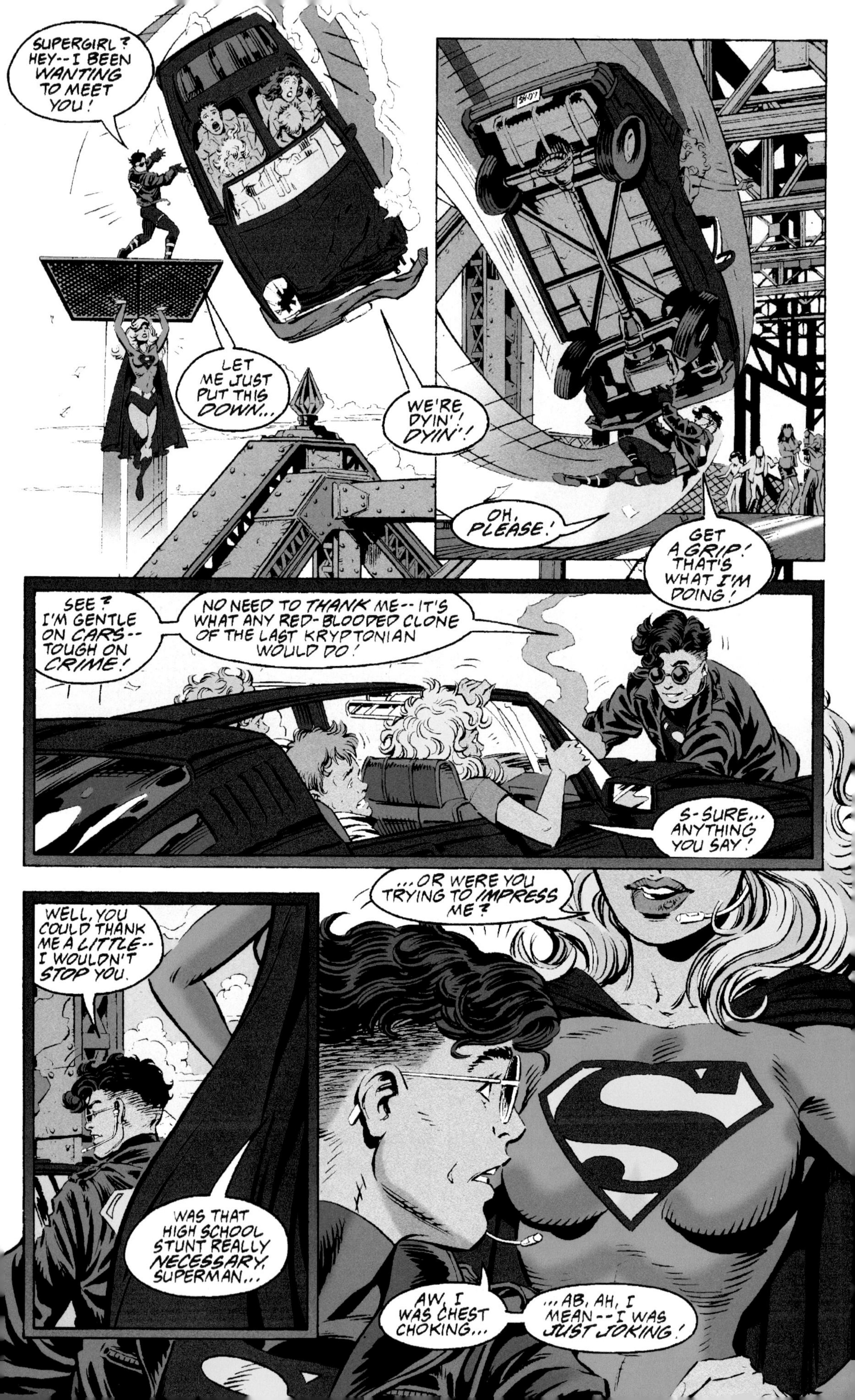
SUPERGIRL? HEY-- I BEEN WANTING TO MEET YOU!
LET ME JUST PUT THIS DOWN...
WE'RE DYIN'! DYIN'!
OH, PLEASE!
GET A GRIP! THAT'S WHAT I'M DOING!
SEE? I'M GENTLE ON CARS-- TOUGH ON CRIME!
NO NEED TO THANK ME-- IT'S WHAT ANY RED-BLOODED CLONE OF THE LAST KRYPTONIAN WOULD DO!
S-SURE... ANYTHING YOU SAY!
WELL, YOU COULD THANK ME A LITTLE-- I WOULDN'T STOP YOU.
...OR WERE YOU TRYING TO IMPRESS ME?
WAS THAT HIGH SCHOOL STUNT REALLY NECESSARY, SUPERMAN...
AW, I WAS CHEST CHOKING...
...AB, AH, I MEAN-- I WAS JUST JOKING!

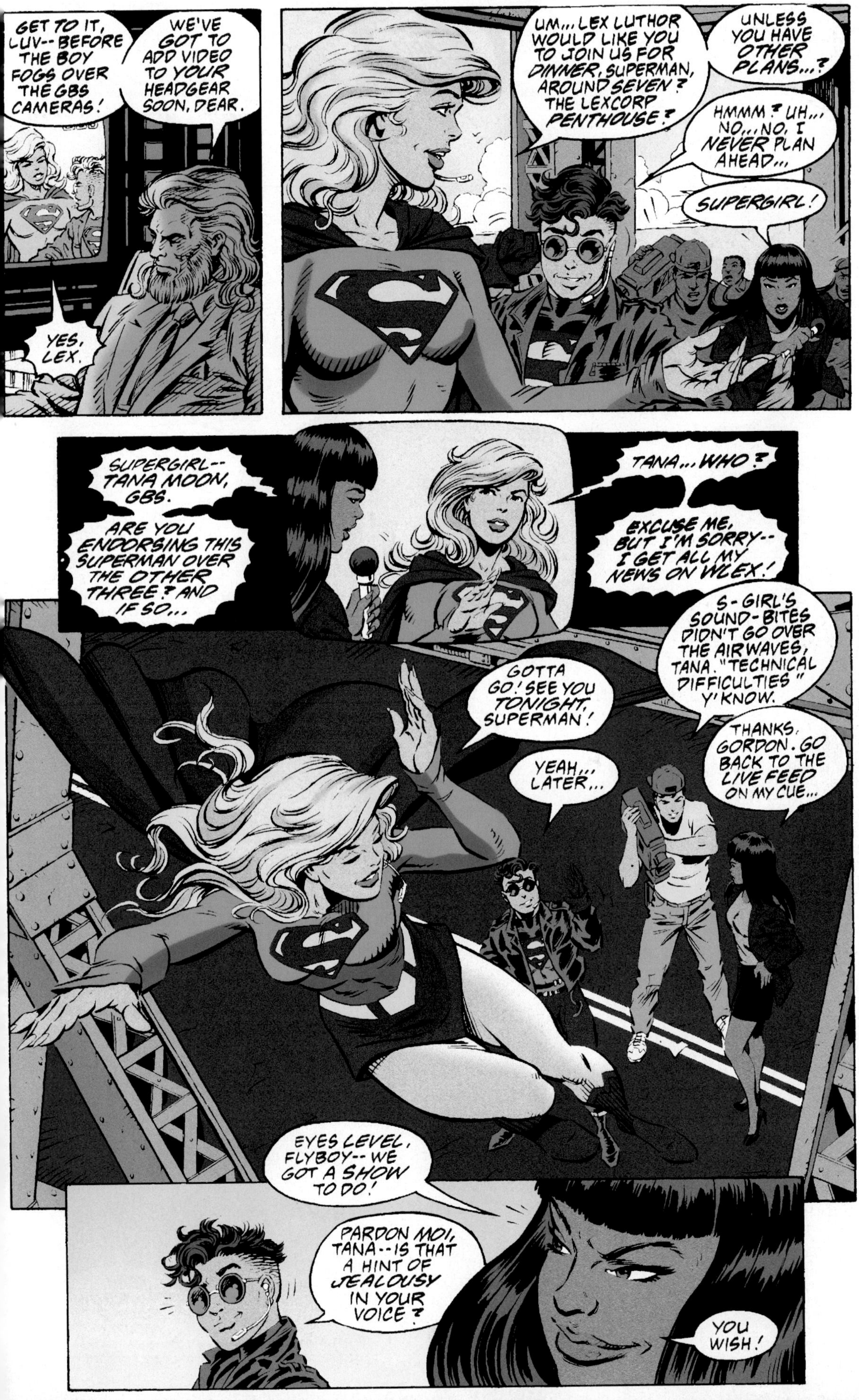
GET TO IT, LUV-- BEFORE THE BOY FOGS OVER THE GBS CAMERAS!
WE'VE GOT TO ADD VIDEO TO YOUR HEADGEAR SOON, DEAR.
YES, LEX.
UM... LEX LUTHOR WOULD LIKE YOU TO JOIN US FOR DINNER, SUPERMAN, AROUND SEVEN? THE LEXCORP PENTHOUSE?
UNLESS YOU HAVE OTHER PLANS...?
HMMM? UH... NO... NO, I NEVER PLAN AHEAD...
SUPERGIRL!
SUPERGIRL-- TANA MOON, GBS.
ARE YOU ENDORSING THIS SUPERMAN OVER THE OTHER THREE? AND IF SO...
TANA... WHO?
EXCUSE ME, BUT I'M SORRY-- I GET ALL MY NEWS ON WLEX!
GOTTA GO! SEE YOU TONIGHT, SUPERMAN!
S-GIRL'S SOUND-BITES DIDN'T GO OVER THE AIRWAVES, TANA. "TECHNICAL DIFFICULTIES" Y'KNOW.
YEAH... LATER...
THANKS, GORDON. GO BACK TO THE LIVE FEED ON MY CUE...
EYES LEVEL, FLYBOY-- WE GOT A SHOW TO DO!
PARDON MOI, TANA--IS THAT A HINT OF JEALOUSY IN YOUR VOICE?
YOU WISH!

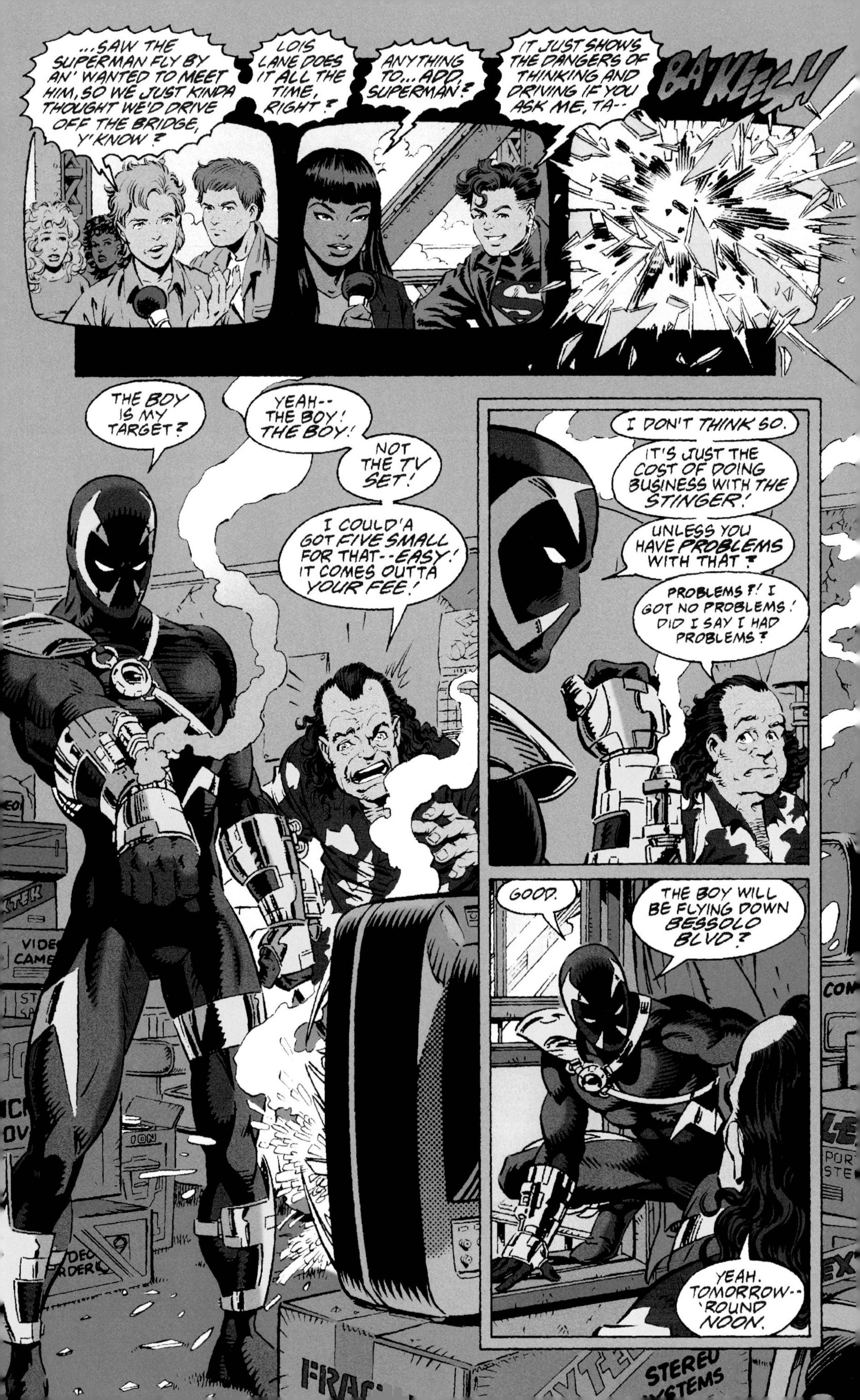
...SAW THE SUPERMAN FLY BY AN' WANTED TO MEET HIM, SO WE JUST KINDA THOUGHT WE'D DRIVE OFF THE BRIDGE, Y'KNOW?
LOIS LANE DOES IT ALL THE TIME, RIGHT?
ANYTHING TO... ADD, SUPERMAN?
IT JUST SHOWS THE DANGERS OF THINKING AND DRIVING IF YOU ASK ME, TA--
BA-KEESH
THE BOY IS MY TARGET?
YEAH-- THE BOY! THE BOY!
NOT THE TV SET!
I COULD'A GOT FIVE SMALL FOR THAT--EASY! IT COMES OUTTA YOUR FEE!
I DON'T THINK SO.
IT'S JUST THE COST OF DOING BUSINESS WITH THE STINGER!
UNLESS YOU HAVE PROBLEMS WITH THAT?
PROBLEMS?! I GOT NO PROBLEMS! DID I SAY I HAD PROBLEMS?
GOOD.
THE BOY WILL BE FLYING DOWN BESSOLO BLVD?
YEAH. TOMORROW-- 'ROUND NOON.
STEREO SYSTEMS

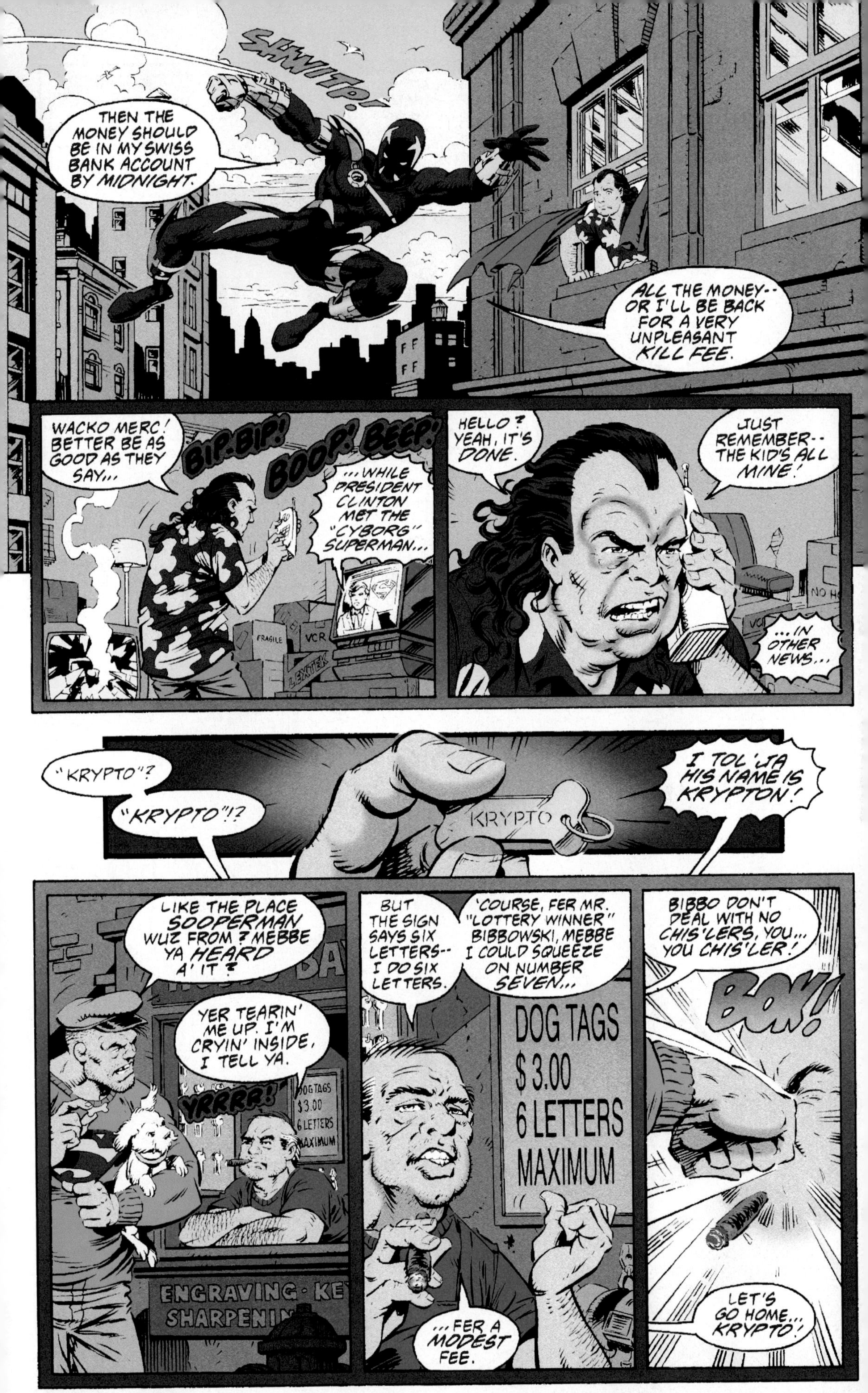
SHNITP!
THEN THE MONEY SHOULD BE IN MY SWISS BANK ACCOUNT BY MIDNIGHT.
ALL THE MONEY-- OR I'LL BE BACK FOR A VERY UNPLEASANT KILL FEE.
WACKO MERC! BETTER BE AS GOOD AS THEY SAY...
BIP-BIP! BOOP! BEEP!
...WHILE PRESIDENT CLINTON MET THE "CYBORG" SUPERMAN...
FRAGILE
VCR
LEXTEK
HELLO? YEAH, IT'S DONE.
JUST REMEMBER-- THE KID'S ALL MINE!
...IN OTHER NEWS...
"KRYPTO"?
"KRYPTO"!?
KRYPTO
I TOL'JA HIS NAME IS KRYPTON!
LIKE THE PLACE SOOPERMAN WUZ FROM? MEBBE YA HEARD A' IT?
YER TEARIN' ME UP. I'M CRYIN' INSIDE, I TELL YA.
YRRRR!
DOG TAGS $3.00 6 LETTERS MAXIMUM
ENGRAVING · KE
SHARPENIN
BUT THE SIGN SAYS SIX LETTERS-- I DO SIX LETTERS.
'COURSE, FER MR. "LOTTERY WINNER" BIBBOWSKI, MEBBE I COULD SQUEEZE ON NUMBER SEVEN...
DOG TAGS
$ 3.00
6 LETTERS
MAXIMUM
...FER A MODEST FEE.
BIBBO DON'T DEAL WITH NO CHIS'LERS, YOU... YOU CHIS'LER!
BOK!
LET'S GO HOME... KRYPTO!

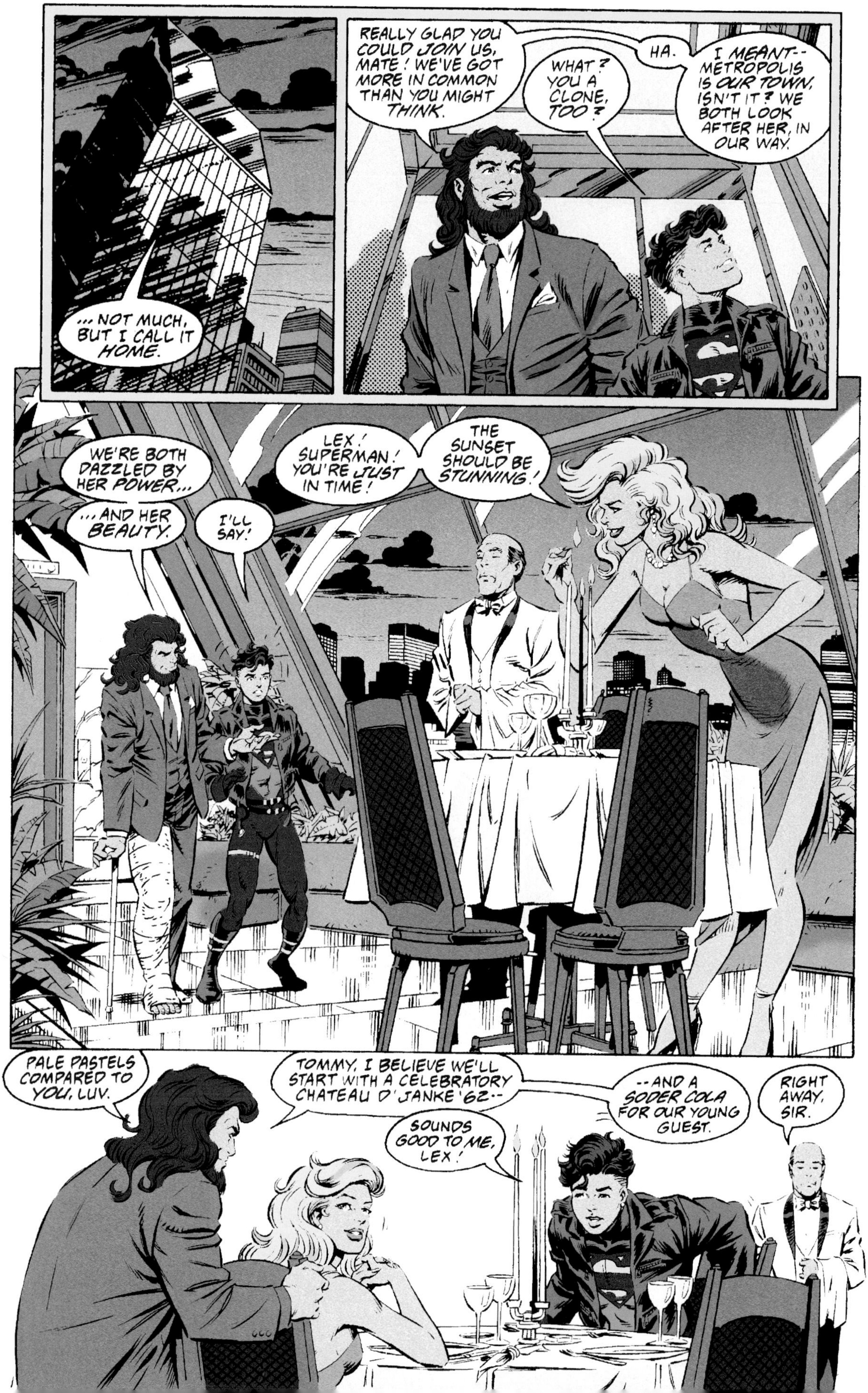
...NOT MUCH, BUT I CALL IT HOME.
REALLY GLAD YOU COULD JOIN US, MATE! WE'VE GOT MORE IN COMMON THAN YOU MIGHT THINK.
WHAT? YOU A CLONE, TOO?
HA.
I MEANT-- METROPOLIS IS OUR TOWN, ISN'T IT? WE BOTH LOOK AFTER HER, IN OUR WAY.
WE'RE BOTH DAZZLED BY HER POWER...
...AND HER BEAUTY.
I'LL SAY!
LEX! SUPERMAN! YOU'RE JUST IN TIME!
THE SUNSET SHOULD BE STUNNING!
PALE PASTELS COMPARED TO YOU, LUV.
TOMMY, I BELIEVE WE'LL START WITH A CELEBRATORY CHATEAU D'JANKE '62--
SOUNDS GOOD TO ME, LEX!
--AND A SODER COLA FOR OUR YOUNG GUEST.
RIGHT AWAY, SIR.

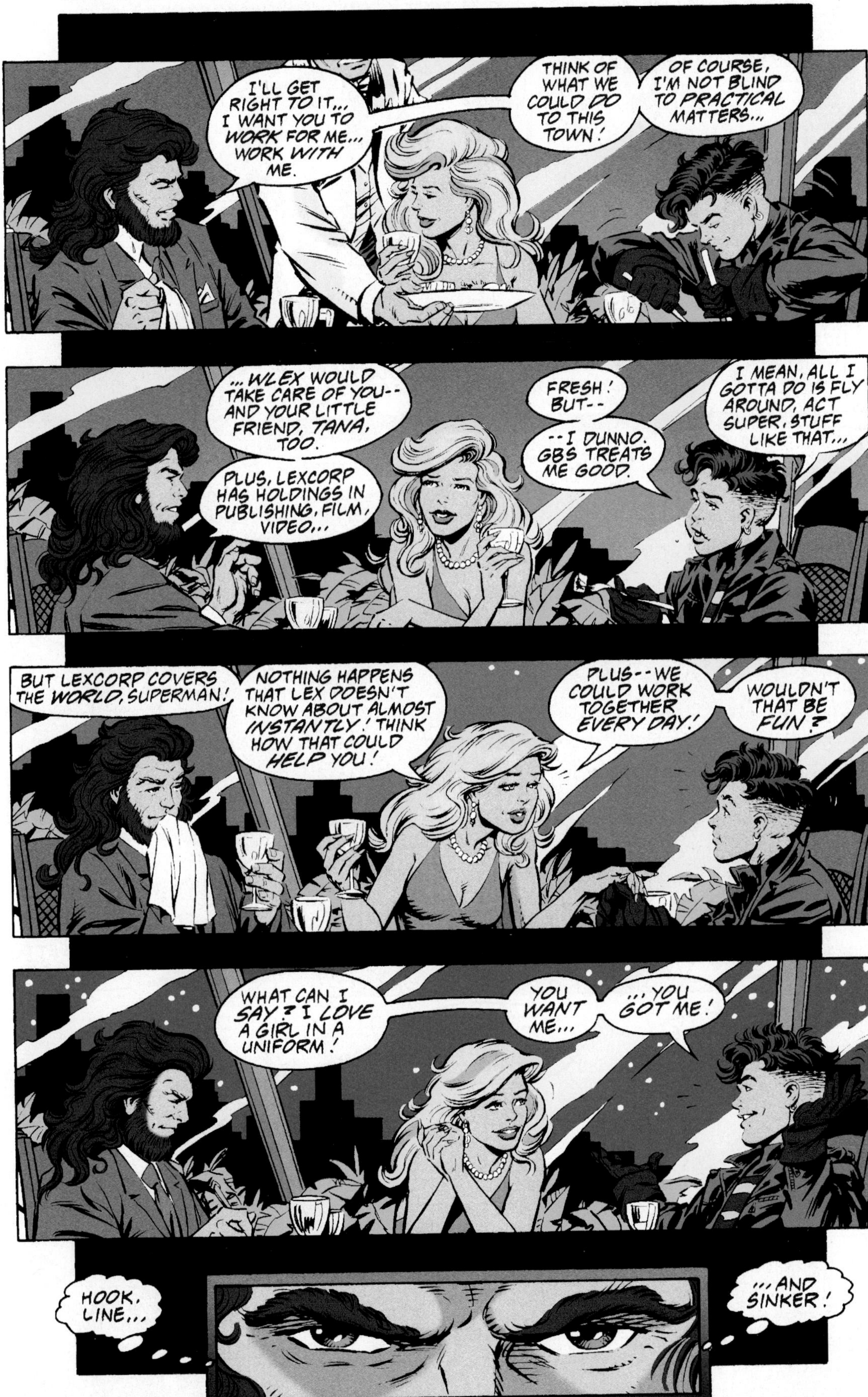

I'LL GET RIGHT TO IT... I WANT YOU TO WORK FOR ME... WORK WITH ME.
THINK OF WHAT WE COULD DO TO THIS TOWN!
OF COURSE, I'M NOT BLIND TO PRACTICAL MATTERS...
...WLEX WOULD TAKE CARE OF YOU-- AND YOUR LITTLE FRIEND, TANA, TOO.
PLUS, LEXCORP HAS HOLDINGS IN PUBLISHING, FILM, VIDEO...
FRESH! BUT--
--I DUNNO. GBS TREATS ME GOOD.
I MEAN, ALL I GOTTA DO IS FLY AROUND, ACT SUPER, STUFF LIKE THAT...
BUT LEXCORP COVERS THE WORLD, SUPERMAN!
NOTHING HAPPENS THAT LEX DOESN'T KNOW ABOUT ALMOST INSTANTLY! THINK HOW THAT COULD HELP YOU!
PLUS--WE COULD WORK TOGETHER EVERY DAY!
WOULDN'T THAT BE FUN?
WHAT CAN I SAY? I LOVE A GIRL IN A UNIFORM!
YOU WANT ME...
...YOU GOT ME!
HOOK, LINE...
...AND SINKER!

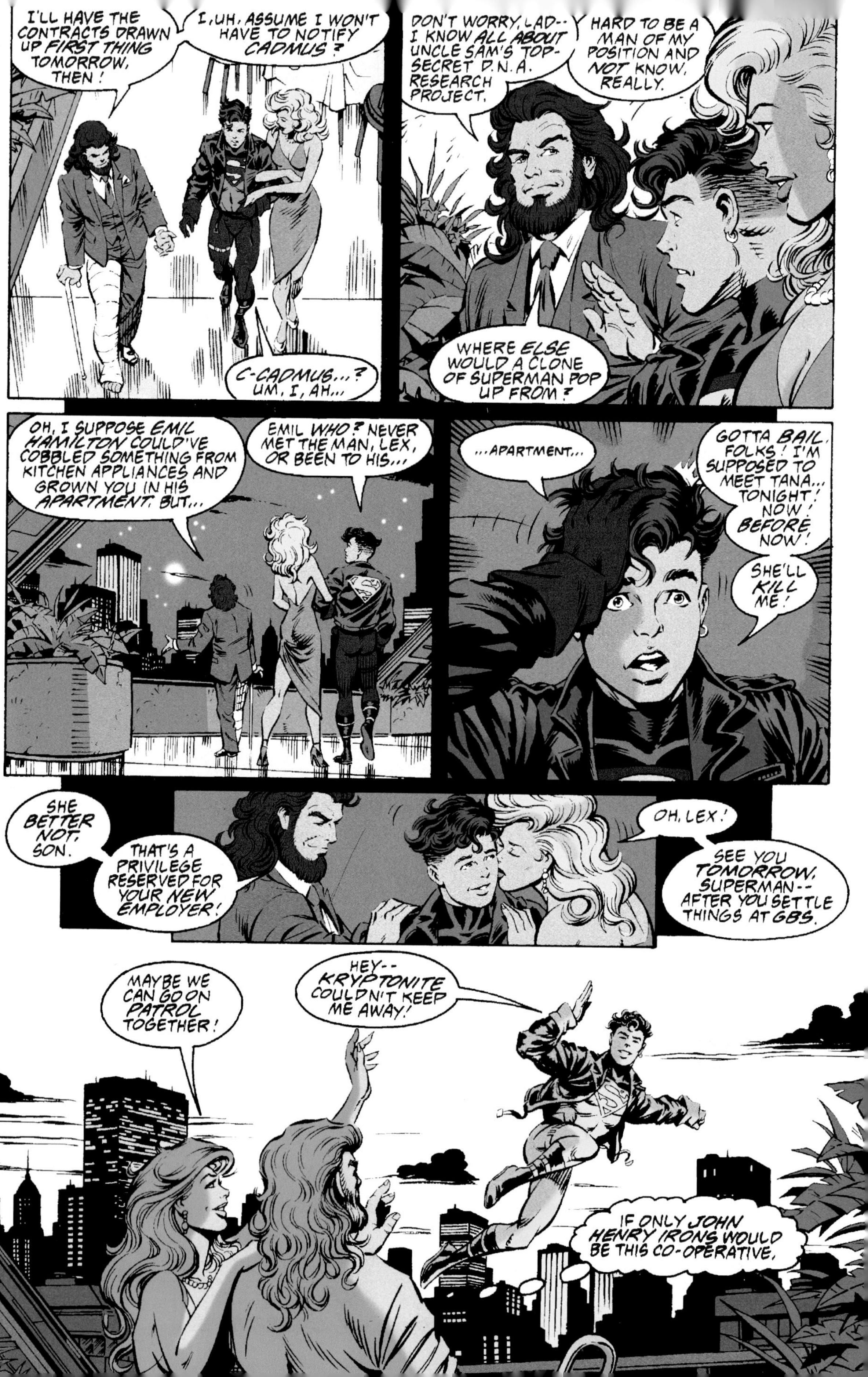
I'LL HAVE THE CONTRACTS DRAWN UP FIRST THING TOMORROW, THEN!
I, UH, ASSUME I WON'T HAVE TO NOTIFY CADMUS?
C-CADMUS...? UM, I, AH...
DON'T WORRY, LAD-- I KNOW ALL ABOUT UNCLE SAM'S TOP-SECRET D.N.A. RESEARCH PROJECT.
HARD TO BE A MAN OF MY POSITION AND NOT KNOW, REALLY.
WHERE ELSE WOULD A CLONE OF SUPERMAN POP UP FROM?
OH, I SUPPOSE EMIL HAMILTON COULD'VE COBBLED SOMETHING FROM KITCHEN APPLIANCES AND GROWN YOU IN HIS APARTMENT. BUT...
EMIL WHO? NEVER MET THE MAN, LEX, OR BEEN TO HIS...
...APARTMENT...
GOTTA BAIL, FOLKS! I'M SUPPOSED TO MEET TANA... TONIGHT! NOW! BEFORE NOW!
SHE'LL KILL ME!
SHE BETTER NOT, SON.
THAT'S A PRIVILEGE RESERVED FOR YOUR NEW EMPLOYER!
OH, LEX!
SEE YOU TOMORROW, SUPERMAN-- AFTER YOU SETTLE THINGS AT GBS.
MAYBE WE CAN GO ON PATROL TOGETHER!
HEY-- KRYPTONITE COULDN'T KEEP ME AWAY!
IF ONLY JOHN HENRY IRONS WOULD BE THIS CO-OPERATIVE.

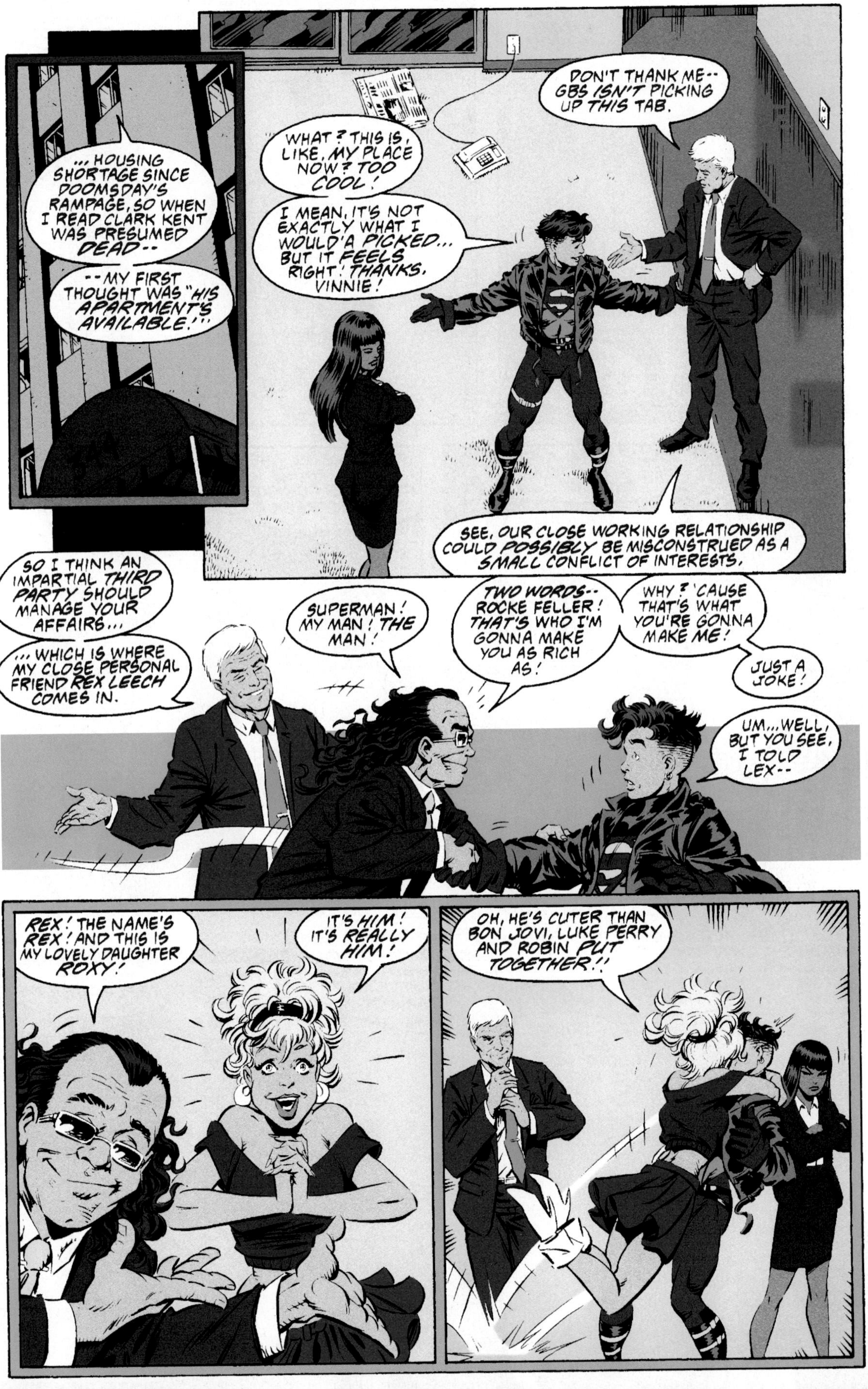
...HOUSING SHORTAGE SINCE DOOMSDAY'S RAMPAGE, SO WHEN I READ CLARK KENT WAS PRESUMED DEAD--
--MY FIRST THOUGHT WAS "HIS APARTMENT'S AVAILABLE!"
WHAT? THIS IS, LIKE, MY PLACE NOW? TOO COOL!
I MEAN, IT'S NOT EXACTLY WHAT I WOULD'A PICKED... BUT IT FEELS RIGHT! THANKS, VINNIE!
DON'T THANK ME-- GBS ISN'T PICKING UP THIS TAB.
SEE, OUR CLOSE WORKING RELATIONSHIP COULD POSSIBLY BE MISCONSTRUED AS A SMALL CONFLICT OF INTERESTS.
SO I THINK AN IMPARTIAL THIRD PARTY SHOULD MANAGE YOUR AFFAIRS...
...WHICH IS WHERE MY CLOSE PERSONAL FRIEND REX LEECH COMES IN.
SUPERMAN! MY MAN! THE MAN!
TWO WORDS-- ROCKE FELLER! THAT'S WHO I'M GONNA MAKE YOU AS RICH AS!
WHY? 'CAUSE THAT'S WHAT YOU'RE GONNA MAKE ME!
JUST A JOKE!
UM...WELL, BUT YOU SEE, I TOLD LEX--
REX! THE NAME'S REX! AND THIS IS MY LOVELY DAUGHTER ROXY!
IT'S HIM! IT'S REALLY HIM!
OH, HE'S CUTER THAN BON JOVI, LUKE PERRY AND ROBIN PUT TOGETHER!!

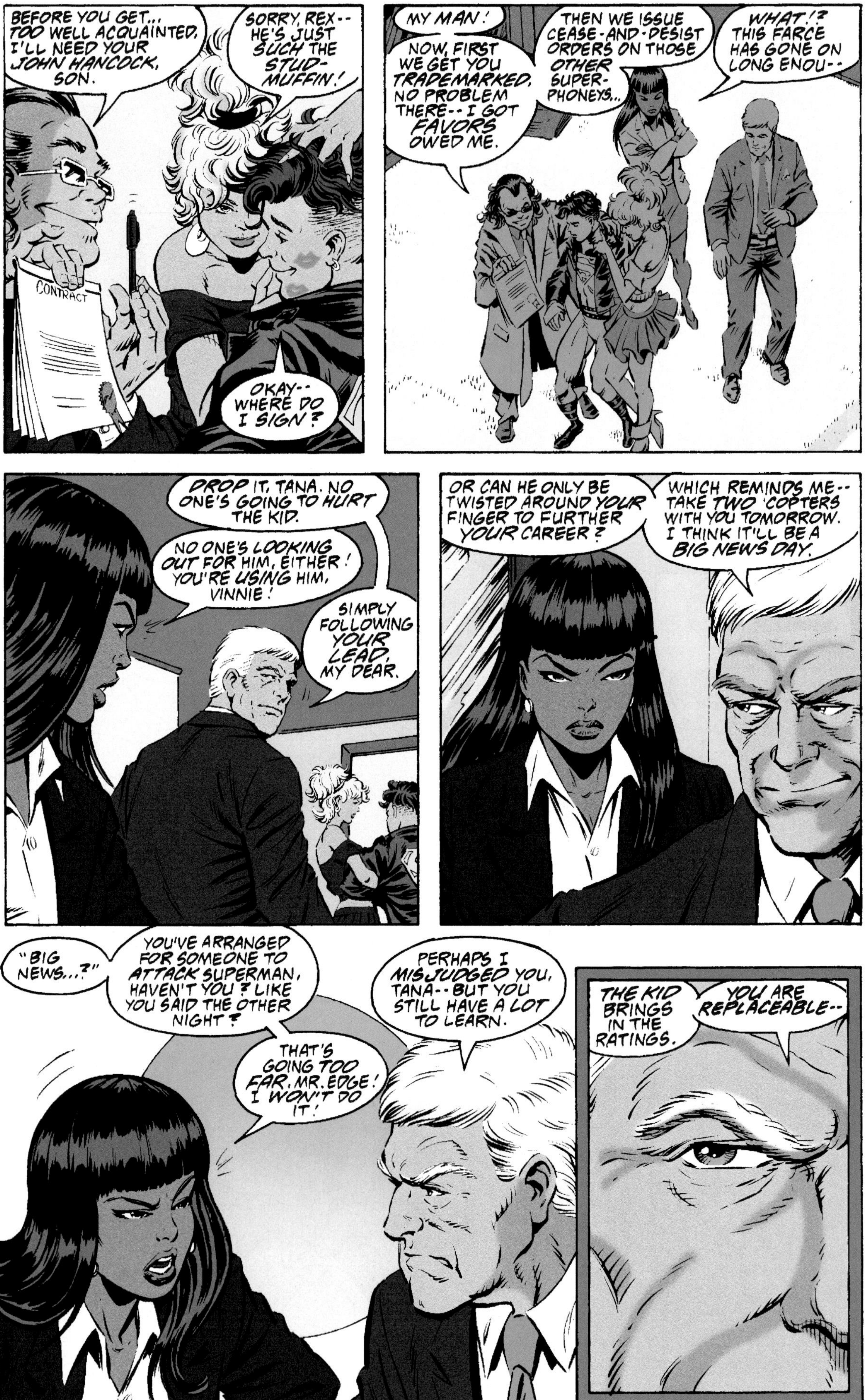
BEFORE YOU GET... TOO WELL ACQUAINTED, I'LL NEED YOUR JOHN HANCOCK, SON.
SORRY, REX-- HE'S JUST SUCH THE STUD-MUFFIN!
CONTRACT
OKAY-- WHERE DO I SIGN?
MY MAN!
NOW, FIRST WE GET YOU TRADEMARKED, NO PROBLEM THERE-- I GOT FAVORS OWED ME.
THEN WE ISSUE CEASE-AND-DESIST ORDERS ON THOSE OTHER SUPER-PHONEYS...
WHAT!? THIS FARCE HAS GONE ON LONG ENOU--
DROP IT, TANA. NO ONE'S GOING TO HURT THE KID.
NO ONE'S LOOKING OUT FOR HIM, EITHER! YOU'RE USING HIM, VINNIE!
SIMPLY FOLLOWING YOUR LEAD, MY DEAR.
OR CAN HE ONLY BE TWISTED AROUND YOUR FINGER TO FURTHER YOUR CAREER?
WHICH REMINDS ME-- TAKE TWO 'COPTERS WITH YOU TOMORROW. I THINK IT'LL BE A BIG NEWS DAY.
"BIG NEWS...?"
YOU'VE ARRANGED FOR SOMEONE TO ATTACK SUPERMAN, HAVEN'T YOU? LIKE YOU SAID THE OTHER NIGHT?
THAT'S GOING TOO FAR, MR. EDGE! I WON'T DO IT!
PERHAPS I MISJUDGED YOU, TANA-- BUT YOU STILL HAVE A LOT TO LEARN.
THE KID BRINGS IN THE RATINGS.
YOU ARE REPLACEABLE--

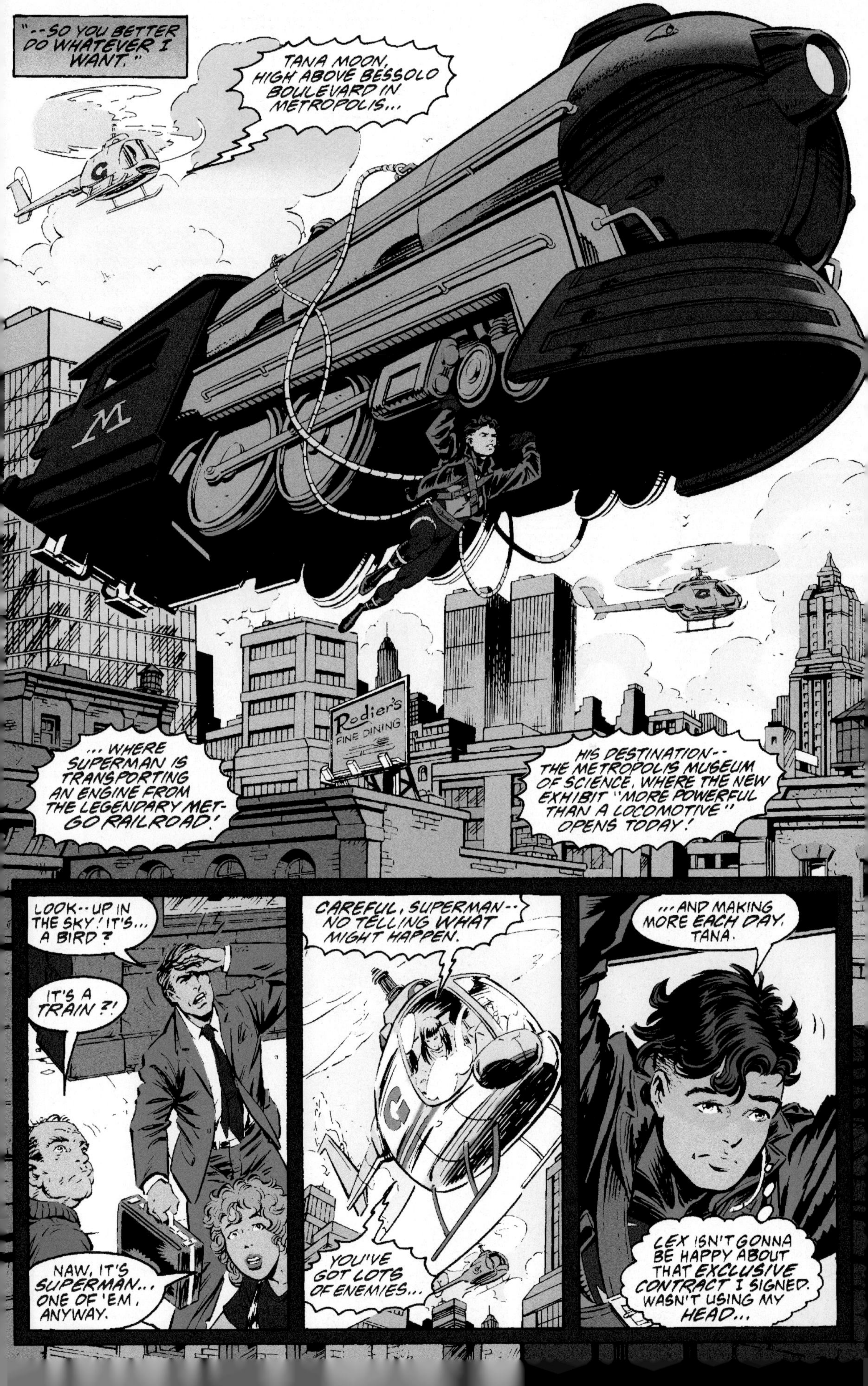
"--SO YOU BETTER DO WHATEVER I WANT."
TANA MOON, HIGH ABOVE BESSOLO BOULEVARD IN METROPOLIS...
... WHERE SUPERMAN IS TRANSPORTING AN ENGINE FROM THE LEGENDARY MET-GO RAILROAD!
HIS DESTINATION-- THE METROPOLIS MUSEUM OF SCIENCE, WHERE THE NEW EXHIBIT "MORE POWERFUL THAN A LOCOMOTIVE" OPENS TODAY!
Rodier's FINE DINING
LOOK--UP IN THE SKY! IT'S... A BIRD?
IT'S A TRAIN?!
NAW, IT'S SUPERMAN... ONE OF 'EM, ANYWAY.
CAREFUL, SUPERMAN-- NO TELLING WHAT MIGHT HAPPEN.
YOU'VE GOT LOTS OF ENEMIES...
...AND MAKING MORE EACH DAY, TANA.
LEX ISN'T GONNA BE HAPPY ABOUT THAT EXCLUSIVE CONTRACT I SIGNED. WASN'T USING MY HEAD...

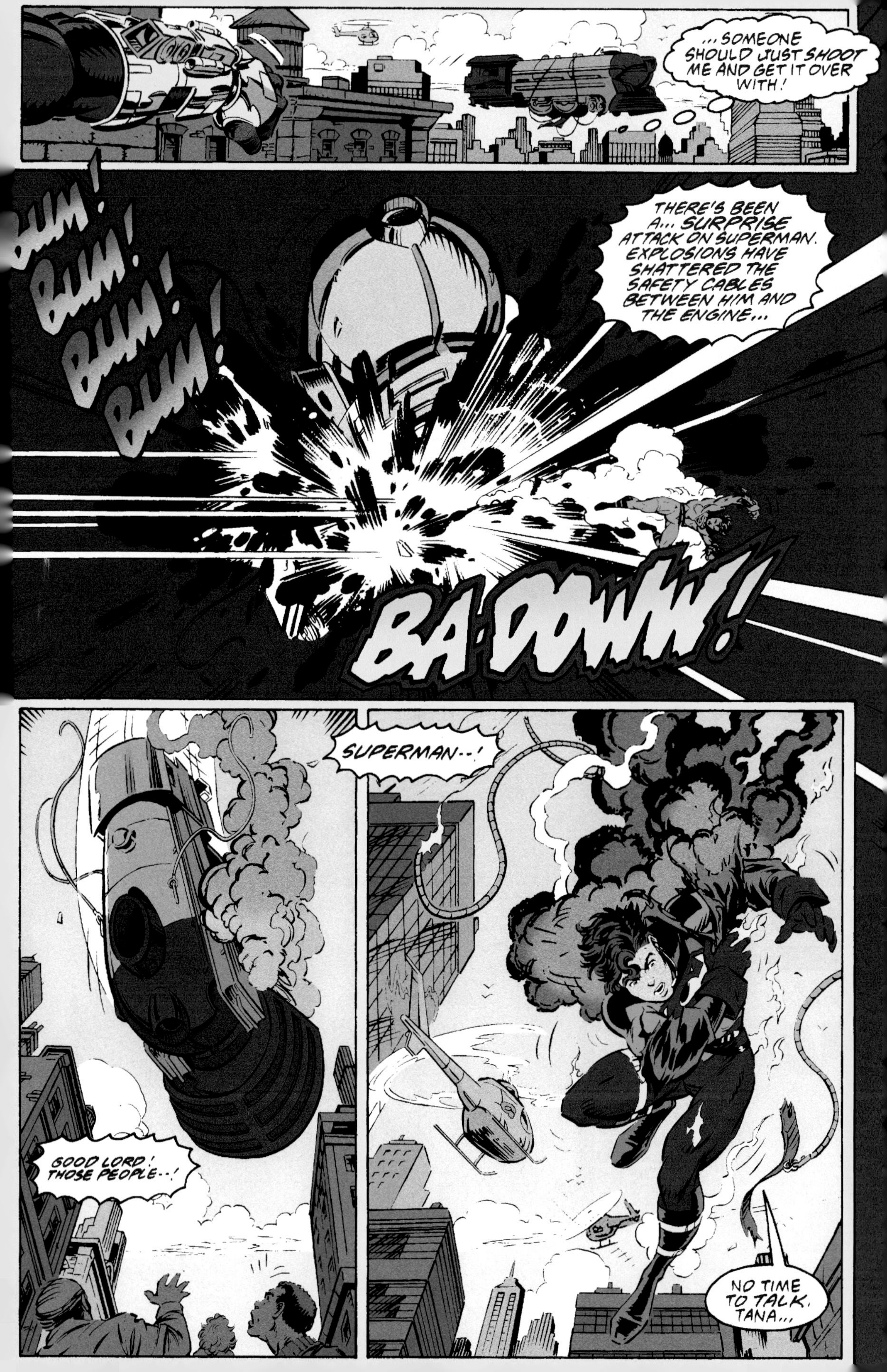
...SOMEONE SHOULD JUST SHOOT ME AND GET IT OVER WITH!
BLIM! BLIM! BLIM! BLIM!
THERE'S BEEN A... SURPRISE ATTACK ON SUPERMAN. EXPLOSIONS HAVE SHATTERED THE SAFETY CABLES BETWEEN HIM AND THE ENGINE...
BA-DOWW!
GOOD LORD! THOSE PEOPLE--!
SUPERMAN--!
NO TIME TO TALK, TANA...

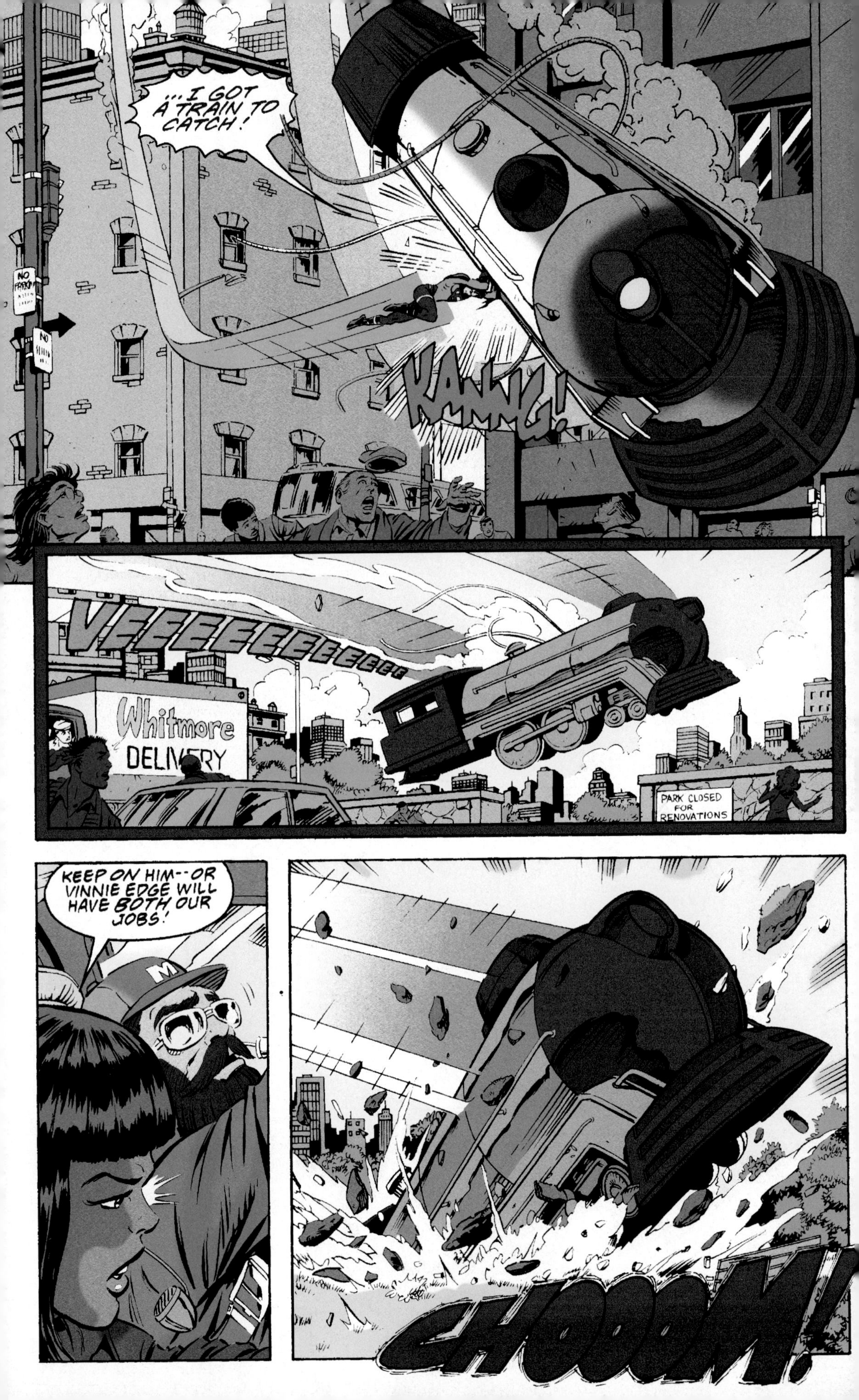
...I GOT A TRAIN TO CATCH!
NO PARKING
KANNG!
VEEEEEEEEEEEEE
Whitmore DELIVERY
PARK CLOSED FOR RENOVATIONS
KEEP ON HIM--OR VINNIE EDGE WILL HAVE BOTH OUR JOBS!
CHOOOM!!

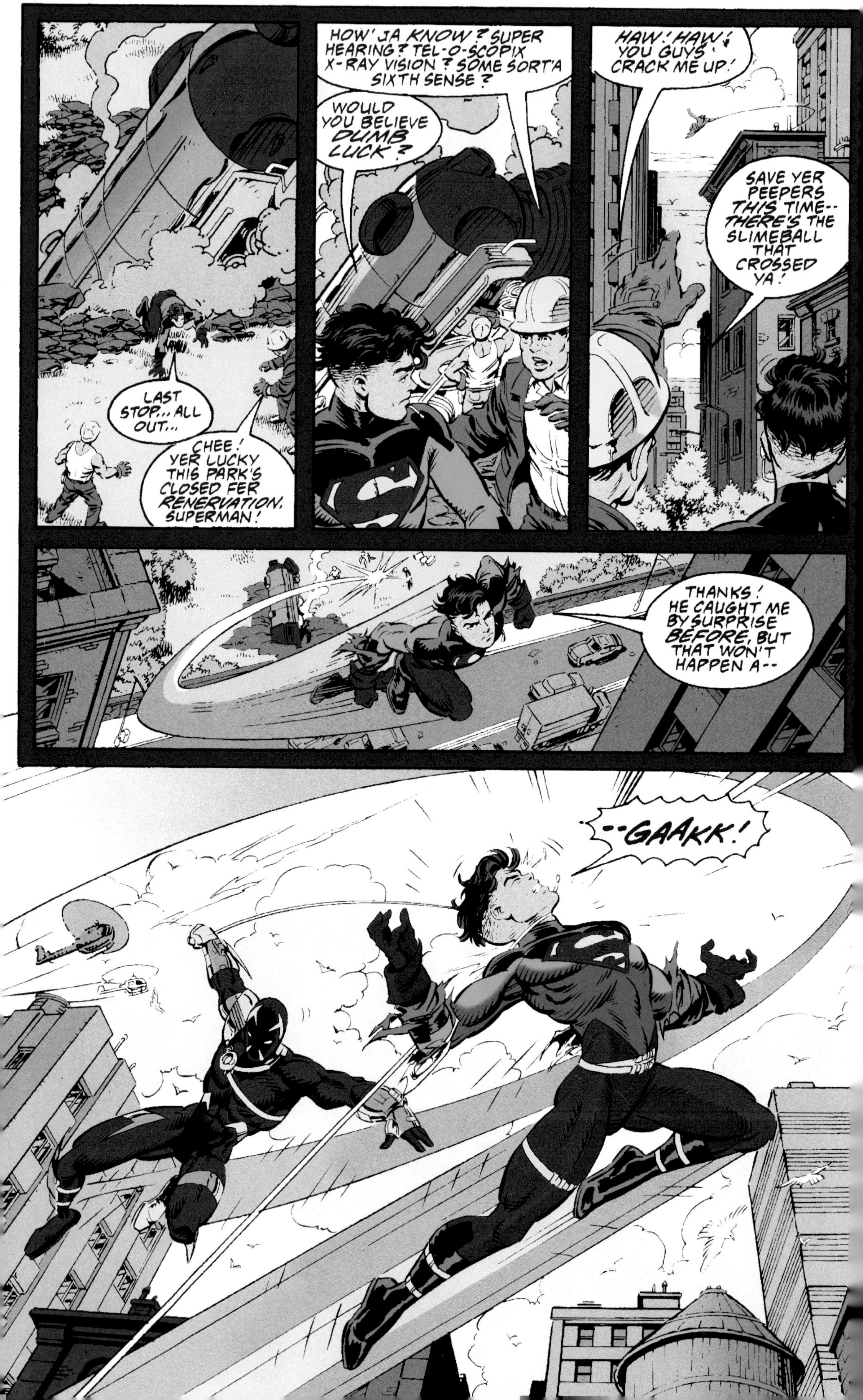
LAST STOP... ALL OUT...
CHEE! YER LUCKY THIS PARK'S CLOSED FER RENERVATION, SUPERMAN!
HOW'JA KNOW? SUPER HEARING? TEL-O-SCOPIX X-RAY VISION? SOME SORT'A SIXTH SENSE?
WOULD YOU BELIEVE DUMB LUCK?
HAW! HAW! YOU GUYS CRACK ME UP!
SAVE YER PEEPERS THIS TIME-- THERE'S THE SLIMEBALL THAT CROSSED YA!
THANKS! HE CAUGHT ME BY SURPRISE BEFORE, BUT THAT WON'T HAPPEN A--
--GAAKK!

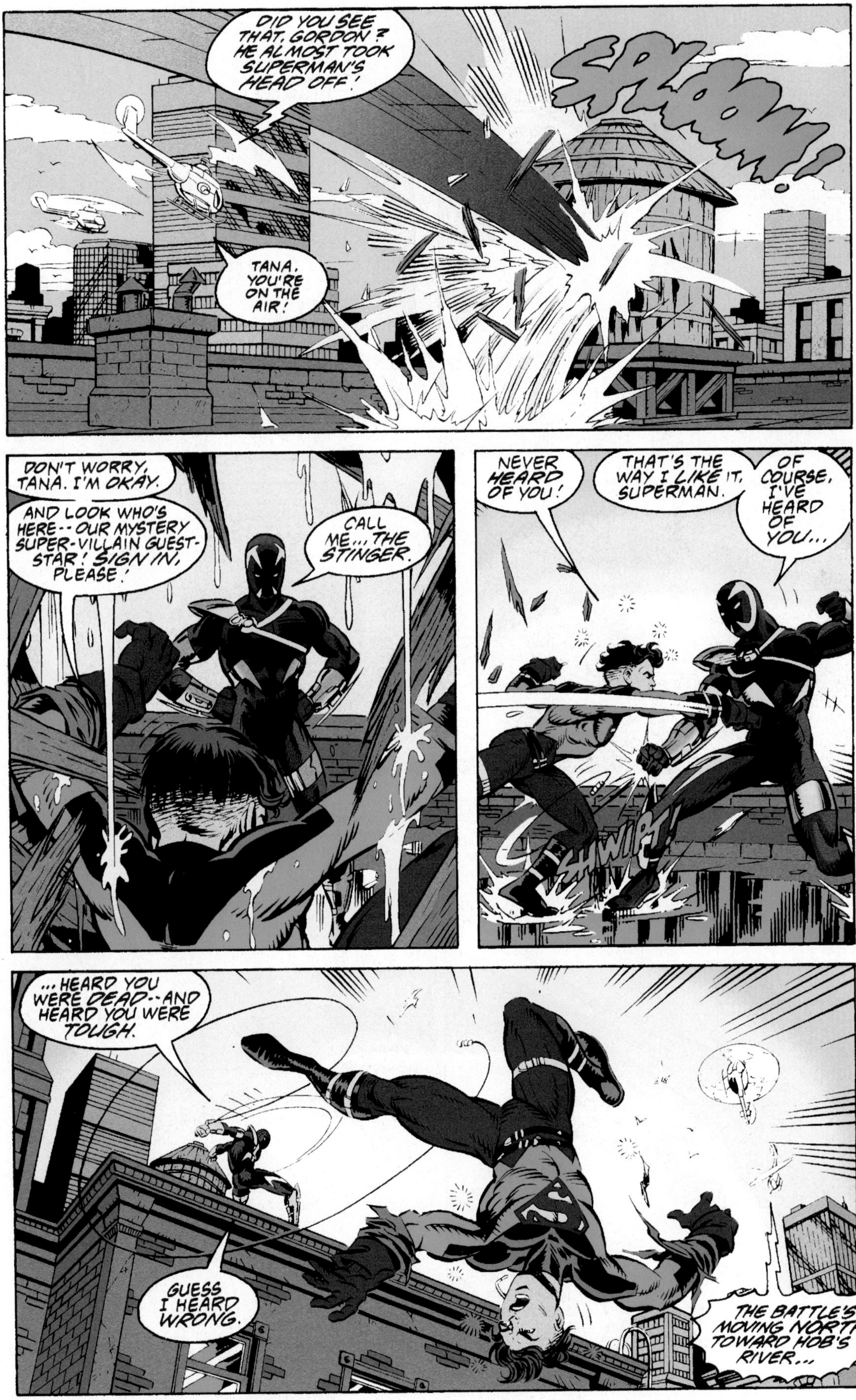
DID YOU SEE THAT, GORDON? HE ALMOST TOOK SUPERMAN'S HEAD OFF!
SPLOOM!!
TANA, YOU'RE ON THE AIR!
DON'T WORRY, TANA. I'M OKAY.
AND LOOK WHO'S HERE-- OUR MYSTERY SUPER-VILLAIN GUEST-STAR! SIGN IN, PLEASE!
CALL ME... THE STINGER.
NEVER HEARD OF YOU!
THAT'S THE WAY I LIKE IT, SUPERMAN.
OF COURSE, I'VE HEARD OF YOU...
SHWIP!
...HEARD YOU WERE DEAD--AND HEARD YOU WERE TOUGH.
GUESS I HEARD WRONG.
THE BATTLE'S MOVING NORTH, TOWARD HOB'S RIVER...

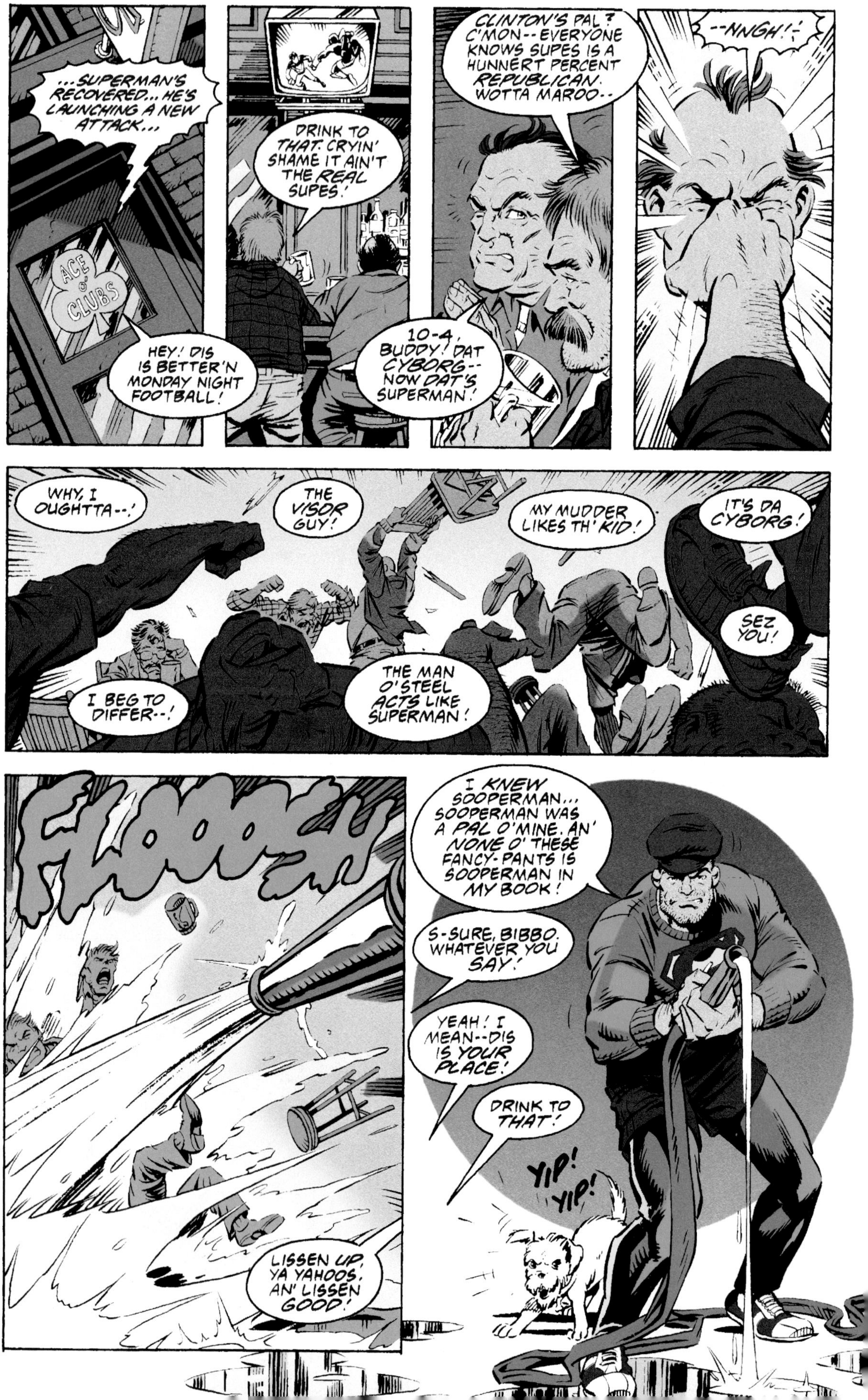
...SUPERMAN'S RECOVERED... HE'S LAUNCHING A NEW ATTACK...
ACE o' CLUBS
HEY! DIS IS BETTER'N MONDAY NIGHT FOOTBALL!
DRINK TO THAT. CRYIN' SHAME IT AIN'T THE REAL SUPES!
CLINTON'S PAL? C'MON--EVERYONE KNOWS SUPES IS A HUNNERT PERCENT REPUBLICAN. WOTTA MAROO..
10-4, BUDDY! DAT CYBORG--NOW DAT'S SUPERMAN!
--NNGH!--
WHY, I OUGHTTA--!
THE VISOR GUY!
MY MUDDER LIKES TH' KID!
IT'S DA CYBORG!
SEZ YOU!
I BEG TO DIFFER--!
THE MAN O'STEEL ACTS LIKE SUPERMAN!
FLOOOSH
LISSEN UP, YA YAHOOS. AN' LISSEN GOOD!
I KNEW SOOPERMAN... SOOPERMAN WAS A PAL O'MINE. AN' NONE O' THESE FANCY-PANTS IS SOOPERMAN IN MY BOOK!
S-SURE, BIBBO. WHATEVER YOU SAY!
YEAH! I MEAN--DIS IS YOUR PLACE!
DRINK TO THAT!
YIP! YIP!

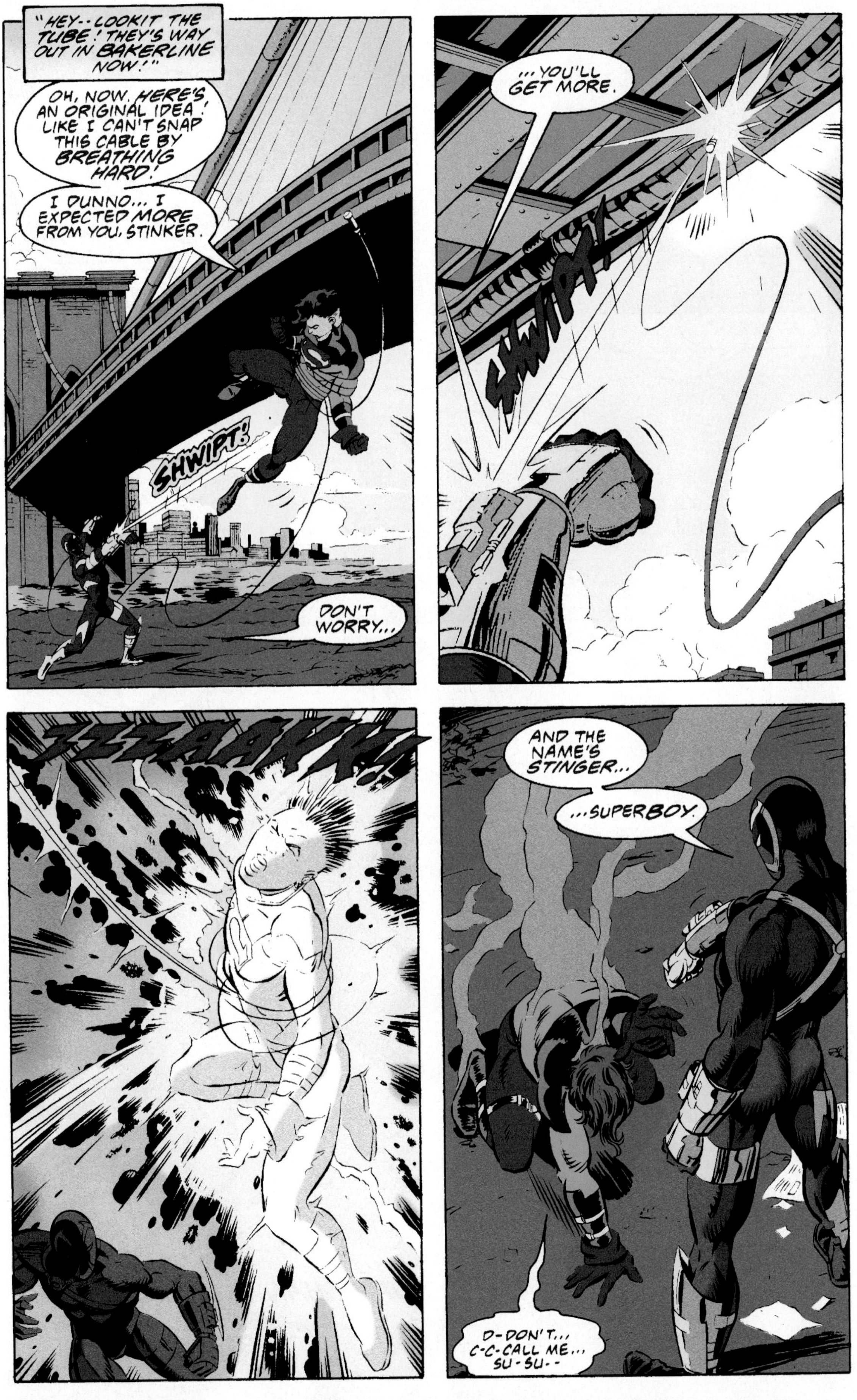
"HEY--LOOKIT THE TUBE! THEY'S WAY OUT IN BAKERLINE NOW!"
OH, NOW. HERE'S AN ORIGINAL IDEA. LIKE I CAN'T SNAP THIS CABLE BY BREATHING HARD!
I DUNNO... I EXPECTED MORE FROM YOU, STINKER.
SHWIPT!
DON'T WORRY...
...YOU'LL GET MORE.
SHWIPT!
AND THE NAME'S STINGER...
...SUPERBOY.
D-DON'T... C-C-CALL ME... SU-SU--

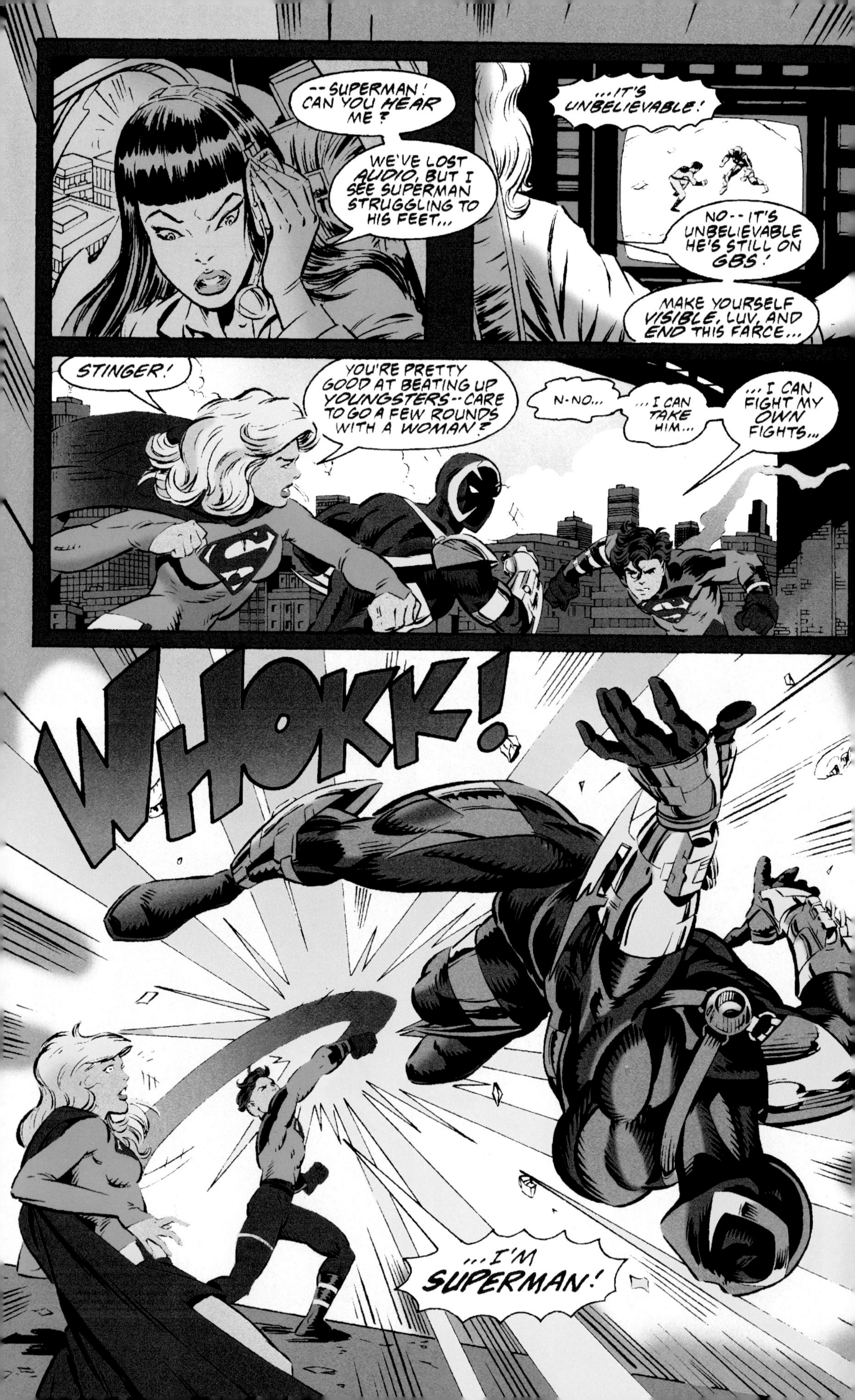

--SUPERMAN! CAN YOU HEAR ME?
WE'VE LOST AUDIO, BUT I SEE SUPERMAN STRUGGLING TO HIS FEET...
...IT'S UNBELIEVABLE!
NO--IT'S UNBELIEVABLE HE'S STILL ON GBS!
MAKE YOURSELF VISIBLE, LUV, AND END THIS FARCE...
STINGER!
YOU'RE PRETTY GOOD AT BEATING UP YOUNGSTERS--CARE TO GO A FEW ROUNDS WITH A WOMAN?
N-NO...
...I CAN TAKE HIM...
...I CAN FIGHT MY OWN FIGHTS...
WHOKK!
...I'M SUPERMAN!

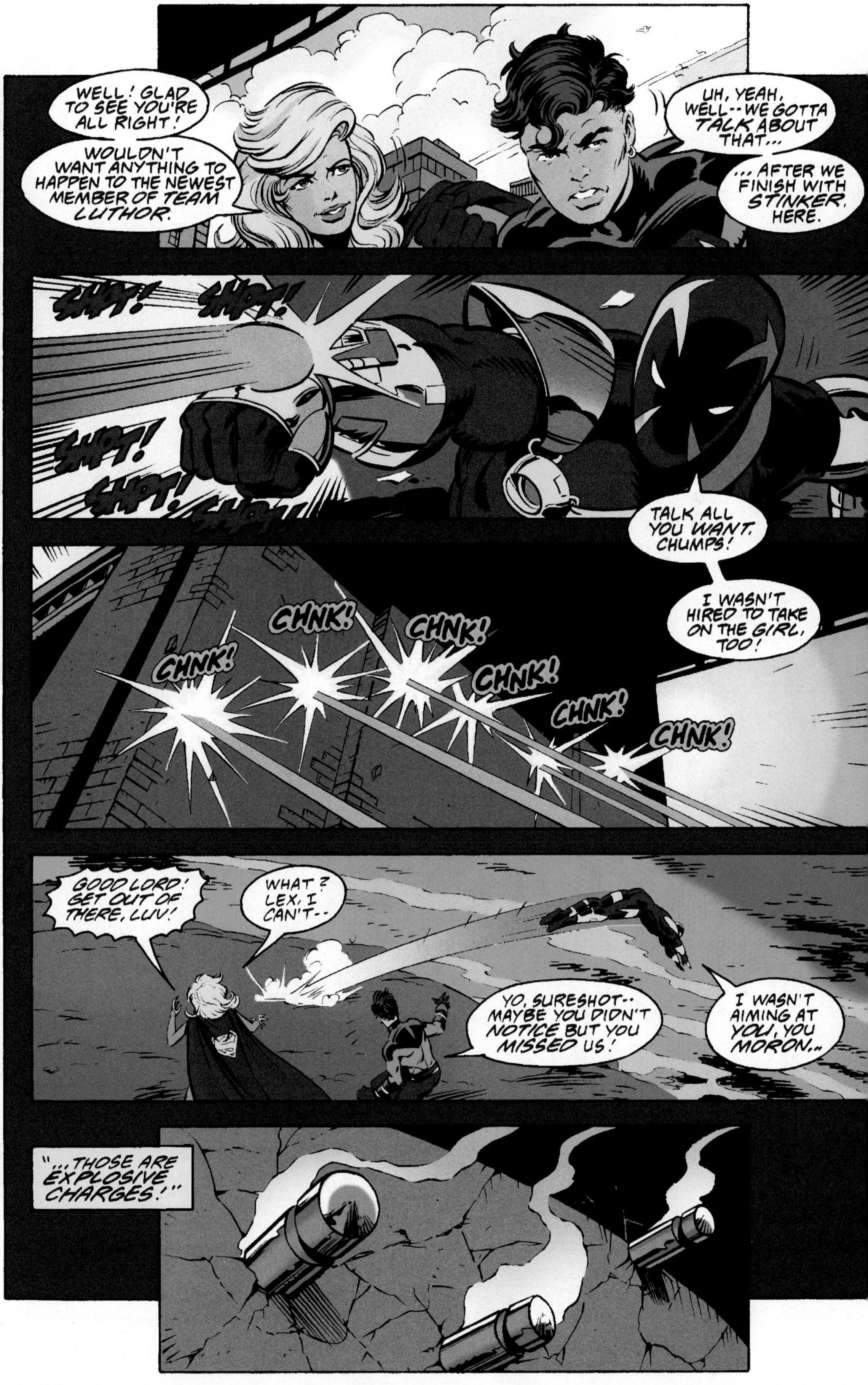
WELL! GLAD TO SEE YOU'RE ALL RIGHT!
WOULDN'T WANT ANYTHING TO HAPPEN TO THE NEWEST MEMBER OF TEAM LUTHOR.
UH, YEAH, WELL--WE GOTTA TALK ABOUT THAT...
...AFTER WE FINISH WITH STINKER HERE.
SHPT! SHPT!
SHPT! SHPT!
TALK ALL YOU WANT, CHUMPS!
I WASN'T HIRED TO TAKE ON THE GIRL, TOO!
CHNK! CHNK! CHNK! CHNK! CHNK! CHNK!
GOOD LORD! GET OUT OF THERE, LUV!
WHAT? LEX, I CAN'T--
YO, SURESHOT-- MAYBE YOU DIDN'T NOTICE BUT YOU MISSED US!
I WASN'T AIMING AT YOU, YOU MORON...
"...THOSE ARE EXPLOSIVE CHARGES!"

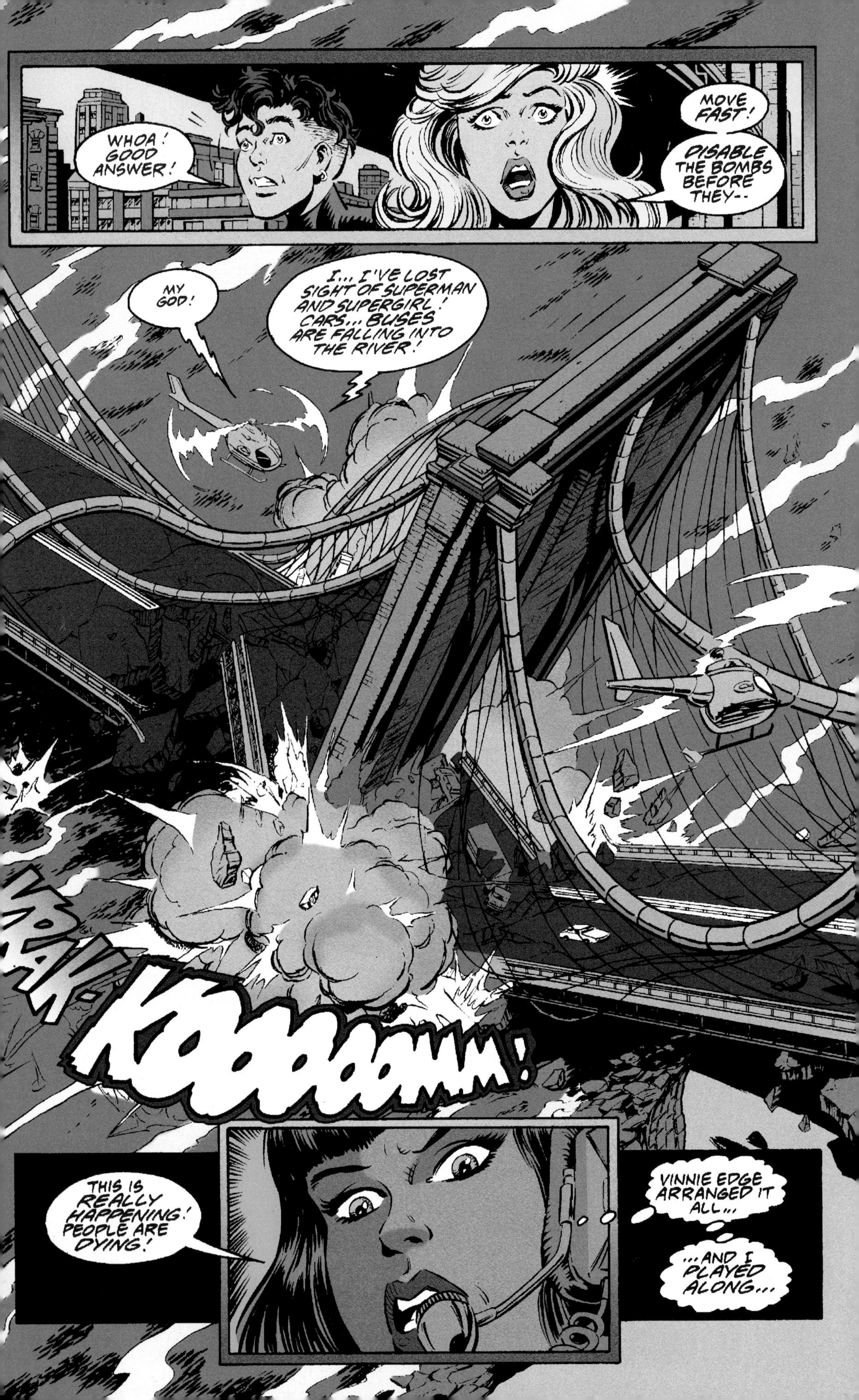
WHOA! GOOD ANSWER!
MOVE FAST!
DISABLE THE BOMBS BEFORE THEY--
MY GOD!
I... I'VE LOST SIGHT OF SUPERMAN AND SUPERGIRL! CARS... BUSES ARE FALLING INTO THE RIVER!
KRAK-KOOOOOMM!
THIS IS REALLY HAPPENING! PEOPLE ARE DYING!
VINNIE EDGE ARRANGED IT ALL...
...AND I PLAYED ALONG...

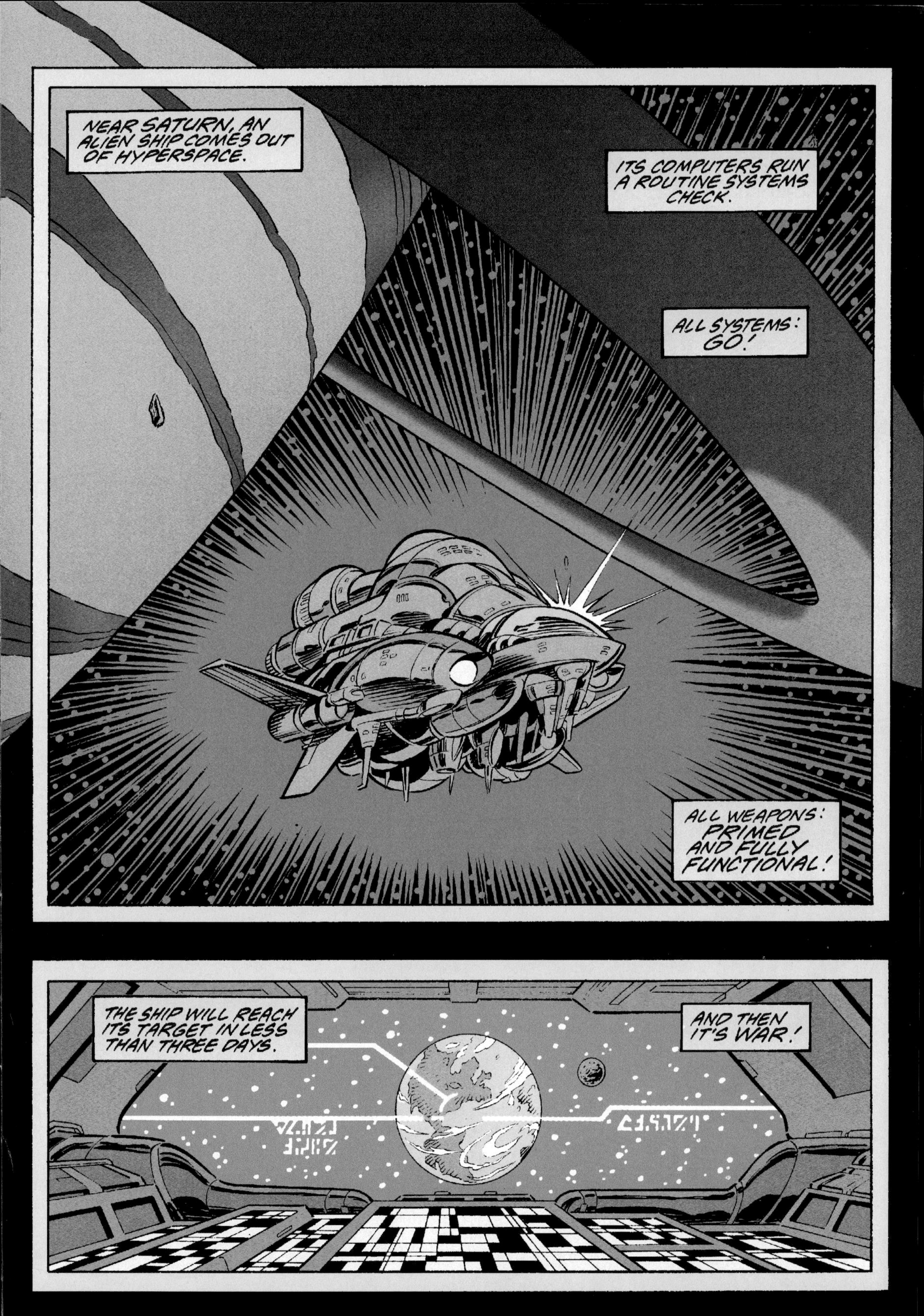
NEAR SATURN, AN ALIEN SHIP COMES OUT OF HYPERSPACE.
ITS COMPUTERS RUN A ROUTINE SYSTEMS CHECK.
ALL SYSTEMS: GO!
ALL WEAPONS: PRIMED AND FULLY FUNCTIONAL!
THE SHIP WILL REACH ITS TARGET IN LESS THAN THREE DAYS.
AND THEN IT'S WAR!

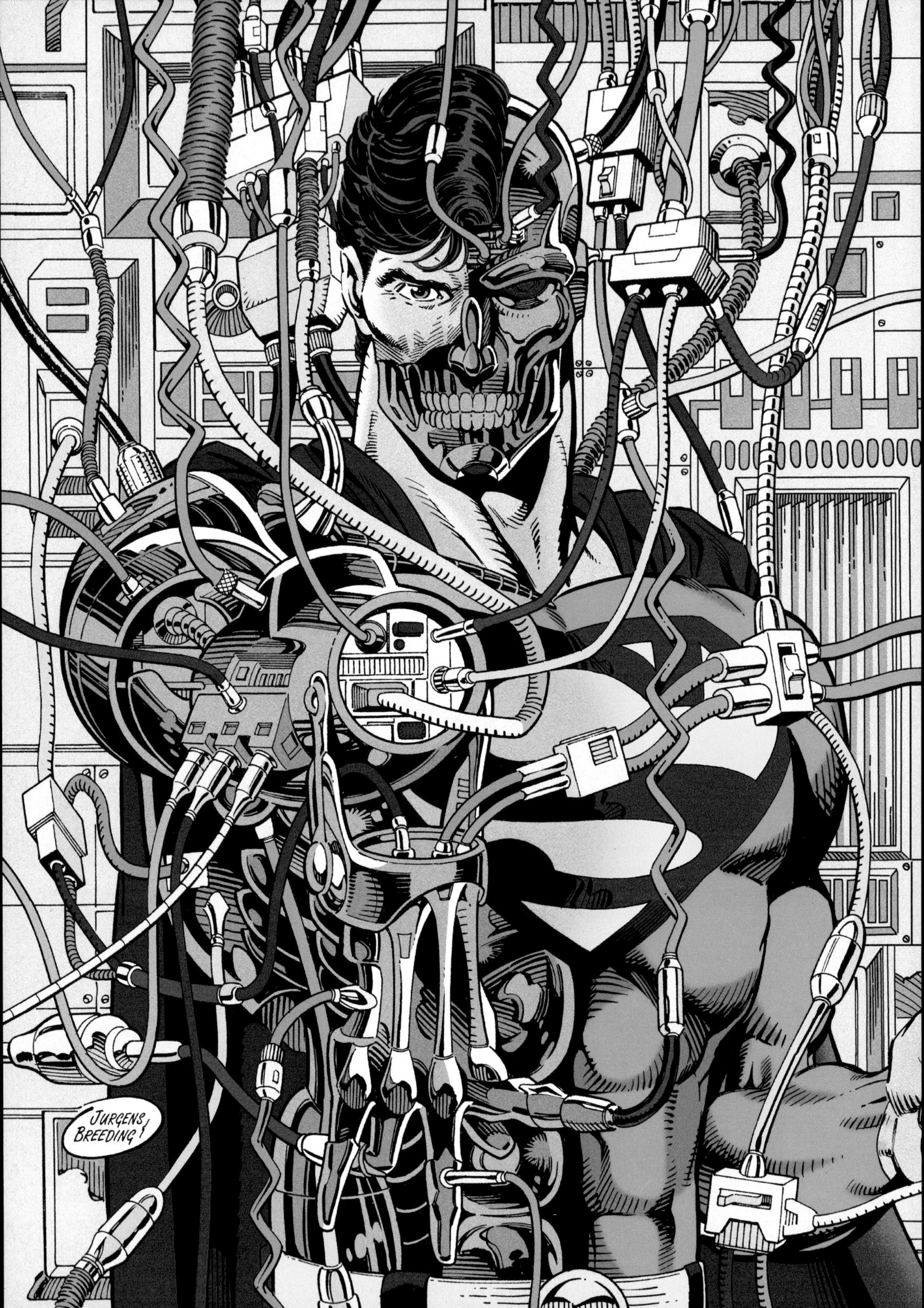
JURGENS
BREEDING

THE MAN OF TOMORROW by **Dan Jurgens** and **Brett Breeding**

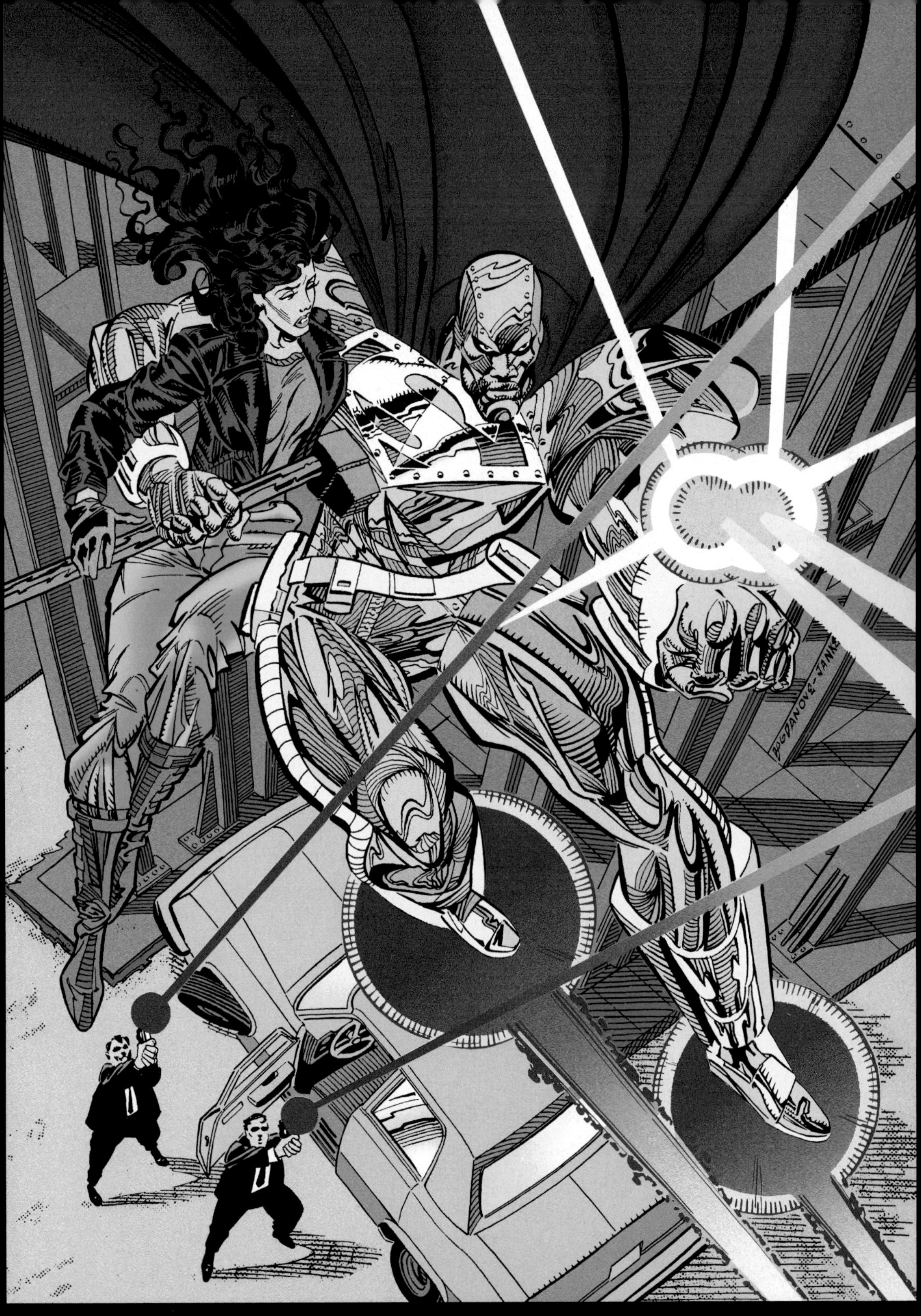
BOGDANOVE-JANKE

THE MAN OF STEEL by **Jon Bogdanove** and **Dennis Janke**

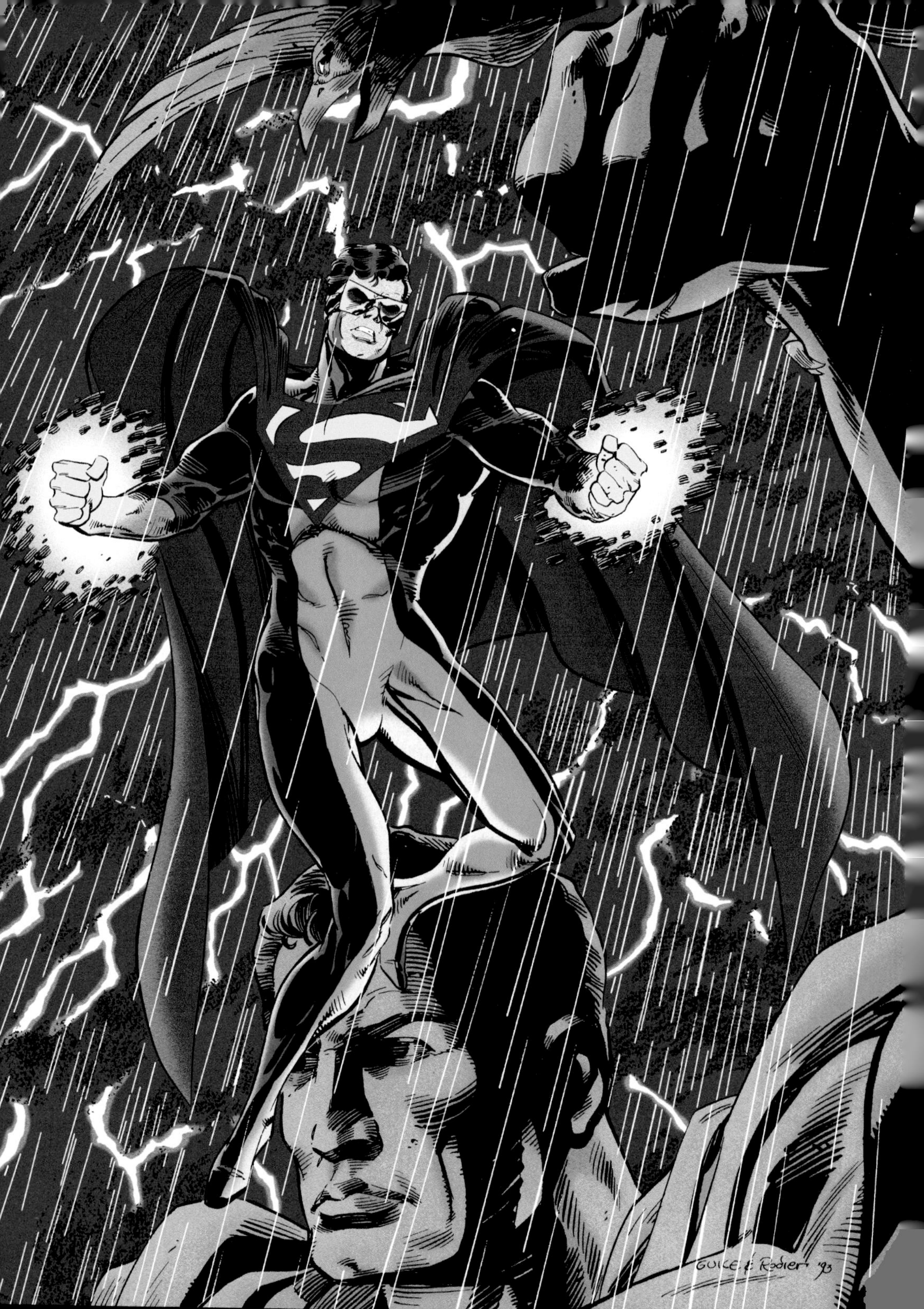
GUICE & Rodier '93

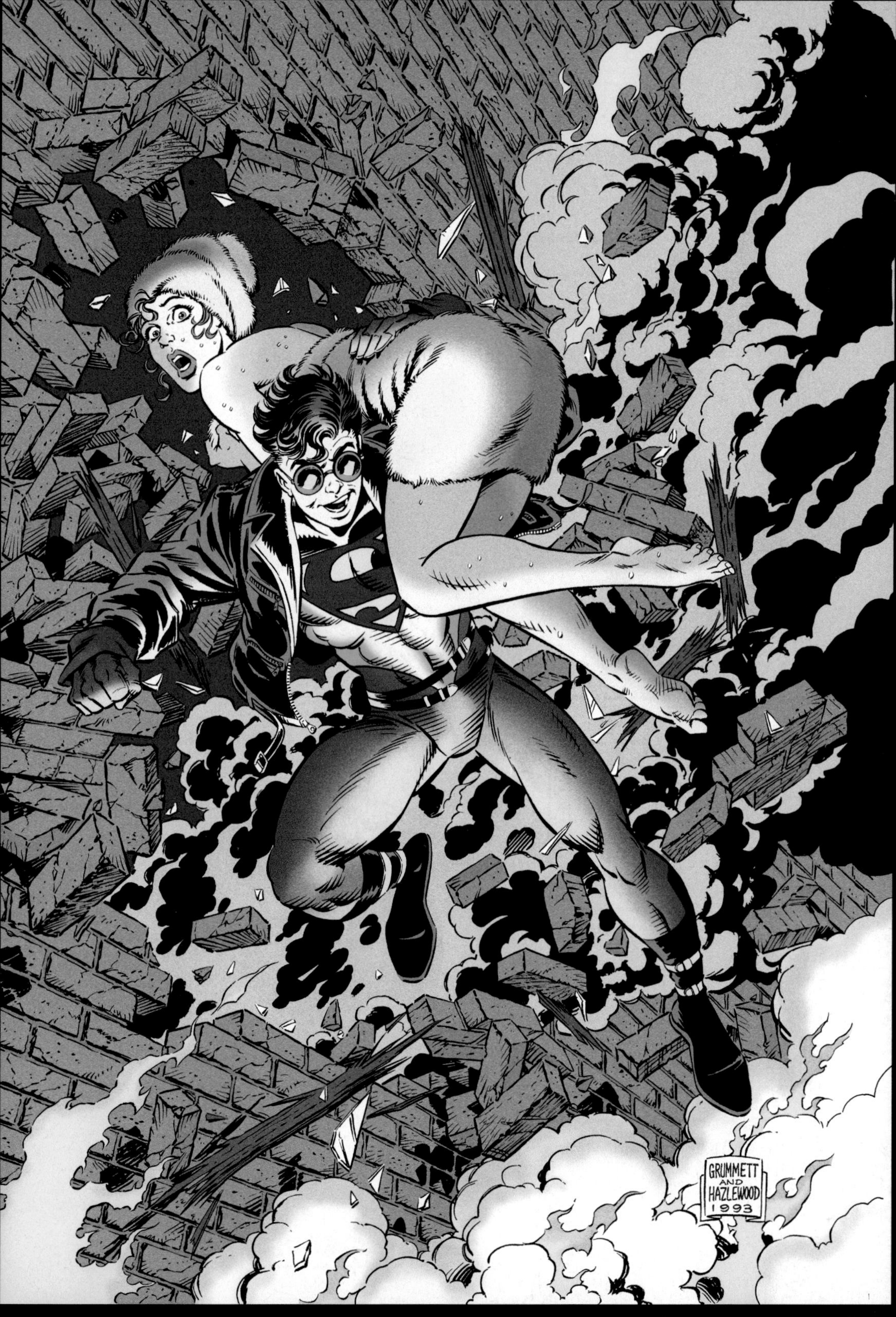
GRUMMETT AND HAZLEWOOD 1993

SUPERBOY by **Tom Grummett** and **Doug Hazlewood**

Mike, Jen, et al:

Here's my design for the "Kryptonian" Superman Replacement.

As you can see, it keeps the basic black body-suit look of the Krypton Man/Eradicator minus the high-tech ruffles. As a matter of fact, the main body suit is one piece, covering our new guy from temple to toes.

The cape ~~attaches~~ attaches to the big S-Emblem which is stapled directly to our new guy's chest. No, wait! I was just kidding...the Emblem is held there electromagnetically or some such way.

The visor attaches to the ear cups of the Flash-Gordon-like headpiece. The eyes should be visible as little more than shadows...think Wally Wood...to heighten the mystery.

So? Vat chu tink?

Roger

ATTENTION : MIKE CARLIN
RE: "MR. KICK-BUTT"

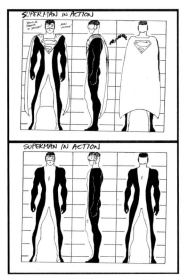

SUPERMAN IN ACTION

SUPERMAN IN ACTION

Letter and sketch above by Roger Stern for the design of the "Kryptonian" Superman.
Sketch right by Guice of the new Eradicator design.

SHORT CROPPED HAIR

SCAR TISSUE ON FACE

• THINK "EASTWOOD" IN THE MOVIE UNFORGIVEN

THIS GUY IS ONE MEAN S.O.B / COMPLETELY COLD IN POSTURES

ARROGANT STANCES

ROUGH/WEATHERED FACE ... LOOKS LIKE HE'S BEEN THRU HELL!

JACKSON GUICE /1993

THE NEW
ERADICATOR!

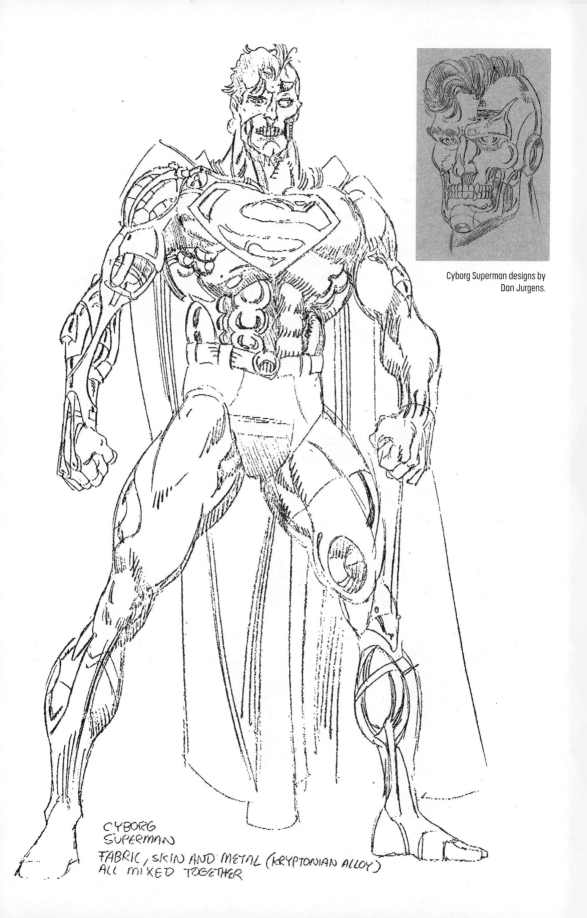

Cyborg Superman designs by
Dan Jurgens.

CYBORG
SUPERMAN
FABRIC, SKIN AND METAL (KRYPTONIAN ALLOY)
ALL MIXED TOGETHER

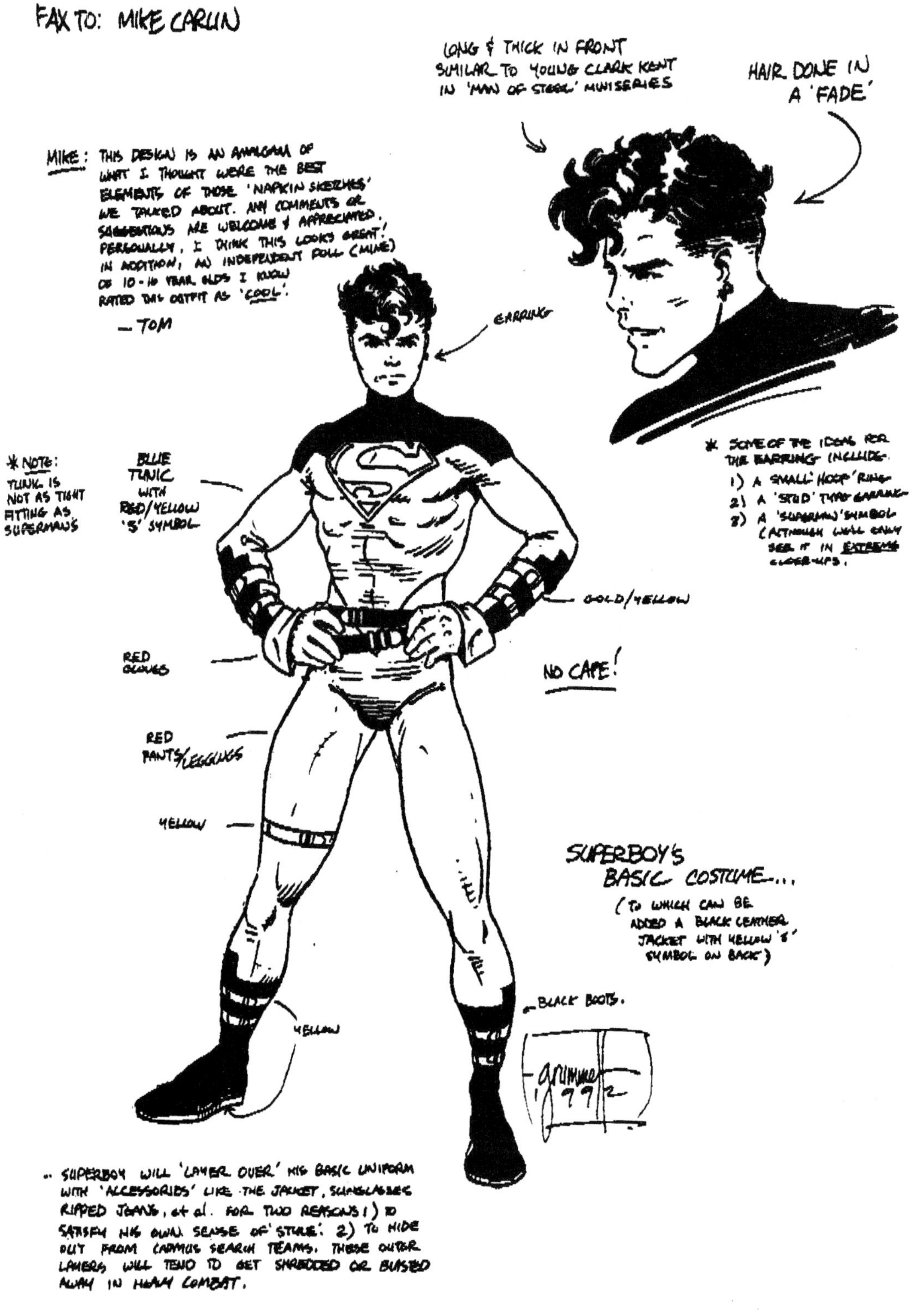
FAX TO: MIKE CARLIN
LONG & THICK IN FRONT SIMILAR TO YOUNG CLARK KENT IN 'MAN OF STEEL' MINISERIES
HAIR DONE IN A 'FADE'
MIKE: THIS DESIGN IS AN AMALGAM OF WHAT I THOUGHT WERE THE BEST ELEMENTS OF THOSE 'NAPKIN SKETCHES' WE TALKED ABOUT. ANY COMMENTS OR SUGGESTIONS ARE WELCOME & APPRECIATED. PERSONALLY, I THINK THIS LOOKS GREAT! IN ADDITION, AN INDEPENDENT POLL (MINE) OF 10-16 YEAR OLDS I KNOW RATED THIS OUTFIT AS 'COOL'.
— TOM
EARRING
* SOME OF THE IDEAS FOR THE EARRING INCLUDE:
1) A SMALL 'HOOP' RING
2) A 'STUD' TYPE EARRING
3) A 'SUPERMAN' SYMBOL (ALTHOUGH WE'LL ONLY SEE IT IN EXTREME CLOSE-UPS.
* NOTE: TUNIC IS NOT AS TIGHT FITTING AS SUPERMAN'S
BLUE TUNIC WITH RED/YELLOW 'S' SYMBOL
GOLD/YELLOW
RED GLOVES
NO CAPE!
RED PANTS/LEGGINGS
YELLOW
SUPERBOY'S BASIC COSTUME...
(TO WHICH CAN BE ADDED A BLACK LEATHER JACKET WITH YELLOW 'S' SYMBOL ON BACK)
BLACK BOOTS.
YELLOW
GRUMMETT '92
.. SUPERBOY WILL 'LAYER OVER' HIS BASIC UNIFORM WITH 'ACCESSORIES' LIKE THE JACKET, SUNGLASSES RIPPED JEANS, et al. FOR TWO REASONS 1) TO SATISFY HIS OWN SENSE OF STYLE. 2) TO HIDE OUT FROM CADMUS SEARCH TEAMS. THESE OUTER LAYERS WILL TEND TO GET SHREDDED OR BLASTED AWAY IN HEAVY COMBAT.

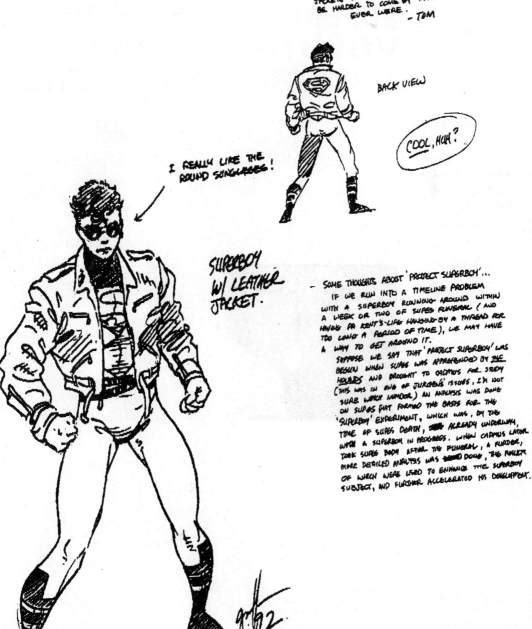

NOTE TO KARL/MIKE: IF WE ASSUME SUPERBOY GENERATES THE SAME AURA THAT HIS ADULT COUNTERPART DID, HIS CADMUS-MADE SUPERBOY OUTFIT WILL BE INDESTRUCTIBLE. HOWEVER THIS PROPERTY WOULD NOT EXTEND TO HIS LEATHER JACKET, WHICH, LIKE SUPERMAN'S CAPE, WILL TEND TO SHOW SOME WEAR & TEAR. I VISUALIZE A SCENE WHERE SUPERBOY SURVIVES A MASSIVE EXPLOSION IN AN ATTACK, AND SAVAGELY RETALIATES TO AVENGE HIS JACKET! ("YOU GOONS RUINED MY JACKET! I'M GONNA KILL YA!") SINCE MA KENT ISN'T LIKELY TO BE SEWING LEATHER JACKETS (IF AT ALL) THEY'LL BE HARDER TO COME BY THAN SUPES' CAPES EVER WERE. — TOM

BACK VIEW

COOL, HUH?

I REALLY LIKE THE ROUND SUNGLASSES!

SUPERBOY W/ LEATHER JACKET.

— SOME THOUGHTS ABOUT 'PROJECT SUPERBOY'...
IF WE RUN INTO A TIMELINE PROBLEM WITH A SUPERBOY RUNNING AROUND WITHIN A WEEK OR TWO OF SUPES FUNERAL (AND HAVING PA KENT'S LIFE HANGING BY A THREAD FOR TOO LONG A PERIOD OF TIME), WE MAY HAVE A WAY TO GET AROUND IT.
SUPPOSE WE SAY THAT 'PROJECT SUPERBOY' WAS BEGUN WHEN SUPES WAS APPREHENDED BY THE HOUNDS AND BROUGHT TO CADMUS FOR STUDY (THIS WAS IN ONE OF JURGENS' ISSUES, I'M NOT SURE WHICH NUMBER) AN ANALYSIS WAS DONE ON SUPES THAT FORMED THE BASIS FOR THE 'SUPERBOY' EXPERIMENT, WHICH WAS, BY THE TIME OF SUPES DEATH, ALREADY UNDERWAY, WITH A SUPERBOY IN PROGRESS. WHEN CADMUS LATER TOOK SUPES BODY AFTER THE FUNERAL, A FURTHER, MORE DETAILED ANALYSIS WAS DONE, THE RESULTS OF WHICH WERE USED TO ENHANCE THE SUPERBOY SUBJECT, AND FURTHER ACCELERATED HIS DEVELOPMENT.

"It's fresh air. I like this all-too-human Superman, and I think a lot of you will, too."
—SCRIPPS HOWARD NEWS SERVICE

START AT THE BEGINNING!

SUPERMAN: ACTION COMICS VOLUME 1: SUPERMAN AND THE MEN OF STEEL

SUPERMAN VOLUME 1: WHAT PRICE TOMORROW?

SUPERGIRL VOLUME 1: THE LAST DAUGHTER OF KRYPTON

SUPERBOY VOLUME 1: INCUBATION

"BELIEVE THE HYPE: GRANT MORRISON WENT AND WROTE THE SINGLE BEST ISSUE OF SUPERMAN THESE EYES HAVE EVER READ."
— USA TODAY

GRANT **MORRISON**   RAGS **MORALES**   ANDY **KUBERT**